THE
# UNITED STATES PONY CLUBS MANUAL OF HORSEMANSHIP

Also by Susan E. Harris

*Horsemanship in Pictures*

*Grooming to Win, Third Edition*

*Horse Gaits, Balance and Movement*

*The United States Pony Club Manual of Horsemanship:*
*Basics for Beginners / D Level, Second Edition*

*The United States Pony Club Manual of Horsemanship:*
*Intermediate Horsemanship / C Level, Second Edition*

# THE UNITED STATES PONY CLUBS MANUAL OF HORSEMANSHIP

ADVANCED HORSEMANSHIP/HB - A LEVEL

Second Edition

Written and Illustrated by

Susan E. Harris

and

The United States Pony Clubs, Inc.

John Wiley & Sons, Inc.

Copyright © 2014 by Susan E. Harris and the United States Pony Clubs, Inc. All rights reserved.

Howell Book House /Wiley General Trade, an imprint of Turner Publishing Company

No part of this publication may be reproduced, stored in a retrieval system or transmitted in any form or by any means, electronic, mechanical, photocopying, recording, scanning or otherwise, except as permitted under Sections 107 or 108 of the 1976 United States Copyright Act, without either the prior written permission of the Publisher, or authorization through payment of the appropriate per-copy fee to the Copyright Clearance Center, 222 Rosewood Drive, Danvers, MA 01923, (978) 750-8400, fax (978) 750-4744. Requests to the Publisher for permission should be addressed to Turner Publishing Company, 424 Church Street, Suite 2240, Nashville, Tennessee, (615) 255-2665, fax (615) 255-5081, E-mail: submissions@turnerpublishing.com.

Trademarks: Wiley, the Wiley Publishing logo, and Howell Book House are trademarks or registered trademarks of Wiley Publishing, Inc., in the United States and other countries, and may not be used without written permission. All other trademarks are the property of their respective owners. Wiley Publishing, Inc., and Turner Publishing Company are not associated with any product or vendor mentioned in this book.

Limit of Liability/Disclaimer of Warranty: While the publisher and author have used their best efforts in preparing this book, they make no representations or warranties with respect to the accuracy or completeness of the contents of this book and specifically disclaim any implied warranties of merchantability or fitness for a particular purpose. No warranty may be created or extended by sales representatives or written sales materials. The advice and strategies contained herein may not be suitable for your situation. You should consult with a professional where appropriate. Neither the publisher nor author shall be liable for any loss of profit or any other commercial damages, including but not limited to special, incidental, consequential, or other damages.

Turner also publishes its books in a variety of electronic formats. Some content that appears in print may not be available in electronic books.

Cover design: Mike Penticost
Cover photograph: Courtesy of The United States Pony Clubs and Shelley Mann
Book design: Lissa Auciello-Brogan

Library of Congress Cataloging-in-Publication Data

Harris, Susan E.
  The United States Pony Club manual of horsemanship. Advanced horsemanship / by Susan E. Harris.
     pages cm
  Includes bibliographical references.
  1. Horsemanship. 2. Ponies.  I. United States Pony Clubs. II. Title.
  SF309.H365 2014
  636.1'6--dc23
                         2014025673

ISBN: 978-1-11813-350-7 (paperback), 978-1-11823-869-1 (e-book)

Printed in the United States of America
14 13 12 11 10 9 8 7 6 5 4 3 2 1

# Contents

Foreword   vii

A Note from the United States Pony Clubs, Inc.   ix

About the U.S. Pony Clubs, Inc.   xi

U.S. Pony Clubs Mission Statement   xiii

Notes about the USPC HB through A Levels   xv

About This Book   xvii

**Part 1:** Riding, Training, and Teaching   **1**

  **1** Biomechanics and Movement of the Horse   3

  **2** Principles of Riding on the Flat   34

  **3** Dressage and Training Principles   66

  **4** Jumping   115

  **5** Cross-Country Riding and Jumping   172

  **6** Longeing   208

  **7** Bitting, Tack, and Presentation   247

  **8** Teaching Horsemanship   285

**Part 2:** The Horse   **325**

  **9** Systems of the Horse   327

  **10** Conformation and Soundness   371

**11** The Foot and Shoeing   394

**12** Conditioning and Exercise Physiology   415

**Part 3:** Horse Care and Stable Management   **431**

**13** Feeds and Nutrition   433

**14** Health Care, Diseases, and Veterinary Knowledge   488

**15** Stable and Facility Management   552

**16** Bandaging   579

**17** Travel Safety   599

Index   617

# Foreword

One of the great mysteries of life is the process of growing up. It seems only a blink of an eye ago that I was 8 or 9 and I heard my mother discussing starting a Pony Club with my instructor Hilda Gurney. As is the case with most kids, I went hoping for some fun with my friends. What I found was a system that required that I take on the responsibility of learning horsemanship. Of course, the rigor of ratings, rallies, and organized lessons was a new environment that seemed unreasonable at first. The idea of taking time off from madly galloping around the hills to attend unmounted lessons on topics that ranged far and wide seemed like cruel and unusual punishment. However, as is usually the case with kids who develop a love for all things horses, I found myself gradually immersed in a universe that added immeasurably to every aspect of my life for the next 50 years. The skills and attitude developed by the Pony Club system gives young people a foundation that helps them to grow into productive adults. This book is a compilation of knowledge regarding the art and science of horsemanship. This knowledge lies at the core of Pony Club. The basic principles contained here are timeless and lay before the young rider a pathway to understanding horses that can last a lifetime. Not every young person getting involved with horses and Pony Club will stay for a lifetime. My wife Lisa and I grew up in the same Pony Club, and now have a Pony Club of our own filled with 8- and 9-year-old kids just like we were many years ago. But every person, young or old, will benefit from the time they spend in Pony Club.

Kids, horses, and dreams . . . big or small . . . it all starts here.

*Brian Sabo*

# A Note from the United States Pony Clubs, Inc.

The first requests from U.S. Pony Club members for a manual of their own were received when The United States Pony Clubs, Inc. was founded in 1954. By 1994, it was determined that there was need for a text that matched our standards, used terms specific to North America, and was written at a reading level comfortable for the majority of our members.

This new edition of *The United States Pony Clubs Manual of Horsemanship, Advanced Level*, reflects the updated standards and advances in both riding and equine knowledge.

Author and illustrator Susan E. Harris, an experienced and successful riding instructor, has received guidance from the USPC Standards and Curriculum Committee, Instruction Council members, various national examiners, and others who have helped supply current data and information in order to help bring this manual to completion. We wish to thank the following people who contributed to the knowledge and development of this edition:

> Claire Harmon, USPC Vice President of Instruction, USPC National Examiner, USEA ICP, for content and coordinating input from consultants and committees
>
> Consulting veterinarian Stacy Anderson, DVM, MVSc, DACVS-LA, USPC National Examiner
>
> Brian Sabo, USEA Level 4 Instructor, for his help in the Cross-Country Riding and Jumping chapter, and for writing the Foreword
>
> Nancy Ambrosiano
>
> Trenna Atkins, "S" Level Dressage Judge
>
> Jakki Avery, USPC National Examiner, HIS Judge

Katy Barglow, PhD, USPC National Examiner, "r" Dressage Judge, USDF Gold Medalist

Kevin Bowie, USPC National Examiner

Karen Brown, USPC National Examiner

Stephanie Caston, DVM, DACVS-LA

Laurie Chapman-Bosco, MDE., PAS, USPC National Examiner

Melissa Dabadie, USPC Chief Horse Management Judge

Alita Bunny Hendricks, USPC National Examiner, Chief Horse Management Judge

Laura Johnson, BS, MS

Karen Kalck McCormick, DVM, DACVIM-LA

Richard Lamb, USPC National Examiner, USEA ICP

Jane Manfredi, DVM, MS

Kimberley McDonald, USPC National Examiner

Sarah Morgan, USPC National Examiner

Vicki Hammers-O'Neil, USPC National Examiner, USDF Certified Instructor, 4th Level

Connie Riker

Natalie Shaw, USPC National Examiner

Keri Thomas, DVM

Clair Thunes, BSC, MS, PhD Nutrition

Kim Lowman Volmer, USPC National Examiner

Kayla Wafful

Deb Willson, USPC National Examiner

Josh Zacharias, DVM, MS, DACVS-LA, DACVSMR, Farrier

Although we do not claim to cover all special interest areas, we have carefully listened to and considered all suggestions. Plainly, this manual represents several years of research. We hope young riders everywhere will enjoy Susan Harris's exceptional work as much as we do.

# About the U.S. Pony Clubs, Inc.

Pony Club started in Great Britain in 1928 with 700 original members. By 1992 there were more than 125,000 members in 27 countries, making it the largest junior equestrian group in the world. The United States Pony Clubs are made up of Clubs and Centers throughout the country, where we teach Sportsmanship, Stewardship, and Leadership through Horsemanship. Thousands come to learn and enjoy horse sports with the United States Pony Clubs.

The three volumes of the USPC Manual of Horsemanship are written especially for Pony Club members and for the volunteers who lead and teach them, but they will also be helpful to anyone who wants to learn or teach good horsemanship. In these manuals, the emphasis is on how children learn, rather than on subject matter alone. They stress progress along a continuum of learning instead of mere acquisition of facts.

The manuals provide an introduction to the curriculum of the U.S. Pony Clubs, and are written to help young people meet the current U.S. Pony Clubs Standards of Proficiency. However, the levels of proficiency required by the standards cannot be achieved by book work alone. Practical hands-on learning is essential, as is good mounted instruction at all levels. As in any course of study, effective teaching and learning require outside reading and supplemental material. Content from the U.S. Pony Clubs' most recently published standards and reading lists, and individual teachers' resources, will be necessary to augment this textbook.

Pony Club supports the ideal of a thoroughly happy, comfortable horseperson, riding across a natural country, with complete confidence and perfect balance on a horse or pony equally happy, confident, and free from pain or bewilderment.

# U.S. Pony Clubs Mission Statement

### *The USPC's Mission*
The United States Pony Clubs, Inc. develops character, leadership, confidence, and a sense of community in youth through a program that teaches the care of horses and ponies, riding, and mounted sports.

### *Core Values of the USPC*
- *Horsemanship* with respect to health care, nutrition, stable management, handling, and riding a mount safely, correctly, and with confidence.

- *Organized teamwork* including cooperation, communication, responsibility, leadership, mentoring, teaching, and fostering a supportive yet competitive environment.

- *Respect* for the horse and self through horsemanship, for land through land conservation, and for others through service and teamwork.

- *Service* by providing an opportunity for members, parents, and others to support the Pony Club program locally, regionally, and nationally through volunteerism.

- *Education* at an individual pace to achieve personal goals and expand knowledge through teaching others.

- ***Sportsmanship, Stewardship, and Leadership through Horsemanship***

For more information about the U.S. Pony Clubs, or if you would like to join or start a Pony Club or Center in your area, please contact:

> The United States Pony Clubs, Inc.
> The Kentucky Horse Park
> 4041 Iron Works Parkway
> Lexington, KY 40511
> 859-254-PONY (7669)

The following trademarks are owned by the United States Pony Clubs, Inc., and are protected by Registered Trademark ®: USPC, United States Pony Clubs, and design (official seal).

# Notes about the USPC HB through A Levels

Everyone joins Pony Club as an unrated member and progresses through the lower-level certificates (D-1 through C-2) at their own pace. These certifications are tested by a local Pony Club examiner. The HB through A certifications are national tests, administered by the National Testing Committee. The requirements for each certification are called the Standards of Proficiency.

The D certificate is an introduction to riding, establishing a foundation of safety habits and knowledge of the daily care of pony and tack. The C Pony Club member is learning to become an active horseperson, to understand the reasons for what he is doing, and to develop a competence in horse care and riding that will enable a lifetime of pleasure in a variety of equestrian sports.

National certifications require a much greater depth of knowledge and proficiency than the earlier certificates. Successful candidates are competent, all-around horse people, active members of USPC who participate in a variety of Pony Club activities. They are also thoughtful leaders who set an example for all levels.

In addition to its instructional programs, the USPC offers a variety of activities at Club/Center, Regional, Inter-Regional, and National levels for team and individual participation. These activities include Eventing, Dressage, Hunter Seat Equitation, Show Jumping, Games, Polocrosse, Tetrathlon, Polo, Quiz, and Western. Foxhunting, vaulting, and driving are other resource activities that many members are involved in.

*Note: Achieving a certification does not necessarily qualify a Pony Club member for participation in any horse sport. To compete safely or qualify as a team member for a particular activity, further study, preparation, and specialized coaching may be necessary.*

# About This Book

This book is written for Pony Club members, instructors, and others who want to develop their horsemanship and horse management skills and knowledge to advanced levels. It follows the standards and system of instruction of the U.S. Pony Clubs, Inc., and is based on the fundamentals taught in the USPC D and C Levels and covered in the previous USPC Manuals of Horsemanship: *Basics for Beginners/D Level* and *Intermediate Horsemanship/C1-C2 Level*. Part One of this book covers horse biomechanics and movement, riding on the flat, dressage, jumping, cross-country jumping, longeing, tack and bitting, and teaching horsemanship. Part Two includes equine systems, anatomy and physiology, conformation, the foot and shoeing, and conditioning and exercise physiology. Part Three covers horse management, including stable and facility management; nutrition; diseases and health care; bandaging; and travel safety.

To get the most out of this book, you need to know the material covered in the first two manuals. Certain topics covered there are not repeated here, and the riding skills taught at this level are based on a foundation of proficiency in the basic and intermediate skills and knowledge. Even if you are already an experienced horseperson, reviewing the first two manuals will help you check your basics and be consistent in the progression of your riding, training, knowledge, and teaching. To prepare for the USPC's H-B through A certifications, you must also be familiar with the USPC Standards of Proficiency and must study additional sources.

> *This book is not intended as a substitute for professional advice and guidance in the field of horseback riding. A person should take part in the activities discussed in this book only under the supervision of a knowledgeable adult.*

# Part 1

# Riding, Training, and Teaching

# 1

# Biomechanics and Movement of the Horse

Horses are amazing creatures, uniquely designed to avoid predators in the wild. As riders, we use the athleticism of the horse to perform in competitions and for other purposes, rather than to avoid a predator. Through selective breeding, the athleticism of horses has improved dramatically since horses were first domesticated long ago.

The skeletal framework determines the horse's conformation and much of his athletic ability. The muscles move the skeletal framework by acting in pairs to flex and extend joints. The suspensory apparatus of the limb allows the horse to store potential energy due to the elasticity in the tendons and ligaments of the lower leg. This potential energy allows the horse to move efficiently and, at times, flamboyantly. It is critical to review the skeletal and muscle systems (see Chapter 9, "Systems of the Horse") to better understand the anatomical intricacies involved in the biomechanical movement of the horse.

## Movement of the Horse

Horses are athletes; they are only useful because of their ability to move. Good movement is efficient, athletic, and appropriate for the discipline; it allows a horse to reach his full potential. Poor movement is unattractive, makes it uncomfortable to ride, and is potentially damaging to the horse.

Different breeds, types, and individual horses have different kinds of movement, which make them suitable for a particular purpose. Regardless of type, all horses share the same basic anatomy and principles of movement. In addition, there are certain basic qualities that are essential to good movement and soundness in all horses.

## Good Movement

Good movement depends on a horse's conformation, soundness, and correct muscle use. It is affected by shoeing, footing, and the way the horse is trained and ridden.

## How a Horse Moves

When a horse moves, his hindquarter muscles provide the power that pushes him forward. The deep muscles of the back and spine stabilize the back and transmit the thrust to the rest of his body. The abdominal muscles, along with the deep inner back muscles, called the *psoas group*, flex the *lumbosacral joint*, lift the back, and allow the hindquarters and hind legs to come under the barrel to create power, propelling the horse forward. With every stride, the muscles of the hindquarters flex the joints of the hind legs and swing them forward to take a stride.

The deep muscles of the neck stabilize the base of the neck and help the horse to arch his neck, raise his forehand, and change his balance. The muscles at the top of the neck raise and extend the head and neck. The muscles on the underside of the neck flex the neck downward and the pectoral muscles help to extend the forearms. The lateral muscles (on the sides of the neck) bend the neck sideways.

The muscles of the shoulder, neck, and arm rotate the shoulder blades, and flex and extend the shoulder and elbow joints. Along with the forearm muscles, they help the forelegs flex, swing forward, absorb shock, and carry weight. The *suspensory apparatus* also helps to carry the horse's weight, absorb shock, and support the fetlock joint, and aids in the rebound effect, which helps each foot leave the ground and allows the horse to move efficiently.

The front legs of the horse are not connected to the body by bones (such as the human collarbones), but through the muscles of the shoulder and chest that suspend the horse's trunk between the shoulder blades; this complex of muscles is called the *shoulder sling*. These muscles include the *serratus group, rhomboideus, trapezius,* and *pectoral group*. These muscles are important in stabilizing the chest and shoulders during movement. When the lumbosacral joint is flexed, they also can help the horse lift the base of his neck, raising and arching the neck and shifting his balance upward and backward.

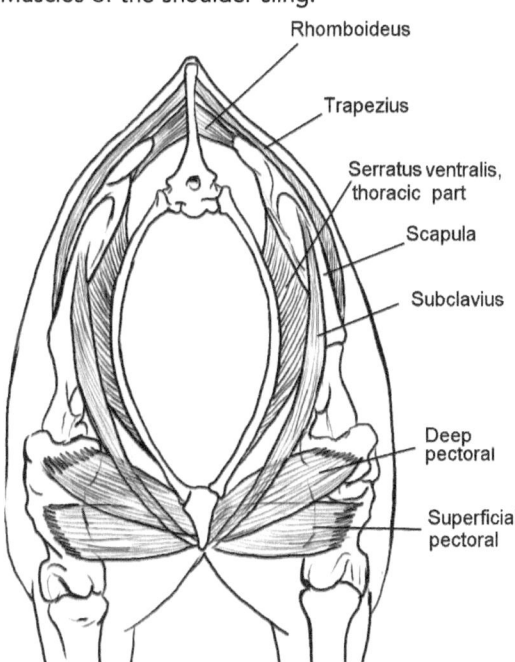

Muscles of the shoulder sling.

## The Circle of Muscles

The *circle of muscles* is a series of muscles and muscle groups that determine the horse's posture and use of his body when in movement, especially when carrying a rider. It is made up of certain deep hindquarter muscles, back muscles, neck muscles, and abdominal muscles, as well as some components of the shoulder sling.

In good movement, the circle of muscles works in harmony; each muscle group performs its function without becoming overstressed or underused. Poor movement and incorrect riding breaks up the smooth functioning of the circle of muscles and puts more stress on some muscle groups. This is less efficient, hampers the horse's athletic ability, and may eventually lead to soreness, poor muscle development, and unsoundness.

The muscles of the spine (several layers of deep muscles on each side of the back, connecting the vertebrae of the croup, loin, back, and neck) help to stabilize the spine and transmit the power (thrust) to move the horse forward. These muscles, along with the hindquarter muscles, create a *chain of muscles* on each side of the spine, from hind leg to poll.

The circle of muscles is attached to the framework of the skeleton at the spine, ribs, sternum, and pelvis. The *lumbosacral* joint is an important

The skeleton and dorsal ligament system.

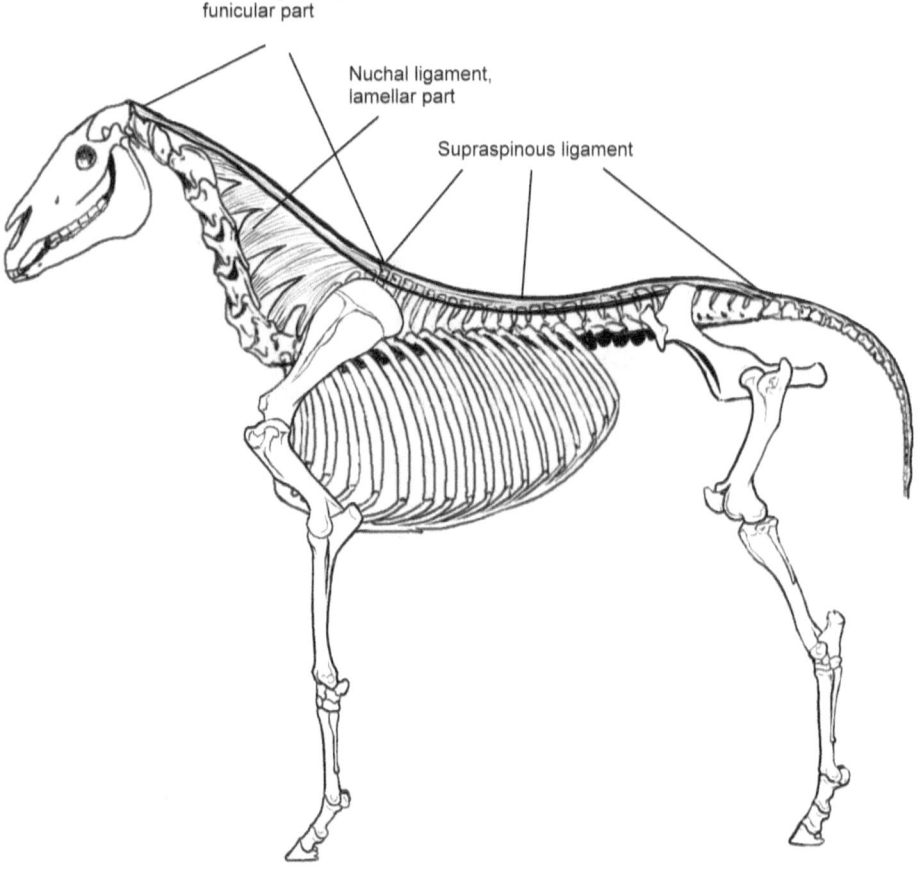

element that allows the pelvis to flex or tilt slightly forward, bringing the horse's hind legs and hindquarters underneath him.

The dorsal ligament system, consisting of the nuchal ligament, which runs from the withers to the poll and to each of the cervical vertebrae, and the supraspinous ligament, which runs along the top of the spinous processes of the dorsal, lumbar, and sacral vertebrae, is also an important structural component.

The movement at the base of the horse's neck is based on the movements of the last cervical vertebrae (C6 and C7) and the first thoracic vertebra (T1), as well as the surrounding muscles, whose actions are influenced by the tilt of the pelvis. The movement that occurs in this area allows the horse to stretch his head and neck out, which is necessary for balancing, correct stretching, and for the horse to reach forward into contact with the rider's hands.

The key components of the ring of muscles are the deep muscles of the top and base of the neck, the back, the hindquarters, and the abdominal muscles.

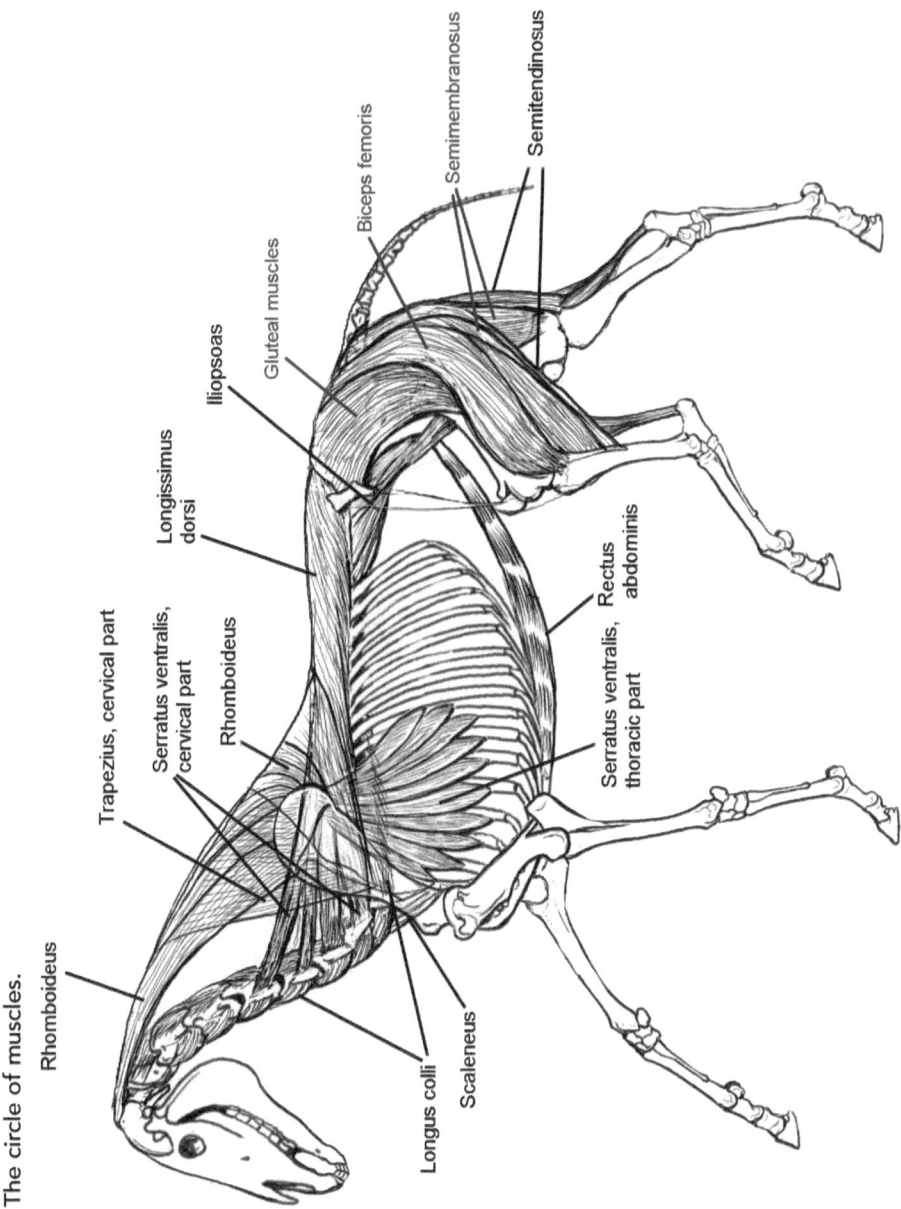

### Muscles of the neck:
- *Rhomboideus:* When it contracts, it causes the base of the neck to sink and brings the head up, resulting in a "ewe" or "swan" neck. However, if a horse has a tilted pelvis and engaged hind end, this muscle can help lift the base of the neck and also influences the scapula.

Muscles of the neck.

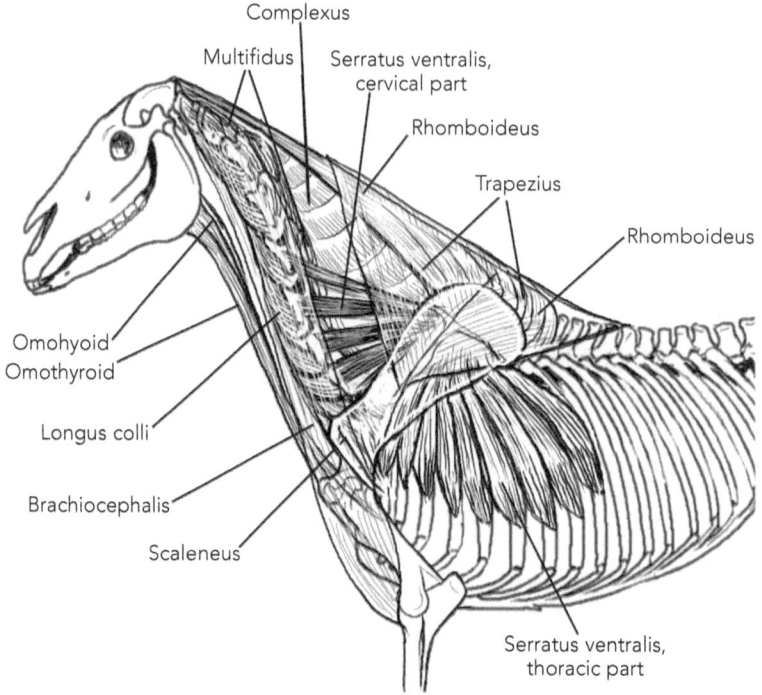

- *Cervical trapezius:* Similar effect as the rhomboideus, but it acts to a greater degree on the base of the neck and elevates the scapula.
- *Longus colli:* Runs along the underside of the cervical vertebra. When it contracts, it allows the base of the neck to elevate if the abdominal muscles are contracting and the hindquarters are engaged. It is weaker than the rhomboideus and cervical trapezius, so those muscles must be relatively relaxed for it to contract maximally.
- *Scaleneus:* Assists the *longus colli* in raising the base of the neck.
- *Serratus (ventralis and thoracis):* This is the primary muscle to counteract gravitational forces on the trunk and is a key player in the *shoulder sling*. It is the largest muscle of the forelimb and attaches to the inner side of the scapula. It lifts the base of the neck and withers when contracting, if the abdominal muscles are engaged.

**Muscles of the back, trunk, and hindquarters:**
- *Longissimus dorsi:* When a horse is at rest, if this muscle contracts, the back hollows. If the horse is in motion with a correctly tilted pelvis and engaged hind end, with contracting abdominal muscles, then it can actually lift the back and withers.

BIOMECHANICS AND MOVEMENT OF THE HORSE 9

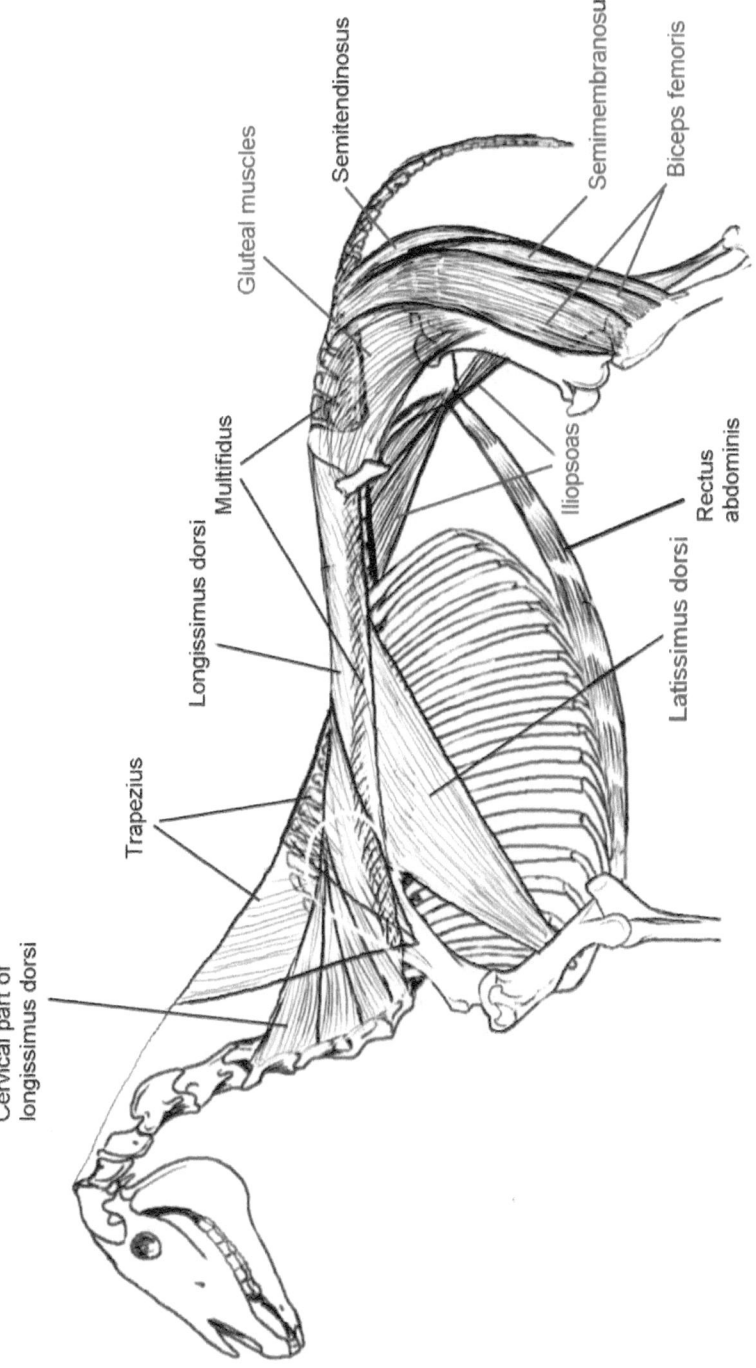

Muscles of the back, trunk, and hindquarters.

- *Iliopsoas:* When this muscle contracts, the bottom of the pelvis tips forward due to flexion of the lumbosacral joint, allowing the horse to engage his hindquarters.
- *Rectus abdominus:* When this muscle contracts, the back comes up because the underline of the horse contracts and the spine arches slightly (like doing an abdominal crunch).
- *Multifidus:* When this muscle contracts, it stabilizes the vertebrae during the dorsoventral (up and down) motion of the back.
- *Muscles of the hindquarters:* Involved in creating thrust.
- *Semitendinosus and semimembranosus muscles:* Provide an important connection from the coccygeal vertebra (base of the tail) and pelvis (ischium) to the back part of the hind limb by inserting on the back of the tibia. They help to stabilize the back end of the circle of muscles and create the thrust that propels the horse forward.
- *Biceps femoris muscle:* This muscle originates from the pelvis and coccygeal vertebra and inserts onto the patella and ligaments of the stifle joint. It is involved in flexion and extension of the stifle joint and extension of the hip joint necessary to create thrust.
- *Gluteal group:* These muscles are powerful hip extensors that are also important in creating thrust and stabilizing the hindquarters during collection and jumping.

**Dorsal ligament system:**
- *Nuchal ligament:* This fan-shaped ligament attaches the thoracic dorsal spinous processes (the withers) to each of the cervical vertebrae and the

Dorsal ligament system and effect on top line.

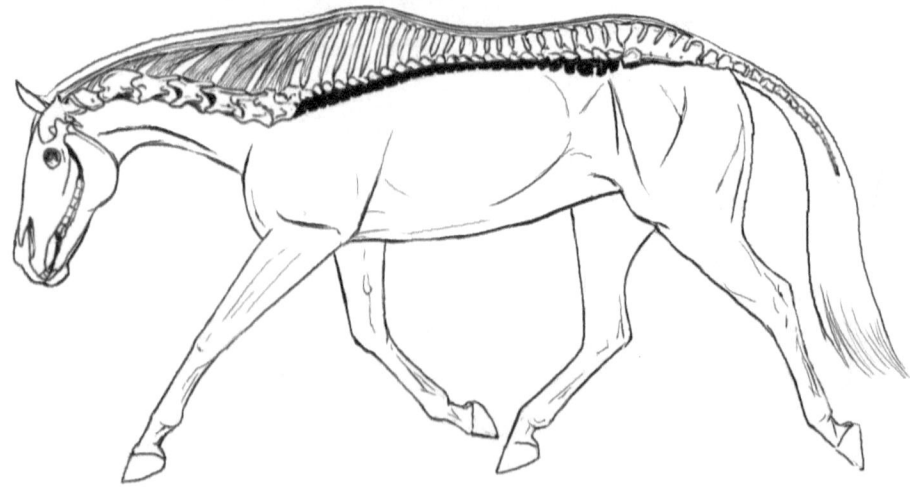

Major muscle groups in motion.

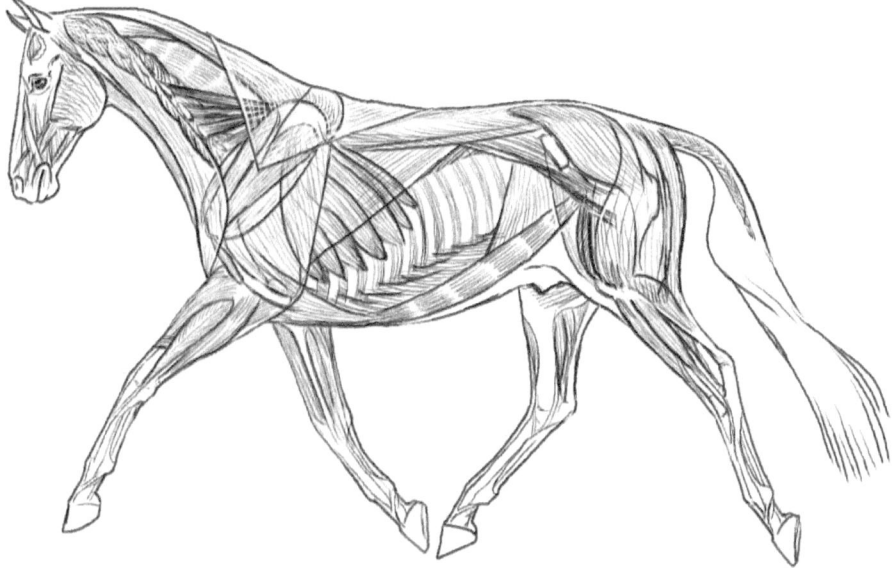

skull, to support the neck. When the head is lowered, it pulls on the bones of the withers and back, affecting the horse's balance.

- *Supraspinous ligament:* This ligament attaches at the first thoracic vertebra and extends back to the coccygeal vertebra (the base of the tail). It supports the back. It connects to the top fibrous portion of the nuchal ligament.
- *Sacral ligaments:* These ligaments attach to the pelvis so that it is directly attached to the spine.

# The Suspensory Apparatus: Creation of Potential Energy

The *suspensory apparatus* is a system of ligaments and tendons in the lower leg that support the fetlock joint as it extends during the *loading phase* of the stride. Because each limb carries most of the weight of the horse during the loading phase, the suspensory apparatus is necessary to prevent the fetlock joint from overextending or sinking too far toward the ground, which also helps absorb shock. The elastic structures of the suspensory apparatus contribute to a rebound effect, which helps the foot leave the ground at each stride. The suspensory apparatus is essential to the horse's ability to move and bear his own weight, even at a standstill. Injuries to the suspensory ligament and flexor tendons cause serious problems because the horse depends on these structures for normal weight bearing. One reason these structures are slow to heal is because they are under constant strain and load in a standing horse.

The suspensory apparatus is the same in the front and hind legs. Structures of the suspensory apparatus are:

- *Suspensory ligament:* Large ligament that runs down the back of the cannon bone from the back of the knee or hock (carpal or tarsal) bones to the proximal sesamoid bones, then separates into two lower extensor branches that run diagonally forward to the common digital extensor tendon.

- *Distal sesamoidean ligaments:* Ligaments that run down the back of the pastern, from the proximal sesamoid bones, which work with the suspensory ligament to support the fetlock. They attach along the palmar (back) aspect of the first and second phalanges (long and short pastern bones). (See Chapter 9, "Systems of the Horse," page 345.)

- *Deep digital flexor tendon:* This inner tendon runs behind the carpal bones, behind the fetlock joint, and below and under (*distal and*

Tendons and ligaments of the lower foreleg. Structures of the lower hind leg.

Fore limb

Hind limb

*palmar/plantar* to) the navicular bone, fastening to the underside of the coffin bone. It is a continuation of the *deep digital flexor muscle* located above the carpal joint (knee) or tarsus (hock).
- *Superficial digital flexor tendon:* This outer tendon runs from behind the carpal bones, behind the fetlock joint, and attaches to both the long and short pasterns. It is a continuation of the *superficial digital flexor muscle* located above the carpal joint.
- *Proximal sesamoid bones:* Two small bones at the back of the fetlock joint that form a "pulley" through which the flexor tendons pass behind the fetlock joint.

## The Phases of a Stride

A *stride* is a sequence within a gait during which all four legs complete a step. Each leg completes the following cycle of movement:

- *Landing (impact):* The hoof touches the ground and begins to receive the weight of the horse.
- *Loading:* The horse's body continues to move forward and his center of gravity passes over the hoof. This is when the fetlock joint fully extends, putting strain on the flexor tendons and suspensory ligament.
- *Stance (support):* The *flexor structures* (muscles and tendons) pull the limb back into a *normal weight-bearing position*. The horse's center of gravity moves ahead of the hoof.
- *Breakover (thrust):* The hoof begins to leave the ground at the heel, and the weight-bearing surface shifts toward the toe. The deep digital flexor tendon is still being stretched at the beginning of this phase, as it helps to rotate the coffin bone at breakover (the moment when the toe of the hoof "breaks over" and leaves the ground). The upper joints of the limb flex to facilitate lifting the hoof.
- *Swing:* The limb swings through the air and straightens in preparation for landing.

# Biomechanics of the Dressage Horse

The biomechanics of the horse is the study of how a horse moves. It is a study of the gravitational forces exerted on the muscles and the skeleton of the horse in motion, and how muscles, bones, tendons, and ligaments work together to produce movement with and without the influence of a rider.

Phases of a stride (hind leg).

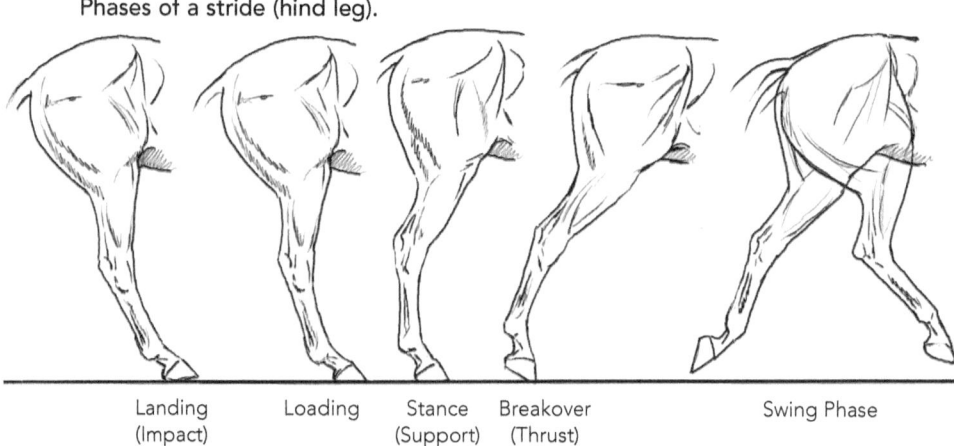

| Landing (Impact) | Loading | Stance (Support) | Breakover (Thrust) | Swing Phase |

Riders and trainers must understand biomechanics in a practical way in order to train and ride horses to make them stronger and to achieve their best performance without causing damage, pain, or stress for the horse. Understanding the biomechanics of the horse also helps the rider better understand the correct and most effective timing of the aids.

## The Forequarters

The horse's potential energy, stored in the forelegs, has an important role in regulating his overall balance. The energy stored during the *loading phase* of the stride is unloaded during the *swing phase* of the stride.

The angle of the entire leg relative to the ground at the moment of the *breakover phase* determines the overall direction that the energy from the loading phase is directed, and the amount of energy available for the swing phase. For example, if the foreleg is at or in front of a vertical line relative to the ground, the recoil is upward and backward, shifting the horse's balance upward and backward toward the hind end. However, if the foreleg is behind the vertical at the moment of recoil, the push is forward, shifting the horse's balance to the forehand. If the forelegs do not push sufficiently against the ground at the right moment, the front feet stay on the ground too long, so that it appears that the horse rolls over his front feet and legs onto the forehand.

Top dressage horses have more elbow flexion during the protraction phase of the forelimb, which helps to elevate the carpus. Additionally, these horses have a greater degree of retraction of the forelimb, thus taking longer to retract their forelimbs before entering the *stance phase*.

The front legs of the horse are connected to the body by muscles of the shoulder and chest, called the *shoulder sling*. When these muscles relax and

Action of forelegs against the ground.

Vertical: recoil upward and back

Behind vertical: pushing forward

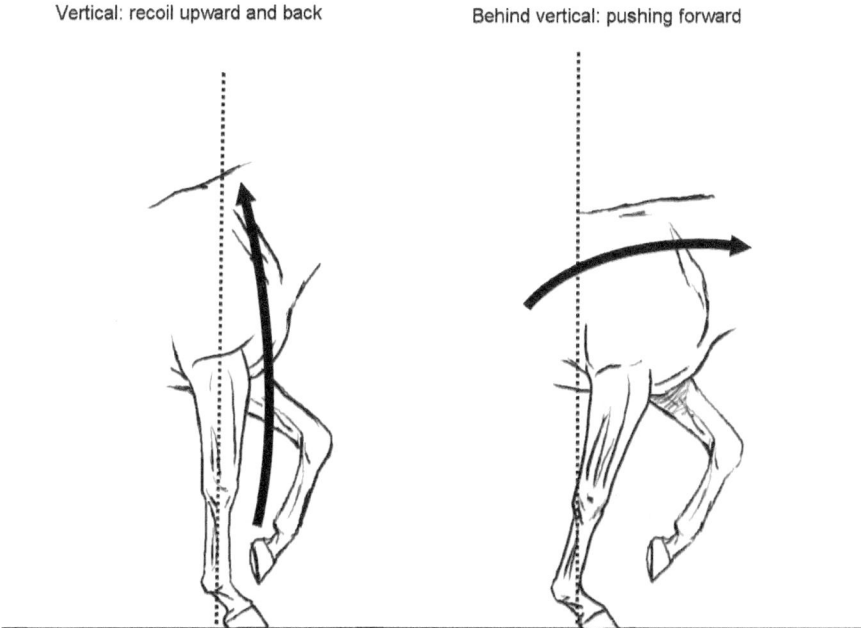

Effect of contraction of shoulder sling muscles.

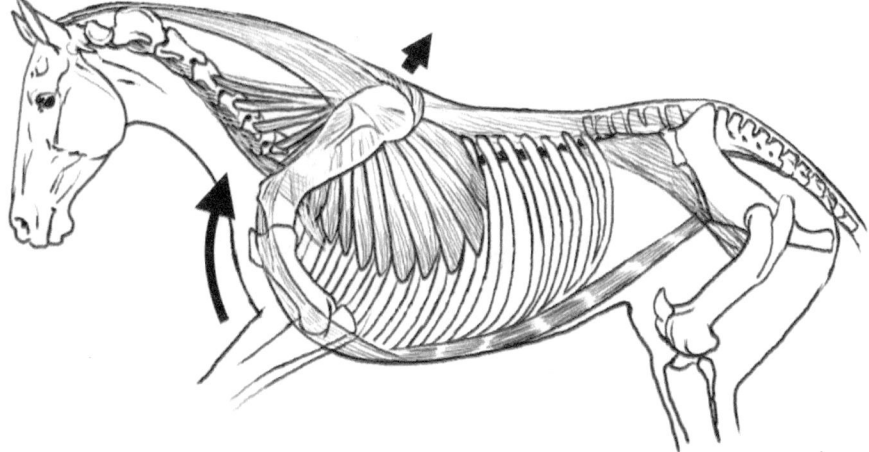

lengthen, the withers sink and the horse's outline appears to be more hollow, downhill, and heavy on the forehand. When these muscles contract, the rib cage is lifted, raising the withers and giving the horse a more "uphill" and balanced position. This is especially important in the gaits containing a moment of suspension, such as the trot and canter, and in collection. The actions of these muscles, along with the suspensory apparatus, also determine how easy the trot is to ride. This elevation of the forehand is more easily obtained if the hindquarters and abdominal muscles are active and engaged.

## The Hindquarters

In addition to storing potential energy in the suspensory apparatus, as in the front legs, the hind legs store energy through *engagement*, the bending of the hip, stifle, and hock joints as the leg bears the weight of the horse in the *stance phase* of the stride. This is not the same as *hock action*, which refers to the flexion of the hocks in the air, as in a Hackney trot, or *reach*, which refers to how far under the hind leg swings, as in a racing Standardbred. Because of the ability of hind legs to provide engagement, they are able to generate thrust and impulsion through the release of energy during the transition from the weight-bearing phases of the stride to the swing phase. Therefore, a horse must have engagement in order to produce *impulsion* (or *thrust*).

During the *loading phase* of the stride in the hind limb, the hip, stifle, and hock joints flex, while the fetlock joint extends, causing the leg to compress and absorb concussion. The flexion of the upper joints should be maintained through the *stance phase* of the stride in order to create the greatest amount of energy for the *swing phase*. The amount of energy stored (engagement)

Engagement of the hindquarters.

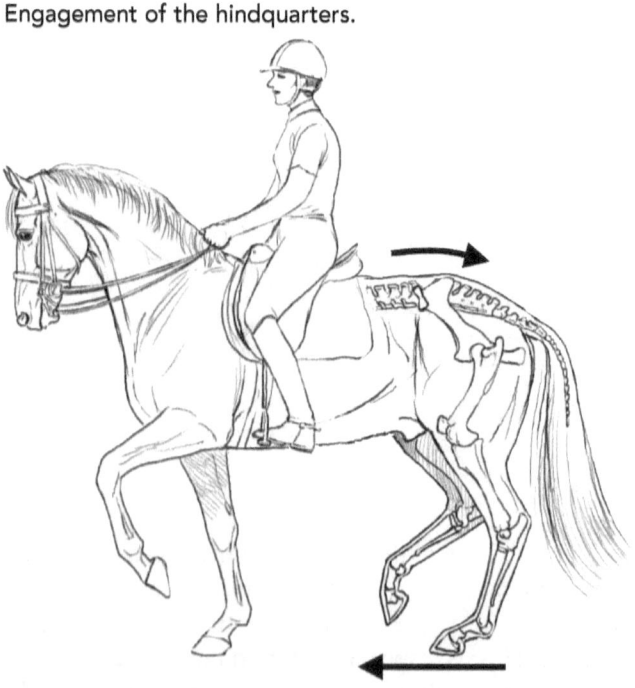

Good and poor use of the hindquarters.

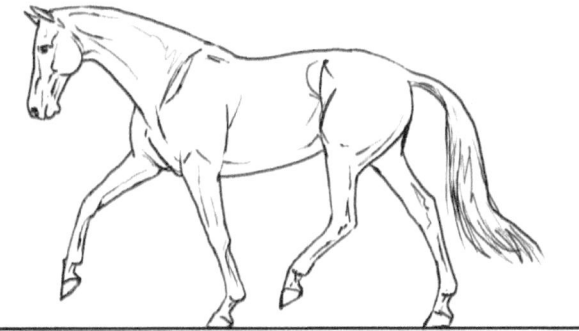

Horse using hindquarters well, with hind legs stepping well under body

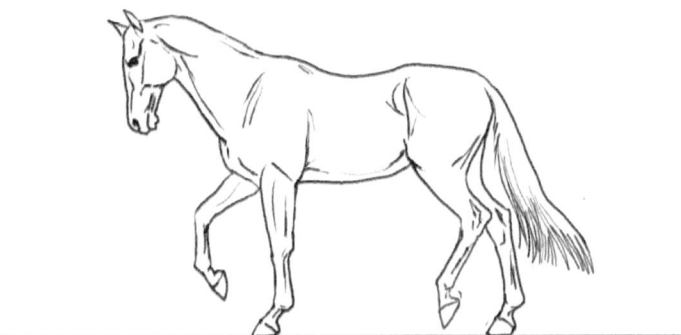

Poor use of hindquarters, with hollow back ans short stride

determines the degree of impulsion the horse moves forward with. Horses can also add stored energy by tilting the pelvis, using the *psoas group* of muscles to flex the *lumbosacral joint* (see Chapter 9). Tilting the pelvis brings the hind legs farther under the body (*protraction*) and closer to the center of gravity, which adds power to the stride and improves the horse's balance. At the same time, the back muscles are stretched and activated to stabilize the energy created by the hind limbs.

As the hip, stifle, and hock joints begin to extend during the *breakover phase*, the hoof pushes against the ground to generate propulsion for the *swing phase*. The release of energy during the breakover phase propels the horse's whole body forward and, to some degree, upward. As the horse's muscles become stronger to allow greater bending of the joints, greater energy can be stored (increased engagement) that ultimately allows the horse to create more upward energy, as required in collected gaits.

For dressage horses, core stability is important for attaining the collected gaits. The key hindquarter stabilizing muscles (for example, *biceps femoris* and *middle gluteals*) should be well developed, whereas muscles more responsible for forward thrust (for example, *semitendinosus* and *semimembranosus)* are less developed. To obtain elevation of the forequarters and collection of the hindquarters, ideally the hind hoof should contact the ground while the hoof is in front of the hip and at the end of the protraction phase of the stride. This is possible if the pelvis is tilted forward by the psoas group of muscles flexing the lumbosacral joint. This allows for the abdominals to contract, and the long muscles of the back, including the multifidus, to lift the back, further stabilizing the core.

As the horse becomes stronger, the muscles of the hind limb can work faster, shortening the stance phase and lengthening the swing phase of the stride, leading to gaits with increased elasticity and suspension as required in the medium gaits.

## The Back

The horse's back connects and coordinates the hind legs (the "motor") with the forelegs. The back consists of the vertebrae and ligaments of the spine and the back muscles (see Chapter 9). The spine has limited lateral (side-to-side) mobility, but can rotate slightly, which gives the rider the feeling of bend in the rib cage. The back also has limited *longitudinal* (up-and-down) mobility, but can give the feeling of rounding and lifting when the abdominal muscles are contracted, the lumbosacral joint flexes slightly, the top line muscles are appropriately and rhythmically contracted, and the *deep epaxial spinal stabilizing muscles* (*multifidus* and *sacrocaudalis lateralis*) are activated. In this way, the back biomechanically acts in a bow-and-string manner, with the vertebrae being the bow and the *rectus abdominis* tensing the bow to flex the back. The circle of muscles and the dorsal ligament system allow the horse to "carry" himself in motion.

Working "through the back" or "over the back" involves a number of factors, including:

- Engagement of the haunches and hind legs
- Rhythmic contraction of both the large and deep epaxial spinal stabilizing muscles of the back, and the support of the abdominal muscles, which lift the back
- Swinging of the back with slight rotation from side to side
- Upward thrust of the front legs
- Stretching forward of the poll, using the dorsal ligament system

In summary, the many parts of the horse (forelegs, back, neck, and hind legs) play a part in the way the horse moves. The bones, ligaments, tendons, and muscles work together to create movement. While muscles are the structures that are most easily developed through training, they are not the only component needed for the horse to move well—all of the parts of the horse must work in harmony and be developed, strengthened, and kept healthy.

You can find more information about the biomechanics of the horse in books, in DVDs, and online. A better knowledge of the factors that create equine movement can only improve the riding, training, teaching, and judging of horses.

## Biomechanics of a Jumping Horse

Jumping horses, particularly in the cross-country phase of eventing, have more need for thrust from the hindquarters than dressage horses. Therefore, the *semimembranosus* and *semitendinosis* muscles are more developed in jumping horses, whereas the *biceps femoris* and *middle gluteal* muscles are less developed than in upper-level dressage horses.

To obtain this forward thrust in jumping horses, ideally the hind hoof contacts the ground while the hoof is directly under the hip and in the retraction phase of the stride. In show jumpers, just before the fence (particularly when the height of the fence is above 1 meter or 3 feet 3 inches) there is a brief period where the engagement and collection needed is similar to that of a dressage horse; however, unlike the dressage horse, this degree of collection is not sustained for long periods of time.

Most jumping horses jump easily from the canter or gallop, where the jump itself occurs during the *suspension phase* of the stride; however, horses can also jump from the other gaits.

Selected muscles important for jumping include:

**Neck and forequarters:**
  *Serratus ventralis, cervicis,* and *thoracis:* These muscles raise the neck when the front limbs are flexed going over the jump and help to support the trunk and forehand of the horse while landing.
  *Triceps:* This muscle in the back of the horse's arm extends the elbow and is important for energy generation in the jumping phase. Good jumpers usually have a well-developed triceps muscle.

**Back and hindquarters:**
  *Longissimus dorsi* and *ileocostalis:* These are long muscles that lie alongside the spine and help the horse round his back over the jump. The saddle rests primarily on the *longissimus dorsi*.
  *Middle gluteal:* This muscle extends from the top of the horse's hindquarters to the *longissimus dorsi*, in the lumbar area. It is very

important in helping the horse to raise itself up on its hind legs during the takeoff phase of the jump.

*Iliacus* and *iliopsoas (psoas group):* The *iliacus* is important for hip flexion in takeoff, over the fence and the first departure stride. *Iliopsoas* is important for flexion of the hip and hind limb protraction on landing.

*Semimembranosus* and *semitendinosus:* These muscles are part of the hamstring group that run along the back of the horse's hind leg and inner thigh. They are important for thrust in the galloping horse. These muscles also help flex the stifle, allowing the hock to flex as well via the *reciprocal apparatus*, so that the horse can jump cleanly over the fence.

Phases of the jump include the second and first approach strides, takeoff, suspension, landing, and the first departure stride. The quality of the first three phases largely determines the success of the jumping effort itself.

**Approach and takeoff:**

The last stride of the approach is shorter and quick when compared to the second approach stride, and it is sometimes a four-beat stride. This is when the horse stretches its neck downward. In the last approach stride, the horse starts to move the forehand upward, slowing the forward motion by braking with the front feet, thus getting ready for takeoff. As the front feet leave the ground, the head and neck are raised. This is followed by both hind hooves contacting the ground simultaneously and equally pushing off from about the same distance from the fence, allowing the horse to move upward and forward. When the hind legs line up together and push nearly simultaneously, there is greater thrust than when the hind legs are separated with one behind the other (called *leaving one leg behind*). This lining up of the hind legs during takeoff makes it easy for the horse to change leads over a jump.

The *stance phase* of the hind limbs is longer in the takeoff part of the jump to allow for greater generation of power. Poor jumpers have higher forces exerted against the ground on both takeoff and landing, which may contribute to earlier wear and tear on the joints.

**Suspension:**

During the jump suspension *(flight) phase*, there is a longer-than-normal stride length in order to clear the jump, compared to the canter strides before or immediately after the jump itself.

During suspension, the forelegs fold to clear the obstacle. This may be done in two ways: The shoulder blade rotates, bringing the knees up in front of the chest, where they are flexed tightly and evenly, or the knees may be flexed but brought backward, with the hooves coming close to or even

# BIOMECHANICS AND MOVEMENT OF THE HORSE

Phases of the jump.

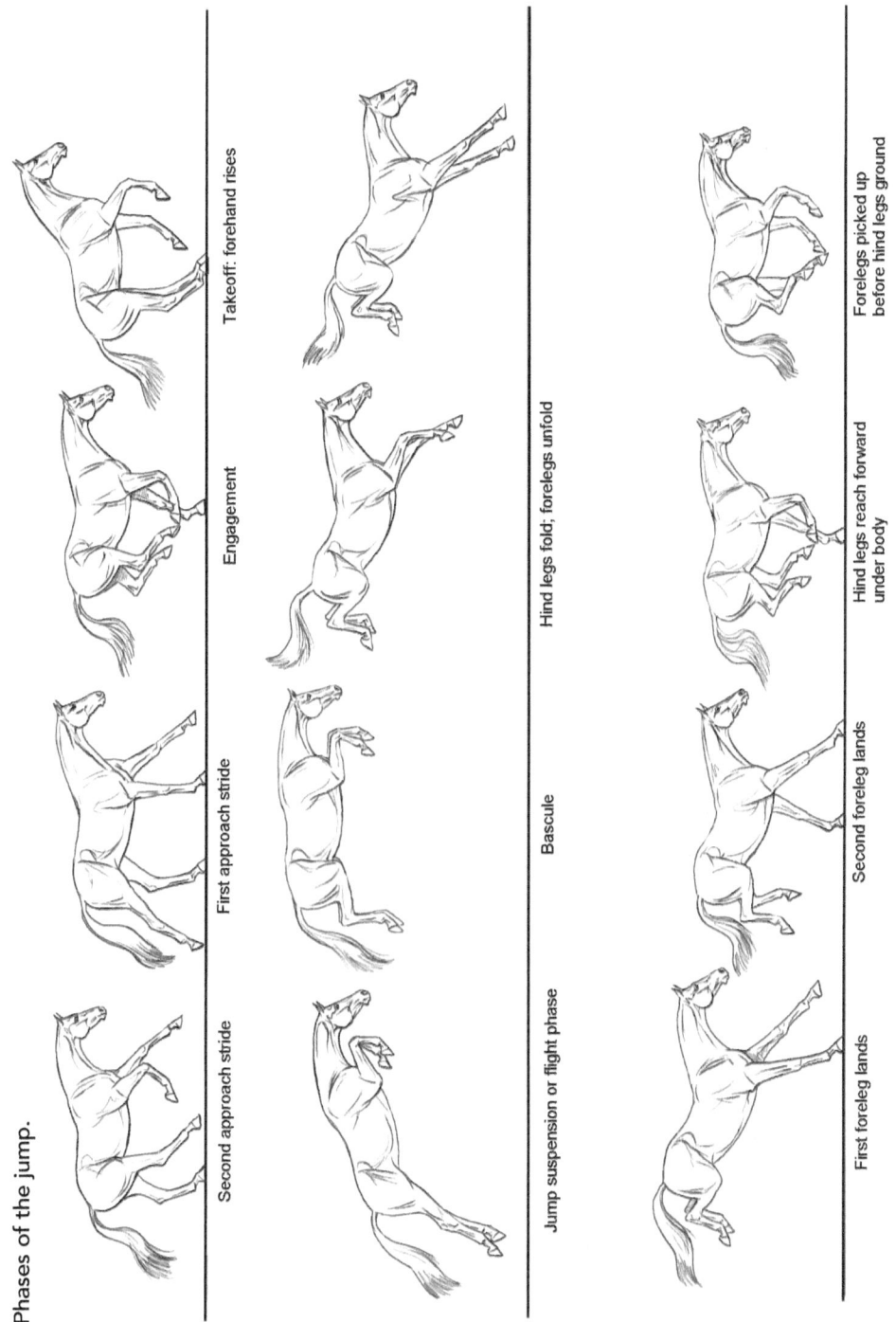

striking the underside of the chest. The former technique is preferred in show hunters, while the latter is often performed by show jumpers, some of whom must wear a chest protector on the girth to prevent injury from their hooves striking the chest.

The hind legs are extended as they leave the ground; as the hindquarters rise, the hind legs flex at the stifle, hock, and fetlock joints, folding the hind legs behind the body.

During the flight phase, the horse stretches his neck forward and lifts and rounds his back in an arc or *bascule*. A horse may show a greater or lesser degree of bascule in a jump, depending on the height and shape of the obstacle, his takeoff point, the rider's balance and influence, and the individual horse's jumping ability and technique. In general, the ability to jump with a good bascule is an important trait in a good jumper and is an important factor to consider when selecting, training, and riding jumping horses.

In the later phase of suspension, the forelegs unfold and reach forward, preparing to land. The hind legs are folded at their utmost as they pass over the highest point of the obstacle. Sometimes a horse may make acrobatic efforts during suspension (reaching forward with the forelegs, bringing the hind legs forward under the body, or twisting) in an effort to avoid hitting an obstacle.

As the horse passes over the last element of the obstacle, his body angles downward and his forelegs reach out toward the ground, while his hind legs remain folded.

**Landing and departure:**
During landing, the forelegs land one after the other; a longer time between the forelegs landing is correlated with a clean jump without hitting the obstacle. The trailing forelimb (the second to land) has the highest forces when landing, which may explain why horses prefer to land on a particular lead to minimize pain, as the forelimbs take most of the impact from landing. The horse's mass pivots over the trailing foreleg as his hind legs are flexed and engaged under his body. The horse rounds his back and engages his hindquarters as his hind legs reach forward toward the ground; it is important the rider stays in balance at this critical point.

Both forelegs are picked up before the first hind leg hits the ground. However, the hind hooves come close to the forelegs, so if a foreleg is delayed in breakover and leaving the ground (as in heavy mud or holding ground), the hind hoof may strike the bulbs of the heel or the back of the foreleg (*overreaching*), resulting in an injury or pulling off a shoe. For this reason, horses often wear bell boots, tendon boots, or other leg protection when jumping.

During the first departure stride, the hind legs push the horse forward in a four-beat rhythm while balance is regained. This stride is shorter in duration; it is actually half of a canter or gallop stride and is called a *half bound*. The following stride is the first complete canter or gallop stride.

# The Gaits

Generally, sport horses that are considered to have good gaits take longer strides, with greater suspension, that occur less frequently (that is, long strides rather than short, quick steps).

## The Walk

The walk has four evenly spaced beats. The sequence of footfalls in the walk is left hind, left fore, right hind, right fore. In the walk the horse always has one or two feet on the ground, so the walk has no moment of suspension, and therefore does not have true *impulsion*. However, the walk should have energy, activity, and should cover ground. When a horse takes long strides at the walk, he should "overstep" (for example, the hind feet step past the hoof prints left by the front feet on the same side).

The purity of the walk is defined by the evenly spaced four-beat rhythm of the footfalls. The counts should be equally spaced as 1, 2, 3, 4, not 1, —2,3,—4; or 1,2, —3,4.

**The goals of the walk are:**
- The regularity of the four-beat rhythm.
- The activity and variety of the lengths of steps in the different walks.
- Movement that flows through the whole body (back, shoulders, and neck).

**Faults in the walk:**
- Loss of pure rhythm, from a slight irregularity of footfalls to a *lateral walk* (where the rhythm of the walk approaches a two-beat gait, and the fore and hind legs on one side of the body appear to move almost together as a camel walks, similar to pacing). In a lateral walk, there is no clear "V" shape formed by the front and hind feet on the same side.
- Lack of tracking up or overstepping (may indicate a short or restricted hind stride, lack of thoroughness, or reduced swing in the back). This may also be due to the horse's conformation (for example, long back or short legs).
- Lack of reach of forelegs (freedom in shoulders), even if accompanied by overstep, from tension in the shoulders.
- Lazy, sluggish walk.

Sequence of the walk.

- Short, uneven, or unlevel (steps of varying height) steps.
- Lack of oscillation of the neck, back, and/or rib cage, from tightness or restriction by the rider.

Schooling of the walk should be included in the work. Walking over correctly spaced cavaletti will encourage the horse to lift his legs and reach in the shoulders and hindquarters. A relaxed, free walk in the open also encourages the horse to develop a more ground-covering walk.

## The Trot

The trot is a two-beat gait of alternate diagonal legs (left hind/right fore and right hind/left fore), separated by a moment of suspension. The trot should show free, active, symmetric, and regular steps (regularity).

The quality of the trot is judged by the regularity and elasticity of the steps, the cadence (even rhythm), and impulsion in both collection and extension. This quality originates from a supple back, well-engaged hindquarters, and the ability to maintain lateral and longitudinal balance.

**The goals of the trot are:**
- A pure two-beat rhythm with clear moments of suspension.
- Balance and coordination between fore and hind limb movement.

# BIOMECHANICS AND MOVEMENT OF THE HORSE

Sequence of the trot.

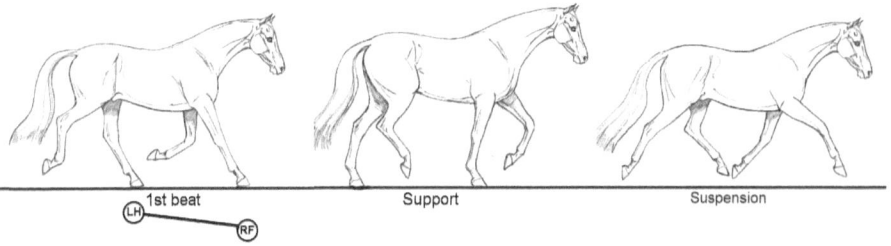

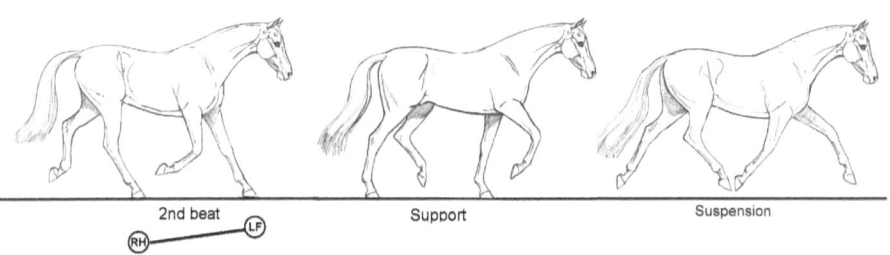

- Reaching leg appears to strike the ground before the cannon bone reaches the vertical.
- The quality of the trot improves when it includes increased scope, reach, range of motion and elasticity, and/or longer periods of suspension.

**Faults in the trot:**
- Minimal suspension—gait appears flat without a distinct swing phase.
- Feet are grounded too long behind body/pivot point (that is, the legs rotate too far behind vertical before leaving the ground—horse pushes out behind).
- Reaching legs strike the ground too near or at the vertical during the impact phase of the stride, resulting in a short stride.
- Front and hind limbs not parallel (fail to cover ground).
- "Broken diagonal," unlevelness or unevenness—dissociation of diagonal legs so that one of the diagonal legs visibly grounds before the other, causing the trot to lose a two-beat rhythm. May indicate that the horse is too much on the forehand, lameness, tension, or *rein lameness*

Faulty trots.

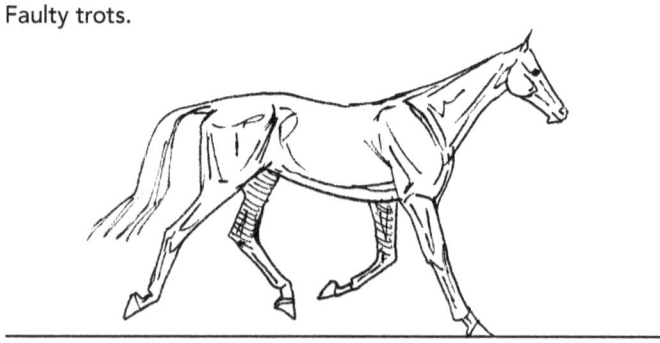

Irregular trot, foreleg landing first

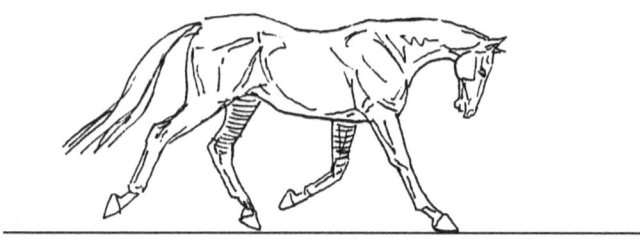

Irregular trot, running on the forehand

- Little articulation of joints.
- Slow, lazy steps or short, quick steps.

Working over cavaletti can be useful to develop length of stride *suspension* (air time), and to help the horse use his body.

## The Canter

The canter is a three-beat gait with suspension and leads. In a right-lead canter, the sequence of footfalls is left hind, left fore/right hind together (*diagonal pair*), right fore, followed by a moment of suspension. The left-lead canter sequence is right hind, left hind/right fore (*diagonal pair*), left fore, moment of suspension. The canter should always have light, cadenced, and regular strides, and should begin without hesitation. The quality of the canter is judged by the regularity and lightness of the steps, the uphill tendency, a cadence originating from acceptance of the bridle with a supple poll, the engagement of the hindquarters with an active hock action, and the ability to maintain the same rhythm and a natural balance during transitions in the gait. The horse should always remain straight on straight lines and properly bent on curved lines.

# BIOMECHANICS AND MOVEMENT OF THE HORSE

**The goals of the canter are:**
- Purity of rhythm—on the second beat, the diagonal pair of legs should appear to strike the ground simultaneously.
- One air phase (of *suspension*) in each stride, after the leading front leg leaves the ground.
- Oscillation of the body between hind and forelimbs is part of the canter mechanics. The head may nod down slightly as the weight is transferred over the forelegs. The rider should take care that the aids that influence the balance are applied at the correct time in the stride, so that they don't restrict the normal head movement.
- The quality of the canter includes scope, reach, range of motion, and elasticity.

**What we want to see in the canter:**
- The inside foreleg should show reach, with the forelegs well separated.
- The hind legs should also show separation, with the outside hind leg appearing to reach past the inner hind leg while still in the air, but before the inside hind leg strikes the ground.
- The feet should leave the ground soon after the cannon bones pass the vertical (the moment when the forelegs are pushing up to shift the balance to the rear).

Sequence of the canter.

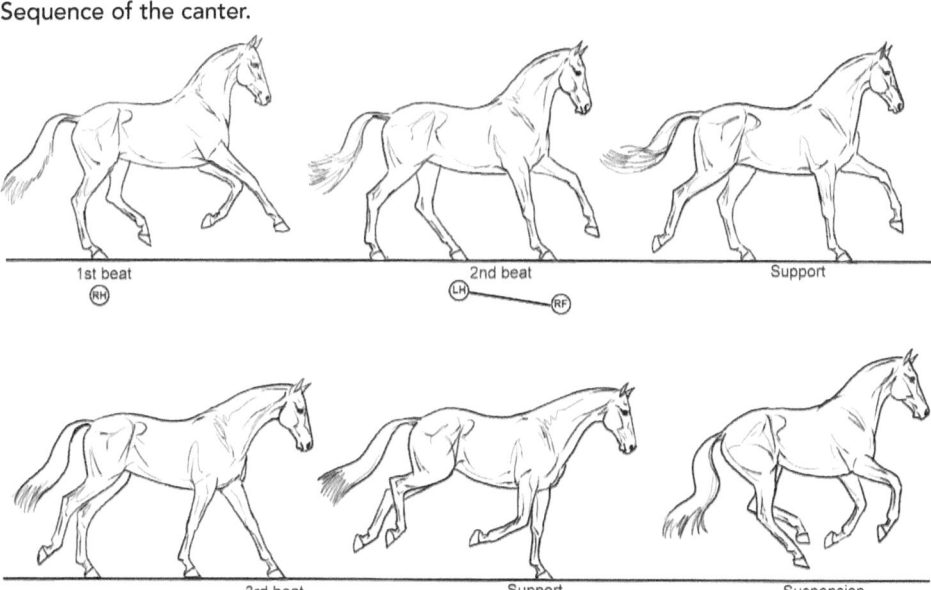

**Faults in the canter:**
- Insufficient suspension phase so gait appears flat (exception: with greater collection the hind legs step under sooner, so the suspension phase becomes smaller).
- Clarity of rhythm lost (loss of cadence), usually because of loss of balance or tension in the back or neck.
- Rolling over front legs onto the forehand, because the horse is not using front legs to push forehand up.
- Excessive rocking movement—some head and neck movement is normal, but too much indicates added weight on the forehand or tension in the neck and back.

**Disunited or cross-canter:**

A *disunited canter* (or cross-canter) occurs when the horse is on one lead in the front legs and the other lead in the hind legs. The order of footfalls may be left hind, right hind/right fore together (lateral pair), left fore, or right hind, left hind/left fore together (lateral pair), right fore.

A disunited canter (or *rotary canter*) is an uncoordinated gait that makes turning and lateral balance difficult, although a horse can jump from a disunited canter. It often occurs when a horse makes an attempt at a flying change but changes only in the front legs. It is a serious fault in the canter.

# The Gallop

The gallop is a four-beat gait with suspension and leads. It is the horse's natural speed gait. In a right-lead gallop, the sequence of footfalls is left hind, right hind, left fore, right fore, followed by a moment of suspension. The left-lead gallop sequence is right hind, left hind, right fore, left fore, followed by a moment of suspension.

Disunited canter.

Sequence of the gallop (left lead).

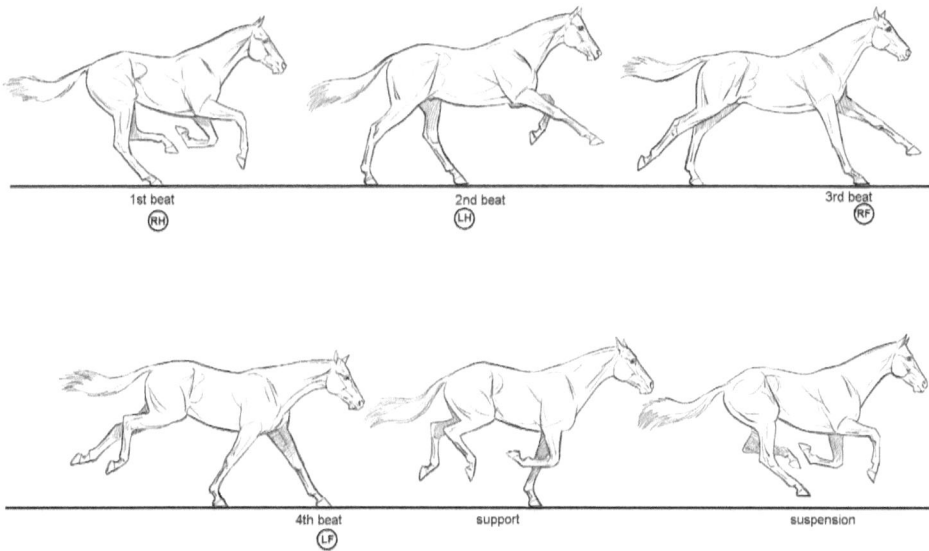

The balance of the gallop is more on the forehand than in the canter; however, a gallop should be rhythmic and balanced, with the hind legs reaching well under the body for speed, power, and balance, especially in event horses, foxhunters, and other horses that gallop and/or jump over rolling natural terrain. A tired or unbalanced horse leans more and more on his forehand as he gallops, making him too heavily balanced on the forehand. This can make it difficult for him to make transitions, turns, shift his balance, or jump safely.

## Movement Problems

There are several *syndromes* (sets of symptoms) of faulty movement that result in inefficient gaits that are hard to ride and may even cause unsoundness. These may be caused by a horse's physical weakness, poor use of the body, unsoundness, conformation problems (see Chapter 10), and especially by incorrect riding and training, and overstressing immature horses. Good riding and training can do much to improve the horse's strength, muscle development, and athletic use of his body.

## On the Forehand

A horse is said to be *on the forehand* when he moves with poor engagement, carrying too much weight on his front legs and making little use of his sling muscles. This can make him clumsy and he may lean on the bit and pull, depending on the rider to support this unbalance. Some horses compensate by raising their head and neck as a method of catching their balance. Moving too much on the forehand is common in green and underdeveloped horses that have not yet learned to balance themselves under a rider; "overbuilt" horses (high in the hips and low in the forehand); weak, tired, or lazy horses; and poorly ridden horses.

There are two common variations of being on the forehand:

**Inactive:** The horse moves slowly or strides short with his hind legs, does not use his hindquarters correctly to reach under his center of gravity, and has a low head carriage. This is also evidenced by a sluggish walk and trot and canter that lack suspension. The horse will easily break down into a lower gait when not constantly reminded by the rider.

To improve, sensitize the horse to lighter but more effective leg aids, then use leg aids and half-halts to ask for balance and energy, engage the hind legs, and rebalance the horse. The goal is for the horse to carry himself, which requires the rider to maintain her own balance and use effective half-halts. Do not allow the horse to lean on your hand, but encourage him to balance up and support himself.

**Too hurried/quick:** The horse does not accept the half-halts and becomes quicker or more hurried in his strides (called *running*). This also tends to make him shorten his strides. These horses are most likely to go with a high head and neck to help their balance, while some over-curl the neck and go behind the vertical, making half-halts even more difficult. A horse that is running or hurried may lose the clarity of the gait rhythm, and his tempo is often too quick and irregular.

To improve, slow the pace, steady the tempo, and work to re-establish physical and mental relaxation. Straight lines tend to encourage running, so it is better to work on bending lines and circles. Use half-halts in rhythm with the gait and frequent transitions to help the horse rebalance himself. When the pace becomes slower and steadier, use tactful leg aids to encourage better engagement of the hind legs, making corrections if the horse starts to hurry again.

## Inverted (Hollow, Above the Bit)

The horse moves with a stiff, hollow back; a high head; short, quick, and irregular steps; and poor engagement. He throws his head up and pokes his nose out, making correct contact impossible. His movement is stiff, irregular, and difficult to ride, and instead of walking he may jig or pace. His stiff, hollow back may cause soreness in his back and hind legs, which adds to his tension and makes him more difficult to control. This is common in hot, nervous horses that are overexcited, but the problem can also be caused by pain or fear, an ill-fitting saddle, unsoundness, rider stiffness, poor seat and/

## Faulty Movement Syndromes

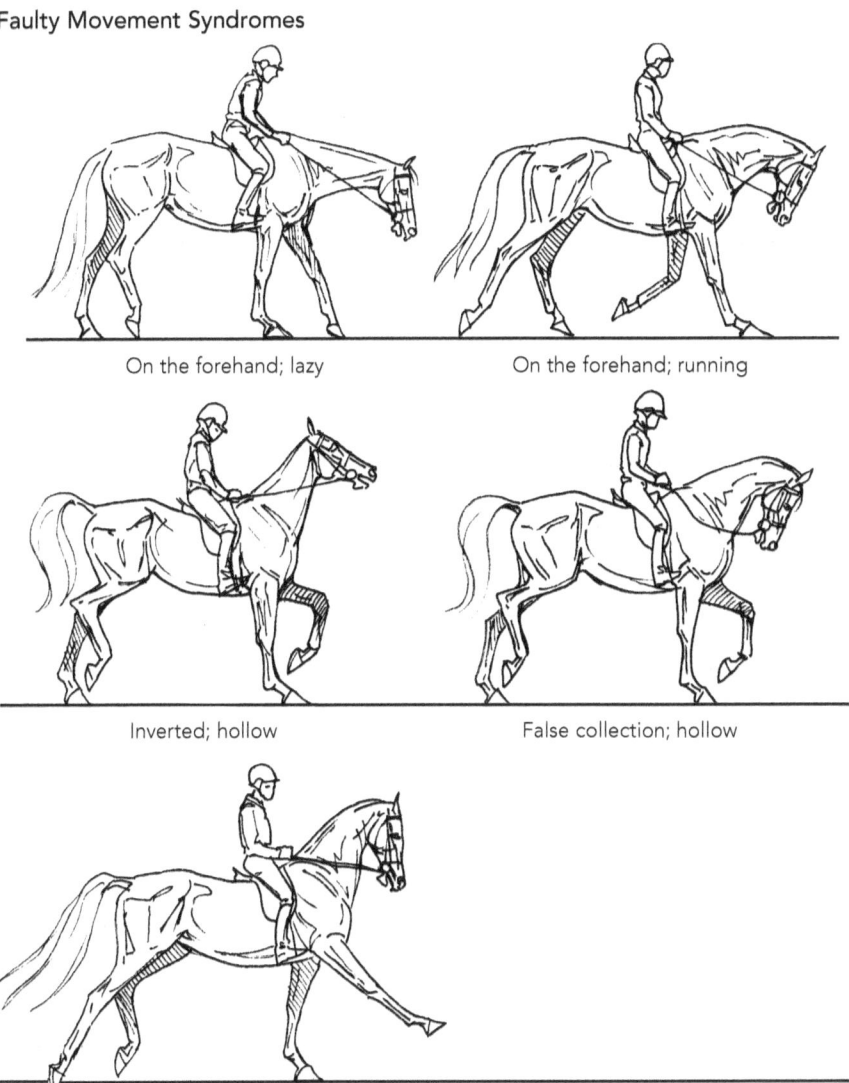

On the forehand; lazy

On the forehand; running

Inverted; hollow

False collection; hollow

False extension

or hands, or in young, undeveloped horses that are uncomfortable and unbalanced under the rider's weight.

To improve, work on restoring calmness, comfort, and better rhythm so the horse can unlock his tense muscles and make better use of his hind legs and his circle of muscles. This will bring his back up and allow him to reach forward to the bit. Just getting the head down is not the answer, and may result in a false frame if forced. The rider must ride in balance and use tactful aids to slow and steady the tempo, then ask for longer strides; his hands must be gentle and sympathetic, especially when the horse begins to take contact with the bit. Check the saddle fit and make sure the bit is mild and comfortable. Cavaletti work (if done calmly and in rhythm) can help the horse learn to engage his hind legs, round his back, and stretch his neck out and down.

## False Collection (Hollow, Behind the Bit)

The horse moves with short, irregular strides and poor engagement. His back is tense and hollow, and he draws back from the bit, retracting his neck and evading contact. Like the inverted horse, he may take pacey steps instead of walking and is stiff, uncomfortable, and difficult to ride; his trot becomes irregular and his canter may have four beats. At faster gaits, he may over-flex his neck and drop his chin against his chest, making control difficult. This problem is often caused by misguided efforts to force a horse into collection by working from front to back or through the misuse of severe bits, draw reins, or pulling hands. This problem is similar to that of the inverted horse in that the horse needs to relax, find his rhythm, and restore his engagement and use of his circle of muscles. However, it is harder to cure when a horse has learned an incorrect response: to retract his neck, over-flex, and withdraw from the bit.

To improve, re-establish relaxation, ride in balance, slow the tempo, and encourage longer strides and better engagement of the hind legs to bring the back up and encourage the horse to reach out and take contact with the bit. It requires skill, work, and patience to solve this.

## False Extension (Hollow, Stiff, and Irregular)

The horse moves with energetic but stiff, irregular steps. His back is hollow, and his hind legs go *out behind* (they swing farther out behind than they reach forward). In the trot, his front legs may extend stiffly forward with toes pointing up (toe flipping or "goose-stepping"), and the diagonal pairs of legs begin to dissociate (the hind legs take shorter steps than the forelegs). His canter is irregular, often with four beats. His neck is stiffly retracted, and he does not use his circle of muscles in harmony. The horse may exhibit *rein lameness*, a strained, irregular gait caused by incorrect riding. This type of movement is often seen when a horse is driven forcibly against a harshly restraining hand. It causes soreness and damage to the back, stifles, and hocks.

To improve, work on getting the horse back to a longer, more natural frame and regain rhythm, relaxation, engagement, and the use of his circle of muscles. Cavaletti work may help if done calmly and in rhythm.

Rehabilitating a horse with this problem requires a good and perceptive rider who can recognize the warning signs of tension and incorrect movement, especially when asking for more advanced work.

## Crookedness (One-Sidedness)

The horse moves slightly sideways, with his head, shoulder, or hip carried to one side. This restricts his freedom of movement, interferes with impulsion, and causes stiffness and difficulty with lateral balance, especially in turning. The horse takes a stronger contact with the bit on one side (stiff side), and tends to avoid contact on the other (hollow side). He may tilt his head instead of flexing correctly at the poll. This problem often occurs when a horse is weak in one hind leg; he protects the weaker leg by moving slightly sideways, and avoids carrying as much weight on it as he should, especially in collected movements. This makes it more difficult for him to turn or bend in one direction, and he may have difficulty taking one lead at the canter.

All horses are asymmetrical (one-sided) to some degree, and all horses have a naturally stiff side and a naturally hollow side; one of the goals of training is to develop the horse's two sides as equally as possible. However, a horse that habitually moves crookedly should be checked by a veterinarian to determine whether unsoundness is a factor.

To improve, the crooked horse needs to strengthen the muscles of his weaker side and become more supple on his stiff side. He must learn to engage both hind legs equally, and be able to carry more weight on his weaker hind leg (especially in turns, cantering, and lateral work). He must also learn to carry his weight more equally on both shoulders, remaining upright and bending instead of leaning in a turn, and to take equal contact on both reins.

Correct turning, bending, and lateral work can improve a horse's straightness and lateral balance. Use half-halts to balance the horse before, during, and after each turn or corner, and use both inside and outside aids to help him move with correct alignment (hind legs following in the tracks of his front legs) through the turn. The rider must be careful to ride in good balance, without collapsing in the hip or rib cage; leaning; or sitting unevenly. Lateral work such as leg-yielding, shoulder-in, travers, and renvers can strengthen and supple the horse and develop his ability to use his hind legs more equally. Working over cavaletti on a curve (properly spaced and ridden) can be beneficial. Improving straightness and equal development is a process that requires good riding and choosing the right exercises to help the horse.

# 2

# Principles of Riding on the Flat

The purpose of flat work is to improve your horse's suppleness, responsiveness to the aids, and way of moving, making him more obedient, better balanced, and easier to ride on the flat, over fences, and in the open. Flat work is also essential for the rider's development and fitness, and for improving his skills.

It's important to ride correctly, with good form, when schooling. Everything you have learned has a purpose—to make it easier for your horse to feel, understand, and carry you well.

## Physical and Mental Preparation for Advanced Riding

### Physical Fitness

Advanced riding is physically demanding. You must be strong and fit enough to maintain your position in motion, and your muscles and joints must be supple enough to absorb shock and follow the horse's movements. You must be able to ride actively for long periods without tiring. Being fit also decreases your chances of injury.

As you train for cross-country riding, you may need additional fitness work besides riding and stable work for strength, endurance, weight

## Faulty Movement Syndromes

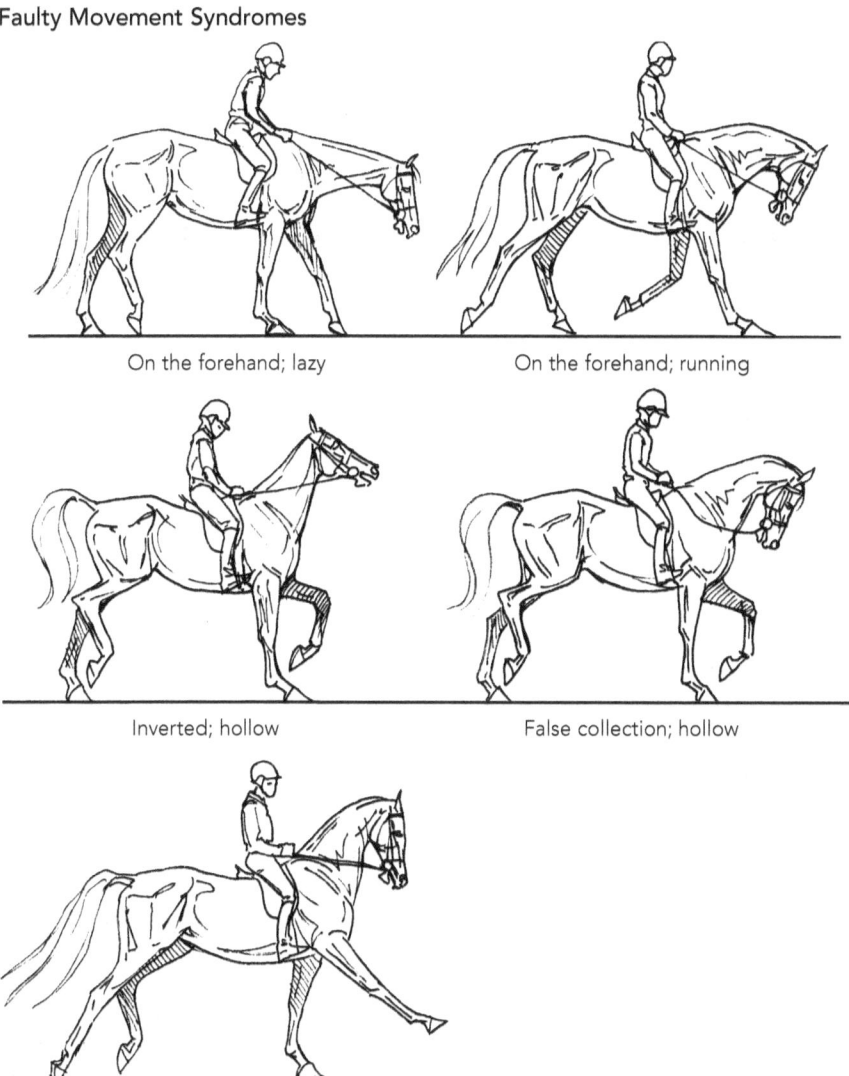

On the forehand; lazy

On the forehand; running

Inverted; hollow

False collection; hollow

False extension

or hands, or in young, undeveloped horses that are uncomfortable and unbalanced under the rider's weight.

To improve, work on restoring calmness, comfort, and better rhythm so the horse can unlock his tense muscles and make better use of his hind legs and his circle of muscles. This will bring his back up and allow him to reach forward to the bit. Just getting the head down is not the answer, and may result in a false frame if forced. The rider must ride in balance and use tactful aids to slow and steady the tempo, then ask for longer strides; his hands must be gentle and sympathetic, especially when the horse begins to take contact with the bit. Check the saddle fit and make sure the bit is mild and comfortable. Cavaletti work (if done calmly and in rhythm) can help the horse learn to engage his hind legs, round his back, and stretch his neck out and down.

## False Collection (Hollow, Behind the Bit)

The horse moves with short, irregular strides and poor engagement. His back is tense and hollow, and he draws back from the bit, retracting his neck and evading contact. Like the inverted horse, he may take pacey steps instead of walking and is stiff, uncomfortable, and difficult to ride; his trot becomes irregular and his canter may have four beats. At faster gaits, he may over-flex his neck and drop his chin against his chest, making control difficult. This problem is often caused by misguided efforts to force a horse into collection by working from front to back or through the misuse of severe bits, draw reins, or pulling hands. This problem is similar to that of the inverted horse in that the horse needs to relax, find his rhythm, and restore his engagement and use of his circle of muscles. However, it is harder to cure when a horse has learned an incorrect response: to retract his neck, over-flex, and withdraw from the bit.

To improve, re-establish relaxation, ride in balance, slow the tempo, and encourage longer strides and better engagement of the hind legs to bring the back up and encourage the horse to reach out and take contact with the bit. It requires skill, work, and patience to solve this.

## False Extension (Hollow, Stiff, and Irregular)

The horse moves with energetic but stiff, irregular steps. His back is hollow, and his hind legs go *out behind* (they swing farther out behind than they reach forward). In the trot, his front legs may extend stiffly forward with toes pointing up (toe flipping or "goose-stepping"), and the diagonal pairs of legs begin to dissociate (the hind legs take shorter steps than the forelegs). His canter is irregular, often with four beats. His neck is stiffly retracted, and he does not use his circle of muscles in harmony. The horse may exhibit *rein lameness*, a strained, irregular gait caused by incorrect riding. This type of movement is often seen when a horse is driven forcibly against a harshly restraining hand. It causes soreness and damage to the back, stifles, and hocks.

To improve, work on getting the horse back to a longer, more natural frame and regain rhythm, relaxation, engagement, and the use of his circle of muscles. Cavaletti work may help if done calmly and in rhythm.

Rehabilitating a horse with this problem requires a good and perceptive rider who can recognize the warning signs of tension and incorrect movement, especially when asking for more advanced work.

## Crookedness (One-Sidedness)

The horse moves slightly sideways, with his head, shoulder, or hip carried to one side. This restricts his freedom of movement, interferes with impulsion, and causes stiffness and difficulty with lateral balance, especially in turning. The horse takes a stronger contact with the bit on one side (stiff side), and tends to avoid contact on the other (hollow side). He may tilt his head instead of flexing correctly at the poll. This problem often occurs when a horse is weak in one hind leg; he protects the weaker leg by moving slightly sideways, and avoids carrying as much weight on it as he should, especially in collected movements. This makes it more difficult for him to turn or bend in one direction, and he may have difficulty taking one lead at the canter.

All horses are asymmetrical (one-sided) to some degree, and all horses have a naturally stiff side and a naturally hollow side; one of the goals of training is to develop the horse's two sides as equally as possible. However, a horse that habitually moves crookedly should be checked by a veterinarian to determine whether unsoundness is a factor.

To improve, the crooked horse needs to strengthen the muscles of his weaker side and become more supple on his stiff side. He must learn to engage both hind legs equally, and be able to carry more weight on his weaker hind leg (especially in turns, cantering, and lateral work). He must also learn to carry his weight more equally on both shoulders, remaining upright and bending instead of leaning in a turn, and to take equal contact on both reins.

Correct turning, bending, and lateral work can improve a horse's straightness and lateral balance. Use half-halts to balance the horse before, during, and after each turn or corner, and use both inside and outside aids to help him move with correct alignment (hind legs following in the tracks of his front legs) through the turn. The rider must be careful to ride in good balance, without collapsing in the hip or rib cage; leaning; or sitting unevenly. Lateral work such as leg-yielding, shoulder-in, travers, and renvers can strengthen and supple the horse and develop his ability to use his hind legs more equally. Working over cavaletti on a curve (properly spaced and ridden) can be beneficial. Improving straightness and equal development is a process that requires good riding and choosing the right exercises to help the horse.

# 2

# Principles of Riding on the Flat

The purpose of flat work is to improve your horse's suppleness, responsiveness to the aids, and way of moving, making him more obedient, better balanced, and easier to ride on the flat, over fences, and in the open. Flat work is also essential for the rider's development and fitness, and for improving his skills.

It's important to ride correctly, with good form, when schooling. Everything you have learned has a purpose—to make it easier for your horse to feel, understand, and carry you well.

## Physical and Mental Preparation for Advanced Riding

### Physical Fitness

Advanced riding is physically demanding. You must be strong and fit enough to maintain your position in motion, and your muscles and joints must be supple enough to absorb shock and follow the horse's movements. You must be able to ride actively for long periods without tiring. Being fit also decreases your chances of injury.

As you train for cross-country riding, you may need additional fitness work besides riding and stable work for strength, endurance, weight

The rider's core muscles. The rider's core muscles.

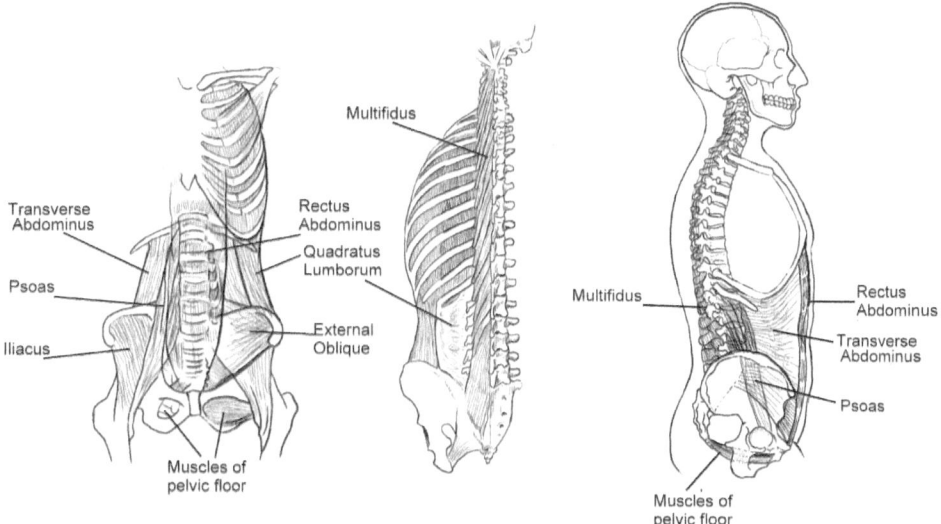

control, or specific skills, especially if you spend much of each day sitting down. This may include aerobic exercise, strength exercises, and body development methods such as Pilates, as well as maintaining a proper diet.

Riders need to be especially fit and strong in their core muscles (the deep inner muscles inside the abdomen). You can strengthen and improve your core muscles through Pilates and similar forms of exercise that target these muscles.

## Mental Preparation

Some considerations for preparation for advanced riding include:

- **Mental preparation,** which can greatly improve your riding and your ability to get the most out of instruction and competition. Important aspects of mental preparation include focus and positive thinking, reminding yourself of what you want to do. It is also important to have a clear intent for what you want the horse to do. Mental rehearsal of your competition rides also prepares your body and mind to repeat movements as you visualize them.
- **Body awareness** helps you to feel what you are doing and release excess muscle tension that keeps you stuck in incorrect habit patterns. This makes it easier to feel your horse's movement and reactions, and to ride with sensitivity, tact, and "feel." Even if you are not aware of how you use your body, your horse is. If you are stiff, crooked, or slightly out of balance, it interferes with his ability to move and carry you well. When

**Crooked rider.**

Head tilts

Shoulder low

One arm and hand stronger

Collapsed hip
Uneven weight on seat bones

Elbow, knee, and toe stick out

Stirrup shorter

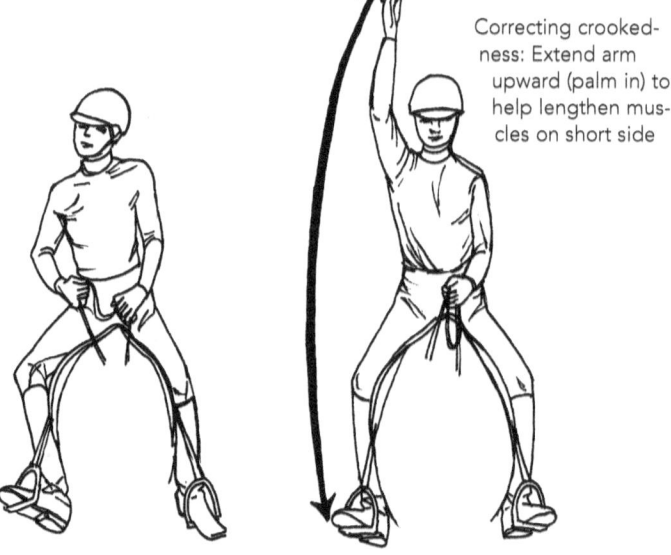

Correcting crookedness: Extend arm upward (palm in) to help lengthen muscles on short side

a rider becomes aware of his body and improves, his horse often improves dramatically.

No rider is perfect, so you may not realize when you are riding with an incorrect habit pattern, such as tilting forward or rounding your back. In addition, no one is perfectly symmetrical; we all have a stronger side (and arm and leg). This can cause you to ride unevenly, or to use your aids more strongly on one side.

Ways to improve your body awareness include breathing deeply to remove tension, becoming aware of any contraction in your muscles, and letting your joints be free to absorb the horse's motion. Looking at your position in a mirror or watching videos of yourself, along with your instructor's assessment, can help you make corrections.

Progress in riding takes goals, organized effort, and self-discipline. Your attitude can influence your moods and motivation, which in turn affects how well you ride and achieve your goals.

# The Rider: Working On the Flat

## Seat and Position

At the B and A levels, you must be able to ride with a secure, supple, and independent seat at all gaits, with and without stirrups. (At the C3 level, you

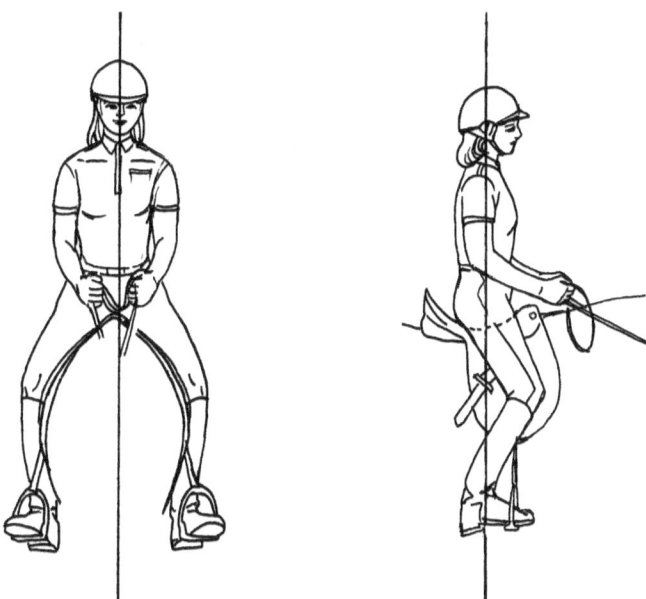

The balanced seat.

should be developing an independent seat in a good basic balanced position, with a secure base of support.) Your seat must follow the motion of the horse smoothly, without stiffness, tension, or loss of balance, which interfere with the horse's movement and your ability to apply the aids.

A rider is in balance with his horse when their balance or centers of gravity are united so they work together as one. Riding in balance requires a correct and balanced position and a supple seat that adapts easily to the horse's changing balance.

For a review of the balanced position, please refer to the *USPC C Level Manual*, pages 4–8.

## Developing the Sitting Trot

You can sit the trot only when your horse moves correctly, with a round, swinging back. A tense, hollow back causes a high head and a stiff gait, which is uncomfortable for both of you. This prevents the horse from using his hind legs well, responding correctly to seat aids, or working *through his back* and *on the bit*.

A tense, hollow back and high head may be caused by:

- Lack of independent seat in the rider, which creates stiffness and bouncing.
- Lack of elastic contact, or the rider hanging on the reins.

Moving round versus moving hollow.

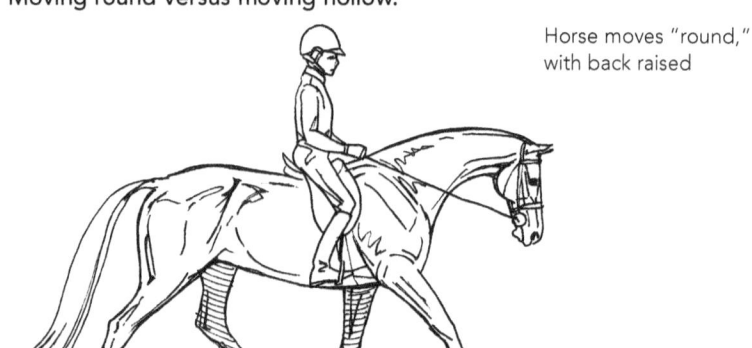

Horse moves "round," with back raised

Horse moves "hollow," with back dropped

- Lack of level balance, or the horse carrying too much weight on the forehand.
- An ill-fitting saddle (especially one that pinches the shoulder muscles).
- Soreness in the horse's back, hind legs, or other physical pain.

## Riding Without Stirrups at All Gaits

Riding without stirrups at all gaits should be done routinely. Work without stirrups must be done correctly to be safe and beneficial. (For details on work without stirrups, review the *USPC C Level Manual*, pages 8–11.)

# Advanced Use of the Aids

At the C3, B, and A levels, you should ride your horse "on the aids" while you develop feel, timing, and "educated aids." ("On the aids" means that the horse is paying attention and responding correctly to all your aids.) If you give an aid at the correct point in the stride, your horse can respond easily. If you give the aid at the wrong time, he cannot respond even if he wants to. This can lead to confusion, resistance, and training setbacks. In order to time your aids correctly, you must understand the gaits and the order in which the horse moves his legs, and be able to feel the moment when he can respond to your aids. (See Chapter 1, "Biomechanics and Movement of the Horse," for more information on the rhythm of the gaits.)

## *Leg Aids*

Correct leg aids develop from a correct seat and leg position. Your inner legs gently "embrace" the horse with a continuous soft, passive contact; the horse must learn to accept this gentle contact. Riding with a constant muscular squeeze, nagging with repeated but ineffective leg aids, or "slapping" the legs at every stride irritates the horse, teaches him to ignore normal leg aids, and impairs your seat.

For more about specific leg aids, including position and technique, please review the *USPC C Level Manual*, pages 15–19.

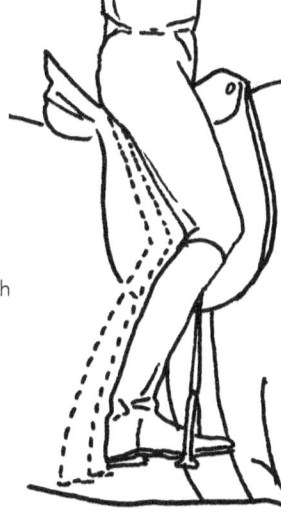

Leg aid positions.

1. Normal position
2. Inside leg behind girth
3. Outside leg behind girth

### Seat Aids

Seat aids develop from a correct, supple, and balanced seat, when the horse is developing *thoroughness*, his back is round and swinging, and he is accepting the rider's seat.

- **Driving seat aid.** For a more active driving aid, used to send the horse forward, the pelvis tilts and the seat "tucks" slightly forward and downward, lengthening the spine and sending the knees down and the lower legs down and back against the horse's barrel. When using this driving seat aid you must be careful that its effect is to send the horse forward, not drive the horse's back downward. If the horse's back is not "up," using a driving seat aid will make it more hollow.
- **Unilateral (one-sided) seat aid.** A unilateral seat aid engages one seat bone (usually the inside seat bone) more strongly than the other. This aid can be valuable in bending and lateral work as well as other movements; however, the rider must be careful to keep the seat centered and balanced.

### Rein Aids

Good rein aids are developed from a correct and balanced seat, while maintaining the elasticity of the contact. Correct rein aids cannot be given unless the horse is ridden from *back to front:* The rider's legs ask for energy from

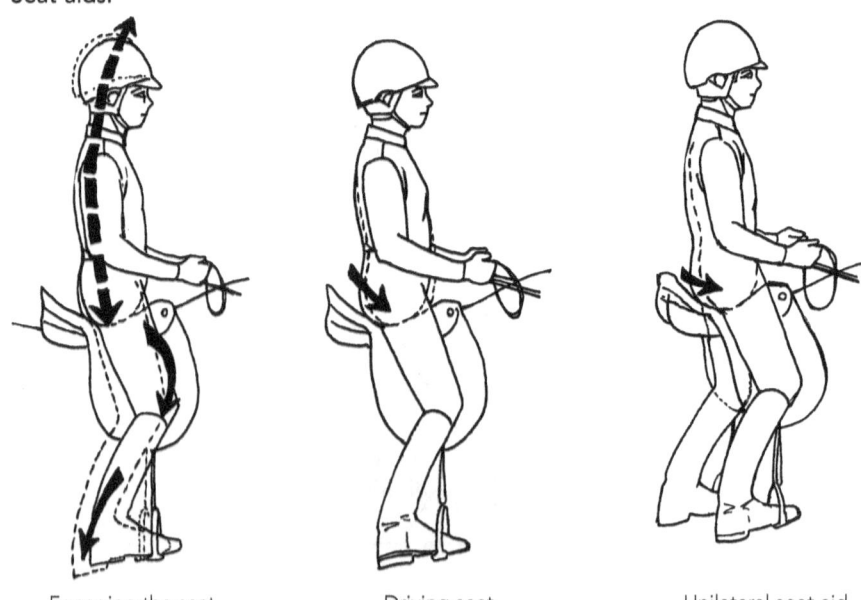

Seat aids.

Engaging the seat     Driving seat     Unilateral seat aid

the hindquarters, the seat regulates the energy as it goes through the horse's back, and the hands receive and regulate the energy. Remember that rein contact is *not* achieved by taking back with the hands, but is created by energy (impulsion) from the hindquarters through a supple back, causing the horse to reach forward into the bit. Riders must be reminded of the negative tendency to do too much with the reins and too little with the legs and seat.

For more information on rein aids, please see the *USPC C Level Manual*, pages 23–28.

### Actions of the Hands

The hands *act* when they increase rein tension to ask for reducing the pace or gait, a halt or rein back, a half-halt, a change of direction, or a change in the position of the horse's head or neck carriage.

The rein aids have the following actions:

- **The asking rein** consists of either closing the fingers momentarily, or for a stronger effect, turning the hand inward from the wrist. It asks the horse for a response, such as a turn, a bend, or a flexion. If the horse does not respond immediately, the hand should yield and the asking rein should be repeated as required.
- **The yielding rein** returns the rein to the normal position and contact after the horse yields, or before repeating the "asking rein."

The leg-seat-hand connection.

- **The non-yielding rein** contains the energy momentarily, or can resist the horse's efforts to push his head forward, or pull the rider's hands forward by the action of the hands closing, without altering their position, until the horse yields to the bit and becomes lighter in the hand. However, the hands do not act in a backward direction or continue their action for too long. The rider's contact must resume elasticity when the horse yields.
- **The regulating or guarding rein** complements the action of the inside asking rein, especially when asking for lateral flexion in the poll. It permits the horse to flex laterally in response to the inside asking rein, but prevents the horse from overbending laterally. To use a regulating rein aid, the rider yields his outside rein just enough to allow the correct amount of flexion at the poll or bend in the neck.

## The Five Rein Effects

These rein effects can be used in several ways to influence the horse's direction and positioning:

1. **The opening** or **leading rein** is the rider's primary rein aid, and is most commonly used for basic bending, turns, and circles. It gently takes the horse's head in the desired direction with a rein aid that leads to the inside, so the horse's shoulders will follow. The opening rein does not apply pressure backward, but to the side. This effect is used for horses at all stages of development and training, but is especially useful in the earlier stages. It is easily understood by the horse, its effects are straightforward, and it can safely be employed both at slower gaits as well as at speed.

   To apply an opening rein aid, briefly rotate your hand outward away from the horse's neck so that your fingernails are on top and your thumb points in the direction of the turn. This brief rotation of your hand changes the pressure on the bit sideways and outward in the desired direction of travel. The outside hand must move forward enough to allow the horse to follow the opening rein.

   This rein effect can affect the horse's lateral flexion but has little or no direct effect on the horse's longitudinal flexion and is not involved in collection.

2. **The direct rein** applies pressure straight back, affecting the hind leg on the same side by restricting the impulsion on the side on which it is used. If applied with both hands, it asks a horse to rebalance, slow, or stop. If used with one hand, it asks him to bend and turn in that direction. This rein has a powerful stopping and/or collecting effect on the horse in that it causes him to rebalance himself toward one or both hindquarters.

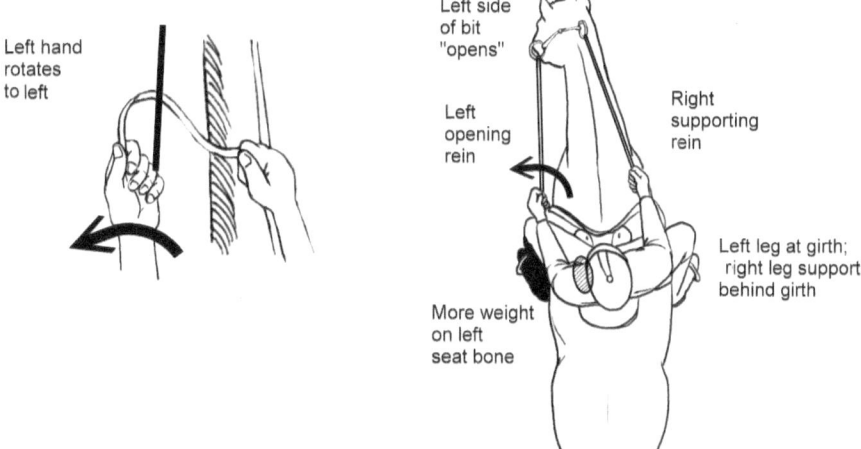

Opening rein.

To apply a direct rein aid, your hand comes into position somewhere in front of your hip and resists the horse's forward movement by closing your fingers and resisting momentarily; if necessary, you may momentarily flex your wrists inward, then relax back to a soft fist. By fixing your hand momentarily, the horse rewards himself instantly when he gives or answers the aid. Always relax your fingers as soon as your horse begins to give to your hand.

**Note:** Using this rein for bending and turning causes a tendency for the horse to swing his hindquarters outward, requiring a stronger outside leg aid. It can also cause a *clashing of the aids* if the direct rein is used in conjunction with a forward-driving leg and/or seat, as the hands are saying "stop" and the legs/seat are saying "go."

3. **The neck rein** or **bearing rein** creates a one-sided rein effect, making it effective for horses and riders of all levels. These rein aids affect the horse's direction and lateral flexion, but not his balance or collection. These rein effects can also produce various degrees of counter-bending and loading of the opposite shoulder, and can be used to momentarily straighten a crooked horse.

The neck rein and bearing rein are very similar, but not exactly the same aid. A neck rein works primarily by the touch of the rein against the horse's neck, with minimal or no backward bit pressure. A bearing rein is a more powerful aid that pulls backward and against the neck, resulting in stronger bit pressure and more counter-flexion at the poll.

Direct rein (both).

Direct Rein of Opposition
Both hands

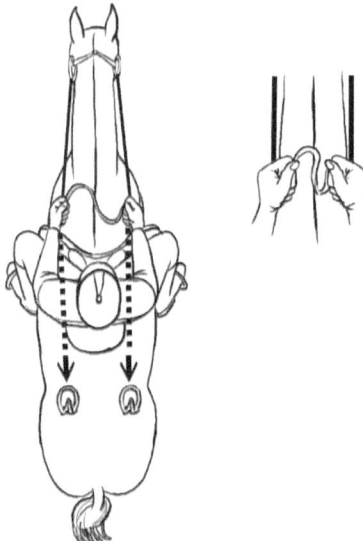

Direct rein/bending rein (one hand).

Direct Rein of Opposition
One hand (bending)

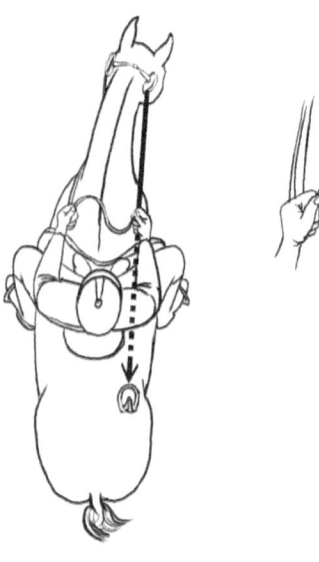

Because these two rein aids are very similar, the terms "bearing rein" and "neck rein" are often used interchangeably, but they are actually different rein effects, especially in Western riding.

The neck rein or bearing rein is also a partner rein for the opening rein when used in the same direction (for example, both to the left). This has the effect of bending the horse slightly to the side on which the neck rein is being used, shifting the horse's balance to the opposite shoulder, so that the horse is inclined to move forward and slightly sideways.

To apply a neck rein or bearing rein, keep your thumb up, and move the rein toward the direction you want the horse to go, bringing the rein into contact with the neck and the corner of the mouth. The horse should flex his head slightly to that side, while his neck and shoulders move away from the rein pressure, shifting his weight forward and away from the neck rein aid and loading the opposite foreleg. Be careful not to move your hand across the center of the neck or pull backward, which can cause the horse to tip his head sideways.

**Note:** A true *neck rein* is light, brief, and acts primarily from the rein contact with the horse's neck. A *bearing rein* is a stronger aid, causing stronger pressure on the bit, greater lateral flexion at the poll, and creating a more powerful effect.

## PRINCIPLES OF RIDING ON THE FLAT

Neck rein / bearing rein.

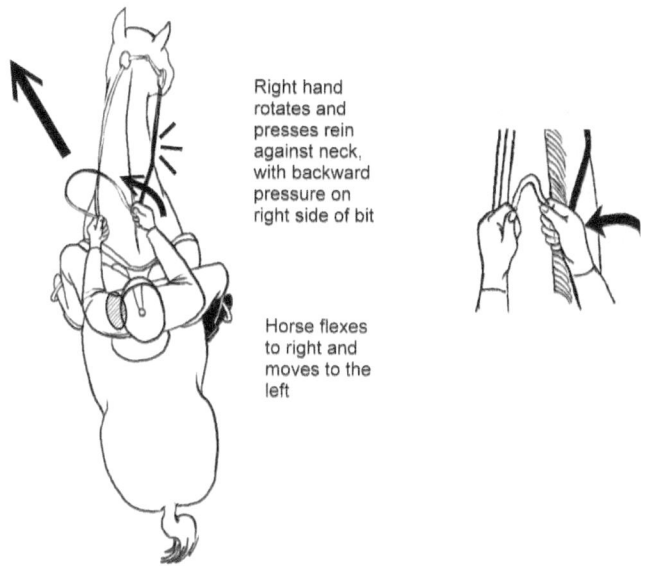

Neck rein in conjunction with opening rein and direct rein.

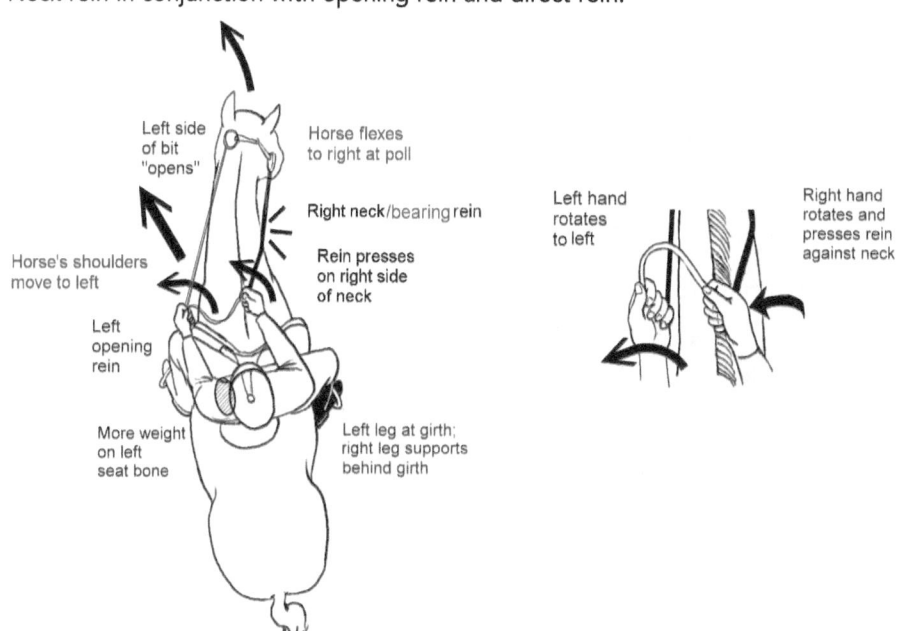

## Indirect Reins of Opposition

All reins of opposition affect the hind legs. It is important to understand that reins of opposition have a restricting and somewhat collecting effect on the horse, so they should be used thoughtfully in terms of how much pressure is used and when they are appropriate. An indirect rein aid can only be used by one hand at a time. Using two indirect rein aids at once would be conflicting aids and would confuse the horse.

4. **Indirect rein of opposition in front of the withers** is used to position the head and neck, to encourage bending, and to move the shoulders laterally. It acts on the shoulders and makes the horse turn by shifting his shoulders in the opposite direction from the rein aid (for example, a right indirect rein would move the left shoulder away from the rein aid, with the haunches moving to the right). It can also be useful in lateral movements such as shoulder-in and renvers, but it should be used to make small corrections only.

   To apply an indirect rein of opposition in front of the withers, your hand should be in front of the withers, and without crossing the neck, move it toward the horse's opposite shoulder, offering resistance by closing your fingers and moving your hand slightly in the direction of your center. Your hand should remain in front of the withers throughout the aid. Pulling backward on the rein makes the aid too strong and could unbalance the horse.

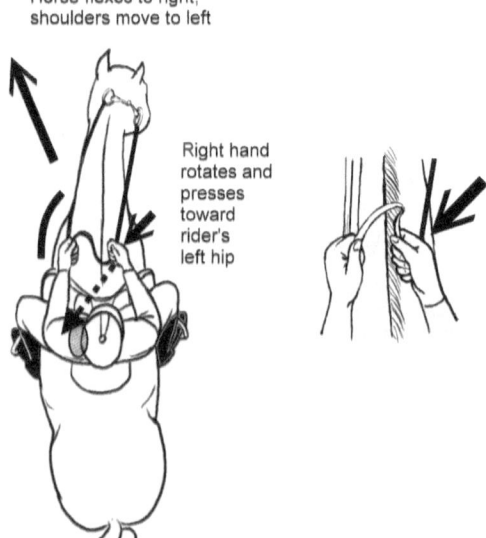

Indirect rein of opposition in front of the withers.

Horse flexes to right, shoulders move to left

Right hand rotates and presses toward rider's left hip

5. **Indirection rein of opposition behind the withers** is important in executing more advanced movements, as well as helping balance a horse on circles and in turns. It causes the horse to load the outside hind leg, as well as the outside shoulder, and to move forward and sideways in the direction that the rider's leg dictates, such as in a half-pass. It is a powerful rein effect and must be used judiciously and with tact, and should be reserved for advanced riders and the more technical movements of dressage.

To apply an indirect rein of opposition behind the withers, bring your hand behind the withers in the direction of the horse's opposite hip (without crossing the center line of the horse's neck), and close/resist with your hand. This rein is *not* pulled toward the outside hip, but is simply positioned in line with it, while you close your fingers and resist with your hand.

# Putting the Horse On the Aids and "On the Bit"

## Where Contact Begins: Making the Connection

*Connection* occurs when the energy and activity from the hind legs is transmitted through a supple, swinging back and top line, with the horse reaching forward at the poll, seeking contact with the rider's hands, and accepting the

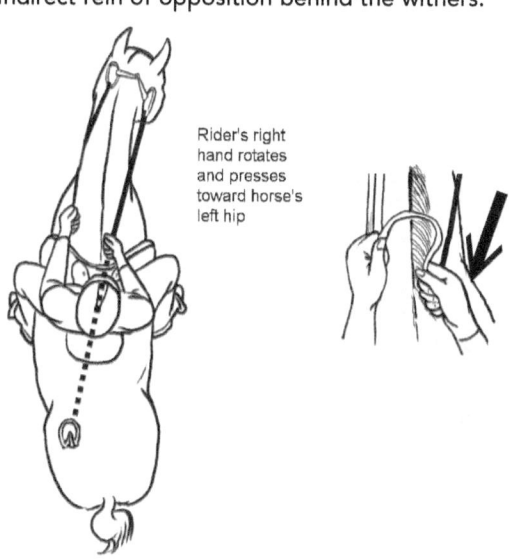

Indirect rein of opposition behind the withers.

Rider's right hand rotates and presses toward horse's left hip

Making the connection.

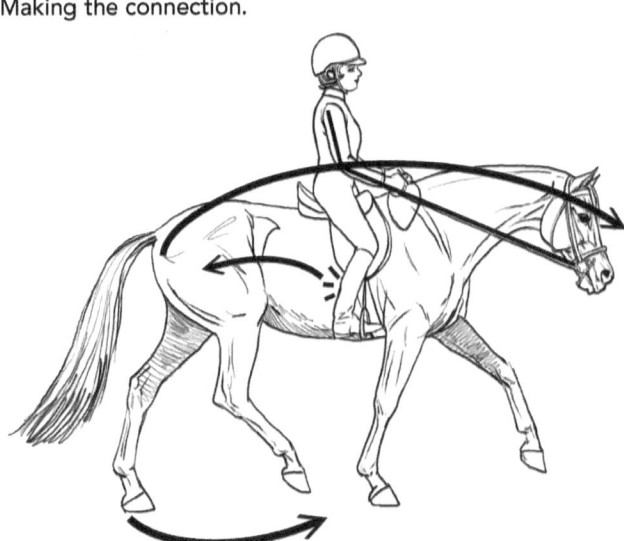

bit. A *connected* horse should develop *throughness*. This means that the aids of the rider go *through* the horse without meeting stiffness or resistance, so that the rein aids affect the hind legs, and the energy from the hind legs goes through the top line into the rider's contact.

## Accepting the Bit (Accepting Contact)

When a horse accepts the bit, he is willing to flex at the poll, which brings his face closer to the vertical, and show lateral flexion when asked by the rider. He will carry his head with the poll at the highest point and with a closed mouth, but he softly chews the bit.

## On the Bit

The horse to be considered to be *on the bit* when he accepts the bit and the aids go reliably *through* the horse. The horse seeks the bit, showing the amount of self-carriage and engagement needed for the movement. If the horse is on the bit, he is always willing to stretch down, maintaining contact and staying round, whenever the rider allows him to take more rein. A horse might appear to be on the bit, yet if he does not stretch his head to meet a giving rein, or if he can evade a half-halt, he is not truly on the bit. When the horse is on the bit he works *through his back* by lifting and rounding his back, and he goes forward with regular strides, good engagement, and free forward movement.

## Accepting the bit.

- Poll is the highest point of the neck.
- Horse reaches forward to the bit with light, steady contact.
- Relaxed jaw
- Closed mouth
- Horse chews the bit softly.

## On the bit: correct and incorrect.

On the bit: round and moving forward from behind.

Correct

Incorrect: "head set"; not round, riding from front to back.

Incorrect

**Resistance to the bit.**

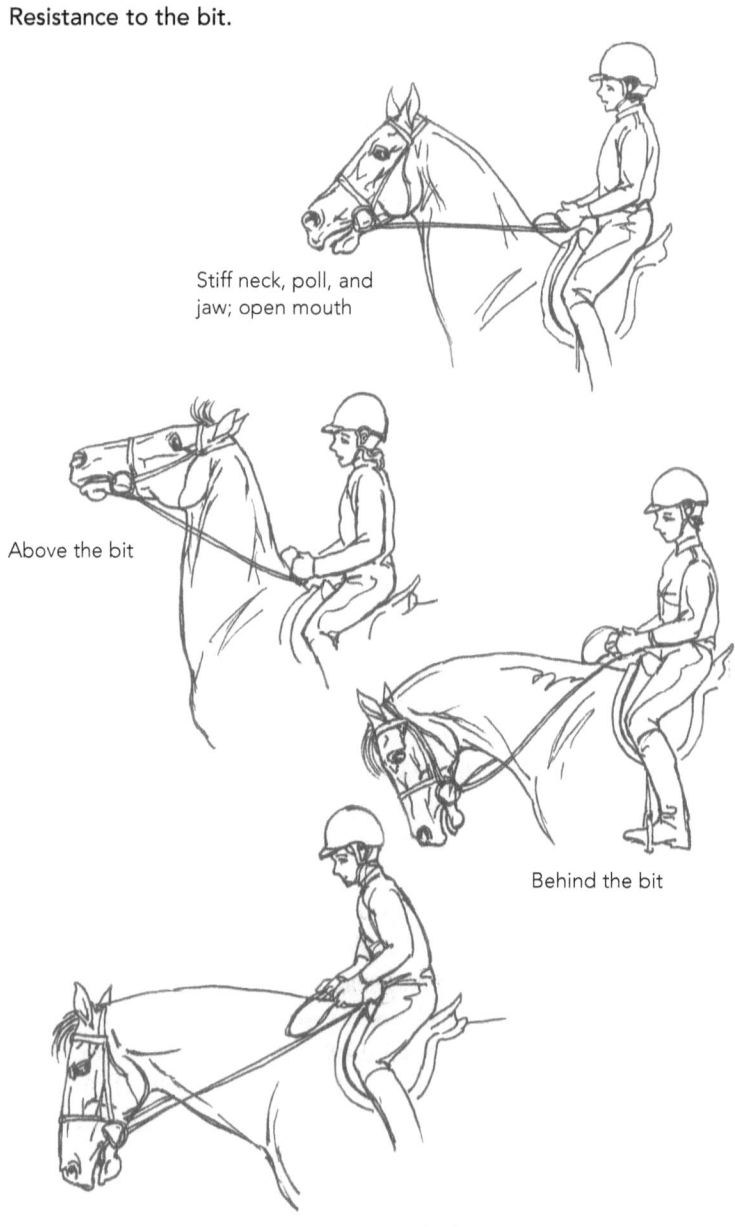

Stiff neck, poll, and jaw; open mouth

Above the bit

Behind the bit

Leaning on the bit

Riding a horse on the bit has nothing to do with a *head set* (a fixed, vertical position of the head). *Setting the head* with see-sawing hands, severe bits, or control devices only creates a *false frame*, which prevents the horse from using his body and moving correctly, and going truly on the bit.

## Resistance to the Bit

Resistance to the bit is a distress signal. Some common signs of resistance are head tossing, pulling, leaning on the bit, carrying the head too high (*above the bit*), tucking the chin in too far (*overbending*), opening the mouth, or refusing to take any contact with the bit (getting *behind the bit*).

The most common reason for resisting the bit is a lack of training of the horse and/or rider, but mouth pain can be problematic as well.

## Bending and Lateral Balance

Bending is another aspect of keeping the horse correctly aligned, both in his spine and body and with his hind legs following in the tracks of his front legs. Correct alignment is called *straightness,* even when it refers to bending correctly on a curved or circular track.

When moving on a curved track, the horse's inside hind leg must engage and bend its joints more, carrying more weight, and his outside hind leg must swing farther. The rib cage rotates slightly to the outside, and the muscles on the outside stretch further.

When a horse bends correctly, his inside hind leg reaches well forward (*engages*) at every stride, his back comes up, and he stays balanced, without leaning. His hind legs follow in the tracks of his front legs, and he looks in the direction of the turn. He keeps his weight in the center, "standing up" instead of leaning through turns, which improves his balance. He maintains the same pace, rhythm, and tempo, without speeding up, slowing down, or breaking gait. When he turns like this, he is well-balanced and can keep moving forward with energy and power (*impulsion*).

All horses have a natural tendency to bend more easily in one direction. This results in a *stiff side* (the side on which he finds it harder to bend), and a *hollow side* (the side to which he tends to over-bend). (For a discussion of the stiff side and the hollow side of the horse, please see Chapter 3, "Dressage and Training Principles.")

### Riding the Horse into the Outside Rein

Riding the horse *into the outside rein* enhances control, straightness, bending, and engagement. The outside rein receives and regulates the impulsion from the hindquarters, momentarily supports the balance of the horse, and controls the amount of bend.

The horse should reach for the outside rein. Your inside rein indicates the direction in which he should look and move. Your outside leg, behind the girth, guards to be sure that the horse's outside hind leg does not escape outward. Your inside leg, close to the girth, asks the horse to engage his inside hind leg, and reminds him not to fall in. Your outside rein must remain

Bending: The horse bends around the rider's inside leg, softening on the inside and stretching on the outside, showing roundness, engagement, and free forward movement.

elastic, with brief squeezes regulating the bend, balance, and impulsion. However, the outside rein can only regulate what it receives; if your leg fails to send your horse forward and out, and there is no stretch into your outside hand, you have nothing to work with. If you pull or have too strong a contact on the outside rein, your horse may become crooked or counter-bent.

### Stretching Down

Stretching *down and out* (also called *chewing the bit out of the rider's hands*) is an exercise to demonstrate and improve contact, relaxation, swinging through the back, and stretch of the top line and neck.

The willingness of a horse to reach down and out into contact shows the horse has confidence in the rider's hands and is proof of good work. It should be used in warm-up, during work as a rest and reward between more difficult movements, and when finishing work, to allow the horse to stretch his muscles.

To stretch down correctly, the horse must engage his hind legs to support the extra weight that is transferred to the forehand as he stretches. This creates a continuous stretch from the tail over the lifted back and round neck out to the poll. Snatching at the bit, dropping contact, or poking his nose out are *not* correct stretching, and show that the horse is not properly on the aids. Dropping the contact or allowing a loop in the reins are not correct riding of the stretching exercise.

# PRINCIPLES OF RIDING ON THE FLAT

Riding the horse into the outside rein.

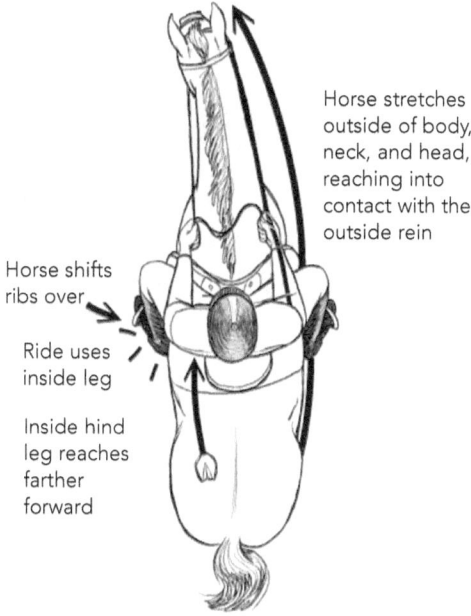

Horse stretches outside of body, neck, and head, reaching into contact with the outside rein

Horse shifts ribs over

Ride uses inside leg

Inside hind leg reaches farther forward

To ask your horse to stretch down and out, first be sure your horse's balance and impulsion are sufficient, and keep your legs and seat active as you gradually allow him to take your hands forward and down, as far as he is willing to go. If he is willing to stretch further, you can allow the reins to slip gradually through your fingers, but be careful not to drop the contact. The horse should "follow the bit down," maintaining contact, with his poll softly flexed; he may chew the bit as he stretches (hence the phrase "chewing the bit out of the rider's hands"). When he has stretched down and maintained contact for a few strides, continue to support the rhythm with your seat and leg aids as you smoothly shorten your reins and bring him back to a normal frame.

## Inside and Outside

It is important to understand the concept of inside and outside, especially in lateral work. *Inside* refers to the direction in which the horse is bent, *not* the inside or center of the ring. *Outside* refers to the outside of the bend, *not* the outside of the ring or track.

There are certain movements in which the horse may be bent toward the track or the outside of the ring. In this case, the "inside" aids are still those on the side toward which the horse is bent, and the "outside" aids may be on the side toward the center of the ring.

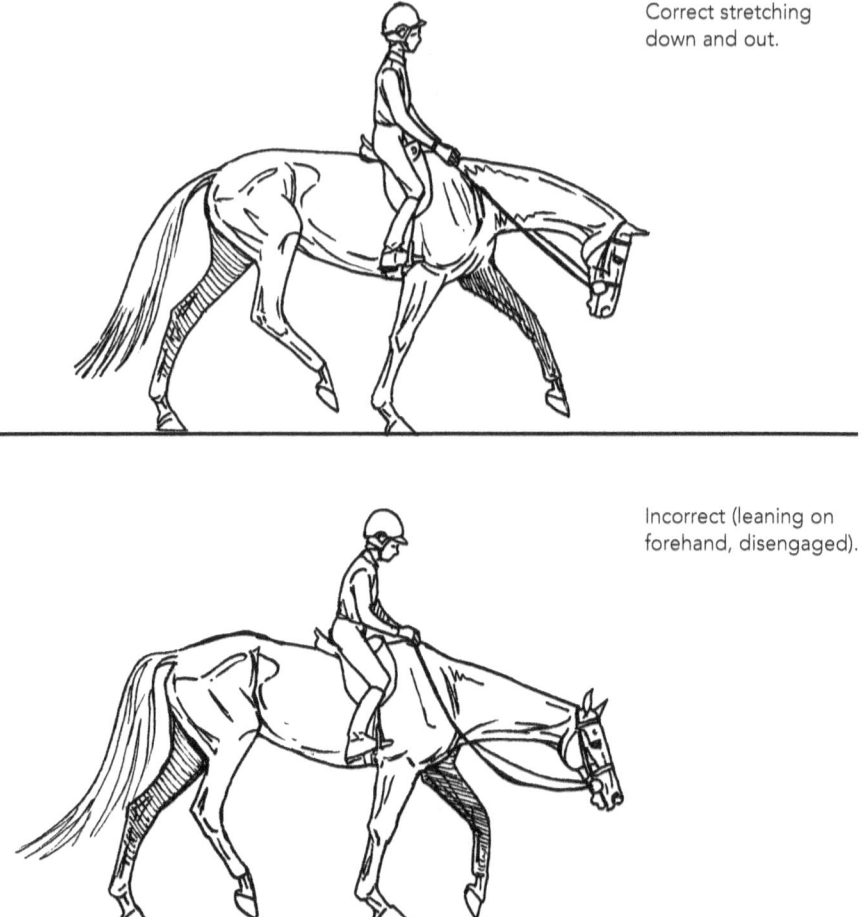

Correct stretching down and out.

Incorrect (leaning on forehand, disengaged).

### Inside and Outside Aids

Correct seat, leg, and rein aids help your horse turn, track, and bend correctly. The inside aids are the seat bone, leg, and rein on the inside of a bend or turn. The outside aids are those on the outside. Your inside leg (close to the girth) keeps him moving forward, asks him to bend, and prevents falling in. The inside rein asks him to look in the direction of the turn. The outside rein and outside leg behind the girth set a limit on how far out he may go and how much he bends, and keep him on the line of travel.

### Releasing the Inside Rein

There are two different types of this inside rein release:

1. A momentary release with the inside hand, moving the hand forward up the neck to make a loop in the rein, and sometimes patting the horse's

neck briefly with the releasing hand, is used as a reward and to encourage relaxation.

2. For more advanced horses and riders, a momentary release of the inside rein is used to test balance, rhythm, and self-carriage. This differs from the stretching rein because the hand goes up the neck, rather than toward the bit. It is important to be able to correctly support the horse with the seat and leg during this release. The horse should not change his balance or outline during this release.

To release the inside rein, move your inside hand, holding the rein, forward toward the bit on a straight line to the bit, while your outside rein maintains the same steady contact. Do this smoothly but fairly slowly, so that you don't surprise the horse. You can give him a single pat on the neck, as long as it does not make you lean forward or alter your position. Re-taking the contact is the most sensitive time, so take care to smoothly re-establish contact with the horse's mouth.

### Timing the Aids

In order to be reliably effective, the rider's aids should be in rhythm with the horse's footfalls, so they can accentuate, enhance, or diminish different aspects of each stride, as needed.

The correct timing of each aid is dictated by the horse, by the moment he is in his stride, as well as by the lateral swinging of his rib cage and the longitudinal swinging of his back. The best time for the rider to influence

Release with inside rein.

the direction and reach of a specific leg of the horse is when the leg is in the air. It is easier to connect a specific leg to the ground for a longer moment when the leg is bearing weight.

Here are some tips for learning to time aids correctly:

- Know when the horse is moving each hind leg. This is important so you know when to apply your leg aid to get the effect you want.
- For more forward movement or greater engagement, apply the leg aid as the hind leg (on the same side) is pushing off the ground, so it can respond with greater thrust and by swinging more forward through the air.
- To move laterally, apply the leg aid as the hind leg is pushing off to convert the step into a sideways step.
- To lengthen stride in the walk, apply the leg aid as the hind leg on the same side is pushing off and leaving the ground. This can be done as alternating leg aids (left, right, left, right). In addition, the horse must be allowed to *oscillate* his head and neck (allow the head and neck to move forward and back) in the walk.
- In the trot, posting on the *outside diagonal* (outside foreleg and inside hind leg) lets you feel the push of the inside hind leg as it helps you rise. Applying a brief inside leg aid *as you begin* to *rise* will affect the inside hind leg as it pushes off and swings forward.
- If you post on the *inside diagonal* (inside foreleg and outside hind leg), you can apply an inside leg aid as you *sit,* catching the moment when the inside hind leg pushes off and swings through the air. This can be useful for leg-yielding in rising trot. In the sitting trot, the rider should consider which hind leg his leg aids will affect.
- In the canter, the outside hind leg moves first, followed by inside hind and outside fore together, then inside fore. It has an up-and-down rocking motion. The "up" moment, when the forehand rises, is when the hind legs reach forward and strike the ground. The horse then becomes level when the inside hind and the outside foreleg touch the ground. The "down" moment, as the head and forehand drop, is when the leading foreleg strikes the ground.
- In the canter, the horse can rebalance himself best if you half-halt during the "up," as the forehand rises. At that moment, you can also affect the pushing upward motion of the outside leg to improve balance. If you half-halt on the "down," the hind legs are already in the air and moving backward and cannot be affected, except for the horse to change leads or gait.
- It is important not to allow your contact to become stronger when the horse's head and neck reach out in the "down" moment, but allow your

**Timing leg aids.**

Leg aid affects hind leg on the same side

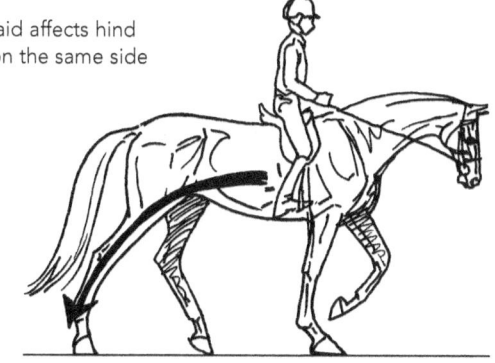

Apply leg aid as hind leg pushes off

contact to follow the natural motion of the head and neck. As the horse becomes more collected, this head and neck motion will become less.

## Half-Halts

The purpose of a half-halt is to signal the horse to prepare for a movement, to rebalance the horse more onto his hindquarters, and to increase the engagement of the hind legs.

When applying a half-halt correctly, your core muscles engage and your sacrum and tailbone drop down, flattening your lower back a little, with a

## Timing aids in posting trot.

Using left leg aid as left hind leg is pushing off; posting on right diagonal

Using left leg aid as left hind leg is swinging forward; posting on left diagonal

## Pattern of footfalls in canter.

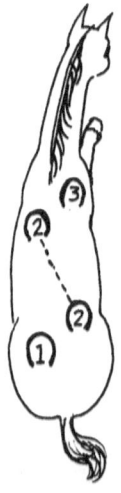

Right lead

Left lead

Timing aids in canter.

slight rotating motion of your pelvis. Your seat "opens," which allows the horse to round up his back and deepens your seat. Your knees release as your legs sink down and back under your seat, making a stronger contact on your horse's barrel. Your spine briefly lengthens, your shoulders widen, and your elbows sink.

The timing of half-halts is very important. To make a good half-halt, you must know how your horse moves and changes his balance. It is important to know where his legs and feet are in each stride to correctly influence his balance. The half-halt must be given at the moment in the stride when the horse can do what you are asking.

An example is the timing of half-halts in the canter. In order to improve balance and engagement, the correct timing is to give the half-halt at the first part of the stride after the suspension phase, when the hind legs are on the ground and can be influenced to bend their joints more, in order to develop greater thrust. If you want the horse to keep cantering, you must allow the canter to proceed after your initial half-halt, and repeat the half-halts as needed rather than create more weight in the reins at the moment the horse is on his front leg, when he can do nothing about changing his balance. If you maintain a half-halt for too long, the horse is likely to halt because you are not allowing him to go forward, or at the least he will probably transition to trot.

For a description of the half-halt, please see the *USPC C Level Manual*, pages 18–19.

## Making Transitions

A rider would always like to have a transition happen at exactly the spot where he requested it, but the quality of the transition is even more important than the accuracy. The quality of the transition depends on the horse's balance before, during, and after the transition, and maintaining the correct rhythm, energy, and tempo in the gaits before and after the transition. In downward transitions, the horse's balance and the degree to which he steps under his

Half-halt.

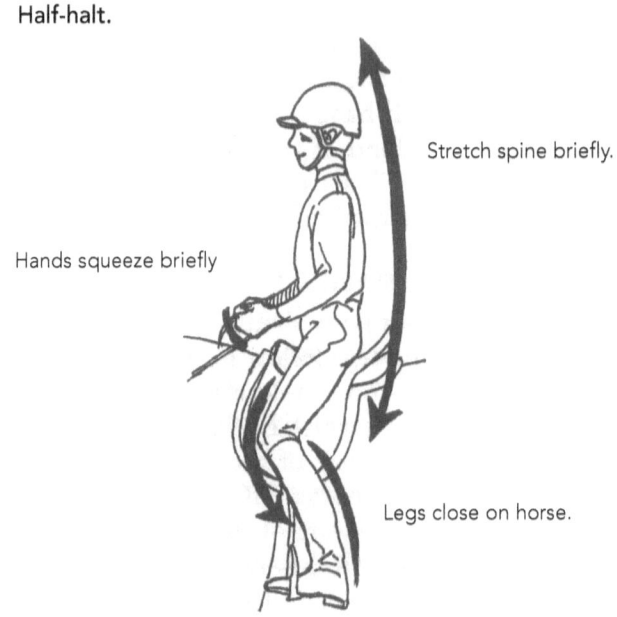

Hands squeeze briefly

Stretch spine briefly.

Legs close on horse.

body with the hind legs are good indications of engagement. A prompt, active upward transition to trot or canter is a good indication of impulsion.

It is very important to prepare for any transition with half-halts, so the horse is ready for the change. The better the preparation, the better the transition will be. There are many types of transitions used in flat work and dressage, including transitions between the gaits (such as from walk to canter, or trot to walk) and transitions within the gaits (such as collected trot to medium trot, or medium canter to extended canter, and back to collected canter). Riding good transitions between gaits or within the gait is a good way to improve the horse's engagement, balance, suppleness, and impulsion, showing that he is listening to your half-halts and is in front of your driving aids.

When preparing a horse for a transition, you must be aware of any deviation from straightness, which can cause stiffness, crookedness, and spoil the transition and the quality of the movement after the transition. The horse's shoulders should stay in front of the hind legs, and his hind legs should travel in the tracks of his front feet. In more advanced exercises, the rider may sometimes place the horse "in position" (with a very small bend, in order to align the inside foreleg with the inside hind leg), or even in a slight shoulder-fore position (with the horse's inside shoulder placed very slightly to the inside of the inside hind leg), for greater engagement. However, riding with too much "position" or over-bending the neck to the inside can block the engagement of the inside hind leg and impede the impulsion.

## Trot-Walk-Trot

This exercise consists of approximately ten strides of trot, three strides of walk, then ten strides of trot. It can improve your horse's balance, impulsion, and responsiveness, but you must stay in balance and time your aids correctly. Start with posting trot; on the last five strides, sit the trot, use half-halts, and prepare to walk. On the *first* step of walk, immediately rebalance and ask for the trot. At first, your horse may not understand that he must trot, walk, and then immediately trot again. With a few repetitions, he will learn to rebalance in the trot to be ready to walk, and to "keep his motor running" by maintaining impulsion and balance during the brief walk phase.

## Halt-Trot

To trot from a halt, without walking steps, you must use repeated half-halts to engage your horse's hind legs, build his energy, and contain it until he really wants to move forward. Practice trot-walk-trot transitions until he is alert, on the aids, and in front of your legs. Then halt and give brief half-halts until you feel his energy building. When you close your legs, engage your seat, and ask for trot, think of your horse "springing" into a trot, with power from his hindquarters going through his round back and neck into your hands. You must soften your fingers to allow him to go forward, but without slackening the reins or falling forward.

## Trot-Halt

To halt from a trot without walk steps, you must half-halt effectively and rebalance the trot for several strides, until your horse is able to engage his hind legs, shift his balance back, and tuck his hindquarters under him as he completes the last step of trot. Because a horse stops with one diagonal pair of legs, then the other, your rein aids must be given as a "one-two," timed with the outside and inside shoulder.

## Canter Departs

There are three types of canter departs, which require progressively higher levels of riding and training. All three must be executed with clear, coordinated aids and at the right level of training. The horse should always be prepared for a canter depart with one or more half-halts.

Canter departs are developed progressively. A very green horse usually canters from the trot, using an angled canter depart and outside lateral aids. As he becomes better balanced and responsive to the aids, he can canter from a working trot, with diagonal aids and a straighter canter depart. A trained, supple, well-balanced horse can canter from the walk, using inside lateral aids, which result in a more precise depart and a straighter, more collected canter.

- **Outside lateral aids.** These are leg and rein aids on the same side (the outside). The horse's head is flexed slightly at the poll to the outside, and the outside leg is applied about 4 inches behind the girth. This aid activates the outside hind leg and frees the inside shoulder, helping the horse to take the inside lead. It is clear and simple for green or unschooled horses, but it produces an outside bend and a crooked canter.

    An *angled canter depart* reinforces the outside lateral aids, especially for green horses. The horse is angled slightly into the rail before asking for the canter. The visual aid of a wall or corner guides him into a slight turn as he begins to canter, making it easier to take the inside lead. It also discourages him from running onto his forehand.

- **Diagonal aids.** The diagonal aids for a canter depart are the outside leg, applied about 4 inches behind the girth, and the inside rein aid. The outside leg activates the outside hind leg to begin the canter, and the inside rein indicates the lead and asks the horse to look in that direction. This is a natural step from outside lateral aids and an angled depart, as it uses the familiar outside leg aid, but results in a straighter canter depart and canter. Its disadvantages are the lack of a true bend (looking in the direction of the lead is not bending), and lack of precision in beginning the canter.

    A more sophisticated version of diagonal aids prepares the horse with outside leg behind the girth, then adds a slight push with the inside seat bone, along with the inside rein. This is a more precise aid, resulting in a better balanced depart and more prompt response. It also prepares the horse for the more advanced inside lateral aids for the canter.

- **Inside lateral aids.** Advanced canter departs are executed with inside lateral aids, which allow you to address the horse's balance, bend, and engagement, and to ask the horse to strike off more precisely with his hind legs. They establish a slight bend (or "position"), which indicates the lead. This is important in cantering from the walk, in the counter-canter, and in changes of lead.

    For an inside lateral depart, the horse must be on the aids. Prepare by asking for a slight bend in the direction of the lead you want, using half-halts. Your inside leg, applied close to the girth, inside direct rein aid, and a slight push of your inside seat bone ask for the canter, while your outside aids (outside leg behind the girth and outside rein) act as supporting aids.

Canter aids (right lead canter).

Outside lateral aids: outside leg, outside rein

Diagonal aids: outside leg, inside seat bone, inside rein

Inside lateral aids: inside leg, inside seat bone, inside rein

Precise timing is crucial in this canter depart. The horse begins a canter depart by balancing for an instant on his *outside* hind leg. This is followed by the diagonal pair (inside hind and outside fore together), then the inside fore. The outside hind leg must be well engaged to support the horse as he begins the canter. You must time your aids at the instant when he is balanced on his outside hind leg. In the trot, this is when the inside diagonal (inside foreleg and outside hind) touch down. In the walk, it is when the inside shoulder begins to move backward.

## Downward Transitions from Canter

Downward transitions from the canter require especially good balance, suppleness, and timing. The horse must stay round as he engages his hindquarters more, shifts his balance back, and "sits" into the downward transition. If asked to "come back" when he is unbalanced, hollow, or at the wrong point in the stride, he cannot make a good transition, especially to the walk. Ask for the downward transition as the horse's leading leg reaches forward, while his hind legs are in the air and his back begins to round. Give short, clear half-halts, keeping your upper body tall and vertical and your legs back under you. Tipping forward or leaning back, letting your legs swing forward, and pulling makes your horse stiffen against you with a hollow back, spoiling any chance of a round, balanced, and correct transition.

Canter depart: The horse balances on his outside hind leg. Notice the engagement of the inside hind leg, and the upward lift of the forehand.

**Canter-trot-walk transitions.** At first, ask the horse to shorten his canter for several strides, trot for several steps, and then walk. This allows a little more time to rebalance in the trot before the transition to walk. As you and your horse become better at this, decrease the number of trot steps between canter and walk.

**Canter-walk transitions.** Canter-to-walk transitions (without trot steps) require balance and timing, *not* harsher aids. You must shorten and balance the canter for several strides, then give the same aid as for the canter-trot transition clearly and strongly, but without pulling or hanging on the mouth.

## Warm-Up

A proper warm-up is essential for every ride. It begins by establishing a regular rhythm and consistent tempo with energy and activity in all three gaits. Next, the rider should work on suppleness exercises, including circles, changes of direction and figures that are familiar to the horse. During this phase, the relaxation and swing through the back should always be maintained. By creating a better lateral balance through correct use of the aids, the horse should develop better longitudinal balance, allowing him to stretch his top line and reach correctly to the rider's contact. After establishing these steps, the rider will go on to work on the exercises for the day. After work, be sure to include a correct cool-down phase, to bring your horse's pulse and respiration down to a normal range.

## Riding and Evaluating a Strange Horse

Riding different horses is a most important part of your riding education. Each horse is an individual, with something special you can learn from him.

Before riding a strange horse, find out all you can about him. If possible, watch his owner ride him first, and compare the way he goes with that of your own horse. If he seems quicker in his reactions, more sensitive, or nervous, you will have to be especially quiet and smooth in the way you ride while you get to know him.

Before mounting, do a careful tack safety check, adjust the stirrups to fit, and check the girth. Ask the owner if you should carry a whip or wear spurs.

When mounting a strange horse, be especially smooth and quiet. Ask the horse to stand still while you mount and for a few moments afterward while you get settled and get acquainted.

Try out a new horse at a walk at first, making several halts and turns in each direction. Use the lightest and softest aids, increasing them a little at a time if necessary. Don't surprise a strange horse with sudden, strong aids. Give yourself and the horse time to relax and feel confident with each other.

Ride as you would when warming up your own horse. It may take a little practice before you feel that you are in good balance with an unfamiliar horse, especially during transitions. Ride changes of direction and transitions, and don't canter or jump until you feel that you know each other and are working well together. As you ride, try to form your own opinion of this horse, his temperament, training, and way of moving.

Riding someone else's horse is a great privilege, so it is your responsibility to take the best possible care of him. Be tactful; never get rough or fight with him. Pay attention to his condition and bring him back calm and cool. After you have ridden someone else's horse, it is only polite to brush off and put the horse away properly, clean the tack, and re-adjust the stirrups to where they were. It's also important to be polite and tactful when giving your opinion of someone else's horse. Even if you found him difficult to ride, find something nice to say about him, and thank the owner for letting you ride him!

# 3

# Dressage and Training Principles

In its simplest sense, dressage means "training." Dressage is a basis for training horses of all types. When basic dressage training is completed, a horse should be a pleasure to ride, and is also prepared for specialized training in any discipline. In addition, dressage can be used to improve movement and to rehabilitate horses with poor muscle development, stiffness, or movement problems due to incorrect riding or training. Dressage is important in a rider's education, because it develops a supple, balanced seat, correct and subtle application of the aids, and understanding of movement and training.

Dressage can also be a competitive sport (to Olympic level) or an exhibition of equestrian art. Correct dressage is a gymnastic exercise for the horse, which strengthens and supples him.

Dressage competition is conducted in a standard dressage arena. It is useful to have a dressage arena with letters set up for training purposes at home.

## Principles of Dressage

Dressage is based on classical principles and methods that have been proven over several centuries. These principles, in brief, are as follows:

- The gymnastic development of the horse: developing strength, suppleness, balance, and good movement, based on an understanding of horse

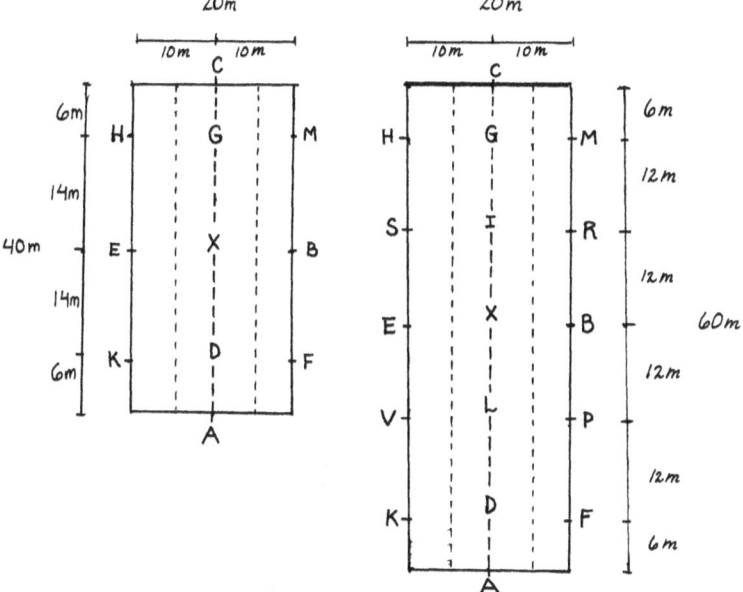

Small and large dressage arenas.

anatomy, movement, and biomechanics. Good dressage makes a horse's gaits more beautiful and pleasant to ride, makes him stronger and sounder, and prolongs his useful life.

- Dressage training is progressive; each stage is based on the foundation of previous work.
- The goals of dressage are harmony, unity, and cooperation between horse and rider, without the use of force. The rider's aids should be so subtle as to be nearly invisible; the horse gives the impression of doing of his own accord what the rider asks.
- A balanced, supple, and independent seat, which permits correct and subtle application of the aids, is essential for dressage training at any level.

## Obedience, Submission, Harmony, and "Throughness"

The goal of dressage is willing cooperation, never domination of the horse by force. The process starts with attention, confidence, and simple obedience, and is further developed and refined throughout the training process. The end result should be a horse and rider who work together in harmony;

Upper-level competition gives Pony Club members an opportunity to apply what they have learned and to polish their skills.

the horse appears to perform of his own free will what the rider asks of him, and expresses his beauty and spirit in his movements.

**Obedience:** An obedient horse is attentive to his rider and complies promptly with his rider's requests to the best of his ability, without evasion or disobedience. In order for the horse to understand and obey, the rider must give clear, correct, and properly timed aids.

**Submission:** Submission means "yielding." The horse yields to the rider's aids willingly, with trust in the rider and without resistance or evasion. Submission is expressed especially in correct flexion of the poll and softly chewing the bit in response to the rider's aids.

**"Throughness":** The horse allows the effect of the aids (especially rein aids and half-halts) to go through his body and influence his hind legs, without being blocked by stiffening or resistance.

## The Training Scale

The Training Scale has evolved as a means to illustrate the different steps that are essential elements in the correct training of a horse. It is important to understand that these elements are interrelated. One step is not supposed to be perfect before attempting the next, but instead, they should be used as a reference for understanding the general progression and development of the horse in his training from young horse to final goals.

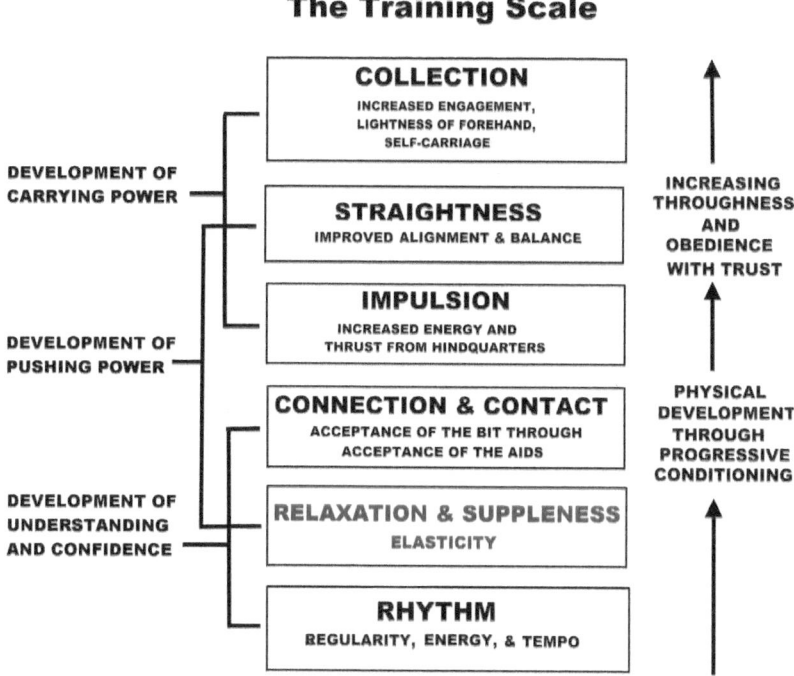

If there are difficulties with more advanced steps on the Training Scale, it is important to return to the earlier steps to be sure that they were maintained in the progression.

## Step 1 – RHYTHM
### with Energy and Tempo

### Rhythm
The *rhythm* of each gait is the sequence and timing of the footfalls (the purity of the walk, trot, and canter) and is the most basic requirement to maintain correct training. The loss of purity in the natural gaits (for example, a lateral walk or a four-beat canter) should be taken as a warning sign that something is going wrong. The rhythm of each gait is discussed later in this section.

### Tempo
*Tempo* is the rate of repetition of the rhythm (quick or slow) in beats per minute. Every horse has his own best working tempo in each gait in which he can move most efficiently but show energy in his movement. This tempo may sometimes be a little faster or slower than the horse would do on his

own. Tempo should remain the same within a gait, even when lengthening or shortening stride.

### Speed

Tempo and rhythm are not the same as *speed*, which is measured in miles per hour, or time it takes to travel between two points. In eventing, speed is expressed in meters per minute, especially in cross-country.

**Practical application of this step:**

- **Rhythm:** Please see discussion of rhythm of each gait in Chapter 1, "Biomechanics and Movement of the Horse."
- **Tempo:** The rider needs to find the correct tempo that allows the horse to relax his top line and swing through his back. A good tempo also enables the horse to move with his forelegs and hind legs well coordinated, and to maintain his balance.
- **Energy:** When the horse begins to relax in a clear rhythm and steady tempo, you can ask for increased energy or engagement, taking care that the other two elements are not lost. The rider must be sensitive to how much energy the horse can handle while staying in balance.

## Correct Rhythm of the Gaits

The gaits used in dressage are the walk, trot, and canter (see Chapter 1, "Biomechanics and Movement of the Horse," for specifics). The paces of the gaits include working, collected, medium, and extended gaits, and will be discussed later in this chapter.

## Step 2 – RELAXATION
### Suppleness with Relaxation and Elasticity

*Relaxation* is essential for good movement. This refers to athletic relaxation, not to laziness.

**Mental relaxation** refers to the horse's mental/emotional state: calmness, without anxiety or nervousness.

**Biomechanical/physical relaxation** refers to the horse's physical state, indicating the absence of muscular tension (contraction) other than that needed for optimal carriage, strength, and range and fluency of movement. Often, physical and mental/emotional relaxation go hand in hand.

Signs of relaxation include:

- Soft expression of eyes and face; ears not stiffly fixed.
- Deep breath (like a sigh) and/or "blowing the nose" (a long, gentle snort); usually observed during warm-up.

- Mouth closed, with lips relaxed; tongue in place under the bit; horse chews the bit softly.
- Relaxation of poll, throat, and neck results in opening of salivary glands, creating a wet, relaxed mouth and a small amount of foam on the lips.
- Tail swings softly in rhythm with the gait, indicating a relaxed, swinging back.
- Muscles contract and relax freely and easily in the rhythm of the gait.
- Horse is willing to stretch his head and neck forward and reach for the contact, moving with a round top line and an elastic, swinging back.

**Suppleness** is defined as the range of motion of joints and the horse's pliability or flexibility. A horse's natural suppleness is largely determined by genetics, but may over time be improved or negatively impacted through riding and training.

**Elasticity** is the ability to stretch and contract the muscles smoothly, shown in each stride, and in the ability to show differences in lengthening and shortening strides, medium, collected, and extended paces.

**Straightness** basically refers to a horse's alignment in motion. He moves forward *on one track* with his hind legs following directly behind his front legs. One of the goals of training is to develop the horse as evenly as possible on both sides.

## *Lateral Balance (Bending)*

*Lateral balance* is the distribution of the weight of horse and rider as equally as possible on the left and right legs. Loss of lateral balance means an increase of weight to one side.

*Bending* is an aspect of keeping the horse correctly aligned in lateral balance, with his hind legs following in the tracks of his front legs. Correct alignment is called *straightness*, even when it refers to bending correctly on a curved or circular track. It is not true that a horse's feet follow each other like a railroad track, although this can be a useful image. In correct bending, the inner hind leg and outer foreleg actually come closer to the horse's midline.

When a horse bends correctly, his inside hind leg reaches (engages) under his center of gravity toward his midline at every stride. This contracts his abdominal muscles, stretching his back and rotating his rib cage slightly to the outside. The outside front leg should reach in the direction of the movement so that too much weight is not placed on his inside front leg, causing him to lean on the inside shoulder. If the outside front leg reaches away from the direction of the movement (to the outside), it is considered to be "falling out." The muscles on the outside of the horse stretch farther, while those on the inside of the bend soften. The horse looks in the direction of the bend (except in shoulder-in) with no tilt of the head and with the ears level.

The aids for correct bending include using the inside leg aids to engage the inside hind leg, asking the horse to flex at the poll to the inside of the bend, guarding with the outside leg that the haunches do not escape outward, and use of outside rein half-halts to adjust balance and direction of the outside shoulder.

All horses have a natural tendency to bend more easily in one direction. This results in a stiff side (the side to which he finds it harder to bend), and a hollow side (the side to which he tends to over-bend). This is partly because one hind leg is stronger than the other. One goal of good riding and training is to strengthen the weaker hind leg, supple the stiff side, and help the horse become as equally developed as possible. This makes him stronger, sounder, more supple, and easier to ride, and also helps keep him sound.

Here's how to identify a horse's stiff and hollow sides:

**Stiff side:**
- The horse prefers not to bend in this direction. He may turn stiffly or counter-bend (bend to the outside) when ridden in his stiff direction.
- The horse takes a stronger contact on the rein on the stiff side.
- When trying to bend to the stiff side, the horse's ribs feel stiff and bulge against the rider's inside leg.
- The horse may lean onto the shoulder on his stiff side.

**Hollow side:**
- The horse prefers to bend or even over-bend in this direction, especially in the neck.
- The horse takes very little contact with the rein on the hollow side.
- When bending to the hollow side, the ribs move away from the rider's leg.
- The horse may move out through the outside shoulder when ridden on the hollow side.
- The horse may fail to put adequate contact on the outside rein when the hollow side is on the outside of the bend.
- The back muscles on the hollow side are less contracted, so the saddle and the rider's seat tend to drop down on the hollow side.
- The hind leg on the stiff side is usually weaker than the hind leg on the hollow side.

It requires work for a horse to bend correctly through a turn. If his rider is not alert, a horse may make mistakes that make him move and bend poorly when he finds turning and bending difficult. These problems are not hard to correct once you are aware of them.

Here are several common mistakes and ways to correct them:

- **Slowing down the tempo or breaking to a slower gait:** Use your legs in rhythm with the gait to maintain the rhythm and tempo.
- **Shortening stride:** In a difficult bend, such as a 10-meter circle, a horse will shorten his strides, especially on the inside of the bend, but should not slow his tempo. Use your inside leg aid to ask for longer strides and maintain the tempo, especially with the inside hind leg.
- **Speeding up the tempo or breaking to a faster gait:** This is usually caused by loss of balance. Use half-halts before and during the turn.
- **Falling in (leaning in):** Use your inside leg more strongly, but be sure the horse moves away from your leg to the outside rein. Check to see that you are not restricting too much with the outside rein to allow the horse to stretch into his outside shoulder. Remember to sit tall and don't lean in yourself.
- **Falling out with his outside shoulder:** Rotate your seat and use a direct outside rein to prevent him from drifting outward. Be careful that the horse is not over-bending his neck.
- **Swinging hindquarters to the outside:** Use your outside leg behind the girth to keep his hind legs tracking behind his front legs, and make sure that your outside rein is not counter-bending the horse, which can make him swing his hindquarters into the same direction.
- **Swinging hindquarters to the inside:** This is common in the canter on the horse's stiff side. Use the outside rein to control the shoulders and the inside leg at the girth to keep the horse on the line.

## *Longitudinal Balance*

The purpose of improving the balance of the horse is to make him more easily influenced by the rider. This is done by shifting more of his balance to the hindquarters, making the forehand more mobile.

A horse working at Training through First Level should move in a *level* or *horizontal balance* (that is, not falling on the forehand). Later, in collected paces, the horse begins to move in a more *uphill balance*, giving the impression of lowering his haunches and lifting his shoulders as if moving up an incline.

*Longitudinal balance* is influenced by the position of the torso of the horse relative to his base of support. Because about 60 percent of a horse's weight is located in his front end, the center of gravity in a standing horse is located just behind the shoulder. As a horse carries more weight on the

Lateral and longitudinal balance of the horse.

hind legs, the center of gravity shifts slightly farther back until it is under the rider's weight in a well-balanced horse.

**Longitudinal suppleness** refers to the ability for the horse to re-adjust his balance smoothly and efficiently. This ability is exemplified during transitions between and within gaits. The best way to improve longitudinal suppleness (balance, engagement, and stretching of the top line) is through transition work, both between and within gaits. Improving lateral suppleness also improves longitudinal suppleness.

**Engagement** is the bending of the hip, stifle, and hock joints as the hind legs bear the weight of the horse during the stance phase of the stride. This allows the horse to store energy, which is released as *impulsion* (or *thrust*) as the hind legs push off from the ground. A horse must have engagement in order to produce impulsion. Engagement is not only the horse keeping the hind legs more under the body, but is greatly influenced by the horse shifting his balance to the rear to load the hind legs.

Engagement is not the same as "hock action" (the flexion of the hocks in the air, as in a Hackney trot), or "reach," which refers to how far the hind leg swings, as in a racing Standardbred.

## Step 3 – CONTACT
### Acceptance of the Bit and Aids

After establishing the first two steps in the Training Scale, the horse should be in enough balance and suppleness through the top line to relax his neck and be willing to reach downward into the rider's hand. It is important that the horse seeks contact with the rider's hand, rather than the rider "taking

Contact: Stretching down into the bit.

backward" to get contact. When the horse seeks contact, the rider can regulate it with the rein aids and the horse begins to *accept the bit*.

**Accepting the bit:** When a horse accepts the bit, his neck relaxes and he is willing to flex at the poll, bringing his face closer to the vertical, and also to show lateral flexion when asked by the rider. He will carry his head with the poll at the highest point and with a closed mouth, but he softly chews the bit. The feel on the reins is light but steady.

Incorrect movement. Horse moves stiffly, with disengaged hind legs and a hollow back. Rider is out of balance, behind the motion, and driving the horse against stiff, pulling hands.

Good acceptance of the bit at First Level. The horse's head is slightly behind the vertical, but the connection from the rider's elbow to the bit is excellent, and the overall outline is correct for First Level.

**"On the aids":** The horse accepts and responds to the rider's leg, seat, and rein aids, causing him to engage his hind legs, round his back, slightly arch his neck, and relax his poll, quietly chewing the bit.

**Submission:** In order for a horse to accept contact, he must also understand the concept of *yielding* or submitting to the aids, including light pressure on the mouth and leg pressure to make him go forward or laterally. A horse cannot accept the aids if he does not understand how to yield to pressure on the bit or move away from the leg aids.

When a horse *accepts the bit* and is *on the aids*, swinging through his back and becoming *through*, we consider him to be *connected* (or *in connection*).

See Chapter 2, "Principles of Riding on the Flat," for more information about contact, connection, and accepting the bit.

## Step 4 – IMPULSION
### Increased Energy from the Hindquarters

Impulsion is thrust, from the releasing of the energy stored by the engagement of the hindquarters, through a back that is free from negative tension, and is shown in the horse's elastic, whole-body movement.

## Lengthening of the Stride in the Trot or the Canter

The horse should cover more ground with each stride. As the horse stores more energy in the engagement stage of the stride, he creates more thrust. The top line should be allowed to lengthen slightly while still maintaining balance, showing *throughness* and elasticity in the lengthened strides, as well as in the upward transitions and when returning to working paces.

## Medium and Extended Trots and Canters

A medium or extended trot or canter has more uphill balance and a longer suspension phase than a lengthening of stride. A prerequisite to medium and extended paces is the development of collection. In the medium paces, the additional pushing power in the lengthened strides requires less time in the phase where the leg is behind the horse's hip, and greater engagement to thrust the horse more powerfully into the air. Ground-covering strides with suspension can depend on the conformation of the horse as well as thoroughness, reach, and elasticity; however, the amount of over-tracking only increases when the thrust from the hind leg engagement carries the horse further during the *suspension* (air time) phase of the stride.

## Hints for riders:

- It is useful to count the number of your horse's strides between two fixed spots, such as the letters M and F. If the horse covers that amount of ground in fewer strides, his strides will have lengthened.
- If you ask for more than the horse is capable of, he may lose his top line connection, raise his head and neck, drop his back and/or go on the forehand, or become hurried in his tempo.
- Working on longer strides in the open can help to develop thrust. On a gentle uphill slope, ask the horse to go forward more without increasing his tempo. The slope will cause the horse to use more muscle in the hindquarters for pushing power. This is strenuous work and must be developed gradually over time.
- Riding over cavaletti, with correct spacing, can also encourage your horse to adjust his strides.

If, when doing these exercises, the horse loses his rhythm, balance, or connection, you should return to more basic work.

## Shortening Stride

Shortening the stride is not just slowing down. To shorten stride correctly, a horse must shift his weight back to his hindquarters while maintaining the same tempo; his strides then cover less ground. It feels as if he "sits down" behind while going forward. Shortening stride helps a horse keep his balance on slippery ground or when going downhill. It is also the beginning of collection and is used to improve longitudinal balance, especially in transitions between gaits and within a gait.

To ask your horse to shorten stride, use half-halts in rhythm with his gait, with brief, rhythmic squeezes on the outside rein. As the horse comes back to you, close your fingers to keep him from stretching out while you use your legs to keep him alert awake and lively. Use your back, seat, and core to help hold the energy beneath you that is created by your legs. Sit up and maintain your balance, keeping your legs back under your seat and on your horse's sides to encourage him to engage his hind legs. If you try to shorten stride by pulling on the reins, or lose your balance instead of rebalancing properly, your horse will learn to resist your hands, hollow his back, and stiffen against you instead of shortening correctly.

## Step 5 – STRAIGHTNESS
### Equal Contact in Both Reins

One of the goals of dressage work is to have the horse become equally supple to both directions and take contact with the bit equally on both sides. Straightness is necessary in order for the weight to be evenly distributed over the two halves of the body. It is developed through systematically training and suppling both sides of the body.

From the earliest mounted lessons, it is a goal for the horse to travel with his body correctly aligned, so that the haunches follow the shoulders on the line of travel on straight lines, circles, and turns. Straightness can also refer to the correct alignment as in reference to the arena, as in leg-yields.

**Straightness.** If the horse is straight, the hind legs will push exactly in the direction of the center of gravity. The restraining aids will pass through the horse correctly via the mouth, poll, neck, and back to the hindquarters, and will act on both hind legs equally.

A horse can only become straight if his rider's weight is balanced equally on either side of the horse's back. The rider must be careful to ride in good balance, without collapsing in the hip or rib cage, leaning, or sitting unevenly. Use half-halts to balance the horse before, during, and after each turn or corner, and use both inside and outside aids to help him move with correct alignment through the turn. Riding over cavaletti on a curve (properly spaced and accurately ridden) can be a useful exercise. Improving straightness and equal development is a long process, and it requires good riding, including a straight rider, and choosing the right exercises to help the horse.

This phase and the next phase, collection, work to straighten the horse's spine by improving the rider's control of the horse's shoulders and his balance through the use of lateral work and other exercises.

This horse and rider demonstrate straightness on a diagonal line.

## Training Methods to Increase Straightness

**Riding "in position."** A horse (seen from above) is shaped like a triangle; his shoulders are narrower than his hindquarters. He naturally tends to move with his outside shoulder and hip parallel to the fence, causing him to move with his inside hind leg more to the inside of the track and reducing the weight carried by the outside hind limb. In order to move truly "straight," his shoulders and front legs must be brought inward just enough to line up with his hind legs. This is called "riding in position."

To ride in position, the rider positions the shoulders slightly to the inside so that the inside front leg is directly in front of the inside hind leg. The rider very slightly increases her weight on the inside seat bone while turning her entire upper body, including both arms, very slightly (less than 5 degrees) to the inside. This causes the outside rein to be closer to the horse's neck and shoulders and the inside rein to be slightly away from the neck and shoulders. The inside leg maintains its position at the girth, while the outside leg is slightly behind the girth. The outside supporting rein and leg are important to maintain straightness through the horse's body and neck.

If you ride toward a mirror "in position," you should not see the horse's inside hind leg as it will be directly behind the inside front leg, and the neck and head will be straight with no flexion.

Straightness and riding in position.

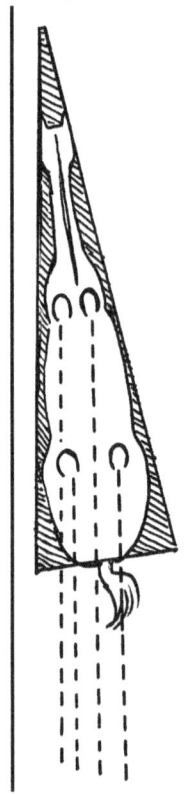

Horse moves crookedly when outside shoulder and hip are aligned with the track

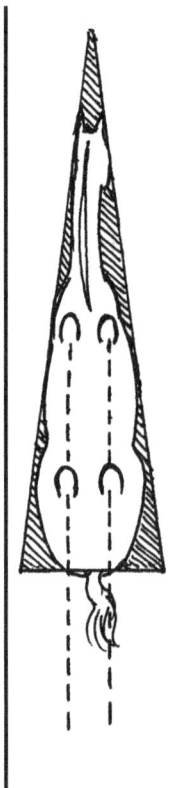

Riding "in position" to the right, horse is bent slightly to the right, bringing shoulders in line with hind legs

## Shoulder-Fore

Shoulder-fore is a preliminary exercise that prepares the horse for the shoulder-in. It is ridden with the same aids as shoulder-in, but with less bend and a smaller angle to the wall or track. Instead of moving on three tracks as in a shoulder-in, the horse's front legs are moved only slightly off the track, so that the track of the inside hind leg goes between the tracks of the forelegs.

Shoulder-fore has less collecting effect than shoulder-in, but it can be useful as an intermediate step between leg-yielding and shoulder-in. It can also be useful in straightening the canter, especially for horses that are not yet able to canter in shoulder-in without becoming stiff.

The aids for shoulder-fore are the same as for shoulder-in (please see page 97).

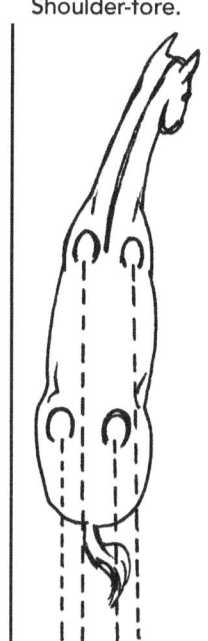

Shoulder-fore.

## Step 6 – COLLECTION AND LIGHTNESS

**Collection**

This is a state in which the horse is gathered together, moving with short, suspended strides in an uphill balance, without sacrificing impulsion. The horse's frame is shorter, with the neck arched. As he progressively begins to become more comfortable carrying his weight on his hindquarters, his forehand will become lighter and more mobile.

In the collected paces the strides become shorter and higher, but without losing impulsion or energy. When a horse moves in collection with impulsion,

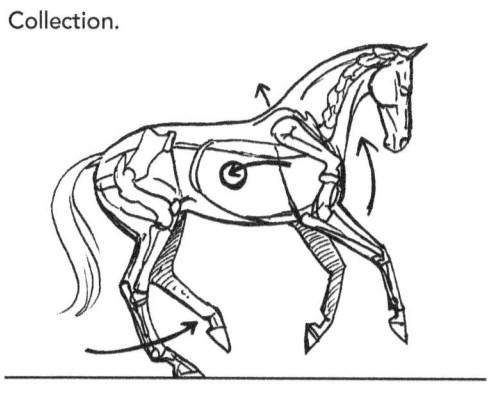

Collection.

suppleness, and the right degree of self-carriage, he is light, athletic, and able to move in any gait or direction at the slightest indication. Lightness is highly dependent on good riding and harmony between the horse and rider.

Collection can only be achieved by a horse that has developed all the other qualities that come before it on the Training Scale. If any of those elements are lost when trying to collect the horse, the rider should move back down the scale to reinforce whatever elements are inadequate. Collection cannot be forced without creating discomfort, resistance, and poor movement, all of which can ruin a horse's training.

**Outline (Frame)**

The outline, balance, and carriage of the horse depends on his level of training and what he is doing at the moment. His *outline* (or *frame*) is determined by the horse's ability to engage his hind legs and round his back, and by the resulting carriage of his head and neck. Don't confuse the terms "outline" or "frame" with the horse's head and neck position, otherwise known as a "headset." The horse must never be shortened more in front of the rider (that is, in his head and neck) than he is shortened behind the saddle (that is, engaged and "sitting down" in the hindquarters). Be careful that you do not become fixated on the horse's head and neck position—dressage is not about a headset or a "frame."

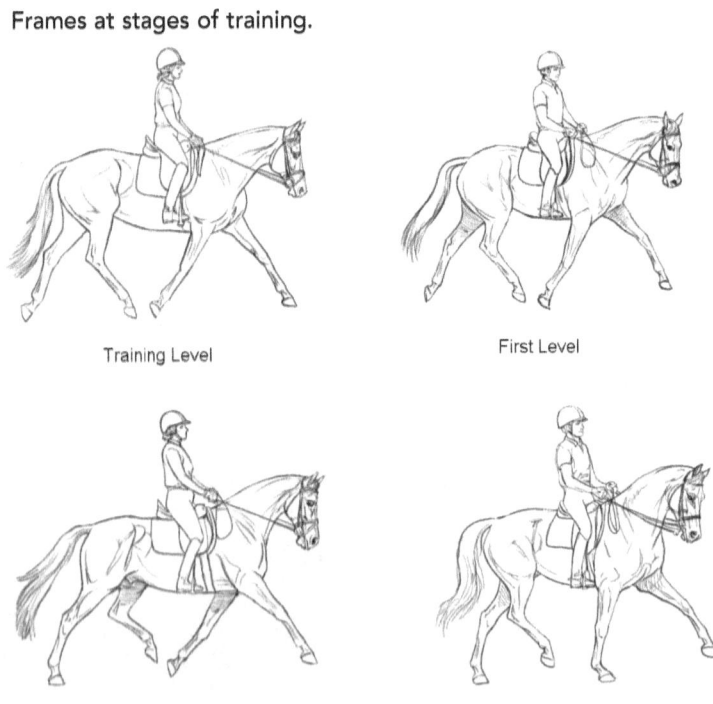

Frames at stages of training.

Training Level

First Level

Second Level

Third Level

### Development of Frames in Stages of Training

A Training Level horse should work in a *level balance* (that is, not traveling downhill or on the forehand) and show acceptance of the bit. He is asked to maintain this balance and bit acceptance through simple transitions (walk to trot, trot to canter, canter to trot, walk to halt) and large circles, demonstrate his willingness to stretch forward and downward when asked, and "chew the reins out of the hands." As the horse develops, he becomes stronger and better balanced, and begins to develop thrust, which allows him to lengthen his outline and his stride. A First Level horse is able to demonstrate lengthening of stride in the trot and canter, and to maintain his balance and connection in slightly more difficult figures (smaller circles and leg-yields) and transitions (trot-halt-trot).

Through further training, the horse becomes better able to engage his hind legs under his body, raise his back, and shift his balance to the rear. This collection is reflected in the more "uphill" tendency of a Second Level horse, that is able to show true medium gaits (as opposed to lengthenings) and stay balanced in smaller circles, lateral movements (shoulder-in and haunches-in), and more difficult transitions (walk-canter-walk).

A Third Level horse is confirmed in uphill balance, and can maintain it through more difficult lateral movements (half-pass) and flying changes of lead. He has the balance to show a greater change in outline and stride length, demonstrating both medium and extended gaits. Correctly done, this training process through the levels should enhance the horse's strength, suppleness, athleticism, and natural gaits.

## The Paces Within the Gaits

Paces are the variations within the gaits. These definitions are found in the current USEF Rule Book – Dressage section, and apply to Dressage Specialty tests as well as Eventing tests. In all variations within a gait, the rhythm and sequence of footfalls should remain the same.

## The Walk

**Medium walk:** A clear, regular, and unconstrained walk of moderate lengthening. The horse, remaining on the bit, walks energetically but relaxed, with even and determined steps, the hind feet touching the ground in front of the hoof prints of the fore feet (overstepping). The rider maintains a light, soft, and steady contact with the mouth, allowing the natural movement of the head and neck.

**Free walk:** The free walk is a pace of relaxation in which the horse is allowed complete freedom to lower and stretch out his head and neck. The

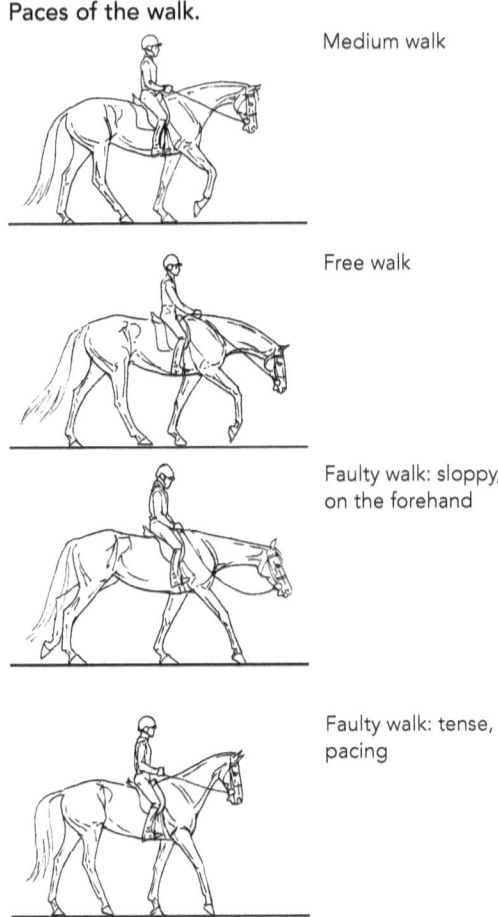

Paces of the walk.

Medium walk

Free walk

Faulty walk: sloppy, on the forehand

Faulty walk: tense, pacing

degree of ground cover and length of strides, with the hind feet over-stepping clearly in front of the hoof prints of the front feet, are essential to the quality of the free walk.

**Extended walk:** The horse covers as much ground as possible, without haste and without losing the regularity of the steps. The hind feet over-step, touching the ground clearly in front of the hoof prints of the fore feet. The rider allows the horse to stretch out his head and neck (forward and downward) without losing contact with the mouth and control of the poll. The nose must be clearly in front of the vertical.

# The Trot

**Working trot:** This is a pace between the collected and the medium trot, when a horse's training is not yet developed enough and ready for collected

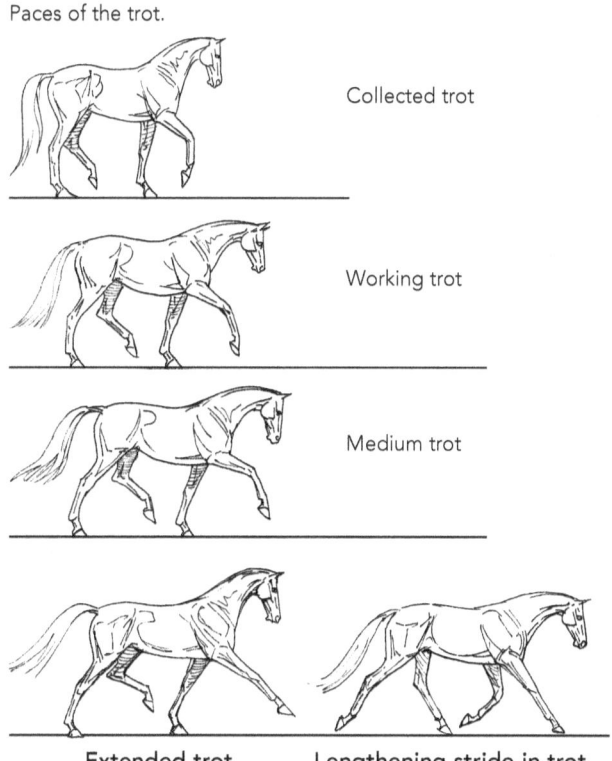

Paces of the trot.

Collected trot

Working trot

Medium trot

Extended trot    Lengthening stride in trot

movements. The horse shows proper balance and goes forward with even, elastic steps and good hock action, remaining on the bit. The expression "good hock action" underlines the importance of impulsion originating from the activity of the hindquarters.

**Lengthening of stride**: In some tests, *lengthening of stride* is required. This is a variation between the working and medium trot in which a horse's training is not developed enough for medium trot. The lengthening of stride is developed through increased thrust and impulsion required of a horse at First Level.

**Collected trot:** The horse, remaining *on the bit*, moves forward with the neck raised and arched. The hocks, being well-engaged and flexed, must maintain an energetic impulsion, enabling the shoulders to move with greater mobility, thus demonstrating complete self-carriage. Although the horse's steps are shorter than in the other trots, elasticity and cadence are not lessened.

**Medium trot:** This is a pace of moderate lengthening compared to the extended trot, but "rounder" than the latter. The horse goes forward with clearly lengthened steps and with impulsion from the hindquarters, but without hurrying. The rider allows the horse to carry his head a little more in front of the vertical than in the collected and working trot, and to lower his head and neck slightly. The steps should be even, and the whole movement is balanced and unconstrained.

**Extended trot:** The horse covers as much ground as possible. The steps are lengthened to the utmost as a result of great impulsion from the hindquarters, but without hurrying. The rider allows the horse to lengthen the frame and gain ground while controlling the poll. The fore and hind legs should reach equally forward in the moment of extension, and the fore feet should touch the ground on the spot toward which they are pointing. The whole movement should be well-balanced, and the transition to collected trot should be executed smoothly by taking more weight on the hindquarters.

## The Canter

**Working canter:** This is a pace between the collected and the medium canter, in which a horse's training is not yet developed enough and ready for collected movements. The horse shows natural balance while remaining on the bit, and goes forward with even, light, and active strides and good hock action. The expression "good hock action" underlines the importance of an impulsion originating from the activity of the hindquarters. The horse must maintain suspension (or "jump") in each stride.

**Lengthening of strides:** In some tests, "lengthening of strides" is required. This is a variation between the working and medium canter in which a horse's training is not developed enough for medium canter. The lengthening of stride is developed through increased thrust and impulsion required of a horse at First Level.

**Collected canter:** The horse, remaining *on the bit*, moves forward with the neck raised and arched. The hocks, being well-engaged, maintain an energetic impulsion, enabling the shoulders to move with greater mobility, thus demonstrating self-carriage and an uphill tendency. The horse's strides are shorter than in the other canters, without losing elasticity and cadence.

Good versus poor canter.

**Medium canter:** This is a pace between the working and the extended canter. Without hurrying, the horse goes forward with clearly lengthened strides and impulsion from the hindquarters. The rider allows the horse to carry his head a little more in front of the vertical than in the collected and working canter, and at the same time allows the horse to lower his head and neck slightly. The strides should be balanced and unconstrained.

**Extended canter:** The horse covers as much ground as possible. Without hurrying, the strides are lengthened to the utmost. The horse remains calm, light, and straight as a result of great impulsion from the hindquarters. The rider allows the horse to lengthen the frame with a controlled poll and gain ground. The whole movement should be well-balanced, and the transition to collected canter should be smoothly executed by taking more weight on the hindquarters.

# Schooling Figures

(For diagrams and descriptions of changes of direction and schooling figures, please review pages 44–48 of the *USPC C Level Manual*.)

## Changes of Direction

In changes of direction, the horse should adjust the bend of his body to the curvature of the line it follows, remaining supple and following the indications of the rider without any resistance or change of gait, rhythm, or tempo. Corners should be ridden as one-quarter of a circle appropriate to the level of the test (10 meters at Training and First Levels, 8 meters at Second and Third Levels).

Changes of directions can be executed in the following ways:

- Right-angled turn including riding through the corner (one-quarter of a volte of approximately 6 meters)
- On the short or long diagonal
- Half-circles with change of rein
- Turn on the haunches
- Serpentine loops

## Ring Figures

The figures required in dressage tests are circles, voltes, serpentines, and figure of eight.

**Circles and voltes:** A volte is a circle of 8 to 10 meters in diameter. If larger than 10 meters, it is a circle.

**Serpentine:** A serpentine with alternating loops consists of half-circles connected by a straight line. When crossing the center line, the horse should be parallel to the short side of the arena. The straight connection varies in length depending on the size of the half-circles. A serpentine with one loop on the long side of the arena is executed with a 5-meter or 10-meter distance from the track, as specified in the test.

**Figure of eight:** This figure consists of two voltes or circles of equal size (as prescribed in the test), joined at the center of the eight. The rider should straighten the horse an instant before changing direction at the center of the figure eight.

## Stretching the Frame

This exercise gives a clear expression of the throughness of the horse and demonstrates his balance, suppleness, obedience, and relaxation. In order to execute the exercise of "stretching on a long rein" correctly, the rider must lengthen the reins as the horse stretches gradually forward and downward. As the neck stretches forward and downward, the horse's mouth should reach to a line level with the point of the shoulder, or even lower. The horse must keep an elastic and consistent contact with the rider's hands; the reins must not loosen or drop contact. The gait must maintain its rhythm and tempo, and the horse should remain light in the shoulders (not falling on the forehand) with a swinging back and with the hind legs well engaged. During the re-take of the reins, the horse must accept the contact without resistance in the mouth or poll.

Good stretching down.

This horse is stretching down well. However, the rider should look up and not lock her hands in place.

# Work on Two Tracks and Lateral Movements

In work on two tracks and lateral movements, the horse moves sideways as well as forward. Work on two tracks includes simple sideways movements such as leg-yielding. Lateral movements refer to moving sideways and forward with bend.

The aim of this work is to:

- Improve the horse's obedience to the aids of the rider.
- Supple all parts of the horse, thereby increasing the freedom of his shoulders and the suppleness of his quarters as well as the elasticity of the bond connecting the mouth, poll, neck, back, and haunches.
- Improve the cadence and bring the balance and gaits into harmony.
- Improve and test collection.

Lateral work can benefit a horse only when it is correctly taught and ridden. The horse must keep his rhythm, balance, and connection. If he becomes tense, hollow, irregular, or loses his desire to go forward, stop the lateral exercise and re-establish the basics. If a horse has difficulty with a lateral movement, he may not be physically ready for it. Try a simpler version of the exercise, and don't ask for too many steps at once.

To ride lateral work, you must be aware of your inside and outside aids. When doing lateral work, you use one set of aids to ask the horse to move sideways and the other aids to regulate the movement, telling him to stay in balance, how far to move, and when to stop moving sideways. You also use half-halts to keep him in balance so that he can step sideways in a coordinated way. In each movement, you must be clear about how to use each aid and what it does, and you must coordinate it with the other aids.

You must ride in good balance as well, without leaning, twisting, or collapsing to one side. You must also learn how to apply your left and right aids evenly, instead of over-using the aids on your stronger side. This requires a ground helper with an educated eye, preferably your instructor, to help identify your weaknesses. Mirrors are also helpful to assess the quality of the lateral movement in real-time.

## Basic Two-Track Exercises

These exercises can improve your horse's suppleness, balance, straightness, and response to your leg and seat aids, and they are the foundation for more advanced work. They also teach you to coordinate your aids and help you understand how they work. Beginning two-track work is done with a straight horse, with flexion at the poll only. This initial work teaches the horse to move sideways as well as forward in response to the aids.

**Turn on the forehand:** The purpose of this exercise is to supple the horse and teach him obedience to the aids. In this exercise, the inside of the horse is the side *from* which the horse yields (that is, the horse is flexed at the poll to the right, which is the inside, when the haunches move to the left). The horse moves around the inside front leg. The outside front foot steps forward and around the inside forefoot, which remains active in the sequence of footfalls. The hind feet move on a curved line, with the inside hind foot striking the ground in front of the outside hind foot.

Your horse has already learned to move sideways from pressure, both on the ground and when you are mounted. (Please see the *USPC C Level Manual*, pages 30–33.) The turn on the forehand is the next step in teaching him to move sideways in a more controlled way from leg pressure.

To begin, ask for only a quarter-turn on the forehand (90 degrees) or less. Your horse should take three or four steps to complete the turn. His inside hind leg should cross over in front of the other hind leg with each step. If the inside hind leg crosses behind the other hind leg, he is trying to back up.

Riding the turn on the forehand at the rail of the ring helps the horse understand what you want him to do. The rail acts as a guide and keeps him

Turn on the forehand.

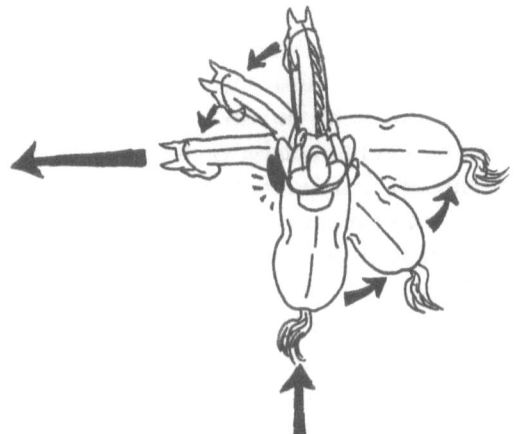

Ride straight to the rail and halt.

Inside leg behind the girth asks for each step.

Ride straight forward after turn.

from walking forward instead of turning. To start a quarter-turn, ride across the ring and make a square halt facing the rail, leaving enough room so that your horse will not bump into the rail as he turns.

Flex the horse slightly away from the direction in which his hind legs should move while keeping his neck straight. (To move his hind legs right, flex him slightly to the left. The left side is the inside, and your left seat bone, leg, and rein are your inside aids. The right side is the outside, and your right seat bone, leg, and rein are the outside aids.)

Swivel your body and look slightly to the inside (left), and give a brief direct rein aid with your inside (left) hand. Use your inside (left) leg aid 3 or 4 inches behind the girth to ask the horse to step sideways with his hind legs. Your outside (right) rein and leg should be in contact with the horse but should remain quiet. Give a brief leg aid and direct rein aid to ask for each step, and relax your aids as your horse responds. At first, pause between steps and give him time to rebalance himself and prepare for the next step. Later, you can ask him to make several steps in succession, but he should never hurry sideways too fast or out of control. When your horse takes the last step of the quarter-turn, he will be facing straight down the track. Pat him and ride forward, to encourage free forward movement.

When performing a turn on the forehand, you must sit in balance in the center of the saddle. If you lean forward or shift your weight to one side, it will confuse your horse, and he cannot make a good turn. Wait until he finishes one step before asking for the next. If you rush him or apply the leg aid too long, he may take too big a step sideways and hurry through the turn. Keep contact with your horse's mouth, but don't use too strong a rein aid. This can make him back up.

After you can perform a turn on the forehand in one direction, try it the other way. This exercise is usually easier for a horse in one direction and more difficult in the other, needing extra practice.

**Spirals:** Riding spirals is a simple way to improve your horse's lateral balance and his response to the inside and outside aids at the walk and trot. This builds on the simple Forward-and-Out exercise your horse has already learned. (Please see the *USPC C Level Manual*, pages 30–31.)

Start by riding a 15-meter circle at a walk. (It helps to ride the circle in the end of a dressage arena or to set up markers that show you the correct size circle.) Your horse must move forward in good rhythm, paying attention to your aids and bending correctly, with his hind feet following in the tracks of his front feet.

To spiral out, use your inside aids (inside leg near the girth and inside indirect rein) to ask your horse to move sideways and outward a little with each stride. Your outside aids should be in contact with your horse. You use them to keep him from moving sideways too much on any step, falling out (leaning on his outside shoulder), or rubber-necking (bending his neck too much to the inside). It should take several steps to achieve the 20-meter circle. When the circle is large enough, use your outside aids (outside supporting rein and outside leg behind the girth) to stop moving sideways, and ride forward on the circle. Practice this exercise in both directions at the walk and later at the trot.

Timing your aids correctly will help your horse learn to cross his hind leg over and step sideways. You need to give the leg aid when the horse's hind leg is reaching forward and swing through the air—that's when he can reach farther forward and cross it over. In the walk, give the leg aid with your inside leg when the rib cage is swinging outward. In the posting trot, apply an inside leg aid as you rise to catch the inside hind leg in the air. (It is also possible to change to the inside diagonal for this exercise, which allows you to use your inside leg aid as you sit down.)

Spiraling in means gradually making the circle smaller by moving in a little more toward the center with each stride. This is a little more difficult than spiraling out, because the horse must step inward while bent to that side, which requires more balance and an elementary degree of collection.

To spiral in, start by riding a 20-meter circle. Sit deep and tall and rotate your body toward the center, using your outside leg on your horse's side behind the girth. Your inside aids maintain contact, keep the bend, and keep your horse from cutting in too quickly, or falling in by leaning on his inside shoulder. Gradually spiral in until the circle is 15 meters in diameter (about three-fourths the size of the original circle). Use your inside aids to tell your horse when to stop spiraling in and to move forward on the smaller circle.

When your horse can spiral outward and spiral inward in both directions, you can alternate these exercises. Always ride forward for at least several

Spiral in and spiral out.

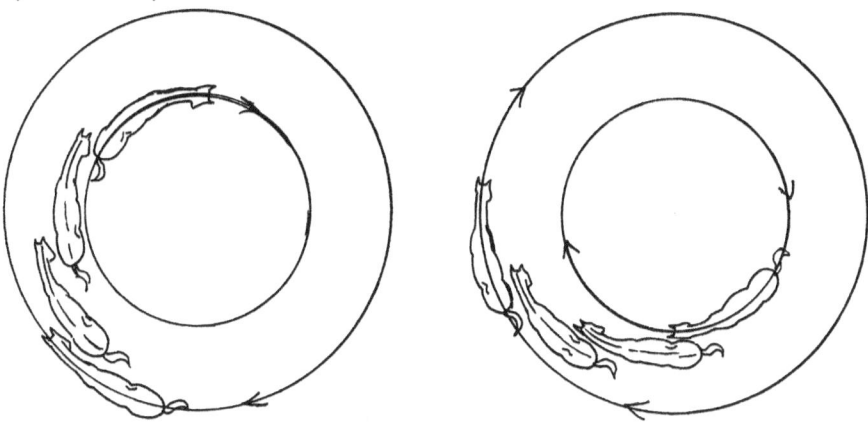

strides between lateral exercises, and ride forward afterward to establish free forward movement.

(**Note:** This movement should not be confused with a leg-yield. While spiraling inward and outward resembles a leg-yield in some ways [the horse moves laterally in response to the rider's active leg aid], it is not a true leg yield because the horse is bending around the rider's inside leg. In a true leg yield, the horse's body is straight, with a slight flexion only at the poll.) Spiraling in and out is a good precursor to shoulder-in and eventually, to haunches-in.

**Leg-yielding:** The horse is straight, except for a slight flexion at the poll away from the direction in which he moves, so that the rider is just able to see the eyebrow and nostril on the inside. The inside legs pass and cross in front of the outside legs. Leg-yielding can be included in the training of the horse before he is ready for collected work. Later on, together with the shoulder-in, a more advanced movement, it is the best means of making a horse supple, loose, and unconstrained to improve the freedom, elasticity, and regularity of his gaits and the harmony, lightness, and ease of his movements. Leg-yielding can be performed on the diagonal, in which case the horse should be parallel to the long sides of the arena, although the forehand should be slightly in advance of the hindquarters. It can also be performed along the wall, in which case the horse should be at an angle of about 35 degrees to the direction in which he is moving.

To ask a horse to leg-yield, use your inside aids (a short squeeze with your inside leg close to the girth, and a brief squeeze of your inside hand) just as his inside hind leg lifts into the air to begin stepping forward. Your outside hand may give a small opening rein aid to lead your horse in the right direction. Immediately after using the inside aids, give a brief half-halt to keep him straight and in balance so that he steps sideways instead of just going faster. Your outside aids should be in contact with your horse, ready to tell him "That's far enough" after each step.

When you ride a leg-yield, you must keep your horse straight and rebalance him after each step. You must sit up straight and even, not lean or twist, and you must remain in the center of your saddle, not letting your seat slide to the outside. Too much inside rein can cause the horse to over-bend his neck instead of flexing at the poll. If your horse doesn't pay attention to your leg aids or doesn't step sideways enough, you may have to tap him with a dressage whip beside your leg, or touch him gently with a spur. (Ask your instructor, to be sure you are using your aids correctly and not confusing your horse.)

When you can leg-yield easily at a walk, you can try the same exercise at a sitting trot. It's especially important to use good half-halts to keep your horse straight, in balance, and paying attention, and not to trot too fast. Remember to half-halt after each sideways step to keep the horse from going faster. After three or four steps, ride forward in a posting trot and reward him with a pat. If this exercise proves difficult, return to the spiral and turn on the forehand exercises.

**Leg-yielding from the quarter line to the rail:** Turn down the quarter line of the arena and make sure your horse is moving straight for several strides before you begin to leg-yield. Your horse should remain parallel to the long side of the arena. Ask him to leg-yield toward the rail for three or four strides, then ride straight forward. If your horse begins to angle toward the track or loses his balance and coordination, ride straight forward for a few strides before asking him to leg-yield outward again.

Practice this several times; then change directions and try leg-yielding from the other leg. Gradually the angle can be increased by leg-yielding from the center line to various points along the rail.

You will probably find one direction easier than the other. This is related to the horse's hollow and stiff sides (as discussed earlier in this chapter). Generally, the horse moves easily away from the hollow side, although he may tend to fall through his outside shoulder or over-bend his neck. It is often more difficult to move the horse away from his stiff side, but easier to keep him straight.

When this exercise can be performed easily in both directions, you can progress to the next exercise.

**Leg-yielding along the wall:** The horse moves forward and sideways at an angle to the wall (about 35 degrees). His body is straight and his head is flexed slightly at the poll, away from the direction in which he moves.

Leg-yielding along the wall may be performed with the head toward the wall, or with the tail toward the wall. (Don't confuse this with shoulder-in: In

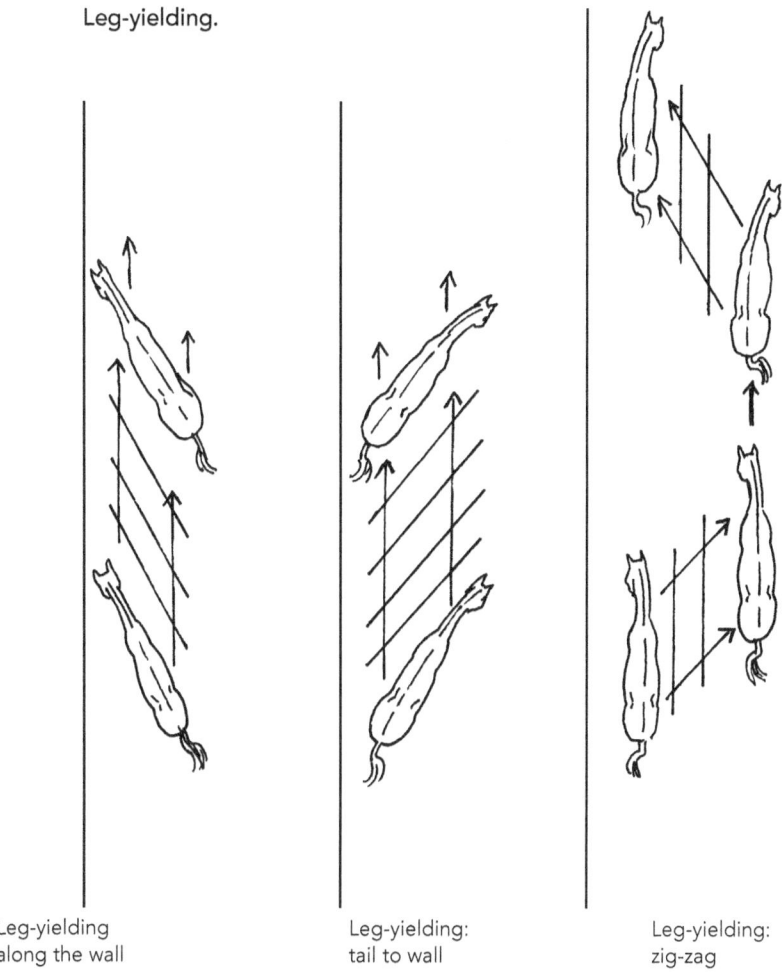

Leg-yielding.

Leg-yielding along the wall

Leg-yielding: tail to wall

Leg-yielding: zig-zag

leg-yield, the horse is straight in the neck and body with just a slight flexion at the poll, and both the front and hind legs cross, whereas in shoulder-in, the horse is bent away from the direction of travel, and only the front legs cross.)

**Leg-yielding on the diagonal:** The horse moves forward and sideways along a diagonal line. His body is straight and parallel to the long side of the ring, and he flexes slightly at the poll, away from the direction in which he moves.

In a variation of this exercise, the horse is asked to leg-yield from the wall to the center line or quarter line, to straighten for a stride, and then to leg-yield back to the wall (a zig-zag). (Don't confuse this with a half-pass, a more advanced movement, in which the horse is bent in the direction of the movement.)

Leg-yielding on the diagonal, moving from right to left. The horse is straight, with a slight flexion at the poll to the right. The horse shows good flexion and reach in front but should stretch into contact more.

## The Lateral Movements

Lateral work is two-track work done with bend. In the easier lateral movements (shoulder-in), the horse is bent away from the direction of travel. In more advanced lateral movements (haunches-in, renvers, half-pass, and turn on the haunches), the horse is bent in the direction of travel. The direction of the bend is always considered the inside. The aim of lateral movements is to develop and increase the engagement of the quarters and thereby also the collection.

The bend or flexion must never be exaggerated so that it impairs the balance and fluency of the movement. In the lateral movements the gait should remain free and regular, maintained by a constant impulsion, yet they must be supple, cadenced, and balanced. The impulsion is often lost because of the rider's preoccupation with bending the horse and pushing him sideways.

**Shoulder-in:** This exercise is performed in collected trot, and can be used in training to develop a collected trot from the working trot. The horse is ridden with a slight but uniform bend around the inside leg of the rider, maintaining cadence, at a constant angle of approximately 30 degrees to the track. The horse's inside foreleg passes and crosses in front of the outside foreleg; the inside hind leg steps forward under the horse's body, following the same track as the outside foreleg, with the lowering of the inside hip. When viewed from the front, the horse is on "three tracks"—the outside hind is one track, the inside hind and outside fore are the second track, and the inside fore is the third track. The horse is bent away from the direction in which he is moving.

The aids for the shoulder-in include using the inside rein to create an inside flexion in the poll, and an inside opening rein to bring the shoulders in off the track. The rider's inner leg (at the girth) asks for engagement of the inside hind leg and for the horse to not continue in off the track onto a circle, but rather to step sideways down the long side of the arena. The rider's outside leg (slightly behind the girth) guards that the haunches do not swing out but keep the bend. The rider's outside rein guards that the outside shoulder does not escape too much down the track but allows the outside foreleg to reach down the track. The outside rein should not create a counter-bend or create a tilting of the poll by being too restrictive.

Some common problems are insufficient angle, with the horse only bending at the neck; or too much angle, creating a leg-yield (this is common when the rider moves the inside leg back to keep the haunches out). If the horse loses his bend, rhythm, or impulsion, ride a 10-meter circle and continue the shoulder-in after finishing the circle, remembering that the shoulder-in is really just the first step of a circle before moving down the track.

**Haunches-in (travers):** This exercise can be performed in collected trot or collected canter. The horse's forehand remains on the track and the quarters are moved inward. His outside legs pass and cross in front of his inside legs. The horse is bent in the direction in which he is moving. He is slightly bent around the inside leg of the rider, but with a greater degree of bend than in the shoulder-in. The horse moves with a constant angle of approximately 35 degrees in relation to the track. When viewed from the front or behind, he moves on four tracks (outside fore on the first track, inside fore on the second track, outside hind on the third track; inside hind on the fourth track).

To begin the travers, the horse's hindquarters must leave the track, or after a corner or circle, they may already be placed to the inside. At the end of the travers, the quarters are brought back on the track without any counter-flexion of the poll or neck, as one would finish a circle.

To apply the aids for the travers, the rider places her outside leg behind the girth and asks the outside hind leg to step inward, under the body, while the inside leg and the inside seat bone maintain the bend, asking the horse to rotate his rib cage to the outside and to engage his inside hind leg. The inside rein (indirect rein, in the direction of the horse's outside hip)

Shoulder-in.

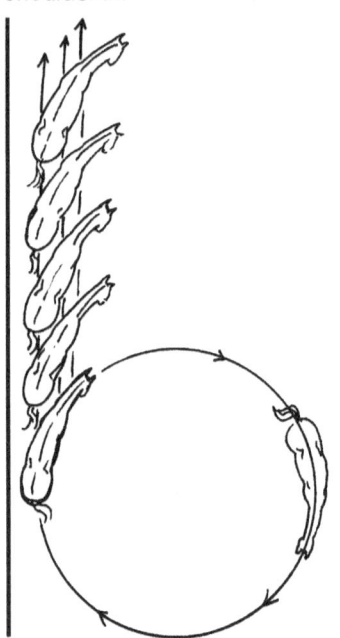

Circle, follow by shoulder-in

Aids for shoulder-in

1. Outside supporting rein (regulates bend)
2. Outside leg behind girth (holds hindquarters on track)
3. Inside rein (positions forehand and maintains bend)
4. Inside leg at girth (bends horse and maintains lateral movement)

Incorrect: Inside rein overbends the neck

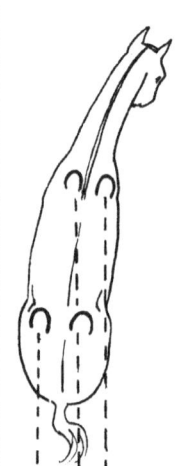

Shoulder-in on three tracks

A good shoulder-in. The horse moves on three tracks with front legs crossing, showing roundness, correct angle, and bending.

asks the horse to keep looking straight down the track, and the outside rein regulates the bend.

To begin a haunches-in to the left, start with a 10-meter circle to the left. As you complete the circle, use your inside (left) leg, seat bone, and a small amount of rein to keep the bend to the inside (left), while your outside (right) leg asks the hindquarters to stay inside of the front legs instead of returning to the track.

Some common problems include pushing too much with the outside leg, causing the rib cage to go against the inside leg; and the rider falling to the outside, causing the haunches to fall out or the bend to be lost. The rider should sit in the middle of the horse, with the weight shifted slightly in the direction of the movement. The head and neck of the horse should be parallel to the long side of the arena, with the horse looking down the track with his ears level (not over-bent in the neck or tilting his nose to the outside). Any problems with basics are best corrected by riding another circle or riding straight ahead out of the travers.

**Renvers (haunches-out, tail to the wall):** *Renvers*, or *haunches-out*, is the same as haunches-in (travers), except that the horse moves with his hindquarters on the track and his shoulders toward the inside of the arena. He is bent around the rider's inside leg, and looks in the direction of the

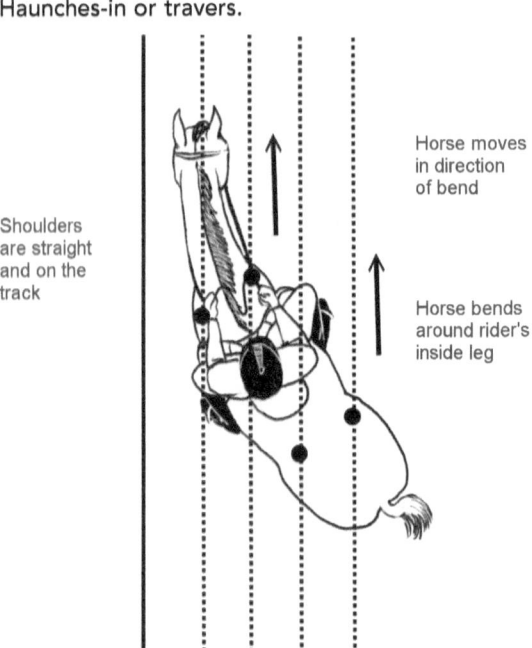

Haunches-in or travers.

Horse moves in direction of bend

Horse bends around rider's inside leg

Shoulders are straight and on the track

movement. ("Inside" refers to the bend, not to the center of the arena.) The aids are the same as for haunches-in; only the horse's position in relation to the track differs.

Renvers, like haunches-in, is a collecting movement. Renvers is more difficult than the travers because the horse does not have the rail or wall next to his shoulder as a reference point.

The goal for renvers is to show a fluent lateral movement on a straight line in collected trot, with a greater degree of bend than in shoulder-in. The fore and hind legs cross, and balance and cadence must be maintained.

In going from shoulder-in to renvers or renvers to shoulder-in, position of the horse's body relative to the track remains the same, but the bend changes. This is a difficult movement but an excellent suppling exercise and a test of response to the aids for advanced horses and riders.

**The turn on the haunches:** The turn on the haunches is a movement in which the forehand moves in even, regular steps around the horse's inside hind leg, maintaining the rhythm of the walk. The horse bends in the direction of the turn. His inside hind leg may advance in an arc up to 1 meter in diameter under him; the outside hind leg should step toward the bend and direction of the turn. Turns on the haunches may be executed as quarter-turns (90 degrees), half-turns (180 degrees), or full turns (360 degrees).

# DRESSAGE AND TRAINING PRINCIPLES

Renvers.

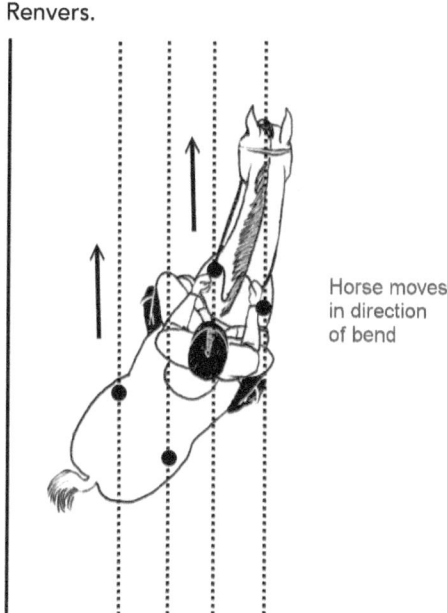

Horse moves in direction of bend

Comparison of shoulder-in, travers, and renvers (three tracks).

Shoulder-in  Travers (Haunches-in)  Renvers (Haunches-out)

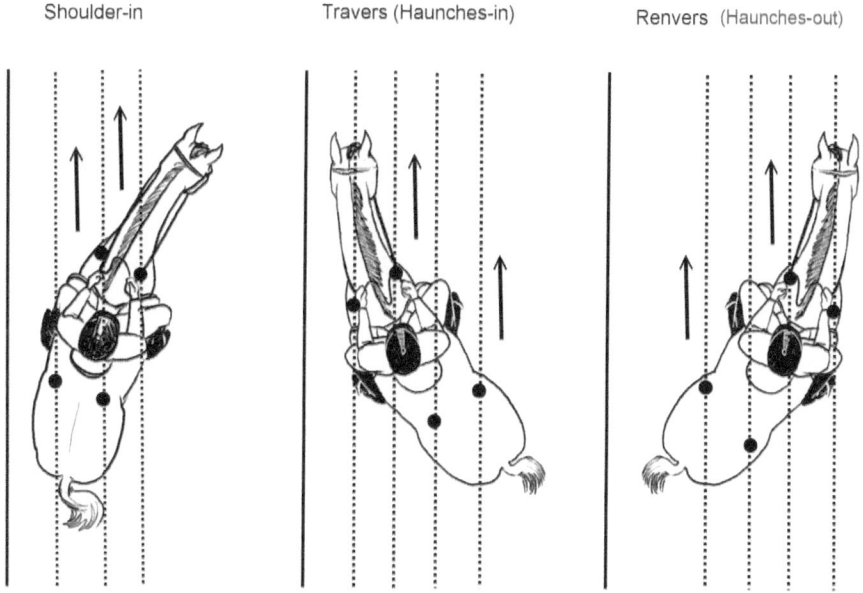

Turn on the haunches: the horse bends in the direction of the turn.

To perform a turn on the haunches, the rider collects the walk and rides *in position*, with a very slight bend in the direction of the turn. To begin the turn, the rider applies a half-halt with the seat and outside rein aids. The rider's outside leg aid, and turning of the rider's shoulder, along with weighting the inside seat bone, cause the horse to turn. The rider's outside rein and inside leg work together to control the bend (which is minimal) and to maintain the regularity of the walk and balance in the turn.

Faults in the turn on the haunches include backing up; losing the rhythm of the gait; pivoting on the inside hind leg; losing balance (as evidenced by uneven, hurried, or irregular steps); the haunches falling outward or stepping sideways; and the hind legs separating rather than staying engaged under the horse. Another common fault is the horse counter-bending from overuse of the rider's outside aids. The rider must keep her weight to the inside. This can be difficult, as the momentum of the movement tends to throw the rider to the outside, which encourages the horse's haunches to fall out. Don't try to make the turn smaller than the horse is ready for; this often leads to loss of the walk rhythm or activity ("sticking"). The turn on the haunches can be a difficult movement to learn, as it combines elements of haunches-in on a small circle with elements of shoulder-in (moving the shoulders around the haunches). Riding alternate shoulder-in and haunches-in on a 10-meter circle is an excellent way to test the basics before attempting turns on the haunches.

Turn on the haunches.

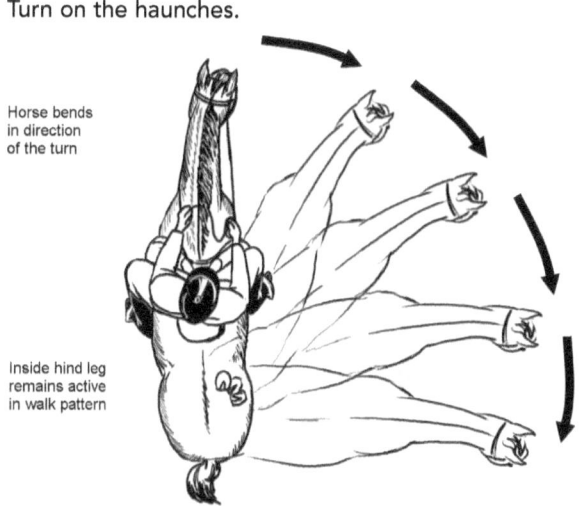

**Half-pass:** This movement is a variation of travers, executed on a diagonal line instead of along the wall. It can be performed in collected trot or collected canter. The horse should be slightly bent around the inside leg of the rider and in the direction in which he is moving. The horse's body should be nearly parallel to the long side of the arena, with the forehand slightly in advance of the hindquarters. The bend in the half-pass increases with the steepness of the diagonal (that is, there is less bend in a half-pass on the long diagonal of the arena than on a short diagonal line). The horse should maintain the same cadence and balance throughout the whole movement. In order to give more freedom and mobility to the shoulders, it is very important that the impulsion be maintained, especially the engagement of the inside hind leg.

In the half-pass in trot, the outside legs pass and cross in front of the inside legs. The canter half-pass is performed in a series of forward/sideways strides.

The aim of the half-pass in trot is to show a fluent collected trot movement on a diagonal line, with a greater degree of bend than in shoulder-in. The fore and hind legs cross, and balance and cadence are maintained.

The aim of the half-pass in canter is to demonstrate and develop the collection and suppleness of the canter by moving fluently forward and sideways without loss of rhythm, balance, or softness, and with submission to the bend.

To prepare for a half-pass, ride a 10-meter half-circle to the center line. Maintaining the same bend as on the 10-meter circle, apply the same bending aids (inside leg at the girth, outside leg behind the girth, inside rein leading the forehand toward the inside, and outside rein supporting and

Half-pass, left to right. The horse shows good balance and lateral reach, and there is harmony between horse and rider.

controlling the bend), but shift a little more of your weight to the inside of the bend without leaning, twisting, or collapsing your inside hip. Use repeated outside leg aids in rhythm to send the outside hind leg forward and sideways. If the horse begins to lose his balance, bend, or rhythm, or if his hindquarters begin to lead or trail, ride straight forward.

Faults in the half-pass include loss of rhythm, impulsion, cadence, or bend; loss of position (haunches leading or trailing); and tilting the head. If the rider brings her outside leg too far back, the horse may evade by bringing his haunches too far in. Too strong an outside leg can move the rib cage to the inside, against the bend. The rider must be careful to keep the engagement and forward steps of the inside hind leg and to maintain the suspension in the gaits.

## Other Movements

### Counter-Canter

Counter-canter is a canter on the lead opposite the direction the horse is tracking (for example, left lead if tracking right). The horse is slightly flexed toward the side of his leading legs. Counter-canter improves the horse's balance, straightness, and suppleness by encouraging the inside hind leg ("inside" here refers to the lead, not to the arena) to carry more weight to propel the horse around the turn. Counter-canter improves the quality of the canter and prepares the horse for flying changes. The horse must not be over-bent in the neck or forced to canter on a turn that is too difficult for his level of training, balance, and suppleness.

To ride a counter-canter, start by riding a regular canter on the correct lead, with the horse flexed to the inside only enough to make him straight. Your normal bending aids keep the horse in the same lead and maintain his flexion in the direction of the lead. Start by riding a shallow single loop to the quarter line and back to the track, maintaining the slight bend toward the side of the leading leg during the loop. You should feel as if the horse "stands up" and remains vertical through the corners and the loop.

You can progress to a deeper single loop (from the track to the center line and back to the track), and then to a 3-loop serpentine, then to changing the rein while maintaining the same lead, and finally to cantering around the ring and in circles in counter-canter. If the horse struggles, trots, or does a flying change, return to a simpler exercise. Never punish a horse for doing a correct flying change, even if not asked for—quietly make a transition to trot or walk and return to the counter-canter.

Be careful not to lean sideways, over-bend the horse toward his leading leg, or bend him the wrong way in counter-canter. Ten-meter circles in true canter, interspersed with the counter-canter, can help the horse maintain and improve his balance.

## Changes of Lead

Changes of lead require good balance, straightness, and timing. The horse must rebalance himself and straighten, bend slightly in the direction of the new lead, and push off into the canter without losing his balance or rhythm.

Before you can begin changes of lead, your horse must be able to make good canter departs on either lead on a straight line, and good transitions from canter to trot or walk. At first, he may need to trot for six or seven strides or longer in order to rebalance and be ready to depart on the new lead. As his balance, straightness, and transitions improve, he can perform more advanced changes of lead.

**Change of lead through the trot:** This is a change of lead where the horse is brought back into the trot and after a few trot strides, is re-started into a canter with the other leg leading. Ideally, three to five trot steps are performed, but the smoothness and straightness of the transitions is most important.

**Simple change of lead at the canter:** This is a movement in which, after a direct transition out of the canter into a walk, with three to five clearly defined walk steps, the horse makes an immediate transition into the other

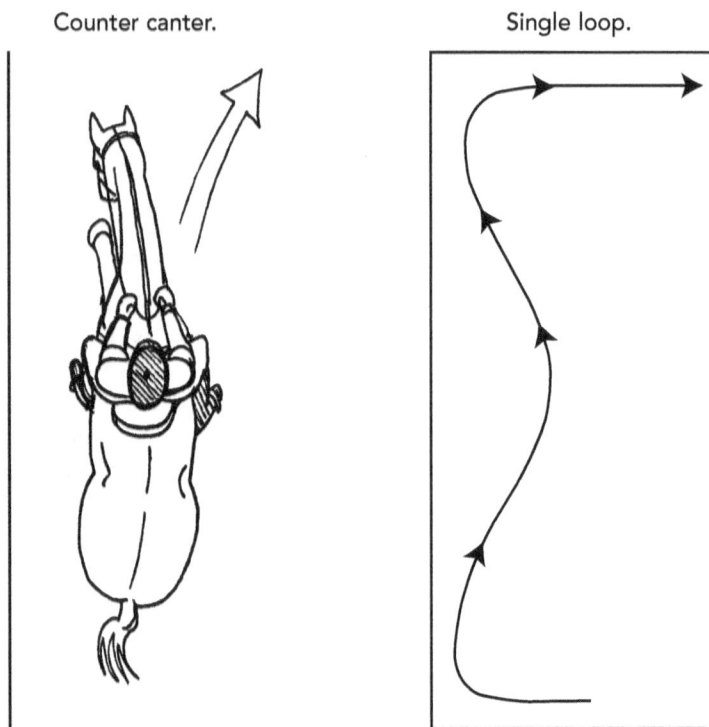

Counter canter.

Single loop.

canter lead. This movement requires the ability to collect the canter for a clean canter-walk transition with no trot steps. Correct preparation with rebalancing half-halts is essential. As in the change of lead through trot, the quality of the canter, walk, and transitions is more important than the number of strides. It is often easiest to introduce canter-walk transitions from a 10-meter canter circle, using the circle to help shorten the stride and collect the canter before the transition to walk. The walk-to-canter transition comes from an active walk and a horse that is clearly responsive to the canter aid.

**Flying change of lead:** The flying change is performed in one stride, with the front and hind legs changing at the same moment. The change of the leading front and hind legs takes place during the moment of suspension; therefore, maintaining suspension or "jump" in the canter is important for flying changes. The rider's aids should be precise and unobtrusive. Flying changes of lead can also be executed in series at every fourth, third, second stride, or at every stride (*tempi changes*). The horse, even in a series of changes, remains light, calm, and straight with lively impulsion, maintaining the same rhythm and balance throughout the series. Enough impulsion must be maintained so as not to restrict or restrain the lightness, fluency, and ground cover of the flying changes in series. The aim of flying changes is to show the sensitivity, obedience, and response of the horse to the aids for the change of lead.

To ask for a flying change, prepare the horse with half-halts, straighten him, and then give the aids for the new lead just before the moment of suspension (as the leading foreleg strikes the ground). You must stay in balance, but your seat lightens a little to allow the back to round up as the horse changes his lead. Don't lean too far forward, tip sideways, or give too strong a leg aid.

Flying changes are advanced movements that require good preparation, balance, and coordination. A horse must be able to do good simple changes of lead (through the walk) and counter-canter fluently before he can learn to do flying changes. However, if a horse has a naturally good canter, some trainers teach the flying change earlier, before the counter-canter on tighter lines is fully established, to avoid later confusion in case the horse thinks he is always supposed to counter-canter.

**The rein-back:** This is a rearward diagonal movement with a two-beat rhythm but without a moment of suspension. Each diagonal pair of legs is raised and returned to the ground alternately, with the forelegs aligned on the same track as the hind legs. During the entire exercise, the horse should remain on the bit, maintaining his desire to move forward. The steps are counted as each foreleg moves back. After completing the required number of steps backward, the horse should show a square halt or move forward in the required gait immediately.

A correct rein-back is a test of obedience to all the aids and shows that the horse accepts the bit without resistance, moves straight, and is supple in his back and hind legs. It requires the horse to put more weight on his hindquarters and bend the joints of his hind legs more. This can improve his engagement and balance, but can easily overstress his back, hocks, and stifle joints if it is practiced too much or incorrectly, or if it is forced.

Because it is a fairly difficult movement, a horse should not be asked to rein-back until he reaches the point in his training where he is ready to do it. He must respond to all your aids (seat, legs, and hands); go forward while accepting the bit; and respond properly to half-halts. If a horse resists the bit, is difficult to halt, or is not calm and cooperative, he is not ready to rein-back. Rein-back should not be used as a punishment!

To apply the aids for a rein-back, at the halt, your legs and seat ask him to move, but you "close the door" with a holding (non-allowing) rein aid. As the horse meets your holding hands, his forward movement becomes a rein-back; his impulse to move forward is let out backward.

Steps of rein-back.

1st beat LF & RH

2nd beat RF & LH          Halt          Moving forward

As soon as the horse begins to yield and move backward, your hands must lighten without losing contact. Both legs (an inch or two behind their normal position) act as supporting aids, keeping the horse straight as he steps back. Your body should stay in a vertical balance, without leaning forward or backward, but you should lighten your seat a little by transferring some of your weight to your thighs. This allows your horse to round up his back and engage his hind legs so he can step backward easily. If you lean back, drive your seat bones into his back, or pull, you will cause him to hollow his back, resist your aids, and rein-back badly, if at all.

To stop the rein-back and move forward, sit deep, engage your seat and leg aids, and lighten the rein contact. In a good rein-back, your horse should remain balanced and in front of your legs, so that he is willing and able to move forward immediately at any time.

Faults in the rein-back include the horse anticipating, resisting, or hurrying the movement; resisting or evading the bit; moving crookedly; or backing with inactive or dragging front or hind legs. These are usually caused by rider faults such as halting or reining-back "all in the hands," sitting too heavily or out of balance, failure to use supporting leg aids, or leaning forward.

## Stages of Training

Basic training is broken down into progressive stages. There is no absolute timetable for completing these stages; instead, it depends on the maturity of the horse; the skill and experience of the trainer and rider; and circumstances such as the horse's health, soundness, and mental attitude. Training must progress gradually at a pace appropriate for the individual horse, starting with a foundation of correct work and moving on only when the horse is fluent, confident, and physically ready for the next step. Rushing the early training or skipping ahead to advanced movements without proper preparation will handicap the most talented horse, and can result in a horse with mental, physical, and/or performance problems.

While even very young horses can benefit from daily handling and ground training to develop confidence, obedience, and manners, they are not physically or mentally mature enough to be ridden regularly before the age of three, and even later for slow developers. Training horses too young and too hard jeopardizes their future soundness and careers.

Basic training (on the flat) is broken down into the following progressive stages.

**Manners and basic ground handling:** The young horse is taught to lead; tie; have good manners during grooming, foot care, and other handling; and load in a trailer. The object is to develop confidence, obedience, and manners. This type of handling is best carried out from a very early age.

Ground training may include round pen work, work in hand, parallel leading, longeing, ground driving (long lining), and sometimes driving (to cart). Some trainers introduce the young horse to simple obstacles in hand at this stage to build confidence, lessen spookiness, and develop trust in the trainer and a good learning attitude. The object is to establish respect, trust, and obedience to body language, voice commands, and whip and rein signals; to introduce the bit, bridle, surcingle, saddle, and other equipment; and to develop confidence, obedience, and free forward movement.

**Starting under saddle (backing):** The young horse learns to accept a rider on his back, at a walk and later at the trot and canter, making simple transitions and turning. The object is to establish confidence, calmness, obedience, and basic control, and to familiarize the horse with carrying a rider. Sometimes this is carried out first on a longe line, Some trainers use a quiet, experienced horse to accompany the young horse and give him confidence.

**Basic training under saddle:** Introduces the young horse to being ridden at the walk, trot, and canter, with simple aids and basic control. The object is to establish calmness and relaxation, teach the horse to carry the rider's weight while moving comfortably and calmly in a long frame, establish free forward movement, and have the horse accept the rider's weight and simple aids. Exercises include working walk, trot, and canter; simple turns; and large circles.

**Novice/Training Level:** The object is to establish relaxation, confidence, and develop a horse that is supple and moves freely forward with a clear and steady rhythm, accepting contact with the bit. Exercises include medium walk, working trot, and canter; free walk; 20-meter circles; basic bending and changes of rein; halts through the walk; canter to trot and trot to canter; and stretching the frame on the 20-meter circle.

**First Level:** The object is to confirm the previous work and in addition, develop the thrust to achieve improved balance and throughness, and maintain a more consistent contact with the bit. In addition to the gaits and paces of Training Level, exercises include lengthening the stride in the trot and canter. Other movements at this level are 10-meter circles and half-circles; halt-trot and trot-halt transitions; lengthening stride in trot and canter; leg-yielding; change of leads through the trot; and introducing the counter-canter through a shallow loop at the canter, maintaining the same lead.

**Second Level:** The object is to improve the previous work, so that the horse, having achieved the thrust required in First Level, now accepts more weight on the hindquarters (collection); moves with an uphill tendency, especially in the medium paces; and is reliably on the bit. A greater degree of straightness, bending, suppleness, throughness, balance, and self-carriage is required than at First Level. Work includes collected trot and canter; medium walk, free walk, and medium paces of trot and canter; canter transitions from the walk; simple change of leads; counter-canter; 10-meter circles; shoulder-in; travers; renvers; turns on the haunches; and rein-back.

**Third Level:** The object is to confirm that the horse, having begun to develop an uphill balance at Second Level, now shows increased engagement and thrust, especially in the extended paces. Transitions between collected, medium, and extended paces should be clearly defined and performed with engagement. The horse should be reliably on the bit and should show greater straightness, bending, suppleness, throughness, balance, and self-carriage than at Second Level. New movements included are half-pass in the trot and canter, flying changes, and showing a clear release of both reins for four to five strides on a 20-meter circle.

## Work in the Open

Work in the open should be included in the basic training as soon as the horse is calm and obedient to simple aids. The young horse should be ridden out in company with a quiet, older horse that will give the youngster confidence and set a good example. For nervous horses or those that are overwhelmed by new sights and sounds, begin with short, quiet walks, accompanied by a "babysitter" (an older, quiet horse) while cooling out at the end of training sessions, or even leading the horse out to "see the sights" on foot. For safety's sake, ride in a secure area (preferably an enclosed field), and never ride alone.

As the horse becomes accustomed to riding outside and his training progresses, his training should be carried on outside as well as in the ring. Riding over natural rolling terrain in all gaits will improve his balance and fitness, and teach him to handle footing, terrain, and simple natural obstacles. The more time he spends moving freely forward in natural conditions, the better for his later training, especially if he is to become a hunter, jumper, or event horse, or simply an all-around pleasure horse.

For more details on riding, training exercises, and jumping in the open, see Chapter 4, "Jumping," and Chapter 5, "Cross-Country Riding and Jumping."

## Work over Cavaletti and Ground Poles

The purpose of cavaletti work for dressage horses is to improve the swing in the back, suppleness, throughness, and balance. Ground poles or cavalatti are often utilized in the warm-up phase of everyday work, and rather than being used as a separate exercise, they are incorporated into other figures, including circles and transition work. During cavaletti work, the rider should sit lightly to encourage the horse's back to lift and swing, but should maintain an active connection (and bend, in circle work) and continue to ride with the elements of the training scale in mind.

**Walk poles:** Walk poles should be set for the horse's normal stride length (typically 2'6" to 3' apart). Work over walk poles encourages relaxation, looseness of the back, bending of the joints, and activity. If set slightly longer, they can be used (carefully and gradually) to develop a longer, more ground-covering walk. Walk poles are excellent for horses that tend to lose the rhythm in the walk (that is, become lateral), as series of steps over the poles helps to maintain an even four-beat walk rhythm. For a more advanced horse, walk poles might be used before or after a canter-walk-canter or free walk-medium walk-free walk transition, or in the preparation for a turn on the haunches, to improve the purity and activity of the medium walk.

**Trot cavaletti:** Trot cavaletti may be used on a straight line or on a circle. Straight cavaletti are usually set either at a single-stride distance of approximately 4' to 4'6" apart, or allowing a stride in between, at approximately 8' to 9', or alternating between these two settings. Straight cavaletti can be gradually raised (start by raising alternate ends of the poles, then raise both ends to 3" to 6") to help develop cadence and swing through the back. When

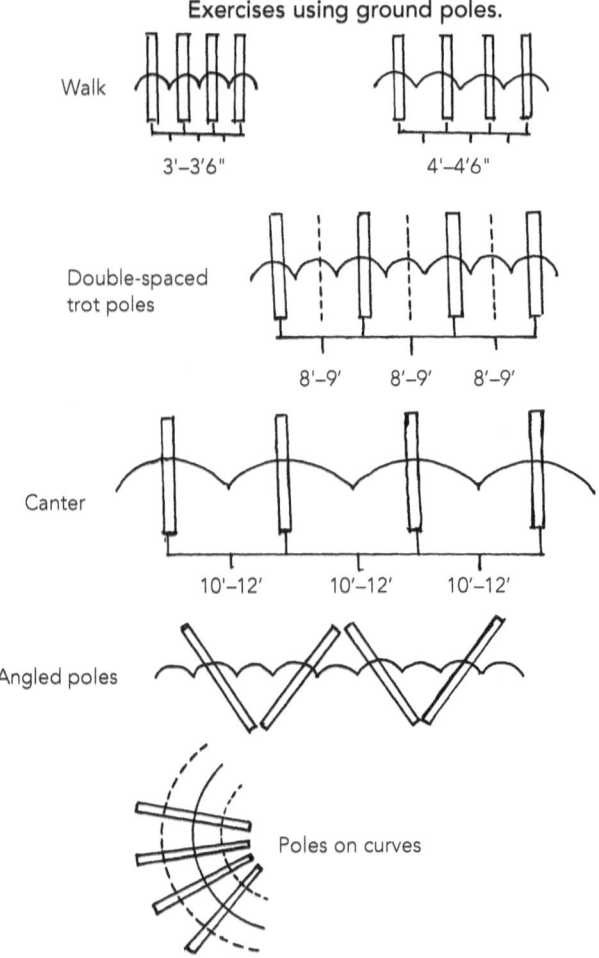

Exercises using ground poles.

using raised cavaletti, the distance between the poles may need to be shortened 2" to 3" to accommodate the increased effort of the horse raising his legs higher through the raised poles.

As with walk poles, trot cavaletti can also be used to improve the quality of the trot before or after a transition to walk or canter.

Cavaletti or ground poles on a circle should be ridden on an accurate curved line and can be used to develop bending and suppleness. They are usually set at 2'5" apart on the inside and 6' apart on the outside, for an approximately 15-meter circle; the inner ends of the poles are set closer for a 10-meter circle and farther apart for a 20-meter circle. Additionally, by riding a little more to the inside or the outside, circle poles can help develop lengthening and shortening of the stride. It is especially important for the rider to ride an accurate line over the cavaletti when riding cavaletti or

More exercises using ground poles.

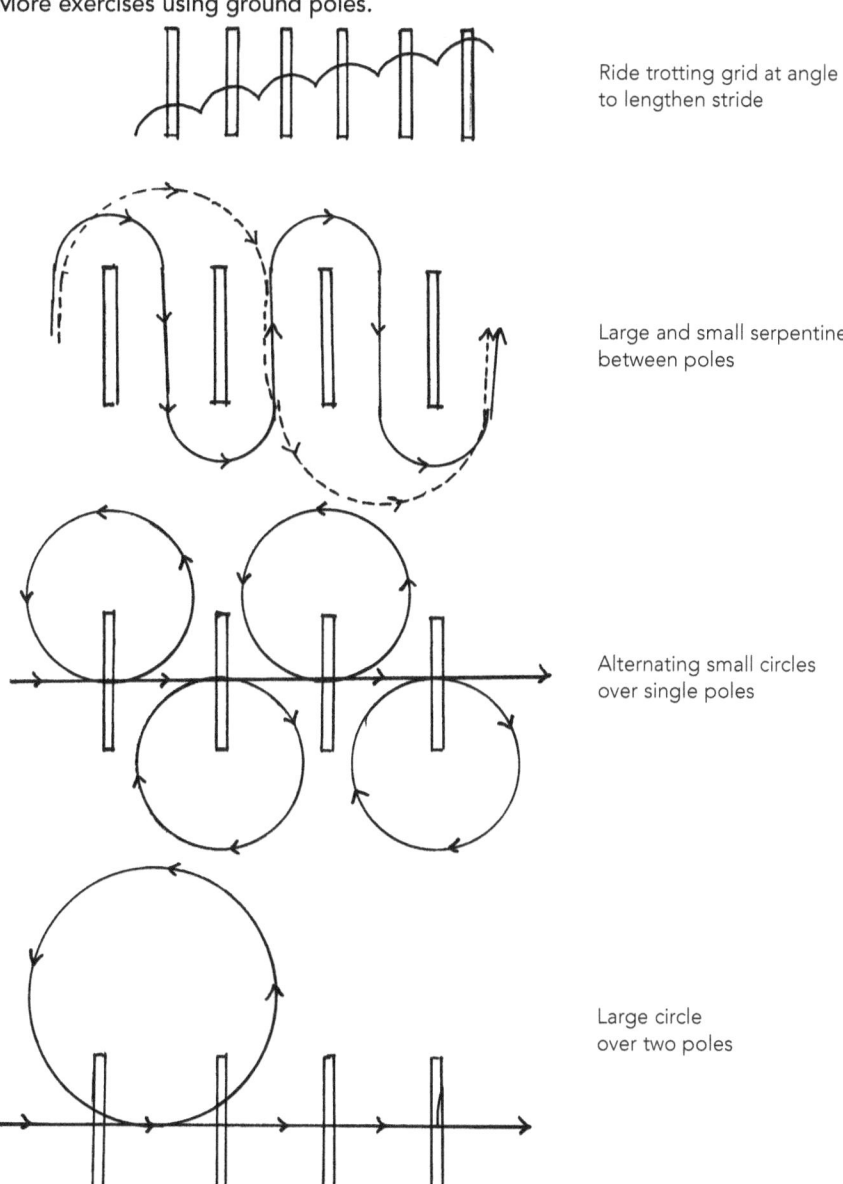

Ride trotting grid at angle to lengthen stride

Large and small serpentines between poles

Alternating small circles over single poles

Large circle over two poles

ground poles on a curve, because any deviation may cause the horse to take irregular steps. Poles painted with a center stripe make it easier for the rider to plan and ride an accurate curved line.

**Canter cavaletti:** Canter cavaletti are typically set on a straight line approximately 8' to 9' apart, and usually work best when raised 6" to 9" off the ground on both ends to improve the energy, jump, and suspension in the canter. Even a single cavaletti is useful for this purpose. To ride a canter cavaletti line, the rider must be able to place the horse properly at the first pole (rather like seeing a correct takeoff distance while jumping). For developing lengthening and shortening in the canter, two cavaletti or poles may be set at a 48' or 60' distance, then canter the two with various numbers of strides in between. This ensures that the horse is truly lengthening the stride, instead of only quickening. Canter poles can also be used on a circle, like those in the trot.

# 4

# Jumping

## Good Jumping Performance

A good jumping performance is more than just jumping higher, faster, more difficult fences, or winning in competition. It is jumping with better security, confidence, and control, and, especially, riding over fences in good form and classic style. This is not riding just to look pretty, but with the balance, strength, smoothness, and control that allow you to ride different horses well and help them give you their best athletic performance.

Good jumping is safer, smoother, and easier for both horse and rider, and unites them. It feels wonderful and is beautiful to watch!

Here are some qualities of a good jumping performance:

**In the horse:** During the approach, the horse moves straight and freely forward, with good balance and rhythm. He adjusts his stride to meet the fence at the best takeoff spot. During takeoff, he engages both hind legs equally and pushes off powerfully. His shoulders rotate up and forward as he brings his forelegs up and folds them tightly. His neck and head stretch out and down, and his back rounds in an arc, or *bascule*. His hind legs fold up tightly and evenly, and he lands lightly, in good balance. He goes forward smoothly, powerfully, and in stride.

Over a course, a good jumper moves freely forward with a steady, even pace, adjusting his stride as necessary for good takeoffs. He turns in balance and follows the best track of the course accurately. He has extra *scope* (jumping ability) when needed. He is calm but energetic and willing, and his performance flows smoothly.

Good performance of horse and rider over a jump.

**In the rider:** A good jumping rider rides in balance with his horse, with eyes up, keeping an elastic contact with his horse's mouth. He lets the thrust of takeoff close the major angles of his body, aligning his shoulders more or less over his knees and toes, with his seat close to the saddle. His legs stay directly under him, with lower legs in contact with the horse's sides and heels down. His hands and arms follow the horse's mouth, keeping an elastic connection with a straight line from elbow to the bit throughout the jump. During landing, he stays in balance over his feet and absorbs the shock down through his ankle, knee, and hip joints.

A good jumping rider is effective and positive, riding smoothly and quietly, without roughness or extra movement. He uses his hand, leg, and seat aids independently, and he is in balance with his horse at all times, never interfering with his horse's efforts.

# The Jumping Seat

## Form Follows Function: Seat, Position, and Stirrup Length

*Form follows function* is an old saying about riding style. It means that the *function*, or the job you do, determines the *form*, or the way you ride when you do it. You must have the right position, balance, and riding skills for the kind of riding you are doing, because correct and functional riding allows your horse to do his job safely, efficiently, and to the best of his ability. A classical dressage position is the wrong seat for show jumping, and a good cross-country galloping position won't help you ride a good dressage test. Good basics in the Balanced Seat will adapt to special kinds of riding.

Position and stirrup lengths.

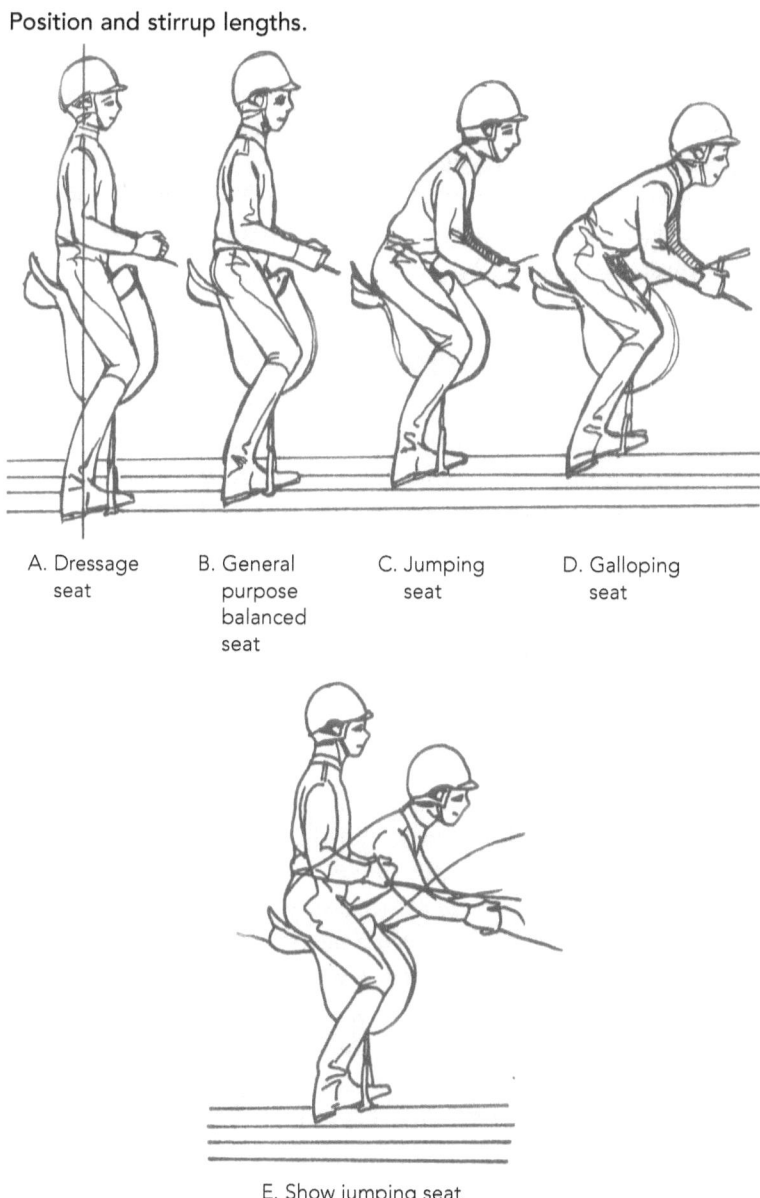

A. Dressage seat  B. General purpose balanced seat  C. Jumping seat  D. Galloping seat

E. Show jumping seat

There are different basic positions and stirrup lengths for different kinds of riding:

- **For basic jumping, schooling over ground poles, smaller fences, and cross-country hacking:** The rider sits close to the saddle, with shorter stirrups than for flat work (top of ankle bone), resulting in sharper angles at ankle, knee, and hip joints. His angles close (shoulders over knees and feet) in a secure position. The rider's seat stays close to saddle but not directly on the horse's back. His weight is supported down into the whole leg, with elastic ankle, knee, and hip joints. The rider's lower leg is the base for his own balance as well as the means for creating a balanced horse, moving straight with good rhythm and impulsion.

- **For jumping larger fences, equitation, and course work:** Shorter stirrups may be used when jumping bigger fences, so the rider's seat is higher above the saddle to give the horse more freedom during the jumping process. This causes sharper angles at the ankles, knees, and hip joints.

## Jumping Seat

The jumping seat is the position used over fences. It is in no way a rigid, "posed" position; the rider's position changes to adapt to the balance of the horse. In jumping, shorter stirrups are necessary for balance and security; they create greater angles at the ankle, knee, and hip joints. These angles help absorb the thrust of the takeoff and the shock of landing, and allow the rider to stay in balance.

The legs remain in place against the horse's side, but the body angles (especially the hip angle) open and close to go with the movement and balance of the horse. As in all seats, the rider's angles must be balanced: feet under the center of balance, with stirrup leathers vertical. The hips and seat are behind this vertical line; the head, shoulders, and knees are ahead of it.

## Full Seat, Half-Seat, and 2-Point Position

A rider may ride in a *full seat* (fully seated in the saddle, as in a dressage seat) or a *half-seat* (balanced in a jumping or galloping position, with the seat out of the saddle). The full seat is also called *3-point contact*, meaning that three points of the rider (both legs and the seat) are in contact with the horse. The half-seat is called *2-point contact* or *2-point position*, because the rider's seat (the third point) is off the saddle. The rider's *body angle* (the angle between the thigh bones and the upper body, at the hip joint) may vary in either of these seats, according to the balance of horse and rider and what the rider is doing.

## Light Seat

The light seat is a seat halfway between the dressage seat and the jumping seat. It is useful in schooling jumping horses on the flat and over cavaletti

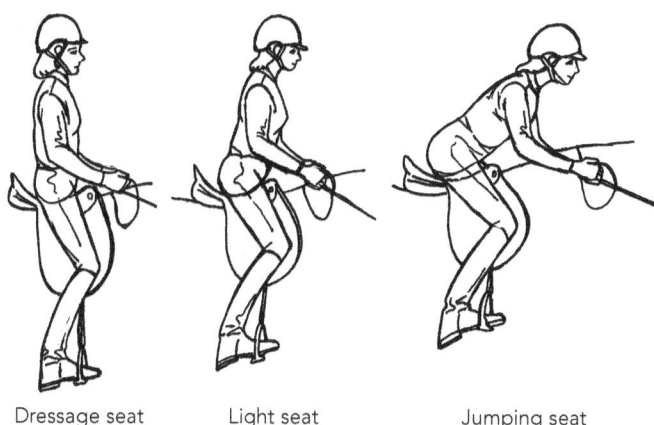

Dressage seat    Light seat    Jumping seat

and gymnastics, when you frequently change from flat work to jumping, for hacking and cross-country riding, and for riding young horses whose backs are not yet developed enough to carry the rider in a dressage seat. It is used quite often on a course to allow horses to canter freely forward between jumps. It offers security and allows you to be light on the horse's back.

In a light seat, the front part of your seat bones stay in contact with the saddle, and your upper body is angled slightly forward. This places more of your weight on your thighs, knees, and stirrups, and lessens the pressure of your seat bones in the saddle. This allows you to quickly and smoothly change from a light seat to a jumping seat (seat out of the saddle) or a full seat (sitting down in the saddle), and to change your body angle to influence your horse. When riding in a light seat, your stirrups will be shorter than dressage length (at the ankle point), but not as short as when jumping larger fences.

## Parts of the Seat

The rider's seat can be divided into four parts: *lower leg, pelvis area, upper body,* and *arms and hands*. All parts must work together to create a functional whole. In this section, we discuss a functional seat for jumping and riding over fences.

### Lower Legs

The lower legs and feet must be placed under the center of the body, with stirrup leathers vertical. While the joints and angles of the legs must be flexible, the legs should remain securely in place on the horse's sides, even when the upper body angle changes. A lower leg that moves forward and back indicates lack of body strength, correct balance and independent seat, and a weak base of support. Unsteady lower legs are often caused by pinching with the knees.

- **Stirrup placement:** Stirrup irons are placed under the ball of the foot (at the balance point of the foot). Irons should be perpendicular to the horse's side, crossing underneath the foot at an angle, with the outer branch of the iron near the base of the little toe. The angle of the foot depends on rider's conformation; approximately the same angle as that of rider's knees and thighs.
- **Feet and ankles:** The heels must be down, but must sink downward and backward, not be pushed forward or jammed down, locking the ankles. The ankles must flex under the rider's weight and absorb thrust and shock. They should not be rolled inward or outward; either causes stiffness.
- **Calves:** They must be stretched down and back, with the inner calf in contact with horse.
- **Knees:** Knees should be flexible, not pinching; gripping knees cause pivoting, unsteady lower legs.
- **Stirrup length:** Correct stirrup length for jumping varies with the size of the jumps. At the basic adjustment (for ordinary jumping, up to 3'), the stirrup should hang to the point of the ankle bone. Stirrups should be raised one hole for each foot the fences are increased in height.

### Pelvis Area (Thighs, Seat, and Pelvis)

The weight is more toward the front of the seat bones than in other seats. Shorter stirrups result in the seat being suspended over the seat of the saddle, but the seat bones should remain close to the saddle (not forward over the pommel).

The seat, with light and following contact with the saddle, can be used as an aid for communication with the horse. In 3-point contact, the weight is distributed between inner thighs and seat bones. In 2-point contact, the weight is distributed between the lower inner thighs and knees and should flow down through the rider's leg and into the calf and heel; the seat bones are clear of saddle.

The upper body should act as a unit, neither stiff nor sloppy. The *core muscles* (the deep inner muscles of the back and abdomen) are important for integrity and alignment of the upper body. *Body angle* refers to the angle between the thighs and the torso; this angle opens and closes at the hip joints and is important for balance and control.

- **Hip joints:** Open and close freely; hip joints control the angle between the upper body and the legs.

- **Back:** Flat, straight (neither excessively hollow nor rounded).
- **Chest:** Carried high and open (not contracted at upper chest and collar bones).
- **Shoulders:** Shoulders and collarbones hang wide and freely over ribs (shoulders not hunched, rounded, or contracted).
- **Head and eyes:** Eyes look ahead to focal point over center of fence. Head is balanced (not looking down or tilted to one side).

### Arms and Hands

The arms and hands are connected to the body by the *shoulder girdle*, which consists of the collarbones, shoulder blades, and shoulder joints. Supple and elastic joints of the shoulder girdle, arms, and hands are crucial to riding with a light, steady contact, and preventing stiffness, tension, and accidental jerks on the horse's mouth. The rider's arms and hands must become independent from his body and balance, in order to give light and correct rein aids.

- **Straight line from elbow to bit:** Important for contact and correct release. May be broken upward, but not downward.
- **Upper arms:** Move freely from shoulder joints; close to body.
- **Elbows:** Flexible; close to the body. Elbows out indicates too-long reins, flat hands, and tension in upper arms, shoulders, and chest.
- **Wrists:** Straight.
- **Hands:** Holding reins in a soft fist, with fingers closed (open fingers can lose grip on the reins or can be sprained). Knuckles between vertical and 30 degrees inside vertical.

## The Rider's Angles

In jumping, the angles of your legs and body enable you to control your position and balance. They act as springs and shock absorbers, working together to absorb the thrust of takeoff and the shock of landing. The major angles are the *ankle, knee,* and *hip joints*, which control leg and body position and balance; and the *shoulder* and *elbow joints*, which control hand and arm placement, contact, and release.

These angles must close and open automatically, almost like a reflex, as your horse jumps. Correct angles depend on correct stirrup length, a balanced position, and freedom from excessive muscle tension, which locks the joints and causes you to compensate with position faults such as rounding the back. Practice over gymnastics develops your ability to use your angles correctly and to allow the horse to close and open your angles as he jumps.

The rider's angles.

# Improving Your Jumping Seat

## Core Strength and Muscle Fitness

Core strength refers to the deep inner muscles of your abdomen and back and their ability to support your spine and keep your body stable and balanced. Core strength is essential for security, balance, and flexibility, and helps your body remain secure and balanced even when challenged by a quick, powerful, or unexpected movement of your horse. It is the basis for a safe, secure, and independent seat, especially over fences. Because jumping involves large, quick, and powerful movements of the horse, the rider's balance is less stable than in riding on the flat, but it is even more important to have a secure and functional seat.

Inadequate core strength leaves a rider's balance vulnerable to the bounce, thrust, and forces of the horse's movement in jumping. This causes the rider to compensate (unconsciously) with position and technique faults such as rounding the back, standing up too far forward, gripping and pivoting on the knees, or falling back and hitting the saddle.

Core strength can be developed by exercises that balance and strengthen the whole body, using the inner muscles of the abdomen and back. Exercise methods that specialize in core development off the horse, such as Pilates work, can be very useful for riders in developing core strength, flexibility and overall strength and fitness. It is difficult to reach true athletic fitness through riding alone, and most riders need to do some kind of fitness training in addition to riding. Many riders find that their riding improves and

Jumping with good form and balance. Rider demonstrates good angles at ankle, knee, hip, and upper body, but line from elbow to bit is broken slightly upward.

riding problems become easier to fix when they become fitter and improve their core strength.

## Correcting Rider Jumping Faults

Nobody is perfect, so you undoubtedly will have faults or mistakes in your jumping that need correcting. Rider jumping errors, however minor, don't just look bad, they handicap a rider and his horse, especially over bigger jumps. Most of these problems are unconscious habits that start when a rider uses a wrong technique or tries to cope with a jumping problem. These errors must be addressed, because they work against the horse's jumping efforts and can cause problems in his jumping and confidence, and put the rider at risk.

Most rider jumping faults have a common cause: a weak base of support and/or core muscles. Another common problem is incorrect muscle development and muscle memory—that is, you have been practicing a skill incorrectly and it has become a bad habit. Lack of fitness can also cause problems; if you are out of shape or out of practice, you will need to go back to a lower level of jumping while you regain your fitness and skills.

The longer you have had a bad habit, the longer you will have to work to change it. The first step is *awareness:* realizing what you are doing. This may involve a timely comment from your instructor or seeing yourself in a photo or on a video. The next step is *correction:* learning a technique to correct the bad habit. This may mean changing your stirrup length or learning a new way of doing something. Then you must *practice* doing it the correct way so that it becomes a new habit. You will need to repeat an exercise that will help you learn a correct technique and make it a habit. At first, the new (correct) way will feel strange because your body is still used to your old (incorrect) habit. The more you practice, however, the more familiar the new procedure will become, and it will eventually turn into a good habit. It takes time and practice to re-train your muscle memory and strengthen the correct muscles, so that the correct habit becomes easy.

Here are some common rider jumping faults and ways to correct them.

**Weak base of support:** Also seen as **heels up** and **unsteady, loose or swinging lower legs,** especially at the canter. A rider with these faults is insecure and out of balance over jumps, especially during landing, which can upset the horse. Possible causes for this fault include:

- Tight, pinching knees that cause the rider to pivot at the knee.
- Too-long stirrups, which do not give the rider enough support to absorb shock and use the lower leg properly.
- Bad habits, due to incorrect muscle development and/or muscle memory (the rider is not using the leg and core muscles properly to make the jumping effort without loss of lower leg security).
- Jumping big fences before basic skills are solid.

**Correction:** Check stirrup length. Practice standing in the stirrups and half-seat at walk, trot, and canter, with weight sinking into your heels, and calves in contact with the horse's sides. Release your knees (relax the knee grip) until you feel your knees sliding up and down a little on the saddle flap as your horse trots. On takeoff, release knees and think "sink": Let your seat sink closer to the saddle, your heels sink down and backward, and your legs sink into your horse's sides. Think of landing with your feet under you on the ground.

**Jumping ahead of the motion; standing up in the stirrups:** This is a dangerous habit, as it can cause refusals and you can easily fall off. Too-long stirrups cause you to stand up instead of folding correctly. Some riders are afraid they will be left behind, so they get ahead of the motion, which is incorrect and unsafe.

**Correction:** Check stirrup length. Practice folding at hip joints (shoulders over knees), keeping the seat close to the saddle. Instead of standing up, sink closer to the saddle and deeper into your heels. When you fold correctly, your seat sinks closer to the saddle as your upper body moves closer to your horse's neck. Let the horse close your angles as he takes off. Jumping low grids without reins and stirrups may help.

**Jumping behind the motion; legs rotate forward:** This is a serious fault because it interferes with the horse; you sit down on his back and catch him in the mouth. This can spoil your horse's jumping style and make him unhappy about jumping. This habit may start if you jump a horse that is too strong for you, or if you jump fences that are too difficult or at too fast a pace for your level. It can also come from trying to get your heels down by shoving them forward instead of letting them sink down and back as they should. Legs that rotate forward show a lack of a strong base of support, and riders who jump behind the motion often lack the core strength to stay with the horse in a good balanced position.

**Correction:** Ride in posting trot with the motion and in half-seat at trot and canter to help your balance and develop strength in your body and legs. Jumping a quiet horse with stirrups, without reins (in a safely enclosed jumping chute) can also help. When you jump, think of landing in your feet—not sitting on your seat. If your horse is strong, work on half-halts and transitions to help make him easier to control.

**Ducking:** When you quickly snap forward into jumping position and fold too far, your chest comes too close to your horse's neck. Instead of letting the horse close your angles as he takes off, you put too much effort into the jump. Ducking disturbs a horse and may make him tense up and get quick. It often results from riding behind the motion during the approach, then trying to catch up on takeoff. Jumping with too-long stirrups can also contribute to this habit.

**Correction:** Check stirrup length and balance. Exercises that help you ride in balance, with your horse during the approach, will help (see correction for jumping behind the motion). Concentrate on keeping your eyes on your target, feeling the horse's rhythm, and relaxing your seat and joints to allow him to close your angles. Breathing out as he takes off may help. It may help to practice a crest-release exercise, supporting your upper body by resting your hands lightly on the neck. Use your core strength to keep your body from folding too far, in order to avoid pushing your horse onto his forehand during the jumping process.

**Round back; hollow back:** A round back is too relaxed and floppy, folding at the waist instead of at the hip joints. Jumping with a round back makes it harder to control your hip angle and balance. It often goes with riding behind the motion or looking down, and it is usually the sign of weak core muscles.

A hollow back is stiff, tight, and tense, with tight, locked hip joints. It can cause you to stand up instead of folding correctly, get ahead of the motion, and collapse forward on landing. Jumping with a hollow back can hurt your back.

**Correction:** Practice sitting closer to your horse and stretching your spine. Practice riding in half-seat and folding into jumping position with a "long back"—keeping your back long and flat, folding at the hip joints, keeping your eyes up, and sinking your seat bones backward toward the saddle as you fold. Posting trot with the motion and riding bounces and

Rider jumping faults.

A. Good jumping position

B. Standing up ahead of the motion, hollow back

A. Behind the motion; leg rotates forward; round back

A. Looking down; pinching knees; leg pivots back; heel up

B. Ducking

simple gymnastics can help you keep your back flat and fold at your hip joints as you sink into your lower leg for support.

## Hands and Releases

The purpose of a release is to allow your horse to use his head and neck freely to balance himself as he jumps. As the horse starts to jump, he stretches his head and neck in a "balancing gesture." He pushes off with his front legs to raise his forehand, tucks up his front legs, rounds his back and stretches his neck over the jump (called a "bascule"), and balances himself as he lands and canters on. If you restrict his neck or hurt his mouth, he will be handicapped in jumping and may lose his confidence. This can

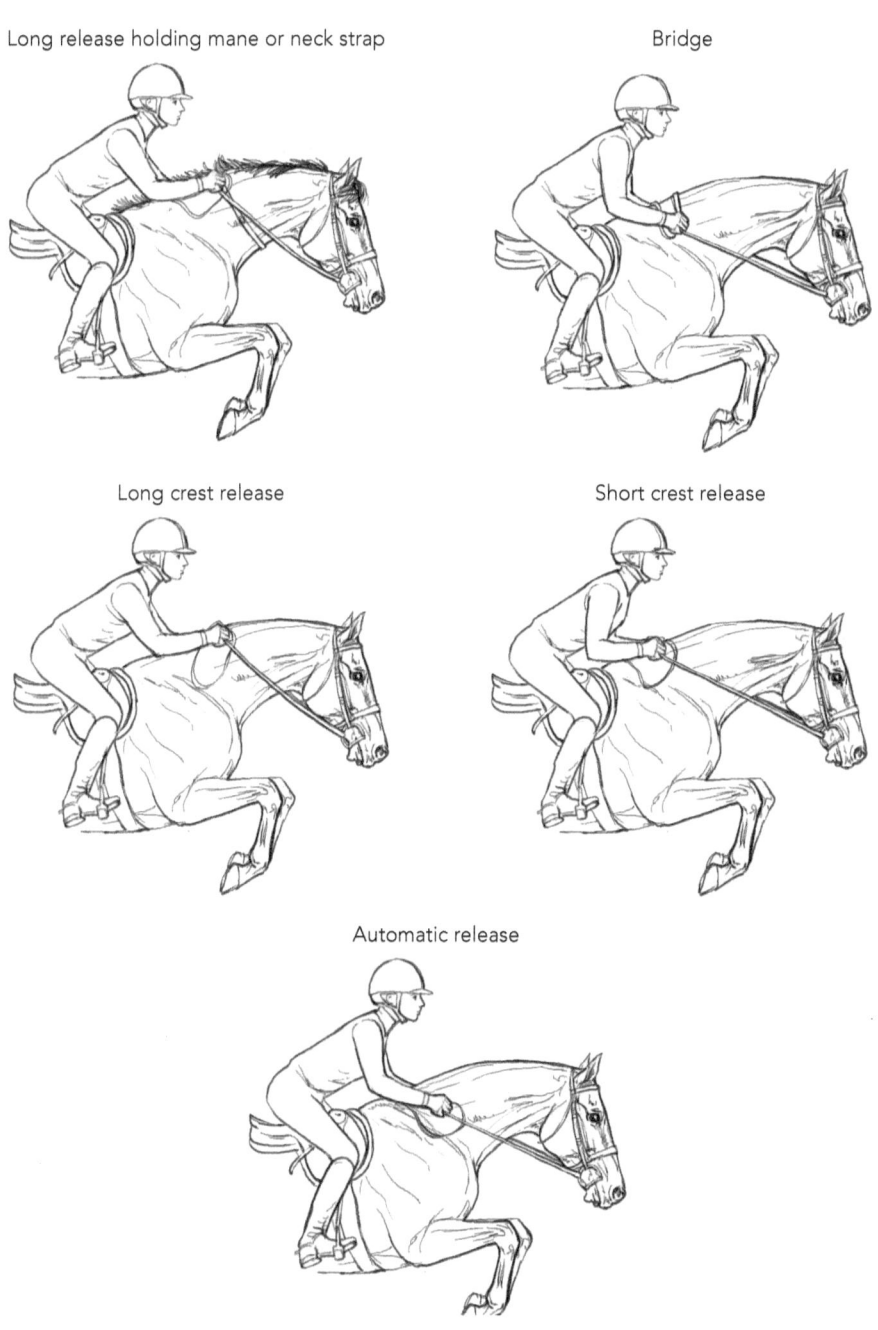

Long release holding mane or neck strap

Bridge

Long crest release

Short crest release

Automatic release

make a horse jump stiffly and awkwardly, make mistakes, tense up, rush his fences, or refuse.

Releasing correctly does not mean abandoning control. Jumping riders say, "The approach belongs to the rider, but the jump belongs to the horse."

This means that you can use all your aids to control your horse on the approach to a jump, but during the jump, you must allow him to use his head and neck freely. If you try to hold him back, slow him down, or discipline him during a jump, you interfere with his jumping efforts. After he lands, you may have to rebalance, correct a swerve, or even stop him.

A correct release allows your horse to make a good jumping effort, stretching his head and neck in a good bascule, while allowing you to stay in control. You should be developing an automatic release, so that you can use it most of the time. However, you must be able to use other releases correctly when the situation requires it.

Various kinds of releases, including the basic release and the long and short crest releases, learning the automatic release, and jumping with a bridge are discussed in the *USPC D Level Manual* (pages 111–112) and the *USPC C Level Manual* (pages 60–61 and 89–90).

## Releases: Special Techniques

**Driving hold for automatic release:** This special way of holding the reins can help you follow the balancing gestures of the horse's head and neck more accurately, and develop a better automatic release when jumping on contact. The rein comes into the hand between the thumb and first finger,

Excellent jumping form, with rider in balance, showing a straight line from elbow to the bit.
Photo credit: Brant Gamma.

Driving hold

Slipping the reins

Knot in end of reins

with the end of the rein coming out of the little finger. Keep your wrists straight and allow the horse to stretch your arms and elbows forward as his neck and head stretch out and down over a vertical, spread, or gymnastic jumping line.

The driving hold is not as effective as a normal rein hold in controlling the horse on the approach, but it is an excellent exercise for advanced riders.

**Slipping the reins:** This is an emergency measure used to keep from interfering with the horse in the event of a peck or stumble, if the rider is left behind, and sometimes on drop fences. The rider keeps his position (or in case of a peck, stumble, or extremely steep descent, may even lean back).

**Rider hand and release faults.**

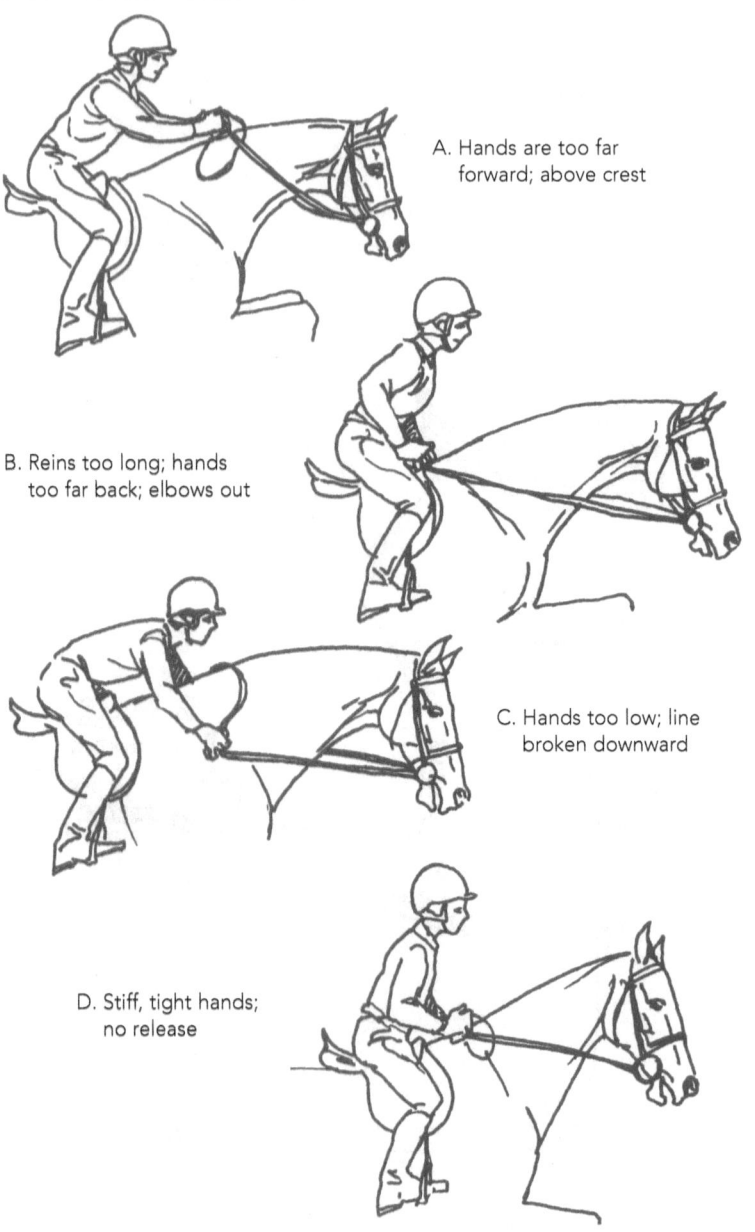

A. Hands are too far forward; above crest

B. Reins too long; hands too far back; elbows out

C. Hands too low; line broken downward

D. Stiff, tight hands; no release

To slip the reins, open your fingers and allow the horse to pull the reins through as far as necessary, even to the buckle. On landing, you must quickly gather your reins and readjust them to a normal length. Because of the delay and temporary loss of control this causes, slipping the reins should be reserved for emergencies.

In situations where the need to slip the reins may arise (jumping cross-country or steeplechasing), the end of the rein should be tied in a knot so that the reins cannot part at the buckle if you should slip them to their full length.

## Improving Your Hands and Release When Jumping

First, adjust the length of your reins so that you can ride with good contact. *Keep a straight line from the bit through your hands to your elbows.* During the approach, use half-halts, not pulls, to keep a steady rhythm, and maintain a light, steady contact until you feel your horse take off. Practice the four basic releases (especially the long release) over ground poles and low, easy jumps. You can begin using the automatic release when you have a more stable position with independent aids. Use trotting poles followed by a cross-rail or a simple gymnastic to steady your horse's stride while you work up to jumping without reins. (This will improve your horse's confidence, too.) Jumping low but fairly wide spreads can help you feel how your horse stretches his neck during the jump, and learn to follow the motion freely with your hands and arms.

Good form and balance over a stadium fence, with eyes up and on a target.

## Jumping Half-Halts

Half-halts can be used in a light seat and in a jumping seat. A jumping rider must be able to use half-halts effectively to call for the horse's attention, rebalance, shorten stride, and engage the hindquarters. However, the way you half-halt must help your horse's jumping, not interfere with it.

Half-halts are most effective in a light seat, because your seat bones are in contact with the saddle.

Here are three kinds of jumping half-halts:

**Half-halt in half-seat:** Your seat bones sink back and downward as your spine briefly lengthens, *keeping the same body angle;* your legs stay under you, sinking back and down into your stirrups and your horse's sides. This half-halt rebalances you while going forward, and calls for the same response from your horse. It can be used in a half-seat or a light seat, when galloping, or during an approach, when in danger of being left behind.

**Opening the body angle (stretching up):** Your body angle opens at the hip joints and your shoulders come back over your seat as you momentarily "stretch up" using your core muscles, and your weight sinks down into your lower leg as your hands momentarily "check" (resist or hold). This is a more powerful half-halt, acting on your horse's back and hindquarters. It is effective in balancing for turns, shortening stride, and engaging your horse's hindquarters. **Caution:** Misusing this half-halt, especially right before a fence, can put you behind your horse and cause you to be left behind when he jumps.

**Half-halt with lifting rein:** The most powerful half-halt, it combines sitting up (opening the body angle) with an upward lift on one rein.

Half-halts in jumping seat.

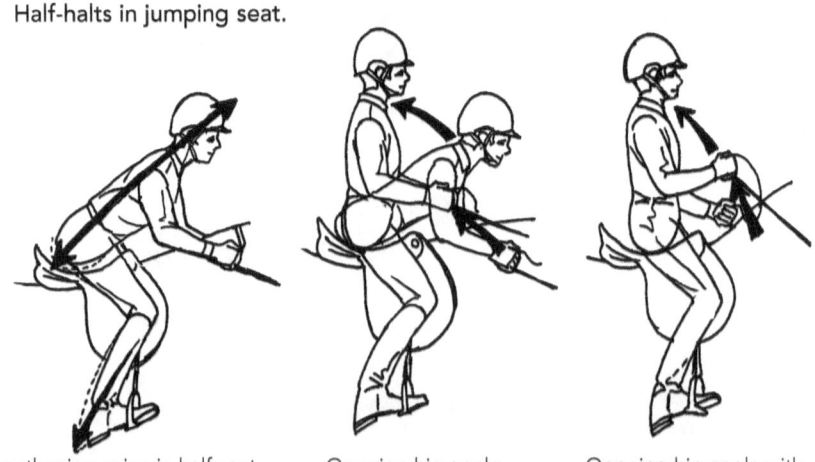

Lengthening spine in half-seat    Opening hip angle    Opening hip angle with upward lift on one rein

The rein (usually the outside rein) is lifted *briefly* upward (not pulling backward); this changes the action of the bit upward into the corner of the mouth and encourages the horse to raise his head and neck. This half-halt acts strongly on the horse's back, hindquarters, and head and neck, for maximum response in rebalancing and "coming back." It is used as an emergency aid; to rebalance a strong, heavy horse that leans on the forehand; and to correct a horse that bucks, bolts, or hangs toward the in-gate or the stable. **Caution:** This half-halt must be used with good judgment, or it can hurt the horse's mouth and negatively impact his training.

# Jumping Challenges and Corrections

## Disobediences

Disobediences (refusals or runouts) must be handled correctly. First, stay in control. If your horse runs out, stop him as soon as possible and turn him back toward the fence, *away* from the direction in which he ran out. In case of a refusal, you may correct your horse briefly in front of the fence with your legs, a cluck, and a tap of your stick. Then take him back to a suitable distance and approach the fence again, being careful to keep your horse on the aids, straight, and in control. It is better to feel strong and sure than to go fast.

If your horse swerved or ran out, you must be prepared to prevent another swerve by using your leg aid on the side he swerves toward, while you steer him straight with your hands. Using a leading rein on the inside and a supporting rein on the outside may help keep him straight. Keep your eyes up and firmly on your target, looking straight over the center of the fence. Use your aids (both hands and both legs) to create a corridor that leads directly over the center of the fence and down the line afterward.

## Reasons for Disobediences

When a disobedience (a refusal or a runout) happens, you must discover the reason and correct the problem before asking the horse to jump again. Here are some common causes of disobediences:

***Rider problems:***
- Getting left behind and catching the horse in the mouth
- Getting ahead of the motion and dropping the horse, or looking down
- Poor turn; crooked or disorganized approach
- Poor judgment: restricting a keen horse too much, or sitting passively on a horse that needs to be ridden positively
- Lack of nerve or determination (horses can tell!)

*Jumping problems:*
- Slippery ground
- Wrong takeoff distance
- Poor balance or lack of impulsion during approach
- Difficulty in seeing or judging the jump, especially when jumping from light into shadow

*Fear caused by:*
- Unfamiliar or spooky-looking jump, or distractions
- Over-facing a horse (asking him to jump fences too big or too difficult for his stage of training)
- Bad experiences, such as a fall, hitting a fence, or a scare
- Pain or bad riding in the past, causing loss of confidence

*Pain from:*
- Lameness or sore back
- Improperly fitted saddle (pinching withers or jabbing shoulders during or after jumping)
- Rough hands
- Bad riding, especially getting left behind or catching horse in the mouth

## Jumping Faults

- **Taking off too close or too far away:** May be caused by a mistake by horse or rider. Often occurs when the horse is out of rhythm, unbalanced, or too much on the forehand during the approach. Sometimes this is caused by the rider's inability to "see a distance" or ride an accurate, balanced approach.
- **Correction:** Teach both horse and rider to find the correct takeoff. Placing poles and/or gymnastics can help the horse become more consistent in taking off correctly.
- **Chipping in (extra stride):** The horse puts in one or more short, quick strides just before takeoff. This may happen when he is out of balance, on the forehand, going too fast, loses confidence, or gets the wrong distance. *Propping* is an exaggerated version of chipping in, when the horse "brakes" suddenly with his forelegs before taking off. This may be caused by riding an approach too fast or making abrupt changes of stride too close to the fence.
- **Correction:** Work on lengthening and shortening stride to make the horse's canter more adjustable. Ride in at a steady pace, not too fast, and do not make last-minute changes of stride or balance. Placing poles or gymnastics may help.

Horse jumping faults.

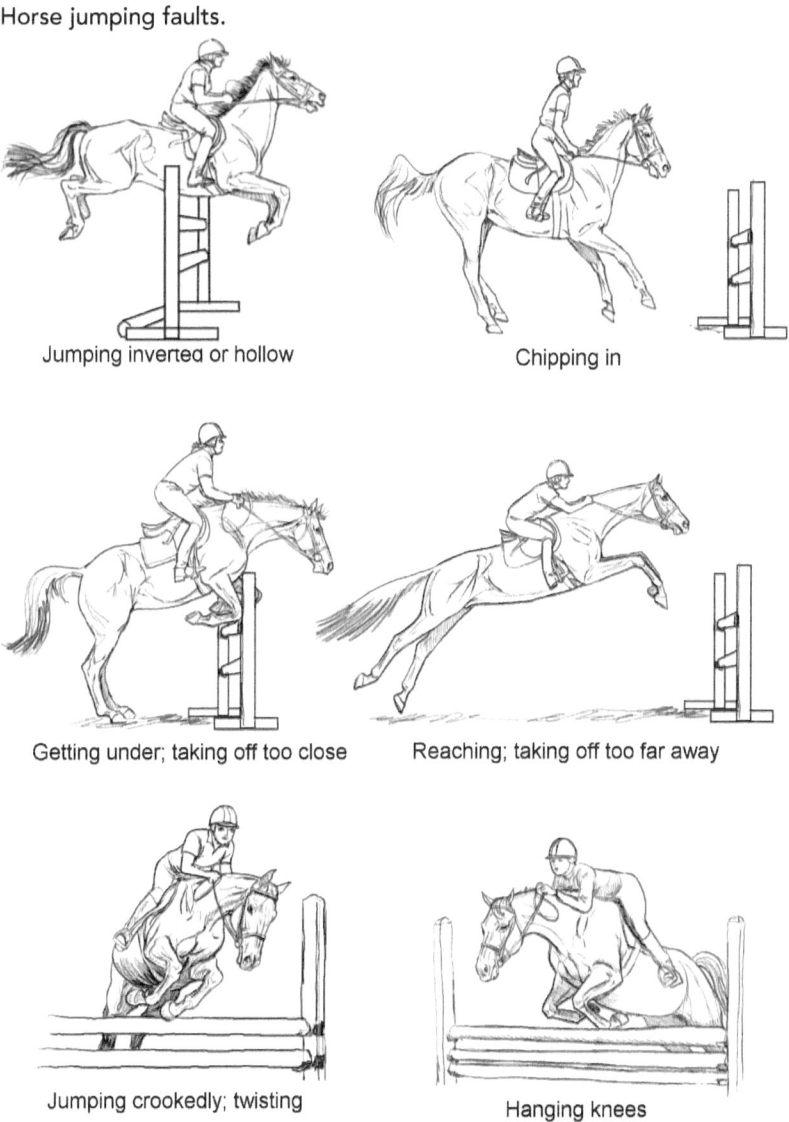

Jumping inverted or hollow

Chipping in

Getting under; taking off too close

Reaching; taking off too far away

Jumping crookedly; twisting

Hanging knees

- **Jumping "inverted" (hollow back, high head):** Usually seen in stiff, tense horses, or when a rider interferes by sitting down on the horse's back or restricting him with the reins. The horse cannot jump with a good arc, or bascule, and cannot fold his front or hind legs well; this may cause him to hit the fence or knock down a rail.
- **Correction:** The horse must be ridden with free use of his head and neck, to rebuild his confidence and develop a better bascule. Work over gymnastics and oxers can help him learn to jump with a better arc.

- **Flattening:** The horse jumps with a flat arc with little bascule. It is similar to jumping inverted but not as pronounced. Horses often jump flat when they are insufficiently balanced without engaging their hind legs well, tired, or going too fast.
- **Correction:** Ride the approach in a balanced, rhythmic, and energetic canter, with impulsion but not speed. The takeoff should be close to the base of the fence. Continue to improve by working over gymnastics and oxers.
- **Hanging knees, trailing hind legs:** Hanging knees mean the forearms point down and the forelegs do not fold properly. It is dangerous, because hitting a fence with the forelegs can cause a fall. Hanging knees may be caused by getting too close to a fence or poor jumping style. Trailing hind legs do not fold tightly and are likely to knock down rails, but they are not as dangerous as hanging knees.
- **Correction:** Jumping ascending spreads (step oxers) gives the horse more time to fold his legs. Work over gymnastics, especially bounces, can help him find a better takeoff distance and teach him to be quicker with his front legs. Make sure the horse has enough impulsion; a dull, tired, bored, or inattentive horse is more likely to hang or trail his legs.
- **Jumping crookedly:** A horse that swerves across a jump, jumps at an angle, or twists sideways in the air is hard to control and to ride in a straight line. Horses that usually jump to one side may be trying to spare a weak or unsound leg and should be checked by a veterinarian. Sometimes a crooked jump is due to rider error: a poor turn, line, or approach.
- **Correction:** Ride a straight line to, over and after the fence. Use ground poles to form a chute on the takeoff and landing side. Cross-rails, Swedish oxers, and jump poles set in an upside-down "V" against the top rail encourage the horse to jump the center of the fence. If a horse habitually swerves in one direction on landing, jump fences on a circle so that he must turn in the opposite direction. (See page 145 for exercises to improve straightness in jumping.)

# Types of Obstacles and Their Effects

## Vertical Fences

Vertical fences require a short, high jump, with accuracy and balance. The horse must jump up and "curl around" a vertical, and must jump cleanly. Large verticals are usually jumped best from a collected stride. Balance,

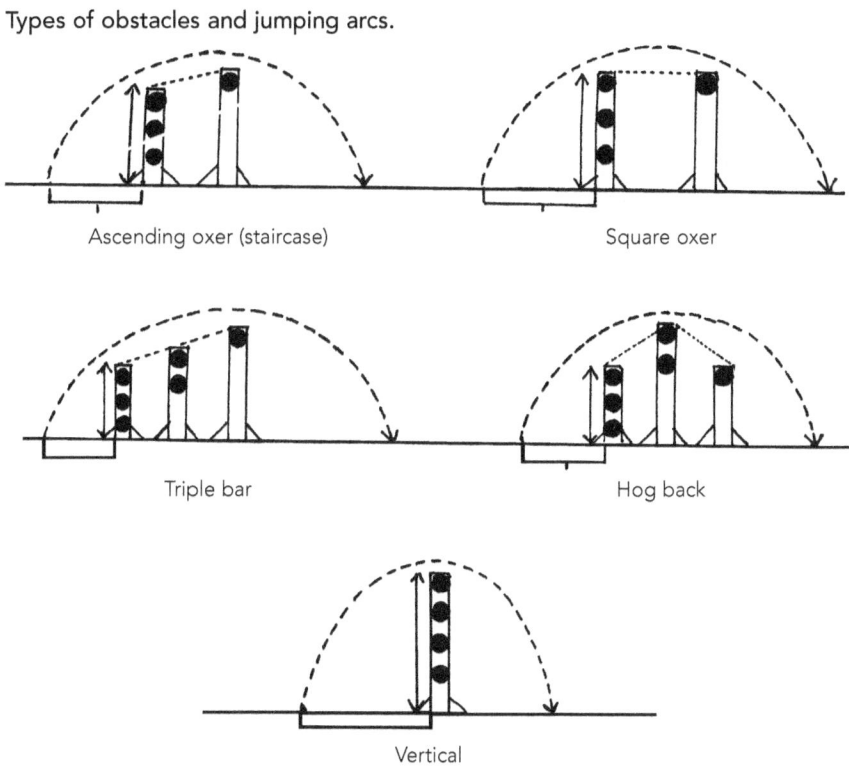

Types of obstacles and jumping arcs.

impulsion, and accurate distance are especially important, and the pace should not be too fast. It is easier to turn in the air or to jump at an angle over verticals than over spread fences.

## Spread Fences

Spreads require a longer, wider jump with greater scope. The horse must extend himself to jump out and across a spread fence, which requires scope and power, and results in a longer arc. The rider must be careful not to restrict the reach of the horse's head and neck, which helps him extend his forelegs, or to sit down and cause him to drop his hind legs too early. When jumping a spread, a horse tends to lengthen his stride and may "flatten out" and get on the forehand; this uses up ground and may cause the distance to the next fence to "ride short." Most horses jump spreads best from a slightly lengthened, powerful stride. It is unwise to jump a spread fence from a long takeoff spot, as this adds to the width of the fence and increases the chances of hitting the back rail.

Spread fences with height as well as width demand scope, power, and a clean, careful jumper. The horse must get his forehand and front legs up enough to clear the first element, extend himself enough to get across the spread, and fold up his hind legs to clear the back rail. The rider must ride a bold but accurate approach, and stay off the horse's back and avoid interfering with him throughout the jump.

Rider interference, jumping high but not wide enough, or miscalculating the takeoff and descending early, can cause a horse to jump into a spread. For safety, the back rail of a spread should only be a single pole, and safety cups or breakable pins should be used on the back rail of an oxer and the middle and back rails of a triple bar.

There are many types of spread fences, with different characteristics:

- **Ascending oxer (step oxer, staircase):** The easiest spread; its upward sloping shape gives the horse more time to fold his legs, while the back rail is easily seen. An inviting fence for green horses.
- **Triple bar:** Like ascending oxers, the upward sloping shape allows more time to fold the legs. The width of a triple bar tends to encourage horses to land with a long stride.
- **Hog's back:** The shape of the fence encourages a round arc and a good bascule. A hog's back must never be built so that the back rail is obscured.
- **Square oxer (equal width and height):** The most difficult type of oxer, requiring a big, powerful jump with scope, width, and height. Requires good folding of both front and hind legs.
- **Swedish oxer (cross oxer):** If jumped in the exact center, it is similar to a parallel oxer, with front and back elements the same height. If jumped at a point where the first element is lower than the back elements, it creates an ascending spread. This is an imposing fence that requires scope and accuracy.

## Jumps with Water

**Water jump:** A wide, shallow ditch or artificial pool filled with water, usually with a small, slanting brush fence on the takeoff side. The far edge is marked by a white strip. Sometimes a single rail is placed over the middle of the water, which encourages the horse to jump it properly.

True water jumps are spreads with little or no height. The horse should take off close to the edge, so as not to make the spread wider. They are usually jumped best from a slightly lengthened stride, but the horse must stay in balance and not fall on his forehand. The rider must allow the horse freedom to stretch fully over the water, but must *not* drop contact before takeoff, which can cause a refusal.

The horse jumps with a good bascule over an oxer.

**Liverpool:** A spread or vertical built over water, it is primarily a mental test; a liverpool is no more demanding than an ordinary jump of the same dimensions, but it is imposing in appearance. An inexperienced horse or rider may look down into the ditch or water, which is distracting and can cause a refusal. You must ride positively, have the horse well in front of the legs, and *not* drop contact on the approach. Liverpools should be jumped from a slightly lengthened, powerful stride with the horse well in hand, not from a flat, over-extended stride.

## Types of Obstacles in Combinations

The types of obstacles in a combination affect the way a combination "rides" because of their characteristic arcs, takeoff, and landing points, and their effects on the horse's stride. Various combinations of obstacles may require extra balance, accuracy, or ability to shorten or lengthen stride.

The distance between elements of a combination is critical. A distance that is too difficult for the horse or rider, or made tricky by the type or size of obstacles, is dangerous. Start with two-stride combinations set with "easy" distances, adjusted to fit the horse's natural stride; this gives the horse some margin for error. You should only increase the difficulty of the obstacles and/or the distances when you are sure of the horse's (and the rider's) capability and confidence.

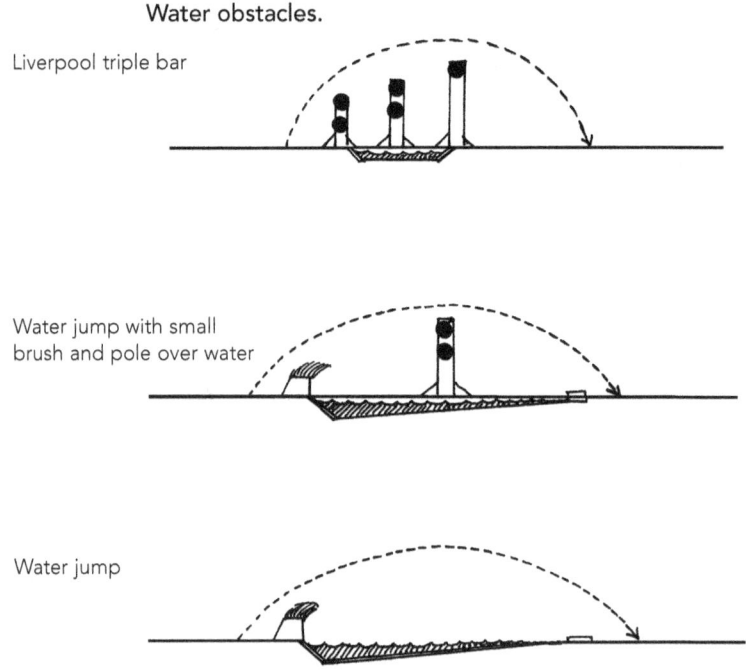

Water obstacles.

Liverpool triple bar

Water jump with small brush and pole over water

Water jump

The distances given in the following examples are average distances for a 16-hand horse with a 12-foot stride, jumping fences approximately 1.0 meter (3'3") to 1.10 meters (3'7"). You must know your own horse's ability, characteristics, and length of stride, and adjust distances accordingly.

**Vertical to vertical:** This combination requires balance, engagement, and accuracy. The horse must land and rebalance, and take a medium-short, round, well-balanced stride to jump the second element clean. If he lands short or loses impulsion after the first element, he may have to take an extra-long stride and may take off too far back or jump flat at the second vertical. It is important to rebalance immediately on landing.

**Vertical to oxer:** The horse must land from the vertical in balance but going forward with a driving stride to jump the spread successfully. If he lands short, loses impulsion, or falls on his forehand, he will have trouble adjusting his stride to take off accurately and with scope enough to clear the oxer. A wider oxer or one with height and spread make this more difficult.

Distances in combinations with various types of obstacles.

| | | One stride | Two strides |
|---|---|---|---|
| Vertical-vertical | | 24'–26' | 34'6"–36' |
| Vertical-staircase | | 23'–25' | 34'1"–35'6" |
| Vertical-parallel | | 23'6"–25' | 34'6"–36' |
| Staircase-vertical | | 24'6"–25' | 34'6"–36' |
| Staircase-staircase | | 22'6–24'6" | 33'6"–35'6" |
| Staircase-parallel | | 23'–24'6" | 34'–35'6" |
| Parallel-vertical | | 24'6"–25'6" | 34'6–35'6" |
| Parallel-staircase | | 22'6"–24' | 33'–35' |
| Parallel-parallel | | 23'–24'6" | 34'–35' |

(These distances are for the average 16-hand horse, with a 12-foot canter stride)

**Oxer to vertical:** This combination demands excellent balance control. The oxer encourages the horse to land with a long stride, possibly on the forehand; he must rebalance quickly and may have to shorten stride to be ready to jump up and "curl around" the vertical.

**Oxer to oxer:** Requires scope, balance, and accuracy. The first oxer may encourage the horse to land on the forehand; you must rebalance without over-shortening his stride, and take off accurately but with power enough to clear the oxer.

## Approximate Distances for Combinations for Ponies

| | Small | Medium | Large |
|---|---|---|---|
| One-stride | 19'–20' | 20'–22' | 22'–24' |
| Two-stride | 29'–30' | 30'–32' | 33'–34' |

Setting combinations with correct distances is important for safety as well as successful jumping. The size, experience, and jumping level of both horses (or ponies) and riders, and the height, spread, and difficulty of the obstacles, must be taken into account. Please see the USPC Show Jumping Rules for Rallies, Appendix V (posted on the USPC website, www.ponyclub.org) for more detailed information on combinations at various heights.

## Some Different Fences

**Airy fences:** Fences without a ground line, or with little or no "filler," are difficult to judge. The horse must be attentive and careful, and must be ridden positively to a good takeoff distance. Horses may over-jump these fences or may "dwell" (hesitate) in the air, which can affect the distance to the next fence. Horses in all jumping disciplines should practice these types of fences, because some modern courses use limited or no ground lines.

**Spooky or unusual fences:** Spooky or unusual fences command a horse's attention and tend to make him "back off," shorten stride, jump high and short, or even refuse. They must be ridden positively but not too fast, with the horse well in front of the legs. Dropping the contact can cause a refusal or a hesitant, awkward jump.

# Gymnastics and Gridwork

*Gymnastic jumping* with ground poles (also called *gridwork*) can help develop a horse's coordination, accuracy, and a good jumping style, and it can correct certain problems. It also focuses the horse's attention, steadies his stride, and can be used for variety and to keep him interested in his work.

Riders benefit from gymnastics as well, especially to learn better rhythm, balance, and timing in order to ride more confidently. Riding gymnastics without stirrups can help to develop a more independent seat with a more secure seat leg, leading to an automatic release.

Basic gymnastics (including distances for horses and ponies) are covered in the *USPC C Level Manual,* Chapter 2.

## General Considerations

Gymnastic exercises can only accomplish their purpose if they are safe and suitable for the needs and level of horse and rider. They must be properly constructed and accurately measured, and must use suitable obstacles and ground poles that will not roll under a horse's foot and cause an accident. Because of the danger of injury to riders and horses, any unused cups should be removed from standards. Poles should be substantial and easy to see, and standards and obstacles must not be capable of trapping a horse's leg.

You will need one or more helpers to adjust poles, obstacles, and distances for gymnastic exercises.

Horses should generally wear protective boots for gymnastics and pole work because of the increased possibility of interference. As in all jumping, the rider should check his stirrup length, girth, helmet, and chin strap before he begins.

Gymnastic jumping is more physically demanding than it appears, because it requires multiple efforts and intense concentration. Horse and rider must be well warmed up first. Be aware of the horse's (and rider's) fitness and fatigue levels, and *stop* jumping before performance and/or attitude begin to deteriorate.

Gymnastics and ground poles should be approached in a steady trot or canter with impulsion. A fast, uneven, or unbalanced approach increases the chances of mistakes and magnifies problems. When possible, grids or gymnastics should be set so that they can be approached from the left or the right, alternating directions.

## Ground Pole Work

Ground poles can be used for attention and variety, to stabilize the stride, improve suppleness, increase activity, develop rhythm and suspension, strengthen the hindquarters, and teach the horse to adjust his strides. They are also used in connection with jumps to teach the horse to take off at the right distance and to jump straight. Quiet work over and around ground poles can help to relax a horse that tends to rush fences.

In these examples, spacing is based on a 16-hand horse with an average stride. You must adjust the spacing to fit your horse's stride so that his feet fall in the middle of the spaces between the poles. Poles can be 10 to 12 feet long and 3 or 4 inches in diameter. Square or hexagonal poles are less likely to roll.

See Chapter 3, "Dressage and Training Principles," for exercises using ground poles. When working over cavaletti and ground poles for jumping, the rider should ride in a half-seat or light seat to encourage the horse to stretch and round his back in a bascule.

Ground poles in connection with fences:

- **Trot poles to small fence (cross-rail), or before gymnastic:** Three to six ground poles spaced at a comfortable distance for your horse's trot (average horse: 4'6"); takeoff distance (last ground pole to base of fence) equals twice the trot pole distance (average horse: 9').
- **"Three-way" trot poles to fence or gymnastic:** Three trot pole grids (spaced as above); center grid leads to fence or grid, with additional grid angled to each side. Rider may choose to angle right or left over trot poles, or go straight over grid and fence. Good for turning and for horses that anticipate or rush fences.

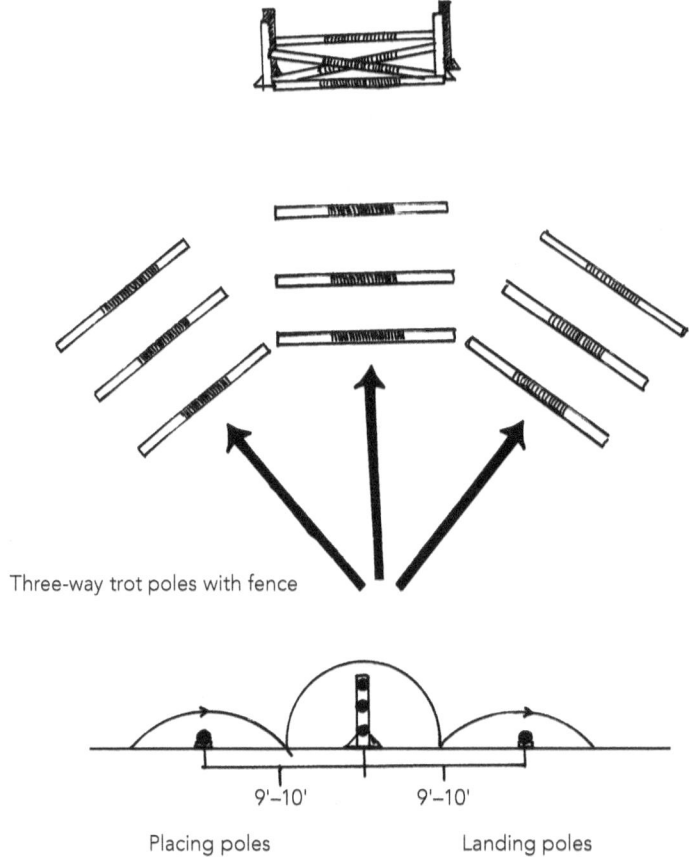

Three-way trot poles with fence

Placing poles      Landing poles

- **Placing pole:** Ground pole placed in front of the base of the fence to help horses learn appropriate takeoff distances. The pole is placed so that the horse steps over ground pole and arrives at a comfortable takeoff spot. A placing pole for a fence approached at a trot should be 8'6" to 9' from the base of the fence, and if approached in a canter, 9' to 11'. Generally, a placing pole should be placed closer to the jump for an oxer and farther away for a vertical.

- **Landing pole:** Ground pole placed approximately one stride (correct distance varies) from the fence on the landing side. Initially the landing pole should be placed farther away from the jump than the takeoff rail to ensure that the horse can land without interference. This encourages the horse to look at the landing spot, make adjustments in the air, and rebalance over the landing pole. This helps to develop bascule and balance on landing, and discourages rushing after the fence; it also teaches the rider to rebalance on landing.

- **Guide pole:** Ground pole placed perpendicular to fence, on takeoff and/or landing side, to prevent the horse from drifting to one side during approach, in the air, or on landing. A chute (two guide poles placed about 6' apart) may be used to keep the horse straight on approach. Be careful when using a chute on the landing side to avoid the horse landing on one of the poles.

## Exercises for Straightness and Turns

Ideally, a horse should jump each fence straight over the center, turn in either direction, and land on either lead with equal ease. He should also fold his legs evenly, without "dropping a leg," twisting, or drifting to one side, as these can cause him to hit a fence. Horses that habitually jump crookedly may be trying to spare a weak or unsound leg; they should be checked by a veterinarian.

Exercises to correct crooked jumping.

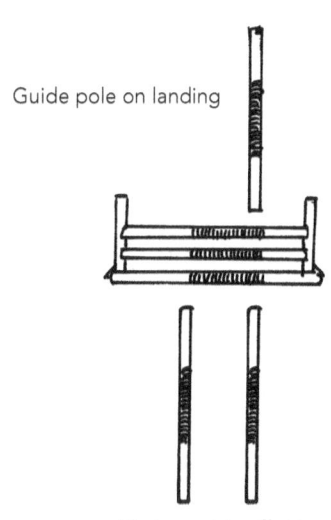

Guide pole on landing

Chute on takeoff side

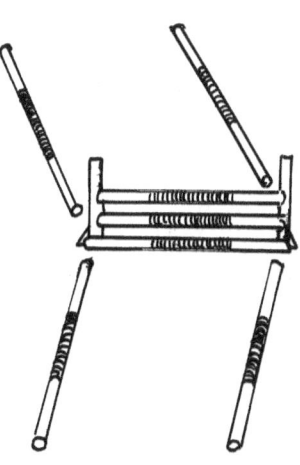

Chute on takeoff side with angled poles on landing side to encourage landing on designated lead

Open vee

Exercises for the crooked or uneven jumper include:

- Guide poles or a chute on the ground before a fence
- Single guide pole (not a chute) on landing side of a fence
- Angled poles (angled against the top rail as an inverted "V")
- Jumping fences on an angle (away from horse's preferred direction)
- Jumping fences on a curve or circle; turning in the air

## Gymnastic Distances

Distances between the elements of a gymnastic affect the horse's length of stride, takeoff point, balance, and rhythm. The distance can make a gymnastic easy, difficult, or impossible. A small variation in distance (as little as 6 inches per stride) can make a big difference in difficulty. Distances should be accurately measured with a tape, not estimated by "eye" or by pacing them off. Measure from standard to standard, from the back of the first element to the base of the second element. Measuring the diagonals (from left standard of the first element to right standard of the second) and making sure the diagonal measurements are equal will keep the fences properly aligned.

A distance may be easy, short, or long. An easy distance is tailored to the horse's natural stride, considering the size and type of obstacles, and the jumping arc they produce. Easy distances develop confidence (in both horse and rider) and confirm the habit of taking off at the correct spot.

Short distances require the horse to shorten his stride and maintain his balance between fences. They encourage a horse to jump "up and around" the fence, be quick and careful with his front end, and engage his hocks more. This results in a rounder jump with more power off the ground, a better bascule, and better folding of the forelegs. Shortened distances also help teach bold horses to wait and maintain their balance, and to jump with impulsion instead of speed.

Too-short distances can be discouraging and even unsafe; horses may get in too close and hesitate or stop, and some horses will try to leave out a stride if the distance is too short for them. Longer distances allow the horse room to lengthen his stride; they favor scope and a longer, flatter takeoff and jumping arc. However, a longer distance can also allow a horse to go on the forehand, increase his speed, and jump fast and flat, or "chip in" with an extra short stride. The rider must keep the horse in balance, maintain the rhythm, and get the horse to lengthen his stride correctly to prevent such problems.

Because of the effects of distances, green horses and horses (or riders) lacking in confidence need gymnastics with easy distances. The next step is to jump slightly shortened distances to develop better balance, engagement, and jumping form. Long distances are used less and must be adjusted and ridden correctly to avoid developing undesirable habits.

## Approaches to Fences

The approach to a fence determines how the horse will jump it. Good approaches demand good riding and control, which must be developed by proper schooling in flat work. To ride a good approach, you must be focused, organized, and ride with clear intent. Indecision, loss of concentration, or last-minute changes can upset and demoralize your horse, and lead to bad jumps, refusals, and loss of confidence.

The elements of an approach are line, pace, impulsion, balance, and distance.

- **Line** is established by your eyes. It extends from the beginning of the approach, over the center of the fence, to a "target" or focal point. A line may be straight, angled, or curved and may include more than one obstacle.
- **Pace** is the speed, rhythm, and tempo at which you jump. The pace must be appropriate for the horse, the jump, and the situation. Maintaining a regular and even pace is more efficient, smoother, and easier for the horse, and makes it easier to see distances and jump in stride.
- **Impulsion,** or energy and desire to go forward, is indispensable for jumping. The horse must be reliably "in front of your legs." Impulsion must be channeled into the best pace, rhythm, balance, and line, or it can degenerate into uncontrollable energy.
- **Balance** refers to the balance of both horse and rider. The horse must be in the right balance for the jump; you must be in balance with him, and influence his balance. Certain situations, such as jumping large verticals, sharp turns before or after the fence, uphill or downhill slopes, jumping at speed, or slippery footing, make good balance especially critical.
- **Distance** refers to the takeoff distance, or the spot where the horse leaves the ground. This is influenced by all the previous elements, and also by the rider's influence on the horse's pace, length of stride, impulsion, and balance. A rider may "rate" a horse to achieve a specific takeoff distance, but this requires skill, accuracy, and the ability to "see a distance," or know where the horse will take off.

## Lines of Approach

An approach may be straight, angled, or curved. Single fences and the first fence in a line are usually (but not always) ridden off a turn or an opening circle. When a fence is followed by a turn or a bending line to the next fence, line and rebalancing immediately after the fence become critical. This is especially important when speed counts, as in a timed jump-off.

Your inside and outside aids (both legs and both reins) create a "channel" that keeps the horse moving straight and accurately along your chosen line. Your aids must be ready to prevent or correct crookedness, sideways movement, drifting out, or falling in while sending your horse forward in rhythm.

- **Straight approach:** A normal approach is a straight line for at least three strides before the fence, and leads directly over the center. Sometimes it is necessary to jump a fence at a point other than the center, in order to jump from good footing or for a better line to the next fence. Accuracy requires concentration and straightness.

    Long, straight approaches (seven strides or more) require good rhythm, timing, and the ability to keep a steady pace and *wait* for the jump. Horses (and riders) need to guard against increasing their pace, leaning on the forehand, and rushing on a long approach, which result in an over-bold approach and a difficult distance.

- **Bending approach:** A bending approach is on an arc, bending line, or circle; you can adjust the distance by tightening or widening the arc. On a bending approach you must establish pace, rhythm, balance, and impulsion early. Your outside and inside aids are especially important to keep your horse from bearing out, letting his hindquarters swing out, or falling in. Look ahead at the jump as you ride the curved line of the approach; over the jump, look ahead to where you are going.

    The following exercise develops your eye for a distance on a bending approach:

    Set up a 25-meter circle, with "gates" (a pair of cones or standards) at three of the quarter points, and a pair of standards with a ground pole at the fourth. Canter the circle; as you pass through each gate, look ahead to the next. Ride each quarter as an even arc, using your aids to keep the pace even and prevent your horse from falling in or bearing out. Work in each direction, then raise the fence to a cross-rail, then a simple vertical. This exercise teaches you to jump "automatically" as you look ahead to the next fence, and prepares you and your horse for turning in the air.

Bending line.

Jumping on a circle.

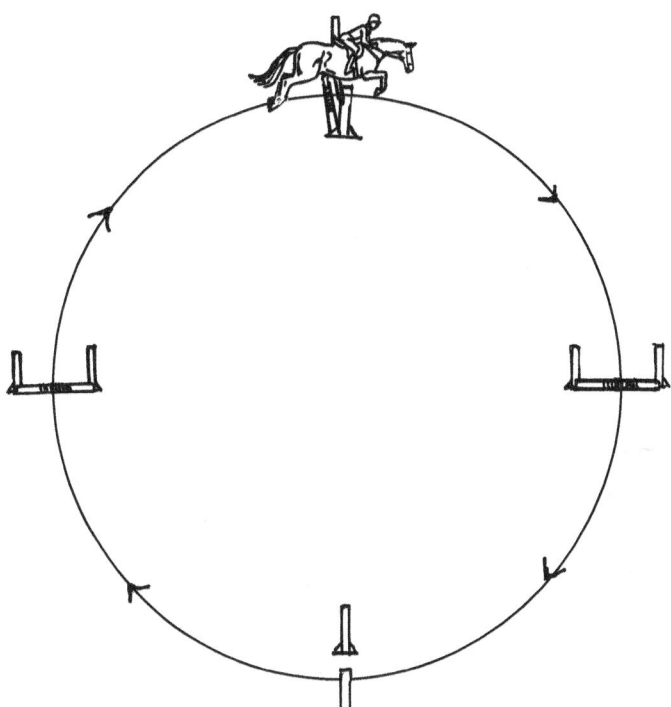

Angled approach.

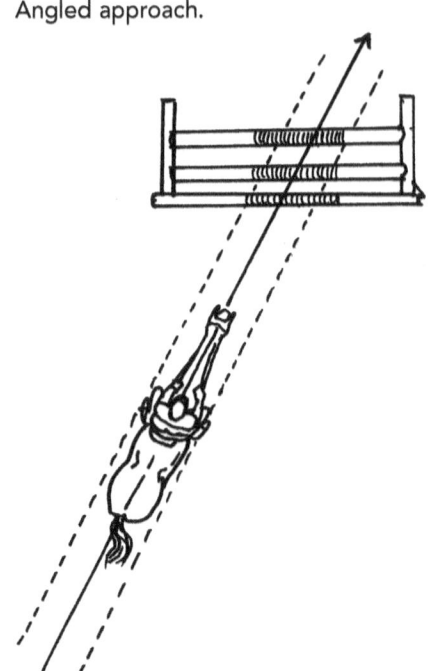

- **Angled approach:** An angled approach follows a line that crosses the fence at an angle. It is used to save ground, or to line up for the next fence. Because an angled approach can invite a runout, it must be ridden very accurately and positively. Choose a focal point to aim for and define your line clearly, using leg and rein aids on both sides to "channel" the horse straight along the line. The pace should be steady but not too fast. Impulsion, with the horse reliably in front of the legs, is essential.

## Leads and Jumping

Leads are important for balance and safety in turns and approaches. Although a horse can jump from either lead on a straight line, turning on the wrong lead handicaps his balance and maneuverability, and can result in an inaccurate approach or even a fall. When a horse is on the correct lead, his inside hind leg is engaged well under him, and he can balance better through turns. On the wrong lead, his outside hind leg is farther forward, and he cannot turn as sharply or as fast. A disunited canter is worst of all: he is uncoordinated;

on one lead in the hind legs and the other lead in front; and may bear out, break to a trot, or even fall if he tries to turn sharply.

Schooling for leads and lead changes in jumping depends on good flat work. The progressive steps are:

**Canter departs on designated lead, along the rail and in the open, without the visual aid of the rail or a corner:** Establish the correct lead on a circle before jumping at canter.

**Improving balance, engagement, and maneuverability in the canter:** Ride circles, turns, and figures of varying size; changing leads through the trot (later, through the walk) when changing direction. Increase and decrease the circle (in both directions). Ride approaches to fences from turns and circles.

**Counter-canter:** Develops straightness, balance, and preparedness for flying changes. Practice counter-canter on straight lines, shallow single loops, and wide, easy turns before and after fences.

**Landing on a designated lead:** Start by trotting a fence on a circle; then trot the fence and canter away from it on the circle. Do this first in your horse's preferred direction, then in his harder direction.

**Turning and changing leads over a jump:** Horses often change leads naturally over a jump, because the effort of lining up their hind legs to jump often causes them to switch leads. You can jump a single vertical as a figure-eight exercise (see diagram), alternating leads.

**Flying change of leads:** The horse changes leads in the air, during the moment of suspension. The horse must change *clean* (hind legs and front legs both change at once) and smoothly, without bucking or speeding up. If he changes only in front, he will be disunited. Some horses will correct themselves and change behind in the next stride or two (this is called a *late change*), but this doesn't always happen.

Figure eight over pole or fence for flying change of leads.

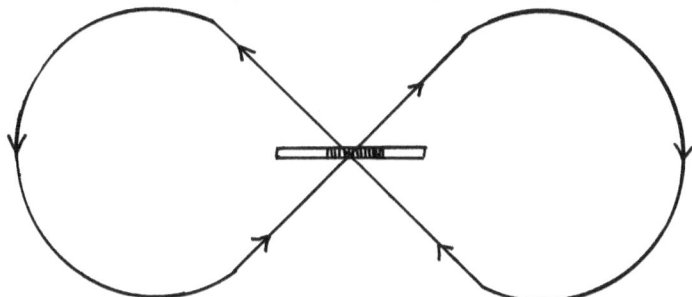

On any horse, you must rebalance (half-halt), straighten the horse, and then give the aids for the new lead:

- New outside leg, about 4 inches behind the girth
- New inside leg, close to the girth
- New outside supporting rein
- New inside rein indicates direction (opening rein)
- Keep your weight in the center (*don't* lean sideways!)

You must give the aids at the right time in the canter stride. Rebalance and straighten the horse on the "up" (as the forehand rises). Ask for the new lead on the "down" (as the head and neck reach out and down); the horse is going into the "jump" or suspension phase, and can change when all four feet are off the ground.

*Never* lean over the inside shoulder, pull the head sideways, or spur a horse roughly to try to make him change—this unbalances and upsets him, and can make him buck or rush off.

Flying changes come easily and naturally to some horses and are more difficult for others. If a horse is green or awkward at changing leads, consider the following:

- You may be making it hard for him to change leads. Are you stiff, out of balance, or throwing your weight from side to side? Are you hanging on his mouth, or unclear with your aids or timing?
- Your horse may not be straight, balanced, or advanced enough in his canter work to do flying changes yet. Go back and review the previous canter work before asking for flying changes.
- He may need more impulsion and better engagement to make the change. If his canter is flat, lacking "jump," his back is hollow, or he is "strung out" and disengaged, he cannot change leads.
- He may not understand what you want. Try making several simple changes (through the walk) at the same spot, gradually decreasing the number of walk steps to a single stride, then ask for the flying change in the same place. You can canter a figure eight over a ground pole, giving the aids for the flying change when the horse is in the air over the pole. When he does change correctly, reward him immediately and generously, and *end the lesson!*

Flying change of leads.

# Jumping Turns

To turn accurately, a horse must engage his hind legs (especially the inside hind leg) well under his body, and have balance and impulsion. Horses often slow down, lose impulsion, or become unbalanced during turns, which can lead to loss of time, a bad jump, a runout, or even a fall. Turns in jumping, especially at speed, require good riding and a horse made balanced and "turn-able" by correct flat work.

## Riding Jumping Turns

In a jumping turn, balance and engagement are all-important. If the horse is on the wrong lead, disunited, or on the forehand, his hind legs are not placed safely and surely, he lacks power, and worst of all, he can easily slip or even fall.

Lateral balance is important, too. It is natural for a horse making a fast turn to lean inward, but if he overdoes this, you can both lose your balance.

When a horse has trouble in a turn, he is likely to bear out (widen the turn), fall out through his outside shoulder, over-bend in his neck, slow down, or break his rhythm and gait. All of these cost time, balance, and impulsion, and can spoil your approach to the next fence.

When riding jumping turns, your body balance, leg aids, and rein aids are critical.

> **Seat and balance:** The tighter the turn, the more vertical you should be, from your feet to your head. This helps you use your weight and balance to keep your horse engaged and balanced. Turning your eyes and rotating your center in the direction of the line adjusts your balance, acts as a seat aid for turning, and makes your rein and leg aids

more effective. Leaning excessively forward or inward can throw your horse onto his forehand and unbalance him.

**Leg aids:** Your inside leg, close to the girth, asks your horse to engage his inside hind leg, to maintain impulsion, and not to fall inward. Your outside leg, stretched back and down, with the heel down, about 4 inches behind the girth, prevents the horse from bearing out or allowing his hindquarters to "skid" to the outside. Both legs help to maintain the bend and the canter lead, and keep your horse moving forward with impulsion.

**Rein aids:** Both inside and outside reins must act together in order to keep the horse moving forward along the line you have selected. The outside rein regulates the pace and is especially important to prevent bearing out or over-bending the neck; the inside rein indicates the direction of the turn and asks for the bend. The inside rein can be used in a brief upward correction for a horse that falls in or leans on his inside shoulder.

## Turning in the Air

Turning in the air can help you save ground, land on a particular lead, or get a better line to the next fence or turn. It is an important skill for riding jumpers or courses in which turning tightly or speed is a factor, and can also be used to correct a horse that drifts sideways or anticipates a turn on landing.

Start with a simple vertical fence (turning across a spread makes it wider and increases the chances of hitting the back rail). Select your line carefully, and know exactly where you want your horse to go as he lands. A good beginning exercise is to set up a fence on a circle, placing pairs of cones or standards at the quarter points (see page 149).

Turning in the air.

To turn in the air:

- Look ahead in the direction of the turn, toward your next focal point. Never look down, as this unbalances you.
- Lead the horse's head in the direction of the turn by applying an opening rein with your inside hand. Move your hand sideways (never backward!); you can also rotate your inside hand briefly (as if "thumbing a ride"). The other hand releases normally (at first, you may need to rest the other hand on the horse's crest for support).
- Shift your weight *slightly* toward your inside knee, keeping the outside leg slightly back. Both legs should stay well under you, and your weight should shift only a little; if you allow your heel to come up or displace your weight too much, you become unbalanced and unsafe.

## Roll-Back Turns

A roll-back turn is a short turn of 180 degrees or more. It is a variation of the turn on the haunches, performed at speed. The horse must engage both

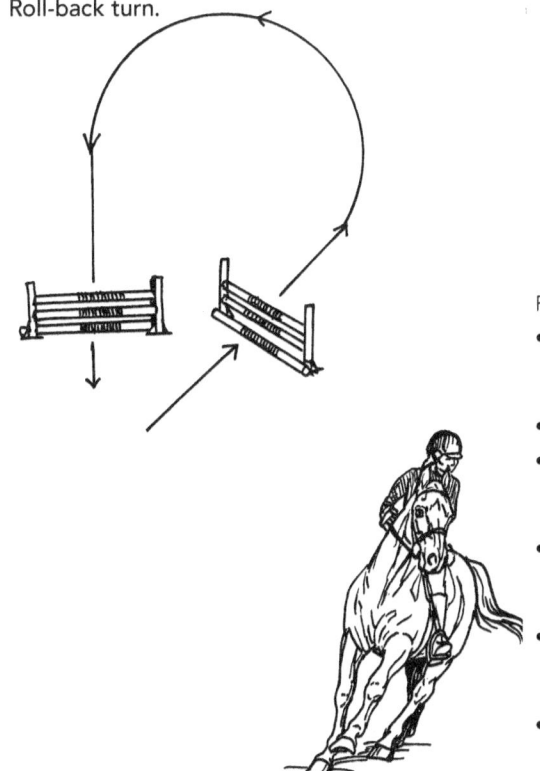

Roll-back turn.

Riding a roll-back turn:
- Open hip angle (to maintain balance and increase effectiveness of aids)
- Look in direction of turn
- Outside leg behind girth (keeps haunches from "skidding" to outside)
- Outside supporting rein (regulates bend, prevents horse from bearing out through outside shoulder)
- Inside leg at girth (asks for engagement of inside hind leg, maintains impulsion)
- Inside rein (leads forehand in direction of turn)

hind legs, but especially his inside hind leg, well under his body. His forehand swings around, making a wider circle than his hind legs, which turn in a very small circle. If he performs the turn well, he comes out of the turn with good balance, extra engagement, and power. If he loses engagement or his hind legs swing outward, he may bear out, lean over his inside shoulder, lose rhythm and engagement, or change to a disunited canter. All of these errors cost time, balance, and the ability to move forward and jump well.

To ride a roll-back turn, you must open your hip angle and stretch up, with your seat bones close to or lightly in the saddle and your legs under your seat. Keep your outside leg back (with the heel down) to control the hindquarters, and look in the direction of the turn. Your inside leg keeps the inside hind leg engaged. Use a firm outside rein to keep your horse from bearing out or over-bending his neck, and use your inside rein to lead your horse through the turn. As you open your hip angle and sit closer to your horse, be sure to stay in balance with a following seat so you do not get left behind as your horse goes forward out of the turn.

A good exercise for roll-back turns is to ride a 15-meter half-circle in reverse (leave the track at an angle and turn back to the track). Ride this first in trot, then in canter (canter on the lead you will turn toward, after leaving the rail). Later, set a fence on the track and ride a roll-back turn to the fence.

## Turning Problems

The following problems often crop up in jumping turns:

> **Loss of impulsion, slowing down:** This is how a horse protects himself when he is not balanced or athletic enough to turn properly, or if he senses indecisive or weak riding. Your legs (especially your inside leg) maintain impulsion and engagement; you must use good judgment about how tightly your horse can turn, considering the footing, pace, and his experience and ability.
>
> **Bearing out (going wide):** A horse bears out to avoid the difficulty of a tight turn, especially if he is unbalanced laterally, going too fast, or if his rider fails to use his outside aids effectively. To correct this, you must be in good balance (it helps to sit up straighter than usual), with an effective outside leg and outside supporting rein. Pulling the horse around with a strong inside rein and inadequate use of the outside aids often causes bearing out.
>
> **Falling in over the inside shoulder (leaning in):** The horse loses his balance inward. This comes from lack of engagement of the inside hind leg, too much weight on the forehand, and often from bending to the outside; it can be caused by pulling the horse around with the reins with insufficient inside leg. The horse needs to engage his hind

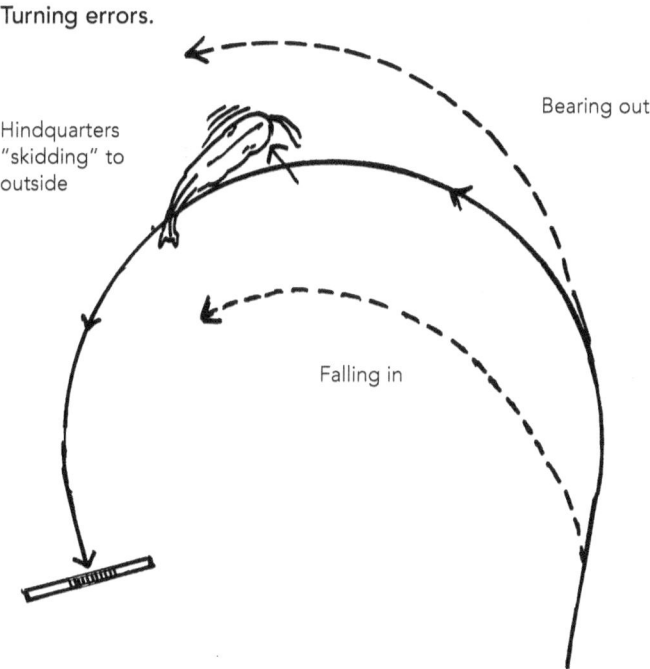

Turning errors.

legs, rebalance himself, and "stand up" around the turn; this takes effective half-halts, inside leg at the girth, and sometimes a corrective upward lift on the inside rein.

**Hindquarters "skidding" to the outside:** The horse loses his balance inward, with inadequate engagement and too much weight on the forehand. He may "dig" with both hind legs together ("rabbit hopping"), instead of engaging his inside hind leg; this can cause him to change to a disunited canter, slip, or even fall. It also costs speed, power, and balance.

Your outside leg and rein connection keeps the hindquarters in line and prevents them from skidding. Use effective half-halts, inside leg for better engagement, and sit up in a more vertical position on tight turns to control the hindquarters and turn in balance.

## Elements of a Jumping Course

Only four elements (basic parts) can be put together to make up a jumping course. Each of these can include different kinds of obstacles and can range from easy to difficult. They are the following:

1. Single fences (or first fence in a line)
2. Related distances (line of two or more fences less than 85 feet apart)

3. Combinations
4. Turns and bending lines

**Single fences:** A single fence is a fence either set by itself or so far from the previous fence that it has little effect on how you jump it. The first fence of a course, a fence following a turn, or the first fence in a new line can be considered a single fence.

To jump a single fence, you must ride accurately and choose the right line. Be very positive when jumping the first fence on a course or a single fence, especially if it looks unusual or is placed so that you are going away from home.

**Related distances:** A related distance is a line of two fences set close enough that the way you jump the first fence affects the number of strides and the way you jump the second fence. Most related distances are three to seven strides, or 96 feet or less.

Elements of a course.

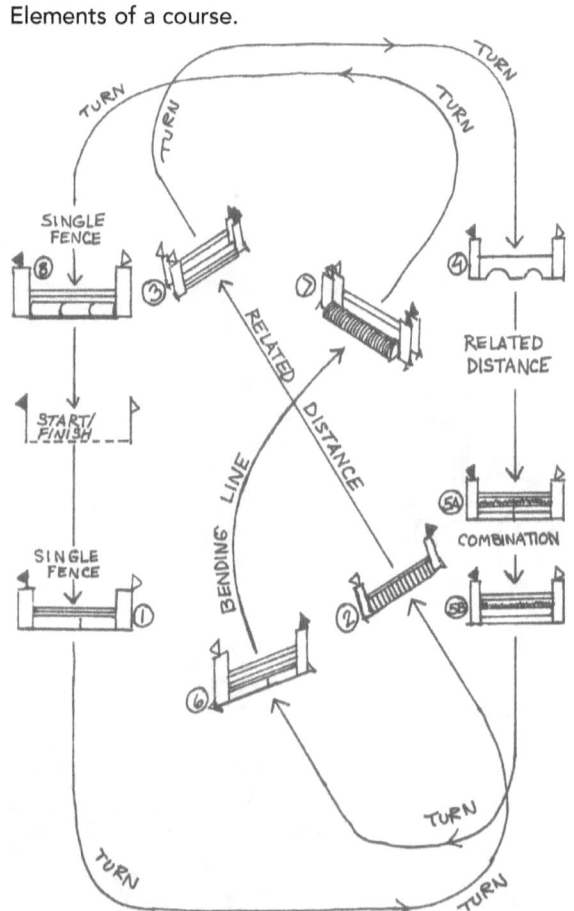

3' vertical—60 feet—3' vertical.
A. 12' canter stride: 6' landing, four 12' strides (48'), 6' takeoff = 60'.
B. 10' canter stride: 5' landing, five 10' strides (50'), 5' takeoff = 60'.
Related Distance: 3' vertical, 60' to 3' vertical.

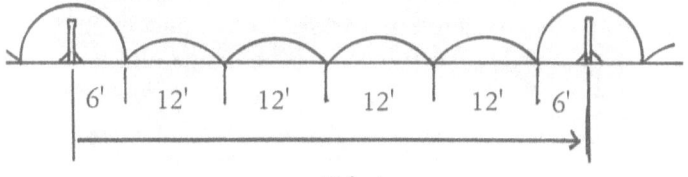

60 feet
A. Ridden with 12' stride:
6' landing, four 12' strides, 6' takeoff

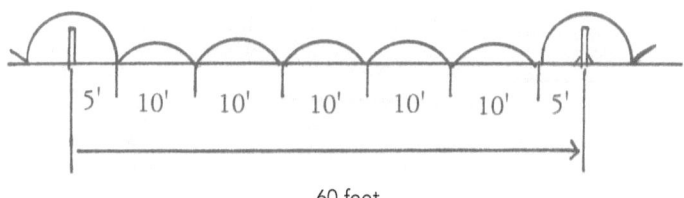

60 feet
B. Ridden with 10' stride:
5' landing, five 10' strides, 5' takeoff

The number of strides in a related distance depends on how the horse jumps the first fence (especially how much space he uses for landing), the length of his strides, and where he must take off for the second fence. Here is an example of a related distance that could be ridden in either four or five strides:

To ride related distances, you must know how long your horse's strides are at an average jumping canter. (The average canter stride for a 16-hand horse is 12 feet.) It's more important to keep good balance, an even pace, and the right length of stride for *your* horse than to insist on riding a certain number of strides in a line. For example, if your horse jumps safely and comfortably with an 11-foot stride, it may not be not sensible (or safe) to push him to try to take 12-foot or longer strides. The faster he goes and the longer his strides, the easier it is for him to lean too much on his forehand, get out of balance, and make a serious mistake. This is especially dangerous when jumping solid cross-country fences.

It is especially important to keep a steady rhythm and to keep your horse's strides even. If he keeps changing his balance and strides, you won't be able to tell when he is going to take off, and you both will have trouble.

Certain conditions can make a horse's strides shorter or longer than usual. This may change the way some fences or lines "ride." Hard, slippery, or muddy ground; an uphill slope; and going away from home can make a horse shorten his strides or lose impulsion. A slight downhill slope, going toward home, or jumping a spread can make him lengthen his strides. When jumping in an indoor arena, horses tend to back off and shorten their strides because of the enclosing walls, making it more difficult to maintain impulsion.

You may have to steady your horse or encourage him to keep an even pace with the length of stride that is best for him. Try to keep your pace even instead of making a big change in his stride close to the takeoff. This disturbs a horse and can result in a bad jump or a refusal.

### Suggested Average Related Distances for Horses
(Average horse stride is 12')

| Stride size | 11'9" | 12' | 12'3" |
|---|---|---|---|
| 3 strides | 47' | 48' | 49' |
| 4 strides | 58'9" | 60' | 61'3" |
| 5 strides | 70'6" | 72' | 73'6" |
| 6 strides | 82'3" | 84' | 85'9" |
| 7 strides | 94' | 96' | 98' |

### Suggested Average Related Distances for Ponies
Small ponies: Up to 12.2 hands
Medium ponies: 12.2+ hands to 13.2 hands
Large ponies: 13.2+ hands to 14.2 hands

| | Small | Medium | Large |
|---|---|---|---|
| **Stride size** | **10'** | **10'6"** | **11'3"** |
| 3 strides | 40' | 42' | 45' |
| 4 strides | 50' | 52'6" | 56'3" |
| 5 strides | 60' | 63' | 67'6" |
| 6 strides | 70' | 73'6" | 78'9" |
| 7 strides | 80' | 84' | 90' |

**Combinations:** A combination is two or more fences in line, placed so close together (with less than 39 feet between them) that there is room for only one or two strides. The obstacles that make up a combination are called

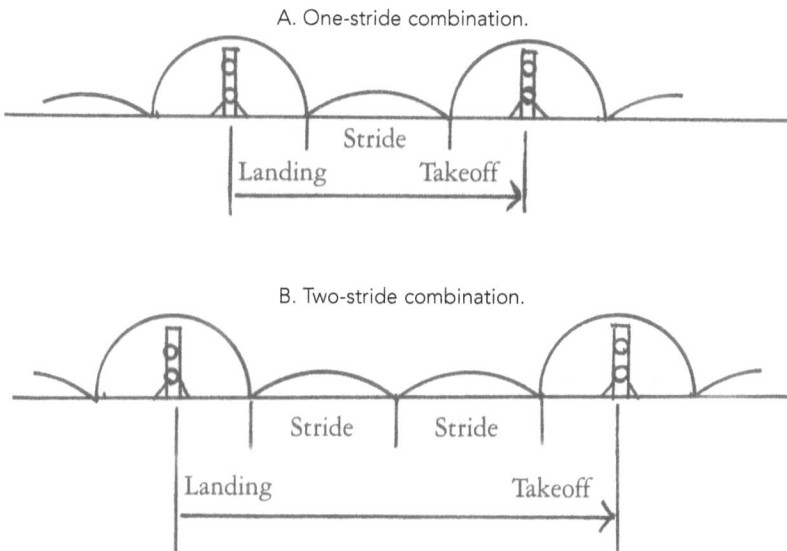

A. One-stride combination.

B. Two-stride combination.

*elements.* A double combination has two jumps or elements; a triple combination has three.

Combinations are really very short related distances. The way your horse jumps the first element, and how much room he uses during landing, determines how much space he has to take one or two strides and take off at the next element. Combinations must be set with distances that are reasonable and safe for your horse's strides and jumping ability. Large, long-striding horses and smaller, short-striding ponies should not be asked to jump the same combination unless the distance is adjusted for each.

In competition, a combination has the same fence number, but each element also has a letter (for example, Fence 10-A and 10-B). If your horse refuses the second or third element of a combination, you must re-jump the entire combination. (For example, if your horse jumps 10-A but refuses at 10-B, you must go back and jump both 10-A and 10-B again.)

The distance between elements in a combination, along with the type of fences, determine how many strides between the element and how the fences must be jumped.

**Turns and bending lines:** Single fences and the first fence in a new line usually involve a turn. The turn, and the line resulting from the turn, can make a jump easy or difficult. A good turn brings you to the jump in good balance and sets up the right line to the next fence. A poor turn brings the horse in at an angle that can make him run out or misjudge the fence. It is usually best to try to jump a fence squarely in the center, as this makes

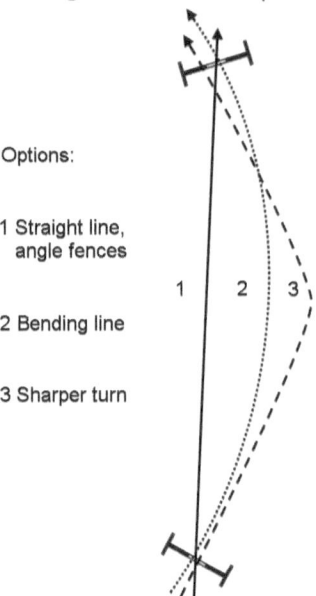

Bending line with three options.

Options:

1 Straight line, angle fences

2 Bending line

3 Sharper turn

a runout less likely. However, there may be times when you must jump one side of a fence to save time, to get the best line to the next fence, or to take off from better footing. In this case, you must be especially careful to ride straight and avoid a runout.

A bending line is a line of two fences, the second of which is not in line with the first. To meet the second fence straight, you must ride the line on a curve. This takes clever riding and good control, and you must choose the best line to ride. If you ride a wider turn, you gain more room and take more strides. Riding a straighter line saves ground and takes fewer strides.

If you enter show-jumping competitions, you must know the rules and enter the appropriate class and level of competition for you and your horse. You will need special coaching to safely prepare yourself and your horse for this type of competition and to help you during the show.

## How to Measure Distances

**Determining your horse's average stride:** Competition courses are designed with an average stride in mind (often 12 feet for average horses). However, you can determine the length of your horse's average stride. This can be done by raking a section of the track smooth, riding over it at a normal jumping canter, and measuring the distance between the first hoof print and the same hoof print in the next stride.

Walking a distance.

Four 3' steps = one 12' canter stride

**Walking a distance:** To walk a distance, you must learn to take a stride that is one-quarter the length of your horse's stride, so four of your strides will equal one canter stride. For example, if your horse's stride is 12 feet, your strides should be 3 feet (36 inches). Use a measuring tape or yardstick to measure until you can take consistent steps of the correct length.

When walking a distance, you must allow for landing from the first fence and takeoff at the next fence. The actual landing distance may vary depending on the jump, the pace, and other factors, but it must be at least as long as the height of the last element of the fence, and it may be longer. A good rule of thumb is to allow two of your strides for landing.

The same rule applies to the space allowed for takeoff at the second fence: It must be at least the same distance as the height of the first element, but it may be longer. Two of your strides is a good average takeoff distance.

To walk a distance between fences, start at the base of the first fence, on the landing side. Take two 3-foot strides for landing space, then take four equal 3-foot strides for each canter stride, counting the canter strides. Allow approximately two 3-foot strides for takeoff, depending on the type of jump and other factors. If you find that the distance is "tight" (short), you may need to shorten your horse's stride or adjust your takeoff spot. If the distance is long, you may need to lengthen his stride, adjust the takeoff point, or add a stride (making all strides shorter) to take up the extra distance.

When walking distances, it is important to be straight and accurate. If you walk from one jump to the next on an angle or do not go straight, it will alter the distance.

# Types of Courses

Different types of courses are designed for various purposes and test certain qualities in horses and riders. While you may or may not compete over all the following types of courses, you should understand their purpose and be able to ride appropriately over each (at a suitable height for the horse).

Working hunter course.

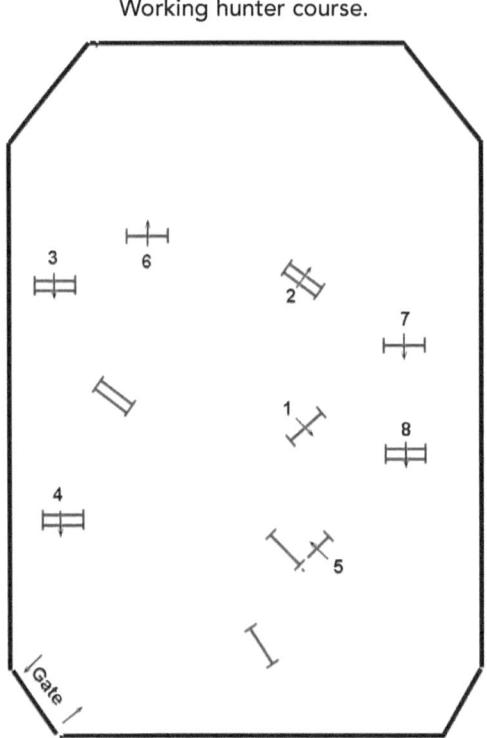

Designed by Phil DeVita for the 2010 Winter Equestrian Festival, Junior Hunter divisions

## Hunter Courses

Hunter courses are designed for a smooth, flowing performance of the horse, demonstrating an even pace over fences simulating those found in the hunting field. In competition, the horse is judged on his performance, manners, and way of going. An even, steady pace; consistently good takeoff distances; good jumping style; long, low movement; and overall smoothness and ease of performance are paramount.

There are two types of hunter courses: traditional and handy. A traditional hunter course consists of single fences, related distances, and includes a combination. Handy hunter courses simulate tricky and difficult hunting country by including more complex elements like hand gallop to a jump, a bending line, roll-back turn, a fence at the end of the ring, or a trot jump. Movement that saves time and ground (handiness) but does not sacrifice performance or style is rewarded by the judge.

Hunter derby competitions are two-phase events. Horses first jump a traditional hunter round. The top 12 exhibitors then ride the handy course. The horse with the best combined score (between the traditional and handy

Handy hunter course.

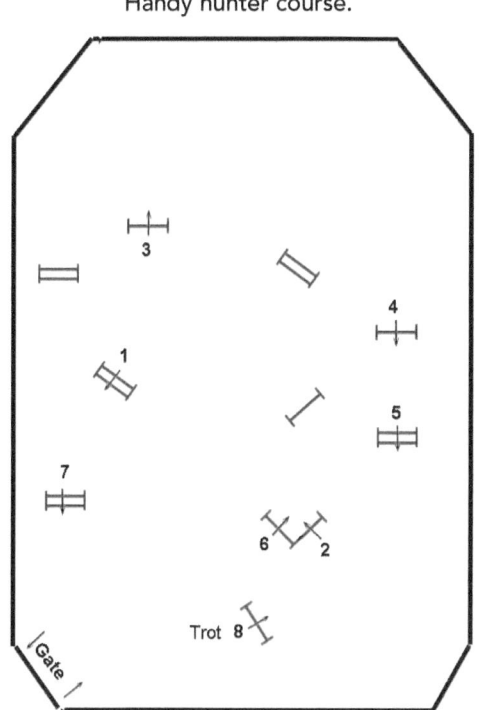

Designed by Phil DeVita for the 2010 Winter Equestrian Festival, Junior Hunter divisions

rounds) wins the derby. An exciting feature of a hunter derby is the high side option fences. Both courses contain at least four fences with high side options. These fences are larger than the other fences on the course. A rider can choose to jump as many (or as few) of the high side options as he feels will best maximize his score. Riders receive one bonus point added to their base score for each high side option successfully attempted. Riders are allowed to walk the course prior to the start of Hunter Derby competitions so that they can properly plan their rides and decide which high side options (if any) are appropriate for their mount to attempt.

## Equitation Courses

Equitation courses are designed to test the skills of the rider. In an Equitation class, the rider is judged on his own and his horse's performance over the course, including correct takeoff distances, accurate lines and turns, form and style, and maintaining an even pace over the course. The rider must be both effective and smooth, with aids as subtle as possible.

Equitation courses may be held over hunter or jumper type obstacles, including verticals and spreads up to 1.15m (3'9"), one or more

## National PHA Medal Equitation Course with test.

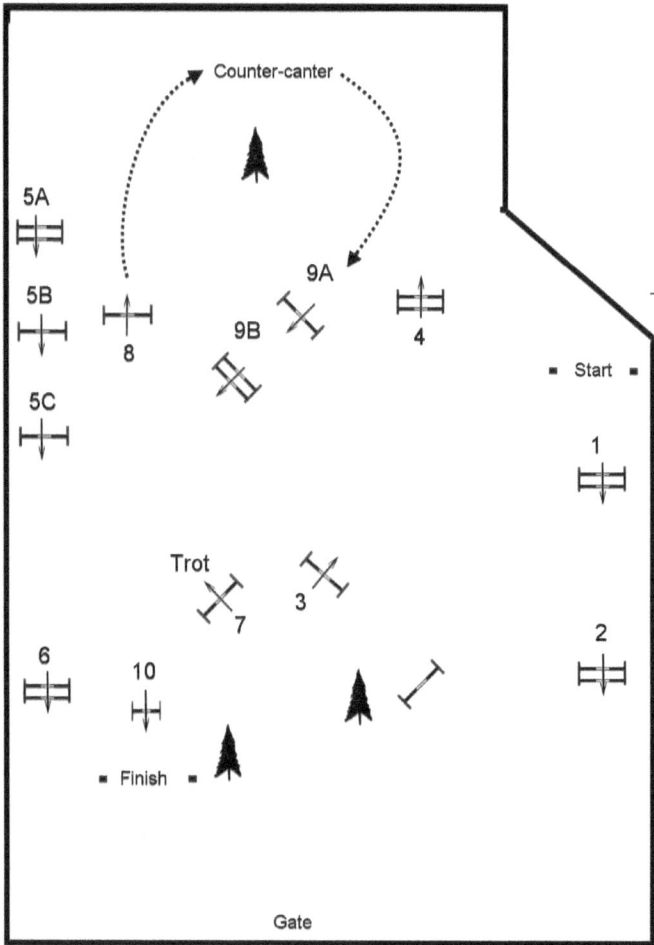

Designed by Steve Stephens for the National PHA Medal Hunter Seat Equitation Class at the 2010 Lake Placid Horse Show

combinations, and at least two changes of direction. Course designers include tests of technical ability (related distances, bending lines, and combinations); precision (narrow fences); and control (ability to lengthen and shorten stride smoothly, ride a specific line, and turn accurately). The horse is expected to be on the correct lead in all turns, so the ability to land in the correct lead and execute smooth flying changes is important.

Equitation classes often require testing the top contenders for ribbons. The type of test that may be required varies, depending on the class specifications. Judges must choose tests from the printed list in the current USEF Rule Book (www.usef.org). They include such tests as hand gallop; turn on the forehand; ride without stirrups; jump obstacles on a figure-eight course;

Jumper course.

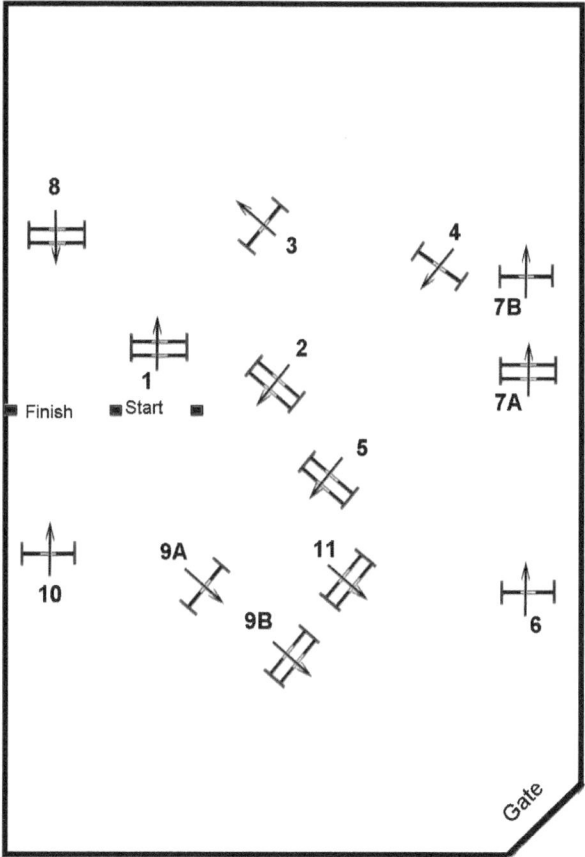

Designed by Steve Stephens for the Amateur Owner Jumper division at the 2010 Winter Equestrian Festival

change horses; or answer questions regarding basic horsemanship, tack, equipment, and conformation.

Specifications for different Equitation Classes can be found in the USEF Rule Book.

## Show Jumping (Jumper) Courses

Show jumping classes are held over a course of show jumping obstacles, including verticals, spreads, double and triple combinations, and many turns and changes of direction. The purpose is to jump cleanly over a twisting course within the time allowed; jumping faults are incurred for knockdowns and disobediences, and time faults for exceeding the time allowed. Riders walk both the course and the jump-off course before a competition to plan their ride.

## USPC Championship jumper course.

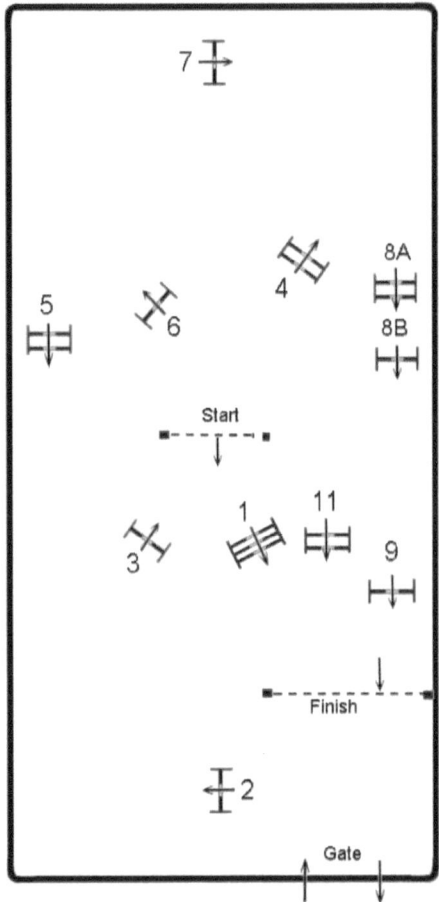

Designed by Bob McCune for the Developing Horse and Rider division at the 2011 USPC Festival Championships

Jumper courses can be highly technical, requiring boldness, scope, power, accuracy, and control; speed is also a factor, especially in jump-off courses and speed classes (in which time counts in the first round). A jumper must jump big, bravely, and fast, but he must also be careful and accurate to avoid knockdowns, and must be balanced and rideable in order to rate and turn accurately. A jumper rider must ride the best line to each fence, saving ground with well-planned turns and lines, and must adjust his horse's stride for each fence and distance, while avoiding knockdowns. In a jump-off, he must balance the need to go as fast as he can and turn as tight as possible against his horse's ability to jump cleanly.

The type of class and how it will be scored must be posted on the course diagram, along with other important information like the *time allowed* (a

Stadium course 1 (eventing).

Designed by Deb Willson

rider's time must be faster than the time allowed to avoid incurring time penalties) and the *time limit* (if a rider is slower than this posted time, he will be eliminated).

Rules for USPC competitions are found in the USPC Show Jumping Rule Book, and rules for USEF competitions are in the USEF Rule Book.

## Stadium Jumping Courses (Eventing)

Stadium jumping is typically the third phase of an eventing competition. This test is similar to an ordinary show jumping competition, but without any attempt to find a "winner" of the test on its own. Its main objective is to prove that the horse and athlete are well trained in the specialist discipline of show jumping. It was originally designed to see if the horse still had the energy, control, ability, and agility to come back after cross-country to complete this course successfully. The nature of the course, its length, the speed demanded, and the dimensions of the obstacles depend on the degree of difficulty of the whole competition.

This jumping test is a single round over show jumping–style obstacles, with a maximum time allowed based on a standard pace appropriate for the level of competition. Knockdowns and disobediences incur penalty points. While exceeding the time allowed will also incur penalty points, it is not a speed event, and there is no bonus for extra speed. There is no jump-off. The

Stadium course 2 (eventing).

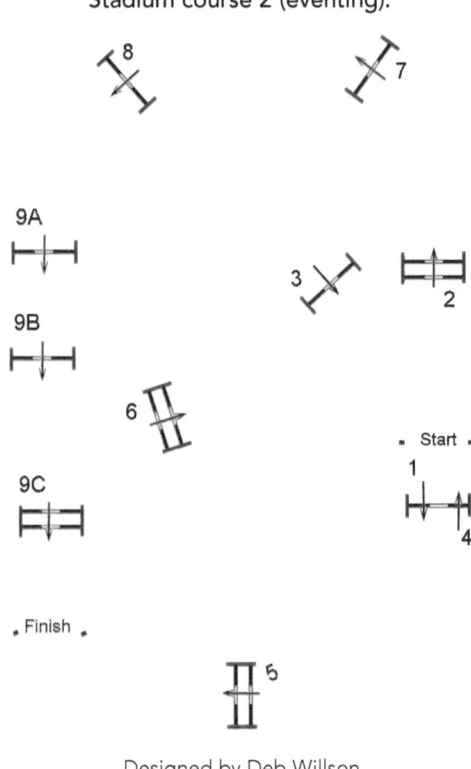

Designed by Deb Willson

penalty score of the show jumping phase is combined with the scores from the dressage and cross-country phases to determine a winner. For more detailed information about the show jumping phase of eventing, refer to the USEF and the FEI (www.fei.org/) Rule Books.

# Walking a Show Jumping Course

Riders walk a show jumping course to determine the best track, balance, and pace to maximize their horse's ability to jump the course clean and within the time allowed. As a rider plans the ride, he must pay attention to the following:

- **Quality of footing.** For example, sloppy or hard footing might encourage riders to choose a more conservative track or pace.
- **Terrain and crown of arena.** The slope of an arena can impact balance and pace.

- **Placement of fences.** Fences placed near outside influences can make it more difficult to maintain a horse's attention. Horses tend to go slower when going away from the in gate and schooling area, and go faster when going toward the gate.
- **Related distances.** Riders must be able to walk measured distances between jumps accurately and discern what pace will be needed, how many and how long their strides will be, and the best track for their horse.
- **Color, shapes, and sizes of fences and materials used.** Different types of fences will affect a rider's choice of track, balance, and pace. For example, a rider might choose to gallop to an inviting oxer set in deep cups, but should balance and ride carefully to an airy vertical set in shallow cups.
- **Sun/shade.** How well the horse and rider can see a jump may change throughout the day as the lighting and shadows change. This can also be affected by weather and the type of arena in which the competition is held.

It is important for riders to walk courses with a knowledgeable instructor who can help them evaluate the course and choose an appropriate riding plan. An experienced coach will give suggestions to help riders avoid problems on the course. A well-ridden plan will seem effortless, with the horse and rider moving positively forward on a well-chosen track, maintaining consistent rhythm, pace, and balance.

# 5

# Cross-Country Riding and Jumping

## Review of Cross-Country Fundamentals

To ride and school safely in the open, over more demanding cross-country fences, a secure seat and effective control are crucial. The sound fundamentals that you have worked hard to develop in yourself and in your horse are your basis for galloping, jumping, and schooling over cross-country fences, and for activities such as eventing, foxhunting, or hunter paces.

## Safety

Safety is the first consideration when riding cross-country. Safety starts with good preparation of horse, rider, and equipment; it requires knowledge and solid skills; and most of all, it depends on good judgment and experience.

- *Never* ride or jump cross-country alone.
- Ride a horse you can control safely in this situation.
- You need the right equipment, it must be in absolutely sound condition, and you must check each item for fit and security before you start.
  - Certified safety helmet, properly fitted, with chin strap snugly fastened; safe and functional riding attire (see page 300 of the *USPC D Level Manual* for details).

- A body protector (safety vest) is required. Vests come in three levels of protection, and must be fitted correctly. It is optional to wear an air vest, but this must be worn with a body protector.
- Jumping-type whip (no wrist loop), spurs (blunt).
- A watch or stopwatch is good for keeping track of time during eventing competition and for assessing speed in galloping work.
- Eventing, or jumping saddle, fitted to horse and rider.
- Bridle properly fitted, with bit suitable for cross-country control. Nonslip reins, knotted at the end. Noseband must not interfere with expansion of the nostrils.
- Martingale or breastplate (optional) correctly adjusted. Rein stops are required whenever a running martingale is used.
- A jumping strap (a neckstrap secured around the horse's neck, which can be made from an extra stirrup leather) can be useful for safety.
- Bell boots and galloping boots provide protection for your horse's legs.
- Check your horse's legs, feet, and shoes before riding cross-country.
- Be aware of footing, terrain, and ground conditions, and check the takeoff and landing before jumping an obstacle.
- Use good judgment about your own capabilities, those of your horse, and anyone riding with you. Be aware of your horse's fitness and fatigue levels, and how he is feeling and performing.

## Rider Fitness

You cannot gallop, jump, or school cross-country safely and effectively unless you are fit enough to ride well for as long as it takes to get the job done. Riding in a galloping position for any length of time is surprisingly tiring; your muscles (especially your core muscles) must be strong, supple, and accustomed to doing their job, and you must be aerobically fit in order to take in enough oxygen. When you are unfit, you pant, your muscles ache, and your arms and legs feel like rubber; you become loose, unbalanced, and insecure; and your control and judgment deteriorate. Fitness is not just a matter of being competitive; it is essential for participating safely in this sport!

Cross-country riders need to be *riding fit* (muscles accustomed to this type of riding) and aerobically fit (which may require other types of fitness work in addition to riding). You must also use good judgment about what you can and should do at your present level of fitness.

Horse and rider equipped for cross-country jumping.

## Review of Seat and Position

The cross-country seat is adapted for galloping, negotiating natural terrain, and jumping solid fences at a cross-country pace. The most important factors are security, balance, and your ability to adjust for different speeds, obstacles, uphill and downhill, and natural conditions you may meet.

Major points are:

- You must be able to ride in 2-point contact (seat above the saddle), 3-point contact (seat in the saddle), and a light seat (seat touching the saddle with upper body angled forward), and be able to shift easily from one seat to another.
- Your feet and legs must stay underneath you, while your knee and hip angles open and close to adjust to the motion of jumping, galloping, and negotiating changes in terrain. Your stirrup leathers should stay vertical to the ground, even though your body angle may change greatly. This is especially important in keeping your balance and absorbing shock when landing from a jump.
- To keep your legs safely under you, you need a secure, well-placed base of support, especially the lower leg. Your calves must lie firmly on your horse's side. They can only do this if your heel is well down and back, with your weight sinking into your ankles.
- In cross-country riding, the stirrup is placed just behind the ball of the foot for extra security.
- The stirrups must be above the ankle point, short enough to create the proper angles in your ankles, hips, and knees, and for you to ride in a good galloping position. Too-long stirrups open your angles, causing

Good versus poor cross-country position.

- Eyes up
- Shoulder over knee
- Hands low, using bridge
- Stirrups correct length
- Lower leg on horse's side
- Heels well down

Weak, unsafe cross-country position.

- Eyes down
- Standing up forward, over pommel
- Stirrups too long
- Reins too long; hands flat
- Knees pinching; lower leg slipping back
- Stirrup on toe; heels up

your leg to pivot backward, and can lead you to stand up forward, lean on the horse's neck, and get ahead of your horse, all of which are dangerous! They also make it extremely difficult to control a strong horse at the gallop. Too-short stirrups put you higher above your horse and may cramp your muscles, but it is better to ride a little too short than too long.

- A cross-country rider must be in balance with her horse. Your horse can gallop and jump most easily when you are *with* him (your center of balance is directly over his center of balance). However, it is safest to ride very slightly "in behind him" for security, balance, and control. This helps you to keep your horse in front of your legs, to keep him

This rider shows confidence and a secure and effective cross-country seat, while allowing her horse freedom to use himself well.

moving reliably forward and prevent hesitation or a refusal. It makes you more secure when adjusting to changes of balance and terrain at speed, and can help you stay with your horse if he should jump awkwardly, hit a fence, or stumble. Of course, this does not mean you should be out of balance or behind the motion, fall back on the saddle, or bump his back, which can handicap your horse and can give him a sore back.

You must never be ahead of your horse, especially when approaching a fence and when jumping. Getting ahead is dangerous, especially over cross-country fences; it can handicap your horse when jumping, and can cause a refusal, fall, or serious mistake. If you are ahead of the motion, any sudden change of balance (such as your horse hitting a fence or landing more steeply than you expected) can send you over his head.

- You must allow your horse freedom to use his head, neck, and balance, and avoid interfering with his efforts, especially when jumping and recovering after a fence. Even if your balance is slightly behind your horse, you can extend your hands and arms, or slip your reins (see page 129). This is called the "allowing arm." Rigid, pulling, or unyielding hands and arms cause horses to become stiff, heavy, and hard-mouthed.

This rider's eyes are up and his arms and hands are excellent. However, his pinching knee has caused his leg to pivot backward and his heel to come up, throwing his shoulders too far forward and leaving him vulnerable if his horse should stumble, hesitate, or need rebalancing on landing.

# Galloping

As you become more experienced and knowledgeable about cross-country riding, you may ride more at the gallop. This may be during activities such as foxhunting, competing in horse trials or eventing, and conditioning your horse for fast work. One thing that should *not* be included is racing your horse. This can ruin his training and endanger you both, and can cause serious injury. Racing requires special race training with an experienced, professional racehorse trainer.

Work at the gallop is fun, but it is also a big responsibility. A horse can be injured much more easily during fast work than in ordinary riding. His tendons and ligaments are under more stress; they lose their strength and elasticity as they get tired. Galloping too fast, too long, or over the wrong kind of footing, especially when a horse is not fit enough, can injure muscles, joints, tendons, or ligaments, and can cripple a horse. Fast work also puts more demands on his heart and lungs, which can be damaged if overstressed.

Many horses get excited by galloping, and may become "hot" and hard to control. They will keep on galloping long after they should have stopped, even if they are hurt or nearly exhausted. You must be responsible for knowing how much galloping is good for your horse; for knowing how fit he is and when he is tiring; and for deciding when and where to gallop, how fast to go, and when to stop.

Your horse must always be warmed up thoroughly before galloping, and he must not be galloped too long, too fast, or too often for his fitness, or on hard ground.

## Galloping Position

The galloping position is essentially the same as the cross-country jumping position. Your balanced galloping position helps your horse to keep his own balance, and puts you in a position from which you can best control him. Your stirrups must be shorter than normal jumping length—above your ankle bone. Shortened stirrups help you stay in balance and keep you from bumping your horse's back. They also make it easier to use your strength to control a strong horse at the gallop. When galloping at the fastest pace (520 meters per minute), your stirrups will be even shorter.

In a galloping position, your seat should be above the saddle and your body must be balanced over your stirrups. This means that your seat is *behind* your feet, and your shoulders are ahead of your feet, just over your knees. Your hands should be down alongside your horse's neck, with the reins in a bridge. *Don't* get so far forward that your crotch is over the pommel of the saddle, or lean out over the horse's neck. Leaning too far forward is unsafe, makes it harder to keep control and stay in balance, and encourages your horse to lean too much on his forehand. This bad habit often shows up in riders who are tired, unfit, or riding with stirrups too long for galloping. On the other hand, you must not let your seat bump the saddle or fall back onto your horse's back, which can happen when you get tired. This makes you unbalanced, tires your horse out, and makes it harder for him to gallop and jump.

To gallop safely, you must be fit yourself. Riding in a galloping position takes fit muscles and good wind, and you may get surprisingly tired from galloping for only five minutes or so. When you get tired, you have difficulty staying in balance and in control. To get yourself fit for galloping work, practice riding in a galloping position at a trot (without posting) for five minutes at a time. You can do this around a ring or, even better, around a field, over rolling ground, or on a trail ride. Gradually increase the time until you can ride at a slow trot in galloping position for up to eight minutes. This exercise helps condition your horse, too.

## Control

Control in the open, especially galloping and jumping, depends on your security and position (especially stirrup and rein length), your fitness, your horse's training, and most of all, your judgment and experience.

Important factors in control are:

- To stay in control you must stay in balance. Use a stirrup length short enough to give you a firm leg and good control of your balance (above the ankle point). Don't topple forward, lean on your horse's neck, or let your legs slip backward.
- Your reins should be short enough to maintain a steady contact when your hands are just above and in front of the withers. Reins that are too long allow your horse to become unbalanced or to ignore you; if your reins are too short, you will hang on your horse's mouth, and may get pulled forward.
- A *bridge* is an option for additional control when galloping and jumping, especially when riding a horse that gets strong or pulls. Riders may choose to use a *single bridge* or a *double bridge*. A *single bridge* has only one rein lying across the neck (the right rein is bridged across the neck and held by the left hand). A *double bridge* has a section of both reins lying across the neck, on top of each other, held by both hands. When your hands are properly placed, with the correct length of rein, the bridge steadies your hands and makes the horse pull against himself, instead of against you. A bridge can also give you support when landing from a drop fence or a jump into water.
- Keep your horse paying attention by asking him to "come back" from time to time by slightly shortening his stride. Never let him gallop flat-out; he may become unbalanced or overexcited and get out of control, and may run into a fence, an obstruction, or rough ground.

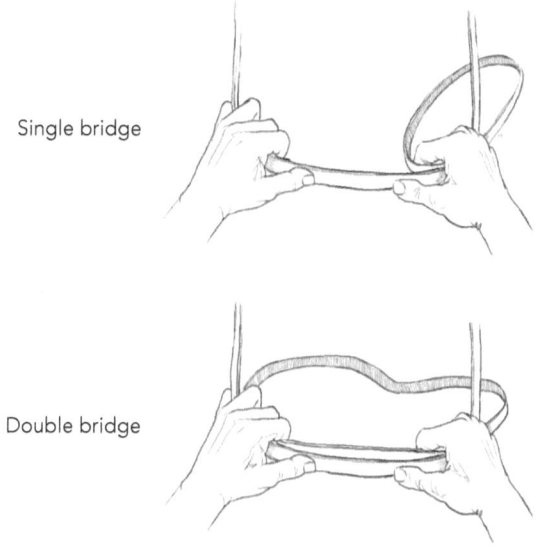

Single bridge

Double bridge

Galloping position, using a bridge.

- To bring a horse back, sink down into a 3-point position, keep your legs on his sides, push your heels down, and "rock back," opening your hip angle and bringing your shoulders back each time you give a rhythmic squeeze on the outside rein. If your horse does not respond to an ordinary rein aid, give a brief lift on one rein, and if necessary, use a pulley rein. (See Chapter 4, "Jumping," for information on half-halts in jumping seat.)
- Use a bit that your horse respects, but don't rely on severe bitting for control. Over-bitting is just as dangerous as under-bitting; remember that horses pull against and run away from pain.

## Balance and Control

In cross-country work, a horse has a natural tendency to get more and more on his forehand when galloping, going downhill, after landing from a jump, and especially when he is tired. If he moves too much on the forehand, his balance "runs away with him": He must move his legs faster to keep up with his balance, and going faster puts him even more on the forehand. This can handicap him when he needs his balance most: on turns, hills, approaches to jumps, takeoff and landing, and changes in terrain and footing.

You must be aware of your horse's balance so you can help him. A horse that is moving in good balance (even at speed) engages his hind legs well at each stride, which makes him feel round and bouncy, as if he were jumping through a gymnastic. He "has his hocks under him," and keeps his balance where he has control of it, so he can turn, adjust his stride, or jump easily, and he feels secure and sure-footed.

An unbalanced horse takes long, flat strides; his hind legs swing far out behind him, but don't engage well under his body. He may lean on the bit

Cross-country control.

Sitting up and rocking back; opening hip joint

Pulley rein:  Brace one hand on neck
Lift up briefly with other hand
Rock shoulders back

and pull, or move with his back hollow and his head high, with short, quick strides. He feels uncontrolled and irregular, and may slip, skid, or stumble on turns or going downhill. He has speed, but not true impulsion; this makes him hard to rate, and he may take off too early or too close to his fences. He may tend to jump flat, hit his fences, and land heavily. A horse going fast and unbalanced into a cross-country fence (especially if his rider is unbalanced, too) is an accident waiting to happen!

To help your horse stay balanced at speed, you must restrain his speed somewhat while asking him to engage his hind legs more. Stay in balance yourself, with your stirrup leathers vertical to the ground, and your legs under your center of balance. Open your hip angle and bring your shoulders

Balance in the gallop.

Well-balanced cross-country gallop with rider in a correct balanced position

Rider leaning too far forward has caused a poorly balanced horse, leaning on the forehand and unsafe

back a little, keeping your legs firmly on his sides, until you feel him respond. You must find the proper gallop at which you and your horse are in balance, and the state of balance in which your horse moves easily and feels maneuverable.

**Caution:** A horse that is seriously unbalanced may be tired, lame, or too inexperienced for the speed and the job he is trying to do. Pushing on with a horse that is not up to what he is being asked to do is not only abusive, but it is also asking for an accident.

## Schooling Your Horse: Control, Safety, and Manners

When you ride in the open and gallop with others, as in foxhunting or riding cross-country with friends, you need especially good control. A horse's herd instinct makes him want to stay with other horses and not be left behind. The faster you gallop and the more horses there are galloping together, the more exciting it is. This may lead your horse to pull, race other horses, or buck from excitement and high spirits. For safety, you must make him pay attention to *you*, and not get carried away by excitement and his natural herd instinct. You must be responsible for keeping him at a safe distance from other horses, as he will not do this by himself.

To keep your horse's attention on you and to keep him balanced, you must ride with good balance and contact. Leaning too far forward or galloping with loose reins lets a horse lean on his forehand, become unbalanced, and get out of control. Every now and then, ask your horse to *come back* by shortening his stride and slowing slightly. When you can shorten his stride easily, you have good control at the gallop. If you ask your horse to "come back" and he does not respond, ask again with stronger aids. Sit up and use a pulley rein several times, if necessary. If he still does not respond, turn in a large circle, gradually making the circle smaller until he comes back under control. Always pull up gradually, as pulling up abruptly can injure tendons or ligaments, especially when a horse is tired.

Before you can gallop with other horses, your horse must gallop well under control on his own. At first, ride with only one other horse that is quiet and easy to control at a gallop. Practice keeping a safe distance (at least four horse lengths) behind the other horse at the walk, trot, and canter. If your horse begins to catch up to the other horse, rock your shoulders back and use a brief pulley rein two or three times until he stays back and keeps his spacing. When you can keep your distance safely and easily at a canter, your leader can move into a gallop for a short distance while you practice maintaining spacing at a gallop.

Galloping beside another horse is exciting to both horses. This can be a good exercise for a lazy horse, but a strong or excitable horse could turn into a runaway. When you gallop beside another horse, ride beside the other rider, not slightly ahead or behind. Riding beside another horse's hindquarters puts you in a position where you could get kicked.

If you are riding cross-country, jumping, or galloping in a group, you must pay attention to other horses and riders. If one horse in the group becomes excited or hard to control or a rider has trouble, the whole group must slow down or stop. Never race past another horse, crowd up close to another horse, or leave a horse and rider behind the group. These can cause a horse to get overexcited, kick, or get out of control. One inconsiderate rider can put all the others in danger, and it can teach horses bad habits as well as ruin the experience for others. (For control exercises for riding in a group, see the *USPC C Level Manual*, pages 99–102.)

If you are jumping with other riders and your horse refuses or runs out, you *must not* block the fence if others are waiting to jump. Move out of the way of any oncoming horses *immediately;* then try again when the fence is clear. If your horse is reluctant to jump a particular fence, it may help to follow another horse over it at a safe distance (at least six horse lengths).

## Galloping over Natural Terrain

When you gallop cross-country, the ground is not always level, and you come across different kinds of footing. Use good judgment and ride at a pace that is safe for the ground conditions. You must slow down to a canter or even a trot or walk to ride safely over some places, while in other places you can safely let your horse gallop on. It is easier for your horse if you set a steady, average pace suitable for your horse and for good control, and stay at that pace when conditions allow.

- *Rolling terrain:* Galloping over rolling terrain is fairly easy, as long as you remember to keep your balance. When going downhill, rock your weight slightly backward and slow to a balanced canter or a slow gallop. Uphill, keep your horse steady and stay up off his back; letting a horse run fast uphill tires him quickly. In steep places, slow to a balanced trot or walk when going down, and keep a slow, sensible pace when going up.
- *Narrow, twisting trails:* Keep to a slow gallop or canter, and be alert for low branches, tree roots, or sharp turns around trees. Your pace must be slow and balanced enough so that you can turn easily.
- *Heavy ground and deep sand:* Deep, soft ground such as deep sand or plowed fields is very hard on a horse's legs and tires him quickly. If you gallop into heavy ground suddenly, he can injure a tendon. If possible, stay to the edge of plowed fields and ride on the *headland* (the unplowed edge). If you must cross deep, soft ground, come back to a walk or trot.
- *Holes and rocks:* In some areas, you may find outcroppings of rock, groundhog holes, or ground squirrel holes. Slow to a speed at which you and your horse can see a hole in time to avoid it, and stay in balance so that he can recover if he should stumble. Groundhog or ground squirrel holes are usually on the side of a hill or near hedgerows. There will be two or more holes, and some holes may not have a telltale pile of dirt around them. Go around the whole area, if possible.

- *Hard ground, slippery ground, mud, and bog:* None of these conditions is safe for galloping. Slow to a trot or, at most, a slow canter. If the ground is very slippery or mud is very deep and boggy, walk. Beware of frosty ground, which may be frozen hard with a thin, very slippery layer of mud on top. The ground may stay frozen (and very slippery) in a shady area, in the woods, or behind a tree or wall, even after the ground in the open has thawed. *Never* gallop on or even alongside a paved road!

## Improving Your Knowledge of Pace

Your speed is called *pace*, and you must be able to gallop at two standard speeds: a slow gallop and a faster cross-country gallop, and also ride at a brisk cross-country trot. An average cross-country pace for C Level eventing is 350 to 400 meters per minute, or 13 to 15 miles per hour. A slow gallop is 300 meters per minute, or about 11 miles per hour. A brisk trot is 240 meters per minute, or just under 9 miles per hour.

You should be able to recognize and ride specific paces at a steady gallop, depending on the level at which you are training and competing. These paces may include:

- 220 meters per minute (trot)
- 350 to 400 meters per minute (medium center)
- 350 to 450 meters per minute (gallop)
- 350 to 520 meters per minute (gallop)

Check the USPC Standards of Proficiency for your specific certification to see what is required at your level.

At first, you must learn to recognize the first two (slower) galloping speeds and maintain a steady pace in good balance at the gallop. Later, as you and your horse become fit and more experienced in galloping work, you may work at the faster paces used at more advanced levels of eventing, eventually working up to the top pace of 520 meters per minute.

Do not be in a hurry to reach the top speeds. Working at the faster speeds demands a strong, fit, and athletic horse and rider, with excellent judgment and control. Galloping too fast too soon can injure your horse and set back his training.

An important element in cross-country pace is the *coffin canter*, a balanced, shortened, and collected canter that is used to approach cross-country jumps such as a coffin jump. The horse should move in a more active canter with his balance back over his hocks, and should feel controlled but energetic and "bouncy." By minimizing speed and momentum and maximizing vertical lift, the coffin canter keeps your horse slow enough to have time to assess a complex jump such as a coffin jump, and gives him the power, balance, and agility he needs to negotiate the jump successfully.

Practice lengthening to a gallop and shortening and rebalancing your horse to a coffin canter. This pace is an essential skill because speed is not always a good solution when jumping cross-country, especially with today's more complicated "complex-type" obstacles, multiple jumping efforts, terrain factors, and an increased emphasis on safety in our sport.

## Measuring Distance and Time

To develop an accurate sense of pace, you will need to measure out an 800-meter track (half a mile, or 874 yards, or 2,622 feet), or you could lay out a 400-meter track and go around twice. Post a marker (a flag, post, or something easy to see) every 100 meters.

You will need a stopwatch (the type of stopwatch used by event riders is convenient, as it has large buttons and a digital readout that is easy to see). Make sure you know how to work the watch before you time yourself.

If you ride the 800-meter (half-mile) track at an even gallop in the right time, you are going at the right pace. The easiest way to learn to recognize the correct pace is to ride alongside an experienced rider who can show you just how fast you must go.

Although in a combined training event you would start from a standstill from the starting box, when timing your pace you should start about 50 yards before the first marker, so that you have reached your chosen pace when you start to time yourself. Start your watch at the first marker, and check your pace at each 100-meter marker.

Here are times for the **speeds at the gallop:**

- 220 meters per minute (9 miles per hour, trot): 800 meters in 3 minutes, 20 seconds
- 350 meters per minute (13 miles per hour): 800 meters in 2 minutes, 20 seconds
- 400 meters per minute (15 miles per hour): 800 meters in 2 minutes

**More advanced speeds at the gallop:**

- 450 meters per minute (18 miles per hour): 800 meters in 1 minute, 40 seconds
- 520 meters per minute (20 miles per hour): 800 meters in 1 minute, 30 seconds

The following chart will help you identify the time for the various paces.

### Chart 5-1: Times and MPH for Various Paces at the Gallop

| Approx. Pace (meters per minute) | Miles per Hour | Time for 800 Meters (½ mile) | Time for 100 Meters |
|---|---|---|---|
| 220 mpm | 9 mph (trot) | 3 min. 20 seconds | 25 seconds |
| 350 mpm | 13 mph | 2 min. 20 seconds | 17.5 seconds |
| 400 mpm | 15 mph | 2 min. | 15 seconds |
| 450 mpm | 18 mph | 1 min. 40 seconds | 13 seconds |
| 520 mpm | 20 mph | 1 min. 30 seconds | 11.25 seconds |

## Tips for Riding at a Galloping Pace

- To ask your horse to gallop, use your legs in rhythm with his movement to extend his stride. Don't let him scramble with short, quick strides.
- A steady average pace is less fatiguing and less likely to result in injury to a horse than going very fast and frequently pulling up, then speeding up again. You will have to slow down in certain conditions (such as steep slopes, rocks, or mud) and make up time by going faster where the going is good, but don't use up your horse unnecessarily with excessive speed and severe changes of speed.
- On a cross-country course, choose landmarks located at given distances (such as the halfway point). Calculate what your time should be at the marker (considering the terrain and conditions). On course, you can check your watch at the marker to see if you are running slow, ahead of time, or right on your plan.
- Even if your time is slow, *the way your horse feels matters more than the time!* Never get so caught up in trying to make the time that you push your horse at a faster pace than he can handle.

## Recognizing Signs of Tiring

It is very important to be aware of your horse's condition and of how much energy he has left at all times. A horse that is galloping easily, with energy in reserve, is said to be galloping *well within himself.* It is important to recognize when your horse is moving easily, and when he is tiring or reaching his limits.

When a horse starts out, he maybe fresh, eager, and full of energy, and he may want to run. You must save his energy early on in order to have enough left to finish your ride safely, in good condition, but without wasting time or going unnecessarily slowly. Save energy by going slowly up hills and over deep or difficult ground, and by keeping a steady, reasonable pace over good ground. Don't gallop all-out; this tires a horse very quickly. Remember that heat and humidity will tire your horse much more quickly than normal weather conditions.

Stay aware of your horse's breathing. He will naturally breathe harder when he gallops, but if he begins to breathe extremely hard or loudly, he needs to slow down and catch his breath. Sometimes a horse will take an extra-large breath and then breathe more easily as he gallops. Irregular or very fast breathing means he needs to rest right away.

As a horse gets tired, he leans on his forehand, his strides feel heavier, and it becomes harder to keep him balanced. A tired horse tends to make mistakes when jumping, and may fumble his takeoff, jump flat, hit his fences, or land heavily. All these are signs that your horse needs to slow his pace, take a breather, or even stop.

While some horses slow down as they get tired, many get caught up in the excitement and will keep going until they are exhausted, if you let them. Don't assume it's okay to keep going just because your horse is willing to go on. You must use good judgment to keep him safe. Never abuse his courage by letting him gallop on until he is exhausted or injured.

## Cross-Country Jumping

At previous levels, you learned how to develop the skills you and your horse need to jump different types of cross-country fences. As you advance, you will jump different types of fences, gradually increasing the degree of difficulty, and adding new types of fences.

### The Horse's Jumping Form

Cross-country jumping horses must jump with good balance and in safe, functional, and efficient form. Good jumping style allows a horse to jump bigger and more safely, with minimum stress on his legs, wind, and muscles. It also helps a horse to remain in balance and to recover quickly from the effort of jumping, changes of terrain, or unexpected occurrences such as a slip or hitting a fence. Most of all, good jumping form is safer for both horse and rider, and diminishes the chances of hitting a fence, making a mistake, or falling.

Cross-country jumping, especially at speed, tends to encourage horses to jump fast and flat. Schooling over gymnastics and cross-country fences should focus on teaching the horse to maintain his balance and roundness, while moving confidently and reliably forward to his fences. He must also

Good and poor cross-country jumping form.

Jumping flat (poor)

Jumping with good form

be schooled to keep and improve his responsiveness and attention to his rider, to jump straight, and to land in balance, rebalance quickly and easily, and lengthen and shorten stride.

## Problems in Cross-Country Jumping

Problems may be related to one or more of the following factors:

- **Terrain:** Uphill and downhill terrain and changes of terrain require more effort, affect the horse's balance, and can alter the jumping effort required for an obstacle.
- **Rider confidence and experience:** The horse gets his confidence from the rider, so it is essential that the rider be secure, confident, and ready for the level he is riding. Being overfaced (obstacles too big or too difficult), over-mounted (too much horse), or unprepared can cause bad experiences and accidents to riders and horses.
- **Horse's confidence and experience:** Inexperience, rider hesitation, or a previous bad experience with a certain type of fence can impair a

horse's confidence. Horses need to learn how to handle different types of cross-country fences through patient, progressive schooling. Some horses are temperamentally unsuitable for this type of work.

- **Pace:** Speed tends to make horses jump flat, and can compound balance, timing, and control problems. A sensible pace is appropriate to conditions, the fences, terrain and footing, and the horse's and rider's capabilities and fitness.
- **Control:** Some horses become overexcited, strong, or difficult to control, especially when jumping at speed or in company with other horses. Effective bitting (sometimes in conjunction with a particular noseband or martingale) and good, confident riding are essential.
- **Fatigue:** A tired horse tends to gallop on the forehand, jump flat, hit his fences and land heavily, and is harder to balance; he has less energy and scope than when fresh. Fitness, proper conditioning, and intelligent management of pace are important in staving off fatigue and jumping safely when a horse is tiring.
- **Balance:** Terrain, speed, fatigue, and rider balance all may encourage a cross-country horse to run on his forehand. Jumping off the forehand can cause takeoff errors and makes it more difficult to recover from a mistake.
- **Rider error:** Poor balance, timing, or presentation at the fence, or interference with horse's jumping efforts, can defeat even the best jumper.

## Jumping Different Types of Cross-Country Obstacles

In cross-country jumping, it is important to bring your horse into every fence straight, balanced, and *in front of your legs*. This means that your legs have contact with his sides, and if you squeeze them firmly, he will immediately go forward. You must be positive (sure and strong), or he may lose his confidence. For most cross-country fences, it is more important to be in good balance and going forward with a positive attitude than it is to take off at an exact spot.

For safety's sake, never jump cross-country alone. Always have a knowledgeable person with you. You should school over any new cross-country fence, with the help of your instructor, before you gallop over it or ride it as part of a course. To give your horse confidence, it may help to follow a quiet, experienced horse over a new fence. The height and difficulty of the fences must be appropriate for both you and your horse. The way to build confidence is to school over many small cross-country obstacles of different types and never to overface your horse by asking him to jump a fence that is too big or difficult for either of you.

A good, bold jump over a cross-country fence.

Here are some types of cross-country fences:

**Banks:** Jumping a simple bank may require you to jump up, down, or both. More advanced banks may require you to jump down into water, up out of water, or both. Some banks include a ditch on the takeoff side.

It is best to begin with a simple bank that is wide enough for you to jump up, take one or more strides, and then jump down. Shorter banks, with only enough room to jump on, then off, are more difficult, as are banks with a ditch or into or out of water. Approach a bank with plenty of impulsion, but not too fast. You do not want your horse to jump too far and make the jump down difficult, or to try to clear the whole bank! Look up and ahead and keep your legs on so that he keeps going forward. Keep your balance in the middle, your eyes up, and sit up as he jumps down. Remember that you must stay off your horse's back and be in balance throughout the jump for him to be able to use his hindquarters properly in taking off, jumping, landing, and going away from the bank.

**Steps:** Steps are a series of banks, to be jumped up or down. You must keep going in rhythm, as a horse may lose impulsion when jumping up. When going down, find a central balance and keep your weight back, over your legs, with your seat slightly off his back and your eyes up.

**Drop fences:** Jumping a drop fence is like jumping down off a bank, except that you must jump the fence as well. This makes the landing steeper and the drop greater than those you experience when jumping off a bank.

One-stride bank

Jumping down steps

Riding a drop jump

When riding a drop fence you must fold forward on takeoff as you would over a vertical fence. Use a short release and bridge your reins. As your horse begins to descend, open your hip angle and stay vertical to the ground, over your legs. Be careful not to get too far forward, which can pitch you forward on landing, but don't sit back so far or so hard that you drop your horse's hind legs down into the fence or hit his back as you land. You may have to relax your fingers and let your reins slip if your horse needs more rein as you land.

**Mound jumps:** These jumps may be set on top of a mound (a natural or artificial elevation of earth). Trotting and cantering over small mounds will help you learn to adjust your balance as your horse's balance changes from uphill, to a jump, and then downhill. It is important to keep your legs under your body and keep your balance in the center (never ahead of your horse) as you negotiate the mound. The next step is to trot, and then canter, over a simple log placed on a mound.

**Downhill jumps:** You have already practiced riding downhill approaches and small downhill jumps. Larger downhill jumps are ridden the same way, much like drop jumps. Good balance during the approach is most important. Be sure that your horse goes forward straight, in good balance, with his hocks well under him. Downhill sloping ground makes a jump lower, but the landing will be longer and steeper. Ride a downhill jump as you would a drop jump, staying back in a central balance off the saddle, over your legs, and be ready to rebalance immediately on landing, especially if the downhill slope continues after the jump.

**Uphill jumps:** Jumping an uphill jump is like jumping up a bank, but more demanding. The uphill sloping ground makes the jump bigger and may encourage your horse to take off from too far away. Keep your horse in a bouncy, well-balanced, and slightly more collected canter, well in front of your legs. Never let him gallop uphill leaning on his forehand, with long, sprawling strides. This could make him arrive at an uphill jump dangerously out of balance and without the power necessary to clear it.

Mound jump.

Downhill fence.

As your horse takes off, it is important to stay off his back and loins, allowing him to use his head and neck freely. Do not lean too far forward or jump ahead before the takeoff; this will inhibit your horse's ability to take off cleanly. If you sit down or get left behind, he could drop his hind legs into the fence. Holding the mane or a neckstrap is a good precaution to be sure that you don't interfere with his mouth.

**Trakehners and fences with ditches:** Your horse has already learned to jump open ditches, but he must also learn how to jump a ditch, a trakehner, or a ditch and wall that is part of a fence. Most horses are suspicious of holes in the ground, so you must ride positively, use your legs firmly, and look beyond the jump. If you look down into the ditch or drop contact, your horse may stop.

When the ditch is on the takeoff side, it acts as a ground line and encourages a horse to stand back and jump in good style.

A *trakehner* is a rail over a ditch or angled across a ditch. It is ridden as a jump with the ditch on the takeoff side.

When the ditch is on the landing side, your horse may not see it until the last moment. You must ride this jump strongly so that the pace and the thrust of the jump carry you well out over the ditch.

A *ditch and wall* is a fence with a ditch on the takeoff side, and a wall on the far side of the ditch. An easier version is a ditch with a brush box on the far side. The wall is sloped slightly away from the takeoff side. This fence is shaped like a triple bar without the middle rail, so you should focus on the top of the back element (the wall), and be careful not to look down.

**Coffin jumps:** A *coffin jump* is a combination of obstacles: a fence, followed by a ditch, then another fence. A more difficult type has a fence,

Jumping uphill (right and wrong).

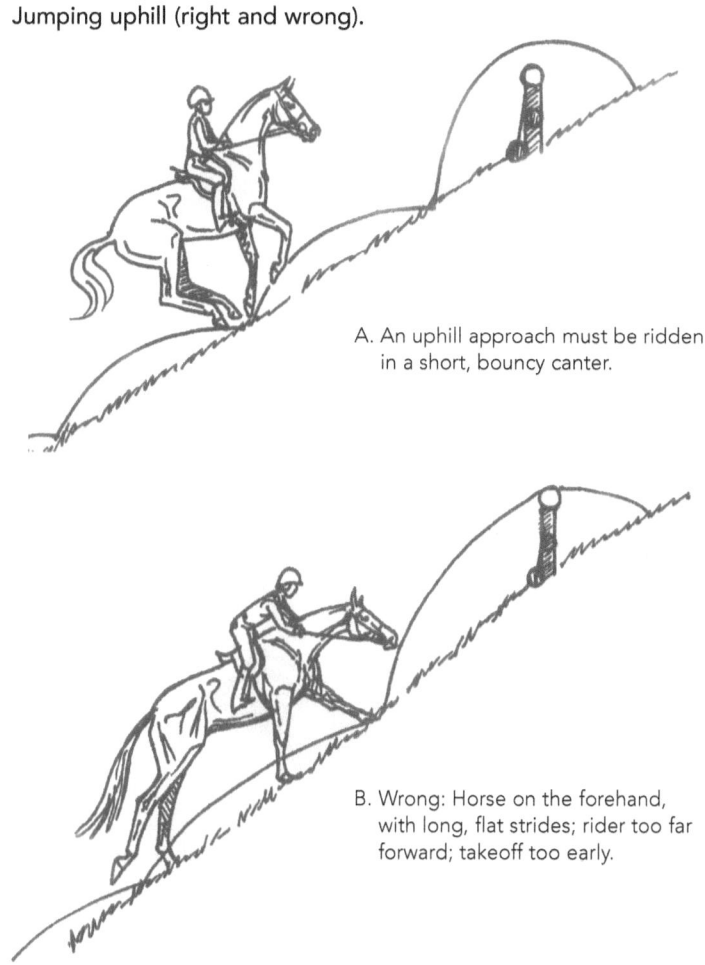

A. An uphill approach must be ridden in a short, bouncy canter.

B. Wrong: Horse on the forehand, with long, flat strides; rider too far forward; takeoff too early.

a downhill slope to a ditch, then an uphill slope to the second fence. The distance from fence to ditch and from ditch to second fence may be a bounce or one or two strides. A *half-coffin jump* is a combination of two obstacles: a fence followed by a ditch, or a ditch followed by a fence.

To learn to jump coffin jumps, begin with a small fence or log two strides from a simple open ditch. Jump this in both directions—first the ditch and then the log, and vice versa. When your horse does this well, add another small log or fence and jump it as a triple.

When jumping a coffin, it's important to approach in good balance and rhythm, with your horse well in front of your legs. Using the "coffin canter," a balanced, lively, but not-too-fast canter, gives him time to see and assess the obstacle and the balance to jump it well. Stay in balance over your legs and let him rock you as he jumps, strides, jumps, strides, and jumps again,

Fences with ditches.

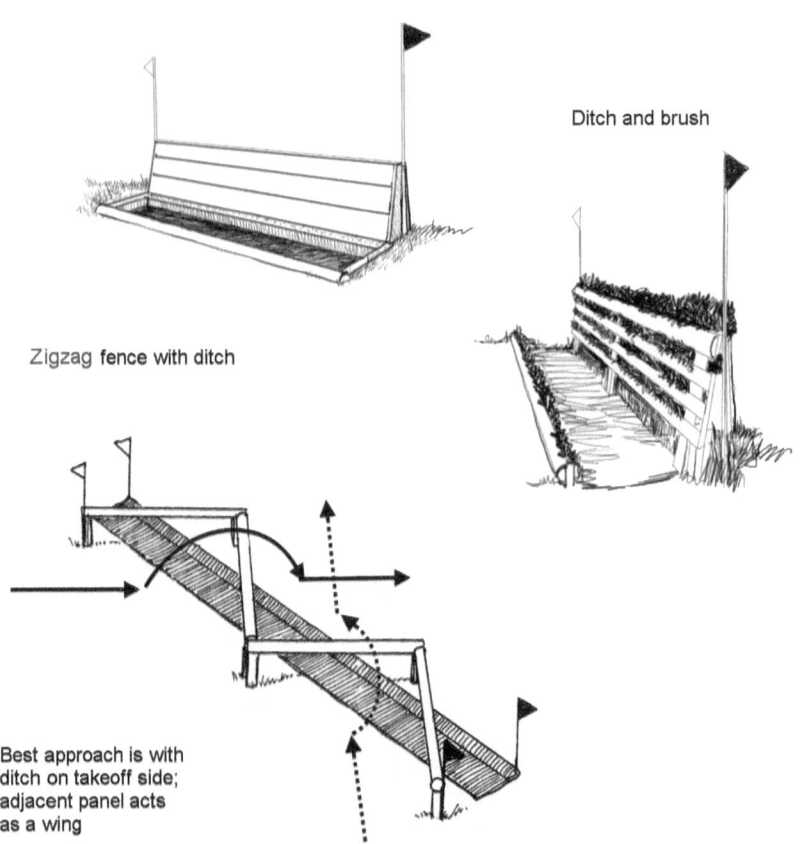

just as when riding a gymnastic. Keep your eyes up and your legs on his sides, and don't drop contact with his mouth.

**Combinations:** You may have to jump a combination of two or three fences placed less than three strides apart. The distance may require two strides, one stride, or a bounce. In cross-country, the elements of a combination are numbered A, B, and C. If your horse should refuse at the second or third element, you may go back and re-jump the whole combination, or you may jump only the obstacle at which the refusal occurred. (This is different from show jumping rules.)

You must be clear about the line you ride through a combination and about the exact spot in which you will jump each element. Drifting sideways or making an inaccurate approach may lead to a runout, or change the distance enough to make it difficult to jump the second element safely.

Coffin jump.

When jumping combinations, you must jump the first element going forward in good balance and rhythm. If you meet the first element right and keep your rhythm, it helps you meet the next element right, too. Cross-country combination fences are usually set at slightly longer distances than those in stadium jumping, to allow for the longer strides your horse takes at a cross-country galloping pace.

*Related distances* refer to obstacles that are not marked or numbered as combinations, but they are set close enough together that the way you jump the first obstacle affects your line, pace, and takeoff at the next obstacle. (This is usually seven strides or less.) You will need to know your horse's average length of stride at various paces, and his capabilities and weaknesses. When walking the course, you should pace off such distances and decide on your best line, the best pace, and any adjustments you will have to make in the related distance.

**Option fences:** An option fence is an obstacle or combination of obstacles that can be jumped in more than one way. There is a difficult way (usually the fastest and most direct line, but with larger or more difficult fences), and an easier way (which often has more turns and a more complicated line, and takes longer, but may have lower or simpler fences). You must decide how to ride this obstacle while walking the course. When deciding which option to take, keep in mind your horse's abilities, experience, and length of stride, and which option would be easiest for him to jump well.

## Jumping More Advanced Types of Cross-Country Fences

### Galloping (Steeplechase) Fences

Galloping fences are designed to be jumped at a faster pace (but *not* a racing pace). They are usually made of brush and slant away from the takeoff side, which makes them easy to judge and to jump. The Steeplechase phase of a Classic three-day event consists of four to six steeplechase fences for

Option fence with short and long routes.

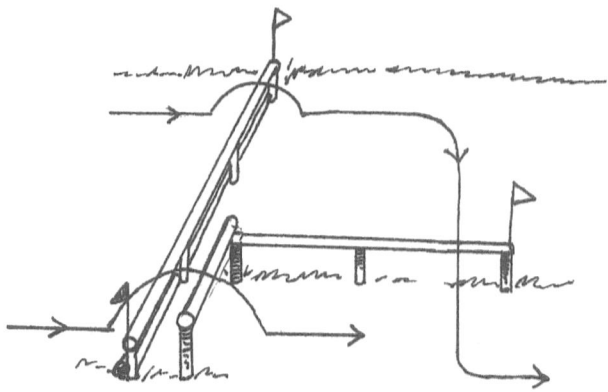

Training Level and five to seven jumps for Preliminary Level, to be jumped at a gallop. The horse must find a suitable galloping pace, balance, and rhythm and jump these fences in stride so that he moves and jumps efficiently, taking less out of himself.

Speed, length of stride, and easy, slanting fences all encourage a horse to move on his forehand and jump flat. When a horse has jumped one or more galloping fences, it can be difficult for him to come back and jump round over a different type of fence. Don't encourage him to fall on his forehand or sacrifice his jumping technique by allowing him to jump too fast, flat, or carelessly over steeplechase fences.

To ride galloping fences, you should shorten your stirrups to the maximum height for you (usually one or two holes higher than normal cross-country length). Close down over your stirrups, but keep your weight centered a little behind your stirrups. This is "insurance" in case your horse makes a bobble while jumping at speed. If you are even the least bit ahead of him, you will be off! Adjust your reins to a good galloping length, and use a bridge.

When riding a galloping fence, keep the horse in good balance and let him move forward to the fence, but don't encourage him to race or overextend himself.

### *Angles, Corners, and Narrow Jumps*
Angles and corners jumps require planning, obedience, and an accurate approach and line. Such fences invite a runout, so you must be clear about the line you will ride, the point at which you will jump, and the line you take after the fence. Ride a consistent line of approach, without weaving or changing your mind. Indecision, drifting, or looking down can spell disaster!

Steeplechase-type fence, jumped with flat arc.

Angles, corners, and narrow fences can be built easily with stadium jumping equipment. This helps you break them down into simple components and easy steps, before jumping fixed cross-country fences. Practice riding schooling fences at angles and keeping the horse in a "channel" between your left and right aids, on the approach and afterward.

**Narrow fences** (also called *skinny* fences) and **chevrons** are a test of accuracy and obedience. Narrow fences are 8 feet wide (at Preliminary Level). A *chevron* is a narrow fence with one or more panels shaped like an inverted triangle. They are sometimes placed on a mound or in a combination, which increases the difficulty. When riding a narrow fence or a chevron, it is important to have the horse in front of your leg and ride an accurate line. Think of your left and right legs and reins creating a channel to keep your horse straight on the line you have selected before, during, and after the jump.

**Narrow zigzag fences** often have an imposing appearance, but are really a series of narrow fences that are connected. Walk the line you have selected, and remind yourself on which side you will need to use stronger aids to keep your horse jumping straight.

Narrow fence and chevron.

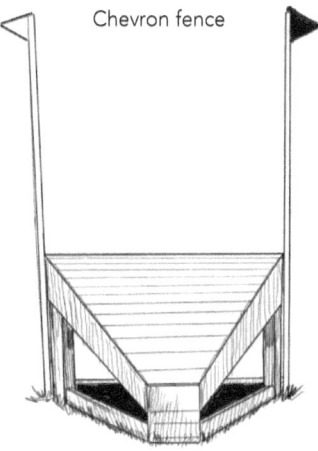

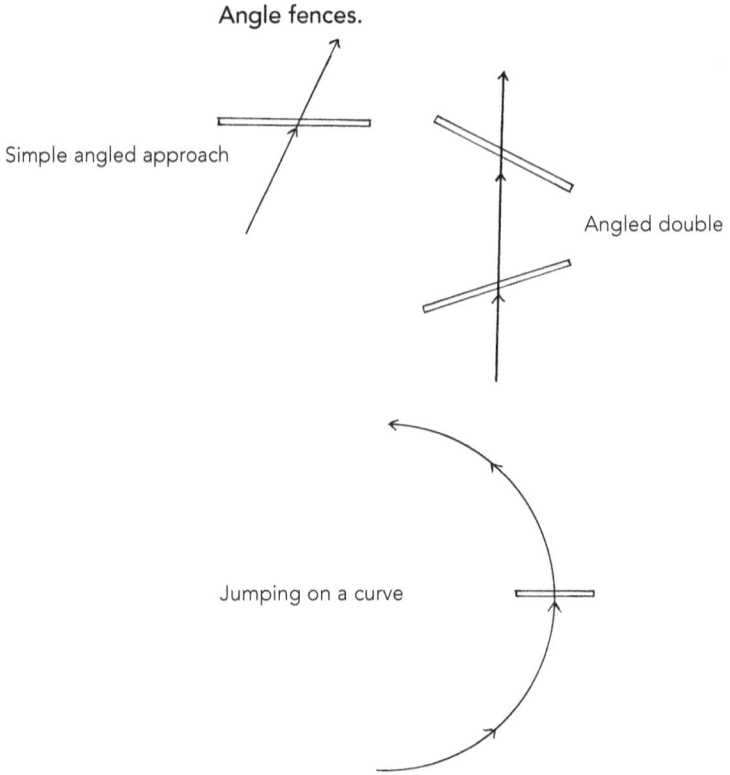

Angle fences.
Simple angled approach
Angled double
Jumping on a curve

**Angles** should be jumped as single fences first. When the horse goes straight and jumps at an angle reliably in either direction, you can move on to variations of angles, such as a pole angled over a ditch, forming a "V." When planning your approach, try to jump as close to the center of the "V" as possible, not out where it is wider. Avoid creating a false ground line by jumping it so that the ditch is on the far side.

**Corners jumped as a spread** are the most difficult type of angled fence, as they ride as a parallel oxer, and the narrow end invites a runout. If you drift even a little, the spread may be impossibly wide, or you may incur a runout or a swerve in the air. Use firm supporting aids on the narrow side of the fence to keep the horse from drifting or falling out in that direction, and use your eyes positively to define your chosen line.

### Option Fences and Combinations

These obstacles require forethought and planning. You can build variations of option fences out of stadium jumping materials, which allows you to practice almost any type of combination you might encounter. This is safer and more versatile than starting out over fixed obstacles. As with corners

Jumping a corner.

and angles, break them down into their components, and practice the components by themselves before combining them.

As a result of your previous work, you should know your horse's capabilities and weaknesses. Does he have a big jump? If so, the option of the single larger fence may be your best choice. Is he limited in scope, but handy? He may handle a trappy turn better than a maximum-size fence. Is he unreliable about jumping certain types of fences, or from a short or long takeoff distance? In schooling at home, you should work on his weak points and on types of fences at which he is inexperienced or needs confidence. In competition, choose the options that make the most of his abilities and avoid his weaknesses whenever possible.

Distances vary considerably in cross-country combinations, as they are influenced by the size and type of fences, the terrain, and the angles and possible routes of approach. Cross-country combinations are usually set slightly longer than their counterparts in the ring, because the horse will be moving at a stronger pace outside. When evaluating distances, remember that factors that tend to make a horse lengthen his stride (such as a slight downhill grade or a long gallop beforehand) may make the distance ride shorter than it appears.

When riding a combination, you need balance, impulsion, and rhythm, and your horse must go straight. It is usually better to have a bit more impulsion than you need than not enough, but don't let it escape into speed. Most combinations need to be ridden with a balanced, bouncy stride; it may help to imagine that you are riding through a gymnastic as you approach the first element.

Bank and ditch combination.

| Approach in balanced, round, but not overextended canter | Rider's angles close and open with horse's motion | Be careful not to get behind or ahead of the motion | Maintain contact without interfering with horse's use of his head and neck | Keep leg firmly on to keep horse moving forward |

**Bounce fences:** These are a type of combination, and are often found in conjunction with option fences. A cross-country bounce is set at a longer distance than in the schooling ring because of the extra pace and impulsion.

Bounce fences require a horse to engage his hind legs and jump off his hocks with impulsion and accuracy. Approach a bounce as if you were riding a gymnastic, and keep the rhythm. Don't commit your body very far forward at a bounce; instead, keep your balance more central, over your feet, and let your horse rock you as his front end rises, dips, and rises again.

### Drop Jumps and Sunken Roads

*Drop jumps* are fences with a lower landing. A *sunken road* is a drop jump, followed by a jump up a bank.

Bounce fence.

Rider remains balanced over his leg as his angles open and close with the motion of the horse

At previous levels, you jumped simple banks, steps, and drops; now you will encounter fences with more height and a larger drop on the landing side. The horse is usually not aware of the drop until takeoff, or until he is nearly across the obstacle. It is important to keep him reliably in front of your leg and on the aids during the approach; if you drop the contact or lean forward, he may drop his head, see the drop, and hesitate or refuse.

A drop should not be ridden too fast and flat, or the horse will jump with too flat an arc and may stumble or have trouble regaining his balance on landing. On the other hand, if you over-shorten his stride or lose impulsion on the approach, he may hesitate and then lurch over with a steep, nearly vertical landing. A springy trot with good impulsion or a round, bouncy canter is the best approach.

When a horse jumps down a drop, you have to cope with an extra-long descent, much like landing from a big fence. You may also have to absorb more shock on landing. Bridge your reins, slide your leg and foot forward, ahead of the girth, and keep your head and eyes up. Keep your stirrup leathers perpendicular to the ground, and stay back over them. On a big drop, you may have to lean well back, but your seat should remain off the saddle for optimum balance. In this case, let the reins slip through your fingers to the knot at the buckle (see Chapter 4, "Jumping," page 129).

Jumping a drop off a ramp or ledge is like riding a step or jumping down off a bank. It is best approached in a steady, impulsive trot. As with a drop fence, be prepared to balance in the middle or even to lean back if necessary, and to slip your reins.

### *Drop Jumps into Water*

Drops into water present some special problems. The horse cannot judge the depth of the water he is jumping into, or see the bottom, so he must be ridden positively to the fence, and must not be allowed to drop his head or get behind the legs. Landing in water exerts a sudden, strong drag on the horse,

Sunken road.

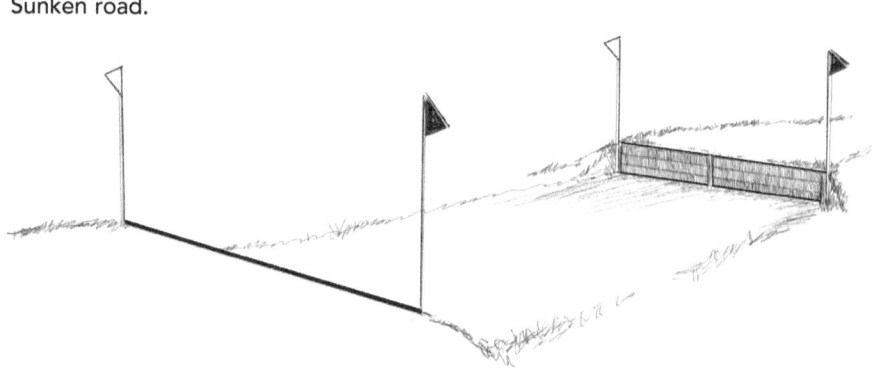

Drop into water.

Takeoff: close hip angle but don't get forward    Descent: open hip angle; slip reins    Landing: stay back, vertical to ground    Maintain balance during recovery

slowing him suddenly. If you jump into water too fast or while leaning forward, this effect is magnified and can send you right over the horse's head! In addition, the horse must make a strong effort to recover his balance and stride in the water; this often feels like a buck or a jump, and can further unseat a rider already loosened by the drop. Finally, the horse must exit the water, often over an additional jump out. You must be able to ride in strongly; keep your balance during the drop, landing, and recovery; and reorganize the horse in time to jump out safely. This takes an extremely secure seat, good timing, and support from the rider.

When jumping a drop into water, the approach and seat are essentially the same as for a large drop. A strong leg position, with the heel well down and the leg in front of the girth, is an essential part of your *safety seat*. Stay back as you descend and land; keep your balance in the center of the horse, with your feet still a little in front of you, during the recovery; and regain your reins as quickly as you can.

Before jumping drops into water, practice water crossings and jumping into and out of water, as described in the *USPC C Level Manual*, pages 110–111. Practice drop fences and steps also, until you are confident and competent in leaning back over your legs, slipping your reins, and recovering your reins and balance on landing.

### *Water to Water Jumps*

A water to water obstacle is a jump that requires you to take off from water and land in water. These fences require balance, power, and extra thrust on takeoff, because of the drag of the water against the horse's legs. They should be ridden at an impulsive trot or a collected, balanced canter. As the horse lands in the water, the drag of the water may slow him abruptly, so

Water to water obstacle.

you should ride them as you would a drop into water, being careful not to get ahead of the motion.

## Cross-Country Courses

You may ride a cross-country course as part of a horse trial, an eventing competition, a Pony Club rally, or just to learn and have fun. To ride a course, you and your horse must be fit and able to jump all the fences on the course, and to ride safely at an appropriate pace. The fences must be suitable for you and your horse—not just the height, but also the degree of difficulty. In competition, you are not allowed to practice over any of the fences. At home, for practice, you should school your horse over each fence individually before you ride them all as a course. Some facilities hold "schooling days" when you can school your horse over their cross-country obstacles with the help of your instructor. This is an excellent opportunity to learn how best to ride different cross-country obstacles that you may not have at home.

**Caution:** Before you think about entering a horse trial, eventing competition, or Pony Club rally, you will need extra instruction and coaching to help you and your horse get ready to compete safely. This is not the kind of competition to enter "just for the experience"!

Riding a cross-country course demands more fitness and different riding skills from stadium jumping. You must be able to handle the galloping pace, the differences in terrain and footing, jumping into and out of shade, riding up and down hills, and negotiating different cross-country obstacles. You *must* be able to ride and jump with control at a safe pace, because galloping and jumping in the open can make some horses very excitable, especially if they are allowed to go too fast. A cross-country course is much longer than a stadium-jumping course (usually more than a mile, with 15 or more fences), so you must be fit, strong, and able to think and stay in control for a longer and more demanding ride. Your horse must also be fit enough to handle the pace and the length of the course as well as the jumps.

## Walking a Cross-Country Course and Developing a Riding Plan

Before you ride a cross-country course, you should walk it at least twice and develop a riding plan. The official meeting and course walk give you the official information about the course and a general idea of the layout of the course.

Walk the course a second time, preferably with your coach. Many good competitors like to walk it a third time, just to be sure. Plan your ride from start to finish, deciding what pace you will ride over each part and noting difficult terrain or places where you must slow down. Plan to save ground wherever you can, but be sure to stay on course. You must know exactly where the course starts and finishes, and the location of any flags that mark turns in the course.

Decide the exact pace, line, and angle at which you will jump each fence. Look for landmarks to keep you on the line you have chosen. Take note of anything that could make a fence more difficult, such as a slippery spot, places where you must jump from sunlight into shadow, or anything that might look spooky to your horse. Remind yourself about jumps that need

Pony clubbers walk a cross-country course.

extra balance, such as drop fences and downhill fences. For combinations or option fences, walk through all possible options and decide on the best way to ride the obstacle. However, once on course, circumstances may change so that you must change your plan. (For example, if the ground is cut up or very slippery, you may have to jump a fence at a different spot.) Keep in mind the time of day you will ride and the position of the sun. This can create shadows that make the fences look different and can change the way you ride them.

## Tips on Riding a Cross-Country Course

- Your horse must be properly warmed up before jumping cross-country. Check your girth, stirrups, rein length, and chin strap before you start.
- Always ride strongly and positively to the first fence. Because it is going away from home, your horse may not want to jump.
- Keep a steady pace that allows your horse to move freely forward in good balance but under control. Slow down in plenty of time for downhill slopes or difficult ground, and don't race wildly up hills or on level ground.
- About 8 to 10 strides from each fence, steady your horse and be sure he is balanced and paying attention to your aids. It is better to come into a fence a bit slowly, increasing your stride as you get closer, than to gallop in too fast and have to check or try to rebalance right before the fence.
- To keep your horse balanced and maintain a lively, steady canter during the approach, imagine that you are riding a gymnastic during the last few strides before each fence.
- Keep contact with your horse's mouth and keep him in front of your legs, but wait for the fence to come to you—don't anticipate and rush to get there.
- You make better time riding accurate lines and saving ground than by galloping fast and wide.
- Pay attention to your horse's rhythm, balance, and energy. If he feels tired, slow down and help him balance, especially on hills. Never risk hurting your horse by going faster or farther than he is fit to go.
- As you get tired toward the end of the course, stay in balance and don't lean on your horse's neck or let your seat bump down into the saddle. When you cross the finish line, slow down gradually.

It is very important to take care of your horse properly immediately after you finish a cross-country course, and later on. See the *USPC C Level Manual,* pages 236–246, for more information on cooling out and caring for your horse after hard work.

# 6

# Longeing

Ground training is a very important part of horsemanship. Good ground training teaches obedience, respect, trust, and cooperation, and helps to establish a good working relationship between trainer and horse. It can improve a horse's movement, help develop his muscles correctly, and affect his attitude and behavior under saddle as well as in the stable.

Whenever you handle a horse, you are practicing ground training. If you insist on certain behavior at some times and ignore it at others, this confuses the horse and undermines his training and respect for you as his handler. Good horsemanship and successful training require correct and consistent handling at all times.

Before a horse can be trained to longe or be schooled in any of the methods described here, he must be properly trained to lead, stand still when asked to, and respond to simple signals and voice commands. (Please review these subjects in the *USPC D* and *C Level Manuals*.)

This chapter includes information about longeing, equipment, and techniques; training horses to longe; and longeing to improve the horse's way of going. Longeing to train the rider (longe lessons) is covered in Chapter 8, "Teaching Horsemanship."

An introduction to longeing, including equipment, safety, and basic principles, is found in the *USPC C Level Manual*, Chapter 10. Before you can progress to the more advanced longeing discussed here, you must know this material and have practiced the basic skills until you can perform them with ease.

## Longeing with the Bit

For ordinary longeing, it is best to attach the longe line to the nose ring of a properly fitted longe cavesson. This permits good control without endangering the horse's mouth or interfering with the contact. However, it is sometimes desirable to longe with direct contact with the horse's mouth. This must be undertaken only by a handler who is experienced in longeing correctly, and only with a horse that is well trained to longe. Longeing a green or difficult horse with the longe attached to the bit can pull severely on the mouth, causing pain, damaging the horse's training, and injuring the mouth.

Methods of attaching the longe line to the bit are described and illustrated in the *USPC C Level Manual*, pages 290–293. The longe line must be attached to the bit in such a way that it is secure and will not twist, bind, or result in excessive or uneven pressure on the horse's mouth. The longe must be unfastened and changed to the inside whenever you change directions.

## Longe Line Attachments to the Bit

**Longe attached to bit and noseband.** This can be done by attaching the longe line to a short strap that runs through the bit ring and the noseband, or using a longe line with a buckle end, or a snap end large enough to encompass the noseband as well as the bit ring (see the following figure). This method permits direct contact with the bit while preventing the bit from being pulled sideways through the mouth. This method also transfers some of the pressure to the noseband instead of to the bit alone. It can be used with a regular cavesson or the cavesson element of a flash noseband, but should not be used with a dropped noseband or figure eight noseband.

**Longe wrapped around inside bit ring and attached to outside bit ring.** Pass the longe through the inside bit ring, wrap it once around the inside bit ring, and then pass it under the chin and clip it to the outside bit ring. Be cautious when using this method. This gives a direct connection to the bit on both sides of the mouth. If you have a horse that pulls hard, this method may cause the two rings of a snaffle to pinch together with a severe "nutcracker" action, causing the joint of the snaffle bit to hit the soft palate of the horse's mouth. In some instances it may not release the nutcracker action, causing discomfort.

**Longe over poll (gag bit effect).** The longe is run through the inside bit ring (from outside to inside), over the poll, and fastened to the bit ring on the opposite side. **Caution:** This arrangement acts as a gag bit, pulling the bit upward into the corners of the mouth and pressing against the poll. It is quite severe, and must be handled carefully to avoid injury to the mouth.

This method is used when maximum control is needed, such as when longeing a strong-willed horse that pulls, when longeing in the open, or when safe control is essential, as when giving a longe lesson. It must only be used by a handler who is expert at longeing and has excellent hands. If used in conjunction with side reins, this attachment can give conflicting messages to the horse, who is being told to raise and lower his head at the same time.

**V- or Y-shaped longe line devices.** These devices are made of leather or nylon. While they make it easy to connect the longe line to the bit rings, they may not provide the best connection with your horse's mouth. Some models are too long and too heavy, which interfere with good contact and can be distracting and even dangerous. If the center ring doesn't slide, it puts more pressure on the outside bit ring than the inside. These attachments should be used with care on horses that are well-schooled at longeing, as they do not provide a clear connection to the horse's mouth.

*Do not* attach the longe to the inside bit ring alone; the bit can be pulled sideways, through the mouth, which can injure the mouth and damage the bridle.

Methods of connecting the longe line to the bit.

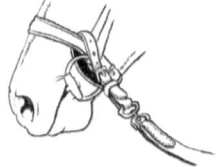

Longe attached to bit and noseband

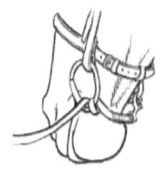

Longe wrapped around inside bit ring and attached to outside bit ring

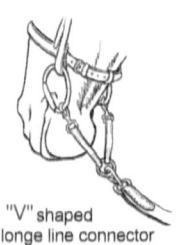

"V" shaped longe line connector

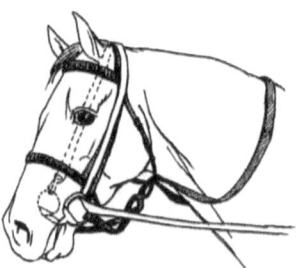

Longe line run through inside bit ring, over poll, and attached to outside bit ring (gag bit effect)

# Longeing Equipment

Basic longeing equipment (including longe lines, whip, cavesson, and snaffle bridle), its fitting, and use are introduced in Chapter 10 of the *USPC C Level Manual*. Other longeing equipment discussed in this section includes surcingles or rollers, side reins, and various types of bitting and training devices. The person longeing should wear a helmet, watch, gloves, and sturdy shoes.

## Surcingle or Roller

A surcingle or roller is a band equipped with rings for side reins, long reins, and so on. Used over a saddle, it provides attachments for side reins. Used alone, it may be used to provide an attachment for side reins, or to accustom a green horse to girth pressure.

When used alone, a surcingle should be fitted as carefully as a saddle, avoiding pressure on the spine or digging into the shoulder blades; a saddle or surcingle pad, or both, should be placed under the surcingle. When used over a saddle, the stirrups may be removed, or they may be tied up and the surcingle passed through the stirrup irons to prevent them from banging on the saddle. Be careful not to pinch the horse's skin between the girth and surcingle.

## Side Reins

Side reins are used to help a horse accept and reach into the contact, improve the top line of the horse, and help the horse learn to carry himself in a comfortable frame. The horse learns to yield or "give" to the bit and side reins while at the same time reaching into contact with the bit, accepting the head and neck position they create. Additionally, work in side reins can help to re-school a horse that has been poorly ridden or one that is changing disciplines.

Properly adjusted side reins encourage a horse to keep his neck and spine correctly aligned. They stabilize the base of the neck, which discourages "rubber-necking," or over-bending the neck sideways. Side reins should never be too tight, as some horses object and will run backward or rear to try to free themselves, risking injury.

Using side reins, or at least an outside side rein, can be helpful for control of a naughty or very fresh horse who tries to turn in, strike out, buck, or pull away on the longe line.

Types of side reins include:

> **Solid side reins.** These reins are made of leather or webbing without stretch or give. Some trainers prefer solid side reins because they

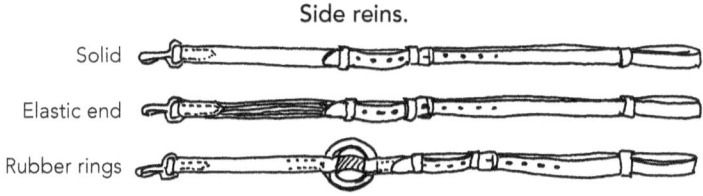

Side reins.

provide a positive connection to the bit. Solid side reins can be quite severe and should only be used for advanced longeing and work in hand. Care must be taken to avoid letting the horse lean on them or get behind the bit.

**Side reins with rubber rings.** *Rubber rings* (or "*donuts*") are inserted in the side reins, which allows the side rein to have more give. The donut side rein is useful for a horse that is less confirmed in the contact. Usually they have a solid piece inside the rubber ring that limits the amount of stretch. However, they add weight to the side reins, and if adjusted too loosely, the rubber donuts may bounce, putting inconsistent pressure on the horse's mouth.

**Elastic end side reins.** *Elastic ends* allow more stretch than rubber rings, for a lighter and more elastic contact with the bit. Although these may be useful for extremely sensitive horses, many trainers believe they encourage horses to pull.

## Adjustment of Side Reins

Side reins must be adjusted correctly for their purpose and for the horse's level of training. All types of side reins are generally attached to the bit or cavesson and girth or surcingle so they are parallel with the ground. They should be used only minimally in the walk, as they may inhibit the balancing gestures of the horse's neck, shorten his stride, and spoil his walk. During warm-up, side reins are usually adjusted quite long if they are used at all, so they do not inhibit the horse's ability to stretch his neck and back. Some horses warm up best with no side reins or long side reins, while others warm up better with the guidance of the side reins. In a typical longeing session, the side reins are shortened as the work progresses, as the horse warms up and comes to a better balance. Side reins must never be shortened so much that the horse is forced to retract his neck or to carry his face behind the vertical.

**Normal-length side reins** are adjusted so that the horse makes contact with the bit when his head and neck are in a normal position for his conformation and level of training. His face should be about one hand's breadth in front of the vertical.

## Adjustment of side reins.

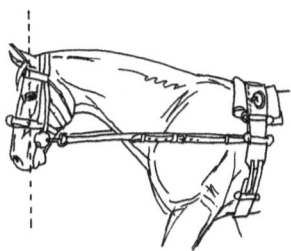

*Basic adjustment:* head at normal height for horse, face slightly in front of vertical

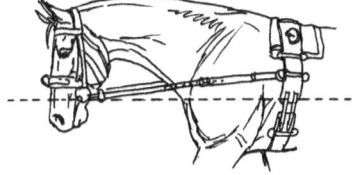

*Long adjustment:* mouth level with point of shoulder, face slightly in front of vertical

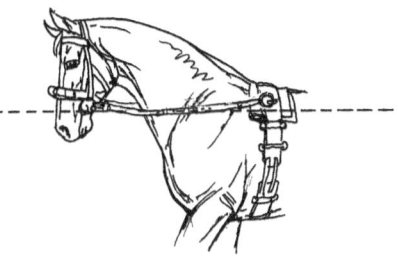

*Short adjustment:* mouth level with point of hip; face at or near vertical

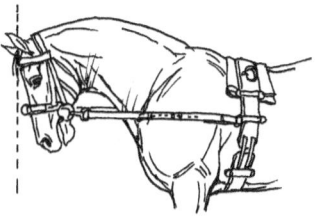

*Incorrect adjustment:* flexion behind poll, face behind vertical

**Longer side reins** are used in the early stages of training. They are adjusted so that the horse can stretch his neck and lower his head, and make contact with the bit with his mouth approximately on a level with the point of his shoulder.

**Shorter side reins** are adjusted to maintain contact when the horse works in a shorter frame in collected gaits, with his face at or near the vertical. Sometimes a trainer will attach shorter side reins at a higher point on the surcingle (closer to where a rider's hands would naturally be) to aid in collection. They are used only for advanced horses, and only for short periods of concentrated work. Shorter side reins do not create collection; instead, they are adjusted to conform to the horse's increased ability to shift his balance to the rear, lower his haunches, and stay collected.

Different well-known and respected trainers have different thoughts on side rein lengths when comparing the adjustment of the inside side rein to the outside side rein. For most horses, both side reins should be of equal length. Sometimes the inside side rein may be temporarily shortened (two or more holes) when used to train a laterally stiff horse, but you run the risk of the horse subsequently falling out through his outside shoulder while appearing to be bending, or he may over-bend his neck rather than his entire body ("rubber-neck"). For a laterally stiff horse, an overly shortened inside side rein can also cause the horse to tip over onto the inside shoulder and push his haunches out on the circle. Ultimately, these evasions to true bending can inhibit the engagement of the inside hind leg.

Sometimes, when starting a green or nervous horse, only the outside side rein is attached, so the horse is less likely to feel trapped and panic or rear. The longe line becomes the inside rein and encourages the horse to reach into the outside side rein. Using only the outside side rein is also helpful with horses that try to turn in on the longer.

In the beginning, adjusting the outside side rein slightly shorter, or longeing with only an outside side rein, can sometimes encourage a horse to stretch into the outside rein. If it is shortened too much, however, this can cause a horse to bend his neck to the outside and fall in on the inside shoulder.

In addition to the length of side reins affecting the horse's connection to the bit and quality of movement, so does the height of the attachment of the side reins to the longeing surcingle, saddle, or girth. Lower placement encourages a young or green horse to "seek the bit" and stretch through his top line, and to develop his *circle of muscles* (see page 5) when longed with proper engagement of the hind legs. However, this placement can sometimes cause a horse to lean on the forehand, so the longer must be aware of how the horse is using himself. As the horse strengthens his back and moves up to more challenging levels of flat work and dressage, the point of attachment of the side reins can be raised. This higher placement of the side reins

Attachment of side reins to surcingle or saddle.

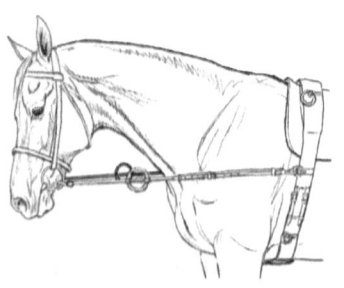

Lower attachment for green horse

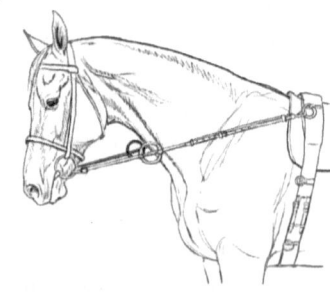

Higher attachment for advanced horse

is appropriate for a horse that is stronger in his top line and more advanced in his training, working with a greater degree of engagement in the hindquarters and lightness in his forehand required for collected gaits.

Always adjust both side reins before attaching them to the bit. Before attaching them initially, adjust the side reins so the snap at the end of the side reins reaches to the level of the horse's nose, with the horse's neck in a natural position. The adjustment of the side reins can be fine-tuned once they have been attached. Fasten the outside side rein first, then the inside—that way you are in a position to immediately send the horse forward if necessary. As soon as the side reins are attached, the horse should move forward. If forced to stand still with short side reins or during adjustment, some horses may lean on the bit, get behind the bit, or become upset, even to the point of rearing.

When a horse has finished working, the side reins should be removed immediately, so the horse can stretch freely while cooling down. The inside side rein should be removed first, followed by the outside one.

**Caution:** *Never* use side reins when jumping, as they restrict a horse's use of his head and neck over a jump and can cause a jab in the mouth, loss of confidence, or even a fall.

## Sliding Side Reins (Lauffer Reins or Vienna Reins)

*Sliding side reins* run from an upper surcingle ring through the bit ring and back to a lower surcingle ring on each side, forming a triangle. *Vienna reins* are "V"-shaped and go from the girth out between the front legs, then split and go through the bit on each side, and attach to the surcingle on either side. Sliding side reins can also be adjusted as Vienna reins, going from the girth, between the front legs, through the bit, and back to a surcingle ring.

Sliding side reins allow a horse to maintain contact with the bit in a range of positions, particularly as he lowers his head and stretches his neck. Unlike regular side reins, they do not tighten or loosen as he changes the position of his head and neck. They can be useful for horses that have too high a head carriage, or are tight in the back and do not know how to stretch forward and down.

Sliding side reins should be adjusted so that the horse can make contact with the bit when he carries his neck slightly arched, with his face at or slightly in front of the vertical. Early in training, they are attached to the middle and lower surcingle rings. At a later stage, they may be attached to the upper and middle rings.

**Caution:** Sliding side reins are advanced training equipment and must be used only by trainers who understand their proper adjustment and use, and have advanced longeing skills.

Sliding side reins/Vienna reins.

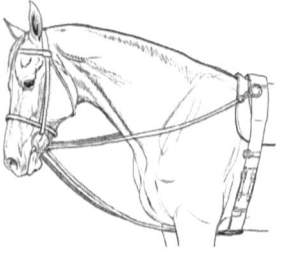

1st adjustment: between forelegs

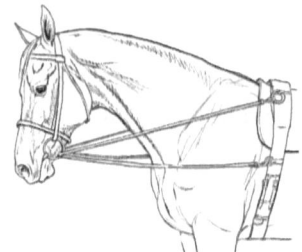

2nd adjustment: to side of surcingle or girth

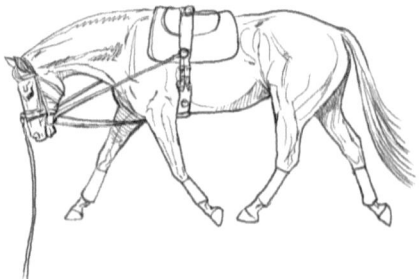

Horse can stretch down while maintaining contact

## Training Devices

All training devices such as side reins and draw reins are intended to develop a specific head and neck carriage. Training devices work by applying pressure when the horse deviates from the desired head and neck position, and reducing or eliminating pressure when he returns to it. In theory, the horse should learn to move in a correct posture and should develop the muscles that facilitate this way of moving.

Unfortunately, if used without skill and knowledge, these devices can act like hard hands, or riding a horse incorrectly "from front to back." A horse may *set his head*, assuming a fixed head and neck position that relieves the pressure, but if he does this with his back hollow or his hind legs trailing, his balance, movement, and muscle development suffer. If a device is adjusted incorrectly or too tightly, the horse cannot find relief from the pressure, causing tension, stiffness, and pain, which can ruin his movement and attitude. It also leads to the development of defenses devices such as leaning on the bit, retracting the neck, over-flexing, or shortening the stride, and even to violent resistance such as rearing or falling over backward. Incorrect use of bitting devices is abusive and can cause muscle soreness, physical damage, or serious accidents.

*Because of the dangers of these devices, they should be used only by experts who are extremely knowledgeable about horse training, movement, and muscle development.* Any training device must be introduced tactfully and adjusted gradually to the point where it works best. The horse must be longed correctly, with careful attention to rhythm, relaxation, engagement of the hind legs, and good movement. Most experts who are capable of using such devices without causing harm have little use for gimmicks; unfortunately, these devices are too often used by less knowledgeable trainers in search of a quick fix. In such hands, they are all too easily abused.

*Elastic poll pressure devices and "neck stretchers"* are commonly used (and abused) training devices. These devices apply pressure on the poll and the bit in a downward and backward direction, with some elasticity. They encourage a horse to lower his head and flex his poll and neck. *Disadvantages:* Although the give of the elastic makes these devices less rigid than some others, they can encourage a horse to over-flex, flex behind the poll, pull on the bit, or become heavy on the forehand, especially if misadjusted or if the horse is not longed correctly.

The *chambon* is another commonly used device. It applies pressure to the poll and mouth when the horse raises his head; the horse is free to stretch forward and down. The chambon teaches the horse the correct response to bit pressure—to reach toward the bit. It is a useful device for horses that hide behind the bit. Correct use of the chambon encourages a horse to lower and extend his head and neck, while raising and rounding his back. As a result, the horse develops his back muscles properly.

*Disadvantages:* Chambons can cause soreness in the neck muscles. The horse may go on the forehand if not longed correctly. Therefore, it is important that the horse is allowed to move to figure out his balance with his neck reaching out and down. Cantering in the chambon should only be done by an experienced trainer, and then only when the horse is confident and consistent in his work at the walk and trot. It takes weeks of correct and consistent work to develop the muscles and movement so that the horse carries himself and does not go on his forehand.

The horse must be taught to respond correctly to the pressure of the chambon (lowering his head) in hand; otherwise, he may resist violently when he feels the pressure, even to the point of rearing or falling over backward. The chambon is only used for longeing, not for riding.

The *de gogue* is a variation of the chambon, which can be much more restrictive, especially if misused. The chambon is intended to be used only for longeing, while the de gogue is used while riding. Pony Club riders should not use de gogues at any level, and the use of restrictive devices is strongly discouraged.

There are various kinds of bitting harnesses that are used for longeing, including bitting rigs and the Pessoa System. These devices consist of a

Training devices (all devices mentioned).

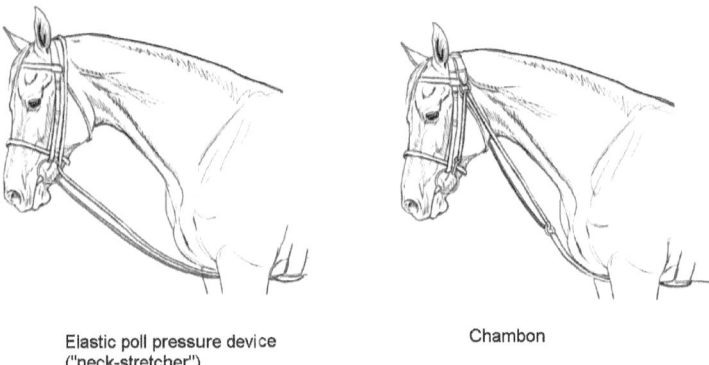

Elastic poll pressure device ("neck-stretcher")

Chambon

surcingle with attachments at different heights for side reins. Some also incorporate a *breeching* (a strap that goes behind the horse's buttocks). *These devices should be used only by experts*, as they can cause a horse to become over-bent, behind the bit, resistant, or "set" the head in a rigid position if they are misadjusted or misused.

## Improving Longeing Technique

Good longeing is largely a matter of communication between trainer and horse, using body language, gestures, timing, tone of voice, and a consistent vocabulary of commands. This relates to the way horses naturally communicate with each other. Besides commands, cues, and learned responses, you communicate qualities such as confidence, relaxation, authority, energy, and awareness. Negative attitudes such as fear, anger, impatience, inattention, and indecisiveness are also easily picked up by the horse.

### Communicating with the Longe Line

The longe line is a means of communication between handler and horse, as the reins are in riding. Light, consistent contact should be maintained at all times when longeing.

It is important to develop skill in handling the longe line. Practice letting out the longe (allowing it to run through your loosened fingers) as the horse moves out onto a larger circle, and taking in the longe (picking up additional folds), until you can do this easily with either hand. For safety, always keep the excess longe in folds, not loops that could coil around your hand, and never let the longe slacken dangerously or drag on the ground, where the horse or the longer could get caught in it.

Maintaining contact can be a challenge with a horse that counter-bends and falls in, or one that falls in and out on an inconsistent circle. The consistency and steadiness of the contact should improve as the session progresses and the circle becomes steadier. The longer must react quickly to correct a horse falling in and be able to rapidly shorten and lengthen the line while maintaining even contact, to stay safely in control.

Your *body language* (posture, gestures, and the way you use your body) convey your mood and intentions to your horse. This is also communicated by touch, through your handling of the longe line and whip.

> **Mental attitude.** Body language starts with mental attitude. Clear intent, which means making a clear decision about what you intend to do and what you intend the horse to do, is especially important. Your attitude of quiet confidence and clear, positive intent gives the horse confidence and encourages him to accept you as his leader.
>
> **Posture and movement.** Your posture and the way you move communicate your attitude and intentions to the horse. In general, the longer's shoulders should be in a line parallel to the horse's body. A submissive posture (eyes lowered, head turned away, shoulders rounded, backing away from the horse) conveys a submissive or even fearful attitude. An aggressive posture (looking directly at the horse with shoulders squared, head up, moving toward horse) conveys dominance or even an attack. It is easier to get a horse to move in balance if you are balanced with good posture than if you slouch or lean. Deep breathing improves your posture and helps you project confidence and calmness.
>
> **Body placement.** Your placement in relation to the horse is extremely important in longeing. (See the *USPC C Level Manual*, page 301, for a discussion of the "control triangle.")

Body language.

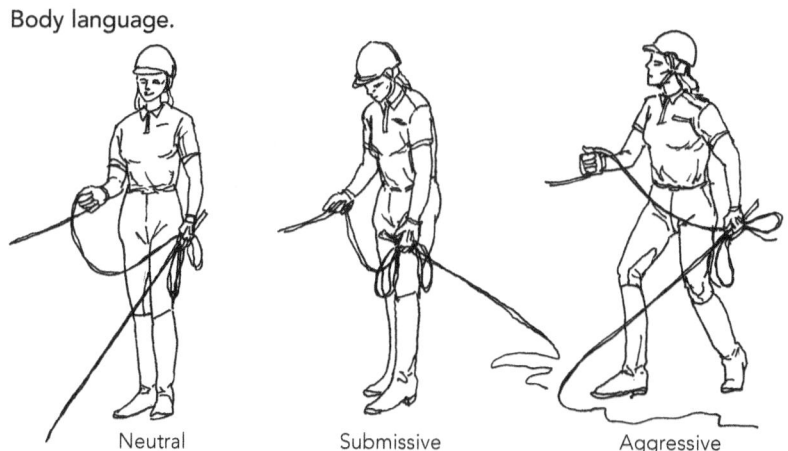

Neutral　　　　Submissive　　　　Aggressive

When longeing, you must be aware of the "control point." This is a point on the horse (usually located slightly behind his shoulder) at which he reacts to your body placement and movements. The person longeing should normally stay opposite the control point; getting behind the control point drives the horse forward, while getting ahead of this point encourages the horse to slow down or stop.

**Gestures.** Gestures are movements of your body, limbs, and whip. Horses understand gestures, as they use them in communicating with other horses. A gesture may be small or large, gentle or vigorous, all of which affects the horse's reaction to it. The longe whip is a driving aid (a substitute for the rider's leg) when longeing. It is carried in the longer's hand and is therefore an extension of his arm, so it accentuates any gestures he makes. Some horses react more strongly to gestures (particularly whip gestures) than others, so start with small, controlled gestures to see how each individual horse reacts. (Specific gestures for longeing are described in the *USPC C Level Manual*, pages 299–301.)

**Importance of posture and hand and arm positions.** As in riding, "good hands" in longeing depend on good posture; balance; and shoulder, arm, and hand positions. Your upper body carriage should be the same as when you are riding. Good balance and posture make it easier to handle the longe line effectively and longe safely. If you slouch or lean forward, you are unable to give clear and correct rein aids, and you can be pulled off balance by a resisting horse. Leaning back against the horse causes a heavy pull on the longe; therefore, this posture should only be used as a momentary defensive measure when a horse pulls hard or tries to bolt.

The long muscles of your back and the muscles at the back of the upper arm stabilize your arm and help you resist if a horse pulls. Your upper arm should hang close to your ribs, with a natural bend at the elbow, as if you were riding. The forearm, wrist, and hand should be held so that the longe forms a straight line from your elbow to the cavesson or bit. Carrying your longe hand too high is tiring and makes your touch stiff, while dropping your arm too low pulls downward against the horse. Bending the wrist or pulling the longe hand inward causes a continuous pull and may teach the horse to pull against you.

**Rein aids on the longe.** The longe line should be treated as a rein, both in maintaining a light, steady contact and in giving rein aids. As in riding, rein aids should be applied as a brief change of pressure in a specific direction, *not* as a pull or jerk. It is important to keep the horse moving forward on the track of the circle in order to maintain the contact.

Specific rein aids for longeing and their effects are discussed in the *USPC C Level Manual*, pages 297–298. You should practice all the rein aids on the longe line until you can use them fluently and easily as needed.

**Waves in the longe line.** *Waves* (sometimes described as *snake lines* because they make the longe line move like a snake) can be used as signals. There are two variations:

1. *Horizontal wave:* This is made by moving the longe hand (holding the longe) forward and backward, causing a sideways "wave" to travel out through the longe line to the cavesson or bit. It causes a brief backward effect of the longe line on the cavesson or bit. Horizontal waves are used as a half-halt and are used in conjunction with a voice command to ask the horse to slow down or halt.

2. *Vertical wave:* This is made by moving the longe hand up and down, causing a vertical wave in the longe line to run outward to the cavesson or bit. It causes a brief up-and-down effect on

Applying a "wave" with the longe.

Vertical wave.

Horizontal wave.

the cavesson or bit, and the approaching vertical wave is seen by the horse's inside eye. Vertical waves are used (along with pointing the whip toward the shoulder) to ask a horse to move outward or to stop cutting in on the longeing circle.

When applying a wave, you must slacken the line a little and give it a gentle flip (horizontally or vertically) to send the "wave" out through the longe line. At the end of the wave, the snap or longe fastening may give a short "snap" up and down or backward, against the cavesson ring or bit ring. This must be done in a controlled way so as not to surprise the horse, cause a severe jerk on the cavesson or bit, or risk hitting him in the face with a loop of the longe.

You should not try to apply a wave until you have completely and correctly established your basic longeing skills. Making waves with the longe line takes practice, but once mastered, it can be very effective.

## Handling the Whip

The longe whip is a means of communication, not an instrument of punishment. It serves as the primary driving aid in longeing, assisted by the voice, taking the place of the rider's leg aids.

The longe whip may be used in several ways:

**Pointing the whip.** Most whip signals are given by pointing the tip of the whip toward a precise spot, or by moving it in a gesture.

**Running out the lash.** The lash may be run out toward a specific point on the horse, keeping it close to the ground. This is accomplished with a quick turn of the wrist, moving the tip of the whip to flick the lash outward, toward the horse.

**Touching with the whip.** Touching the horse with the lash of the longe whip is a strong driving aid to send the horse forward. The lash may be lightly tossed upward, run out to lightly flick the horse, or (rarely) applied with a stinging snap. This last should be used only as a last resort, to stop a serious disobedience.

The lash should usually be applied on the barrel, between the spot where a rider's leg would touch the horse and the haunches. If used on the hind legs or hindquarters, it encourages forward movement but may provoke kicking. Using the whip on the shoulder (to correct cutting in) should be reserved for experts, because of the danger of striking the horse in the head or eye.

For safety, the lash should be kept close to the ground and applied in a forward and upward direction. Striking downward or swinging the lash wildly can cause it to wrap around the horse's legs or get caught on the tack or under his tail, with dangerous results. The lash must *never* be used near a horse's head, because of the danger of striking him in the eye.

**Snapping the whip.** This practice should be avoided when possible, especially if other horses or riders are nearby. Snapping the whip can frighten other horses in the vicinity. Occasionally, an audible snap or crack may be necessary to send an obstinate horse forward. This should be done well behind the hindquarters and close to the ground, by moving the tip of the whip forward, then quickly backward.

## Importance of the Circle

Longeing is work performed on a circle. You can only evaluate and improve a horse's movement when he works consistently on a circle of a given size. If he keeps changing the shape and size of the circle, his movement is inconsistent and you have less control. The most effective way to maintain a circle is for the longer to serve as the pivot point in the center of the circle. The more the longer moves around, the less consistent the pivot point, and the more inconsistent the circle will be.

In the early stages of longeing, the longer walks in a small circle as the horse works in a larger circle (parallel longeing). This keeps the longer closer to the horse, where his signals are more effective. In more advanced training, the longer pivots in the middle of the circle, providing a fixed center point for the circle.

In an alternative method, the longer stands at the center of the circle, with a handler walking with the horse to reinforce any aids the longer gives. The handler gradually moves farther away, until the horse moves forward on the longeing circle without a helper.

Ultimately, the goal is to train the horse to longe with the longer standing at the pivot point. When a horse moves around a longer who is fixed and centered in the circle, it is longeing in the most effective manner.

**Going forward on the circle.** The first requirement is to establish forward movement on a circle, even if this requires parallel longeing or help from an assistant, as described above. If the horse hangs back, hesitates, or turns around, longeing cannot be accomplished.

**Roundness of the circle.** A longeing circle must be perfectly round for best effect. Horses may change the shape of the circle by cutting in or falling out. They usually do this at the same place (often toward the stable or away from a spooky object).

Tips for handling circle problems:

- *Falling out:* Longe in an enclosed ring (preferably a round ring), or create a barrier (using safe materials) on the side where the horse pulls outward. Correctly adjusted side reins help keep a horse from falling out through the outside shoulder. Before he reaches the spot where he falls out, begin applying direct rein aids in rhythm with the steps of his inside hind leg. In difficult cases, using the double longe (see the next section) may help.
- *Cutting in:* Before the horse reaches the point where he usually cuts in, send him forward by using the longe whip in rhythm with his inside hind leg. When he tries to cut in, point the whip toward his shoulder and say "Out." It may help to shorten the longe line and move closer to the horse (parallel longeing) briefly, so that your body language can be used to send him outward. You may also apply a "vertical wave" of the longe to send him outward.

**Size of the circle.** A longeing circle must be large enough for the horse to move evenly and in good balance for his stage of training, but small enough for good control. The smaller the circle and the faster the gait, the harder it is for the horse to keep his balance and track correctly. Longeing on a small circle, especially at fast gaits, puts extra stress on joints and muscles and increases the risk of injury, especially in immature or unfit horses. However, too large a circle makes it harder to keep control.

In early training, the longeing circle should be about 60 to 20 meters (66 feet) in diameter. As the horse's balance and strength improve, he may be longed on slightly smaller circles at the walk and trot (approximately 15 to 18 meters, or 50 to 60 feet, in diameter) or spiraled in and out. Sometimes the beginning of a canter circle may be briefly increased to 25 to 30 meters, to establish contact and balance.

**Tracking correctly on a circle.** Tracking correctly (tracking "straight") on a circle means that the horse's hind legs follow in the tracks of his front legs. This keeps his neck and spine properly aligned and allows him to bend correctly. (See Chapter 1, "Biomechanics and Movement of the Horse," for more information.)

Horses often move crookedly on circles. Judging the degree of bend from the center of the circle (longeing position) takes practice. From this point of view, the horse often appears more bent than he actually is. An observer on the outside of the circle can help you determine the true degree of bend and straightness.

A horse may carry his shoulder to the inside, swing his haunches out, or carry his haunches to the inside. Many horses bend their necks too much to the inside or the outside. To some degree, this is due to the one-sidedness that is found in all horses. This problem must be addressed in order to strengthen and supple the horse, and develop his ability to move correctly in both directions.

Start by establishing your circle in a quiet, steady trot with even rhythm and tempo to allow the horse to establish the track before asking for engagement or more forward movement. Only when the horse is steady and confident can you improve straightness in tracking on the longeing circle.

Tips to improve tracking straight on the longeing circle:

- Correctly fitted side reins discourage a horse from looking out of the circle, bending his neck too much to either side, or "popping" a shoulder. Longe on a large enough circle (approximately 20 meters). Too small a circle makes crookedness worse.
- Use the longe whip to increase the activity in the hind legs. Crookedness is often related to poor activity and engagement of the inside hind leg.
- Keep the speed slow and the rhythm and tempo steady. If a horse leans inward instead of staying vertical or "standing up" and tracking properly, he is probably going too fast for the size of the circle.
- Horses that swing their haunches out may benefit from work with a double longe, which helps to keep the hindquarters in line (see below).

## Double Longeing

The double longe is often used in preparation for long-reining or ground driving. It can be helpful in longeing horses that persistently swing the haunches out, travel crookedly, or turn in to face the handler.

Double longeing requires two longe lines or long reins, a longe cavesson, and a surcingle. For safety's sake, tie the horse's tail up in a mud knot to avoid catching the longe line under the tail.

**Caution:** Before double longeing, the horse *must* be accustomed to feeling the pressure of a longe line around his hindquarters, croup, hocks, and tail, on both sides, without fear or resentment.

In double longeing, the inside longe line is attached to the inside ring of the longe cavesson and runs straight to the trainer's hand. The other longe line is attached to the outside cavesson ring, and passes through the middle or lower surcingle ring, around the hindquarters, and back to the trainer's hand. The outside longe line may need to be extra long to fit around the haunches of the horse. (If no surcingle is available, tie a ring to the stirrup or girth at shoulder height.) When changing direction, the horse must be stopped and both longe lines reattached in the inside and outside positions.

Double longe.

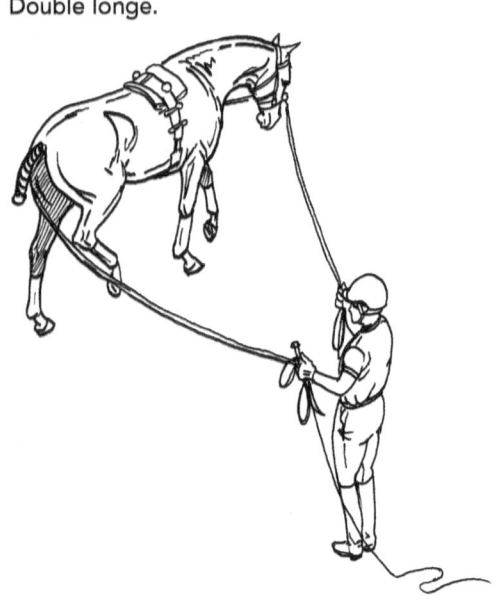

Tail tied up to prevent catching longe on tail

**Caution:** The longe lines or long reins should not be fastened together, as this creates a dangerous loop in which the handler and/or horse could become entangled. Be careful not to allow the extra folds of longe line to hang down in dangerously large, sloppy loops.

The horse is started off in a straight line with the trainer walking behind. After the horse has become accustomed to the two lines and thoroughly accepts them, the trainer gradually walks on a smaller circle to accustom the horse to the pressure of the outside line as outside aids affecting the gaskin, hock, and quarters in general. As work proceeds, the size of the circle can be carefully increased.

The inner longe is handled as usual, keeping a light contact with the inside of the horse's nose. The outer longe must be handled with a light, steady contact along the horse's side and around his hindquarters, to keep his hind legs following in the tracks of his front legs. The horse's head must not be pulled to the outside. **Caution:** Don't let the outside longe drop too low, where it could become entangled in the hind legs, or lift it high enough to get caught under the tail.

# Longeing Young Horses

Longeing puts lateral stress on a horse's legs and joints, which increases with speed, duration, and on smaller circles. A young horse's immature bones and joints are especially vulnerable to injury from too much or incorrect longeing, or from accidents if the horse acts up. Horses are also more easily overstressed mentally by too-long or demanding training sessions. Work in hand and free longeing are less stressful and safer for immature horses than longeing too much or too soon. When longeing young horses, protective boots for the horse are recommended, and training sessions should be short, no more than 20 minutes.

Foals should never be longed, as they are especially vulnerable to neck injuries if pulled violently sideways. Yearlings can be longed at slow gaits for short periods, but must not be overstressed. Two-year-olds (and some yearlings) have nearly reached adult weight, but their bones and joints are still immature. They can be longed lightly, but it is better to vary the training program with work in hand, free longeing, and ground driving or long-lining instead of daily longeing.

# Longeing for Various Purposes

## Longeing for Exercise

Longeing can be used to exercise a horse in place of riding. Because longeing is harder work than it appears, and is especially stressful on unfit or immature joints, you must assess the horse's level of fitness and keep the longeing workload within his limits. Twenty minutes should be the maximum for a fit horse; young or unfit horses should be longed for 10 minutes or less, increasing gradually as the horse's fitness improves.

Always longe on good footing, warm up slowly, and warm down at the end of the session. Work equally in both directions (or slightly more in the horse's difficult direction), and use a watch or timer to keep track of how long he has worked in each direction and the total time.

## Longeing to Settle a Fresh Horse

Longeing can settle a fresh horse or relax a tense horse before riding. This is especially important when a student's horse is too fresh to ride safely. It is best to longe with the saddle and bridle in place (with a cavesson and side reins added). For some horses, starting with long or normal-length side reins helps them to focus on the longer's aids. **Caution:** Fresh horses may kick, so follow safety procedures carefully and stay alert!

Start out as quietly as possible (at a walk, if the horse will cooperate). If the horse is very fresh, it is better to allow him to trot slowly than to fight him about walking. Do not allow bucking and running, because it increases the risk of injury, and because a horse should associate longeing with obedience, not wild, undisciplined behavior. Instead, emphasize developing steady rhythm and tempo, relaxation, and free forward movement. If a horse needs to run, buck, and play, it is safer for you and the horse and better for his training to turn him out rather than to let him run and buck on the longe.

## Longeing an Unfamiliar Horse

When longeing an unfamiliar horse, your primary goals are to assess his movement, attitude, and level of training, and to establish a rapport that will allow you to work with him. Safety precautions are always important, but especially so when working with an unfamiliar horse. Be careful not to get into a position in which you could be kicked, and always treat an unfamiliar horse as if he were a green horse until you ascertain otherwise.

Before longeing, show the horse the longe whip, then run it gently over his body, noting his reactions. Practice parallel leading with halts and transitions to see if he responds to voice commands and to establish rapport. You can then proceed to parallel longeing, followed by regular longeing. Note which direction is easier and which is more difficult, and be alert to keep him from stopping and turning around when working in his difficult direction.

As you longe, assess the horse's gaits, level of relaxation, acceptance of the contact (side reins), as well as his longitudinal balance and lateral suppleness. Consider his temperament and willingness to cooperate with you.

Some categories a horse might fall into are:

- **Well-schooled:** Familiar with longeing, supple and responsive, able to move correctly in all gaits, accepts the aids and responds correctly.
- **Balance and movement problems:** Obedient but stiff, crooked, or unbalanced (usually more so in one direction). May not be able to canter safely on the longe.
- **Green:** Unbacked, or never longed before.
- **Problem horses:** Difficult attitude (tense, "hot," fearful, stubborn, lazy, and so on) or bad habits (balking, bolting, turning around, kicking, and so on).

# Longeing to Improve the Horse
## Longeing for Obedience and Discipline

Longeing is an effective way to teach a horse to pay attention, respond to signals, and learn how to learn. It provides a safe way to establish obedience, respect, and rapport, especially with difficult or spoiled horses.

When longeing for obedience, you must read the horse's intentions accurately. Remember the three-second rule: For a horse to associate a behavior with reward or correction, reinforcement must take place within three seconds or less. You must be prepared to reward or correct instantly, depending on the horse's behavior. One well-timed reinforcement can work wonders; rewarding or correcting even a few seconds too late will have negative results.

Work on one behavior at a time (for example, moving forward promptly in response to a voice command). Be clear and consistent in giving signals, and be ready to act instantly. If the horse resists or acts up, you may need to escalate your corrections (for example, from pointing the whip to snaking it toward the horse, a light touch, or even a sharp crack). Be ready to reward instantly and generously as soon as the horse begins to move in the right direction.

## Longeing to Improve Movement

Longeing may be used to improve the horse's gaits, balance, and movement. Good longeing technique, along with careful observation and an "educated eye" for movement, can lead to improvement in muscle development and performance under saddle. Good longeing, like good riding, should follow the Training Scale, working on Rhythm, Relaxation, Connection, Impulsion, Straightness, and Collection. However, the lower-level elements (rhythm, relaxation, and connection) are more easily addressed in longeing than the upper-level qualities (impulsion, straightness, and collection), which require a trainer with an advanced understanding of these elements and how to work on them in longeing.

The following components are basic to good movement. They should be assessed on an ongoing basis, as they are always interrelated. At any given time one element may need more of the longer's attention than the others. None of these components should be focused on without staying aware of the complete end product.

> **Rhythm and tempo.** Regular rhythm and a good working tempo come first. *Running* gaits are tense and quick, with short strides; too slow a tempo goes with lazy, dragging gaits and a broken or shuffling rhythm. An inconsistent horse that changes from slow to quick and back again cannot move well. When a horse finds the right working tempo, his rhythm becomes clear and steady, he can swing his legs freely in rhythm, and he breathes evenly. This leads to relaxation and better movement.
>
> To improve rhythm and tempo, keep the circle round and consistent in size. Counting to yourself helps to emphasize the rhythm and helps you time your aids correctly. To coordinate the applications of the aids, watch the inside hind leg. The aids (half-halts or whip signals) should be applied as the inside hind leg pushes off and swings through the air.

For a tense, quick horse, longe at a slower trot on a slightly smaller circle (about 18 meters). Encourage a slower tempo with gentle half-halts in rhythm with the motion of the inside hind leg, and quiet, soothing voice aids. For a lazy horse, point the whip toward the inside hind leg each time it swings forward, and use a stimulating voice command such as a cluck or the word "Come" or "Hup."

**Relaxation, calmness, and looseness.** Good working relaxation depends on both mental calmness and athletic relaxation or "looseness" of the muscles. This is only possible when the horse develops a steady working tempo. Mentally tense horses need to calm down and pay attention to the trainer, instead of overreacting to distractions in the environment.

To develop calmness, the trainer's attitude and demeanor are especially important. Breathe deeply; use a quiet, soothing tone of voice; and apply longe line aids with a gentle, relaxed touch in rhythm with the gait. Avoid excessive or large movements of the whip, and use the whip quietly and tactfully. If possible, longe in an enclosed ring, away from distractions.

Athletic relaxation and looseness of the muscles develop only when the horse warms up and settles into a good working tempo. Watch for the following signs that indicate the horse is becoming physically and mentally relaxed:

- The eyes are soft and the ears are not held stiffly.
- Taking a deep breath, like a sigh.
- Blowing through the nose in a long, gentle snort.
- Stretching down with the head and neck and relaxing the back.
- Chewing the bit softly.

**Impulsion and engagement.** The development of pushing power comes from an increased activity of the hindquarters, within the correct tempo and with relaxation, and from the horse's desire to move forward. This results in a swinging back that transmits power from the hind legs and allows the horse to carry himself in balance. The horse works "though his back," becoming a "back mover" instead of moving stiffly as a "leg mover."

Do not be in a hurry to ask for tracking-up until after relaxation and a steady, consistent tempo have been established. Tracking-up and subsequent engagement develop gradually as the horse builds confidence and strength. The mechanics of the hindquarters will change as the horse connects more correctly into the contact and develops strength.

Moving round vs moving poorly.

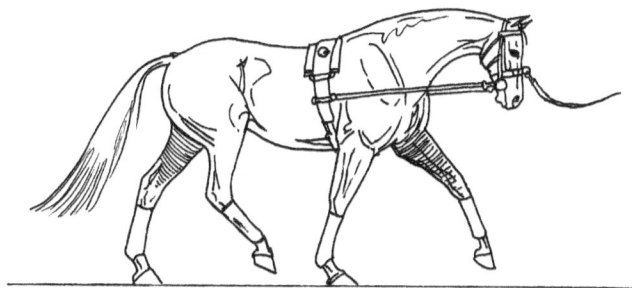

Moving well: round, tracking up, with good engagement

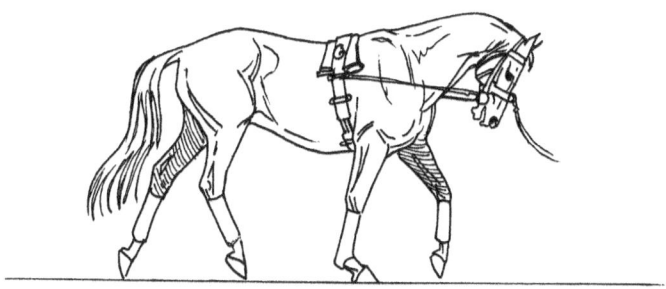

Moving poorly: hollow back, overbent, moving with stiff, constrained steps

To move forward better, the horse must take longer, more powerful strides with his hind legs—*not* run faster with short, quick steps. A horse can only reach farther as the hind leg swings through the air, not when it is grounded and bearing weight. Point the whip at the inside hind leg as it pushes off the ground and swings forward to encourage a longer stride in the same tempo.

Developing pushing power and confirming the horse's desire to carry himself is hard work. Engagement and forward movement require work; a tired, sore, or lazy horse will move with short strides and poor engagement. Tense, quick, running strides; inconsistent tempo; and tension in the back prevent good engagement. A lazy horse may need to be enlivened with strong driving aids (stepping toward the hindquarters, snaking the whip toward the hindquarters, or touching him with the lash) to urge him forward.

**Stretching and use of the back.** In order to carry a rider comfortably, a horse must move with a swinging back that is slightly rounded. This is the result of the engagement of the hind legs at each stride, the downward stretch of the horse's neck, and the use of his abdominal muscles. It requires a good working rhythm and tempo, relaxation and looseness of the muscles, and free forward movement.

Stretching down is a good exercise to develop a rounded, swinging back. To do this, the horse must stretch his head and neck down in a slight arch, seeking contact with the bit. Increasing the activity of the hind legs (while maintaining the same balance, rhythm, and tempo) encourages him to stretch down in a "rainbow" arc, with a round, swinging back and a softly rounded neck.

You can encourage stretching down by using sliding side reins, which allow the horse to keep contact with the bit without tightening as he stretches. At the same time, you can encourage greater activity of the hind legs by pointing the whip at the inside hind leg as it swings forward; this causes the horse to bring his back up.

When a horse stretches correctly, he stays in balance and steps through with his hind legs—falling onto the forehand *is not correct stretching*. His head and neck should not poke stiffly out and down in a straight line, nor should the underside of his neck bulge. His neck should be stretched, slightly rounded, and arched, but he should not be over-bent or behind the vertical. His hind legs should be more active, not less, and he should seek contact with the bit instead of evading it.

**Balance and transitions.** Work on the longe requires more balance than ordinary movement. Young and unschooled horses often have trouble keeping their balance on the longe line, especially at the canter. A well-balanced horse "stands up" or remains upright, bending around a circle. Leaning inward, pulling, stumbling, or breaking gait show that the horse is out of balance and possibly going too fast for the size of the circle. Fear, tension, or lack of engagement may cause a horse to rush, which further handicaps his balance. Therefore, only a well-schooled horse with good balance should be cantered on the longe.

Balance on the longe requires good engagement of the hind legs (especially the inside hind) and appropriate speed for the size of the circle. The horse must learn to bring his hind legs under him and shift his balance to the rear, so that the hind legs carry more weight instead of simply pushing it forward. This requires strength and coordination, as well as engagement, rhythm, and correct tempo.

To help a horse improve his balance on the longe, he may be fitted with side reins, adjusted correctly for his conformation and level of training. These discourage him from falling in or out with his shoulders, and act as a passive restraint on his speed. The longeing circle should be small enough to discourage excessive speed, but large enough for the horse to track correctly, find balance, and bend comfortably for his stage of training. Longe at a trot that allows the horse

Correct versus incorrect stretching down.

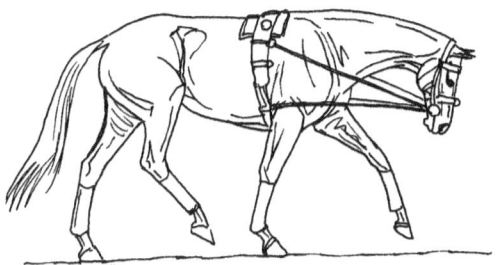

Correct stretching down: round, well engaged

Incorrect: hollow, disengaged, leaning on forehand

to find his balance—not too big, but not a shuffling jog trot—using half-halts in rhythm with the inside hind leg, until he remains upright instead of leaning or pulling.

Frequent transitions, correctly executed, will improve longitudinal balance and strengthen the hindquarters. The horse must balance and rebalance himself for each downward transition and push off with his hindquarters in each upward transition. Work on trotting for ten to twelve strides and then walk for three or four strides. Repeating these transitions in both directions serves to improve a horse's longitudinal balance, provided that the horse continues to accept the contact of the side reins. With repetition, the horse learns to stay in balance in the trot in order to be ready to walk, and to keep his engagement in the walk as he anticipates the trot transition.

Before a horse is able to canter on the longe, he must develop strong enough muscles to strike off into canter and stay in balance in canter on a circle (20 meters or larger). If he leans or travels crookedly at the trot, he is not yet ready to canter. More work on transitions, engagement, and tracking correctly on the circle will gradually develop his balance and strength. Before cantering a horse on the longe, be certain you have accurately assessed his level of training and the stability of his balance in trot.

**Suppleness, straightness, and lateral balance.** Suppleness refers to a horse's ability to shift his balance forward, backward, and laterally. It is not simply flexibility, which is the ability to bend the joints. Although a supple horse must be flexible, a horse can become too flexible and "rubbery" (especially in the neck) if he loses his forward movement or is pulled sideways.

Straightness (in longeing) refers to the horse's ability to track correctly (the hind legs following in the tracks of the front legs) on a circle. It also relates to his ability to develop impulsion and to carry weight equally with both hind legs and both front legs. Horses are not naturally symmetrical; like people, they all have one side that is naturally shortened (the *hollow side*) and one side to which it is difficult for them to bend (the *stiff side*). The hind leg on the hollow side is usually weaker, and often does not track accurately behind the foreleg on that side. The muscles of the ribs on the stiff side are less flexible, so it may cause discomfort when this side is on the outside and the horse must stretch these muscles. The horse will also have more difficulty in shortening the muscles through the rib cage when this side is on the inside. Never force a horse to bend more than he is ready and able to, especially on his stiff side.

One of the goals of training is to develop the horse as evenly as possible to overcome this natural crookedness. This requires frequent changes of direction and extra attention to the correctness of the work on the horse's weaker side or difficult direction.

Correctly adjusted side reins, longeing on a circle of appropriate size, keeping the circle round, and frequent changes of direction are all helpful in developing suppleness. (See the section "Importance of the Circle," page 223.)

Spiraling in and out on a circle is an exercise to improve lateral balance and suppleness. Starting with a 20-meter circle, the horse is brought in on a smaller circle (approximately 12 to 15 meters) by applying a direct rein repeatedly, in rhythm with the gait, while taking in the longe line a little at each stride. Longe a few times around the smaller circle, taking care to maintain the horse's rhythm, balance, and impulsion, and then send the horse gradually back out to a 20-meter circle by pointing the whip toward the girth at each stride (as the hind leg pushes off and swings forward), while letting the longe out. You may also use vertical waves of the longe line as a signal to move outward. The horse should move forward and out slightly at each stride, not outward all at once. This exercise should be practiced in both directions, with emphasis on the horse's more difficult side.

## Improving Acceptance of the Bit

Longeing can be used to educate a green horse to accept the bit or to improve a horse with problems in this area. First, make sure that the horse's mouth is comfortable. The horse should be fitted with a smooth snaffle bit with a mouthpiece that suits his mouth conformation (see Chapter 7, "Bitting, Tack, and Presentation"), a saddle or surcingle, and side reins of equal length. Make sure the bridle is properly adjusted so it does not inhibit correct flexion and relaxation of the jaw.

Sliding side reins may be helpful for horses that are tense, high-headed, or tight in the back, while horses that are overly sensitive in the mouth may do better with elastic side reins. Use a longe cavesson to avoid unintentionally interfering with the contact or pulling on his mouth.

After warming up without side reins, adjust the side reins so that the horse can make contact with the bit when the front of his face is about one hand's width in front of the vertical, with his mouth at approximately the level of the point of his shoulder. Longe at a trot with a steady, moderate tempo, and encourage the horse to take longer strides with his hind legs, without quickening or rushing. As he develops pushing power, he will stretch his back and reach out and down with his head and neck. If the side reins are correctly adjusted, the horse makes gentle contact with the bit.

It is particularly important not to over-shorten the side reins or to cause the horse to "set his head," retract his neck, or over-flex at the poll. However, side reins that are adjusted too long make it impossible for a horse to make contact with the bit while moving in good balance. In fact, some horses will be afraid of the inconsistent contact caused by excessively long side reins and fail to move forward into the contact.

Signs of progress include:

- Gently chewing the bit, a relaxation response that produces foam in the mouth.
- Stretching the neck and back, showing more roundness in the back, while continuing to reach well forward with the hind legs.
- A more steady and consistent, but not rigid, head carriage.
- Indications of relaxation, such as a rhythmically swinging tail, breathing in rhythm with the strides, and gently snorting or "blowing his nose."
- Progression in the development of balance as a result of meeting and giving to the side reins.

## Improving the Canter

For most horses, cantering on the longe is more difficult than trotting because it requires more balance, strength, and suppleness. Correct longeing can greatly improve the horse's canter work under saddle. It must be introduced gradually, however, and kept within the horse's capabilities.

Before cantering on the longe, the horse must longe well at the trot, tracking correctly and moving with good balance, impulsion, and correct bend. He must not lean or pull against the longe or travel crookedly. He may be fitted with side reins, adjusted for normal longeing (with his face about a hand's width in front of the vertical). More advanced horses can canter with shorter side reins (face nearly vertical, mouth on a level with the point of the hip), but they must be able to maintain good forward impulsion and balance in a more collected frame.

Practicing a series of transitions (trot-walk and walk-trot) improves the horse's balance and impulsion in preparation for the canter. Asking him to strike off into canter from a well-balanced walk or trot results in a better balanced canter than if he runs into it from a fast trot. The horse should strike off into canter on a circle smaller than 20 meters, then move outward, correctly bent, to canter on the larger circle. Give a clear signal that means "Canter," not a signal that could be mistaken for a command to speed up the trot. If he misses the canter depart, bring him back to balance in a well-balanced walk or trot before trying again.

Keep the circle round but large enough for good balance at the canter (at least 20 meters). You may need to revert to parallel longeing in order to make the circle large enough and to stay closer to the horse, so he is more aware of your aids. Longeing in a ring with a fence or a barrier supports your outside aids and helps to prevent the horse from pulling or falling out.

Emphasize the *jump* (suspension) in each canter stride by gesturing with your whip toward the inside hind leg as it reaches forward, but take care to not nag with the whip. The horse must respond to the whip aid and maintain his forward impulsion on his own. If the horse hollows his back or moves crookedly (counter-bent or leaning in), his power and balance will suffer, the canter becomes "flat," and it may degenerate into a four-beat canter. Too-restrictive side reins, trying to slow the canter down too much, or cantering on too small a circle for the horse's level of training can lead to this problem. (For more about canter work on the longe, see page 241.)

## Teaching a Horse to Longe

Teaching a horse to longe (whether a green or unbroken horse or a trained horse that has never been longed) requires confidence, patience, and experience in training and handling horses, as well as in longeing. You will also need a safe place to work (an enclosed ring with good footing), and an experienced assistant can also be helpful.

The early stages of longeing are of vital importance, as this is where you make your first real impressions on the horse, gain his respect, and teach obedience to the voice. This lays the foundation for future progress in the horse's training. Longeing can be a great help in developing a well-mannered horse, as well as strengthening muscles, increasing balance and impulsion, and bringing an unbroken horse into condition for riding.

## Equipment

A longe cavesson is an essential piece of equipment for control and to avoid damaging the horse's mouth, along with a 33–35-foot longe line made of cotton webbing (*not* the type with a chain end) and a longe whip. Boots or bandages are highly recommended to protect the horse's legs in case he hits himself as he is finding his balance. Later, you may need a saddle or surcingle, a snaffle bridle, and side reins.

The longer should wear gloves and a watch (to keep track of the duration of the longe work), safe footwear (boots or shoes with flat heels and without spurs, which can get caught on the longe line and trip you), and a safety helmet.

## Prerequisites

Before you can begin training a horse to longe, he must have been taught good manners during ground handling, tacking up, and so on. He must be taught to lead from both sides, and to halt, walk, and trot in response to voice commands. He should be accustomed to seeing a longe whip, and should accept being gently touched with the whip all over his body without fear.

Introduce the longeing equipment first (during grooming is a good time). Adjust the cavesson; try on boots or bandages, and let the horse see and sniff the longe whip before rubbing it gently over his neck, body, and legs. Work patiently and quietly to make it a pleasant experience. This should be repeated as often as necessary until the horse accepts the equipment with an unconcerned attitude.

Using the longe equipment, practice leading and transitions until he responds correctly to voice commands, especially halting. Be sure to work from both sides, and on a circle in both directions.

Next, practice parallel leading (leading from a distance of 4 or 5 feet, then 10 to 12 feet from the horse) on both sides. (For more about parallel leading and parallel longeing, see *the USPC C Level Manual*, pages 284–285.)

## Procedure (with Assistant)

The easiest way to begin longeing a green horse is to work with an assistant. (The assistant must be an experienced horseperson who can lead correctly and who will follow directions.) The assistant can help give the horse confidence, prevent the horse from making mistakes, and help establish control. However, one drawback is that the horse's attention may be divided between the assistant and the trainer instead of on the trainer alone.

The assistant's job is to keep the horse on the track of the circle and to assist the trainer in any way necessary to help the horse learn the aids for longeing. The assistant leads the horse from the outside of the circle, using a lead line attached to the same ring on the cavesson as the longe line. This must be done as unobtrusively as possible, without distracting the horse's attention from the trainer's signals. The assistant never speaks to the horse, but may give the horse a reward (a tidbit) when directed by the trainer. Eventually, the assistant "fades away," doing less and moving farther from the horse, until the horse is longed entirely by the trainer.

To move the horse forward, the trainer should give the voice command "Walk on" and point the whip at the horse's hocks. If necessary, repeat the command and the gesture with the whip. The assistant should move forward with the horse, keeping the lead loose; if the horse does not understand, the assistant leads him forward. When halting, the trainer should give the voice command "Whoa," step slightly forward (opposite the horse's shoulder), and quietly lower the whip tip toward the ground or, less commonly, move the whip forward so that it points to a spot in front of the horse's head. As the command "Whoa" is given, the assistant simply stops walking; if the horse continues to move, he runs against the pressure of the assistant's lead line and the longe line. By walking on the outside of the circle, the assistant can keep the horse from turning in or out. (Some horses work better with the assistant on the inside. However, it is easier for the horse to see the trainer's signals when the assistant is on the outside.)

Make your voice commands in two-syllable expressions. For example, say "Wa-alk" or "Tr-rot." Additionally, when giving commands for an upward transition, make the pitch or intonation of your voice go from a lower to higher pitch, and make commands for downward transitions go from a higher to lower pitch. Some trainers also like to use a verbal half-halt aid just before asking for a transition, usually "And" or the horse's name, also said with either a rising or lowering intonation.

Practice walking and halting at various places on the circle, with the trainer giving all voice commands and words of praise. When the horse responds consistently to voice commands without any help from the assistant, the lead line may be tied around the horse's neck, while the assistant continues to walk alongside without holding the lead. If necessary, the lead line may be used to make a correction. When the horse responds correctly, the lead line may be removed and the assistant is no longer needed.

Practice longeing at a walk, performing halt-walk transitions in both directions, both with the assistant and eventually with the assistant "fading away." Keep the training sessions short (10 to 15 minutes), to avoid going beyond the young horse's short attention span. Since the best reward is stopping work, always end the lesson with something that the horse has done well.

Once the horse learns to walk, halt, and walk forward on the circle without an assistant, he can be introduced to trotting and further longe work, as described in the following section.

## Procedure (Single Handler)

If you don't have an assistant, or if you prefer to work by yourself, you can teach a horse to longe by progressing from parallel leading to parallel longeing, and eventually to true longeing. Without the help of an assistant, it is even more important to work in an enclosed area of suitable size (ideally, a round pen or longe ring about 60 feet in diameter).

Begin by parallel leading (leading from a distance of 4 to 10 feet), walking a circle of a size that results in the horse moving on a 60-foot circle. Practice halting and walking on, using the voice commands described in the previous section. Then move out to a distance of 10 to 15 feet and switch to the position for parallel longeing. In this position, you can point or gesture with the whip more effectively to keep the horse moving forward on the 60-foot circle.

When longeing a green horse, it helps to stay slightly behind the control point to keep him moving forward.

When the horse moves forward on the circle easily for several revolutions, prepare to halt. Move forward, ahead of the control point, and quietly lower the whip or move it so that it points at a spot in front of the horse's head, as you give the command "Whoa." Keep the whip low and quiet (omit the forward whip gesture if it worries the horse). If the horse does not stop, guide him straight into the wall or a corner, so that he has to halt without turning. Walk out to the horse to reward him with a pat and perhaps a tidbit; never bring him in toward you to halt him, or he may learn to turn in whenever he wants to stop working, which is not safe because the longer loses the ability to control the hindquarters.

You can gradually let out the longe and move farther away, but you will probably need to continue parallel longeing with a shortened longe line for a while in order to stay close enough for good control. (But walk a circle that is round and large enough to keep the horse working on a 60-foot circle.)

It is important to remember that the ultimate goal is to be able to longe the horse from the center of a perfect circle, so that the trainer remains stationary in the center and pivots with the horse. To longe like this shows that you are in complete control of the horse from the ground, he is "between your aids" (the longe line and longe whip), and he has achieved sufficient training to be balanced and obedient. Ultimately, suppleness, relative straightness (correct alignment), and more advanced qualities of movement can only be achieved from longeing a horse on a perfectly round circle, which is impossible to create while moving around and parallel longeing. In addition, constant parallel longeing is similar to constantly overusing your leg aids, which can cause a horse to become dull to the leg aid. The goal is for the horse to move freely forward on the longe, as if under saddle, without constant nagging from your body position.

## Trotting

When the horse walks on and halts promptly in response to voice commands, you can introduce trotting. Give the command "Tr-rot" and point the whip toward his hocks, or give it a small shake if necessary. Repeat if necessary, and praise immediately when he trots.

Let the horse trot several times around the circle; if he is slightly tired, he will be more willing to walk when you ask him to. Give the command "Wa-alk," and move forward, slightly ahead of the control point, keeping the whip low and quiet. You can give brief, gentle "check and release" aids and/or horizontal waves with the longe line (see page 221), but try to use voice commands and body language, and avoid pulling on the longe any more than is absolutely necessary. Pulling inward too much may make the horse turn in or bend his neck sideways instead of teaching him to come back to the walk on command. If he has difficulty learning this, go back to the walk and practice until the horse halts more easily.

## Lengthening and Shortening Stride Within a Gait

The horse should be taught to lengthen and shorten stride within a gait on command. To increase the stride, use a short, sharp "cluck" or a command like "Come" or "Hup" once with each stride, while pointing the whip toward the horse's inside hock as the hind leg swings forward. To slow the gait, use a command like "Easy" or "Steady," and give short, repeated half-halt aids with the longe line in rhythm with the gait if the horse fails to respond sufficiently to your voice aid. It may also help to push the horse outward toward the corner or wall, or to move him in on a slightly smaller circle, just enough to encourage him to shorten his stride a little. Praise him immediately when he responds even a little. At first, the horse will probably slow down or speed up the tempo when asked for a change of speed. With practice and correctly timed aids, he will learn to lengthen and shorten his stride instead of simply speeding up or slowing down.

## Spiraling In and Out

A horse needs to learn how to spiral inward and outward on the longeing circle, stepping slightly sideways at each stride. Since most horses are more inclined to cut in or fall inward on their inside shoulder, spiraling out should usually be taught first. This also helps the horse learn to move on the longeing circle with better lateral balance, "standing up" instead of leaning inward. It will also be useful when you are ready to develop canter departs on the longe.

To teach a horse to move outward, start by using your body language to push him out. Shorten the longe line very slightly and step toward the horse with a determined posture, giving the voice command "Out." If the horse fails to respond, you can create vertical waves in the longe line as you point the whip toward the horse's shoulder. When the horse moves outward with his shoulder, relax your posture, quiet the longe line, and praise him. Practice at a walk (in both directions) until he responds consistently, then practice in a trot.

Spiraling inward is usually easier. When the horse is working steadily at a walk or trot on a 60-foot circle, give half-halts on the longe line in rhythm with his gait. As he shortens his stride, gradually shorten the longe line so he comes in to a slightly smaller circle. Be careful not to pull too hard or pull his head and neck inward, or he may over-bend to the inside, lean inward, or stop and turn to face you. Horses that are inclined to over-bend or turn their head to the inside may do better with side reins, or with one outside side rein.

Practice spiraling in and out, gradually enlarging and reducing the circle, to help improve your horse's balance and responsiveness. The horse will need extra work spiraling in and out on his stiff side.

## Cantering on the Longe

Don't try to canter a green horse on the longe until he is working well at the trot (see the section "Improving the Canter," page 236).

To ask for a canter, shorten the longe and temporarily bring the horse onto a smaller circle, while establishing a balanced trot. Remain standing still and ask the horse for the transition to canter. Walking with the horse teaches poor canter departs because the horse is allowed to drift through the outside shoulder; however, occasionally you may need to take a step toward the horse with a strong posture to reinforce your canter transition aids while maintaining contact with the longe line. Give the voice command "Can-ter" and make a circular gesture with the whip, moving it forward and upward toward his stifle. As he begins to canter, encourage him to move outward onto a 20-meter circle, or a somewhat larger circle if necessary. Praise him immediately if he canters, and encourage him to keep cantering, even if only for a few strides.

If the horse has difficulty taking the canter, do not try to drive him into a canter by making him trot faster. This produces a rushing, unbalanced trot from which it is almost impossible to canter correctly.

One way to overcome this problem is to longe the horse over a single ground pole or a small jump. This often causes him to land cantering on the correct lead. As he canters on, shift the circle slightly, to avoid jumping the obstacle again.

Cantering on one lead is a sign of one-sidedness. Cantering on the wrong lead is usually a sign of poor balance. It also may be caused by the trainer pulling the horse's head inward as he begins the canter, or allowing the horse to drift through his outside shoulder as he moves into the canter. The horse often requires more suppling work at the trot in his difficult direction in order to improve his ability to strike off on the correct lead. If caused by a momentary lapse of balance or a mistaken signal, bring the horse back to a better balanced trot and try again. Do not allow him to continue on the wrong lead. Do not try to make him change leads without first bringing him back to a balanced trot.

Cantering disunited (on one lead in the front legs and the other in the hind legs) often happens when a horse is too much on the forehand or when his head is pulled inward. As his hind legs swing to the outside, he is likely to go disunited. (This can also happen when a horse tries to execute a flying change and fails.) A disunited horse should be brought back to the trot and rebalanced before cantering again. He needs more work on tracking correctly, and on "standing up" (remaining vertical and bending) instead of leaning inward. Enlarging the longeing circle may help.

## Handling Longeing Problems

**Longeing away from home.** You may need to longe a horse to settle him in a strange place or before a competition. Before you can longe safely away from home, your horse *must* be well schooled at home, and you should be able to longe him safely in the open. At a competition, clinic, or rally, there may be very little safe space in which to longe. Sometimes the only available space is not level. Use good judgment about where you longe and whether longeing is feasible at all, given the footing and conditions. Do not monopolize the schooling area or longe in an area that is too busy to be safe, or where your longeing will be in the way of other riders warming up. You may have to longe in a smaller circle than usual (if so, do less than usual, because the work is harder for your horse), or in the open.

Especially in the open, keep the work slow and emphasize steady rhythm, stretching, and quiet obedience. Keep his attention on you by timely use of transitions, voice commands, longe line, and whip, and watch for signs of relaxation and loosening up (chewing the bit, blowing his nose, and stretching his neck and back). Discourage bucking and playing.

Don't overdo longeing, especially when warming up for a competition.

**Disobediences.** If a horse bucks or bolts, place one foot in front of you, bend your knees, and keep your shoulders back. Use short, strong half-halts and firm voice commands. A horse that kicks should be corrected with a sharp, displeased voice and a swift upward jerk on the longe line.

A horse whose obedience is questionable should always be longed in an enclosed ring, with no riders present. Don't allow him to drag you around! If a horse is too strong for you to hold, let him go rather than take chances with your safety or his. It may be necessary to change the equipment, such as adding side reins.

**Evasions.** A horse that does not go forward and a horse that comes in on the circle (often practiced simultaneously) is evading your control and the work of longeing. Use the command "Out" and point or shake the whip at his shoulder, as you step forward on the line of the whip, then drive him forward from behind. Increasing or decreasing the size of the circle for one round may also help.

A more serious type of evasion is turning the head in and swinging the quarters out, swinging around to face the trainer, or even whirling around to change direction. These horses may be green, spoiled, or extremely one-sided.

This type of evasion is more common when a horse is worked without side reins, which is a good reason for using them. He should be fitted with correctly adjusted side reins, with the outside side rein short enough to discourage him from bending his neck too much and popping his outside shoulder out. Send him forward strongly, so that he cannot shorten stride, hesitate, or stop. In difficult cases, using the double longe may be helpful.

If the horse succeeds in stopping, facing you, or begins backing away, follow him while maintaining contact until he is stopped by reaching a wall or other barrier, and then step back, opposite his hindquarters, and send him forward. You may need to temporarily shorten the longe, move closer to him, and move in a circle (parallel longeing) until he moves willingly forward on the longeing circle without stopping. Horses usually try this evasion in the same spot, so be aware of any signs of hesitation or shortening stride as he approaches that point and send him forward if you notice him sucking back. Be careful not to get ahead of the control point, which can provoke this behavior.

Some horses stop and whirl around, especially after changing directions or when longed in their difficult direction. Stop the horse and reposition him (lead his head around until he is facing in the correct direction), and then send him forward. This action must be taken promptly and firmly, but not roughly. Avoid "rewarding" the horse with a rest or a release of pressure until he is moving forward again in the correct direction. A horse with this problem should be longed in a longeing ring or round pen, if possible. Some horses do better with side reins or a single side rein on the outside, or with a double longe. Going back to basics, such as longeing with an assistant on the outside, may be necessary with a green or spoiled horse.

**Stubborn horse.** When longeing a calm but stubborn horse (one that refuses to move forward, frequently stops, or has no respect for the whip), stop and analyze the situation. Make sure there is nothing nearby that is distracting or worrying the horse. Have an assistant stand as the pivot point while you go out toward the horse and hold the longe line and parallel longes. This allows you to motivate the horse sharply without "chasing" the horse around or compromising the circle. If there is no assistant available, work the horse with parallel longeing, but only as briefly as necessary so that you do not "nag" the horse to go forward with your body language. Use the whip close enough to his hocks to make him respect it and move forward. Stay close enough to reach the horse with the whip, even if you have to walk a large circle.

In order for your training tactics to be successful, the horse must eventually move forward and out onto a full-size longeing circle, without continuing parallel longeing indefinitely. To motivate a stubborn horse to move forward without compromising your longeing position, you will need a longe whip that is long enough to reach him even when he is out on a 20-meter circle. A standard longe whip can be lengthened by tying a 6-foot braided bootlace to the end of the lash.

When motivating a stubborn horse, the longe whip should be used in a manner similar to the way you would use artificial aids when riding a horse of this type—give a command and reinforce with the whip promptly, firmly, and appropriately, but never in a nagging manner.

If nothing else works, try having an experienced rider ride the horse on the longe line, applying leg aids each time you give a voice command.

**Lazy horse.** A lazy horse avoids the work of longeing (and therefore, its benefits) by putting forth the least effort he can get away with. It is all too easy to fall into a pattern of nagging, so that you do more and work harder while the horse pays even less attention to you. Instead, insist on a prompt response to your aids by using the whip immediately when he fails to respond, as sharply as necessary to command his attention and awaken his energy. Shorten the longe line and momentarily walk a circle closer to him so that you can reach him with the whip. It may be necessary to hit him once across the back of the rump, hard enough to make him respect the whip. As with a stubborn horse, do not fall into the habit of constant parallel longeing, as this will desensitize the horse and foil your attempts to motivate him. Lazy horses do better when kept busy with frequent transitions and different exercises, using brief sessions that end as soon as the horse is responding appropriately to your aids.

**Bored horse.** Horses easily become bored with longeing because of the repetitive nature of the work. A horse that suddenly becomes uncooperative may be bored. Keep longeing sessions short; keep the horse's attention by varying gaits, making frequent transitions, changing directions, and spiraling in or out. Longeing over a single ground pole can also restore a horse's interest. Try longeing in different locations, and avoid a fixed routine.

**The horse that won't stop.** Some horses do not halt well on the longe and will continue forward instead of responding to "Whoa." They may be strong, rushing, nervous, stubborn, or may not know how to respond to half-halts and the "Whoa" command.

Give firm half-halts (even short, sharp tugs) on the longe line to slow and rebalance his gait before asking him to halt. It may be necessary to shorten the longe line and bring him in on a smaller circle to get his attention, or as with a rushing horse, it may be necessary to use a "body block" or direct him into a fence, wall, or corner (which must be too high to jump), giving a voice command to halt just before he is forced to stop.

This horse should go back to work in hand or longeing basics, possibly with an assistant leading from the outside, to make sure he understands that he must stop when he hears "Whoa."

**Falling in.** The horse, especially when longeing to his stiff side, counter-bends and falls in on the circle, putting slack in the longe line. He may be going too fast (*running gaits*), *counter-bending* (head to the outside), or trying to evade work by cutting in on the circle. If a horse is rushing, he must first be slowed down and brought back to a slower and steadier speed and tempo. To correct this, you must establish the contact in order to apply half-halts with the longe line. Shorten the line (even if the circle becomes momentarily smaller or you must temporarily go back to parallel longeing) and send the horse firmly forward and out by pointing or shaking the longe whip toward his shoulder. Once the contact is re-established, apply firm half-halts to regulate the speed and ask the horse to bend as you continue to ask him to move outward on the circle. The horse should have extra practice in spiraling out and responding to whip and longe line aids asking him to move outward. Adjusting the outside side rein slightly shorter may also help (see page 214).

**One-sided horse.** If a horse longes well in one direction but consistently resists in the other, treat him as though he were a green horse. When longeing in his difficult direction, ask for only a little work at a time. When he becomes more comfortable longeing in his difficult direction, he should be worked *slightly* longer on that side to achieve equal suppleness on both sides.

A one-sided horse should be checked by a veterinarian to determine whether lameness, soreness, or faulty vision in one eye might be the cause of his difficulty.

**Frightened or difficult horse.** Do not attempt to longe a really frightened or extremely difficult horse. If a longeing session degenerates into a rodeo performance, the danger of injury to both you and the horse is too great, and the horse will learn nothing of value.

**Problems caused by handler.** Many longeing problems are caused by the handler's mistakes or lack of skill. In these cases, the solution is to improve yourself. Some common handler errors are:

- Not teaching control, as in "Whoa" or "Halt," first.
- Nagging (especially with constant parallel longeing).
- Incorrect technique with longe or whip.
- Dwelling too long on one thing or exercise.
- Poor timing; misreading the horse.

Proper longeing skills allow the longer to effectively train the horse through work on the longe. When longeing, safety is of the utmost importance and should never be compromised. An ongoing assessment of the horse's gaits, his level of acceptance of the contact, and his desire to move freely forward with a clear rhythm and steady tempo is necessary to achieve success. When used with correctly fitted equipment and proper technique, longeing gives the trainer another tool for developing the horse to his fullest potential.

# 7

# Bitting, Tack, and Presentation

This chapter covers bits and bitting; tack and miscellaneous equipment; and the care, storage, and temporary adjustment of tack. You can find more information about tack (types of tack, tack care, condition and safety, fitting to horse and rider, and selection) in the *USPC D Level Manual* (pages 150–154 and 258–297) and in the *USPC C Level Manual* (pages 149–165 and 308–311).

C Level Pony Club members and up are expected to be able to prepare and present themselves, their tack, and their horses correctly for formal and informal occasions. The details of formal and informal attire and turnout inspection are covered in the *USPC D* and *C Level Manuals*.

# Bits and Bitting

Modern humane bits are designed to influence and control horses using pressure, not pain. However, any bit can cause pain and damage the horse's training if it is used or fitted incorrectly, especially in the hands of a rider trying to ride a horse in activities beyond her level. There is a wide variety of bits designed for different purposes, ranging from mild to severe in their effects.

## Pressure Points

Bits and control devices (such as hackamores) work on specific pressure points on the horse's head. There are internal pressure points (those inside the mouth) and external pressure points (those on the horse's head). Pressure on different points has specific effects:

### Internal Pressure Points

| Pressure Point | Characteristic Effects |
| --- | --- |
| Tongue | Encourages flexion and yielding of the jaw, chewing and activation of salivary glands, producing foam. The tongue cushions the effect of the bit on the bars. The edges of the tongue are more sensitive than the center. Some horses have extremely thick, sensitive, or scarred tongues and cannot tolerate excessive tongue pressure. |
| Bars (bones of lower jaw, in the interdental space) | Encourages flexion, yielding of the jaw, flexion at the poll, and lowering the head. The bars may be wide and flat (less sensitive) or sharp and thin (more sensitive). The bars become thinner and sharper lower in the mouth. Excessive pressure on the bars can result in bone spurs. |
| Corners of the lips | The skin is flexible and less sensitive than the tongue and bars. Pressure here encourages the horse to extend his head and neck, and sometimes raise his head. |
| Roof of the mouth (palate) | Less sensitive than the bars but very soft. Palate structure varies greatly and the bit must not create excessive pressure. Too much pressure here tends to encourage the horse to open his mouth, tuck his chin into his chest, or put his tongue over the bit. When the port of a curb bit touches the roof of the mouth, it acts as a fulcrum, causing the cannons of the bit to press more strongly against the bars. |

| External Pressure Points | Characteristic Effects |
| --- | --- |
| Chin/curb groove (under the chin) | Pressure on this spot alone tends to cause the horse to raise his head. When applied by a curb chain in conjunction with a curb bit, it acts as a fulcrum, creating more pressure on the bars. |
| Sides of jaws | Lateral pressure here exerts a guiding effect, encouraging the horse to turn his head to the left or right. Pressure against the cheek teeth can be painful, especially in young horses that are cutting teeth. |
| Bridge of nose | Pressure encourages horse to flex at the poll. The point where the nasal bone and cartilage meet is especially sensitive to pressure. Nosebands placed too low can interfere with breathing, so care must be taken to fit the noseband above the nasal folds. |
| Poll | Poll pressure encourages the horse to lower his head. Poll pressure by itself is not significant unless combined with the pressure of a curb, gag, pelham, Kimberwicke, or some snaffles such as the hanging cheek (Baucher) snaffle. When using bitless bridles or hackamores, poll can be combined with other head pressure points to encourage lowering of the head. |

# Severity of Bits

The severity of a bit depends on the following factors:

| Factor | Explanation |
| --- | --- |
| Direct pressure or leverage | Direct-pressure bits apply the same degree of pressure in the mouth as that applied to the reins. Leverage bits multiply the pressure. Length of shank, tightness of curb chain, and ratio of upper shank to lower shank affect leverage and hence, severity. |
| Shape of mouthpiece | Smooth, flexible mouthpieces that conform to the shape of the mouth are milder than rigid, angular mouthpieces or those shaped to concentrate pressure on a particular portion of the mouth. |
| Thickness of mouthpiece | Thicker mouthpieces distribute pressure over a wider area; thin mouthpieces concentrate it. |
| Surface of mouthpiece | Smooth or soft mouthpieces are milder; twisted, serrated, or sharp-edged mouthpieces are more severe. |
| Pinching effect | Jointed bits (especially those with long cannons) have a pinching effect on the mouth. |
| Auxiliary devices | Dropped, crossed, or flash nosebands and control devices (such as martingales) make the effect of the bit more severe by limiting the horse's options (such as opening his mouth or raising his head). Some (such as draw reins and running martingales) act directly on the bit and change its effect. |

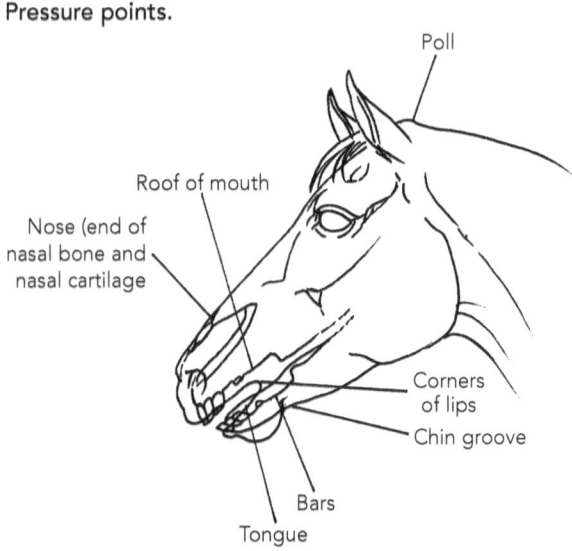

Pressure points.

Any bit used to provide control in USPC activities must do so without causing pain or injury to the horse. It is important to remember that *any* bit can be severe if used severely or fitted improperly.

## Mouthpiece Materials

Mouthpieces may be made of or covered in metal, rubber, hard rubber, leather, or synthetic materials. Different materials can have different effects on a horse's mouth. Mouthpieces may be made of or covered in metal, rubber, hard rubber or vulcanite, or leather; or synthetic materials such as nylon, plastic, Nathe, or Happy Mouth™. Some materials are soft or hard and warm or cold. Their taste can be sweet, flavored, or neutral. Softer materials are milder in effect, but some horses prefer or dislike certain materials:

- Rubber is soft and gentle on the bars and tongue. It usually has a metal or nylon core. Vulcanized rubber is a hard rubber coating, which is baked onto the mouthpiece. This process makes the rubber stronger and less prone to flaking than non-vulcanized rubber.
- High-tech plastics, used in brands such as Nathe and Happy Mouth™ bits, are also soft and flexible. Some have an apple flavor or scent added to encourage acceptance.
- Stainless steel is long lasting, smooth, and easy to keep clean. It is usually very shiny.
- Copper is believed to stimulate the flow of saliva, either with a completely copper mouthpiece or with copper inserts or rollers. (However,

acceptance of the bit and correct flexion at the poll are better ways to stimulate the flow of saliva.) The term "sweet" refers to the action caused by copper in the metal that causes the horse to salivate due to the taste. "Sweet iron" is a mixture of copper and iron.

- Nickel silver is inexpensive, but is weaker than stainless steel. It can break, chip, and develop rough edges easily.
- German silver is a composition of copper, zinc, and nickel, which is intended to stimulate salivation. It is generally heavier than other metal bits and has a brassy color.
- Aurigan silver is an alloy, which is 85 percent copper 15 percent zinc and silicon, which makes it 100 percent nickel-free. It causes horses to salivate, has a distinctive sweet taste, and is a light brass color.
- Titanium is strong, extremely light, resistant to pitting, and nonmagnetic. It also encourages salivation and can be produced in various colors.
- Aluminum is lightweight and easy to maintain, but wears out quickly. It has a drying effect on the mouth and may cause discomfort for the horse.
- Leather (rare today) and latex wrapping are sometimes used to cover a mouthpiece, decreasing the severity of the bit. Both are easily damaged and difficult to keep clean and disinfected, and should be replaced often.

## Selecting a Bit

Every discipline has rules regarding which bits are legal (permitted under the rules) and which are not. Check the current USPC discipline Rule Books for acceptable bits for each discipline.

When selecting a bit, you should consider the following:

- Use the least severe bit possible.
- The horse's age, experience, and level of training.
- The rider's skills and experience.
- The discipline and activity, and the level at which the horse is competing or being ridden in that activity.
- The horse's mouth conformation, including size and shape of lips, tongue, and bars, the height of the horse's palate and any injuries or peculiarities of the mouth. A horse with sharp bars and thin skin usually needs a softer bit than a horse with wide, flat bars and thick skin. Thick mouthpieces may be uncomfortable for horses with small, shallow mouths. A horse with a thick, scarred, or sensitive tongue may need a mouthpiece that relieves the tongue from excessive pressure. Therefore, every time a new bit is tried, it is important to check the fit and comfort of that bit for the individual horse.

- The size and proper fit of the bit. A snaffle bit should have ⅛ to ¼ inch of space outside the lips; a pelham, Kimberwicke, or curb should have ¼ inch on both sides of the mouth. A too-narrow bit may pinch the lips and cause abrasions. Snaffles that are too wide have a severe nutcracker action, and the center joint may hit the roof of the mouth. Curbs that are too wide tend to rock and bear unevenly on the bars, which can cause the horse to tilt his head. (For correct fitting of bits, see the *USPC D Level Manual*, page 284.)
- The horse's temperament and response to the bit, including any problems (getting behind the bit, above the bit, and so on), and his preference for a particular bit or mouthpiece material.

In addition, keep in mind any factors that may require stronger bitting for safe control, such as doing fast work, riding outside in a group, cross-country jumping, or foxhunting. When bitting a strong horse or a horse that pulls, remember that horses tend to pull against or run away from pain. Often a milder bit (sometimes in conjunction with a martingale or some variety of dropped noseband) gets better results than a more severe bit.

## Measuring, Sizing, and Buying a Bit

To determine the correct size bit for your horse, you can use a piece of string or a ½-inch dowel stick about 12 inches (30 cm) long. Tie a knot about 2 inches (5 cm) in on the string or mark the dowel with a permanent marker. Put the string or dowel in your horse's mouth, with the knot or mark against the lips on one side. Mark the opposite side with a marker or little piece of tape. Measure this with a tape measure and write down the measurement.

The height of the palate is important for selecting bit width. Palate height is approximated by the distance between your horse's upper and lower jaws at the level of the corners of the lips. This should be measured on each side, as they can be different. A horse with a low palate or shorter distance between his upper and lower jaws may find a thick bit uncomfortable. Your vet can help safely measure this distance when she floats your horse's teeth. In adult horses, the average diameter space is 27.4 mm and in adult ponies it is 24.9 mm.

Take a tape measure and your horse's mouth measurements along when you go out to buy a bit or look for one online. Regardless of the bit you choose, it should sit in the middle to upper third of the interdental space, both with and without rein tension. A bit that sits too high may cause increased pressure at the corners of the lips, and if it sits too low, the horse has an increased tendency to lift the bit with his tongue or it may strike the canine teeth.

# Types of Bits

## Direct-Pressure, Non-Leverage Bits (Snaffles)

A non-leverage bit applies the same amount of pressure to the mouth as is applied to the reins. A direct-pressure bit has the reins fastened directly to the mouthpiece or noseband, making it easy to use the bit in a lateral direction without tilting it or distorting its effect.

A snaffle bit is a direct-pressure, non-leverage bit that consists of two rings connected by a mouthpiece. (**Note:** A snaffle bit may or may not have a jointed mouthpiece, and a bit with a jointed mouthpiece is not necessarily a snaffle.)

Types of snaffle rings include:

- **Loose ring.** Allows the mouthpiece to slip around the ring and rotate freely, encouraging the horse to relax his jaw, chew the bit, and make foamy saliva. If the holes are large, loose rings may pinch the corners of the lips.
- **Egg butt (barrel head).** Extended joint prevents pinching of the lips. Bit is more stable in the mouth and rotates less freely than loose ring.
- **Dee ring (racing).** Joint extended to upper ends of the "dee." Non-pinching, but tends to fix the bit in the mouth. The sides of the dee have a lateral guiding effect when used for turns.

Snaffle bit ring.

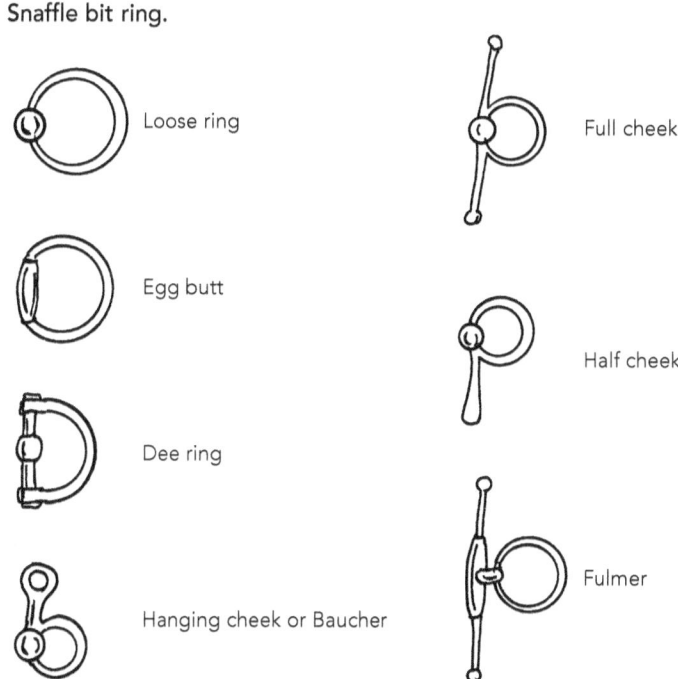

**Full cheek.** Cheeks extend up and down from mouthpiece, preventing the bit from slipping sideways through the mouth and exerting lateral control for turns. For safety, "keepers" may be used, which make it less easy for the horse to catch the upper cheekpieces of the bit on an obstruction. If used, they fix the bit in the mouth and tend to concentrate pressure on the bars and tongue. If keepers are used on a full cheek snaffle, the bit should be placed slightly lower in the horse's mouth.

**Half cheek.** Has upper or lower cheeks only. Its effect is similar to that of full cheeks; lower cheek bits are used in driving and racing bridles to prevent cheeks from becoming caught on the harness or starting gate. Upper cheek bits (with or without keepers) are permitted in dressage.

**Hanging cheek (Baucher).** Snaffle ring with upper cheek and bridle ring. Tends to fix the bit in the mouth, concentrating pressure on the bars. Sometimes used as preparation for a curb.

**Fulmer.** Full cheek with loose ring. Permits more free play than conventional full cheek, but has lateral guiding effect.

## Snaffle Mouthpieces

**Single-jointed, standard weight.** The most common type; acts on tongue, lips, and bars with "nutcracker" action. Mild to moderate.

**Thick (hollow mouth, German).** Usually single-jointed; spreads pressure over a wider surface. Some horses have small mouths that cannot accommodate an extra-thick bit. Mild.

**Double-jointed (French mouth).** Has smooth, "bone-shaped" center link. Lies flat on tongue; reduces pinching effect; flexibility makes it milder and encourages chewing and jaw relaxation. Mild.

**Dr. Bristol.** Double-jointed like French snaffle, but has a flat rectangular plate instead of a rounded center link. The bit should be placed so that the plate lies flat on the tongue; if put in backward, the edge of the plate lies against the tongue, creating severe pressure. Its effect is similar to that of French snaffle, but with more tongue pressure.

**Mullen mouth (half-moon, bar snaffle).** Unjointed, solid mouthpiece with slight curve. Places pressure on tongue and bars across width of bit. Some horses tend to lean against a solid mouthpiece. Mild.

**Roller (roller mouth, single roller, cherry roller, magenis).** Rollers encourage chewing, activation of tongue, and relaxation of jaw, especially in horses inclined to stiffen the jaw. Sometimes used to pacify a nervous horse.

Snaffle mouthpieces.

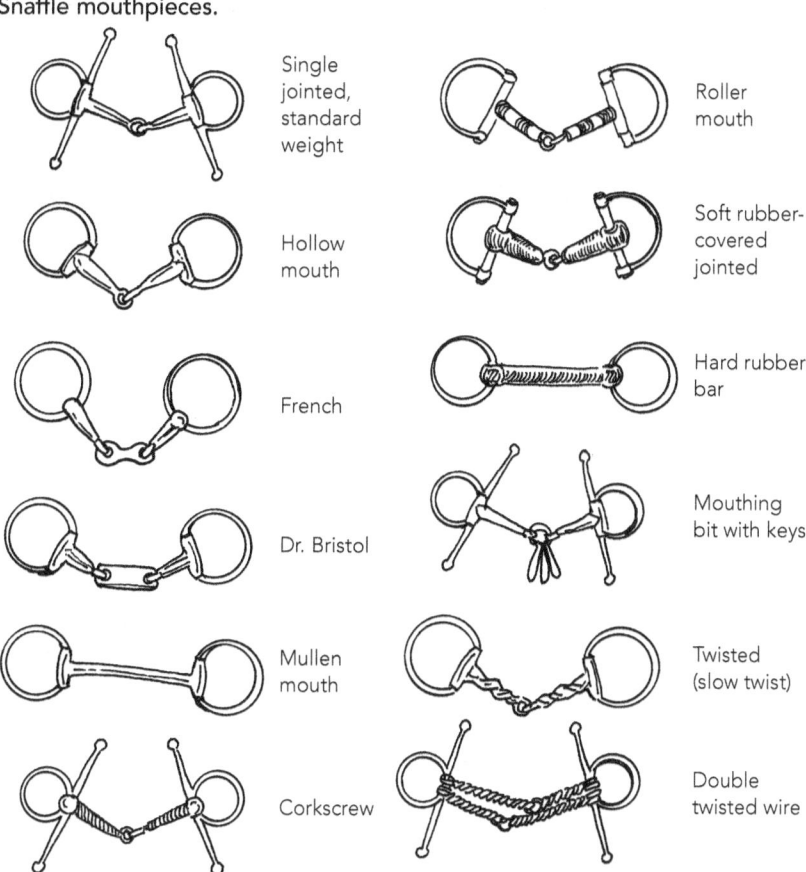

Rotating. The two arms of the mouthpiece meet within a central barrel that allows a swiveling motion but does not permit any nutcracker action. The central barrel allows independent side movement of each side of the mouthpiece. Rotating bits have less rotational movement than other bits with increased rein tension. Pinching of the tongue or protrusion toward the palate is avoided. There are different port heights; the higher the port, the more tongue relief is provided. The height of the horse's palate should be taken into account when choosing a port height. Myler bits (one type of rotating bit) generally sit higher in the horse's mouth, so care should be taken that they are not too close to the second premolars.

Waterford. Made up of five to nine linked pieces that act as a chain in the mouth. Due to the many joints, the waterford has many bumps, which can act as pressure points. The idea is that its great flexibility will discourage the horse from leaning on it. Used primarily on strong horses.

**Mouthing bit (key bit).** Has keys that dangle from a center link. The keys lie on the tongue, encouraging the horse to mouth and play with the bit and relax his jaw. Used to introduce young horses to the bit.

**Twisted (slow twist).** Edges create clearly defined pressure for a stronger effect. Severe.

**Corkscrew (serrated).** Many sharply twisted edges create a serrated mouthpiece that acts strongly on bars, tongue, and corners of lips. Severe.

**Twisted wire (single or double).** Thin mouthpiece and edges of twisted wire concentrate the pressure for a severe, abrasive effect. A double twisted wire mouthpiece has offset angles that act severely on tongue, bars, and corners of mouth. Severe.

**Double mouth ("W" or "Y" mouth).** Double mouthpiece with offset joints creates sharp angles, which act strongly on bars, tongue, and corners of mouth. Severe.

There are many other special types of bits and mouthpieces designed for special purposes or specific mouth problems. The use of severe bits by Pony Club members of any level is strongly discouraged, even if a particular horse sport allows them.

## Leverage Bits (Curbs)

Leverage bits multiply the pressure applied to the mouth (that is, 1 or 2 ounces of pressure on the reins creates several ounces of pressure in the mouth.

A **curb bit** is a type of leverage bit that uses lever action to engage a curb chain or curb strap. Curb bits multiply the pressure applied to the mouth by means of the shank and the curb chain. An upper shank that is 1 inch long above the mouthpiece and 3 inches below the mouthpiece equals a 3:1 ratio (for example, 1 pound of rein pressure equals 3 pounds of pressure in the horse's mouth). Curb bits are usually used with a snaffle rein or a snaffle bit (as in a double bridle), as when used alone they tend to produce over-bending or over-flexion at the poll.

Curb bits, pelhams, and Kimberwickes are the most commonly used leverage bits, although there are also gag bits and certain other combination bits and hackamores that employ leverage.

The parts of a curb bit and their functions are:

**Shanks.** Side pieces that form the lever arm of the curb, having a ring for the bridle at the top and for the rein at the bottom. The leverage (and severity) increases with the length of shank and ratio of upper shank to lower shank. A longer lower shank in relation to upper

Parts of curb bit.

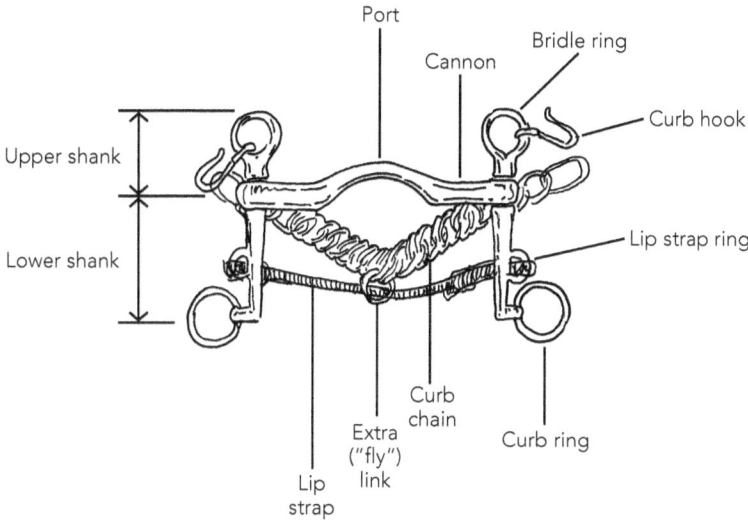

shank increases the leverage and the pressure on the curb groove and bars. A longer upper shank has less leverage and mouth pressure, but increases the pressure on the poll.

The length of shank varies from very short shanks ("Tom Thumb") of 2 inches or so to long shanks (5 inches or longer). Most shanks are 4 inches or less.

**Mouthpiece.** Applies most pressure to the bars of the mouth through the cannons. Some include a port (a raised center portion). Curb bits may have a solid, swivel, or sliding mouthpiece. Swivel shanks and sliding mouthpieces provide more looseness and flexibility and may encourage some horses to chew the bit and relax their jaws.

Curb mouthpieces include:

- *Mullen mouth (half-moon):* Distributes pressure evenly across tongue and bars.
- *Low to medium port:* Puts most pressure on bars; port provides some tongue relief.
- *High port:* Port provides tongue relief; concentrates pressure on bars. High ports may touch the roof of the mouth, acting as a fulcrum that increases the pressure on the lower bars.
- *Jointed:* Breaks at center joint with strong "nutcracker" effect, squeezing sideways on bars. (Not to be confused with snaffle bits, which do not have leverage.)

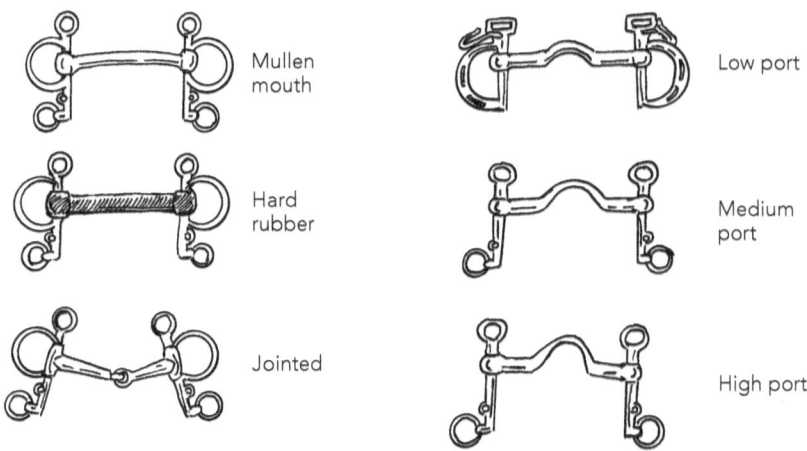

Mullen mouth

Low port

Hard rubber

Medium port

Jointed

High port

**Curb chain (or curb strap).** Attached to the upper shanks (usually by curb hooks), passes under the curb groove at the back of the chin. Acts as a fulcrum for the lever arm of the curb bit. The curb chain must be smooth, flat, and correctly adjusted for the bit to work properly.

**Lip strap.** A small strap attached to the lower shanks, passing through the extra link of the curb chain. It prevents the horse from reaching back with his lip to grab the shank of the bit, and keeps the curb chain from being lost when it is unfastened.

## Adjustment of Curbs and Pelhams

Curb bits (including pelhams and related bits) must be adjusted correctly in order to work as they are designed to do. They should rest in or near the corners of the mouth, without a wrinkle. The bars are thinner and sharper lower down, so placing a curb lower in the mouth makes its effect more severe.

The curb chain must lie flat against the curb groove, and should be adjusted so that the bit rotates 45 degrees to tighten it against the jaw. If adjusted tighter, the curb "grabs" and acts too severely with very little pressure. If too loose, the bit "falls through" with insufficient pressure and the curb chain may pinch the corners of the lips. On a pelham bit, the curb chain is sometimes run through the snaffle ring before being hooked to the curb hook. This prevents it from pinching the corners of the lips, but it somewhat inhibits the ability of the snaffle ring to swivel laterally.

A lip strap is buckled through the extra link ("fly" link) of the curb chain, snugly enough to prevent the horse from reaching back with his lip to grab the shank of the bit.

Adjustment of curb and pelham bits.

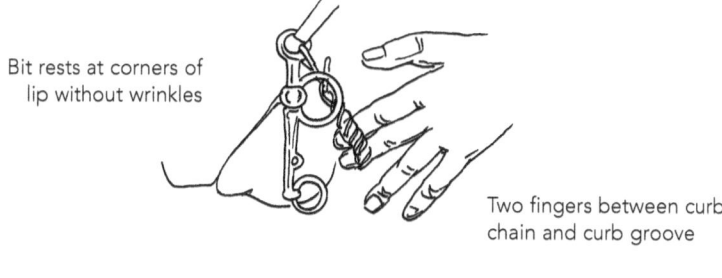

Bit rests at corners of lip without wrinkles

Two fingers between curb chain and curb groove

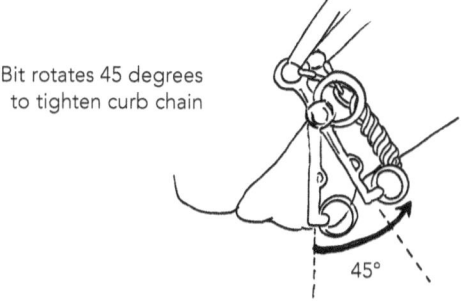

Bit rotates 45 degrees to tighten curb chain

45°

## Double Bridle (Weymouth)

A curb bit is almost never used alone. It is combined with a *bradoon* to make a double (or Weymouth) bridle. The bradoon has smaller rings than a regular snaffle (a maximum of 8 cm in diameter) and is placed above the curb bit and curb chain. Snaffle reins are wider than curb reins, which makes it easier to identify the reins by feel.

In a double bridle, the bradoon is placed high against the corners of the lips, creating one or two wrinkles. The curb bit and curb chain are placed below it. The bradoon must not drop low enough to become caught under the mouthpiece of the curb, which would be extremely uncomfortable.

## Combination Bits (Pelhams and Kimberwickes)

Several types of bits are a compromise between the action of a snaffle and the effects of a curb bit. They include pelhams and Kimberwickes (or Kimblewickes). A pelham has curb shanks equipped with upper (snaffle) rings at the mouthpiece and double reins. As in a double bridle, the snaffle rein is slightly wider than the curb rein.

Pelhams and Kimberwickes come in a variety of mouthpieces; the most common include half-moon (Mullen mouth); low, medium, and high ports; and jointed mouthpieces. The length of shank varies from very short shanks ("Tom Thumb") of 2 inches or so to 5 inches or longer.

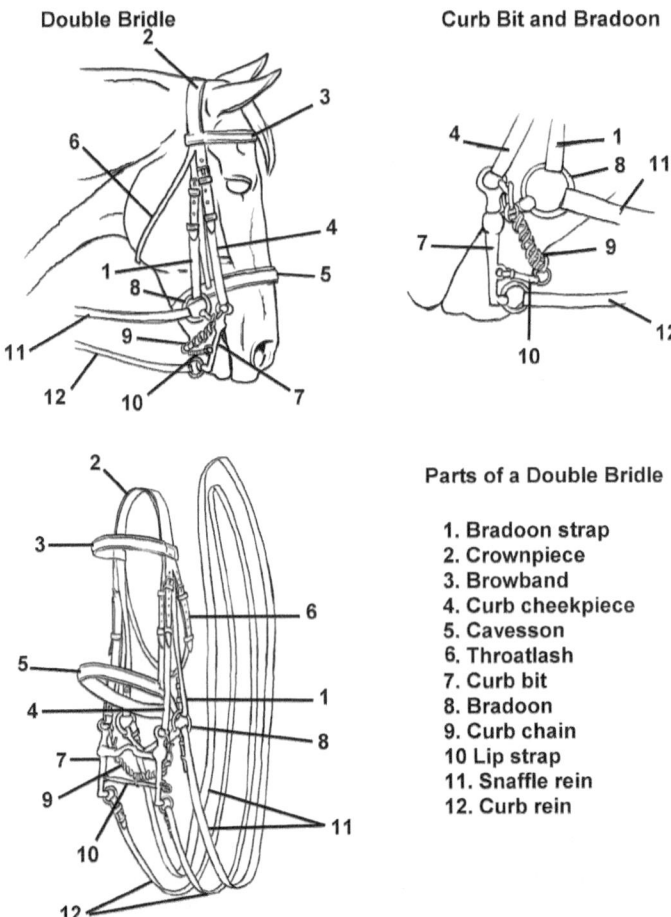

**Parts of a Double Bridle**

1. Bradoon strap
2. Crownpiece
3. Browband
4. Curb cheekpiece
5. Cavesson
6. Throatlash
7. Curb bit
8. Bradoon
9. Curb chain
10 Lip strap
11. Snaffle rein
12. Curb rein

When riding with a pelham, the snaffle rein is normally carried on the outside and underneath the fourth finger; the curb rein is carried inside the snaffle and lies between the ring finger and the fourth finger.

The snaffle rein should be slightly shorter, while the curb rein maintains a lighter contact. This allows the snaffle to act first and protects the horse from accidental overuse of the curb. If equal pressure is applied to both reins (snaffle and curb) at once, each prevents the other from acting with a clear curb or snaffle effect, resulting in an indistinct general pressure.

When a pelham is used with a single rein and a bit converter, also known as roundings (short, rounded leather straps connecting the curb and snaffle rings on each side, to which a rein is attached), the effect is neither clearly curb nor snaffle. This is acceptable for relatively simple activities, but not for control or schooling beyond a very basic level. Riders above the beginner level who need to use a pelham should learn to use double reins correctly.

A Kimberwicke has dee-shaped rings without a shank and a single rein. The Uxeter Kimberwicke has slots in the rings that fix the rein in position, creating a stronger curb effect than when the rein slides freely around the ring. When the rein slides freely around the ring, the curb effect is minimal and the bit acts more like a snaffle.

Pelhams and Kimberwickes and their adjustment are described in the *USPC D Level Manual*, pages 284–286.

## Gag Bits

Gag bits are related to snaffles, but employ leverage for increased severity. They concentrate pressure simultaneously on the corners of the lips and the poll, raising the horse's head to avoid the pressure.

Most gag bits can (and should) be equipped with double reins: a snaffle rein, which allows the bit to be used as an ordinary snaffle; and a gag rein, which is only brought into play when necessary.

Gag bits are severe; they are most often used to retrain spoiled horses or to manage strong pullers in speed events such as polo, cross-country jumping, or show jumping. They should only be used by experienced riders.

Types of gag bits include the following:

- **Gag snaffle.** Resembles a snaffle bit with rings inserted in the top and bottom of each snaffle ring. Special cheekpieces made of rounded leather or rope pass through these rings, terminating in a ring for the reins. When pressure is applied, the bit rotates and slides upward, causing strong pressure simultaneously on the corners of the mouth and the poll.
- **Elevator bit.** A variety of gag bit, with a snaffle mouthpiece and cheeks or shanks with bridle rings at the top of the upper shank and rein rings at the bottom of the lower shank. The bit rotates, putting pressure on the lips and poll simultaneously, encouraging the horse to raise his head.
- **Dutch gag.** Resembles the elevator bit, but has three or more rings in place of cheeks. Its severity can be adjusted by placing the gag rein on a higher or lower ring.

Some other examples of gag bits are the American, Balding, Cheltenham, and Duncan gags.

## Combination Bridles

There are a variety of combination bridles with different degrees of severity.

The Myler combination bit is based on the Myler bitting system. A mouthpiece with short shanks is connected to a nylon cord and leather noseband. Contact with the reins creates pressure on the nose, back of the jaw,

Types of gag bits.

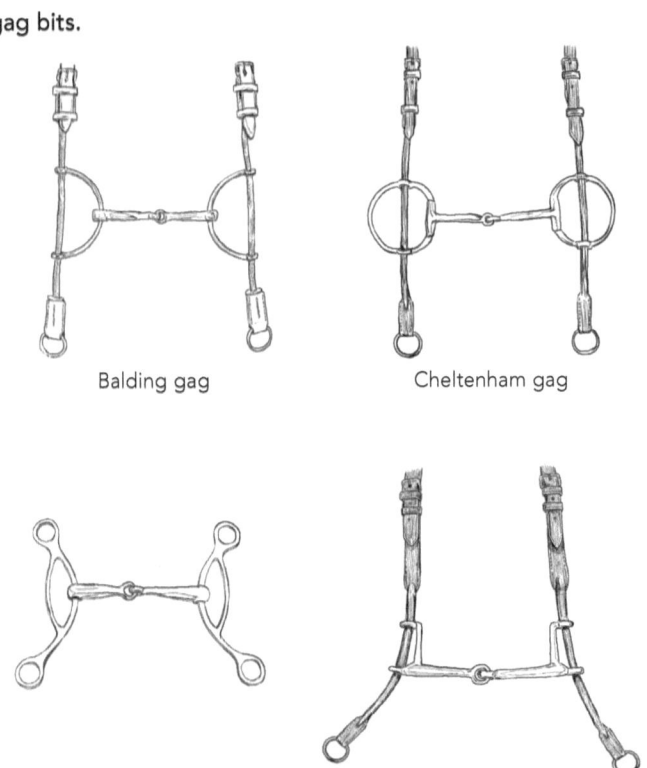

Balding gag

Cheltenham gag

American gag

Duncan gag

and then the poll. This combination system can be used with several types of snaffle mouthpieces with various size ports.

Another combination is the American gag with a German-style hackamore. The strong poll pressure combines with a lifting action on the lips and corners of the mouth. It is most commonly used on show jumpers.

Some combination bridles can serve more than one function, such as the Micklem Multibridle, which combines three main pieces of equipment in one: a bridle, a longe cavesson, and a bitless bridle.

## Nosebands and Their Adjustment

**Cavesson noseband:** The most common and simplest type of noseband, it is designed for use with a snaffle, pelham, Kimberwicke, or double bridle. When correctly fitted, it should have little to no action on the horse's head. You should be able to fit one to two fingers under the noseband and one to two fingers between the bottom of the projecting cheek bones and the top of the noseband.

There are many other types of nosebands designed to keep a horse from opening his mouth or crossing his jaws, or pulling the bit. These nosebands increase the effect of the bit by preventing the horse from opening his mouth to evade its action.

**Dropped or drop noseband:** This noseband encircles the nose just below the end of the nasal bone, with the chin strap in the chin groove. It should be fastened below the bit, with its cheekpieces in front of the bridle cheekpieces. If it is too low, it can interfere with the horse's breathing. If it is too high, it will push the bit into the horse's mouth and pinch the corners of the lips. You should be able to fit one to two fingers between the nosepiece and the face to allow for relaxation of the lower jaw.

The dropped noseband can increase pressure on the nose and lower jaw. It is more severe than a flash noseband (see below) because it puts pressure on the sensitive pressure point at the end of the nasal bone. It should never be used with a standing martingale or for cross-country where breathing is demanding.

**Flash noseband:** This noseband employs a standard English cavesson with an extra strap (the "flash") that adds the function of a dropped noseband. The lower strap, or flash, should pass well above the nostrils (at least four fingers between the flash and nostrils). The strap runs around the nose below the bit and under the chin groove. A loop on top of the cavesson noseband holds the flash strap. The buckle of the flash should rest on the side of the horse's nose, not underneath the chin.

One problem with a flash noseband is that the flash tends to pull the front of the cavesson down, so the cavesson should not be adjusted too loosely. Additionally, the cavesson should be adjusted high enough on the horse's head (typically, two fingers below the facial crest) to allow the flash to encircle the horse's nose and mouth well above the nostrils. There should be one to two fingers between the flash strap and the horse's face. The cavesson also allows for the use of a standing martingale (attached to the cavesson, never to the flash). A flash noseband can cause some restriction in breathing, although this is less likely if it is correctly fitted.

**Crank noseband or Swedish cavesson:** This noseband is similar to a regular cavesson, but it is heavily padded across the nose and under the chin. The chin strap is doubled back on itself to act as a pulley when tightening. It can be adjusted tightly to help keep the horse's mouth closed.

If a crank noseband is too tight, the horse cannot relax his jaw and it can squeeze against the horse's teeth, causing pain. It is often used on a double bridle because the double bridle cannot use a dropped or flash noseband.

**Hanoverian noseband or crank noseband with flash attachment:** This combination of a crank noseband with a flash attachment allows a much tighter fit, decreasing the ability of the flash to pull the cavesson down the nose, and assisting in keeping the horse's jaw closed. As with the regular crank noseband, it must not be overtightened.

**Figure eight, Grakle, or crossover noseband:** This noseband acts over a wider area, which makes it more effective in preventing a horse from crossing its jaw. It is made up of two long leather straps that cross over the bridge of the nose with a pad beneath the crossing on the nose. If properly fitted, this noseband does not restrict the horse's breathing, making it ideal to use for cross-country or galloping work. The side straps (along the cheeks) of this noseband should be adjusted high enough that the crossover point on the nose is located at the level of the bottom of the facial crest. This prevents it from crossing too low over the nose, which could impair airflow into the nostrils.

**Mexican or high ring figure eight:** This noseband is similar to the figure eight noseband, but is adjusted higher. It lies above the cheekbones on the side and the crossover point sits higher on the face. It should not be used with a standing martingale.

**Kineton noseband:** This noseband has an adjustable leather strap fitted to a metal loop ("U" loop) on each side. The loops are hooked around the mouthpiece of the bit. There is no strap to keep the mouth closed. When the reins are used and pressure is put on the bit, it is transferred through the "U" loops, which creates pressure on the nose, the bit, and the sides of the mouth. It is only used with a snaffle bit. It cannot be used with a martingale.

**Lever or combination noseband:** This noseband has half-moon metal pieces that go on each side of the horse's face. The front strap is adjustable and fitted like a dropped noseband. The top strap runs under the jaw and the bottom strap goes under the chin groove. It combines the action of a dropped noseband and a figure eight noseband, and is useful in preventing a horse from crossing his jaws.

## Bridle Accessories

**Poll padding:** This padding is created to sit on top of the poll so that it removes the pressure point created from the two pieces of leather (crownpiece and cavesson) that sit on top of the poll.

**Chin guard or curb chain guard:** Padded foam rubber sleeve that fits under the chin strap of a cavesson noseband or under a curb chain, for comfort.

Types of nosebands.

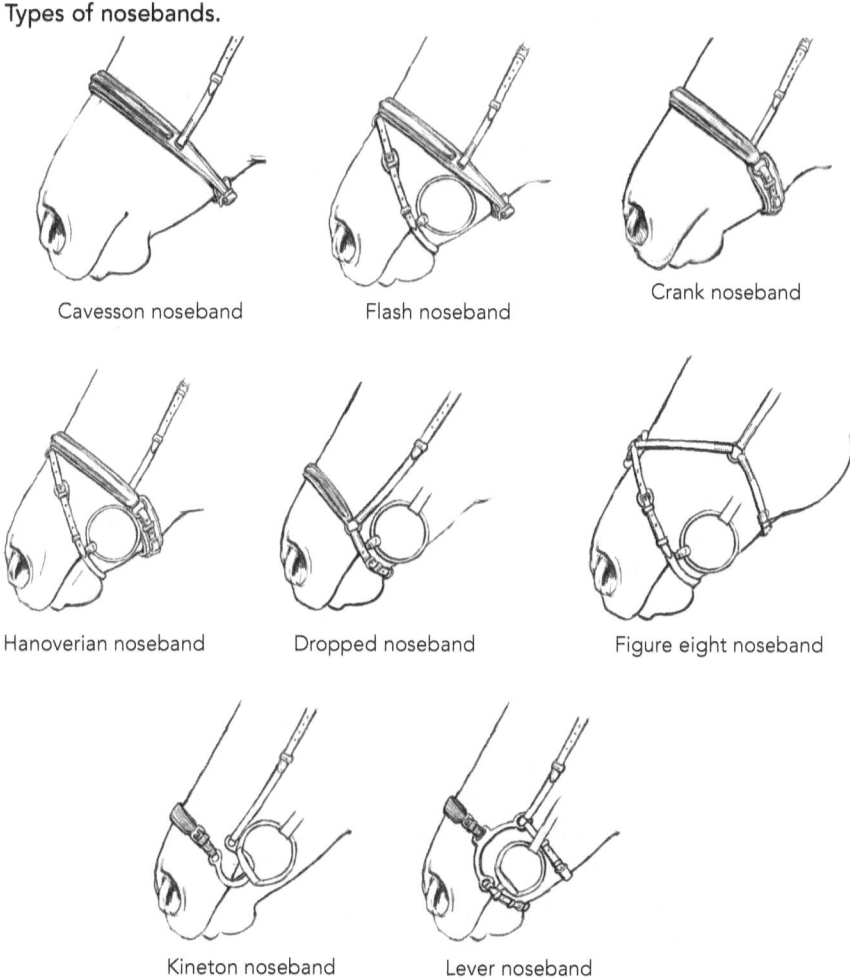

**Bit guards:** Flat rubber circles with holes in the middle that fit around the mouthpiece of a bit, next to the lips. These are used as a temporary measure to prevent a bit from pinching or make a too-large bit fit better.

**Bristle bit guards or bit burrs:** These leather circles with bristles on one side are designed to fit on only one side. The purpose is to encourage a horse to move away from the discomfort of the bristles in a particular direction.

**Australian cheeker (Sure-Win bit holder):** A "Y"-shaped rubber piece that attaches to the crownpiece and runs down the center of the horse's face, ending in circles that fit around the mouthpiece of the snaffle bit. This attachment can help keep the bit up in the mouth, preventing a horse from putting his tongue over the bit.

## Hackamores and Bitless Bridles

Depending on the type, bitless bridles and hackamores can work on the nose, chin, poll, and sometimes the entire head, instead of the mouth. Although they may not be as common as other bits, they are used in lessons, training, show jumping, eventing, western, endurance, and on games ponies. They are also useful for beginners who don't have steady hands; and for training young horses, retraining spoiled horses, and for horses whose mouths have been injured or who have difficulty in accepting a bit.

A hackamore should be adjusted so that the noseband rests on or slightly above the point where the nasal bone ends and the cartilage begins. If placed lower, it cannot cut off the horse's breathing, but it may interfere with the expansion of the nostrils, irritate his muzzle, and lead to head tossing. The chin strap of a leverage hackamore should be adjusted so that the shanks rotate 45 degrees to tighten it, or for non-leverage hackamores, so that two adult-sized fingers can be slipped between the jaw and the chin strap.

The two basic types of hackamores are leverage and non-leverage.

**Leverage hackamores (mechanical hackamores).** These employ a noseband, curb strap or chain, and shanks. Their action is similar to that of a curb bit, except that pressure is applied to the nose and curb groove instead of the mouth. They range from moderate to severe, depending on the construction of the noseband and length of shank. Like curb bits, they encourage flexion at the poll, but are not as effective for turning as direct-pressure devices, as a lateral pull tends to tilt the shank and dig the upper shank into the side of the horse's face.

**Non-leverage hackamores.** These consist of a noseband and chin strap with rings placed on the sides of the noseband. Pressure causes the noseband to rotate and tightens the chin strap, but there is little or no leverage. Because the rings are on the side of the nose, they are more effective for turning, especially when using an opening rein. Non-leverage hackamores include leather-covered jumping hackamores, side-pull hackamores, and western bosals.

**Western bosal:** A bosal is a traditional western non-leverage hackamore (or jaquima). It is made of braided rawhide and fitted to balance on the horse's face. The heel knot adds weight to the bottom of the bosal, causing it to fall away from the horse's chin except when the reins are briefly tightened to give a signal. A bosal may be supported by a headstall with a fiador (a rope throatlatch that supports the hackamore at the heel knot) or used with a simple headstall alone. The reins are tied to the bosal, often incorporating a long mecate, or tie rope. A bosal is used with a light, skilled touch and release, to develop a neck-reined western stock horse. It is not suitable for riding on contact.

**Cross-under bitless bridle (Dr. Cook, Spirit Bridle):** In a cross-under bitless bridle, each rein connects to a strap that passes through a ring on the side of the noseband, crosses under the horse's jaw and up the cheek on the opposite side, where it connects to the headstall. This type of bridle uses no bit but places pressure on the side of the horse's jaw and on the nose. It can create additional pressure on the poll and under the chin when a strong pull of the reins is applied.

Because there is no bit, the horse is unlikely to brace his jaw or neck against the reins.

Bitless bridles and hackamores.

Leverage jumping hackamore

Non-leverage hackamore noseband

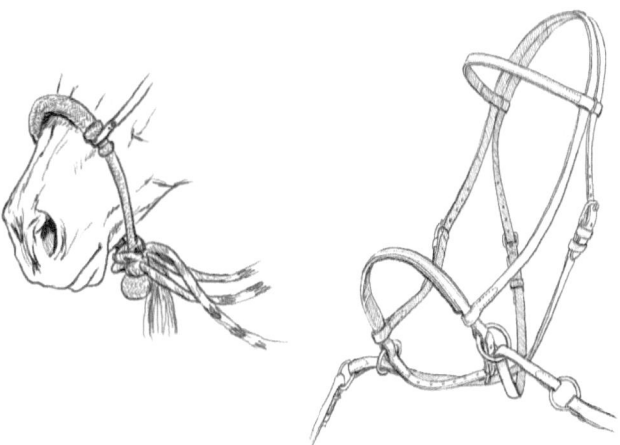

Western bosal              Cross-under bitless bridle

## Training Devices or Aids

Because of the dangers of these devices, they should be used with care. Assistance from a knowledgeable horseperson is recommended. An upper-level Pony Club member should develop and demonstrate skill and good judgment in using this equipment. The following are examples of training aids.

**Draw reins or running reins:** Draw reins are auxiliary reins that are used to position the horse's head or prevent the horse from flipping his head. Draw reins can be used in two positions:

1. Running from the girth, between the front legs, through the rings of the snaffle bit, and back to the rider's hand
2. Attached to the girth on each side near the bottom of the saddle flaps, running forward through the snaffle bit rings, and back to the rider's hand

Draw reins should always be used along with a regular rein, and should only be used on a snaffle bit.

Draw reins multiply the effect of the bit and the rider's hands by adding leverage, and also by the position and angle of the rein. It is deceptively easy to force a horse's head into a false position with draw reins, because it requires little pressure on the reins to do so.

Ideally, draw reins should be adjusted so there is about 2 inches of slack in the draw reins when the horse is working with correct contact and his head is carried properly. In this position, the draw reins simply say "no" to attempts to throw the head up or out into an incorrect position. However, the rider must be able to ride the horse into good balance and carriage, use her seat and aids correctly, and not use the draw reins to pull the head in, especially behind the vertical. Draw reins tend to give the rider a false feeling of light contact with the horse's mouth, when the horse may actually be over-flexing or getting behind the bit. They should only be used by advanced riders, preferably for short periods only, and under the supervision of a trainer who knows how to use them correctly.

If misused, draw reins can result in an over-bent horse that goes behind the bit with his face behind the vertical, his neck flexed incorrectly at the third vertebra, retracting from the bit and curling his neck while going on the forehand. They can inhibit the natural balancing gestures of the horse's head and neck, especially at a walk. Draw reins are dangerous for jumping, as they can prevent the horse from using his head and neck for balance, takeoff, and landing.

**German martingale or Market Harborough martingale:** A combination of draw reins and a martingale, it consists of a long split strap that runs from the girth, between the front legs, through the snaffle bit rings, and then snaps to rings on the reins. If the horse tries to raise or extend his head beyond the point to which the martingale is adjusted, it results in backward and downward pressure of the bit against his mouth. The effect is similar to that of draw reins, except that the draw reins are attached to the snaffle reins and the rider cannot pull the draw reins any tighter than they have been adjusted. If the rider lengthens the reins, the martingale reins are loosened, too.

A German martingale should be adjusted so that the martingale reins are equal, and there should be a minimum of 2 inches of slack in the martingale reins when the horse's head and neck are properly positioned, and the rider has light contact with the horse's mouth. The horse's face should always be in front of the vertical.

Like draw reins, a German martingale can give a rider a false feeling of light contact when the horse is actually over-bent. They should be used only under the supervision of a trainer who knows how to adjust and use them correctly.

**Elastic poll pressure device or "neck-stretcher":** Made of elastic cord that goes over the horse's poll, through the snaffle bit rings, and back to the girth. It does *not* stretch, lengthen, or develop the neck, but applies pressure to the poll and the bit, encouraging the horse to lower his head and flex his neck. It encourages the horse to "set" his head, and many horses learn to flex at the third vertebra instead of at the poll and go behind the vertical.

If used, it should be adjusted so that there are at least 2 inches of slack in the cord when horse's head and neck are correctly positioned, and his face is in front of the vertical. It should never be used for jumping.

# Miscellaneous Equipment

## Breastplates and Breast Collars

Breastplates and breast collars are used to prevent the saddle from sliding back. They are often necessary on horses with large shoulders and flat, narrow ribs. Breastplates or breast collars are used for extra security in show jumping or eventing, in which the added pace, jumping efforts, and terrain changes may make the saddle more prone to slipping than in ordinary riding.

Because breastplates and breast collars are potential sources of irritation and sores for the horse, and can restrict the movement of his shoulders, they should be used only when necessary, and must always be correctly adjusted.

Types of breastplates and breast collars (and their adjustment) include the following:

**Hunting breastplate.** Used in foxhunting, endurance, and polocrosse to stabilize the saddle. Consists of a yoke (neck straps and wither strap), adjustable breast strap (which passes between the front legs and encircles the girth), and two adjustable straps, which buckle to the dee rings of the saddle. A martingale attachment (standing or running) may be attached to the center ring of the yoke. The breast strap and/or neck straps are sometimes covered with fleece to prevent chafing.

The best type of breastplate has adjustable buckles on each side of the neck straps. The breast strap and the two connecting straps that attach to the saddle dees are also adjustable.

A breastplate must keep the saddle from sliding back, but must not bind or restrict at the chest, shoulders, or between the forelegs. When correctly adjusted, you should be able to fit a fist between the chest and the center ring of the yoke, or one hand (sideways) between the wither strap and the withers. The breast strap must be slightly slack, and the buckle must not rub the horse's sensitive skin between the front legs.

**Caution:** Consider the fit of the saddle when using a breastplate that attaches to the saddle dees. If the saddle does not fit correctly or slips back too far, or if the breastplate is too tight, the breastplate may pull the front of the saddle down, digging the tree points into the muscles and causing severe discomfort.

**Breast collar (eventing, polo, or racing style).** Consists of a chest strap of leather, webbing, or strong elastic, buckled around the first billet of the girth. A wither strap adjusts the height and keeps the breast collar from slipping down. Some have a slot at the front to accommodate a martingale. The breast strap may be covered with fleece to prevent chafing.

Breast collars hold the saddle more securely than hunting breastplates, so they are preferred for events in which a weight pad is carried, and for polo.

A breast collar should run horizontally from the chest to the girth, not angled upward. It must not be placed so low as to interfere with the points of the shoulders, nor so high as to press against the bottom of the windpipe. You should be able to slip a fist between the chest and the front of the breast strap, and between the wither strap and the withers. A split-end girth, which is divided for the first 10 inches to accommodate the breast collar straps, is best for placing the connecting straps securely.

Five-point breastplate.

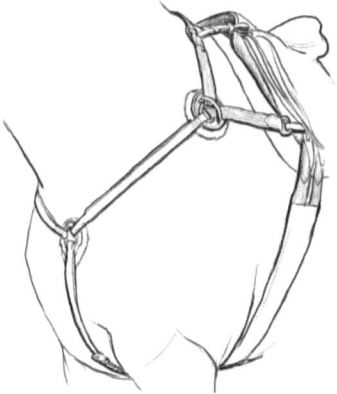

- **Elastic breast girth.** A breast girth is similar to a breast collar, but it attaches instead to the dee rings of the saddle, or to a special loop that is attached to the stirrup bars. The breast strap is made of heavy elastic, and there is no wither strap. Breast girths are used mostly in show jumping, as they restrict the freedom of the shoulders less than other types of breast collars.

  An elastic breast girth can be adjusted more snugly than a breast collar, and it is placed at the base of the neck. It should not restrict the horse's breathing by pressing on the base of the windpipe.

- **Five-point breastplate.** A combination of a breast collar and a breastplate, with padding at the key pressure points. It has extra security, but allows free movement of the shoulders when jumping.

# Crupper

A crupper is a strap attached to a saddle, harness pad, or surcingle, connected to a padded strap that passes under the horse's tail, used to prevent the saddle or surcingle from slipping forward. Cruppers are most often used on small, round-backed ponies and on mules.

To put on a crupper, double up the skirt of the tail and slip the tail-piece over the tail. All hairs must be freed from underneath the tail-piece before attaching the crupper to the saddle.

A crupper should fit snugly enough to keep the saddle from slipping forward, but not tightly enough to irritate the horse or abrade the skin of the dock. It must be kept clean and soft. A stiff, dirty crupper, hair caught underneath the dock, or too tight a crupper may make the dock tender, cause sores, and lead to kicking.

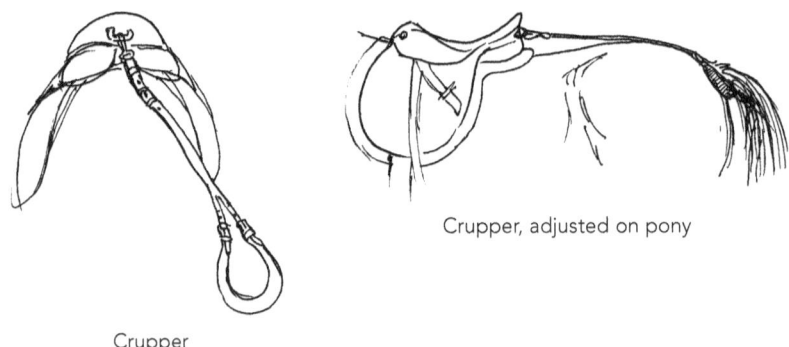

Crupper

Crupper, adjusted on pony

## Temporary Adjustment of Ill-Fitting Tack

When teaching or assisting with Pony Club activities, it is sometimes necessary to make a temporary adjustment of ill-fitting tack so that it can be used safely. Any such adjustments must be made so that the tack is safe for the rider and comfortable for the horse, and should be strictly temporary.

It is also important to consult the rider's instructor, trainer, or parents before adjusting tack, unless immediate safety is involved. Be sure that the child and the parent understand that the adjustment made in their presence is only temporary, and that they both understand what needs to be done to make the tack fit correctly in the long run.

## Tool Kit

A simple tool kit makes temporary "fixes" and emergency repairs to tack much easier. It helps to carry the following items whenever you teach or assist at Pony Club activities:

- Leather punch with assorted size tubes
- Sharp knife (a utility knife with an awl is especially useful)
- Sharp, heavy-duty scissors
- Duct tape
- Self-sticking padded tape (such as Vetrap™ or Sealtex™ latex tape)
- Bath towel
- Pieces of foam rubber (2" thick, size of a saddle pad)
- Several pieces of neoprene or hiker's sleeping pad material (¼" thick, 6 × 12")
- Girth extender
- Rubber bit guards

# Saddle Fit

Padding a saddle is never as satisfactory as having the saddle sized and stuffed to fit the horse correctly. Any temporary extra padding should be placed over the saddle pad, not next to the horse's skin. Sometimes a thick, non-crushable western saddle pad will make a saddle usable (temporarily) when nothing else works.

### Saddle Resting on Withers

**Caution:** This condition will quickly cause a severe wither sore, which can lead to fistula (a deep sore draining down into the space between the spinous processes of the withers) if not corrected. A horse must *never* be ridden with the saddle resting on the withers.

**Problem:** Tree too wide or panels flat in front. (**Note:** Check for broken tree; do not use saddle if tree is broken.)

**To fix:** Pad both sides of the back, leaving a clear channel over the withers and spine. If available, a back protector pad may help. Padding must stay in place and keep saddle clear of withers and spine when rider is mounted. Do not stuff padding between the arch of the saddle and the withers, as this increases the pressure. For a long-term solution, the saddle should be restuffed to fit until it can be exchanged for a saddle with a tree that fits.

### Too Low in Cantle

**Problem:** Rear panels flat or tree too narrow; places the dip (the lowest point of the seat) too far back instead of in the center of the saddle. (**Note:** If tree is too narrow, saddle cannot be used. Raising the back of the saddle will drive the tree points into the horse's shoulders and back muscles, causing soreness.)

**To fix:** Use a lift-back pad or folded towel to raise the cantle until the dip of the seat is in the center. Make sure saddle does not pinch the shoulder blades and that padding is smooth, even, and effective when rider is mounted.

### Leathers Too Long

**Problem:** Not enough holes to adjust stirrups for rider.

**To fix:** Unbuckle stirrup leather and wrap buckle end around top of iron once, then re-buckle. One wrap usually equals about 1½ holes. Leathers should have holes measured and punched at correct length.

### Girth Too Short

**Problem:** Girth too short to leave at least one spare hole below the buckles on both sides.

**To fix:** Use girth extender, buckled to billets.

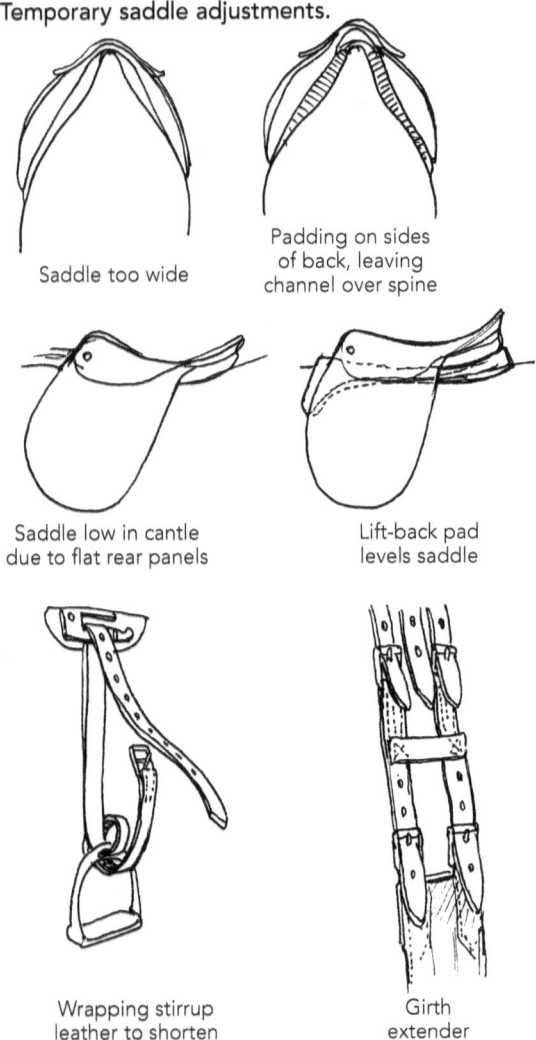

Temporary saddle adjustments.

Saddle too wide

Padding on sides of back, leaving channel over spine

Saddle low in cantle due to flat rear panels

Lift-back pad levels saddle

Wrapping stirrup leather to shorten

Girth extender

### Saddle Slides Forward

**Problem:** Tree too wide, front panels flat, and/or conformation of horse's back (especially roach back or built downhill). Tree points jab horse or pony in shoulders; rider may sit tilted forward, with hollow back.

**To fix:** Place saddle at "lock-in" point (hollow behind shoulder blades). Use neoprene pads, back protector pad, or folded towels to fill in space at sides of back so that saddle sits level, with dip in center. If available, a crupper may be used (but horse must be accustomed to crupper before riding).

# Bridle

## *Too Large*
**Problem:** Cheekpieces and/or crownpiece too long; no more holes to adjust height of bit.

**To fix:** Tie a knot in each cheekpiece, then buckle to crownpiece. Cheekpieces (or bridle) of proper size should be obtained.

## *Bit Too Wide*
**Problem:** Bit slips from side to side; if jointed, it acts with severe pinching effect, and center joint may strike the roof of the mouth. If unjointed, bit acts with uneven pressure and may cause horse to tilt his head.

**To fix:** If only slightly too wide, rubber bit guards may take up some room. If bit is excessively wide, do not use.

Temporary bridle adjustments.

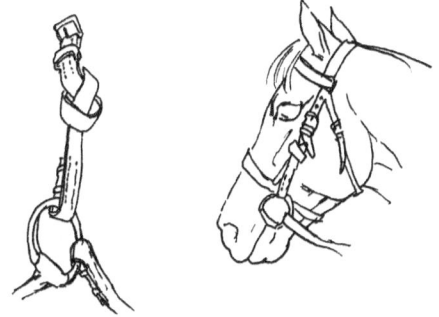

Shortened too-large bridle with knot in cheekpiece

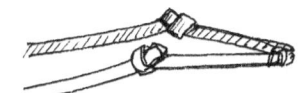

Shortening reins with knot in each rein

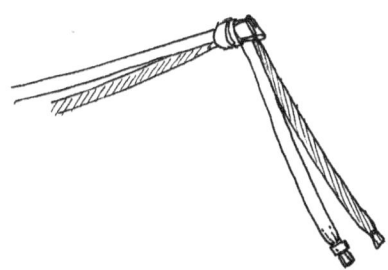

Shortening reins with knot in doubled end of rein; unbuckle rein to prevent loop that could catch rider's foot

### Bit Rubs Sores at Corners of Mouth

**Problem:** Loose ring snaffle with large hole, or bit too narrow; pinches or rubs corners of mouth, causing sore lips. Curb chain adjusted too long, catches a fold of lip as bit rotates.

**To fix:** For loose ring bits, use rubber bit guards. If bit is too narrow, do not use. If curb chain pinches, adjust chain correctly. Curb chain may be run through snaffle ring (on pelhams and Kimberwickes) to keep it away from corners of mouth.

**Caution:** A horse must not be ridden with a bit touching an open sore. Try using a hackamore or bitless bridle while sores are allowed to heal.

### Rubs or Sores from Bridle

**Problem:** Improperly adjusted tack, rough leather, or sharp edges abrade the skin.

**To fix:** Readjust the tack so that pressure is removed from sore spot. Rough or sharp edges can be padded by wrapping with crepe or rubber tape.

Adjustments to bits and bridles.

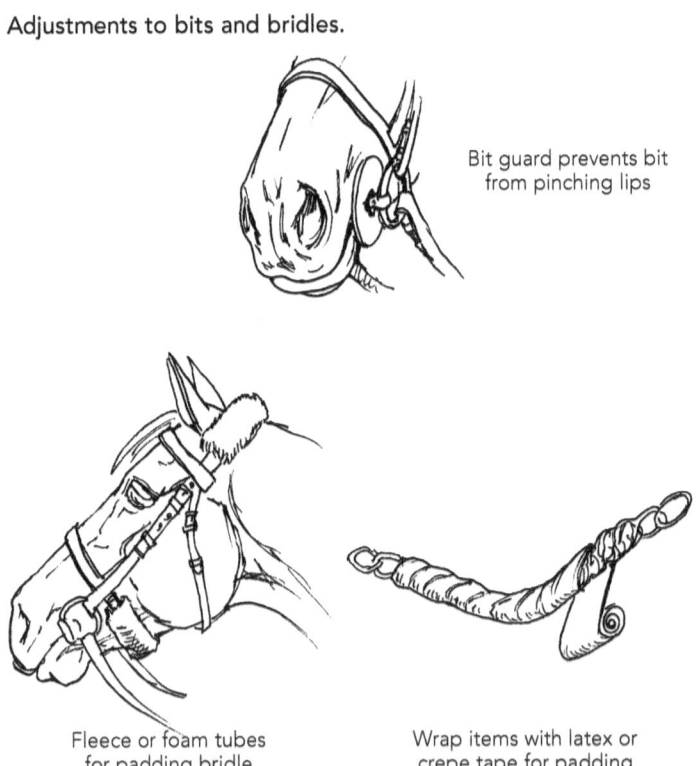

Bit guard prevents bit from pinching lips

Fleece or foam tubes for padding bridle

Wrap items with latex or crepe tape for padding

### Reins Too Long

**Problem:** Extra rein forms dangerous loop in which rider can get caught, or horse's feet may be entangled in the excess in case of a stumble or fall.

**To fix:** Tie reins in a knot, taking up extra rein. If reins are tied, they should be unbuckled to prevent a dangerous loop. For children with small hands, unbuckle the reins and tie a knot in each rein to avoid a large knot at the withers. Then re-buckle the reins.

## Storing Tack

Tack and equipment are expensive and must be stored properly to prevent damage from excessive heat, dryness, dampness, mold/mildew, or rodents.

Leather loses a little of its fat content each day because of the effects of the atmosphere, especially as it dries. It is better for leather to be used daily and properly cared for (cleaned, conditioned, and sealed) than for it to sit unused for long periods.

Tack must be stored in a well-ventilated room, protected from dust, dampness, dryness, and excessive heat, and secure from rodents. Tack should be stored on racks that allow it to keep its proper shape. Creases cause leather to crack and weaken, and dry rot may develop, especially in creases.

When leather tack must be stored for a long period, it should be dismantled and thoroughly cleaned and conditioned or oiled, and any repairs taken care of. Apply a preservative such as leather dressing, glycerin saddle soap, or Lederbalsam, and wrap the leather in newspaper or cloth (pillowcases or old towels work well), which, unlike plastic, allow the necessary circulation of air. Coat any metal parts with petroleum jelly to prevent rust or corrosion. Saddles should be stored on a saddle rack, covered with a breathable saddle cover.

A stable is not the best place for long-term storage of unused tack, as it may be subject to dampness, mold, dust, or rodents. A dry closet is a better choice.

Saddle pads, blankets, bandages, and washable girths should be cleaned or laundered before storage. Dirty items are prone to mildew, rot, and moth damage, and are more attractive to rodents. Woolen items should be placed in plastic bags with moth repellent and stored in trunks or closets.

## How to Figure Eight a Bridle

Clean, wrapped bridles create a look of professionalism and polish in any well-organized tack room. When storing your bridle, keep it neat and tangle-free with this method:

1. Hang the bridle on a hook by the crownpiece.
2. Unbuckle the throatlatch and wrap it counterclockwise around the bridle and reins 1½ times, while looping the reins through the

throatlatch. Slip the end of the throatlatch through the keepers only; do not buckle.

3. Take the unbuckled noseband (and the flash, if one is used) and wrap it once around the bridle and fasten it in the front by slipping the end through the keepers only.

## Selecting Leather

Always buy the best tack and leather that you can afford. Leather is judged by its thickness and ability to hold more fat, and should feel smooth, flexible, and substantial, not flabby or greasy to the touch. The best leather comes from the butts of the hide and is closest to the backbone of the animal. Leather from the belly is generally flabbier and more fibrous, with more blemishes and scars. The rough side of the leather should not feel rough or fibrous; a good piece of leather should feel smooth. Most leather used in tack is full-grain cowhide, because it is the strongest and the grain is uniform and closely packed together.

How to figure eight a bridle.

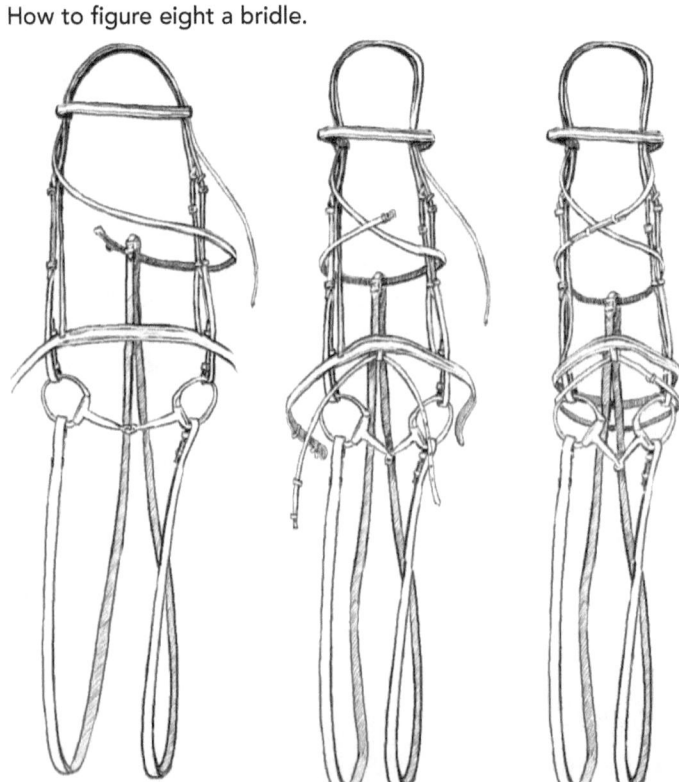

Well-tanned leather has a higher fat content than inferior leather, which allows it to keep its flexibility and "life" during use. New leather may have a whitish substance on the surface. This is called "bloom" and results from fats, oils, and waxes coming to the surface. It is easily removed when you clean the tack and break it in.

## Reclaiming Neglected Tack

Tack that has been neglected or that has come out of long-term storage may need special treatment to reclaim it.

First, inspect the tack for condition and repair, and decide whether it can be safely reconditioned, or if certain parts must be replaced. If it is cracked, weakened, or shows signs of dry rot, it may not be reclaimable. Pay special attention to billets, reins, bit fastenings, stitching, holes, and stress points—any point where the leather is folded or where it meets metal.

Next, remove any mold with a damp rag, using a new rag as often as needed to avoid spreading the mold. A small amount of apple cider vinegar added to your water will help kill mold spores and prevent the mold from returning. Carefully clean the stitching, cracks, and crevices (a toothbrush works well). Then clean the leather with a leather cleaner such as castile soap, Murphy Oil Soap, or Hydrophane Saddler's Leather Care. The tack should be conditioned by applying pure neatsfoot oil, Horseman's One Step cleaner, olive oil, Lexol Conditioner (brown container), or Lederbalsam. Apply the conditioner to both sides, a little at a time, gently bending the leather back and forth so that it absorbs the conditioner and becomes supple. Don't apply so much oil or conditioner that the leather becomes saturated, which may damage it. Drying the tack in the sun will allow the oil or conditioner to soak in and the tack to dry. The sun's ultraviolet light also helps to kill mold spores. After the tack is dry, wipe it down and finish by applying glycerine saddle soap to seal the pores of the leather to protect it.

It is better to repeat this process several times, or to use the tack and clean and condition it daily until it becomes soft and supple, than to over-condition it.

## Turnout and Presentation

At this level, Pony Club members are expected to present themselves and their mounts in a neat, clean, correct, and workmanlike manner for all events, no matter how formal or informal. The horse should be in proper condition and show evidence of good ongoing management, including thorough daily grooming and proper shoeing and foot care. Tack must be safe, correctly adjusted, in good repair, and thoroughly clean, with metal parts polished. The Pony Club member should know the correct name of each item of equipment she uses and be able to explain its purpose, how it works, why it is used on her horse, and its proper adjustment.

Pony Club members must know requirements for formal and informal attire, and must appear correctly turned out according to the requirements of the occasion. Check the Rule Book for your discipline (available on the USPC website, www.ponyclub.org) to make sure you are properly turned out. Clothing must be neat and clean, and should fit properly. (For details on everyday attire and formal and informal attire, see the *USPC D Level Manual*, pages 298–306, and the *USPC Horse Management Handbook*.)

In addition, upper-level Pony Club members are expected to be able to evaluate, prepare, and present a strange horse as if for sale. To do this, you must be able to:

- Recognize the horse's breed and/or type, age, and condition.
- Evaluate the horse's conformation, way of going, faults and strong points, and temperament, and discuss the horse's potential uses and limitations.
- Groom and prepare the horse as if for sale (taking into account how this breed or type of horse should be presented).
- Present the horse in hand, showing him to best advantage (showing off his good points and minimizing his faults).
- Present yourself in an appropriate and horsemanlike manner (dressed as if ready to ride, neatly and correctly turned out).

## Preparation

A horse presented for sale should be in good condition, ideally carrying a little extra condition or "bloom." His feet should be in good condition, recently trimmed or shod. Other preparation tips include the following:

- The horse should be spotlessly clean, with a healthy, shiny coat that reflects good daily nutrition and grooming, not coat polish. The mane, tail, and white markings should be shampooed.
- The head, ears, bridle path, and legs should be trimmed, and the mane and tail pulled and/or trimmed according to the breed or type of horse. Hunters, sport horses, and hunter ponies' manes may be braided to show off the head and neck. (See the *USPC C Level Manual*, pages 148–149.) Always get permission before pulling the mane, trimming, or clipping if the horse is not your own.
- The hooves should be clean and may be polished with hoof oil or a non-sticky hoof dressing. If not braided, the mane should be dampened and brushed to lay it on the correct side, and a tail bandage may be used

to shape the hair of the dock. The horse should be presented in properly fitted tack, with the leather clean and supple and the metal parts polished.
- Even though it is the horse that is being presented, a neat, clean, and attractive stable area and an appropriately turned-out handler make a good impression. The handler should wear clean, informal riding attire, with helmet, gloves, stick, and spurs at hand.
- Sport horses should be shown in a correctly fitted bridle, with the leather clean and polished. Young horses or horses of other types may be shown in a leather halter or show headgear suitable for their breed.

## Braiding

Braiding the mane shows off the quality of the horse's head and the line and muscling of the neck. A hunter or sport horse should be braided in the style suitable for his discipline. The tail should not be braided unless the mane is braided, and then only on hunters and jumpers. Some types of braids include the following:

- **Hunter braids:** Twenty to 30 small, flat braids fastened flat against the neck with braiding yarn, usually in the same color as the mane. Forelock is braided. Used on hunters, hunter ponies, and jumpers.
- **Button braids or English plaits:** Fewer and larger braids, doubled and sewn in with braiding thread in the same color as the mane. Forelock is usually braided. Used on eventers, jumpers, and dressage horses.
- **Knob braids:** Similar to hunter braids, but pushed up into a knob on the top. Fastened with yarn, rubber bands, or braid fasteners. Used on jumpers, dressage horses, and eventers. Forelock may be braided or unbraided.
- **Euro braids:** Same as knob braids, but pushed up higher to make a line of braids that stand up above the neck, fastened with rubber bands and white tape or white braid fasteners to accent the crest. Forelock is usually unbraided. Used on dressage horses, especially in Europe.
- **French braid or running braid:** The mane is braided into a single braid, running along the top of the crest or dropped several inches below the crest, from the bridle path to the withers. Forelock is usually unbraided. This is a method of braiding a long-maned horse for sport horse disciplines.

Each of these types of braiding has its own technique. Directions and illustrations for these and other braiding methods can be found in *Grooming to Win, Third Edition,* by Susan Harris (Howell Book House, 2008), or in

USPC supplementary materials. It is important to pull and prepare the mane correctly, measure and part braids evenly, braid neatly and tightly, and fasten each braid correctly and securely. Wetting the mane with water or Quik-Braid helps to keep the hair neat and makes braiding easier. You will need to stand on a stool in order to braid.

## Presenting a Horse in Hand (Showing to Best Advantage)

When presenting a horse in hand, you should show him to his best advantage. This means showing off his best points and minimizing faults or less attractive points. To do this, you must first evaluate his conformation and way of moving. You will also need to practice leading and setting him up (posing) properly.

- Sport horses and ponies are presented on a triangle pattern. The purpose of the triangle is to allow the judge (standing between B and C) to see the straightness of the paces (going away from C and coming back from A to B) and the athleticism and movement from the side (B to C). The horse is shown on the triangle at both the walk and the trot.
- Lead the horse briskly at walk (or trot, as requested), moving straight on the line. Give a preparatory half-halt before stopping, so that he halts squarely with his hocks under him. Turn him away from you, using half-halts to make him turn on the haunches. Give a half-halt to balance him before leading him back to the viewer at a walk or trot (as requested).
- When moving at the walk or trot, stay on a straight line. (Pick an object at a distance and aim for it.) Stay beside the horse's head and neck, and do not look back at him. Run alongside the horse, allowing him to show an athletic, straight, and free-moving walk or trot.
- To "set up," halt and turn to face the horse. Switch the rein or lead shank to your left hand. Back the horse with short steps until his hind legs are squarely under him with cannon bones vertical (one hind leg may be slightly behind the vertical). Then move the forelegs until they are standing squarely, with both cannon bones vertical. Step back (still facing the horse) and encourage him to look alertly forward. (This takes practice!)
- Avoid emphasizing conformation defects (or creating them where they do not exist!) by allowing the horse to stand incorrectly. Don't let him stand base narrow, with front or hind legs too far under him, or camped out in front or behind. Holding the head too high or too low makes the neck appear unattractive and may make the shoulder look straighter than it is.
- Know the breed or type of the horse you are presenting, and how it is properly presented. (For example, Morgans and certain other breeds are

Showing a horse in hand.

posed "parked out," with hind legs stretched backward; Quarter Horses and stock horse breeds are posed "square"; and hunters, sport horses, and Arabians are posed with forelegs vertical and parallel, with one hind leg slightly behind the other.)
- Take advantage of terrain. If possible, pose a horse on slightly rising ground. Never set him up with hind legs on higher ground than the front legs; this will make him appear hollow backed and sickle-hocked.
- Step back and allow the viewer to see the whole horse, including the head. Encourage the horse to look alert, but do not nag at him.

## Evaluating a Horse for Sale

When evaluating a horse for sale, it is important to get a complete picture of the individual horse and to assess his good points, faults, and overall usefulness.

Here are some points to remember:

- Observe the horse in his stall, noting his stable manners and any signs of stable vices.
- Have the horse stood up in hand and evaluate his conformation. Look at his overall outline, balance, and proportions from a distance, then view him from each side, front, and rear. Compare the two sides for symmetry and even muscle development. Make notes on his strong points, conformation faults, blemishes, and unsoundnesses. (See Chapter 10, "Conformation and Soundness.")

- Examine the horse closely, including the mouth and teeth, legs, and feet. Note the condition of his feet and type of shoes. Corrective or therapeutic shoeing may indicate soundness or movement problems.
- Watch the horse move at a walk and a trot straight away from you, toward you, and from a side view. Note the soundness and evenness of stride, freedom of movement, engagement, type of movement, and straightness of movement. Note any movement faults (plaiting, winging in, forging, and so on).
- Observe the horse's attitude, temperament, and stable manners as he is groomed, tacked up, and otherwise handled.
- Watch the horse ridden on the flat and over fences (to his level of training). Evaluate his performance, manners, and way of going under saddle, taking into account the level and experience of the rider.
- Ride the horse yourself to evaluate his level of training, gaits, and rideability. Try the horse under the circumstances in which you plan to use him (with other horses, hacking out, hunting, and so on). (For details on the evaluation ride, see the *USPC D Level Manual*, pages 20–21.) If he will be ridden by someone else, have that person ride him and handle him.
- Ask for all pertinent information, including any warranties. *Always* have your own veterinarian perform a pre-purchase veterinary examination.
- When looking at horses for sale, it is useful to take photos and/or videos of those you are considering (with the seller's permission).

# 8

# Teaching Horsemanship

U.S. Pony Club instructors teach *horsemanship,* which is more than just riding. Horsemanship means teaching skills and knowledge, and especially the attitude, responsibility, and feeling for horses that makes a true horse person. Sharing knowledge and helping others learn and grow is an important part of horsemanship. This helps not only your students, but their horses and ponies as well.

B Pony Club members teach D and C Level riders in dismounted and mounted classes. Upper-level Pony Club members teach all levels, including dismounted lessons, work on the flat and over fences, and coaching and preparation for rallies and other competitions. Chapter 11 of the *USPC C Level Manual* covers an introduction to teaching, including what makes a good teacher, Safety Checks, helping students prepare for inspection, dismounted instruction, and acting as an assistant.

We always teach best what we know best and care about most. Your riding experience will give you insights and ideas to pass on to your students. As you prepare and teach a lesson, you will often find that it helps you understand the topic better yourself.

# Teaching and Learning

## Types of Learning

There are several types of learning:

**Cognitive learning:** Facts and knowledge. (Example: Learning the parts of the horse.)

**Conceptual learning:** Related to cognitive learning, this is learning concepts or ideas and reasons. (Example: Learning safety rules and the reasons for them.) Most schoolwork emphasizes cognitive and conceptual learning.

**Affective learning:** Related to *affect*, or feelings and attitudes. (Example: Learning to treat a horse kindly.)

**Motor skills:** Learning physical skills and movements. (Example: Learning to post the trot.)

**Problem-solving:** Learning to use one's intelligence and creativity to solve problems, both individually and while working with others. (Example: Learning to handle an uncooperative horse.)

**Social skills:** Learning to interact with other people. (Example: Learning to be a helpful, cooperative Pony Club member.)

All types of learning are important, but in riding instruction, sometimes physical skills and cognitive learning (learning facts) can be over-emphasized. The attitudes and values (affective learning) a child develops through learning horsemanship may be more important than how high he jumps or whether he passes a particular certification level. They also increase his ability to work with others, take responsibility, and solve problems.

## Learning Styles

Although we all learn in many ways, each person has a dominant style in which he learns best. Good teachers use a variety of teaching techniques to appeal to as many learning styles as possible:

**Verbal:** Learning through words. Some people understand best when they hear a verbal explanation, read about a subject, or discuss an idea.

**Visual:** Learning through seeing. Visual learners understand best when they see a picture or watch a demonstration.

**Kinesthetic:** Learning by doing or feeling. Kinesthetic learners need to experience what they learn. Some subjects (such as sitting the trot) require kinesthetic learning.

## We learn

*10 percent of what we read;*
*20 percent of what we hear;*
*30 percent of what we both see and hear;*
*50 percent of what is discussed with others;*
*80 percent of what we experience personally;*
*95 percent of what we teach to someone else.*

—William Glasser

## Teaching Methods

The method you choose depends on the subject, ages, and needs of your students; the teaching situation; and the resources available. It is best to use more than one method, because some people understand better with one method than another. Any method you use must be safe, clear, and organized, and must keep your students' interest.

**Explanation:** When telling how to do something, keep it short and simple, to keep students interested and avoid confusion. Be positive: Tell *how* to do something, rather than how *not* to do it.

**Demonstration:** If you're showing how to do something, your demonstration must be brief, clear, and to the point. Practice first to be sure you can demonstrate correctly, and always show good safety procedures as well as the procedure you are teaching. Make sure all your students can see, and explain the steps as you do them.

**Skill drills:** Repetitive exercises or practice, used in mounted lessons, develop motor (physical) skills (such as half-seat position at the trot). Developing the correct motor skills takes the right kind of practice. Use repetition of an exercise instead of making students hold a position or continue an exercise so long that fatigue sets in. Be creative; vary exercises to keep practice interesting and fun.

**Questions and discussion:** Asking questions can strengthen students' grasp of what they already know, and lead students to *discover* what you wish to teach them. By starting with simple questions that students can answer easily, you can ask "leading" questions that lead them to new ideas. Because the students make discoveries themselves, this is a powerful teaching tool.

Discussing a subject should prompt students to think about it, organize their knowledge, and put it into a practical situation. In

Pony Club certification tests, discussing the performance or topic with the examiner lets the Pony Club member present practical knowledge of the subject, instead of merely repeating memorized words or ideas.

Group discussions work best when all members of the group have at least some knowledge of the subject, or on topics about which people have questions and opinions, such as horse behavior. Don't let one or two students dominate the discussion or answer all the questions; use a "round robin" method or call on each person so that everyone has a chance to contribute.

- **Practical lesson:** Students learn by doing, usually with a brief explanation and/or demonstration first. This works well for teaching hands-on skills such as grooming and bandaging. You must have enough equipment for everyone, a safe place to work, suitable horse(s), and be able to supervise all students while they are working. Having students work in teams or pairs may help.
- **Lecture:** Best for introducing a new topic or information on a subject the group is interested in; only for older students and dismounted instruction. Lectures should be *brief, clear,* and *interesting*. Disadvantages are that students may become bored, may not understand, and may "tune you out," and you do not get as much feedback from your students as in other methods. Lectures tend to be used too often; they can be one of the least effective methods of teaching, especially in mounted and practical situations. Try to find ways to involve students, such as asking questions, doing short reviews, or asking for examples. You can make it fun by including a little competition.
- **Role-playing and skits:** They help students to view reality from another point of view and encourage creativity, expression, and social skills (interacting with other people). This method can be great fun, especially for younger Pony Club members. Role-playing is a good way to demonstrate horse behavior.
- **Games and contests:** Games can motivate students while making learning and practice fun. They should involve skills or knowledge you want to encourage (such as keeping all horses on the rail or learning parts of tack), and must be fun for *all* participants, not just the winner. Don't overemphasize competition at the expense of good horsemanship and teamwork. Above all, games must be safe and suitable for the level of the riders.

These are only a few of the instructional methods you might use. Be flexible and creative, and pay attention to each student's response to the methods you choose.

## Your Students

Every student is an individual, with his or her own needs, abilities, interests, and reasons for riding or being in Pony Club. The more interested you are in your students, the easier and more rewarding it is to teach them. Try to put yourself in your students' place. Would you like to have yourself as a teacher? How easy would it be to learn from you?

Good instructors tailor their teaching to the age and level of their students, without ever talking down to them.

Pony Club members range from young children to young adults. Because skills and learning ability develop gradually, different age groups have different characteristics. However, each child develops at his or her own rate. Some will be farther ahead or slower to develop in certain areas than the average for their age group.

> **Young children** (age 6–9) are developing gross motor skills (skills involving large muscle movements) and coordination. They usually have lots of energy and enthusiasm, like to have fun, and need to be kept busy. However, they have short attention spans and can get bored or physically tired quickly. They need help with strenuous or complicated tasks, such as carrying heavy objects and tacking up.
>
> **Preteens** (age 10–12) have better coordination and are developing fine motor skills (skills requiring small or detailed muscle movements). They have longer attention spans than younger children, but not as long as teens or adults. Preteens are usually very much involved with and influenced by their peer group. They may have lots of energy that needs an outlet, but can be shy and sensitive, especially to criticism.
>
> **Teenagers** are in a process of change—physically, mentally, and emotionally. Some have growth spurts and may have difficulty in coordination while learning to cope with their changing bodies. Teens may feel and act like adults, and at other times act like kids. Teenagers are developing and testing their values, beliefs, and goals. They expect honesty and high standards from teachers and leaders, and their respect must be earned, not demanded. Teenagers, especially at the upper levels, are able to handle much more responsibility than younger children. They need to be involved in the process of setting goals and rules, rather than having these dictated to them.

## Setting Goals

Goals are important for teachers and students. They tell you where you are headed and how you know when you get there. They also help you stay motivated along the way.

When planning a lesson or course, goals (educational objectives) tell what you expect your students to accomplish. To be useful, goals must be clear and specific. For example, "riding better" is too vague a goal; "riding with good balance and position at posting trot" is more specific.

Large goals (such as passing a Pony Club certification test) must be broken down into smaller sub-goals that can be attained step by step. This gives a student many small successes along the way, leading to larger accomplishments. They also build confidence and motivation. Setting a goal so high that it seems unattainable, or concentrating only on a goal far in the future, can be discouraging.

Goals must be important to the student. If you set goals that are not important to your student, you will be in conflict and you probably won't get very far. For example, if competition is important to you but not to your student (or vice versa), you are both likely to be disappointed. Children should be involved in the process of setting goals. Each child has his own motivation, goals, and reasons for riding or being in Pony Club. If your teaching helps your students reach their own goals, you will both be successful.

Using the Pony Club Standards of Proficiency and the Flow Charts for each member's next level can help with setting goals, planning curriculum, and keeping track of which skills have been taught and mastered. These can be found on the USPC website at www.ponyclub.org. They should be printed and kept in a notebook or binder by each individual, with progress marked off by the instructor at each Pony Club meeting, clinic, or camp. This is a good way to help members prepare for their next certification and for DCs, parents, instructors, or other club leaders to determine the readiness for each member who may be considering moving up to the next level.

## Physical Education

Like other sports, teaching riding requires knowledge of the human body and how it works. Instructors must study human anatomy and kinesiology (the study of movement) as much as horsemanship and equitation. The popularity of fitness and sport science has made more people aware of fitness and physical training. However, less research has been done about how the human body is used in riding than in other popular sports.

As an instructor, it is important to know how to assess and teach physical skills, and how best to develop your students' abilities. Devising an exercise to strengthen the proper muscles is much more effective than nagging a rider to correct a bad habit.

We all have an imperfect sense of what our bodies are doing, and have unconscious habit patterns that feel natural and normal to us, even when they are incorrect. For example, a person who habitually tilts forward may believe that he is sitting straight up when he is actually leaning forward; when he sits up correctly, he may feel "all wrong," as if he were leaning backward. In addition, human bodies are not perfectly symmetrical; we all have a stronger and a weaker side. This can cause problems in balance, position, and crookedness. Instructors must help their students become more aware of how they use their bodies, and must realize that repeated mistakes do not mean that a student is lazy or disobedient. A picture is worth a thousand words. If a student is struggling to correct his position, sometimes seeing it with mirrors, pictures, or through videos can really help.

Some riders are naturals, gifted with athletic ability, coordination, and "feel." Riding skills come easily to them, but they may not understand what they do or how they do it. Those who lack these gifts can still become excellent riders, but they need good instruction and may have to work harder. Attitude, desire, and the willingness to work hard—not physical talent—are what ultimately determine how far a person will go in horsemanship.

## Sport Psychology

Sport psychology is an innovation in the teaching and coaching of all sports, including riding. It focuses on the mental and emotional side of sports and competition, including teaching and learning, motivation, goal setting, problem solving, and developing the most effective mind-set for training and competition. Sport psychology techniques have helped riding instructors, competitive coaches, and riders from beginners through Olympic competitors, and the field is growing rapidly. Sport psychology can be especially helpful in dealing with the pressures of competition and overcoming fear.

You can learn more about sport psychology through books, audio tapes, and seminars, and there is much information available on the Internet. Some colleges offer courses and workshops in sport psychology.

# What is Good Teaching?

If you think about the best teachers and teaching you have had, you will probably find that many of the following ideas were essentials. You may be able to think of other aspects of good teaching that are important as well.

## Safety First!

Always put safety first, for people and for horses. Learn (and keep learning) about safety procedures, and use Safety Checks. Plan and practice emergency procedures, and always know how and where to get assistance quickly whenever and wherever you teach.

Establish safety rules and procedures, and insist that they are followed. Don't make exceptions, or allow anyone to ride with unsafe attire or equipment, ever!

Consider the age, experience, physical condition, and abilities of each rider. Teach only what students can handle at the present. *Never* over-face a rider or horse! Fear, fatigue, and confusion interfere with learning and cause accidents.

Use your own best judgment. If you have an uncomfortable feeling about letting a student do something, heed that instinct!

There must always be an adult in charge (in addition to the Pony Club instructor) who has a copy of the written safety/emergency procedures and a list of all necessary phone numbers for help in case of an emergency. Students should wear up-to-date USPC medical information at all times.

## Know Your Subject

In order to teach anything, you must understand it. Motivational speaker Les Brown says, "You can't teach what you don't know, and you can't lead where you don't go." To teach riding at any level, you must have experienced it yourself. Teaching "over your head" is foolish and embarrassing; in riding, it is dangerous! For some subjects, knowing your subject may mean researching or looking it up.

## Be a Model

Your students will do what they see you *do,* not what you *say.* Be properly turned out (boots, breeches or khaki type pants with belt, neat shirt [tucked in], watch, neat hair [tied back], and certified safety helmet for riding lessons; neat, appropriate clothes and footwear for dismounted lessons).

Never smoke, chew gum, or use crude language when teaching. Set the kind of example you want your students to follow.

## Discipline and Respect

Safe horsemanship requires discipline: self-discipline, to set a safe example; disciplined riders, who pay attention and respond to you promptly, especially in an emergency; proper and safe behavior from non-riding spectators and helpers; and well-schooled horses that are under control. Riding is too dangerous a sport for sloppiness or lack of discipline.

Discipline doesn't mean punishment or shouting orders; rather, it means having a clear, positive authority and being in charge. To have discipline, you must first establish ground rules, which must be reasonable and easily followed. Your students (and others) must understand that it is important for everyone's safety that they pay attention and do as you say.

Discipline also implies respect: respect for the horse, for others, for the sport, and for oneself. Being punctual, polite, considerate, and neatly turned out shows respect for the instructor, students, and those who make riding and Pony Club possible.

## Be Interested in Your Students

Know each student as an individual. Find out about special problems they may have (such as learning disabilities, or physical or emotional problems). Discuss each student's goals, what he enjoys, how he learns best, and what he finds difficult.

Be patient. What comes easily to one student may be hard for another. Each student has his own abilities and learns at his own rate.

Understand your students' fears: Physical fear (fear of falling or getting hurt) and mental fear (fear of failure, embarrassment, or looking foolish). Never embarrass or degrade a student, or allow others to do so; discuss fears and problems privately.

Accepting a student's fear, without judgment or criticism, is the first step toward conquering it. "Pushing" a fearful student or denying the fear can make it many times worse, and can create a very dangerous situation. Remember that *safety* must come before achievement.

## Be Fair, Honest, and Positive!

Students respect teachers who are fair and honest. Fairness means treating students equally and having respect for every student and horse, regardless of abilities. Give equal attention to each member of the class and never play favorites.

Be specific in your praise: "Your seat is more secure and less bouncy" is more helpful than a meaningless "Good." When you ask a student to try an exercise or training technique, evaluate the results honestly. If your way doesn't work, admit it and try something else.

Teach in positive terms as much as possible. Tell students how to do something, not how *not* to do it. Avoid negatives like "don't" or "stop"; these can put the wrong idea more firmly into a student's mind! Above all, reinforce and build on the good things about your students, their riding, and their horses instead of tearing them down with negative criticism. Remember that skills are learned through success, not failure.

## Break Material Down into Simple Steps

Anything is easier to learn when it is broken down into small steps (sub-skills), and each step is taught thoroughly before going on to the next. This method develops solid skills and builds confidence through success at each step. Trying to teach too much at once or moving ahead too fast can be overwhelming and unsafe. Bypassing essential steps or skimping on correct basics handicaps a student in later work and is dangerous!

When teaching any subject, ask yourself what skills and knowledge are needed first. Review and test these fundamentals before going on to the next step. If a student has trouble, ask yourself if one of his basics is weak, or if the step he is attempting is too big. Break it down into smaller, simpler steps. Remember that each student (and horse) learns at his own rate. Don't rush a slow student through the basic steps, or hold back a student who quickly masters several steps.

## Use Variety to Keep Lessons Interesting

Keep your students' interest by using a variety of teaching methods and exercises. Different methods appeal to different types of learning. Use your creativity and sense of humor!

- Find different ways to say the same thing and express new ideas. Listen to other instructors, read, and write down new exercises or techniques. Ask questions, use analogies, and relate riding to everyday things, such as riding a bicycle.
- Include some independent work in each class. Help students set goals to work on during a period of "free riding," and discuss their work afterward. Give students homework or exercises to practice on their own.
- Use games and challenges (safe and appropriate for the students' level) to encourage skills and horsemanship while having fun.
- Cavaletti, ground poles, cones, and markers can be used for variety and to create interesting exercises. Always use safe equipment, properly spaced for the size and stride of the horses.

## Set Ground Rules

Students cooperate better if they understand *in advance* what is expected of them in any situation. This is especially important with a new student or class. People feel unfairly treated if they are criticized for breaking a rule if they were not told about it first, and ignorance of safety rules is dangerous.

Keep ground rules simple, clear, and few in number. Always give reasons for them. Instead of lecturing, have the group discuss reasons for rules, or even have them formulate the rules themselves. Posting a sign with barn safety rules or giving students a written list of rules can help reinforce the rules, but does not take the place of good instruction.

# Teaching Techniques

To teach well, you must know your material, prepare, and present it in an organized way, using safe and suitable teaching methods and exercises.

## Resources

The *USPC Manuals of Horsemanship* (Book 1, D Level, and Book 2, C Levels), in addition to this book, are excellent references for teaching subjects for different levels. You should also review the USPC Standards of Proficiency for the level you are teaching.

A good instructor is well-read and stays informed of new developments in riding, training, and horse knowledge through books, publications, videos, the Internet, and educational opportunities such as clinics. Many sources of information can be found on the USPC website at www.ponyclub.org. Consulting with other instructors or an expert is another good way to gather information on a subject. Remember that new skills and ideas must be safe and appropriate for your students, and must fit into the USPC Standards. You may also need to practice an exercise or ride a student's horse in order to have firsthand knowledge on which to base your teaching.

## Progression

Good teaching is *progressive;* it moves from simple to complex and from basic to more advanced. Major subjects and large goals are broken down into smaller topics and sub-goals, and these in turn are broken down into smaller lessons and steps to be mastered. This applies to a course of study (such as the USPC Standards of Proficiency), to subjects (such as bandaging), and to lessons.

It is important to know which skills and knowledge are basic and fundamental to your subject, and which should come later.

## Evaluating Students' Level

When starting work with a new student, especially one beyond the beginner level, you must evaluate his basic skills and knowledge, ask questions, and find out whether any of his basics are weak or misunderstood. *Never* assume a rider's skills in one area must be good because of what you see in another area (for example, don't assume he understands and uses the aids correctly because he has jumped a certain height). Before introducing new work, always review the basics and evaluate how well the rider understands and performs them for his level. It is also important to have the student demonstrate skills he says he has mastered, so that you can assess these yourself.

*Failure to learn and practice correct fundamentals becomes a serious handicap to a rider, hurts his progress, and can endanger him, his horse, and those around him.*

## Lesson Planning and Organization

Being organized saves time and makes it easier for students to learn and for you to teach. Poor organization and planning wastes time and leads to confusion and unsafe situations. It can leave students bored and frustrated, and may lessen their respect for the teacher. Be prepared; review the material and plan your lesson. Divide your lesson into sections and steps, and teach the basics first. Have your teaching area and any equipment set up ahead of time. Keep track of the time, and start and finish on time.

No matter how well you plan, you must adapt your teaching to your students' needs and the conditions *at that time*. You may find that a student needs extra help or more confidence, a horse needs more schooling, or the class needs more review and practice before you can safely go on with the lesson you had planned. Weather, ground conditions, and the teaching environment can change, and people and horses sometimes have bad days. Be aware of how your students and horses are feeling and performing, and be ready to modify your plan to make the lesson safe and positive.

It is important to write out a lesson plan on what you plan to teach and what you will need to teach it. A few notes written afterward help in planning the next lesson, recording students' progress, or when bringing in a substitute teacher. The USPC website has information and lesson plans posted under Safety and the various disciplines. A sample lesson plan appears at the end of this section as well.

A well-organized lesson includes the following:

**Equipment needed:** This should include all items you may need to complete the lesson safely. You may wish to include things like a leather punch, whip, your helmet, and game props.

**References:** Sometimes you may need to do some research before a lesson, look up a topic, make notes, and write down sources so you can refer to them again if needed.

**Preparation:** This includes gathering information on lesson material, lesson planning, and physical preparations (collecting equipment, setting up the ring). It also includes necessary information on students, their level, and horses; and safety preparations (survey of teaching area, and any necessary preparation, such as for longeing, games, jumping, or other activities).

**Introduction and Safety Check:** Introduce yourself to your students by giving your name and a brief bit of information about yourself, what Pony Club you are a member of and what certification you hold, as well as what your favorite equine sport may be.

Ask your students to tell you a little about themselves, including their name, age, and level, and their mount's name and age. It is also very helpful to know if they or their mount has had any injury or illness recently.

Ask how long they have been riding this horse or pony, how many days a week they ride, and how often their mount is ridden. These questions will give you an idea of the fitness and/or soundness level of both mount and rider, which is important to think about to determine if you need to adjust your lesson plan. You can have this conversation during the individual Safety Check you conduct with each rider. Stick to the important issues if time is short.

For a further description of what to look for during your Safety Check, please refer to page 311 in this chapter and the *USPC C Level Manual,* pages 308–311. There is also more information on the USPC website on this.

**Warm-up:** Ten to 15 minutes of progressive exercises are needed to warm up horses and riders and get them physically and mentally ready to work. Remember to vary the exercises and change gaits and directions frequently.

**Review and evaluation:** Observe and evaluate riders as they perform skills they already know and review the last lesson's work. Are they competent and confident? Are there any problems? Do they need more practice or review? If riders (or horses) are not ready to go on to the next lesson you have planned, adjust your plan accordingly.

**Explanation:** Explain the day's objective—what you will teach and why. For new work, explain the step or exercise, what it will accomplish, and why it will help. Keep your explanation clear, short, and simple. Don't lecture!

**Demonstration:** Demonstrate, on the ground or mounted (or have an assistant or one of the riders demonstrate, if possible). Visual aids (diagrams, posters, blackboard, marker board, or even drawing in the dirt) can be helpful. Make sure that everyone can see, and that your demonstration is clear, short, and safe.

**Application (trial):** Students apply or try out the new work. This may need to be done individually, as it is easier to watch each student closely and give help or make corrections. Try to devise an exercise or method that is simple to perform and gives students the best chance of success.

**Critique:** Discuss the student's performance. Be positive; praise any success or effort in the right direction. Suggest ways to improve, and why they might work better.

Sometimes the group can be involved in the evaluation process. This can help the other riders learn through observation, but it is important that students know how to give fair and constructive comments.

**Practice and evaluation:** Practice the exercise again, in both directions. Developing "muscle memory" takes repetition. Reinforce what is correct about the exercise; if you dwell on mistakes, it may fix them more firmly in the student's mind.

**Summary:** Review the day's objectives and success. Discuss problems and how to correct them. Assign homework or practice. Ask questions, and ask if students have questions. Ask students what they have learned, and discuss what they did well and what they need to work on.

Review the lesson yourself, and make notes on what you taught, how it went, and what should be covered in the next lesson.

### SAMPLE LESSON PLAN

Topic: _____ Level: _____

Class Size: _____ Time: _____ Location: _____

Students' Names and Ages: _____

Assistant(s): _____

Equipment Needed: _____

References: _____

Objectives: (How will you know when objectives are achieved?) _____

_____

_____

| LESSON PROCEDURE | NOTES TO REMEMBER | (APPROXIMATE LENGTH) |
|---|---|---|
| A. Introductions | | |
| B. Safety Check | | |
| C. Warm-up | | |
| D. Review and Evaluation | | |
| **NEW MATERIAL** | **NOTES TO REMEMBER** | **(APPROXIMATE LENGTH)** |
| A. Explanation | | |
| B. Demonstration | | |
| C. Application (Exercise) | | |
| D. Critique | | |
| E. Practice and Evaluation (Exercise) | | |
| F. Summary | | |
| G. Homework or Practice Assigned | | |
| Other Notes on Lesson _____ | | |

# Teaching Mounted Lessons

## Voice and Communication

Students must be able to hear and understand your instruction. It takes practice to develop a well-controlled voice that carries well and enunciates clearly, especially outdoors.

In order to be heard at a distance, you must learn to *project* your voice correctly. Shouting or raising your voice is very stressful, makes you sound angry, and can strain your vocal cords and make you lose your voice.

Voice projection requires proper breathing. Most people take shallow breaths most of the time, using the upper chest. To project your voice, you must use your diaphragm and abdominal muscles, and breathe from deep down in your chest as you speak.

To learn to project your voice, practice outdoors or in a large indoor arena. Ask a helper to stand at a distance (100 feet or so) and tell you how well you can be heard. Follow these steps:

1. Place one hand over your lower abdomen, below your navel.
2. Take a deep, slow breath, feeling your lower abdomen "fill" and press against your hand as you inhale.
3. Speak a simple phrase such as "Prepare to trot," as you press your hand against your abdomen. Speak slowly and send each syllable out "from the diaphragm."
4. For contrast, try raising your voice. You can feel the strain on your throat and vocal cords; your helper can tell you which method is easier to hear.

Voice is very directional. Place yourself upwind, facing your class, and aim your voice at your students. If you turn away or speak toward the ground, your students cannot hear you.

Think before you speak. If you use fewer words and simple phrases, it is easier to make each one heard. Talking too much and too quickly makes your speech an indistinct babble. It isn't necessary to fill every moment with instruction. Students need some quiet time in order to process and practice what you have told them.

Vary the tone and speed of your voice to add expression and enthusiasm, or to emphasize action or pace. Avoid speaking in a monotone or sing-song rhythm. Enunciate your syllables more clearly than in ordinary conversation; don't mumble. Your tone of voice conveys as much as your words, to horses as well as to students.

Look up and out, and make eye contact with your students. This projects confidence and authority, and makes you easier to understand. Think of yourself as an actor or actress while you instruct, stepping out of your quiet shell and projecting enthusiasm with your interesting voice.

You can reinforce your words with gestures, body language, and other nonverbal communication. This helps students understand even if they fail to hear everything you say.

## Horse Awareness

The safety and effectiveness of your teaching depends to a great extent on your awareness and how well you work with your students' horses. Being a lesson horse is one of the hardest jobs for a horse, as he must tolerate some inevitable rider mistakes during the learning process. Good teaching is considerate of the horse and should improve his training as well as help the student ride better.

Horses used for teaching must be safe and suitable, whether they are lesson horses or owned by students. You must be able to evaluate a horse's level of training and the rider/horse combination, and be sure they can work safely with each other. Sometimes this requires riding the horse yourself.

As an instructor, you are responsible for the safety and well-being of both the horses you use and the riders you teach. You must make sure that each horse is handled, ridden, and worked in a way that is appropriate for him. Be aware of the fit and suitability of tack, and the horse's fitness and fatigue levels.

Monitor each horse's behavior and attitude throughout the class. Your ability to "read" a horse's mood or intentions is an important safety factor. If you notice a behavior trend (such as a horse beginning to act nervous, irritable, bored, or uncomfortable), take action right away. Don't ignore the behavior until it becomes a serious problem.

## Teaching Mounted Group Lessons

Mounted group work may be taught in several ways:

- **As a ride,** working in line behind a leader at a safe distance.
- **Open order,** in which all riders maintain the same gait, direction, and exercise, but they may pass safely, circle, or cut across to maintain a safe distance.
- **Individual work** performed in turn, with the rest of the riders lined up on the rail or in the center.
- **Riders working independently,** for riders at a suitable level, able to work safely and productively on their own.

It is easier to control a group lesson in a clearly defined area. Arena markers (corners, center-line and quarter-line markers, and dressage letters) help to define figures and where movements are to be executed.

Learn to scan your class, frequently checking each student's technique and control, and giving your attention to the whole class, instead of getting overly involved with one student. If you have an assistant, have him give extra help to individuals when necessary. Learn and use students' names, and be sure to observe and communicate with each student individually, even if briefly.

Working as a ride is good for students and horses. Riders must pay attention, use their aids to adjust pace and spacing, and ride accurate corners, lines, and figures. Horses learn to adjust pace and balance, respond promptly, and work quietly in company. Working as a ride behind an experienced leader can enhance control, especially when the riders in a class have different levels and abilities.

Always establish ground rules for safety, and explain your terms and words of command. Make sure your students (and you!) know left from right and understand your directions. Choose an experienced, competent leader who can set a steady pace and ride figures accurately.

Here are some standard terms and practices for group riding classes:

**Spacing:** Maintain a minimum of one or two horse lengths between horses (more at faster gaits). Tell students to shorten stride or go deeper into a corner to maintain a safe distance. If a rider begins to lag behind, he should increase his pace or cut the corner to catch up. Specify whether students may pass, circle, or cut across the ring to maintain spacing, or whether they must keep their places in line.

**Passing:** If passing is permitted, it must be done only to the inside. Never squeeze between a horse and the rail.

**Track:** Riders should ride on the outer track (next to the rail) unless told to do otherwise.

**Direction:**
- "**On the right rein**" means clockwise (right hand toward inside). "**On the left rein**" means counterclockwise (left hand toward inside).
- "**Track right**" means turn right on reaching the track and proceed clockwise (right hand toward the inside).
- "**Track left**" means turn left on reaching the track and proceed counterclockwise (left hand toward the inside).

When working independently, or when an exercise results in one or more riders changing direction, pass left shoulder to left shoulder.

**Halting, making adjustments:** If a rider must stop, he should do so at the center of the ring, out of the way of those continuing to work.

**Directive Terms:**
- "**Leading file**" means the leader.
- "**Form a ride**" means to form up in line behind a leader, keeping one horse length spacing.
- "**Whole ride**" or "**all**" means all together.
- "**In succession**" or "**in turn**" means one at a time.
- "**Go large**" means return to the outer track and continue in the same direction (on the same rein).

**Words of command tell riders four things:**

- **Who** is being given the command ("Whole ride," "In succession," the rider's name, and so on).
- **What** to do ("Turn left," "Prepare to canter," and so on).
- **When** to carry out the command ("Ride, tr—OT," "Canter NOW," and so on). "Leading file, begin" tells the leader to begin the exercise.
- **Where** to carry out the command ("At the K marker," "As you cross the center line," and so on).

Commands must be clear and well timed. Give the preparatory command ("Leading file, prepare to turn left at the E marker") in plenty of time, pause, and then give the command of execution ("Turn left NOW") when the rider arrives at a good place to begin the exercise. If you give a command hastily or too late, the riders will not have enough time to prepare and may act too late or apply their aids roughly. This can also result in dangerous bunching of horses.

Give students plenty of time to prepare for transitions, and use your tone of voice to help them (and the horses) understand your commands. Your voice should rise when you ask for an increase of pace and fall for a decrease of pace, and give cadence when needed.

## Teaching Beginners

Teaching beginners is an important job, because a student's early experiences with horses and riding can make or break his riding career. Good teaching of beginners includes the following goals:

- **Safety:** A safe experience, teaching basic safety practices and the reasons for them, and establishing a safety-conscious attitude.
- **Confidence:** Developing self-confidence, trust in the instructor, and confidence in the horse.
- **Familiarization:** Becoming familiar with the horse, tack, procedures, and vocabulary.
- **Technique:** Learning basic techniques, such as mounting and dismounting, basic position, holding the reins, and applying simple aids.
- **Control:** Learning to control the horse and use simple aids.
- **Horse care and handling:** Learning safe and simple basics of handling and caring for the horse, and treating the horse kindly and responsibly.
- **Enjoyment:** A pleasant experience tailored to the student's age, personality, and individual needs.

## WHAT YOU WILL NEED

- Student must wear safe and suitable attire (not necessarily riding clothes), including a properly fitted ASTM/SEI safety helmet and safe footwear. (See the *USPC D Level Manual*, page 300.)
- A suitable horse or pony—quiet, patient, and not too big or too small for the rider.
- Tack fitted to the horse or pony and the rider, neck strap, lead line, and longeing equipment if teaching a longe lesson.
- A safe place to work, preferably an enclosed ring (60 × 120 feet is a good size).
- Review the *USPC D Level Manual*, especially Chapter 2, "Basic Riding on the Flat" and Chapter 5, "Handling, Leading, and Tying Your Pony"; and the current USPC Standards of Proficiency, which can be found on the USPC website at www.ponyclub.org. There you will also find lesson plans, handout, worksheets, videos, and more to help you on your way to being an instructor.
- If teaching a class, assistants to help students with their horses and to lead horses.

## Introductory Lesson

An introductory lesson should be short, simple, safe, and fun. Its purpose is to introduce children to the instructor and the horse, develop confidence, and teach what they need to know to have a safe and fun lesson. An introductory lesson should include a tour of the stable, tack room, and other areas, and a discussion of safety rules and the reasons for them. The lesson may be dismounted (teaching safety and horse nature, basic handling, simple grooming, tacking up, and so on), or it may include mounting and dismounting, basic position, holding the reins, and walking on a lead line. It is easier and safer to teach the first lessons as private lessons or very small lead line groups, placing the student in a riding class only after he has shown good basic control and can follow directions. If you must teach an introductory lesson to a group of students, you will need good organization, good control of your class, *and assistants to help you, if available.*

### SOME TIPS FOR TEACHING BEGINNERS

- Review the material in the *USPC D1 Level Manual*, especially safety, pony horse handling, and basic riding (found in the USPC D Manual).
- Keep lessons short, simple, and skill-specific. Everything is new to a beginner, and he can become overwhelmed if you try to teach too much at once.

- Teach students why things must be done a certain way, but keep reasons brief and simple.
- Stay close enough to the student and horse for safety and to encourage confidence. (Use a lead line or longe line until students can manage their horses safely by themselves.) Don't leave a beginner alone in charge of a horse, mounted or dismounted.
- When teaching a group, be aware of group control, spacing, horse behavior, and attention to all riders. Don't get stuck on one rider and forget the rest. You must anticipate horse behavior to keep beginning riders safe, as they lack the knowledge, experience, and control to do this themselves.
- Don't ask beginners to perform an exercise or to ride for too long. Unaccustomed muscles tire quickly, so allow frequent short rest breaks.
- Develop a wide range of exercises and activities you can choose from that can be done at slow gaits. This keeps students interested while gradually building foundation skills and practice time. Allowing students to progress to faster gaits too quickly (because they ask to or you run out of ideas) is unsafe and leads to poor learning and abusive riding.
- Keep lessons fun by teaching in small, easy steps; praising any improvement, and incorporating games, creativity, and a sense of humor.
- Emphasize good horsemanship, especially kindness, consideration, and responsibility for the horse.

## Teaching Jumping

Teaching jumping requires a knowledge of safety, good basic horsemanship on the flat, and knowledge and experience in jumping. You must understand the foundation skills and progression in the training of both horse and rider over fences. Teaching jumping requires an educated eye for cause and effect in the performance of horse and rider, and the effect of different obstacles, combinations, and gymnastics.

Over-facing students or horses, or permitting students to try more advanced jumping than they are prepared for, is *dangerous!* The *USPC Manuals of Horsemanship* (D, C, and HB – A Levels) are organized into progressive skill levels, with recommended jumping activities for each level. Instructors should review the jumping skills for the level they are teaching, and also for the previous level.

Before a rider can jump safely at any level, he must have:

- **Safe attire,** including a properly fitted, approved helmet and appropriate footwear (see the Pony Club website and the *USPC Horse Management Handbook* for more information).

- **Safe, properly fitted tack** suitable for jumping.
- **Suitable horse or pony,** sound, well-schooled, and capable of jumping at the level required.
- **Solid basics at the rider's level,** including a secure and correct seat, effective control and use of aids, non-abusive riding, and good balance in full seat and half-seat (jumping position).
- **Confidence** and desire to jump.

Prepare students and horses for jumping by:
- Checking tack, girth, and helmet for fit and safety helmet certification.
- Proper warm-up on the flat.
- Adjusting stirrups to proper jumping length.
- Jumping warm-up, including ground poles, cavaletti, or low fences.

Use safe equipment and jump only on good footing. *Frangible pins* (breakable jump cup pins) add safety and must be used on the back rail of all oxers. Another option is to use $7/16$-inch dowels cut to 6-inch lengths. Remove unused cups from standards, and store extra equipment safely out of the way.

Build solid-looking, inviting fences with safe lines and distances. Gymnastics and courses must be suitable for the horses' size, stride, and training level, and the riders' capability.

Measure distances and/or heights with a tape measure, and check distances in gymnastics by riding through with ground poles, before raising fences. For mixed classes, set two gymnastics, one for ponies and one for horses.

Make exercises progressive: Evaluate students' performance and horses' behavior over a ground pole, cavaletti grid, or low cross-rail. Horses that rush, weave, or trip over a low pole need more schooling or a better approach before fences are raised. This is a good way to check distances, too.

Encourage rhythm, relaxation, contact, impulsion, straightness, free forward movement, and good jumping form in horses and ponies. Relate correct work on the flat to its effect on jumping.

Teach riders the importance of a correct and secure seat, good balance, use of aids, eye control, and release. Relate rider position (and errors) to the horse's performance over fences.

Make sure the rider can develop sufficient impulsion to jump the fence or gymnastic, and that he has control.

If you see a trend developing (such as a horse starting to rush, hang back, or run out), correct it immediately even if it means going back to an easier exercise. If you ignore such tendencies, they get progressively worse and may become dangerous.

Know when to stop. Finish jumping before riders and horses get tired and their jumping deteriorates. Don't allow children to over-jump their horses (including after class and at home).

Refer to the current USPC Standards of Proficiency for basic gymnastic exercises and descriptions of appropriate jumps and courses for each Pony Club certification level. These are available on the USPC website at www.ponyclub.org.

## Teaching Longe Lessons

Longe lessons allow a rider to concentrate on improving his riding without having to control his horse. Their purpose is to:

- Build confidence.
- Improve suppleness, eliminate stiffness, and help the rider follow the horse's movements more accurately.
- Improve a rider's balance, security, and correct position.
- Develop a secure, correct, supple, and independent seat, from which the rider can apply his aids correctly and easily.

Longe lessons can be useful for students of all levels, as long as the instructor is sufficiently skilled, the horse is suitable, and the length and demands of the lesson are appropriate.

The instructor must always pay attention to the following:

**Confidence:** Persisting in spite of fear and tension prevents progress and leads to soreness, bad experiences, greater fear, and potentially dangerous situations. If a student is afraid or tense, go slower!

**Balance:** The rider needs to find a correct balance, with his weight evenly distributed over both seat bones and a balanced pelvis. If he tips forward, backward, or off to the side, especially in transitions, go back to a slower pace and re-establish correct balance.

**Suppleness:** Suppleness is related to balance and confidence. Loss of balance causes a rider to tighten his muscles or grip in an effort to stay on the horse; fear or lack of confidence causes stiffness. Stiffness can disrupt balance.

Whenever confidence, balance, or suppleness are lost, go back to a slower pace, an easier exercise, or even halt in order to re-establish correct fundamentals.

Be aware of fitness and fatigue levels. Longe exercises are tiring; many short repetitions with brief rest periods are better than prolonging an exercise to the point of exhaustion. (This also applies to the horse, who must not be longed too long in one direction or too long or hard in any session.) Longeing a rider until he is so tired that he "gets it" is very hard on both horse and rider and unsafe, and afterward, the rider usually doesn't know what he did correctly.

Requirements for longe lessons:

**Safe longeing area** with good footing, preferably an enclosed ring, with a minimum of distractions. Other riders should not be riding in the immediate area, nor should there be any loose horses or animals turned out in the area.

**Suitable horse or pony,** obedient and well trained to longe, and accustomed to being used for longe lessons. His gaits must be regular, steady, and comfortable, and he must respond to the instructor's commands. *Never try to teach a longe lesson on a green horse!*

**Instructor with knowledge and experience in longeing,** able to longe the horse with complete control, maintaining even gaits and making smooth transitions.

**Correctly fitted longeing equipment,** including:
- Longe line and longe whip; boots or bandages are recommended for the horse.
- Saddle that fits both horse and rider. The saddle may be fitted with a pommel strap (safety strap), which the rider may hold to secure his position.
- Snaffle bridle.
- A longe cavesson fitted correctly over the bridle (with noseband fastened inside the bridle cheekpieces) is the best choice of equipment.
- Side reins may be used to help maintain a steady balance and frame, but only on well-schooled, experienced horses, and *only* by instructors who can fit them correctly and understand their proper use. (Longeing with side reins is an advanced skill, and is not appropriate for most Pony Club longe lessons. Incorrect use of side reins can damage the horse's training and can be dangerous.)
- Both instructor and rider should wear safe and suitable attire, including a correctly fitted certified safety helmet.

The procedure is as follows:

Longe the horse first without the rider, in both directions, until he is settled and obedient.

If side reins are used, they must *always* be unfastened before the rider mounts or dismounts. This is a safety measure that allows the horse freedom of his head and neck, and prevents the rider from getting caught in the side reins while mounting or dismounting.

When the horse is ready, halt and let the rider mount and adjust the stirrups. He should ride on the longeing circle with reins and stirrups (on the longe line) until he is relaxed and confident. At this point, the reins are no longer needed and can be secured over the horse's neck (tied in a knot if they are to be dropped). However, they should always be within reach in case of emergency.

At the halt, show the rider how to rest his hands lightly on the pommel, and how to hold the pommel or safety strap if he begins to lose his balance or feel insecure. **Emphasize that he must never grab the reins to regain his balance.**

At the walk, let the rider get used to the longeing circle and begin to feel the movement of the horse. Encourage him to breathe deeply, to sit deep and tall, to look up and out, and to notice the way the horse moves his seat bones.

Do some simple exercises that help the rider get used to riding without reins, for example:

- Large arm circles, one arm at a time at first.
- Reaching forward to stroke the horse on neck, then back to stroke behind the saddle.
- Arm circles and shoulder circles, both arms at once.
- Stretching both arms up over head, then touching knees, then toes.
- Side swings (see the *USPC D Level Manual*, pages 72–79).

Let the rider practice at posting trot and sitting trot with stirrups to build confidence. Keep the trot slow, steady, and rather lazy.

The next stage depends on the rider's level and needs, and the instructor's judgment. Some students will need more work with stirrups to develop confidence, balance, and security. Others will be ready to go on to work without stirrups.

Depending on the rider's level and fitness, the rest of the longe lesson may consist of more exercises, position work, transitions, and variations of pace. Remember to work equally on both sides for the benefit of both horse and rider. Give frequent short rest breaks to avoid over-stressing the rider's muscles and his concentration. Longeing is hard work; 10 minutes may be plenty for a novice, and 20 minutes is quite demanding for a fit, experienced rider and horse.

When a student is ready to work without stirrups, cross the stirrup irons over (pull the leathers out and fold them flat) or remove the stirrups altogether. Work at the walk until the rider is confident and comfortable in the correct position. Practicing leg exercises (such as leg stretches and ankle circles) and repeating some easy loosening exercises help develop confidence and a secure seat. Remind your student to secure his seat and reposition himself when necessary by holding the pommel or safety strap, rather than by tensing up and gripping with his legs.

Here are some exercises to develop good balance and position without stirrups:

- At halt or walk, stretch both legs slowly downward, slightly backward, and out to the side from the hip joint. Hold for a few seconds, then release and let legs return to the horse's side. Be careful not to arch the back, tip forward, or exaggerate the stretch. This helps to lower the knees, flatten the thighs, and improve the rider's leg position.

- Bring knees and thighs off the saddle (sideways), then allow them to gently fall back into position. Don't take them too far off or hold for too long, or cramping may result. This emphasizes the balance on the seat bones and allows the legs to hang correctly under the body.

- Hold the arms out to the side and somewhat to the rear. Without body movement, bring each heel back and up alternately to touch the hands, in rhythm with the horse's strides. (Be careful not to kick the horse's sides.) This exercise helps to flatten the thighs and lower the knees.

- Practice sitting trot, posting trot, and half-seat without stirrups. (See the *USPC C Level Manual*, pages 8–9.)

Only advanced riders on experienced longe horses should be allowed to canter on the longe. These riders may practice canter transitions and exercises at the canter for short periods.

For advanced riders, it is useful to practice transitions and work in all gaits with the hands in a riding position, as if holding reins. Always be aware of position, balance, and suppleness. Only a rider whose position is basically correct and supple will be able to stay in balance. If a rider becomes insecure or loses his balance and position for any reason, the horse should be brought back to a walk while the rider corrects his position. Even fit, experienced riders should take frequent short rest breaks, which can be used for discussion.

# Safety in Teaching Horsemanship

Safety is always the first consideration when teaching and working with horses. This is especially important with students who have their own horses or ponies and ride on their own between lessons. Only good safety education and making a habit of safe practices will keep students (and others) safe.

As the instructor, you are responsible for the safety of your students. Use your best judgment, and don't hesitate to recheck something or modify an exercise or activity to make it safer, explaining why the change was necessary. You must set an example for your students in safety and good horsemanship, as they will copy what you do, not what you tell them to do.

Safety requires knowledge, experience, proper procedures, and planning to avoid accidents. All good instructors continue to learn about safety, just as they continue to learn about horses and horsemanship. The following section is only a beginning. In addition, you should be familiar with the USPC Standards of Proficiency, the *USPC Horse Management Handbook*, the online safety training, and the current USPC Recommended Reading List, for your own stable and riding activities. First aid and CPR training are essential for riding instructors, and could save a life!

## Safety Checks

Safety Checks are essential for safe riding and teaching, every time you or your student gets on a horse. They also are an important responsibility for instructors. If you fail to check a student's tack or allow him to ride with unsafe equipment, it could lead to an accident, causing injury to the rider, horse, or both. Students should be taught to make a thorough Safety Check themselves before mounting, but this should always be double-checked by the instructor.

Safety Checks include formal tack and safety inspections at all Pony Club lessons, rallies, competitions, and other functions, and your own personal Safety Check of your students, their tack and attire, their horses, and the environment every time they ride.

Details that must be covered in a tack and safety inspection are described in the *USPC Horse Management Handbook,* the USPC Standards of Proficiency, and the *USPC C Level Manual* (pages 308–311). The following checklists include the teaching environment and other factors you should know about for a safe lesson, and emergency procedures.

# A Safety Checklist for Riding Instructors

I. Teaching Environment
   A. Weather (consider: wind, precipitation, storm coming, extreme heat or cold, heat/humidity index, wind-chill factor).
   B. Ring or teaching area:
      1. Clear of obstacles, distractions, or hazards (take down jumps when teaching beginners).
      2. Suitably fenced, with gate closed.
         a) Rings should never be enclosed by rope, chain, or wire, nor should these materials be used for gates.
         b) No posts or projections protruding to inside of ring.
         c) Gate closed, easily seen, does not invite horse to jump out, no diagonal supports above a gate (which can catch rider's arm or leg).
      3. Suitable size, location, and type of area for students, size of class, and type of lesson.
      4. Safe footing.
      5. Riding pathways must be safe, mowed, clear of debris, free of ruts and holes, and footing otherwise appropriate. Jumps must be clear of overhanging branches that may interfere with the rider or horse. Jumps should be in good repair. No machinery in the area. No barbed wire fencing in the area.
   C. Equipment, obstacles, etc.:
      1. Suitable for class and lesson or activity.
      2. Safely constructed (no sharp edges, protruding points, easily visible to horses, fixed or balanced so as not to fall over or roll, constructed so horse cannot become trapped in obstacle).
      3. Correctly set, with suitable distances, ground lines, and footing.
      4. Breakable (frangible) jump cup pins add safety and must be used on the back rail of all oxers. Another option is to use $7/16$-inch dowels cut to 6-inch lengths.
      5. Jump cups removed from standards when not in use.
   D. General:
      1. Avoid noise and distractions (traffic, construction, mowing, and so on).
      2. Spectators, pets, and other nearby activities under control.
      3. Other horses nearby are distracting; they should not be loose in area, tied to ring fence, or allowed to disturb lesson.

II. Horses and Ponies
   A. Suitable for rider (size, temperament, training level, experience).
   B. Suitable for lesson or activity.
      1. Serviceably sound.
      2. Capable of performing lesson requirements safely.
      3. Fit and prepared for the demands of the lesson.
   C. Instructor should be familiar with horse (evaluate horse and rider combination; ride horse if necessary).
   D. Free from bad habits or dangerous behavior (shown by previous behavior); free from unsoundnesses that could cause accidents.
   E. How is horse acting/feeling at present?
   F. Preparation of horse for lesson (turnout, longeing, instructor ride first if necessary).

III. Tack (Must Meet USPC Standards for Tack and Safety Inspections)
   A. All equipment clean, supple, in good working condition and good repair.
   B. Saddle
      1. Fit: No pressure on spine, two to three fingers clearance at withers, no pinching at shoulders, balanced correctly.
      2. Girth:
         a) Tighten gradually to safe level.
         b) Overtightening a girth is as bad as too loose a girth.
         c) Check before mounting, after 10 minutes of work, and before jumping.
      3. Stirrup bar catches in open position.
      4. Stirrups: Correct size for rider.
         a) Too small can trap foot; too large can let foot slip through.
         b) Safety stirrups recommended for small, lightweight riders.
      5. Saddle pad: Smooth, pulled up in front, correctly secured.
   C. Bridle
      Bit correctly adjusted for comfort and control, curb chain flat (not twisted) and adjusted for correct action of bit.
      1. All buckles closed, strap ends through keepers and runners.
      2. All bridle parts sound, strong, and supple, with sound stitching; correctly adjusted for comfort, security, and control; no rubbing or pinching.

3. Noseband correctly adjusted (comfortably snug, not cranked tight, admits two fingers); throatlatch moderately loose, but bridle secure.
4. Reins correct length, no dangerous loop that could catch rider's foot.

D. Breastplates, martingales, boots, and bandages
1. Control devices (for example, martingales) used only by riders educated in their correct use; suitable for horse, level of rider, and activity.
2. Correctly adjusted to individual horse for security, comfort, and effectiveness.
3. Safety equipment:
    a) Always use rein stops with running martingale.
    b) Rubber ring at neck strap of martingale prevents strap from dropping too low near horse's legs.
    c) Boots and/or bandages correctly put on and securely fastened, suitable for activity.

IV. Riders
A. Correctly and safely dressed for riding (according to situation, whether formal, informal, or everyday attire):
1. Medical information carried as required by USPC Rules.
2. Boots or riding shoes with heel and smooth, one-piece sole (no hiking boots, shoes without heels, or soles with ripples, ridges, or deep tread).
3. Certified helmet, properly fitted, chin-strap fastened.
4. Riding pants, breeches, or jodhpurs that allow correct position.
5. Shirt (short or long sleeves, not sleeveless or tank top) or sweater worn tucked in—no loose-fitting clothing.
6. Appropriate clothing for weather (neck warmer, ear warmers), layering in winter; short sleeves, sun protection, ventilated helmet for hot weather; no long or loose scarves. Gloves optional but a good idea.
7. No jewelry that could catch on horse or tack (for example, rings, bracelets, earrings, hair combs). No sharp objects in hair or pockets. No waist packs.
8. No chewing gum or candy in mouth (can cause choking).
9. No wrist loops on crops.

B. Instructor should be familiar with rider and his level of experience, capability, and riding history. Evaluate riders, take history, and keep notes! Any disabilities, fears, or physical or emotional problems that instructor should be aware of? Is rider on medication? Any medical restrictions?

C. How is rider feeling today? Is rider mentally/physically prepared to ride? What is his level of fitness? Any problems or distractions?

D. Is rider familiar with and confident about riding this horse? About this lesson?

E. Has rider mastered prerequisites for this lesson? What skills or basics are necessary to perform successfully?

F. Can instructor communicate effectively with rider? Does rider have enough discipline and attention span to listen, follow instructions, and ride safely?

# Emergency Procedures for Riding Instructors

I. Before an Emergency Occurs
1. Establish emergency procedures; post procedures and have staff, parents, or responsible adults familiarized with them.
2. Have simple first-aid and emergency equipment on hand:
    Fire extinguishers, hoses, buckets.
    First-aid kits (human, equine).
    Blanket and pillows (can be used to keep injured person comfortable and immobilized, if necessary, until medical help arrives).
3. Have a means of communication for emergency (phone, cell phone, emergency signal). Post emergency numbers (911, Fire, Emergency Service or Ambulance, Police, Veterinarian) and how to report an emergency (including directions to facility) by the telephone. Be sure everyone knows how to call for help and report an emergency. (Not all areas are served by the 911 system; other emergency numbers may be needed.)
4. Record emergency numbers for students' parents and obtain signed permission for treatment in case of emergency. Check that each student is carrying his medical information as required by USPC Rules.
5. Take first aid and CPR training, and maintain your certification.
6. Consult with emergency personnel in your area—fire chief, paramedics, civil defense—regarding your facility and emergency

plans. This is especially important in areas that may be threatened by floods, brush fires, tornadoes, or other natural emergencies.
7. Have a designated area where people are to report to in case of an emergency. Conduct fire drills and practice emergency procedures!

II. Specific Emergency Procedures
   A. Falls
      1. Stop the class. (Teach all riders to stop immediately if a rider falls or a horse gets loose.) Other riders halt or emergency dismount; remain under control while instructor helps fallen student. Catching horse is secondary priority.
      2. Keep fallen rider still while you check for injuries. Don't pull him up on his feet.
      3. If it is believed that the rider may have sustained a concussion, he should not return to riding until evaluated by a physician. More information regarding concussion is available on the USPC website under the Safety tab.
         a) If rider appears possibly injured, follow emergency procedures:

         **CHECK:** Is rider conscious? Able to speak? Check if rider is breathing and has a pulse.

         **CALL:** Send someone to call 911 or Emergency Service immediately, then

         **CARE:** If rider is not breathing, check to make sure that their airway is clear, and then begin CPR if trained to do so. If rider is bleeding seriously, apply direct pressure to wound.

         Do not move victim! Bring help to where he is. Reassure him.

         Do not attempt to move limbs, take off helmet or boots, or get victim up—just keep him still and as comfortable as possible.

         The most qualified first-aid person should remain with victim; send someone else to report accident, send for help, and take charge of other riders.

         b) If rider appears uninjured:

         Don't dramatize the situation, but do allow time for the rider to regain composure.

         Ask if he knows what happened and why.

         Explain how to prevent a recurrence before having him try again.

         Watch for signs of fear, shock, or delayed reaction.

Include the rest of the class in the explanation of what happened and how to prevent it. Sometimes watchers are more scared than the one who actually fell.

Allow time to rebuild confidence, and set rider up for success with easier activities before trying same activity again. This allows time for any adrenaline rush to pass and for any injuries to appear that might not be evident at first, and for the rider to relax and be able to think clearly again.

If you must school the horse, do so in a positive manner, not a rough-riding session. Change horses if necessary for rider's confidence.

Never embarrass the rider or allow others to do so. Don't blame the horse, either!

B. Loss of Control
1. *Stop* all other horses, to prevent incident from involving others and escalating. This may help stop the runaway horse, too.
2. Call instructions—short, simple, and clear: "Sit up!" "Pull up!" "Circle!" A well-projected, calm, commanding voice may get through to a scared rider and may even help control the horse. Shrill, panicky screaming makes a bad situation worse!
3. Move to block the horse, but be careful not to cause him to dodge and spill the rider, or injure you or any other person.
4. On the trail—*Stop all other riders!* Leader reverses to face the ride and keeps control; does not leave the ride. Instructor may follow runaway, but at a safe pace—do not chase or horse will go faster. Try to get rider to circle horse to regain control.

C. Heat-Related Emergency
1. *Heat exhaustion and heat cramps:* Symptoms often begin suddenly, after excessive exercise, heavy perspiration, and inadequate fluid or salt intake. Signs and symptoms resemble those of shock and may include:

    Fatigue, feeling faint or dizzy

    Heavy sweating

    Headache, nausea

    Cool, moist, pale skin

    Rapid, weak heartbeat

    Low-grade fever

    Heat cramps

    Dark-colored urine

**If you suspect heat exhaustion:**

Get the person out of the sun and/or heat and into a shady or air-conditioned location.

Lay the person down and elevate the legs and feet slightly.

Loosen or remove the person's clothing.

Have the person drink cool water or other nonalcoholic beverage without caffeine.

Cool the person by spraying or sponging with cool water and fanning.

Monitor the person carefully. Heat exhaustion can quickly become heatstroke (see below).

Call 911 or emergency medical help if the person's condition deteriorates, especially if fainting, confusion, or seizures occur, or if a fever of 104° F (40° C) or greater occurs with other symptoms.

2. *Heatstroke* is the most severe heat-related problem, potentially life-threatening. Heatstroke can result from exercise or heavy work in hot environments, combined with inadequate fluid intake. In heatstroke, the body's normal mechanisms for dealing with heat stress (sweating and temperature control) become inadequate. The main sign of heatstroke is a markedly elevated body temperature, usually higher than 104° F, with changes in mental status ranging from confusion to coma. Skin may be hot and dry but can be moist. Other signs and symptoms may include:

   Rapid heartbeat

   Rapid and shallow breathing

   Cessation of sweating

   Irritability, confusion, or unconsciousness

   Feeling dizzy or light-headed

   Headache, nausea

   Fainting, which may be the first sign in older adults

**If you suspect heatstroke:**

Move the person out of the sun and/or heat and into a shady or air-conditioned space.

*Call 911 or emergency medical help.*

Cool the person by covering with damp sheets or spraying with cool water. Direct air onto the person with a fan.

Have the person drink cool water or other nonalcoholic beverage without caffeine, if he is able.

Horses may also suffer from heat exhaustion or heatstroke, especially if they are working hard in a hot environment with inadequate water intake. Some horses suffer from *anhidrosis,* a condition that interferes with their ability to sweat, especially in hot, humid climates. Early signs of heat stress in horses are lethargy, excessively heavy breathing, panting, and most seriously, a high temperature and a hot, dry coat without sweating. Some horses may appear colicky.

**If you suspect heat stress in a horse,** stop work and get the horse into a cool or shady area; direct a fan on him if available. Remove tack, offer as much cool water as he will drink, and sponge or hose him down with cool water, scraping as you go, until the water running off his body is cool. In more severe cases, the horse should be bathed with ice water or water containing isopropyl alcohol. If a horse is unable to sweat and has an excessively high body temperature or severe symptoms, call for veterinary help immediately.

D. Injured Horse
1. The most experienced horse first-aid person should deal with the horse. Keep spectators and unqualified people away!
2. Keep the horse as calm and quiet as possible while you assess the situation. The calmer you are, the better for the horse.
3. Protect yourself and any helpers from injury. An injured or upset horse can hurt you unintentionally and compound the emergency. Restrain the horse as necessary, but don't take on more than you can handle.
4. Send for the veterinarian if needed. Staff, students, boarders, and others should be taught how to call for help. Tell them exactly what to say (nature of injury, and so on).
5. Keep the horse quiet and apply appropriate first aid until the veterinarian arrives. Take and record vital signs.

# Handling Teaching Problems

## General Suggestions for Handling Problem Situations

Good communication works both ways: from teacher to student, and from student to teacher. Parents must also be included. It is important that students (and parents) feel that they can communicate with you, especially when a problem arises. To do so, they must feel you are fair and honest, you care about them, and you will listen to what they say. This helps them accept communication from you, trust you, and believe what you say.

Many small problems can be prevented from becoming big ones by clear, positive communication early on. Saying nothing and hoping a problem will go away often allows it to get worse.

For good communication, especially about problems, you must make time to talk with students and parents, and listen to their concerns. Choose an appropriate time when you can listen well, giving your full attention. If this is not possible during a lesson, set up a time when you can meet. It may help to paraphrase what you have heard, to see if you understood it (for example, "As I understand it, you are saying _____. Have I understood you correctly?") When handling a problem or enforcing a rule, use positive, not negative statements, and look for ways to solve problems, not to place blame. Avoid scolding, sarcasm, and labeling or name-calling. Instead, state the effect of the behavior ("When you talk instead of paying attention, you can't hear me, and that isn't safe"), and the consequences ("So we will have to stop the class until everyone is ready to pay attention"). Logical consequences work better than punishment, and reinforcing good behavior (with a smile or praise) works best of all.

## Common Teaching Problems and Some Solutions

### Riding Group of Mixed Abilities
- Assign an experienced rider as leading file.
- Try to find a common subject all can benefit from (for example, leg aids), and teach it on several levels. Novice riders can learn from watching more experienced riders, and the better riders can benefit from demonstrating correct work.
- Be careful to give attention to all riders, not just a few.
- An assistant instructor can give extra help to those who need it.
- When you must focus on one or two riders, give the others something meaningful to do, such as watching the other rider's performance. Sometimes more experienced riders may be asked to practice an exercise while you help another rider.

### Unfit Horse or Rider
- Allow a slower pace, non-strenuous activities, and frequent rest breaks.
- Explain to the rider about fitness and why he must limit his activities.
- Make recommendations on how to begin the conditioning process.

### Inexperienced Rider with Green Horse or Pony
- Emphasize the need for patience by the rider, and a gradual training process.
- Recommend that the rider allow a more experienced person to ride the horse regularly.
- Do not allow sitting trot or any activities beyond the horse's level.
- Encourage the horse to find his balance through free, active gaits and lots of walking.
- Give frequent periods of rest and relaxation; don't go on working past the horse's attention span or level of fitness.
- Suggest books on training of young horses.

### Unsafe or Inappropriate Tack
- Make temporary adjustments if possible. Never allow a student to ride with unsafe equipment.
- If the saddle can't be made safe and nothing else is available, allow the student to ride bareback if he is capable.
- Ask if another rider might loan his tack or mount for some riding time.
- Make sure the student and his parents understand what is unsafe and what to do about it. Be tactful, positive, and helpful!

### Bored or Uninterested Child
- Is the rider bored because he is in a class that is not challenging enough? Is he uninterested in riding? Ask the child to express his feelings about the class. Discuss the problem with parents; is there pressure on the child to ride against his will?
- Assign an assistant instructor for individual help.
- If child is shy, introduce him or her to a "buddy" and have them work as a pair. (Have the entire class work in pairs to avoid putting emphasis on the shy child.)
- Try mounted games.
- If a bored student is capable of moving up, try him in a more advanced group.

### Child Unwilling to Try New Activities
- This may indicate fear and/or lack of confidence. Often the child is afraid he will be forced to do something he is afraid to do.
- Break skills down into small steps. Allow the child to learn each step at his own speed until he is confident enough to combine them.

- Assign an assistant instructor for extra help and modified activities until the child is ready to join the group.
- Explain to the student that he will *never* be expected to do something he isn't ready to do, and that it is okay to stop at any point in an activity.

### Fear
- Fear may be physical (fear of falling or getting hurt); mental (fear of failure, embarrassment, or looking foolish); or both. Fear may or may not be based on a previous bad experience.
- Fear is real. Give the student permission to acknowledge his fear. Never deny it, ridicule it, or make him afraid to express his fear. Covering up fear makes a rider stiff and incapable, and his horse will feel it.
- Physical fear requires a slow, gradual process of building (or rebuilding) confidence. Make sure the activity is safe and that the rider has a quiet, reliable horse. Break skills down into easy steps, and build up many small successes. When the rider begins to feel bored with an exercise, encourage him to stretch his own limits a little at a time by trying just a little more than he is comfortable with. He must push himself—if you push him, you may increase his fear.
- Mental fear is related to stage fright or performance anxiety. Like physical fear, it doesn't help to deny it or to say that there is no reason to be afraid. Some students become more comfortable with mental fears if they practice doing what they are afraid of (competing, performing in front of an audience, taking tests) in gradual stages. Sport psychology techniques are often helpful.

### Over-Mounted Student
- Assess the situation and decide whether this horse/rider combination can work safely at any level. If you feel it is unsafe, don't allow the student to continue to ride on that horse.
- Can the horse be made more controllable by longeing, turnout, a change of equipment, or being schooled by a more experienced rider? Is a change of horses possible?
- Limit activities to a safe level (avoid fast gaits, work in the open, and so on).
- Discuss the problem with the student and his parents. Be sure they understand the danger to the child and to others. Seek solutions, such as borrowing a more suitable mount for Pony Club activities.

### Loss of Temper, Rudeness, or Abusive Riding
- Call a halt immediately. Have the rider dismount and take time to settle down before he continues to ride or handle the horse. Be firm, clear, and calm, but insist on compliance.
- Discuss the incident with the rider in private. Does he understand why his behavior is wrong and what the consequences are? What led to it? How can he prevent this from happening in the future?
- Most such incidents occur when a rider is overwhelmed by fear, frustration, or embarrassment, or is unable to control his horse well enough for the activity. While it is tempting to berate a rider for such behavior, yelling, name-calling, and public humiliation do nothing to teach him better behavior, and may make it worse.

### Interfering Parent
Parents sometimes try to intervene in a lesson situation because:
- They are concerned for their child's safety or welfare.
- They want their child to get the most out of the lesson.
- They believe they are helping.

To improve the situation:
- Establish ground rules with parents at the beginning. Listen to their concerns and explain how these will be taken care of (safety, attention to each child, individual goals, and so on). Explain that it is distracting to students (and therefore unsafe) if anyone besides the instructor tries to give instructions during a lesson, and that you cannot teach if this is happening.
- Some children are distracted when their parents watch their lessons. Suggest that parents leave during the lesson, but come back to watch their child show what he has learned at the end of the lesson.
- Enlist the parent for another activity, such as helping with dismounted lessons, lunch, or building jumps.
- Suggest some ways parents can help their child progress, such as supervising practice at home, videotaping, and so forth.

# Part 2

# The Horse

# 9

# Systems of the Horse

The horse's anatomy is comprised of several systems. A system is a combination of parts that work together to perform one or more functions. Although each system has its own unique role, all systems are interdependent and rely on each other. To better understand horse care, nutrition, conditioning, and especially various ailments, we must understand how these systems work.

The body of the horse is made up of the following systems:

1. **Skeletal** (bones and joints)
2. **Muscular** (muscles)
3. **Respiratory** (lungs)
4. **Circulatory** (heart, blood vessels)
5. **Immune** (provides cells that fight infection, lymphatic system)
6. **Digestive** (gastrointestinal tract)
7. **Nervous** (brain, spinal cord, and nerves)
8. **Endocrine** (glands)
9. **Reproductive** (testicles, ovaries, and related organs)
10. **Urinary** (kidneys and bladder)
11. **Integumentary** (skin, hooves, and hair)

In addition to the anatomy and physiology of the various systems, major diseases and ailments that affect each system are listed under each system.

The details of these diseases and ailments, are covered in Chapter 14, "Health Care, Diseases, and Veterinary Knowledge."

# Animal Surfaces – Terminology

Any discussion of the structure and function of animals begins with an understanding of the terms that indicate direction.

- *Dorsal*—pertains to the upper surface of an animal, including the front side of the limbs below the hock and carpus (knee)
- *Ventral*—pertains to the lower or abdominal surface
- *Cranial*—toward the head
- *Caudal*—toward the tail
- *Medial*—toward the centerline of the body
- *Lateral*—away from the centerline of the body
- *Proximal*—closer to the origin or point of attachment
- *Distal*—farther from the origin or point of attachment
- *Palmar*—the back side or tendon surface of the front legs from the carpus (knee) down to the ground
- *Plantar*—the back side or tendon surface of the hind legs from the tarsus (hock) down to the ground

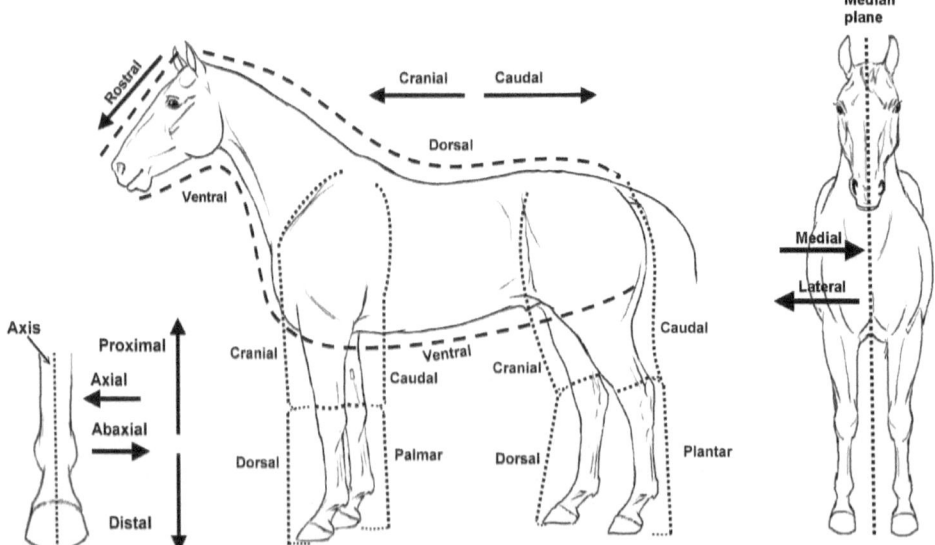

Planes, surfaces, and terminology.

# Systems of Movement: The Skeletal and Muscular Systems

The skeletal system is the framework of the body; its major functions are support, protection of vital organs, production of red blood cells, and with the help of the muscular system, movement. The joints, held together by ligaments, permit movement. Muscles, attached to bones by tendons, move the bones. The foot and lower leg contain special structures adapted for movement, absorbing shock, traction, and protection of the foot.

(The anatomy and function of the foot and lower leg are discussed in Chapter 10, "Conformation and Soundness," and Chapter 11, "The Foot and Shoeing.")

## The Skeletal System

### Bones

The skeleton consists of approximately 206 bones. Bones provide the framework of the body, levers for movement, attachment points for muscles, and protection for vital organs and the spinal cord. Bones are living tissue, with blood vessels and nerves. Red and white blood cells are produced in the marrow of the bones. Bones contain most of the mineral content of the body, especially calcium and phosphorous.

While bone appears to be a hard structure with no visible appearance of change, it does continually remodel. Bone will get stronger as a result of training by increasing the mineral content and density. By the time a horse is mature, minerals make up 95 percent of bone. Of all the structural tissues in the body, bone takes the longest to develop to maximum strength.

Bone also serves as a mineral reservoir, specifically calcium and phosphorus, for the rest of the body. Calcium is a very important mineral for normal body function. It is necessary for normal muscle contraction (smooth, heart, and skeletal), cell function, blood coagulation, and hormone regulation. When the body becomes low in calcium, the bones provide a ready source of this mineral.

Bones can be grouped into four major types:

- **Long bones** support the body weight, act as levers, and provide movement. Examples of long bones are the cannon bones, radius, and femur.
- **Flat bones** protect vital organs, such as those in the head and ribs.
- **Short bones** absorb concussion, such as those in the knee and hock.
- **Irregular bones** such as those of the spinal column, have various functions such as protecting the spinal cord.

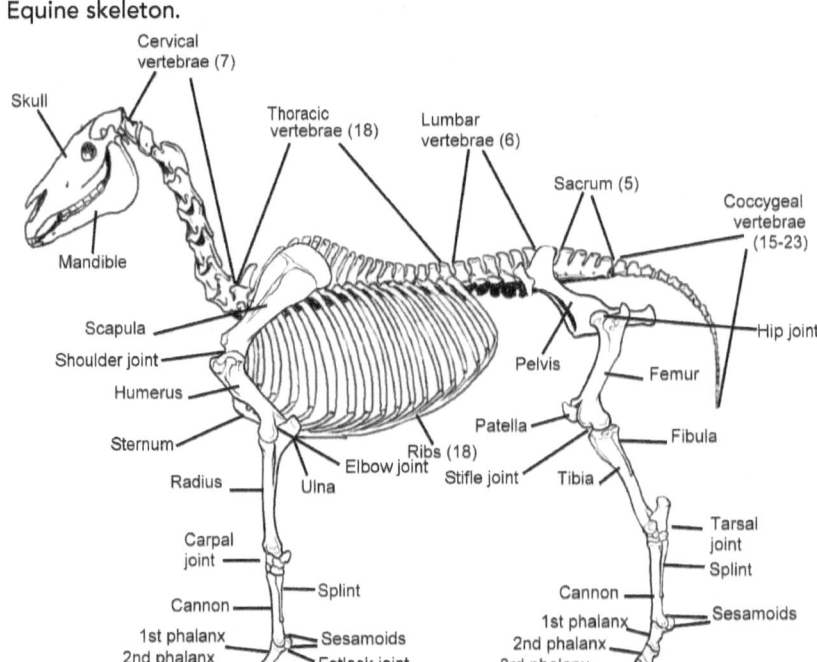

Equine skeleton.

All long bones, except at their points of articulation (where bones meet to form a joint), are covered with a thin, tough membrane called the *periosteum*, which protects the bone and influences its growth. Damage to the periosteum can cause abnormal bony growth, called an *exostosis*, at the location of the injury. The periosteum also contains blood vessels that nourish the bone.

The skeleton can be divided into two major areas: *axial* and *appendicular*. The *axial skeleton* includes the *skull, spine,* and *ribs*. The *appendicular skeleton* consists of the *front and hind limbs,* otherwise known as *appendages*.

## AXIAL SKELETON

- **Skull:** The *skull* is made up predominately of flat bones joined by immovable joints. The skull protects the brain and provides a framework to support the teeth. The *temporomandibular joint (TMJ)* or *jaw joint* allows the *mandible* (lower jaw) to move up and down and side to side for chewing. There is a large opening at the back of the skull called the *foramen magnum,* through which the spinal cord passes.

- **Vertebral or spinal column:** The *spine* is a flexible column of irregular bones bound together with ligaments and cartilage. An elastic cushion separates each vertebra. There is a long passageway though the spinal column called the *neural canal* or *spinal canal* that contains the spinal cord. The purpose of the vertebra is to protect the spinal cord from damage. The bones of the spinal column are divided into five sections:
    - *Seven cervical (neck) vertebrae:* The *cervical spine* is connected to the base of the skull by the *atlas* or *first cervical vertebra*. The joint formed at their connection moves up and down like a hinge, and is known as the "yes" joint. This joint allows the horse to flex at the poll. The atlas joins the *axis* or *second cervical vertebra* at the *atlantoaxial joint*, also known as the "no" joint because it rotates the head and neck from side to side.
    - *Eighteen thoracic (back) vertebrae:* The size of these vertebrae determine the length of the back. The *dorsal spinous processes* (thin bony projections that form the upper surface of the spine) increase in height from the third through the ninth to form the withers.
    - *Six lumbar vertebrae* (usually, but five is not uncommon, especially in Arabians): These vertebrae provide the bridge from the back to the hindquarters and have shorter dorsal spinous processes compared to the thoracic vertebrae.
    - *Five sacral vertebrae* (fused together): These vertebrae attach to the *ilium* of the pelvis to form the *sacroiliac joint*. They also have small dorsal spinous processes.
    - *Eighteen to 23 coccygeal (tail) vertebrae:* These form the tail.
    - *Sacroiliac joint:* This joint is a fibrous but flexible joining of the *sacrum* and the *ilium* of the pelvis. It allows the horse to rotate his pelvis slightly in relation to the spine to create engagement.
- **Rib cage:** The rib cage is integral for the protection of the organs within the thorax, including the lungs and heart. It is designed to allow for expansion of the lungs with each breath (see the respiratory system later).
    - *Eighteen pairs of ribs*, each connected to one of the 18 thoracic vertebrae.
        - Eight pairs of *true ribs*, which connect to the sternum.
        - Ten pairs of *floating or false ribs,* which do not connect to the sternum.
    - *Sternum (breastbone)*, consisting of seven or eight bony segments connected by cartilage. The sternum forms the floor of the thorax or chest cavity.

**Axial skeleton.**

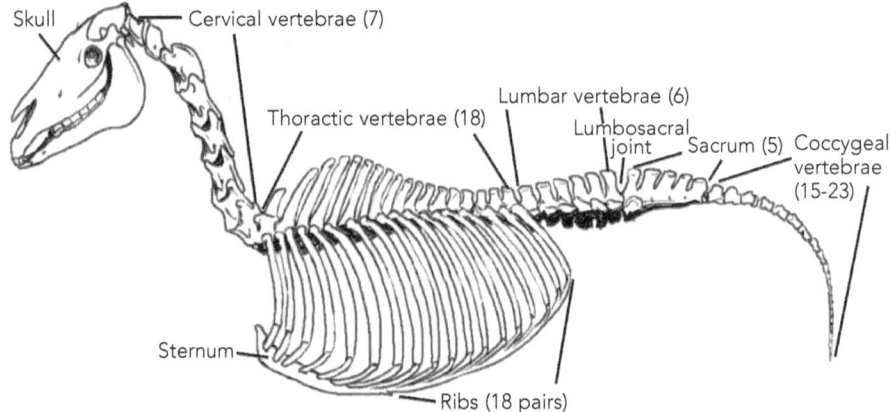

## APPENDICULAR SKELETON

- **Front limbs,** which are not attached directly to the vertebral column by a bony joint.

  - The *scapula (shoulder blade)* is attached by a muscular sling that supports the *thorax* (chest).
  - The *humerus* is mostly hidden by the muscles of the shoulder. The humerus articulates with the scapula above and the radius and ulna below. The proximal (upper) part of it forms the point of the shoulder.
  - The *radius* is the main bone of the forearm.
  - The *ulna* is fused to the upper part of the radius. The proximal part (top), called the *olecranon*, forms the point of the elbow.
  - The *carpus*, or knee, consists of seven to eight bones arranged in two rows to form three joints (proximal to distal: radiocarpal, middle carpal, and carpometacarpal). Similar to the lower hock joints, the carpometacarpal joint has very little movement compared to the other two joints.
  - There are three *metacarpal bones* below the carpus. The middle metacarpal bone, called the *third metacarpus* or *cannon bone*, extends from the carpus to the fetlock. The two smaller metacarpal bones, called the *second and fourth metacarpus* or *splint bones*, are remnants of toes.
  - At the back of the fetlock joint there are two small bones called the *proximal sesamoid bones*. They are completely surrounded by connective tissue and provide an attachment for the *suspensory ligament* to support the fetlock joint.
  - Below (distal to) the cannon bone are the *first phalanx (long pastern), second phalanx (short pastern),* and *third phalanx (coffin or pedal bone).*

- The *distal sesamoid bone (navicular bone)* is behind (palmar to) the coffin bone, and provides a sliding surface for the *deep digital flexor tendon* as it passes under the coffin bone to attach on its bottom (palmar) surface.
- **Hind limbs,** which are attached to the vertebral column at the sacrum via the sacroiliac joint.
  - The *pelvis (hip bones)* is formed by the fused *ischium, ilium,* and *pubis*. The caudal aspect of the *ischium* forms the point of buttock. The wings of the *ilium* form the highest point of the croup and the point of the hip. The pelvis forms a circle that meets at the pubis. The ilium is attached to the spine at the sacrum by a ligament to form the sacroiliac joint.
  - The *femur* is the largest bone in the horse's body. It attaches to the *ilium* on the outside of the pelvic girdle, to form the hip joint.
  - The *patella* is a small bone located on the front of the distal end of the femur. It helps to lock the stifle into place as part of the stay apparatus.
  - The *tibia* is the main bone of the gaskin. It attaches to the femur at the stifle joint and to the hock joint at the *talus*.
  - The *fibula* is incomplete and is fused to the tibia in horses.
  - The *tarsus*, or hock, consists of six bones. The large bone at the back of the joint, the *calcaneus*, forms the point of the hock. The *talus* forms the majority of the joint and connects to the tibia at the *tibiotarsal joint*. There are four main joints in the hock (proximal to distal: tibiotarsal, proximal intertarsal, distal intertarsal, and tarsometatarsal). The two distal joints have little movement and are the most likely to develop osteoarthritis.
  - Below the hock, the bones are the same as the front limb, except that the cannon bones and splint bones are called the *metatarsal bones*.

## Joints
Joints are where bones meet. Some joints are immovable (like the joints of the skull); others permit a little movement or a wide range of movement.

- **Fibrous joints** are immovable, and bones are fused or held tightly together with connective tissue.
- **Cartilaginous joints** are slightly movable joints. They have a pad of cartilage that connects the bones, allowing limited movement due to the minimal elasticity of the cartilage.
- **A synovial joint** is stabilized by a series of ligaments and a fibrous joint capsule that provides the limits to its motion. Inside the joint, the

*synovial membrane* produces a thick, slippery fluid called *synovial fluid*, which lubricates the joint. The *articular cartilage* covers the surface at the ends of bones and allows them to glide across each other smoothly. Because cartilage does not continue to grow after maturity, nor does it heal once damaged or lost, options for treatment are limited. This inability of the cartilage to repair itself following damage ultimately results in the development of *osteoarthritis*, otherwise known as *degenerative joint disease (DJD)*. This is discussed in Chapter 14.

Bone has the ability to adapt and remodel to accommodate progressive loading needed by a horse. Joints, however, have less ability to adapt, but moderate exercise does increase their ability to handle stress.

In areas where a tendon passes across a joint or bony protuberance, a fluid-filled capsule, or *bursa*, cushions and protects the tendon. Chronic irritation of the bursa can result in excess fluid production and soft swelling called *bursitis*.

**The joints of the front leg** are (from top to bottom or proximal to distal):

- *Shoulder (scapulohumeral) joint:* Formed by the scapula and humerus
- *Elbow (radiohumeral) joint:* Formed by the humerus, radius, and ulna
- *Knee joints (radiocarpal, middle carpal, and carpometacarpal):* Formed by the radius, carpal bones (seven to eight small bones that are arranged in two rows), and the three metacarpal bones
- *Fetlock (metacarpophalangeal) joint:* Formed by the cannon bone (third metacarpus), two proximal sesamoid bones, and the long pastern bone (first phalanx)

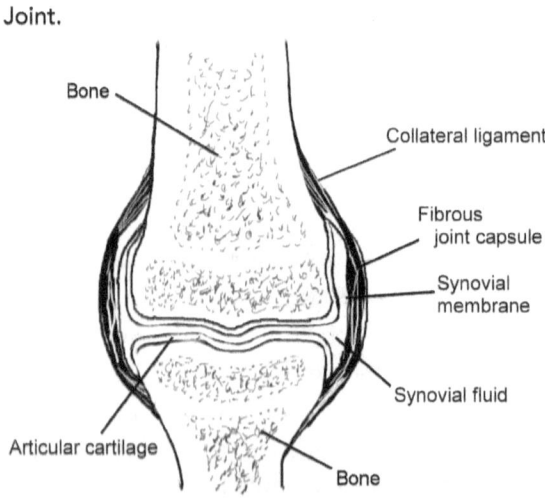

Joint.

- *Pastern (proximal interphalangeal) joint:* Formed by the long and short pastern bones or first and second phalanx
- *Coffin (distal interphalangeal) joint:* Formed by the short pastern bone (second phalanx), coffin bone (third phalanx), and navicular bone (distal sesamoid bone)

**The joints of the hind leg** are (from top to bottom):

- *Hip (coxofemoral) joint:* Formed by the pelvis (ilium) and femur
- *Stifle (femorotibial and femoropatellar) joints:* Formed by the femur, patella, and tibia
- *Hock (tibiotarsal, talocalcaneal, proximal intertarsal, distal intertarsal, and tarsometatarsal) joints:* Formed by the tibia, calcaneus, talus, two rows of stacked tarsal bones, and the metatarsal bones
- *Fetlock (metatarsophalangeal) joint:* Formed by the cannon bone (third metatarsus), two sesamoid bones, and the long pastern bone (first phalanx)
- *Pastern (proximal interphalangeal) joint:* Formed by the long and short pastern bones or first and second phalanx
- *Coffin (distal interphalangeal) joint:* Formed by the short pastern bone (second phalanx), coffin bone (third phalanx), and navicular bone (distal sesamoid bone)

## Ligaments

*Ligaments* are the strong bands of connective tissue that hold joints together. They connect bone to bone. Ligaments are very dense and have a limited blood supply, so an injury to them, such as a sprain, tends to heal slowly. Some of the major ligaments of the horse are:

- The *suspensory ligament* is a very strong, flat ligament running from the back of the knee or hock and upper end of the cannon bone down the back of the leg, in a groove between the splint bones. Just above the fetlock, it divides into two rounded branches that pass downward and connect to the corresponding proximal sesamoid bones. They then continue around to the front of the long pastern where they connect with the extensor tendon, which then attaches to the front of the coffin bone. The suspensory ligament is unique in that it contains muscle fibers in addition to ligament fibers. It is most often injured from repetitive hyperextension of the fetlock joint (when the fetlock drops toward the ground). See Chapter 14 for more information on suspensory ligament injury.

- The *inferior check ligament* is a short, strong ligament running downward and backward from the back side (*palmar aspect*) of the distal carpus and proximal cannon bone to attach to the deep flexor tendon. It is an important part of the *passive stay apparatus* because it assists in locking the carpus, which allows the horse to sleep standing up.
- The *superior check ligament* extends from the *distal and caudal* (lower back) aspect of the *radius* (above the carpus) and attaches to the superficial digital flexor muscle near the junction where it turns from muscle to tendon. Similar to the inferior check ligament, it allows the horse to lock his carpus to rest while standing up (see "Stay Apparatus," page 343).
- *The distal sesamoidean ligaments* attach from the base of the proximal sesamoid bones at the back (*palmar aspect*) of the fetlock joint to the pastern bones, to help "suspend" the fetlock as part of the suspensory apparatus (see "Suspensory Apparatus," page 344).
- The *plantar ligament* extends from the back of the point of the hock to the upper end of the metatarsus, or cannon bone.

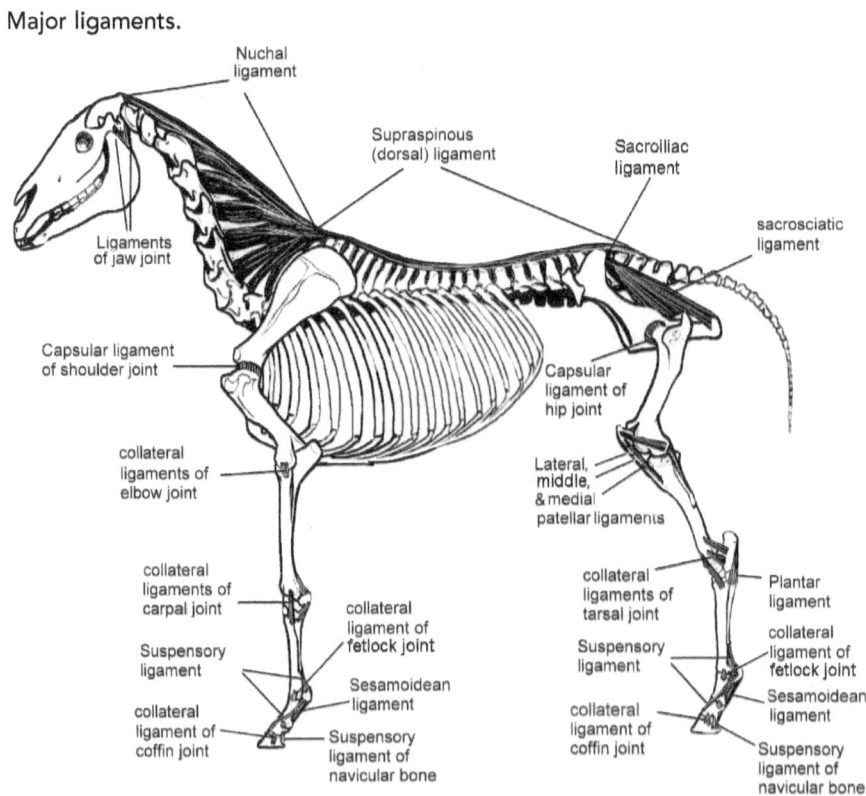

Major ligaments.

Open growth plate; closed growth plate.

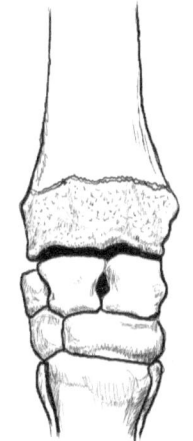
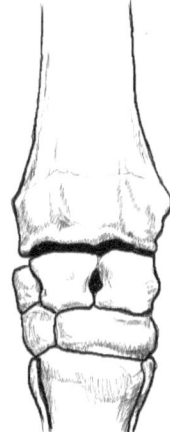

Open growth plate (epiphysis)     Closed growth plate

- The *nuchal ligament* is a fan-shaped ligament that extends from the base of the skull and anchors to the withers, forming the crest of the neck and assisting the muscles of the neck in holding the head and neck in position.
- The *sacroiliac ligaments* attach the sacrum to the ilium of the pelvis and are an integral part of the sacroiliac joint.
- The *sacrosciatic ligament* is made up of a group of ligaments that attach the pelvis to the sacrum.

### Cartilage

*Cartilage* is smooth and firm but flexible. It forms certain structures (like the ears and nose), and covers the *articular surfaces* of bones in joints to allow the bones to move smoothly and help absorb shock.

Cartilage provides a framework in immature long bones. It turns to hard bone as the animal grows and matures at the *epiphyseal plates* (growth plates) found toward the ends of long bones. Radiographs of the growth plates, especially those of the distal end of the *radius*, are sometimes used to determine whether a young horse is mature enough to begin serious work. When the horse is mature, the growth plates will close, reducing the chance of bone injury.

## The Muscular System

The muscle mass of a horse makes up about 45 percent of the horse's weight. Muscle is highly adaptable. With training and conditioning, it adapts to meet the demands of the level of work.

There are three main types of muscle:

- **Cardiac muscle**—found in the heart
- **Smooth muscle**—found in many internal organs, such as the digestive system
- **Skeletal muscle**—muscles that move the bones, usually acting in pairs

### Skeletal Muscles

Because muscles can only pull, not push, skeletal muscles usually work in pairs; one muscle group *flexes* (bends) a joint, and another *extends* it.

Skeletal muscles are made up of many *fibers*, which are arranged in *bundles*. Muscle fibers are controlled by *motor nerves*, which stimulate them to contract or *fire* by means of an electrochemical reaction. When muscle fibers contract, the muscles shortens, exerting a pull. The more muscle fibers involved, the stronger the pull.

Skeletal muscles are attached to bones by a fibrous component, either *tendons* or *fascia*. As a muscle contracts, it pulls against the bone, causing it to move. Muscles are made up of different types of fibers (slow versus fast twitch), depending on their use, and the proportion of fibers can be influenced by conditioning to allow muscles to become more specialized in their function.

The *myostactic stretch reflex* is your horse's insurance policy that he won't overstretch and tear his muscles during exercise. It is controlled by receptors contained in cells that lie parallel to the muscle fibers. These receptors respond to both the speed and strength of the muscle stretching. The greater both of those elements are, the sooner the receptors cause a muscular contraction to stop the stretch, preventing the muscles from tearing.

See Chapter 12, "Conditioning and Exercise Physiology," for more information on muscle cells, muscle fibers, and muscle metabolism.

### Major Muscles and Muscle Groups

Some of the major muscles and muscle groups are:

#### MUSCLES OF THE HEAD AND NECK

- *Masseter:* This large muscle of the jowl is primarily used in chewing.
- *Brachiocephalic:* This long muscle runs from the poll to the upper arm. It is used to extend and raise the forearm and flex the neck from side to side.
- *Rhomboideus and splenius:* These muscles are located along the top of the neck, running to the shoulder blade. They provide muscle definition to the crest of the neck. They are well developed when a horse carries his head and neck properly as a result of correct training.
- *Trapezius:* This large muscle connects the scapula to the neck and back over the withers. Its caudal part supports the front of the saddle and is

involved in moving the shoulders. Its cranial part is involved in neck carriage. The trapezius muscle should be well developed in a fit horse that carries himself properly.
- *Scalenus and longus colli:* These muscles run deep in the neck along the cervical vertebrae. They are important in allowing the horse to carry his long neck in various positions, which is important for an athletic horse. They are an important part of the "circle of muscles" discussed in Chapter 1, "Biomechanics and Movement of the Horse."
- *Serratus group:* These fan-shaped muscles support the base of the neck and the chest cavity. They also allow the horse to shift his weight between front limbs.
- *Pectoral group:* These are the main chest muscles that work to advance the limb and allow a small amount of adduction (moving the front limb toward the chest).

## BACK AND TRUNK MUSCLES
- *Longissimus dorsi:* This is a major deep muscle of the back that supports the vertebra between the neck and pelvis. When it contracts, it extends the back.
- *Abdominal muscles (internal abdominal oblique, external abdominal oblique, transversus abdominus, rectus abdominus):* These muscles of the abdominal wall aid in breathing, support the abdominal organs, and help to raise the back when a horse engages his hindquarters.
- *Psoas group (iliopsoas, psoas minor, psoas major):* Deep muscles from the underside of the lumbar spine to the femur and pelvis; important in engaging the hindquarters by tilting the pelvis.

## SHOULDER MUSCLES
- *Deltoideus, teres major, and teres minor:* These muscles help to flex the shoulder.
- *Supraspinatus and infraspinatus:* These muscles support the scapula, preventing excessive abduction (moving away from the thorax), and help to extend the shoulder joint.
- *Latissimus dorsi:* This muscle runs just behind the scapula. It allows the horse to flex his shoulder.

## FORELIMB MUSCLES
- *Triceps group:* The large muscle group that extends from the back of the scapula to the point of the elbow. They extend the elbow.
- *Biceps brachii and brachialis:* These muscles are located along the front of the humerus, just below the shoulder. They cause flexion of

the elbow and allow the forearm to lift during the swing phase of the stride.

- *Extensor muscles of the lower leg:* These muscles are located on the front of the forearm and end as the extensor tendons; they extend the foreleg.
- *Flexor muscles of the lower leg:* These muscles are located on the back of the forearm and end as the flexor tendons. They oppose the extensor muscles and flex the limb.

## HINDQUARTER MUSCLES

- *Quadriceps (vastus) group:* These muscles start at the top of the femur and end at the stifle; they extend the stifle joint.
- *Biceps femoris:* The outermost muscle of the thigh. It extends the hip and hock, and is involved with both extension and flexion of the stifle.
- *Gluteal group:* The large muscles of the hip that connect the pelvis and femur. They extend the hip.
- *Tensor fascia lata:* A large muscle that runs along the front and side of the femur. It flexes the hip and extends the stifle, allowing the horse to bring the limb forward.

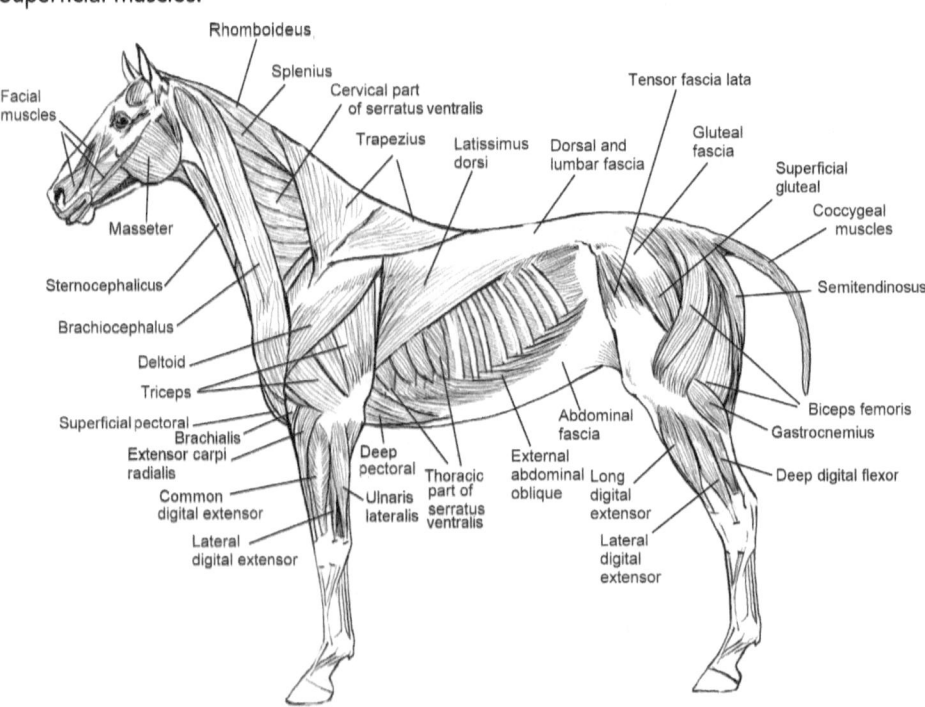

Superficial muscles.

- *Hamstring group (semitendinosus, semimembranosus):* Muscles running along the back of the hindquarters. They extend the hip and hock joint while flexing the stifle. This results in pushing the body forward during the stance phase of the stride.
- *Gastrocnemius and superficial digital flexor musculotendon unit (Achilles tendon):* The large tendon that extends down from the same muscles located on the back of the gaskin. The *gastrocnemius tendon* attaches on the point of the hock, while the *superficial digital flexor tendon* continues down the back of the leg to the lower limb. It extends the hock and flexes the stifle.
- *Extensor muscles of the lower leg:* Located on the front of the gaskin. They flex the hock while extending the lower leg, as part of the reciprocal apparatus.
- *Flexor muscles of the lower leg:* Muscles located on the back of the gaskin. They extend the hock while flexing the lower limb as part of the reciprocal apparatus.

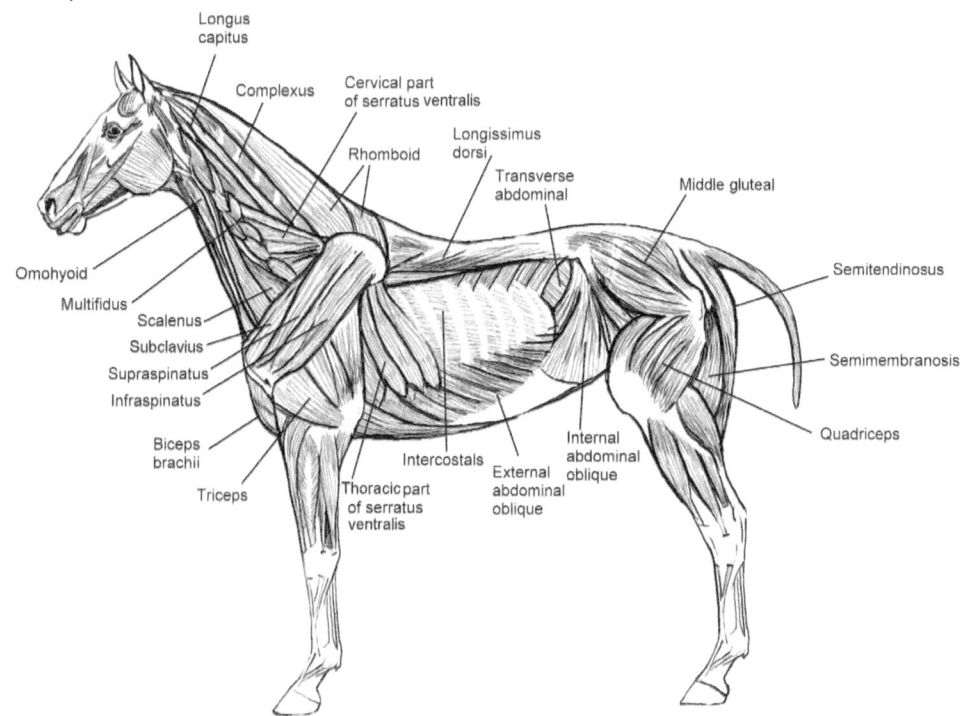

Deep muscles.

### Tendons

*Tendons* are strong, fibrous pieces of connective tissue that connect muscles to bones. Some tendons are wide, flat sheets; others are thick bands or long cables. A *tendon sheath* protects a tendon where it crosses a joint; like a joint capsule, it contains synovial fluid, which lubricates it.

*Fascia* is a thin, tough, and fibrous connective tissue. It encases muscles and lies in wide sheets. Some muscles and tendons are attached to fascia, especially in areas like the back.

- **Flexor tendons:** Tendons that flex the limb:
  - *Superficial digital flexor tendon:* This tendon originates from the *superficial digital flexor muscle* that is located on the *caudal aspect* (back) of the forearm. At the back of the fetlock joint it becomes two branches that attach to the *palmar aspect* (back) of the first and second phalanxes. It is the most *palmar* (superficial) of the flexor tendons as they pass down the palmar aspect (back) of the cannon bone. It is an important component of the stay apparatus by supporting the fetlock joint. When the superficial digital muscle-tendon unit contracts, it causes the knee and fetlock to flex.
  - *Deep digital flexor tendon:* This tendon originates from the *deep digital flexor muscles* that are located on the *palmar* (back) and

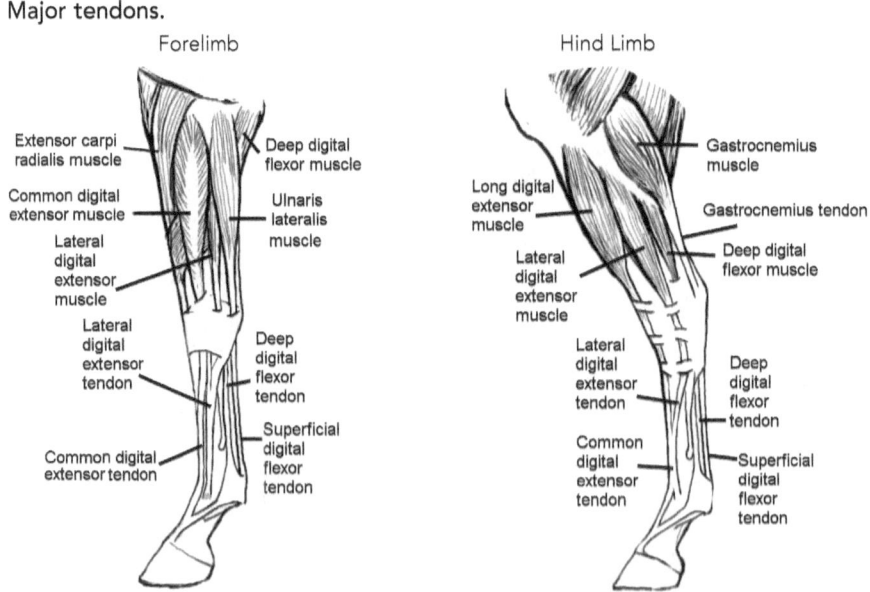

Major tendons.

*lateral* (outside) aspect of the forearm. It attaches to the *palmar* (bottom) aspect of the *third phalanx* (*coffin bone*). It is located underneath the superficial digital flexor tendon as both tendons pass down the palmar aspect of the cannon bone. It is an important component of the stay apparatus by supporting the coffin and pastern joints. When the deep digital muscle-tendon unit contracts, it causes the knee, fetlock, pastern joint, and coffin joint to flex.

- **Extensor tendons:** Tendons that extend the limb:
  - *Extensor tendons:* These tendons originate from the *extensor muscles* located on the *cranial* (front) aspect of the forearm. Below the knee they become the *common digital extensor tendon* that attaches to the *dorsal* (front) aspect of the *third phalanx* (*coffin bone*) and the *lateral digital extensor tendon* that attaches to the lateral aspect of the *first phalanx* (outside aspect of the fetlock joint). Below the hock, they form one primary tendon, the *common digital extensor tendon* that attaches to the dorsal aspect of the *third phalanx*, as in the front limb. When the extensor muscle-tendon unit contracts, it extends all of the joints of the lower limb. Extensor tendons are important to stabilize the limb as part of the stay apparatus, but are less important than the flexor tendons when the horse bears weight. In fact, a horse's extensor tendon can be completely cut and he can learn to move without its assistance.
  - *Gastrocnemius tendon:* This tendon works in combination with the superficial digital flexor tendon in the rear limb to maintain the reciprocal movement of the hind limb (where the hock and stifle must flex simultaneously). If this tendon is cut or ruptured, the horse will have a characteristic "dropped hock" where the stifle can extend and the hock flexes.

## Fascia
*Fascia* is a strong, fibrous, inelastic connective tissue that also connects muscles and tendons to bone. It provides a tough sheath that protects the muscle bundles and holds them together.

## The Stay, Suspensory, and Reciprocal Apparatus
**Stay apparatus of the front limbs:** This system involves the opposing actions of the *extensor* and *flexor tendons* to keep the knee locked. The *triceps* muscles and tendon of the *biceps brachii* muscle keep the shoulder and elbow extended. A fibrous band called the *lacertus fibrosus* also helps to keep the shoulder and knee extended. The *superior check ligament* stabilizes the superficial digital flexor tendon, while the *inferior check ligament* stabilizes the deep digital flexor tendon.

Horse with ruptured gastrocnemius tendon.

**Stay apparatus of the hind limbs:** The *quadriceps muscles* and *ligaments of the stifle* work in tandem to position the patella over the medial aspect of the distal femur to "lock" the stifle into place. This allows the horse to stand using very little muscle energy.

**Suspensory apparatus:** The ability to maintain the fetlock in "suspension" is called the *suspensory apparatus*. It is also considered to be a part of the stay apparatus in the front and hind limbs. It is comprised of the *superficial digital flexor tendon*, the *deep digital flexor tendon*, the *suspensory ligament*, and the *distal sesamoidean ligaments*. (See Chapter 1 for more details on the suspensory apparatus.)

**Reciprocal apparatus of the hind limbs:** Hind limbs are different from the front limbs in that the stifle and hock joints must flex and extend at the same time, unlike the joints of the front limb that can extend and flex independently. This is because the hock flexes in the opposite direction as the stifle, so it is virtually impossible to flex the stifle and extend the hock, or vice versa. The key components to the reciprocal apparatus are the *superficial digital flexor/gastrocnemius unit* on the back of the gaskin and the *peroneus tertius muscle* located on the front of the gaskin.

## Stay apparatus of the foreleg and hind leg.

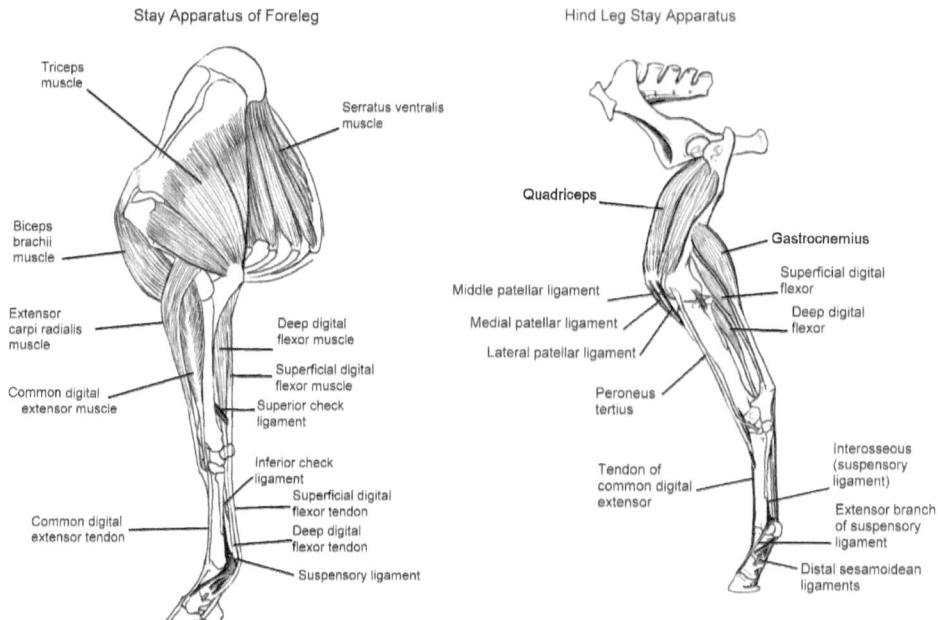

## Reciprocal apparatus of the hind limb.

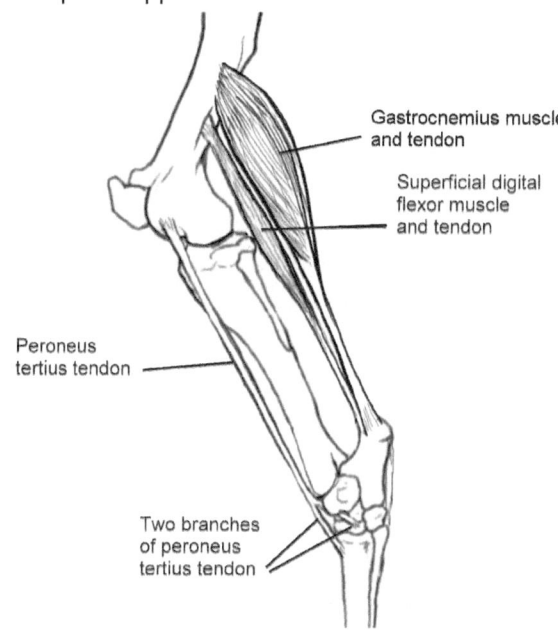

## COMMON DISEASES AND CONDITIONS AFFECTING THE MUSCULAR SYSTEM
- Rhabdomyolysis
- Polysaccharide Storage Myopathy (PSSM)

# The Respiratory System

The major function of the respiratory system is to take in oxygen and to deliver it to the blood. Oxygen is essential to every cell; if the body is deprived of oxygen for more than a few minutes, death results. The respiratory system also removes carbon dioxide, a waste product of metabolism, from the blood.

## The Upper Respiratory System (Head and Throat)

- **Nostrils.** Horses can only breathe effectively through their nose (they are *obligate nasal breathers*), so they do not breath through their mouth as humans do. The *nostrils* are the entrance into the nasal cavity. They can enlarge or dilate to increase the amount of air breathed in when needed, such as during exercise. The hairs inside the nostrils help trap dust and foreign matter. The *false nostril* is located at the top of the nostril. It extends toward the nasal cavity, but has a blind end.
- **Nasal cavities.** This is the primary air passage to the throat. It is lined with a *mucus membrane*, which is important for trapping foreign material and humidifying inhaled air. It is separated from the mouth by the *hard palate,* and farther back, the *soft palate*.
- **Nasal turbinates.** These are very thin, curling bones inside the nasal passages, covered with mucus membrane. Their large surface area helps to warm, humidify, and filter the incoming air.
- **Sinuses.** Air-filled cavities in the bones of the skull, connecting to the nasal cavity; they reduce the weight of the skull and help to warm air as it passes inward.
- **Pharynx (throat).** A common passage for food and air that leads to the larynx.
- **Larynx (voice box).** This structure is made up of multiple cartilage structures to form a specialized short tube, located between the branches of the lower jaw. It contains the *vocal cords*, which produce sound. The larynx controls the air as it goes in and out, and prevents food from entering the *trachea*, with the help of the *epiglottis*.

Respiratory system.

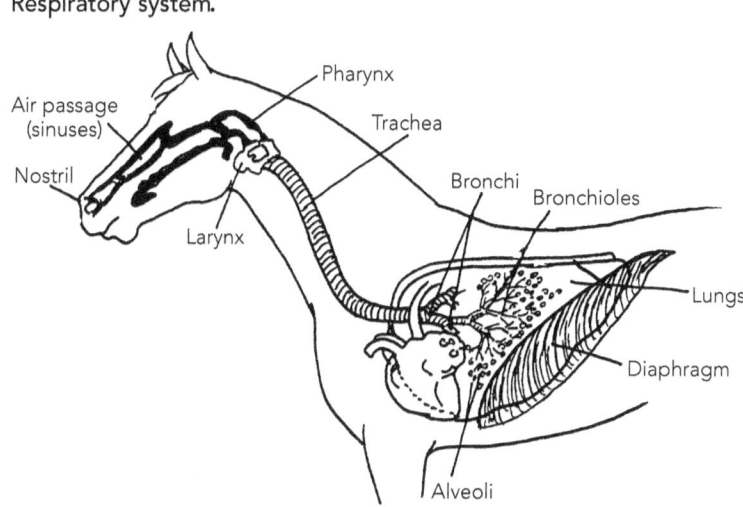

- **Epiglottis.** This "V"-shaped structure flips up to cover the opening of the larynx when the horse swallows. It is critical in preventing foreign material like food or water from entering the lungs through the trachea.
- **Trachea (windpipe).** This long tube made of rings of *cartilage* runs from the larynx to the *lungs*, allowing for the passage of air.

## Lower Respiratory Tract

- **Bronchi.** Within the chest, the trachea divides into two tubes or *bronchi*, with one branch going to each lung. Inside the lung they divide into many smaller passageways called *bronchioles*. The trachea branching into bronchi and then bronchioles can be thought of as a tree and its branches.
- **Lungs.** There are two separate (right and left) *lungs;* elastic, spongy organs that fill the chest cavity. They passively expand to *inhale* air and contract to *exhale* air when the chest muscles expand and contract the chest cavity.
- **Alveoli.** These microscopic *air sacs,* only one cell in thickness, are grouped like bunches of grapes at the ends of the bronchioles. Carbon dioxide and oxygen are exchanged through the walls of the alveoli into the many blood vessels of the lungs.
- **Pleura.** This is the protective covering of the lungs.
- **Diaphragm.** This large sheet of muscle runs from the underside of the backbone to the rib cage, separating the abdomen from the thorax. It is

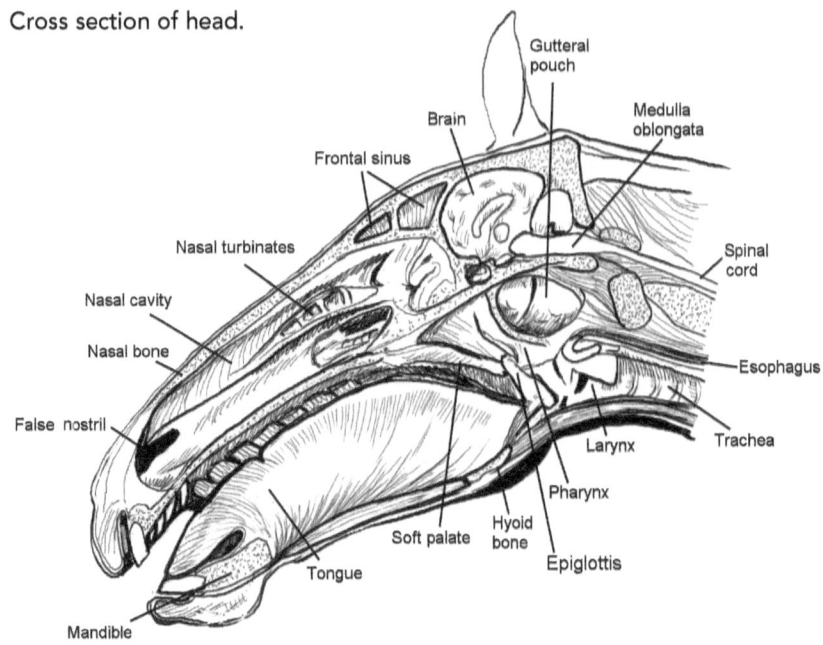

Cross section of head.

the primary breathing muscle, although the muscles of the ribs and abdomen also help. It contracts to inhale air and relaxes to exhale air.

## Breathing

Breathing is the process of moving air in and out of the lungs.

In breathing, the diaphragm contracts and flattens, causing the ribs to expand and making the chest cavity larger. This pulls air in through the nostrils and down into the lungs. As the diaphragm relaxes, it expands and the rib cage contracts, pressing against the lungs and expelling the air. The muscles of the rib cage, trunk, and abdomen also help in this process.

At the gallop, the abdominal muscles work strongly to bring the hind legs forward under the body at each stride. This pushes the abdominal contents (the intestines) forward against the diaphragm and lungs, causing the horse to exhale in rhythm with each stride.

## Points to Remember

The respiratory tract contains *mucus*, which is normally thin and clear. In various respiratory diseases, the amount and quality of the mucus may change.

A *nasal discharge* refers to mucus or matter coming from one or both nostrils. A clear discharge may be normal, especially when the horse first

Respiratory function.

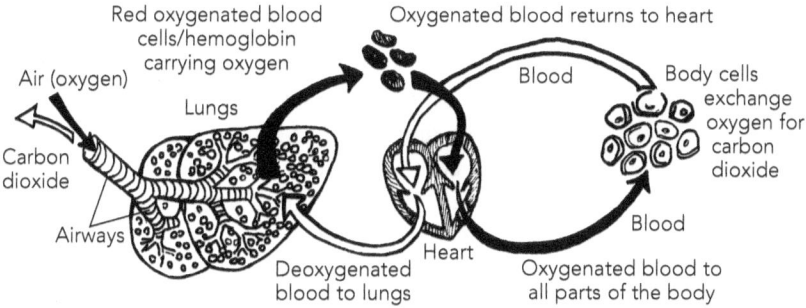

Oxygen exchange.

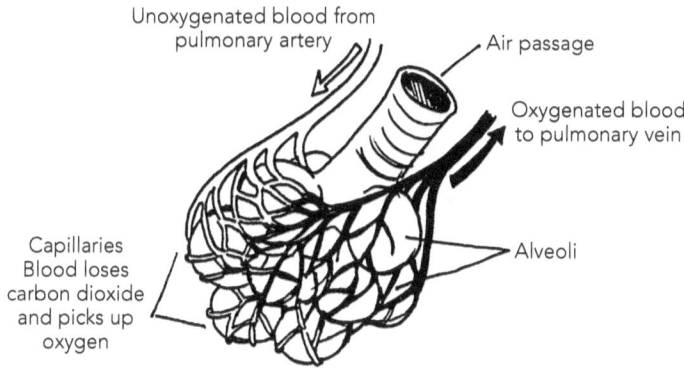

begins work on a chilly morning. A thick, white, reddish, or yellow discharge points to some kind of infection or other abnormality that requires veterinary care. A discharge from only one nostril could indicate a sinus infection, a foreign body, or a bad tooth on the side of the discharge. A discharge from both nostrils usually means a generalized respiratory infection.

A *cough* is a forceful expulsion of air that acts to protect the respiratory tract from inhalation of foreign material. This includes excess mucus, which the body produces in some diseases.

## DISEASES AND CONDITIONS AFFECTING THE RESPIRATORY SYSTEM

- Influenza
- Rhinopneumonitis
- Strangles
- Heaves (recurrent airway obstruction)
- Roaring
- Equine viral arteritis (EVA)

# The Circulatory System

The *circulatory system* is composed of *blood, blood vessels,* and the *heart*. The main function of the circulatory system is transportation. It carries *oxygen* from the lungs to all cells, and *carbon dioxide* from the cells to the lungs. It also transports nutrients and water from the digestive tract to all cells, and carries waste from the cells to the kidneys. Hormones and defense cells are also carried in the blood. The blood and lymph bathe the cells in fluid and maintain the heat of the body.

## The Blood

Blood is made up of several substances:

- **Plasma:** The fluid part of the blood, which is made of *serum* and *platelets* that aid in clotting.
- **Red blood cells:** Cells containing *hemoglobin*, which carries oxygen and, to a lesser extent, carbon dioxide. They are produced in the bone marrow.
- **White blood cells:** Defense cells, which act against harmful *pathogens* in case of disease or injury.

## The Heart

The *heart* is a hollow muscular pump, made of *cardiac* (heart) muscle inside a protective cover called the *pericardium*. The heart has four *chambers* or *internal compartments:*

- **Left and right atria** (upper chambers): Receiving chambers.
- **Left and right ventricles** (lower chambers): Muscular pumping chambers.

The heart pumps the blood by contracting (squeezing) to drive blood from one chamber to another, and outward through large arteries. Deoxygenated blood (which is dark red and depleted of oxygen) carries carbon dioxide from the cells. Blood arrives at the heart through the vena cava, a large vein, and collects in the *right atrium* (the upper chamber). From there it is pumped into the *right ventricle* (lower chamber) through a one-way *valve*. It is then pumped from the right ventricle through the *pulmonary artery* to the lungs, where carbon dioxide is exchanged for oxygen.

The bright red, *oxygenated* blood comes back into the *left atrium* (left upper chamber) of the heart through the *pulmonary vein*. It is pumped through a one-way *valve* into the *left ventricle* (*lower chamber*), which pumps the blood out through the *aorta*, the main artery of the body. The aorta branches into smaller *arteries* to carry oxygenated blood to all parts of the body.

Circulatory system.

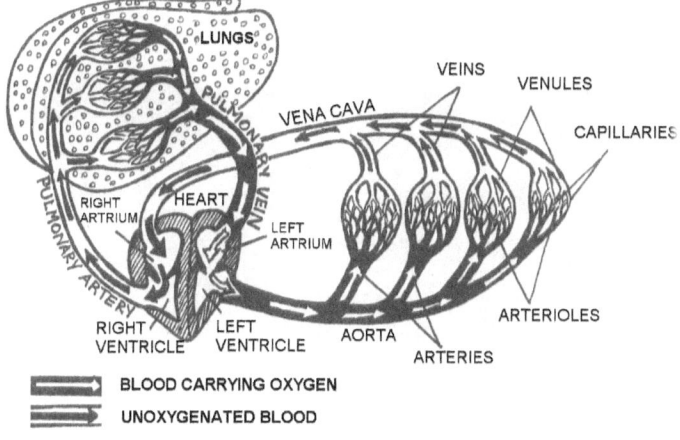

## Blood Vessels

- **Arteries** carry blood away from the heart. The *aorta* is the largest artery. Large arteries branch out into smaller *arterioles*, and finally into tiny *capillaries*.
- **Veins** carry blood back to the heart. Smaller *venules* and *capillaries* combine into larger veins, which eventually flow into the *vena cava*, the largest vein, which carries deoxygenated blood back to the heart.
- **Capillaries** are tiny blood vessels only one cell thick. Oxygen and nutrients are absorbed into the cells from capillaries, and waste products are taken into the bloodstream.

## Points to Remember

The heart is a muscle, and like all muscles it must be kept toned to work efficiently. Like all muscles, the heart must be brought into condition gradually using a properly designed conditioning program (see Chapter 12). A fit heart beats more powerfully, so it can beat fewer times per minute to pump the same amount of blood as an inefficient heart. That is why athletes have a lower heart rate than non-athletes. Since the heart muscle can only rest between beats, fewer beats per minute allows more rest between beats (not to be confused with an abnormal, sluggish heart rate).

Each heartbeat pumps blood out of the heart and into the aorta, then outward through the arteries. Therefore, if an artery is cut, the wound spurts blood with each beat. If a vein is cut, there will be a continuous flow of blood from the wound.

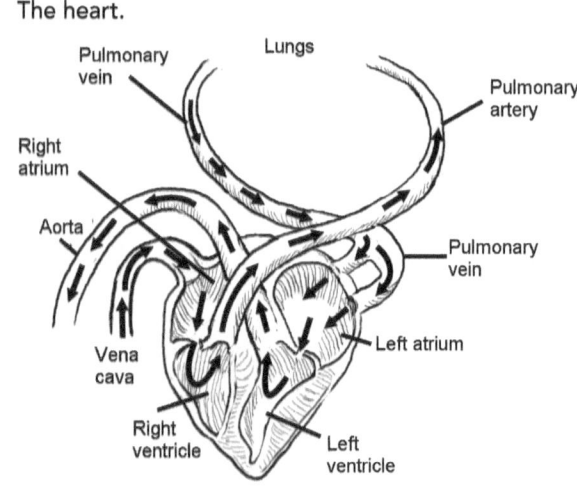

The heart.

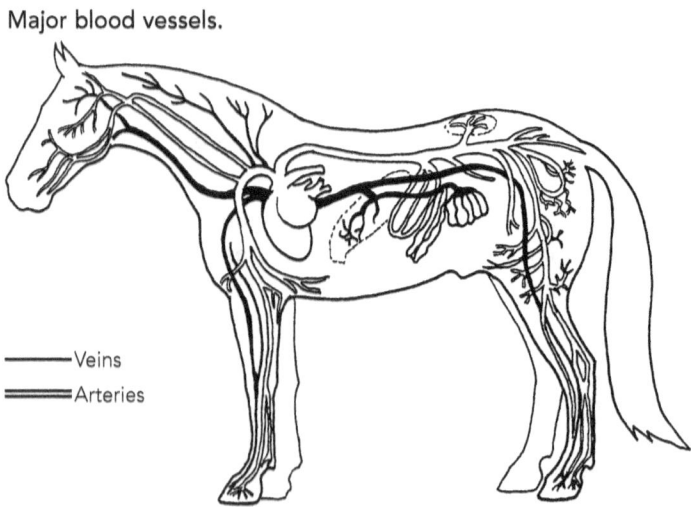

Major blood vessels.

*Arterial* blood pumped away from the heart is *oxygenated* (carrying oxygen) and is bright red. *Venous* blood, which is returning to the heart, is *deoxygenated* and is darker.

## The Immune and Lymphatic System

This system protects the body against harmful invaders such as bacteria, viruses, fungi, toxins, and internal parasites. It detects disease-causing organisms and works to neutralize or kill them so that they cannot damage the body. Sometimes the immune system is too reactive and causes damage to the body instead of repairing it.

The *lymphatic system* consists of:

- **Lymph:** A clear fluid containing white blood cells, which bathes all the cells of the body.
- **Lymph vessels:** Thin-walled vessels that transport the lymph throughout the body, and often run parallel to veins. All lymph ultimately drains into the *vena cava*.
- **Lymph nodes:** Bean-shaped masses of lymphatic tissues, which filter the lymph and produce *lymphocytes* and *antibodies* (defense cells) to cope with infection.

## DISEASES AFFECTING THE CIRCULATORY AND IMMUNE/LYMPHATIC SYSTEM

- Equine infectious anemia (EIA)
- Equine viral arteritis (EVA)
- Passive edema of the legs (stocking up)
- Lymphangitis
- Strangles (purpura hemorrhagica)
- Immune-mediated diseases such as periodic ophthalmia

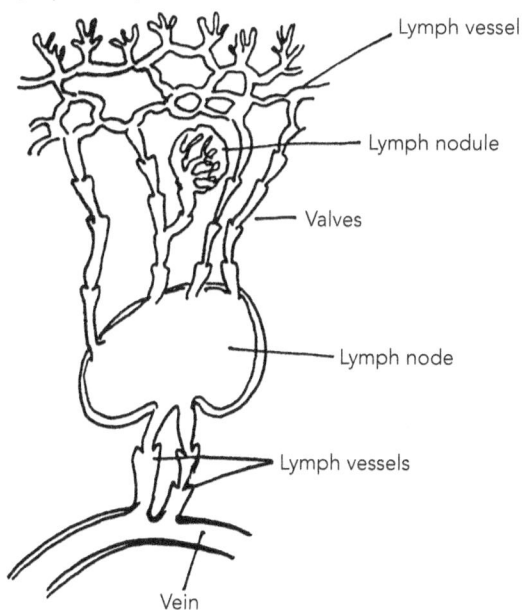

Lymphatic system.

# The Digestive System

The function of the *digestive system* is to take in (*ingest*) food, break it down into usable form, extract most of the nutrients from it, and excrete the waste. The digestive system consists of a long tube (over 100 feet long in most horses) called the *alimentary canal*, running from the mouth to the anus. It also includes the teeth (which grind food) and certain organs like the pancreas and liver (which help in processing nutrients).

## Parts of the Digestive System

- **Mouth:** The *lips, incisors* (*front teeth*), and *tongue* pick up and bite off food (as in grazing). The *molars* (back teeth) chew the food and begin the mechanical breakdown.
- **Salivary glands:** Produce *saliva* that is added to moisten the food and to begin to break down starches. The horse has three major salivary glands—the *parotid, sublingual*, and *submaxillary*.
- **Saliva:** Released when a horse takes food into his mouth. It contains large amounts of sodium bicarbonate; when the saliva enters the stomach, the sodium bicarbonate acts as a buffer against stomach acid, helping to prevent too much acid from building up, which reduces the risk of developing gastric ulcers. The more a horse chews, the more saliva he produces and the better able he is to buffer the acid in his stomach. Saliva also contains an *enzyme* called *amylase* that begins to break down starches in the ingested food.
- **Tongue, pharynx, and epiglottis:** These structures aid in swallowing. The *tongue* moves food toward the back of the mouth and packages it for swallowing. The *pharynx* is the area between the *soft palate* (roof of the mouth) and the opening to the esophagus. It works with both the respiratory and digestive systems. The *epiglottis* is the flap that covers the opening to the windpipe during swallowing.
- **Esophagus:** A muscular tube that carries food to the stomach via wavelike contractions called *peristalsis*. Food can move only one way (toward the stomach) in horses.
- **Stomach:** A muscular sack, holding approximately two to four gallons, which churns the food and saliva to a liquid form. It works best when no more than two-thirds full. *Hydrochloric acid* and the enzymes *pepsin, renin*, and *lipase* are secreted in the stomach and help with the chemical breakdown of food.

    A protective substance called *mucin* is secreted in the *glandular portion* of the stomach that makes up the lower two-thirds of the entire stomach. Mucin is not secreted in the upper one-third of the stomach (the *non-glandular region*), so if this portion of the stomach comes into contact with gastric acid, there is the risk of developing gastric ulcers.

In a natural setting horses graze constantly on high-fiber feeds. Within the stomach, the fiber forms a *raft* on top of the acid and other stomach contents, helping to prevent it from splashing up onto the lining of the upper unprotected section of the stomach. When domestic horses are fed infrequently or the level of forage in the diet is reduced, they have less of a protective raft and are more likely to develop stomach ulcers.

- **Pyloric valve:** The liquid that exits the stomach is called *chyme*. This valve controls the flow of food from the stomach to the small intestine.
- **Pancreas:** Produces and releases *pancreatic juices*. Pancreatic juice is alkaline to counter the acidity of the stomach, and it contains the enzymes *trypsin* and *amylase*, which further help break down proteins and starches. The pancreas also releases *insulin* into the bloodstream to regulate blood sugar levels.
- **Liver:** Converts *amino acids* into *proteins*, stores *glycogen* (a form of sugar or energy), regulates the nutrients carried in the blood, and produces *bile* (a digestive fluid that is secreted continuously into the *duodenum* because horses do not have a gallbladder), which aids in the breakdown of fats.
- **Small intestine:** Consists of three parts: the *duodenum, jejunum,* and *ileum*. The lining of the small intestine is covered with *villi*, small hair-like projections that increase the surface area for absorption of nutrients. The enzymatic digestion of fats, simple carbohydrates, and

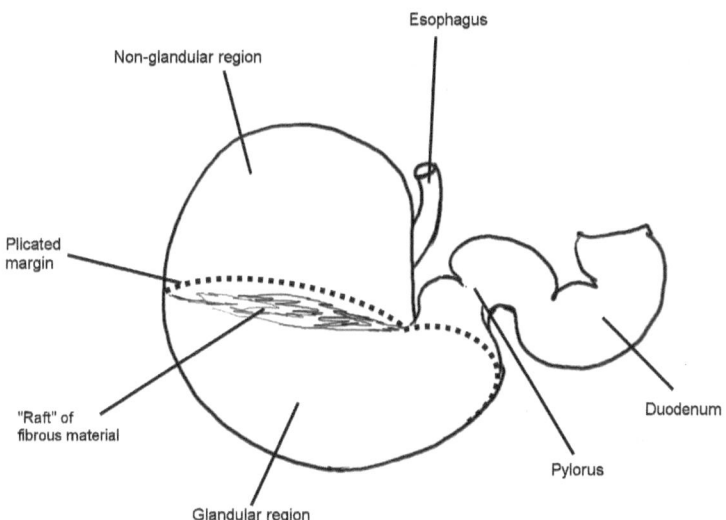

Parts of the stomach (glandular and non-glandular regions).

proteins in the diet occurs in the small intestine, with enzymes being secreted from the intestinal lining. The end products of this digestion (for example, *glucose* and *amino acids*) are absorbed from the small intestine into the bloodstream, where they are carried to various destinations around the body. The fat-soluble vitamins in the diet and most minerals are also absorbed in the small intestine, making it the major site of nutrient absorption.

The three parts of the small intestine are:

- *Duodenum:* Approximately 3 feet long. Ducts from the pancreas and liver secrete digestive juices (*pancreatic juice*, containing the enzymes *trypsin* and *amylase*, and *bile*) into the duodenum. This changes the food from an acid concentration to a more basic form, and the added enzymes further aid in the breakdown of proteins, fats, and simple carbohydrates.
- *Jejunum:* The main part of the small intestine; approximately 60 to 70 feet long. Most nutrients are absorbed into the bloodstream from here.
- *Ileum:* The final part of the small intestine; about 2 feet long. At the end of the ileum is a valve-like structure that controls the flow of food into the cecum.

- **Large intestine:** Consists of four parts: the *cecum, large colon, small colon,* and *rectum.* It holds 60 percent of the volume of the digestive tract. It primarily functions in fermentation of feed and absorption of the by-products of fermentation. *Structural carbohydrates* (such as cellulose) found in forages cannot be digested by enzymes because the enzymes in the small intestine are not capable of breaking the bonds holding these molecules together. Therefore, these carbohydrates, along with any other undigested and unabsorbed nutrients, intestinal secretions, and cells that have sloughed off of the intestinal tract, pass into the cecum.

  Living in the horse's large intestine are millions of "friendly" bacteria and other microorganisms. These bacteria break the complex bonds holding together the structural carbohydrates found in forages. They utilize these carbohydrates for their own benefit, as an energy source to grow. During this process they release *volatile fatty acids (VFAs)* which are absorbed through the lining of the large intestine into the bloodstream. The horse is able to convert these VFAs into forms of useful energy, such as glucose. In fact, horses fed only forage receive most of their energy by converting VFAs to usable glucose.

Other by-products of this microbial fermentation include B vitamins; as a result, it is very unusual for horses to suffer from B vitamin deficiencies.

Rapid changes in the diet can negatively impact this population of bacteria, resulting in gas production, loose manure, and colic. Therefore, all dietary changes should be made slowly over at least 10 to 14 days in order to give the bacteria time to adapt.

The parts of the large intestine are:

- *Cecum:* A large blind pouch approximately 4 feet long; it holds about 8 gallons. It contains bacteria that break down cellulose through fermentation and manufacture some B vitamins.
- *Large colon:* A large, folded-over tube 10 to 12 feet long. It weighs 50 to 75 pounds when it is full of ingested food. Further fermentation takes place here. Most of the by-products of fermentation, VFAs, are absorbed here.
- *Small colon:* A tube 8 to 10 feet long. Some water is extracted here, and the remaining material, which is waste, is formed into fecal balls or manure.
- *Rectum:* A "holding chamber" approximately 1 foot long. It ends at the anus, a circular muscle called a *sphincter*, to control defecation.

Digestive tract.

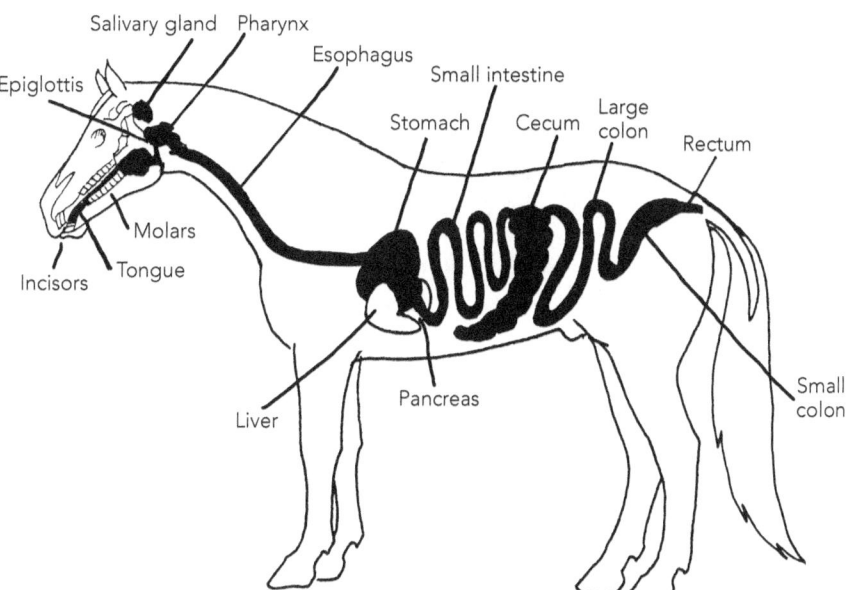

## Points to Remember

*Peristalsis*, the muscular contractions of the intestine, move food and digestive juices along the digestive tract. Peristalsis produces *gut sounds*. Lack of gut sounds or increased gut sounds may be indications of colic or other digestive disorders such as diarrhea.

The manure can give an indication of how well the digestive tract is working. For example:

- Whole grains in the manure mean that feed is not being chewed properly. This could be due to bad teeth or to "bolting" the feed.
- Hard, dry fecal balls may indicate the horse is not drinking enough water.
- Diarrhea can be due to many causes, including parasites, lack of digestive enzymes, bacterial infection in the gut, change of diet, or nervousness.
- Parasites can sometimes be observed in the manure.

### DISEASES AND AILMENTS AFFECTING THE DIGESTIVE SYSTEM
- Colic
- Choking
- Enteritis
- Laminitis
- Potomac horse fever
- Gastric ulcers

# The Nervous System

The nervous system provides "command and control" functions for the body by receiving, sorting, and transmitting *nerve impulses*.

The nervous system has three parts or branches:

- **Central nervous system:** Includes the *brain* and the *spinal cord;* controls all aspect of the body.
- **Peripheral nerves:** The *nerves,* which run to the muscles and all parts of the body.

  These include:
  - *Sensory nerves:* Nerves that receive *stimuli* (changes in the environment such as heat, cold, touch, sound, smell, and taste) and transmit them to the brain.
  - *Motor nerves:* Nerves that transmit instructions to the muscles.

- **Autonomic nervous system:** Controls the functions of the internal organs of the body, allowing the heart to beat, the lungs to breathe, digestion to take place, and so on without the need for conscious awareness. The *sympathetic* and *parasympathetic* systems operate reflexes and "automatic" reactions, such as shivering from cold, and are designed to regulate each other.

## Nerve Cells and Their Functions

The basic nerve cell is called a *neuron*. The body of the cell has branches called *dendrites*, and long fibers are called *axons*. The junction between one neuron and another (where one neuron's axon touches another's dendrite) is called a *synapse*.

The nervous system works like a relay system. Information is passed from neurons to muscles, or from one neuron to another through chemicals. Nerve impulses travel down axons through the dendrites to the synapses, which release a chemical called *acetylcholine* that activates the synapse of the next nerve in the chain of communication. *Acetylcholinesterase* breaks down the acetylcholine to stop the nerve impulse when it is no longer needed. Some diseases and toxic chemicals interfere with this process,

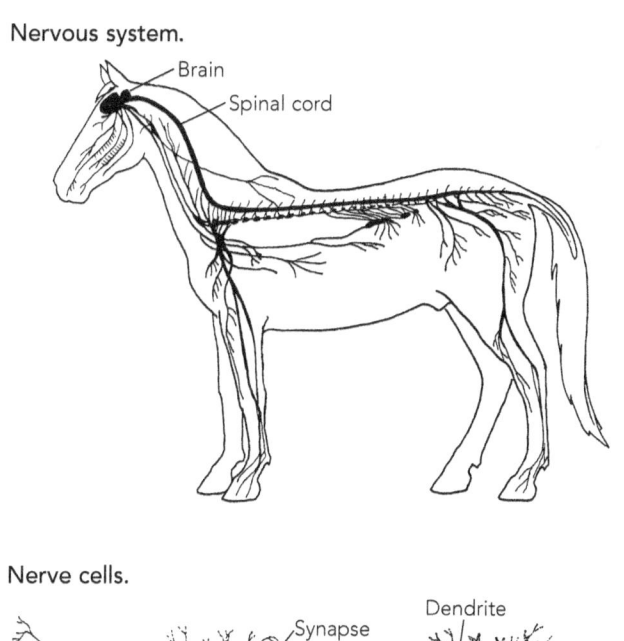

Nervous system.

Nerve cells.

resulting in continuous stimulation (for example, tetanus) or prevention of stimulation of the nerve impulse (for example, botulism).

## Points to Remember

Many pesticides (including certain fly sprays, some dewormers, and flea and tick dips used on dogs) are *cholinesterase inhibitors*. These are cumulative substances, meaning they can build up in the system until they cause damage. If an animal receives too much of a cholinesterase inhibitor (possibly by being exposed to an overdose or a combination of these products), it can block the release of cholinesterase in his nervous system, resulting in muscle spasms or seizures due to the continuous flow of acetylcholine. It is important to read the ingredients and product warning labels, and follow directions carefully when using fly spray, dewormers, insecticides, and pesticides. Also, wait at least 10 days before allowing horses to graze on pastures that were treated with pesticides containing *organophosphates*.

Signs of nervous system dysfunction vary by their location within the system. There is a large difference in clinical signs exhibited by the horse, depending on where the problem is located within the nervous system (for example, brain versus spinal cord). Veterinarians "localize" the problem using specific tests. In general, problems involving the brain cause changes in behavior, vision, and mental ability, while problems involving the spinal cord and peripheral nerves cause changes in coordination and the strength and purpose of limb and body movement.

DISEASES AFFECTING THE NERVOUS SYSTEM
- Tetanus
- Equine encephalomyeletis
- Rabies
- Botulism
- West Nile virus
- Equine protozoal myelopathy (EPM)

# The Endocrine System

The *endocrine system* consists of *glands* that secrete hormones. *Hormones* are chemical substances produced by various organs of the body. They are the regulators of almost all body functions. They are carried in the bloodstream and act on other organs to alter normal body processes such as conserving water, regulating blood sugar (glucose), responding to stress, or altering the metabolism. The endocrine system often works with the *autonomic nervous system* to regulate changes within the body.

In general, a hormone is released from one organ and affects the cells of another *target organ*. Once the change has been made by the target organ, the first organ recognizes that the change has been made and discontinues release of its hormone. This is called *negative feedback*. The ultimate goal of the endocrine system is to maintain *homeostasis*, or maintenance of a stable condition within the body.

The major endocrine glands, the hormones they produce, and their major effects are listed in the following table.

## Chart 9-1: Endocrine Glands, Hormones, and Effects of Hormones

| Gland | Hormone | Acts On | Effects |
|---|---|---|---|
| Pituitary | Follicle-stimulating hormone (FSH) | Ovary | Stimulates follicle development and estrogen production |
| Pituitary | Luteinizing hormone (LH) | Ovaries/ leydig cells Testes | Stimulates ovulation, development of corpus luteum ("yellow body") in ovary, and estrogen production |
| Pituitary | Prolactin | Mammary glands | Milk production (lactation) |
| Pituitary | Growth hormone (GH) | Overall metabolism | Growth and increase of tissue size; regulates protein and carbohydrate metabolism |
| Pituitary | Thyroid-stimulating hormone (TSH) | Thyroid | Stimulates thyroxin secretion |
| Pituitary | Adrenocorticotropic hormone (ACTH) | Adrenals | Stimulates cortisol secretion |
| Pituitary | Vasopressin (ADH) | Arteries, kidneys | Raises blood pressure by increasing water resorption in kidneys |
| Pituitary | Oxytocin | Uterus, mammary glands | Stimulates uterine contractions in foaling; stimulates "milk let-down" from udder |
| Pituitary | Melanocyte-stimulating hormone (MSH) | Melanocytes | Stimulates cells with pigmentation |

*continued*

| Gland | Hormone | Acts On | Effects |
|---|---|---|---|
| Pancreas | Insulin | Cells | Controls blood sugar |
| Thyroid gland | Thyroxine | Cells | Controls rate of metabolism |
| Adrenal glands cortex of kidney | Cortisol | Liver, kidney, white blood cells, fat, muscle | Responds to stress and increases blood sugar; affects carbohydrate, fat, and protein metabolism; suppresses immune system |
|  | Aldosterone | Kidneys | Controls levels of salt and water in blood and tissues to ultimately affect blood pressure |
| Adrenal medulla of kidney | Adrenaline (Epinephrine) | Whole body | Fight or flight response: increases heart and respiratory rate; stimulates sweating; increases blood flow to muscles while decreasing blood flow to internal organs |
| Ovary (follicle) | Estrogen | Uterus and reproductive system | Causes estrus behavior, conditioning of reproductive organs, development of mammary tissue |
| Ovary (corpus luteum or "yellow body") | Progesterone | Uterus and reproductive system | Prepares reproductive tract for pregnancy or diestrus; during pregnancy protects corpus luteum to maintain pregnancy |
| Uterus | Prostaglandin | Corpus luteum of ovary | Stops corpus luteum from secreting progesterone, which results in ovulation |
| Testes | Testosterone | Male reproductive system, overall | Male sex hormone; stimulates libido, sperm production, sexual behavior, and secondary sex characteristics (muscle development) |

## DISORDERS AFFECTING THE ENDOCRINE SYSTEM
- Equine Cushing's disease (pituitary pars intermedia dysfunction)
- Insulin resistance
- Equine metabolic syndrome

# The Reproductive System

The functions of the reproductive system include *sexual behavior, mating, gestation or pregnancy, birth*, and *lactation* (production of milk).

## The Reproductive System of the Stallion

The reproductive organs of the stallion are designed to produce sperm and place it within the mare, where it can unite with an egg. *Sperm* are the male reproductive cells.

The *testes* (or *testicles*) are the organs in which sperm (male reproductive cells) are produced and stored. They function best at a temperature slightly lower than the internal body temperature, so in mature males, they are located outside the body in a sac called the *scrotum*. The sperm finish maturing in the *epididymus*.

*Testosterone* (the male sex hormone) is also produced in the testes. This hormone produces secondary sex characteristics (such as the enlarged crest and deeper voice of a stallion) and influences sexual behavior.

Before birth, the testes are located in the abdomen. They descend into the scrotum through the *inguinal canal*. Both testes should have permanently descended by the age of 12 months. A male having one or more testes retained in the abdomen or caught in the inguinal canal is called a *cryptorchid*.

*Castration* (or *gelding*) involves the surgical removal of both testes. This makes the gelding infertile and removes the source of testosterone, so it

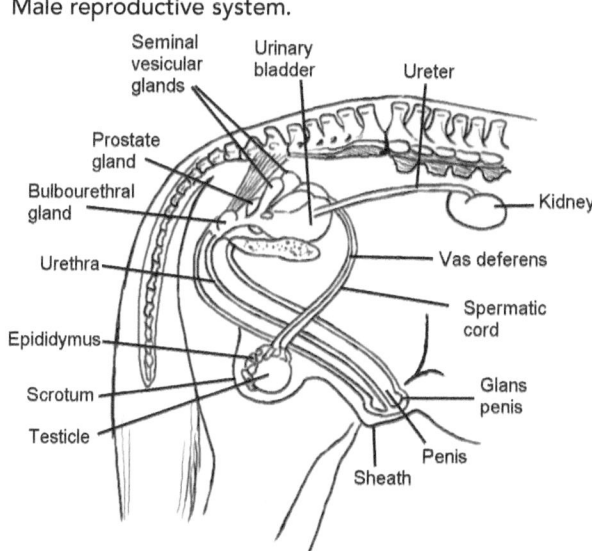

Male reproductive system.

usually (although not always) limits male sexual behavior. It is usually performed when the colt is a yearling, but may be done at other times at the owner's discretion.

During mating, sperm leaves the testicles through the *vas deferens* and is delivered to the *urethra*. It is expelled during *ejaculation*. Substances from the *seminal vesicular gland, prostrate,* and *bulbourethral gland* are added to the sperm to form *semen*. These substances provide nutrients and a protective environment for the sperm as they enter the mare.

The *urethra* allows for the passage of urine and sperm to pass to the outside of the horse. This common tube travels within the penis. The *penis* telescopes upon itself within the sheath. The end of the penis is called the *glans penis*, which is necessary for copulation. A substance called *smegma* accumulates within the folds of the sheath, on the surface of the penis, and in a pouch at the opening of the urethra. This should be removed by periodic cleaning.

The tranquilizer *acepromazine* and the sedatives *xylazine, detomidine,* and *romifidine* cause the penis to relax and hang from the sheath. This facilitates cleaning, and is also a sign that a horse has been tranquilized. See Chapter 14 for more information.

## The Reproductive System of the Mare

The mare's reproductive system is designed to produce an *egg*, which unites with a *sperm* to form an *embryo*. It contains and nourishes the embryo while it develops (*gestation*), and expels it during birth (*parturition*). The reproductive system also includes the *mammary system,* which provides milk for the foal.

The *ovum* (*egg*) is the female reproductive cell. Eggs are produced in the ovaries (there are two, a right and a left). The ovaries also produce the female hormones *estrogen* and *progesterone.*

The *fallopian tubes* lead from each ovary to the uterus.

The *uterus* is the organ in which the embryo implants and grows during gestation. The end of the uterus, located just before the vagina, is called the *cervix*. It is tightly closed, except during estrus.

The *vagina* is the passage from the uterus to the *vulva* (the external opening to the outside of the body). The urethra also opens into the vulva.

### The Estrus (Heat) Cycle

The *pituitary gland* signals the body to release *follicle-stimulating hormone* (*FSH*). This causes the ovary to develop a *follicle* containing an egg (ovum). The ovary then produces the hormone *estrogen*, which stimulates the follicle to open and release the egg (*ovulation*). Estrogen also stimulates receptive behavior (called *estrus,* or *heat*), causing the mare to be receptive to

Female reproductive system.

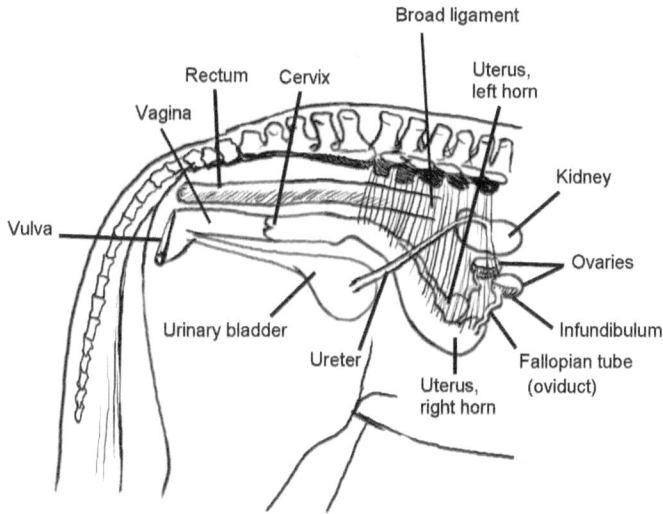

breeding at the time of ovulation. Estrus behavior in mares consists of interest in a stallion, increased frequency of urination, staining of the vulva with a white substance, "winking" or opening and closing of the vulva, and possible behaviorial changes that may affect a mare's trainability.

The remnant of the follicle (which opened to release the egg during ovulation) is called the *corpus luteum (CL)* or *yellow body*. The corpus luteum secretes the hormone *progesterone,* which ends the estrus cycle in one of two ways:

- If the mare is bred and becomes pregnant, it continues to produce progesterone throughout the pregnancy, which helps to maintain the pregnancy and prevents the mare from coming back into estrus.
- If the mare is not bred or does not become pregnant, it produces progesterone for only a few days. After that, the progesterone level drops off and the estrus cycle starts over again, beginning with FSH.

*Gestation (pregnancy)* lasts an average of 335 days.

The *estrus cycle* averages about 21 to 24 days, but the actual period of estrus, during which the mare can conceive, lasts only 3 to 5 days. Mares are *seasonally polyestrus,* which means that they go through many estrus cycles during certain seasons (early spring through late fall), and are *anestrus,* which means they do not cycle during the winter.

This phenomenon is based on the amount of daylight. The increased number of daylight hours beginning in late winter and early spring stimulates the production of FSH. The natural breeding season peaks in spring and early summer, ensuring that most foals are born in the spring, when better weather and natural nutrition are available.

Most fillies begin cycling during the spring of their second year, but they should not be bred until they are three or older, as pregnancy puts a strain on an immature body.

DISEASES AFFECTING THE REPRODUCTIVE SYSTEM
- Rhinopneumonitis (contagious abortion)
- Equine viral arteritis (EVA)

# The Urinary System

The urinary system includes the *kidneys* (and their associated blood vessels), *ureters, urinary bladder*, and *urethra*. It filters out waste materials and excess water from the blood, which are excreted as urine. It also must return all necessary proteins, minerals, and electrolytes to the system, and acts as a buffer in maintaining the proper pH (acidity) of the blood.

## Parts of the Urinary System

- **Kidneys:** The *kidneys* are responsible for filtering the blood to keep the body's electrolytes, pH, and water content balanced. There are normally two kidneys, although an animal can survive with only one working kidney. Each kidney contains millions of *nephrons* (a system of tiny tubules and capillaries), in which filtration takes place.

  Blood is circulated through the kidneys through the *renal veins* and *renal arteries*, which are connected to the aorta and the vena cava.

- **Ureters:** Tubes that carry waste (in the form of *urine*) from each kidney to the *urinary bladder*.
- **Urinary bladder:** A muscular sack that stores the urine until it is excreted.
- **Urethra:** The tube that takes the urine from the urinary bladder to exit outside the body. In a male horse, it goes through the penis. In a female, the urethra exits into the vagina, and the external opening is at the vulva.

## Urine

The waste product of the urinary system is *urine*. Horses excrete a large amount of calcium in their urine, so it tends to be much thicker and cloudier than the urine of other animals. Also, due to other minerals in the urine, it

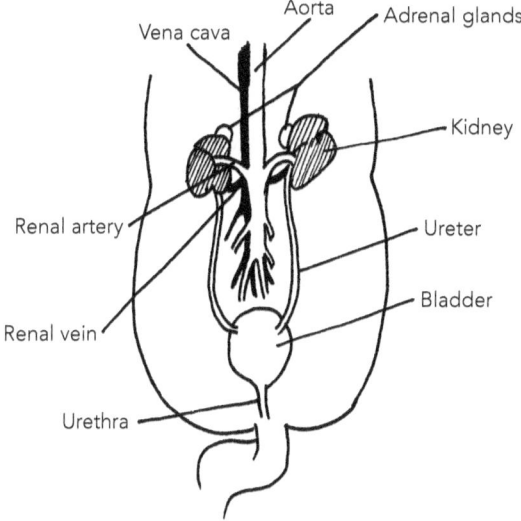

The urinary system.

often turns a bright orange or red when it interacts with materials in the environment, such as snow or certain types of wood shavings.

Horses *posture* to urinate by extending their back legs behind themselves and their front legs in front. This posture is more obvious in geldings. In addition, geldings extend their penis out of their sheath. If a horse "postures" to urinate but nothing comes out, it may be a sign of abdominal pain or a urinary tract obstruction. Horses generally prefer to urinate in footing that will not cause splashing (for example, some horses refuse to urinate in a trailer). Mares that are in estrus may posture to urinate more frequently and only pass a small amount of urine. This is normal.

When horses become dehydrated, they urinate less and the urine may be a darker yellow and cloudier. It is important to monitor the type and amount of urine your horse passes. If you think something is abnormal about the way your horse is urinating, call a veterinarian. Some common reasons to call a veterinarian regarding a horse's urinary tract include very dark brown urine, bright blood in the urine, frequent urination, posturing to urinate and not passing urine, a gelding that does not extend his penis out of his sheath to urinate, or a male horse that cannot retract his penis into his sheath.

## Points to Remember

Although the kidneys excrete waste from the blood, they also filter and retain important nutrients in the blood; otherwise the body would be in a constant state of depletion.

The kidneys work *only* by filtering the blood. They do *not* pick up waste from the large intestine.

The kidneys have a tremendous ability to compensate so they can continue to filter the blood, which is extremely important to maintain normal body function. When an animal has only one kidney, that kidney works overtime. In fact, approximately 75 percent of a kidney must be nonfunctional before blood chemistry will reveal a problem.

Kidney disease is very rare in horses. Horses can form bladder stones due to the high calcium content of their urine. These may cause irritation to the bladder resulting in frequent urination, straining to urinate, or bloody urine, especially after exercise.

## The Integumentary System

The *skin* is the main organ of the integumentary system. It is also the largest organ of the body. It functions as a sheath for the body, protecting against trauma, excessive radiation, and the entry of microorganisms. It also aids in *thermoregulation* (temperature control), excretes waste products, and synthesizes vitamin D. The skin contains *sweat glands, sebaceous (oil) glands*, and *sensory nerves*, which detect pressure, pain, and temperature. The hair coat, mane, and tail grow from the skin and are also part of the integumentary system. The hooves are composed of a specialized form of skin that is hardened by *keratin*.

### Parts of the Skin

There are three layers of skin:

- **Epidermis:** Thin outer layer of skin.
- **Dermis:** Thicker layer below the epidermis that contains most skin structures such as sweat glands and hair follicles.
- **Subcutaneous:** A thin layer of loose fatty material between the dermis and underlying structures (bone or muscle).

The skin contains certain structures, including:

- *Apocrine (sweat) glands*, which secrete sweat.
- *Oil (sebaceous glands),* which secrete *sebum* (skin oil).
- *Hair follicles*, which include the *papilla* (root), the *hair shaft*, and the tiny *erector pili muscle*, which can cause the hair to stand up.
- *Blood vessels* and *nerves*.

Structures of the skin.

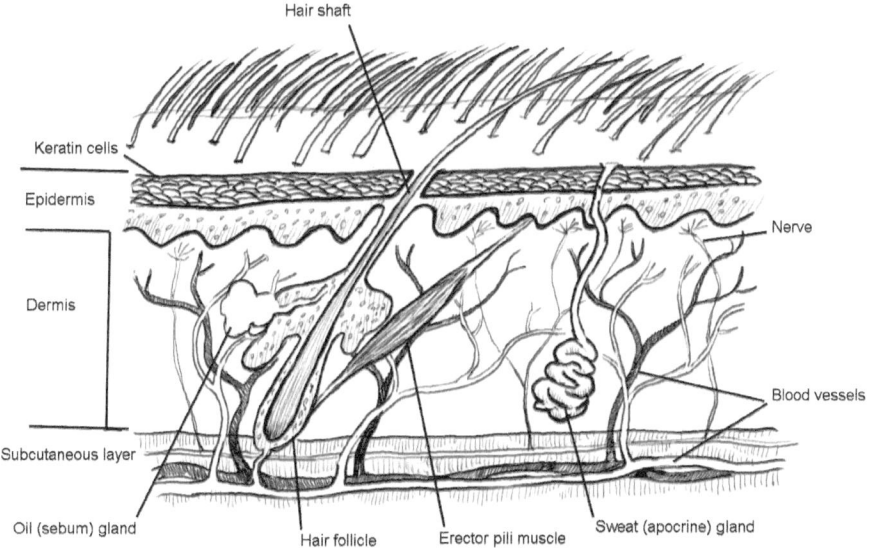

- *Panniculus muscle*, a large, thin sheet of muscle that lies under the skin. This allows the horse to twitch the skin to remove flies and shiver to create heat.

## Points to Remember

The skin has a two-way function: It absorbs sunlight (which it uses to synthesize vitamin D) and heat, and excretes salts and water through sweat. Excess heat is radiated into the air, and the outside air temperature and/or moisture in contact with the skin heats or cools the skin and the body.

The hair coat provides protection from cold, dampness, and insects. Specialized hair features such as *fetlocks*, the *hair inside the ears, whiskers*, and the *mane* and *tail* have protective roles. If this natural protection is removed, the horse will need extra care and is less suited to living and working outdoors.

The winter coat is longer and thicker, with extra-long *guard hairs* that permit water to run off. The skin produces extra sebum (oil), which helps to waterproof the skin and hair coat.

The hairs of the body have tiny muscles (*erector pili muscles*) that permit them to become erect or stand up (called a *staring coat*). This increases the *loft* of the coat, trapping air close to the skin for warmth. A staring coat indicates a horse is trying to keep warm, or a sick horse that may be having chills.

Growth and shedding of the winter coat are determined by hormones released from the *hypothalamus*, a part of the brain that responds primarily to the shortening and lengthening of daylight, and secondarily to the air temperature.

The condition of the skin and hair coat is an indicator of the horse's general health. A healthy horse's skin is supple and pliable, and his hair coat shines with a normal amount of sebum (skin oil). Good grooming, nutrition, and general good health are necessary for healthy skin.

## DISEASES AND CONDITIONS THAT AFFECT THE SKIN
- Warts (papilloma virus)
- Squamous cell carcinoma
- Melanoma
- Sarcoid tumors
- Dermatophilosis (rainrot, rain scald, scratches, grease heel)
- Ringworm
- Bacterial or fungal dermatitis

# 10

# Conformation and Soundness

## Conformation

Conformation affects a horse's strength, athletic ability, and movement. Certain types of conformation favor different kinds of movement; some conformation defects handicap a horse in the way he moves. As a competent horse person, it is important to be able to assess a horse's conformation using a systematic evaluation, in order to determine how each horse's strengths and weaknesses in conformation may affect his athleticism. Particularly when purchasing a horse, one must take into account conformation faults that may lead to later unsoundnesses or complicate training.

A horse's conformation is determined primarily by the shape and proportion of his skeleton. Muscular development may change with condition, but the bones are the primary guide to a horse's conformation. Therefore, when evaluating conformation, you need to be familiar with skeletal anatomy and look at the underlying structure with "x-ray eyes" and not be fooled by superficial appearance, condition, fat, or color.

## Proportions

A horse's proportions (size or length of each part in relation to each other) affect his ability to move. Some examples include:

- Long muscles are able to move a limb farther than short muscles. Length in the neck, shoulder, forearm, croup, and from hip to hock helps a horse take longer strides for his size.
- Shorter is usually stronger. Short, wide, well-developed cannon bones and flexor tendons are stronger than long, narrow cannons. A horse with a long back may have springy gaits and greater scope over fences, but a long back is less able to carry weight and more prone to injury than a short back. Long pasterns are more prone to injury than shorter ones, as they put more stress on the *suspensory apparatus* (*flexor tendons, suspensory ligament,* and *distal sesamoidean ligaments*).
- In the front legs, ideal proportions are long shoulder (*scapula*), medium arm (*humerus*), long forearm (*radius*), short cannon (*third metacarpal bone*), and medium pastern (*first phalanx*). This favors maximum length of stride, strength, efficiency, and range of motion. A short shoulder, long arm, short forearm, and long cannon causes a shorter, higher stride and is less strong.
- A long distance from hip to hock (*hocks well let down*) indicates short, strong hind cannon bones and a more powerful hind leg.

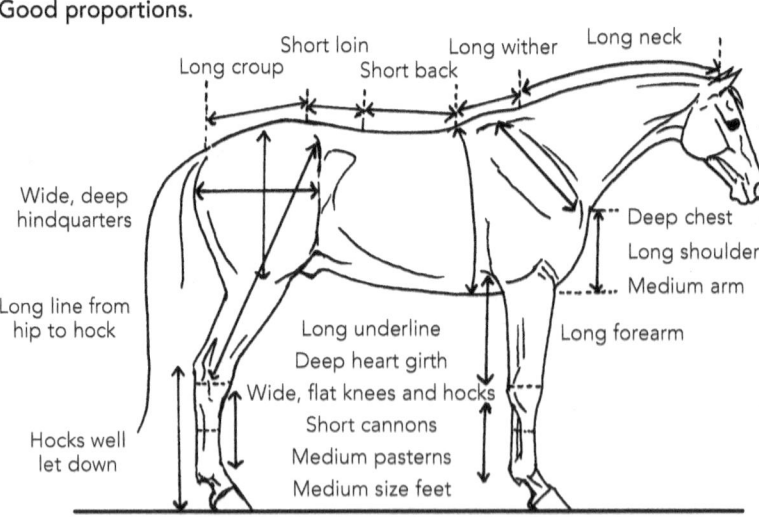

Good proportions.

## Angles

The angles of the major bones affect the range of motion of the joints and the power and efficiency of the horse's stride. Some important angles are:

**Shoulder slope and shoulder angle.** *Shoulder slope* and *shoulder angle* are two different elements. Both are important in evaluating the conformation of the forehand and the potential movement of the horse. It's important to be aware of the skeletal anatomy when evaluating this region. The withers are not connected to the shoulder and have nothing to do with shoulder slope or angle, so the common practice of drawing a line from the point of the shoulder (which is actually the point of the humerus) to some point on the withers does not give an accurate assessment of either shoulder slope or shoulder angle.

When evaluating shoulder slope and angle, the horse should be standing on level ground with the cannon bones vertical. If the horse stands uphill, downhill, or with the foreleg angled forward or backward, it changes both shoulder slope and angle and can result in a false perception of his shoulder conformation.

**Shoulder slope** refers to the angle of the scapula (shoulder blade) to the horizontal, measured as the slope of the spine of the scapula. Ideal shoulder slope is around 45 to 50 degrees, but this varies with the breed and type of horse. The shoulder blade (scapula) rotates with each stride, swinging the entire foreleg forward and back. A sloping shoulder has more range of motion and can swing the foreleg farther forward, which is important for long strides and to bring the knees up in jumping. It also absorbs shock, which makes the gaits smoother. An upright (*straight*) shoulder cannot swing the leg as far forward or up, resulting in a shorter, choppier stride.

**Shoulder angle** refers to the angle of the *scapulohumeral joint* (the joint between the scapula (shoulder blade) and humerus (arm). This angle is measured between the central ridge of the scapula and the humerus. The shoulder angle affects the placement of the horse's foreleg and therefore his balance and movement.

Ideally, this angle should be approximately 90 degrees. If the shoulder angle is too open (greater than 90 degrees), the forelegs are placed more to the front and the shoulder may be too upright. If it is too closed (less than 90 degrees), the forelegs are placed too far back relative to the chest and forehand, predisposing the horse to move more heavily on the forehand and making collection more difficult.

**Hind leg angles.** The hind legs act as levers, which push the body forward and carry weight, especially during transitions and collection.

Shoulder angle and shoulder slope.

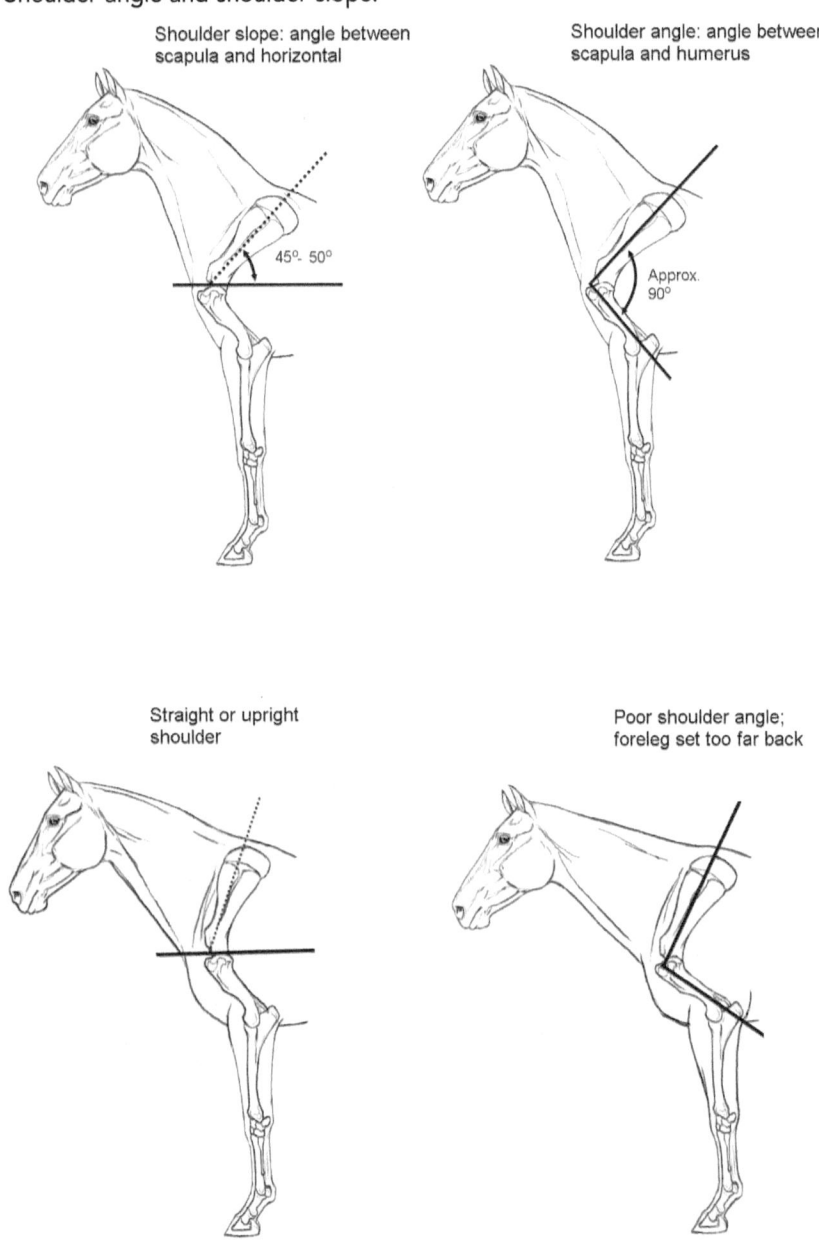

Shoulder slope: angle between scapula and horizontal
45°- 50°

Shoulder angle: angle between scapula and humerus
Approx. 90°

Straight or upright shoulder

Poor shoulder angle; foreleg set too far back

Correct angles make these levers more efficient in pushing and carrying weight.

In the ideal hind leg, a vertical line dropped from the point of the croup runs down the back of the hock, cannon, and fetlock joint. This gives the hocks the best angle. If the hock angle is too acute

Hind leg angles.

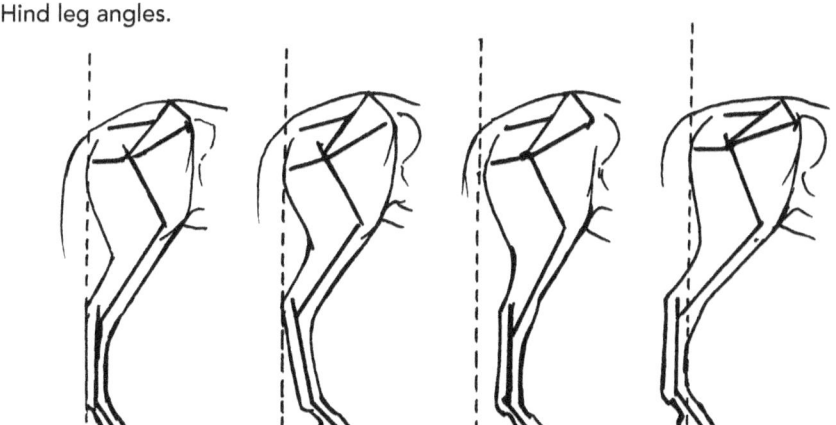

Correct: vertical line from point of buttock passes down hock to fetlock joint

Too much angle: sickle hock

Too open angle: post leg

Camped out behind

(sickle hocks or standing under), they are placed too far under the body to push effectively, and this puts extra stress on structures at the back of the hock. If the hock joint angle is too open (straight hock), it swings forward and backward efficiently but puts extra stress on the hock and suspensory ligament when carrying weight. If placed too far back, the hocks are less able to reach forward under the body, resulting in less engagement and power.

**Angle of pasterns.** Pasterns should be of a medium angle, similar to the shoulder slope (45 to 50 degrees), sloping enough to absorb shock, but not so sloping as to be easily injured or to allow the back of the fetlock joint to strike the ground. The pastern angles in the hind limb are naturally steeper than the front limb (50 to 55 degrees).

Angle of neck.

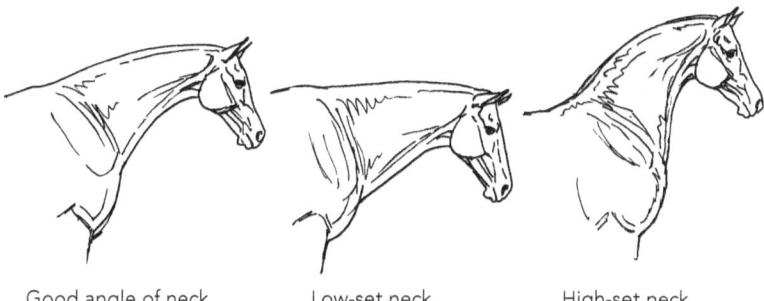

Good angle of neck

Low-set neck

High-set neck

**Angle of neck.** The angle of the neck affects the way the horse naturally carries and uses his head and neck for balance. A low-set neck, which comes out of the front of the chest, results in a low head carriage and a tendency to move on the forehand. A neck set high with an upward angle ("swan neck") encourages flexibility and collection, but makes it easy for the horse to carry his head too high and drop his back. The ideal neck depends on the type and purpose of the horse, but an average angle of neck is best for all-around balance and movement.

## Hindquarter Conformation

**Lumbosacral (LS) joint (coupling).** The *lumbosacral joint* or *LS joint* (the joint between the *lumbar vertebrae* [loin] and the *sacrum* [croup] is important in balance and movement and, with the sacrum, determines the angle of the croup. This area (the loin and LS joint) is called the *coupling*. The LS joint opens and closes during movement, in collection, and in movements such as transitions, jumping, and changes of balance. Ideally, the point of the hip (*tuber coxae*) should be directly underneath the lumbosacral joint. A broad, well-muscled loin and well-placed LS joint is ideal, giving strength to the back and making it easier for the horse to use his hindquarters powerfully in movement, collection, and jumping. A long loin with the LS joint placed farther back is a weaker construction.

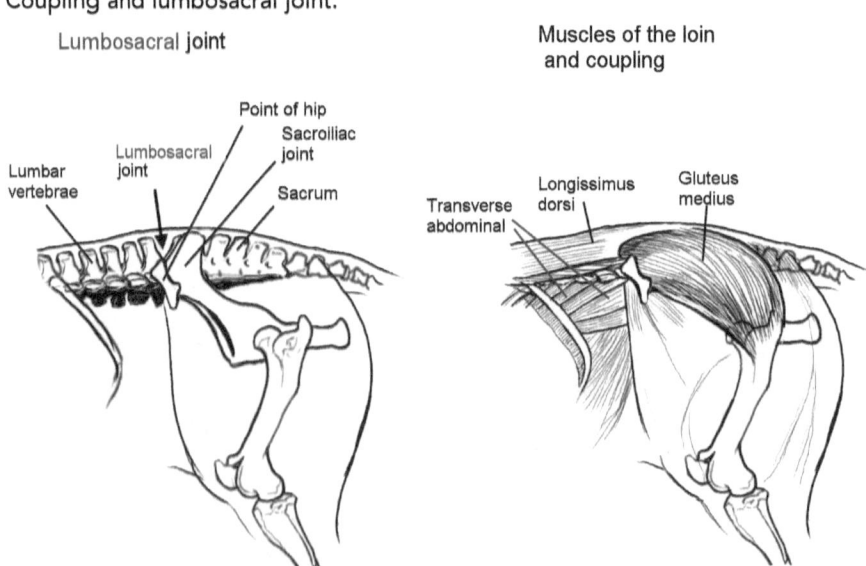

Coupling and lumbosacral joint.

Angles of croup and pelvis.

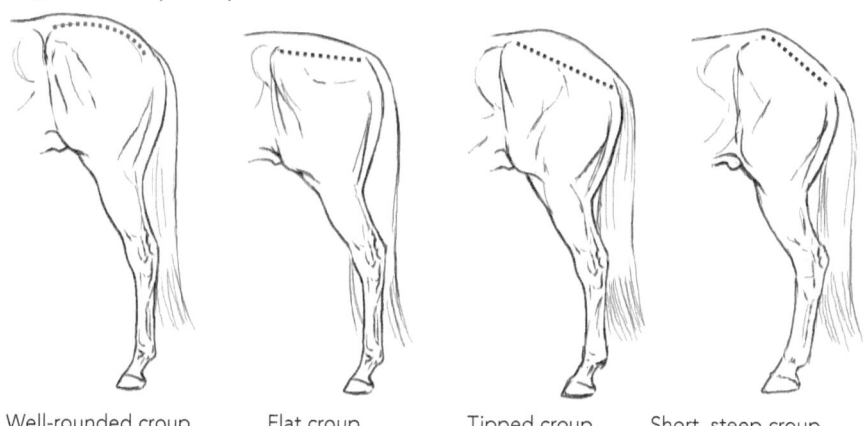

Well-rounded croup · Flat croup · Tipped croup · Short, steep croup

**Angle of croup.** The angle of the croup affects the horse's ability to flex the LS joint, tuck his hindquarters under him, and engage his hind legs for balance and power. An ideal croup is long and slightly rounded, and neither flat nor steep. This allows for good angles, placement, and engagement of the hind legs.

The angle of the croup helps to determine the amount of pushing power a horse will have. A flatter croup allows for a smoother gait and longer strides but with less power, while a steeper croup creates shorter, more powerful strides. An excessively long, flat croup places the hind legs farther back, making it more difficult for the hind legs to reach well forward. This conformation is less problematic in driving horses, so it is more common in breeds that have been developed primarily as carriage horses. A long loin and steep croup are sometimes seen in draft horses that move with short but powerful strides.

Good jumpers and sprinters often have a greater angle in the croup, creating powerful hindquarters. An extremely long, flat croup makes it difficult to do collected dressage work, jump height, or perform western stock work, as it is more difficult to engage the hindquarters.

Length of hip (ilium to ischium) is also important in analyzing the horse's athletic potential. Horses with a longer hip tend to have a more sweeping stride, with more efficient hind leg movement and greater thrust, allowing them to have greater endurance and sustained power, such as in distance racehorses, trotters, and endurance horses. A short hip inhibits muscular attachment and provides a less powerful hindquarter. This provides less thrust for jumping or galloping, and makes collected work difficult.

To assess the angles of the hindquarters, hip, and stifle joints, visualize a triangle on the horse's hindquarters from the point of hip

The hindquarter triangle.

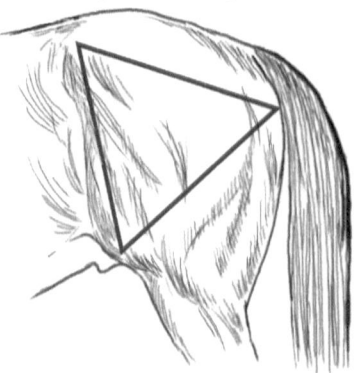

(*os coxae*) to the point of the buttock (*ischium*), and to the stifle (*patella*). An athletic horse generally has a nearly equilateral triangle. If the triangle has a more acute angle at the point of hip, the horse will have more power but a shorter stride because he will have a correspondingly steep croup, whereas if the triangle has a more open angle at the point of the hip, the horse will have less power but a longer stride, because he will have a more level croup. In jumping horses (especially eventers), the distance from the point of hip to stifle should be long, as this will increase the power of the jump.

For more information on conformation, see Chapter 12 in the *USPC C Level Manual*.

## Guideline for Evaluating Conformation

**Determine overall balance:** Before picking out conformational faults, it is important to determine how the horse is balanced. Is the horse built "uphill" or "downhill"? There are a couple ways to determine a horse's longitudinal balance. First, stand the horse on level ground and evaluate how the height of the withers compares to the highest point of the croup. Next, compare the level of the point of the elbow and the point of the stifle. A true uphill-built horse will have withers higher than the point of the croup, and the point of elbow will be level or higher than the point of the stifle.

**Determine overall shape:** Does the horse's body (excluding the neck and head) fit into a square or a rectangle? Ultimately, the horse's overall shape will determine his ability to balance himself. A horse that fits into a square will likely be better proportioned and more balanced than a horse that fits into a rectangle.

Square horse versus rectangular horse.

**Determine overall proportions:** Are the horse's proportions balanced, correct, and harmonious? Does he appear to have a long top line, short underline, and length of neck and leg in proportion to his body length and height? Do all his parts appear to fit smoothly together?

**Determine specific proportions:** This includes evaluating the proportions of specific parts of the limbs, as discussed earlier in this chapter.

**Evaluate leg conformation from the side, front, and rear:** In addition to the points discussed earlier, this includes the assessment of the relative straightness and position of the fore and hind legs relative to the body as discussed in Chapter 12 of the *USPC C Level Manual*.

**Determine hoof conformation:** The hooves should be evaluated for size, balance (from the side and the back of the hoof, both when bearing weight and when it is picked up), signs of wear (for example, flares or dubbed toes), hoof cracks and rings, and the quality of trimming or shoeing. The left and right hooves should be compared to determine symmetry (for example, one hoof may appear more upright than the other, indicating that the horse may routinely bear less weight on the upright hoof).

**Determine the horse's "type" and other conformation points:** Using the information you've gathered in your evaluation, you should be able to estimate the horse's overall type and breed. For example, stock horses tend to be built downhill, have steeper croup angles, heavier muscling, and have lower-set necks compared to Warmbloods that are built level to uphill, with medium croup angles, moderate muscling, and a medium- to high-set neck. In addition, other non-functional conformation points should be assessed, including the shape of the head, size and position of the eyes and nostrils, size of the jowls and throatlatch, set of the tail, size and shape of the withers, and shape of the rib cage.

# Soundness

## Conformation Points That Relate to Soundness

All good conformation is *functional;* that is, it helps the horse to be stronger, sounder, and perform better. However, some points are more directly related to strength and soundness:

- Straight legs (front and rear views)
- Legs correctly set
- Correct angles of shoulder, pastern, and hock
- Short, wide cannon bones with clean, well-developed tendons
- Large, clean, flat joints (especially knees, hocks, and fetlock joints)
- Well-shaped feet, size in proportion to horse
- Short, broad, and well-muscled back and loin
- Symmetry (both sides and limbs appear even and equally developed)

## Conformation Defects and Their Effects on Soundness

No horse is perfect; a horse may have *conformation defects, blemishes,* or *unsoundnesses*. A *conformation fault* or *defect* is a structural problem, which may be hereditary. This makes horses with serious conformation faults poor candidates for breeding. Conformation defects are not unsoundnesses, nor do they always lead to unsoundness. However, serious conformation faults are undesirable because they make it harder for a horse to perform well, put more stress on certain parts, and make it more likely that injuries or unsoundnesses will occur, especially with hard work.

A *blemish* is an acquired defect, such as a scar, that is unsightly but does not affect the horse's usefulness. Some conditions (such as splints) may be classified as unsoundnesses when they are acute and cause lameness, but may subside, leaving only a blemish once they have healed.

*Unsoundnesses* are conditions or injuries that cause lameness or otherwise impair the horse's health or ability to work. Certain conformation defects may weaken a part and predispose a horse to unsoundness, but again, a conformation defect is not an unsoundness and does not always lead to unsoundness. (For more about conformation and unsoundnesses, see Chapter 12 of the *USPC C Level Manual*.)

## Chart 10-1: Conformation Defects and Effects

| Conformation Defect | Effect on Movement and Soundness |
|---|---|
| Base wide | More stress on inside of foot; may lead to ringbone, sidebone, or splints. |
| Base narrow | Causes plaiting, possible interference or stumbling. More stress on outside of foot; may lead to ringbone, sidebone, or splints. |
| Toes in | Causes paddling. More stress on outside of foot; may lead to ringbone, sidebone, or fetlock osteoarthritis. |
| Toes out | Causes winging in, possible interference. More stress on inside of foot; may lead to ringbone, sidebone, fetlock osteoarthritis, or sesamoiditis. |
| Over at the knee | Sometimes associated with contracted tendons. If severe, may cause stumbling. May lead to carpal osteoarthritis. |
| Back at the knee (calf knee) | Extra stress on front of knee joint and flexor tendons. May lead to carpitis, carpal chip fractures, or bowed tendons under strenuous work. |
| Bench knees | Uneven stress on splint and cannon bones. May lead to splints. |
| Knock-knees | Uneven stress on splint and cannon bones and inside of feet. May lead to splints or carpal osteoarthritis. |
| Standing under in front | Tends to move on forehand, may be prone to stumbling, reduces ability to bring knees up when jumping. |
| Camped out in front | Extra stress on flexor tendons and heels. |
| Sickle hock | Hock is less able to extend fully; more stress on plantar ligament. May lead to curb or hock arthritis. |
| Straight hock | Hock is less able to flex and absorb shock, making (post leg) collected gaits more difficult. Extra stress on hock joint may lead to bone spavin, bog spavin, suspensory ligament injury, or thoroughpin. |
| Hocks camped out behind | Horse is less able to engage hocks, making collection difficult, with less speed and power. |
| Cow hocks | Stresses on inside of hock and hind leg; may lead to bone spavin, bog spavin, or thoroughpin. |
| Bowed hocks | Stresses on outside of hock and hind leg; may lead to bone spavin, bog spavin, or thoroughpin. |
| Straight stifle | Angle of stifle joint predisposes joint to stress, stifle joint inflammation (gonitis), and locking stifle. |

*continued*

| Conformation Defect | Effect on Movement and Soundness |
| --- | --- |
| Contracted heels | Lack of frog pressure causes poor circulation; associated with club foot and navicular disease. |
| Flat soles | Causes tender feet; may lead to inflammation of coffin bone (pedal osteitis). |
| Upright pasterns | Increased concussion; may lead to concussion-related ailments such as navicular disease, sidebone, or ringbone. |
| Club foot | Same problems as upright pasterns. |
| Long, sloping pasterns | More stress on flexor tendons and suspensory ligament (may contribute to bowed tendons); fetlock joint may strike the ground, resulting in injury to sesamoid bones. |
| Straight shoulder | Less range of motion in shoulder and foreleg, causing short stride and less ability to fold knees well in jumping. Increased concussion. |
| Mutton withers | Difficulty in fitting saddle and holding saddle in place. May be combined with other faults such as short, upright shoulder or being built downhill. |
| High withers | Difficulty in fitting saddle; prone to wither sores and galls. |
| Long back | Less ability to carry weight; more vulnerable to injury. However, may have more springy gaits and more scope over fences than short back. |
| Short back | Prone to forging, especially if long-legged. |
| Slab-sided | Less room for heart and lungs; may lack endurance. Also, saddle may slip backward. |
| Flat croup | Often associated with hind legs set too far back (camped out behind), causing difficulty in engaging hind legs and in collection, but increases efficiency of movement because fewer strides are required to cover the ground. |
| Short, steep croup | Hindquarters less efficient because of less length of muscle, requiring more strides to cover the ground. Often associated with tipped pelvis, sickle hocks, or standing under. |
| High in hips ("over-built") | Horse tends to move on the forehand; difficulty with balance and especially collection). Saddle may tend to slip forward. |
| Ewe neck | Causes difficulty in flexion and carriage of head and neck (often high-headed). |
| Short neck | Head and neck are less effective as a "balancer" due to decreased lateral suppleness and ability to bend; associated with short stride. |

| Conformation Defect | Effect on Movement and Soundness |
|---|---|
| Too-long neck | May be more difficult to ride on contact, with a tendency (swan neck) to raise or over-flex neck and hollow the back. Roaring (laryngeal hemiplegia) is more common in large horses with very long necks. |
| Parrot mouth | Horse may have difficulty in grazing because upper incisor teeth extend out over lower teeth. If molars are also misaligned, may have difficulty in chewing feed and require more frequent dental care. |
| Undershot jaw | Lower incisors extend beyond upper incisors, making grazing difficult. If molars are also misaligned, may have difficulty in chewing feed and require more frequent dental care. |

# Lameness

Lameness is the leading cause of loss of use of athletic horses in all disciplines. It is a problem that most horse owners will have to deal with at some time. Being familiar with the common causes of lameness and how to determine if a horse is lame is a crucial skill for a horse person to have. See the *USPC C Level Manual*, pages 341–342, for more information about lameness.

## Causes of Lameness

### Arthritis

Arthritis means inflammation of a joint. In horses, arthritis may develop from excessive wear and tear or it may result from a wound involving a joint where bacteria invade a normally sterile environment, causing *septic* (or infectious) arthritis. Both scenarios ultimately lead to the development of bone changes resulting in osteoarthritis.

One of the leading causes of lameness in horses is *osteoarthritis* or *degenerative joint disease*. This disease can occur in any joint and in any limb. Generally, it is caused by excessive wear and tear on the joints from unnatural athletic use. It is a progressive disease that develops throughout a horse's life. Horses with conformation faults of the lower limb are more likely to develop osteoarthritis than horses with ideal lower-limb conformation. Other predisposing causes include *developmental orthopedic disease* (for example, *osteochondrosis*), soft-tissue trauma around the joint, and *joint infection*.

In the early stages of arthritis, the joint becomes inflamed without bone abnormalities. As the inflammation continues, the joint begins to *remodel* (cartilage and bone) and bone abnormalities develop. This is called *osteoarthritis*. Arthritis can also be caused by an acute injury (for example, a sprained joint or a kick from another horse), from infection introduced through a wound, or, in foals, a systemic bacterial infection. If a wound is located near a joint or synovial structure, it should be evaluated by a veterinarian immediately, as early treatment may reduce the chance that septic arthritis will develop.

For the most part, any type of arthritis will eventually lead to the development of osteoarthritis. The degree of lameness a horse with osteoarthritis experiences depends on the severity and the range of motion within the joint. Affected joints that have the greatest amount of mobility (that is, a fetlock joint) suffer the greatest amount of lameness. Horses with osteoarthritis tend to "warm up out of the lameness" and demonstrate a chronic low- to mid-grade lameness.

A lot of research has been performed in the past 20 years searching for therapies to slow the progression of osteoarthritis and potentially cure the disease. Currently, osteoarthritis is treated in a variety of ways. One of the standard methods of treatment is by injection of strong *anti-inflammatories* called *corticosteroids,* with or without *hyaluronic acid* (a substance similar to synovial fluid) into the joint itself. These are known as *joint injections.* Horses can be treated with intramuscular injections of cartilage building blocks called *polysulfated glycosaminoglycans* (*Adquan®*) or intravenous injection of synovial fluid building blocks called *hyaluronic acid* (*Legend®, MAP-5,* among others). Horses can be fed oral cartilage building blocks called *chondroitin sulfate* and *glucosamine* (*Cosequin®, FlexFree,* among others). Recently, veterinarians have attempted to use the horse's own anti-inflammatory products to help slow the progression of osteoarthritis. These products are isolated from a horse's own blood, then injected into the joint. Examples of these products are *interleukin-receptor antagonist protein* (*IRAP*) and *platelet-rich plasma* (*PRP*). Other commonly used therapies include *corrective shoeing* to decrease stress on an affected joint (see Chapter 11, "The Foot and Shoeing") and the judicious use of systemic *nonsteroidal anti-inflammatories* (*NSAIDS*) such as phenylbutazone. (See Chapter 14, "Health Care, Diseases, and Veterinary Knowledge" for more information on drugs used to treat osteoarthritis.)

### Developmental Orthopedic Disease (DOD)

Young horses are susceptible to certain orthopedic (bone and joint) problems due to improper growth. The exact cause of most of the problems in the following list is unknown, but diet, genetics, and exercise are thought to play a role.

- **Osteochondrosis (OCD):** A defect in the ossification of the *joint surface* that causes displacement of an area of abnormal cartilage, or a cyst that remains just below the surface of the joint.

- **Epiphysitis** and **physitis:** A defect in the ossification of the *growth plate* (*physis*) at the ends of long bones that results in inflammation and pain.
- **Wobbler's syndrome:** Cervical vertebral malformation that results in narrowing of the spinal canal, leading to compression of the spinal cord that causes a horse to be *ataxic* (wobbly).

## Common Lamenesses of the Front Limbs

**Bowed tendon:** An injury to the fibers within the *deep digital* and/or *superficial digital flexor tendons*. A "classic" bow that is easily seen from the outside of the horse occurs in the superficial digital flexor tendon, whereas a bowed deep digital flexor tendon results in swelling around the tendons, but not always a classic "bowed" shape.

Different types of injuries to the tendon can occur. These range from *core lesions*, where there is a large circular defect in the middle of the tendon that may extend up and down the length of the tendon, to *partial tears* in the outside surface of the tendon.

Injuries also occur at different locations within the tendon. They usually occur in the cannon bone region; an injury toward the top of the cannon bone is called a *high bow*, injury in the middle is called a *mid bow*, and injury just above the fetlock is called a *low bow*. In extreme cases, the entire tendon can be damaged along the entire length of the cannon bone and the entire flexor tendon area will bow out on the back of the cannon region. The flexor tendons can also be injured at the level of the pastern. This generally results in lameness and little to no swelling, although the flexor tendon sheath may become *effusive* (filled), causing *windpuffs* to form (see "Tenosynovitis," later in this section).

Flexor tendons sustain injury when they are near their physiologic breaking point, which occurs in horses performing at their maximum physical ability (for example, at a full-speed gallop). Racehorses are most likely to "bow" a tendon, but event horses are also susceptible. In addition, horses can bow a tendon after overexertion (such as endurance or long-distance trail riding) or by stepping in a hole in the pasture. Some conformational faults have been loosely associated with horses bowing a tendon. These include long sloping pasterns and long toe/low heel foot conformation.

When a horse bows a tendon, there is immediate swelling in the area of the flexor tendons and the area is sore to squeezing (*palpation*). You should have a veterinarian check your horse immediately, although it may take about seven days for a final diagnosis, using *ultrasonography* to determine the extent of the lesion, because the extent of the initial injury does not stabilize until that time. First-aid treatment includes *aggressive cold therapy* using cold hosing, ice, or a cooling system such as a Game Ready. The horse should be strictly stall-rested and administered non-steroidal anti-inflammatories such as phenylbutazone. A veterinarian will provide further advice as to a controlled rehabilitation program and other therapies such as injecting substances into the tendon to help with healing. Because tendons heal with scar tissue that is not as strong nor as elastic as the initial tendon tissue, horses are at risk of re-injury, especially if a strict rehabilitation program is not followed.

*Bandage bows* occur when a wrap is applied too tightly or with uneven pressure. This causes increased areas of pressure on the structures of the lower limb, including the flexor and extensor tendons. The inner part of the tendon is not damaged as in a true bowed tendon, but the superficial part of the tendon and soft tissues become inflamed, resulting in swelling and pain in the area of the bow. The horse is generally only mildly lame or not lame at all. The horse should not be bandaged and should be treated to reduce inflammation in the area (cold hosing/icing, administration of NSAIDs).

**Bucked shins:** An injury to the front (*dorsal aspect*) of the cannon bone, seen almost exclusively in young racehorses during their initial race training. When a horse gallops, it puts tremendous strain on the dorsal aspect of the cannon bone that causes the bone to remodel in order to become strong enough to accommodate the stress without fracturing. Sometimes, the remodeling process is not fast enough nor adequate, resulting in *microfracture* development within the dorsal aspect of the cannon bone. Pain can develop before this point if the *periosteum,* the bone's outer lining, becomes inflamed. These changes cause obvious pain when the horse is worked or when the area over the dorsal cannon bone is pressed on (palpated). Usually complete fracture will not occur if the training is decreased to allow healing, and then gradually increased to allow the dorsal cannon bone to remodel properly. Sometimes horses develop bone growth from the periosteum (bone lining) that makes the dorsal aspect of the cannon bone bow out more than usual. This is considered a blemish as long as the horse is not lame or sore on palpation.

**Osselets:** This is an antiquated term that was used to describe any bony swellings around the fetlock joint. Traditionally, it was used to describe bony swellings outside of the joint itself (*exostosis of the joint capsule*), but this is a fairly rare occurrence, so the term has fallen out of favor. Horses, especially those used as athletes, can develop osteoarthritis or chip fractures within their fetlock joints. One of the first signs that there is an injury in the fetlock joint is distension of the joint with inflamed joint fluid called *effusion*. The horse will generally be lame and sore when the fetlock is flexed. Chip fractures within a fetlock joint should be removed surgically if they are causing inflammation. Horses with osteoarthritis of the fetlock joint are often treated with intra-articular joint injections of corticosteroids and/or hyaluronic acid and other joint therapies.

**Ringbone:** Osteoarthritis of the pastern (high ringbone) or coffin joint (low ringbone). *High ringbone* is the most common type of ringbone. In its advanced stages, high ringbone can be seen as a characteristic hard lump on the front of the pastern, the result of excessive bone formation (*exostosis*) due to trauma or concussion around the joint. It can occur in the front and rear limbs. Horses with poor lower-limb conformation (for example, short, upright pasterns) are more predisposed to developing ringbone. Poor shoeing or improper hoof balance can contribute to its development. In young horses, it can develop in cases of developmental orthopedic disease where there are bone cysts involving the joint.

As the osteoarthritis worsens, the body attempts to "fuse" the joint by producing bone around the joint to provide stability and therefore, decrease pain. The body is usually unable to completely fuse the pastern or coffin joint, and so the horse remains lame. *Low ringbone* is less common, but results in worse lameness because the osteoarthritis affects the coffin joint, which has much more motion compared to the pastern joint.

Treatment of horses with ringbone is similar to other joints with osteoarthritis. Currently, there are surgical and non-surgical methods that a veterinarian might use to treat the pastern joint that causes the joint to fuse, thereby decreasing pain and allowing the horse to return to work. Unfortunately, there is no definitive treatment for coffin joint osteoarthritis, so those horses often become too lame for athletic use.

**Sidebone:** Ossification of the collateral cartilages located within the bulbs of the heels. It occurs commonly as horses age and is generally not associated with lameness. Horses with larger feet such as draft horses or draft crosses) and horses with conformation faults that cause increased concussion to the lower limb (that is, short, upright pasterns) are more prone to developing large sidebones. Very large sidebones that extend up to the level of the second phalanx may cause injury to the collateral ligaments of the coffin joint. Lameness may also occur when large sidebones fracture, although this is not always the case. There is no treatment, other than proper shoeing and balanced hoof trimming.

**Capped elbow or shoe boil:** A blemish that results from chronic trauma to the *bursa* at the back of the elbow, causing inflammation and a characteristic swelling on the back of the elbow. The swelling can also occur just under the skin without actually involving the bursa. A thick padded boot can be applied around the pastern to decrease the trauma to the area.

**Capped knee:** A blemish similar to a capped elbow, the *bursa(s)* located at the front of the knee (*carpus*) that protect the extensor tendons as they pass over the front of the knee can become inflamed and fill with fluid. The swelling can also occur just under the skin in the front of the knee and not involve the bursa(s).

**Splints:** *Splints* are a result of inflammation of the *periosteum* of the splint bones and subsequent ossification of the *interosseous ligament* that connects the splint bones to the cannon bone with exostosis formation. They generally cause lameness when they first develop (called *green splints*) but become a blemish once the inflammation subsides. Occasionally, they can be problematic after they have ossified because new bone may be produced that interferes with the suspensory ligament, resulting in chronic inflammation of the suspensory ligament. In such cases, the splint bone can be partially removed surgically in order to allow the suspensory ligament to heal. Splint bones can be fractured and not heal properly. In such cases, the non-healed fracture causes pain and part of the splint bone will need to be removed surgically.

Splints are related to conformation abnormalities. Any conformation abnormality that causes uneven stress in the area of the upper cannon bone or along the length of the lower limb predisposes a horse to developing splints. These include bench knees, knock-knees, bow-legged, toed-in, toed-out, base-narrow, and base-wide conformation. Horses that interfere are at risk of developing splints from direct trauma to the bones. Horses can develop splints in the rear or front limbs.

**Suspensory problems:** Injuries to the *suspensory ligament* are common in athletic horses. Similar to tendon injuries, *suspensory injuries* arise when the ligament is overstressed. Unlike tendon injuries, the stress is usually cumulative, occurring over a long period of time, rather than one single event. Front or hind limb *suspensory ligaments* can be affected. Long, sloping pasterns is the primary conformational fault that predisposes horses to developing suspensory injury. In addition, straight hocks are associated with suspensory injury in the rear limbs.

*Desmitis* is inflammation that occurs in a ligament, including the suspensory ligament. The degree of lameness from suspensory injuries has a wide range, as does the degree of injury that can occur. As with tendon injuries, suspensory injuries are classified by their location within the ligament. A *high* or *proximal suspensory lesion* occurs just below the carpus (knee) or tarsus (hock). A *mid-body injury* occurs in the middle of the suspensory ligament at the level of mid-cannon bone. *Branch injuries* occur within the branches of the suspensory ligament just above the fetlock, where the ligament inserts on the top of the sesamoid bones.

Each type of injury heals differently and so is treated differently. Because the top of the suspensory ligament contains both ligament and muscle fibers, these injuries can be difficult to diagnosis with ultrasonography and are often slow and inadequate in healing. Mid-body and branch lesions contain more ligament fibers and so are easier to diagnose with ultrasonography, but also experience similar difficulties in healing as tendons. Suspensory ligament injuries are notorious for healing slowly and poorly compared to tendon injuries, and re-injury can occur.

Initial first aid is similar to that for a tendon injury, consisting of rest, cold therapy, and anti-inflammatories. Unlike tendon injuries, suspensory injuries require more exercise as part of the rehabilitation program because the muscle fibers within the ligament must be strengthened as the ligament heals, and exercise stimulates the ligament to heal with better fiber alignment. Otherwise, treatment is fairly similar and should be based on your veterinarian's recommendations.

**Tenosynovitis:** *Windpuff* is the traditional term used to describe *effusion*, or increased synovial fluid, within the digital flexor tendon sheath; *windgall* is used to describe effusion in the fetlock joint. Because the effusion in both structures is in a similar location near the fetlock joint, many people use the terms interchangeably.

*Tenosynovitis* is the term used to describe inflammation within a tendon sheath. The most common tendon sheath that experiences inflammation is the sheath surrounding the *digital flexor tendons*. This sheath begins in the lower one-third of the cannon region on the back of the leg (front and rear limbs) and continues down to the bulbs of the heel. Its purpose is to protect the flexor tendons as they traverse the fetlock joint.

The digital flexor tendon sheath can become inflamed from chronic trauma as a result of strenuous athletic use and is very common in elderly athletic horses. Effusion in the tendon sheath is usually not associated with lameness unless there is an associated injury to one of the flexor tendons. If the sheath becomes excessively distended, a *carpal tunnel-like syndrome* can develop at the back of the fetlock, where the tendon sheath is restricted by the *annular ligament*. Sometimes, surgery is required to cut the annular ligament and relieve pressure on the structures in the area. Other more serious causes of filling in the digital flexor tendon sheath include injury to the flexor tendons or infection of the tendon sheath.

## Common Lamenesses of the Hind Limbs

**Bone spavin:** Osteoarthritis in the lower joints (*distal intertarsal and tarsometatarsal joints*) of the hock is one of the most common types of osteoarthritis in horses. In severe cases, it can be seen as a hard, bony swelling on the inside and lower part of the hock. When irritated by concussion or stress, *arthritis* (inflammation within the joint) develops, which results in the body attempting to "fuse" the joints by producing new bone (*bone spurs* or *exostoses*) on the edges of the small bones of the hock joints that may become large enough to form a bridge between joints, thereby fusing them. Because these bones are stacked like saucers and have little movement, the body is often successful in fusing the bones together, which stops the pain, and the horse may become sound again. If arthritis occurs in the upper joints of the hock (*proximal intertarsal* and *tibiotarsal joints*), where there is more movement within the joints, the horse will likely remain permanently lame.

Osteoarthritis of the lower hock joints is treated like other types of osteoarthritis (for example, with "hock injections"). There are surgical and nonsurgical methods available to try to increase the rate of fusion of the joint if traditional treatments are unsuccessful.

**Stifle problems:** The *stifle joint* is an incredibly complex joint that is the same as a human knee joint. Fortunately, horses are less likely to injure this joint compared to human athletes. The stifle can be injured during a single traumatic event (such as a kick or a fall over a fence) or as a result of chronic wear and tear. The structures that may be affected include the ligaments of the patella, the structures within the stifle joint, the *menisci*, and/or the cartilage.

One of the more common problems involving the stifle joint is called *intermittent upward fixation of the patella*, or *locking stifle*. This disorder of the *rear limb stay apparatus* results in the horse's patella remaining partially or completely locked in place instead of being released by the contraction of the quadriceps muscles. When the patella locks into place, the horse's leg remains straight for varying amounts of time and when it unlocks, the leg slightly jerks up and forward. Most commonly, the patella only mildly locks and the horse can move the leg completely, but with an abnormal motion of the leg. In severe cases, the leg can be locked in place, which can be distressing to the horse.

Locking stifles are most commonly seen in young horses that have started into training and have weak quadriceps muscles due to lack of conditioning. Horses with very straight hind limbs are at increased risk of developing this problem. See Chapter 12 for more information on conditioning horses with stifle problems.

**Bog spavin:** This is inflammation within the large top joint (*tibiotarsal joint*) of the hock, resulting in increased production of synovial fluid. There is a large, soft swelling on the front and inside of the hock that is usually not hot or painful. It may cause a mild lameness due to increased pressure within the joint, or no lameness at all. Lameness will be more severe if there are concurrent abnormalities in the bones and/or cartilage within the joint (osteoarthritis). The filling within the joint may decrease if work is decreased or the horse is rested, and then flare back up when the work level is increased.

Bog spavin is most commonly seen in young horses that have *osteochondritis dessican*, commonly known as *OCD*. This occurs when there is a defect in the surface of the cartilage due to abnormal development in the joint as a horse grows. The defect results in abnormal cartilage forming within the joint, which then causes the underlying bone to die and detach, often forming a fragment of bone or *joint mouse* that may cause inflammation. Horses with OCD are often not lame and the problem is noticed when they are started into training. The bone fragments should be removed surgically or osteoarthritis may develop. In older horses, bog spavin is usually the result of repeat concussion to the hock joint from hard work and/or poor hock conformation, such as straight hocks. In adult horses, a bog spavin is often considered a blemish, but is a sign of stress in the hock joint. It may cause lameness if too much fluid accumulates that increases pressure in the joint.

**Thoroughpin:** Caused by inflammation within the *tarsal sheath,* which contains and protects the *deep digital flexor tendon* as it passes over the back of the hock. Similar to bog spavin, inflammation causes increased synovial fluid production within the sheath and produces a soft, cool swelling just above the point of the hock. It is usually caused by excessive stress or strain in horses with poor hock conformation; for example, those with sickle or straight hocks. It is generally considered a blemish, but it may be associated with lameness if there is concurrent damage to the soft-tissue structures such as the deep digital flexor tendon or the fibers of the sheath itself.

**Curb (plantar ligament desmitis):** Inflammation of the *plantar ligament,* causing intermittent, mild lameness. It occurs most frequently in Standardbred racehorses and has been associated with sickle-hocked conformation and horses that are stall-kickers. Initial treatment involves reducing inflammation and rest. Despite this treatment having no proven therapeutic benefit, Standardbred racehorses suffering from a curb are often "pin-fired" in the area, resulting in white dots of hair on the back of the hock. After the initial injury has healed, the tissues in the area will usually remain thickened, resulting in a permanent blemish.

**Capped hock:** A blemish caused by chronic trauma (usually associated with stall kicking) that results in inflammation of the *bursa* that protects the *superficial digital flexor tendon* as it passes over the back of the hock. Sometimes the bursa is not involved and the swelling is located just under the skin at the point of the hock.

## Common Lamenesses of the Foot

**Sole abscess:** Abscesses are caused by *anaerobic bacteria* (bacteria that do not require oxygen) creating pus in an enclosed space. Bacteria can be introduced underneath the horn of the sole via puncture (stepping on a nail) or through microscopic cracks in the horn. Once the bacteria have penetrated the sole, they multiply in anaerobic conditions. The body attempts to get rid of them, and pus (the accumulation of inflammatory cells and debris) is produced. The pus and gas produced by the bacteria expand and put pressure on the sensitive tissues of the sole, resulting in severe pain and lameness.

Once the abscess is localized with hoof testers, a veterinarian or farrier will remove the horn of the sole in the area to allow the abscess to drain, which instantly relieves pressure and makes the horse more comfortable. This exposes the area to oxygen, which will kill the anaerobic bacteria. Sometimes, a pocket of pus cannot be located, so the hoof must be soaked in water, usually with Epsom salts, to help draw the abscess to a head.

After the abscess is opened, the hoof is poulticed to continue to draw out inflammation and kill the remaining bacteria.

A wide variety of poultices can be used, ranging from a sugar and iodine mix to Icthammol and Animalintex®. Ask your veterinarian what type of poultice they recommend. Once the area where the sole was removed has dried up and started to harden, a shoe with a pad will protect the area until new sole can form.

Some horses experience sole abscesses more frequently than others. These horses should be evaluated by a veterinarian to assess for an underlying cause. Horses are more prone to abscesses in the spring and fall when pastures and paddocks are muddy, because excessive wetness can compromise the integrity of the sole and lead to bacterial invasion.

**Thrush:** This is an *anaerobic bacterial infection* of the recesses of the foot (the *lateral sulci*). When a foot is not properly cared for or becomes excessively moisturized, *anaerobic bacteria* (bacteria that do not require oxygen) may infect the tissues, resulting in a foul odor and a black or whitish discharge from the structures involved. In severe cases, lameness may occur.

Products containing copper sulfate (such as Koppertox®) are used to dry out the hoof and kill the anaerobic bacteria.

Thrush can be prevented with proper foot care (frequently picking out the feet) and careful monitoring of the feet when the horse is living in a wet environment.

**Navicular syndrome:** This disease complex refers to lameness localized to the heel region of the foot, with or without radiographic changes of the *navicular bone*. The exact cause of navicular syndrome is still under investigation. This syndrome has been redefined now that magnetic resonance imaging (MRI) has given veterinarians the ability to image the soft-tissue structures within the foot. Multiple structures may be involved, including the *navicular bone, navicular bursa, deep digital flexor tendon,* and possibly its *sheath, impar ligament,* and *suspensory ligament of the navicular bone.* (See Chapter 11 for more on the anatomy of the foot).

Horses are usually chronically lame in one or both front feet and show increased lameness when moving in a circle, with the affected foot on the inside of the circle.

Navicular syndrome usually affects both front limbs, so the lameness may switch back and forth between limbs and cause an overall decreased length of stride in the front limbs, which often causes people to think that the lameness is originating in the shoulder. Horses with poor lower-limb conformation resulting in increased concussion to the foot, specifically the heels, are at increased risk of developing navicular syndrome. These faults include under-run and/or contracted heels, upright pasterns, and small feet on a large-bodied horse. Poor shoeing and improper hoof balance may contribute to the development of lameness.

The goal of treatment is to properly shoe the foot to decrease stress in the heel region, often using wedge pads or wedge shoes in a bar or egg-bar configuration. In addition, corticosteroids may be used locally to decrease inflammation in the synovial structures near the navicular bone.

**Corns:** *Corns* are chronic bruising of the *bars of the hoof* that may or may not result in hoof abscesses. They are most commonly seen in horses that are overdue for re-shoeing, where the hoof has grown excessively over the shoe, resulting in increased pressure on the bars because the shoe is not in contact with the hoof wall. Corns are very rare in horses that receive regular farrier care.

**Cracks:** Cracks can occur vertically or horizontally in the horn of the hoof wall in the heel, quarter, and toe. Vertical cracks can extend from the ground or from the coronary band. Vertical cracks extending from the coronary band are due to instability in that area (for example, sheared heels) or from trauma (for example, laceration). Vertical cracks extending from the ground usually occur when the hoof becomes dry and brittle and cracks as a result of concussion in the hoof wall. Horizontal cracks are usually the result of blunt trauma or overstress to the hoof wall. Cracks can cause lameness if they become large enough to cause hoof wall instability and extend into the *sensitive laminae.*

**Laminitis:** This lameness is discussed in detail in Chapter 14.

# 11

# The Foot and Shoeing

## Anatomy of the Foot

The horse's *foot* consists of external and internal structures below the hairline, including the coronary band, from which the hoof wall grows. (The terms *hoof* and *foot* are often used interchangeably; here, "foot" refers to the entire internal and external foot structure, while "hoof" refers only to the external structure.)

## Structures of the Foot

**Coffin bone (pedal bone, third phalanx):** Major bone of the foot; supports the weight of the horse.

**Navicular bone:** Small, rectangular-shaped bone that lies under the back (palmar and distal aspects) of the coffin bone.

**Navicular bursa:** Fluid-filled sac that cushions the deep flexor tendon as it passes over the navicular bone.

**Deep digital flexor tendon:** Crosses the navicular bone and attaches to the underside of the coffin bone.

**Digital cushion:** Spongy structure above the frog. The digital cushion expands and contracts to store and release blood as the horse takes a step, helping to pump venous blood up the leg.

**Coronet:** Junction between hoof and skin.

**Coronary band:** Outer band of hard tissue (horn) just below the coronet that protects the corium, the tissue from which the horn of the hoof grows.

**Corium:** The deep tissue beneath the coronary band, which produces the horn of the hoof that becomes the wall.

**Wall:** The hard outer shell of the hoof. The wall of the hoof supports the horse's weight and is designed to absorb shock. The wall angles backward at each end, forming the bars. These aid in absorbing shock and allowing the foot to expand under pressure. Most of the horse's weight is borne by the walls of the feet.

**Bars:** Formed by the wall folding back on itself near the heels as seen on the bottom of the hoof. They aid in absorbing shock and support the hoof wall as it expands under pressure.

**Insensitive laminae:** Tiny, hair-like tubules that attach the horn of the wall by interlocking or *inter-digitating* with the sensitive laminae. The insensitive laminae is produced by the sensitive laminae.

**Sensitive laminae:** Tiny, hair-like tubules that are attached on the surface of the coffin bone and inter-digitate with the insensitive laminae of the wall. The sensitive laminae have a blood and nerve supply. The interlocking of these two types of laminae suspends the coffin bone in the hoof wall, a strong, hard, protective casing that can flex under pressure.

**Periople:** Thin, varnish-like outer layer of the hoof, which keeps moisture in.

**Sole:** The ground surface of the hoof, inside the wall. The outer layer of the sole is insensitive; the *sensitive sole* is the deep layer next to the underside of the coffin bone, which has a blood and nerve supply. The sole should be arched or concave, not flat.

**Frog:** A rubbery, wedge-shaped structure that lies between the heels. The frog helps to absorb shock and pump blood back up the leg by compressing the digital cushion at each step.

**Lateral commissures:** The grooves on either side of the frog that are cleaned out with a hoof pick.

**Central sulcus:** The small triangular groove or indentation in the center of the frog.

**Lateral cartilages:** Wing-shaped cartilages that extend from the upper sides of the coffin bone and form the flexible bulbs of the heels. They aid in the expansion of the foot and shock absorption.

Inner structures of the foot.

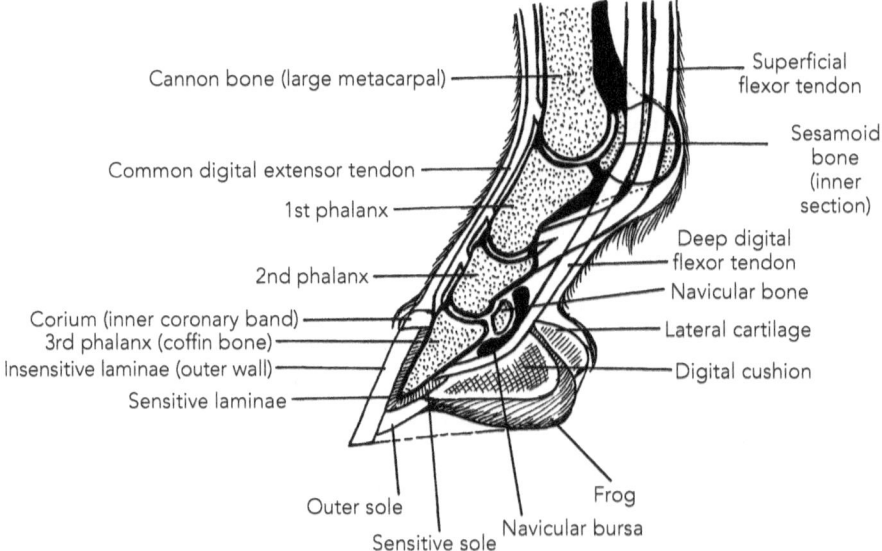

## Functions of the Foot

The design of the horse's foot allows it to perform several important functions: bearing weight, absorbing shock, pumping blood, providing traction, protecting inner surfaces, and allowing for growth and repair of the foot.

**Weight bearing:** The shape and structure of the hoof are designed to bear weight. The *hoof wall* is made up of *tubules* of *horn;* the inside of the wall is made of *horny laminae*, hair-like "leaves" that interlock with the *sensitive laminae* that cover the surface of the *third phalanx* or *coffin bone*, forming a strong attachment, rather like Velcro.

The horse's weight is carried mostly on the hoof wall and on the *frog* and, to a lesser extent, the sole when the hoof sinks into soft ground. The *sole's* main function is to protect the deeper structures of the foot. Ideally, it should be concave, not flat.

**Absorbing shock:** The foot is a major shock-absorbing mechanism, along with the joints and angles of the legs. With each step, the hoof wall expands, especially toward the heels, as the horse bears weight, and contracts as the horse lifts his leg. Elastic structures like the *frog*, *digital cushion*, and *collateral cartilages*, along with expansion of the hoof wall and bulbs of the heels, help the foot absorb shock as it strikes the ground. This reduces the concussion transmitted to bones and joints in the entire leg.

Expansion of the hoof, pumping blood.

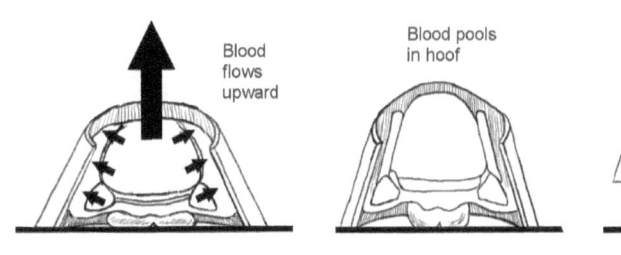
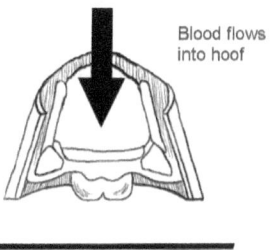

Loading Phase
Expansion of hoof structures

Stance phase

Hoof unloaded

- **Pumping blood:** Because the lower leg and foot have no muscles to aid in pumping blood and are located a long way from the heart, the pumping action of the foot during movement helps blood to circulate in the lower limb.

  Blood enters the foot through the digital arteries. As the horse bears weight on the foot, the digital cushion expands and the collateral cartilages compress against the inner hoof wall, causing blood to pool in the foot. As the horse lifts his leg, the digital cushion shrinks and the collateral cartilages retract away from the hoof wall, causing blood to move up the leg due to hydrostatic pressure. One-way valves within the *digital veins* prevent the blood from returning to the foot.

  This mechanism only works during movement; circulation is impaired when the horse is inactive for long periods. This is why horses may get laminitis in a limb opposite an injured limb. If a horse continuously bears weight on one limb to protect another, the circulation in the limb bearing all of the weight may be compromised, which can lead to damage of the inner lamina of the hoof.
- **Traction:** The ground surface of the foot provides traction on different types of footing. The frog helps prevent slipping on hard or icy surfaces. The concave shape of the sole helps stabilize the foot on soft ground or uneven footing; and the front edge of the hoof digs into the ground as it breaks over.
- **Protection:** The hoof is designed so that tough, insensitive outer structures protect the softer, sensitive parts inside. The outer surfaces of the hoof wall, sole, and frog are insensitive and can tolerate concussion, abrasion, heat, and cold. Each has a sensitive counterpart located deeper, which has a blood and nerve supply. The *periople*

(the shiny outer covering of the hoof wall) seals the hoof, protecting the horn from loss of moisture.

**Growth and repair:** The foot constantly grows, replacing dead cells and those worn away by contact with the ground. The hoof wall grows from the coronary corium, which is located beneath the coronary band and is like the nail bed from which human fingernails grow. The corium produces horn tubules, which make up the horny wall of the hoof. The perioplic corium produces the periople or outer covering of the hoof. The laminar corium (sensitive lamina) produces the insensitive lamina that allows the horn tubules of the hoof wall to slide downward (appearing to grow) without comprising the integrity of the attachment of the hoof wall to the coffin bone. The solar corium (sensitive sole) produces the horny sole (insensitive sole) to protect the bottom of the foot.

The hoof wall grows downward at a rate of about ¼ to ⅜ inch per month. The rate of growth is affected by nutrition, metabolism, health, and climate. Variations in any of these can result in horizontal *growth rings,* which are visible on the hoof wall.

Under ideal natural conditions, the hoof will wear away at the same rate at which it grows. In domesticated horses, this may not happen because they do not encounter hard terrain like horses in the wild. The hoof may wear away faster than it grows, or it may grow faster than it wears down. The horse may then require shoeing or foot trimming.

In addition, the horse's foot grows and wears based on the distribution of weight on the hoof wall. For example, horses naturally bear weight unevenly in the rear limbs due to a slight turning out of the limb (this allows the limb to clear the belly when the stifle flexes and the limb moves forward). Because of this, the hoof becomes asymmetrical as it grows, where the inner (*medial*) hoof wall is more upright and the outer (lateral) hoof wall "flares" out. In a horse with perfect front-limb conformation, the foot will grow relatively evenly. If there is a conformation fault, such as pigeon-toes, then the hoof will grow unevenly. Specifically, it becomes more upright on the part of the hoof bearing the most weight. So, in a pigeon-toed horse, the hoof will be upright on the outside (*lateral*) and tend to "flare" on the inside (*medial*), while the opposite occurs in a horse that toes out. When a farrier trims a foot, he or she corrects these uneven wear patterns. Frequent trimming in barefoot horses is important to keep the foot symmetrical, which promotes proper function and health of the foot.

# The Horse's Foot in Motion

In order to evaluate a horse's movement and the effect of shoeing on his way of going, you must understand the basics of stride and movement.

## Foot Flight Patterns

The *flight pattern* is the path a foot takes as it moves through the air from breakover to landing. Foot flight patterns are determined by leg conformation, the angle and length of the foot, the shape of the foot or shoe, and the weight of the shoe. The horse's breed or type, conformation, natural way of going, soundness, and the balance in which he is ridden can also affect foot flight patterns. The ideal flight pattern represents a sound horse with efficient movement.

To evaluate the flight pattern of each foot, watch the horse walk and trot on a hard, level surface, directly toward you, away from you, and from the side. When watching from the front or rear, focus on one foot at a time; compare its flight path to an imaginary center line. From the side, note the height, shape, and length of the arc. It is easier to see the way the foot lands from the side or rear.

The ideal flight pattern (viewed from the front or rear) is straight and true, without deviating inward or outward. On a level surface, the hoof lands in lateral balance, without twisting, rocking, or one side landing first.

Viewed from the side, the ideal flight pattern is a balanced arc. The foot breaks over easily and is carried at a moderate height (which varies according to breed). The first (upward) part of the flight pattern is equal to the second (downward) part. On hard, level ground, each hoof lands cleanly, with most of the weight on the back half of the foot.

Normal flight path of foot.

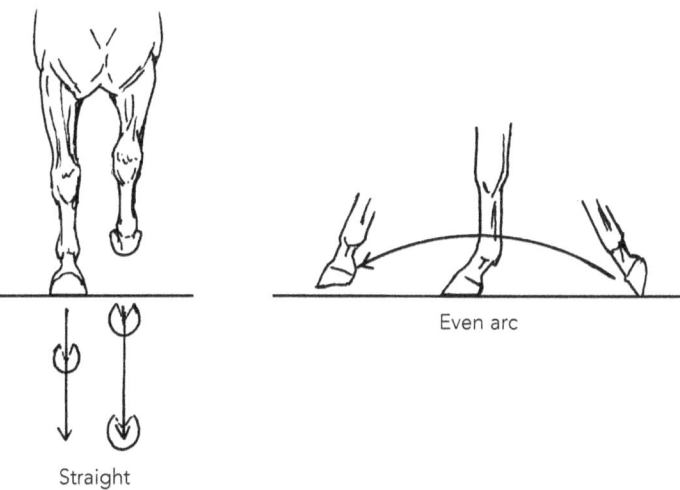

Even arc

Straight

Faulty flight patterns (viewed from front or behind) include:

**Winging in:** The foot breaks over at the inside of the toe and deviates inward. Caused by toe-out conformation, it places uneven weight and concussion on the foot, and can cause interfering.

**Paddling:** The foot breaks over at the outside of the toe and deviates outward. Caused by toe-in conformation, it places uneven weight and concussion on the foot.

**Plaiting:** The foot deviates inward and is placed close to the center line, almost in front of the opposite leg. Caused by base-narrow conformation, it places uneven weight and concussion on the foot and can cause interfering or stumbling.

Faulty arcs of the foot (viewed from the side) include:

**Short initial arc; long, flat landing:** Characteristic of a sloping hoof and pastern angle, with low heel and long toe. The hoof stays on the ground longer, requiring more leverage to break over, causing strain on the flexor tendons and navicular area. The first part of the arc is short and steep; the second part is longer and flatter.

Faulty flight patterns.

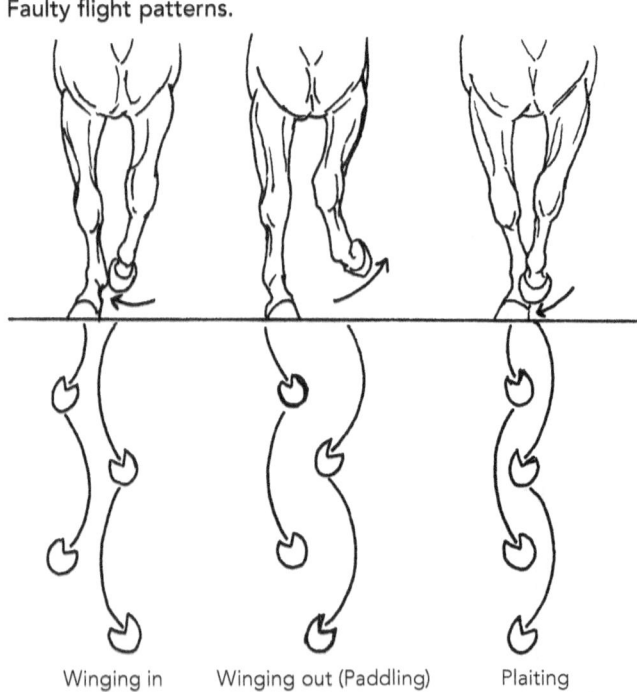

Winging in      Winging out (Paddling)      Plaiting

# THE FOOT AND SHOEING

Arc and hoof angle.

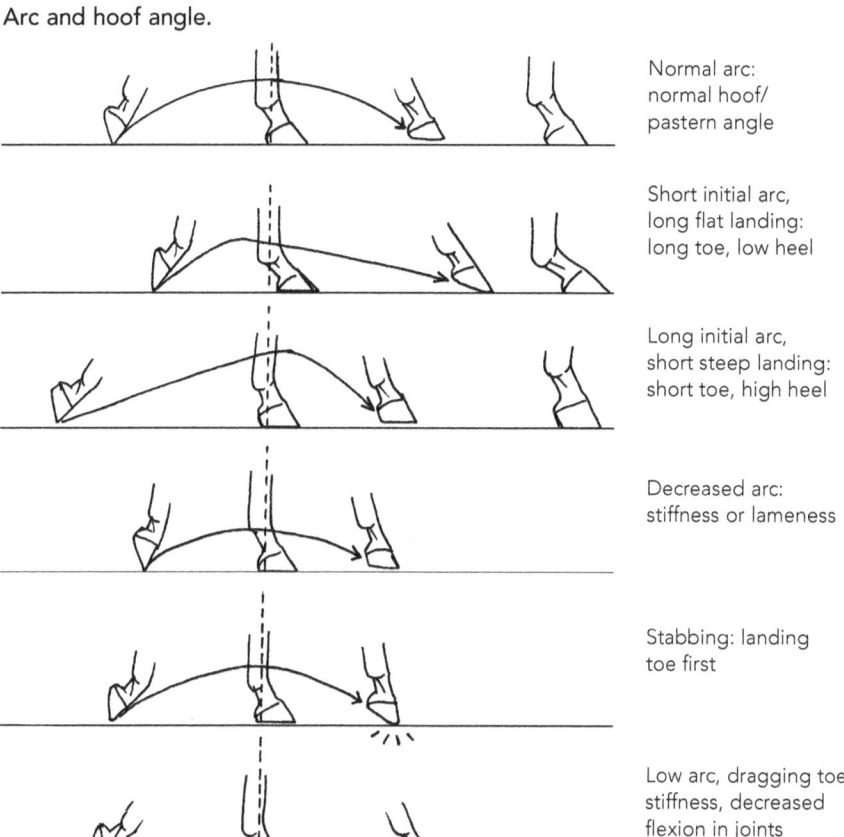

Normal arc: normal hoof/pastern angle

Short initial arc, long flat landing: long toe, low heel

Long initial arc, short steep landing: short toe, high heel

Decreased arc: stiffness or lameness

Stabbing: landing toe first

Low arc, dragging toe: stiffness, decreased flexion in joints

**Long initial arc; short, steep landing:** Characteristic of an upright hoof and pastern angle, with high heel and short toe. The hoof breaks over quickly and the first part of the arc is long and flat. The second part of the arc is short and steep, resulting in increased concussion.

**Decreased arc in one foot:** Characteristic of a lame horse. The foot is carried in a shorter, lower arc, less weight is carried on the foot, and the joints of the leg bend less. If severe, the horse may barely touch the foot to the ground.

**Landing toe-first ("stabbing"):** Characteristic of a horse trying to avoid landing on sore heels. The arc is short and steep, and the horse is prone to stumble.

**Excessively low arc ("dragging the toe"):** Characteristic of a horse that does not flex the joints of the leg sufficiently, often due to lameness, stiffness, fatigue, or moving in poor balance. Some horses also have an inward arc of the swing phase, bringing the leg toward midline and then jabbing the foot outward right before landing. This horizontal arc helps the leg clear the ground during the swing phase, allowing the leg be flexed to a lesser degree.

## Shoeing and Trimming Principles

Good trimming and shoeing aims to keep the horse sound and comfortable, allowing him to move as efficiently as possible for his job, within the limitations of his conformation. Each horse must be shod or trimmed according to his own individual characteristics and needs.

In an ideal situation, when a hoof bears weight, the weight and *concussion* (shock) travel in a straight up-and-down direction due to the forces of gravity. A properly balanced foot distributes concussion and carries weight evenly, without overstressing any part. An incorrectly balanced foot places extra

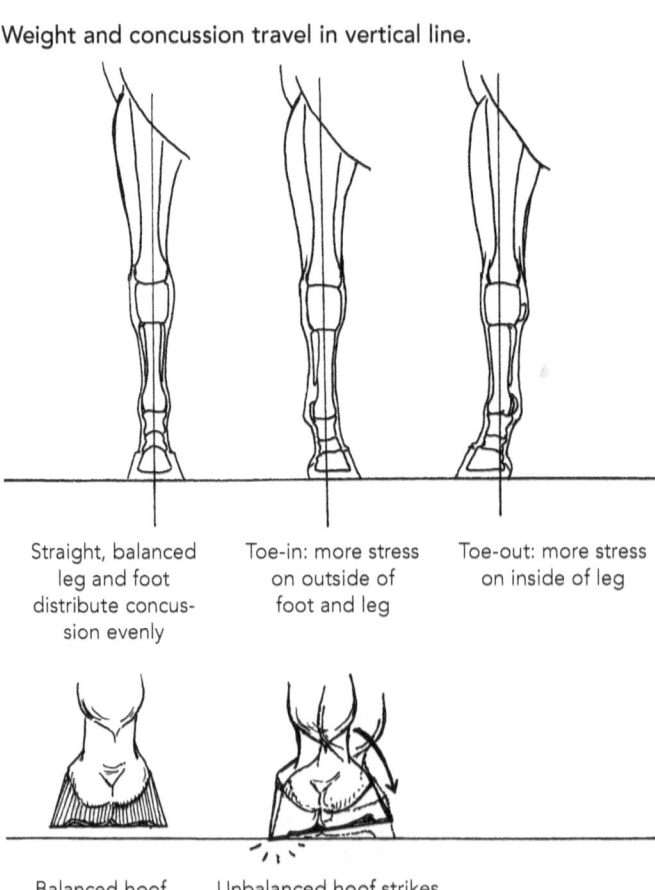

Weight and concussion travel in vertical line.

Straight, balanced leg and foot distribute concussion evenly

Toe-in: more stress on outside of foot and leg

Toe-out: more stress on inside of leg

Balanced hoof lands evenly

Unbalanced hoof strikes on one side first and rocks laterally

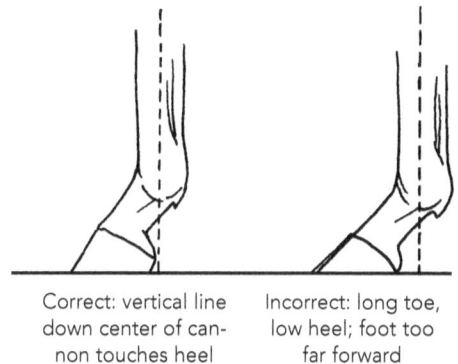

Vertical line from center of cannon touches heel.

Correct: vertical line down center of cannon touches heel

Incorrect: long toe, low heel; foot too far forward

strain and concussion on the parts of the foot and leg due to deviation of gravitational forces. The side of the crooked foot that bears the most weight receives the greatest concussion and strain. An unbalanced hoof strikes on one side first (on the longer side of the hoof wall) and then rocks to the other side, creating uneven stress on the structures of the hoof and lower limb.

The feet should be trimmed (and/or shod) so that they best support the vertical column of the leg. Viewed from the side, a vertical line down the center of the cannon bone should touch the heel of the foot.

A foot should be trimmed so that it lands in good *lateral* or "side-to-side" balance (on a hard, level surface), without twisting, rocking, or landing on one side first.

The angles, balance, and placement of the feet affect the angles of the joints and limbs above them. Incorrect shoeing or trimming causes stress, which can result in injuries and lameness, not only in the feet, but also in structures proximal to (higher than) the feet.

As seen from the side, the angle of the hoof should match the angle of the pastern. This roughly keeps the bones of the pastern and hoof in alignment, although the only definitive way to know that the bones are properly aligned is to take radiographs. A *broken back hoof-pastern axis* is one in which the pastern has a steeper slope than the foot (usually long toe, low heel). A *broken forward hoof-pastern axis* is one in which the pastern has more slope than the foot (usually short toe, high heel); this may be due to a *club foot* or to incorrect trimming. Either places extra stress on bones, joints, tendons, and other structures.

Extra weight tends to increase the arc of the stride (making it higher and shorter), concussion, and the effort needed to pick each foot up. This is why American Saddlebreds and Tennessee Walking horses are fitted with weighted shoes, to make their leg action more pronounced. Draft horses, which have heavy feet, naturally tend to move their legs more vertically

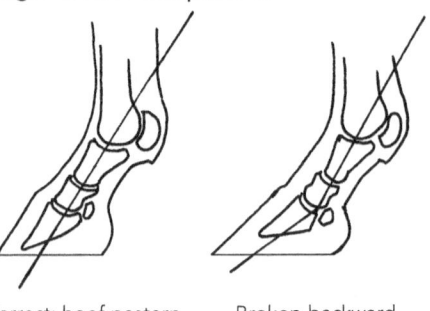

Angle of hoof and pastern.

Correct: hoof-pastern axis matches pastern angle; bones aligned normally

Broken-backward axis: long toe, low heel

Broken-forward axis: short toe, high heel

than horizontally for the same reason. If the horse wings in or out, extra weight will increase this tendency. In general, a horse should be shod with the least weight that is practical, to increase stride length.

A horse's feet change according to his work, way of going, soundness, and other factors. The wear pattern shown by each foot (and/or shoe) is an important indicator of his soundness and way of going.

## Shoeing Tools

A farrier uses many tools when working with a horse's feet. The basic farrier tools (pincers/shoe pullers, nippers, rasp, hammer, clinchers, buffer, hoof knife, and pritchel) are discussed in the *USPC C Level Manual* (pages 249–250).

Some additional farrier tools are:

- *Hoof gauge:* Similar to a protractor; it is used to measure the angle of the hoof.
- *Divider:* Used to measure the length of the hoof.
- *Clinch cutter* or *crease nail puller:* Designed for easy removal of nails. A nail cutter is used to remove clinches, and a crease nail puller is used to pull the nail heads.
- *Shoe spreader:* This tool is designed to spread a shoe slightly at the heels by spreading the branches of the shoe.

## Removing a Shoe

You may have to remove a shoe when a farrier is not available. Removing a shoe is not as easy as the farrier makes it appear, so having a few basic shoeing tools on hand is helpful. You should have a clinch cutter, a driving hammer, pincers, and perhaps a crease nail puller. A rasp, a shoeing stand, and a farrier's apron are also useful.

Here are the steps to removing a shoe.

1. Clean the foot.

   - First, the clinches must be removed or raised from the hoof wall, so that the nails can be pulled without damaging the hoof wall. Pick up the hoof as if you were going to clean it, but put it between your knees so that you can work on the shoe with both hands. Open the clinches by wedging the *clinch cutter* into the bottom of a clinch, then striking the clinch cutter with the *driving hammer* to open it up. At first, keep the clinch cutter at a steep angle to the wall. Then, once you can get it under the end of the clinch, hold it as flat as possible against the wall so that you don't cut into the wall. The clinches will become straightened as they are pushed up with the clinch cutter.

   - Another method to remove the clinches is to extend the horse's leg forward and place the horse's hoof on your knee while you face forward, or rest the foot on a shoeing stand. Then, use the fine side of the rasp to rasp off each clinch until it is even with the hoof wall, taking care not to damage the hoof wall.

2. Next, use the *pincers* (also known as *shoe pullers* or *pull-offs*) to remove the shoe. Place the open pincers around the shoe at the heel, then close the handles and pull the handles down toward the toe and in toward the center of the foot with a rocking motion. Support the toe firmly with your knees. Use the pincers to gradually work the shoe loose as you move toward the toe, working on alternate sides of the shoes until the shoe is loose on the sides of the hoof. You can then hit the shoe back in

Steps in removing a shoe.

place next to the hoof, and the nails will usually stick out and can be easily removed. Or you can place the pincers under the toe and pull back toward the heel to pull the shoe off. Always pull toward the center of the foot to avoid damaging the hoof wall as you remove the shoe. Pulling to the side will crack and damage the hoof walls.

## Materials and Sizes of Shoes

Horseshoes can be made of many different materials: steel, iron, aluminum, titanium, plastic, leather, and more.

Shoes come in many sizes from 000 to 10. The average Thoroughbred size is 1 and the average Warmblood size is 4. Sometimes the size is stamped on keg shoes, but it can vary depending on the manufacturer. Racing shoes/plates are sized differently. A race size 4 should fit a foot that would take a regular size 00 keg shoe.

### Chart 11-1: Horse Shoe Sizes

| Size | Width | Diagonal Length |
| --- | --- | --- |
| 000 | 4¼" | 5" |
| 00 | 4½" | 5¼" |
| 0 | 4⅞" | 5⅝" |
| 1 | 5¼" | 6" |
| 2 | 5½" | 6⅜" |
| 3 | 5⅞" | 6⅞" |
| 4 | 6¼" | 7⅜" |
| 5 | 6⅝" | 7¾" |
| 6-7 | 7" | 8" |
| 8-9-10 | 7⅞" | 9" |

## Trimming and Shoeing to Correct Problems

Proper trimming and/or shoeing can help alleviate pain caused by certain problems and improve a horse's way of going. This requires an expert evaluation of the horse's conformation, way of going, and level of soundness, along with skilled application of special trimming or shoeing techniques. The farrier, veterinarian, and trainer should work as a team in evaluating the horse and deciding on the best way to shoe him to keep him sound during work.

## Corrective Trimming

Corrective trimming in young horses is used to correct certain defects in foot and leg conformation (such as crooked legs) while the horse's bones are still growing. It is most effective in foals and young horses under 12 months of age. The shape and balance of the foot is altered so that the leg gradually grows straighter over many weeks. Corrective trimming to straighten the bones as they grow must be done while the *epiphyseal plate* (growth plate) of the crooked bone is still open, because once the growth plates are closed, the shape of the bone is set.

Crookedness originating near the fetlock should be corrected within six weeks, while crookedness originating from the hock or carpus should be corrected within the first six to nine months of life. Corrective trimming is not always effective, and the foal may require surgery to prevent or accelerate growth at the appropriate location to further straighten the leg.

Radical corrective trimming or shoeing on a mature horse can force the bones out of their normal (although crooked) alignment, causing severe stress on bones, joints, and other structures, and often results in lameness.

## Corrective or Therapeutic Shoeing

Therapeutic shoeing is the use of special shoes and shoeing techniques to help a horse heal after an injury, or to cope with a chronic condition such as navicular syndrome, founder, or arthritis. It is usually done in consultation with a veterinarian.

There is a great variety of therapeutic shoes and shoeing techniques for various ailments and chronic conditions. Some horses may only need therapeutic shoes temporarily for an acute condition such as a foot abscess. Others may require long-term therapeutic shoeing in order to stay sound enough to work.

This type of shoeing is related to corrective trimming and therapeutic shoeing, but is less radical and is usually applied to less severe problems. It consists of adjustments in trimming and shoeing, and the use of specialized shoes, to correct defects in the horse's movement or foot conformation. The purpose is to help the horse move better and work in comfort, not to change his conformation or make his legs and feet appear straighter. If shoeing is used to try to make a crooked limb appear straight, extra stress is placed on the structures of the lower limb, which may contribute to the development of lameness. Many horses need some degree of this type of shoeing, adapted to their needs by an observant and skilled farrier.

Problems such as interfering, forging, over-reaching, stumbling, or dragging the toes can often be helped by special shoes or adaptations such as rolling the toe. Changes in the weight, angle, shape and type of shoe can make a significant difference in the way the foot breaks over, its flight pattern, and how it lands.

In some cases, corrective shoeing must be done at more frequent intervals than usual, such as every four weeks. The extra expense of special shoes and more frequent shoeing should be taken into account when considering the purchase of a horse that has special shoeing requirements.

It is important to know (and record) what size and type of shoes your horse wears, and to take notes on his hoof measurements, angles, and any soundness or movement problems. Remember that his feet may change over time, and so may his shoeing needs.

## Types of Shoes

There are many types of shoes for different purposes. (Basic shoes and features are described in Chapter 8 of the *USPC C Level Manual*.) Shoes may be made in special shapes, usually to correct a problem, with different materials, or with added features. Special shoes (which are often custom-forged) include:

**Bar shoe.** Therapeutic shoe used to apply or relieve pressure on certain parts of the foot. There are different types of bar shoes:

- *Straight bar shoes* are designed to decrease expansion of the heels and support the structures at the back of the foot and at the back of the lower limb. They are used in the treatment of problems such as coffin bone fractures, navicular syndrome, quarter cracks, and suspensory ligament or flexor tendon injury.

- *Heart bar shoes* are used in cases where increased frog support is required, and to decrease the weight-bearing load on the hoof walls. They are often used for horses with laminitis or founder. They must be applied by a skilled farrier; if applied incorrectly, they can cause more harm than good.

- *Egg bar shoes* provide greater support to the structures at the back of the hoof, specifically the navicular apparatus. They are commonly used in horses diagnosed with caudal heel pain and/or navicular syndrome. They can be made from aluminum to decrease their weight, and can be made with a higher heel (wedge) to decrease the pull of the deep digital flexor tendon on the navicular bone. Egg bar shoes may also be used after a horse has sustained a suspensory or tendon injury. These shoes can lead to contracted and/or crushed heels, so they should be used judiciously.

**Trailer shoe.** A shoe with one extended heel, applied only on the hind feet. The extension (⅜" to ¾" and turned out 45°) is usually on the outside and provides lateral support to the foot so that it lands straight. Trailer shoes (sometimes used in conjunction with squared toes) may be used on cow-hocked horses and those that toe out behind. Trailer shoes are not safe to use on horses that paw or kick fences or kick other horses. If a halter is worn, it must be a breakaway type; a horse can get the shoe trailer caught in the halter if he scratches his head with a hind foot.

**Fullered shoe.** A *fuller* is a crease or groove in the ground surface of the shoe. It provides traction and a place to set the nails. It can go completely around or ¾" (all but the toe area).

**Concave shoe.** The internal edge of the ground surface of the shoe is concave instead of perpendicular to the ground. This provides for a better grip and allows dirt to fall out easily. It is used in a variety of disciplines.

**Feather edge shoe (hind preventer).** A shoe with the inside quarter beveled and angled; used to reduce the possibility of interfering and to limit the damage if the horse strikes himself.

**Square toe shoe.** A shoe squared off at the toe, usually used to prevent forging or over-reaching. The squared toe causes the foot to break over sooner by moving the breakover point back on the foot. It may be used on the front, hind, or all four feet. The farrier can alter a normal keg shoe using a forge, or can forge a square toe shoe.

**Rolled toe or rocker toe.** A shoe that is rounded along the thickness of the front of the toe along the ground surface, while the foot surface of the shoe is kept flat. This makes it easier for the foot to break over. It may be used to help prevent stumbling and can also help reduce stress at the tendons of the back of the legs.

**Rockered toe.** A shoe with the toe turned up 45°. It provides a more aggressive reduction of breakover stress than a rolled toe shoe. The foot surface of the shoe is not flat.

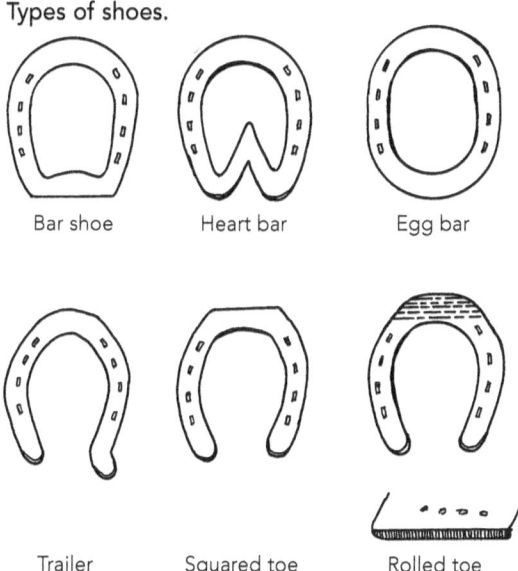

Types of shoes.

Other types of shoes include the following:

**Keg shoe.** A manufactured steel shoe, usually made of steel but can also be made of aluminum. It comes in a variety of standard patterns and sizes. Keg shoes may be heated and shaped or modified, thereby decreasing the time and cost of shoeing.

When fitting a pre-made keg shoe, the farrier must consider the position of the standardized nail holes in relation to the individual horse's white line. If the nail holes are not properly placed, it can cause a nail to be driven inside the white line into sensitive tissue (called *quicking*), which may result in an abscess or lameness. Farriers often modify keg shoes by heating them in a forge, or shaping the shoe "cold" with a hammer and anvil. This decreases the chance of quicking a horse, and can make the shoe as good as a hand-forged shoe.

**Racing plate.** A narrow aluminum shoe for minimum weight, manufactured in several styles. They are very light (aluminum is one-third the weight of steel) but wear out quickly. It is used commonly in race horses where a lighter shoe is needed, or to prevent fatigue. Some have "toe grabs" or a cleat on the toe of the shoe, to give the race horse more traction as he pushes hard with his legs to accelerate.

**Training plate.** Similar to a racing plate, but is usually made of steel for longer wear.

**Aluminum shoe.** These may be used in performance horses to change the arc of the foot flight. Because the shoe is lighter, the horse does not lift his foot as high but maintains a long arc to the foot flight. Many therapeutic shoes are made of aluminum and they come in a variety of shapes.

**Aluminum wide web shoe.** Lightweight manufactured shoe made of aluminum, extra-wide to protect the sole. They are more substantial and longer-wearing than racing plates. Protective steel wear plates at the toe or clips can be added to allow them to be worn longer and add durability. They may be tapped for studs. They are used for horses with sensitive soles to allow more weight-bearing surface at the hoof walls.

**Polo shoe.** A concave, fullered shoe with a higher inner rim (full rim) and beveled outer rim. It provides traction and breakover in any direction. They are used for polo, reining, trail horses, and more.

**Rim shoe.** A concave, fullered shoe with a higher outer rim (full rim). This shoe provides good traction and may be used for polo, reining, eventing, trail horses, and more.

**Sliding shoe (slider).** A shoe with a smooth, flat wearing surface and extended heels. It is most often used on the hind feet of reining horses to allow them to perform sliding stops. The web is usually wider than that of a normal shoe.

# Optional Features

## Pads

Pads are used to protect the sole, reduce concussion, or to treat various problems. Silicone, oakum, or other packing material can be used between the sole and the pad. There are several types of pads:

**Regular pads:** Pads made of leather or synthetic material. They protect the sole and frog and may reduce concussion. They close the foot to mud, stones, and dirt. Silicone or a similar substance is usually applied between the pad and the sole to provide more shock absorption and to prevent debris from getting between the foot and the pad, which might cause bruising.

**Pour-in pads:** These are made by piping a liquid urethane product (for example, Equi-Pak®) that quickly hardens to a rubbery consistency in a regular open shoe or bar shoe to make the solar surface even with the ground. Like regular pads, pour-in pads protect the sole and frog, but unlike regular pads, they conform to the sole of the foot similar to a custom orthotic. They provide greater shock absorption than regular pads because the material absorbs and dissipates concussive energy. They also create a more even distribution of pressure within the hoof and take some weight off of the walls of the hoof, because they cause the sole to bear more weight.

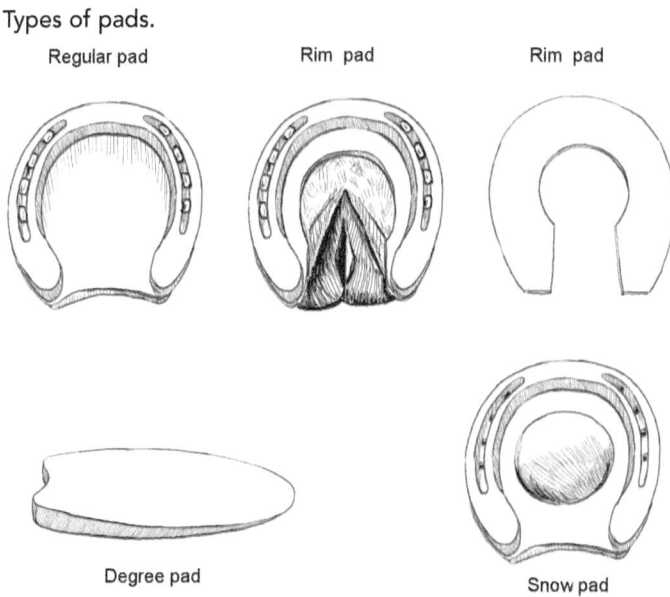

Types of pads.
Regular pad   Rim pad   Rim pad

Degree pad   Snow pad

**Degree pads:** Wedge-shaped pads, thicker at the heel; used to raise the angle of the heel while protecting the sole and reducing concussion. They may be used in horses with caudal heel pain/navicular syndrome or in horses with tendon injuries. Degree pads apply more pressure in the heel area, which can gradually cause the heel to be crushed if they are used for a prolonged period of time or are applied improperly.

**Rim pads or cut-out pads:** Pads that cover the edge of the foot and heels, leaving some of the frog and sole exposed to air. They are used to reduce concussion under the wall of the hoof; provide more depth, thus increasing the concavity of the sole: and if wedged, to alter the angle of the foot.

**Snow pads:** Polyurethane pads placed under the shoe to prevent snow from packing in the hoof. Some are full pads with a convex ball in the center of the pad. Another type is a rim-style pad that is open in the center. These pads flex as the horse moves, popping the packed snow out of the hoof.

## Clips

A shoe may have clips at the toes, quarters, or on the sides (quarter clips) or at the toes (toe clip), which help it to stay on by reducing stress on the nails.

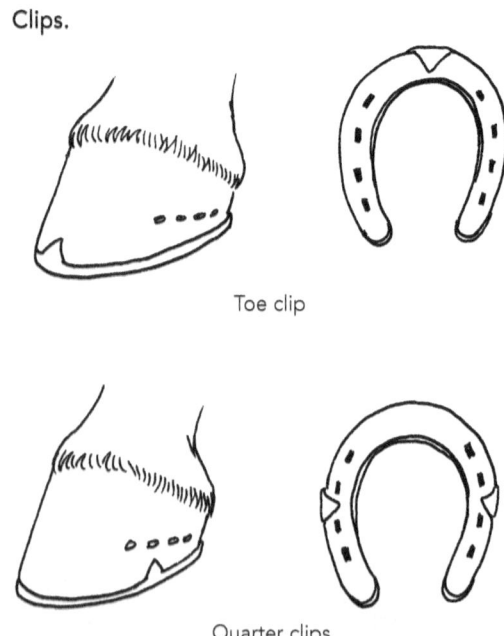

Clips.

Toe clip

Quarter clips

## Traction Devices

Traction devices can be added to shoes to prevent slipping, but remember that almost any type of shoe adds some amount of traction.

**Heels or calks:** Permanent fixtures on the shoe that dig into the ground and help to prevent slipping, especially on grass, mud, or areas with loose footing. Often used on shoes for jumping horses or trail horses in the mountains.

**Borium:** A generic name for tungsten carbide, borium is a super-hard steel alloy that is welded onto the heels and/or toes of the shoe. Borium bites into hard surfaces like pavement, ice, or rock, to prevent slipping. It is especially helpful for carriage horses that pull loads on hard road surfaces or those that ride on icy surfaces in the winter. However, it increases concussion and can inflict severe injuries if a borium-shod horse kicks another.

**Tapped shoes with removable studs (screw-in calks):** Shoes can be tapped (drilled) to receive screw-in studs or calks of various sizes and types. They are used in eventing and show jumping, for security on different types of footing and conditions.

Some studs are driven in without threads and cannot be interchanged.

Studs should be used only when the horse and the activity require them, and under expert supervision, as they can cause injury if used improperly. It is important to use the correct length and type of stud for grass, soft footing, mud, or hard ground. When studs are used, the horse should wear bell boots for protection, in case he steps on himself.

Studs must be removed when the horse is not working on a surface that requires them. A special tool is used to insert, tighten, and remove them. The holes should be plugged with cotton, foam, or rubber plugs with a small amount of oil (WD-40, chainsaw oil, or motor oil), to prevent dirt from filling the holes and ruining the threads.

Traction devices.

Heels or calks     Borium

**Tapped shoes and screw-in studs.**

- Small square road stud
- Short pointed stud
- Long pointed stud
- Medium pointed stud
- Long square stud
- Screw-in plug
- Cotton plug

Shoe tapped to receive screw-in calk

Using tee tap to remove plug and clean treads

Base of tee tap serves as wrench to insert and tighten stud

Shoe with stud in place (on outside heel)

Types of studs include:
- *Road studs:* Small studs for hard surfaces.
- *Bullets:* For use on ground that is fairly firm but soft on top.
- *Blocks:* Square studs for soft, muddy ground.
- *Olympic:* Largest, sharper studs for extremely slippery footing.

**Fullering:** Crease in ground surface of shoe that provides traction.

**Toe grabs:** Strip of steel placed in the toe of a shoe, commonly used on race horses. Toe grabs can reduce traction on hard surfaces such as concrete. They also will raise the toe on these surfaces, causing stress in the heel region and tendons. They can be very dangerous to other horses or people if a horse kicks or strikes.

**Ice or mud nails:** Horseshoe nails with sharp or large heads that provide more traction.

# 12

# Conditioning and Exercise Physiology

Conditioning horses for demanding athletic activities, such as eventing, requires an understanding of exercise physiology and modern conditioning methods. Above all, it requires experience and good judgment. The conditioning program must be adapted to the individual horse and to day-to-day and week-to-week conditions. Close observation of the horse and the advice of an expert are essential.

The material in this chapter is based on that covered in Chapter 7 of the *USPC C Level Manual*. This material, especially the sections on thermoregulation, cooling out, and basic conditioning, should be read in conjunction with this chapter.

## Exercise Physiology

The horse is an athlete by design. He is built to move, and every system contributes to and collaborates with the other systems to produce movement, agility, speed, and endurance. To understand conditioning, it is important to know how the various systems operate during exercise (see Chapter 9, "Systems of the Horse") and how the horse moves (see Chapter 1, "Biomechanics and Movement of the Horse").

## Muscles and Energy Production

Skeletal muscles are the muscles that produce *movement* (*locomotion*). They work by *contracting* or shortening. Skeletal muscles can only pull; they cannot push. For this reason, many skeletal muscles operate in pairs; one muscle flexes or bends a joint, and an opposing muscle extends or straightens it.

Muscles are made up of long, slender muscle cells that make up *muscle fibers*. A muscle fiber contains thousands of tiny thread-like filaments called *myofibrils*. These in turn contain even smaller protein filaments of two types: *myosin filaments* and *actin filaments*.

Muscle fibers are arranged in *bundles* that resemble long strands. These bundles in turn make up the *muscle belly*. Some muscles are simple, with only one muscle belly; others are complex, with several muscle bellies that function together. Muscles are connected to bones by *tendons*, tough bands of connective tissue. Muscle bundles and the muscles themselves are encased in *fascia*, a thin, tough connective tissue. Muscles are supplied with blood vessels (arteries, veins, smaller arterioles and venules, and capillaries). *Glycogen* and *triglycerides*, sources of energy for muscular contractions, are stored in the muscle fibers. *Motor nerves* control muscular movement; *sensory nerves* monitor the amount of tension and stretch in a muscle.

*Contractions* in muscle fibers are produced by a chemical reaction involving calcium that causes bonds between the actin filaments and the myosin filaments to form and release, shortening and relaxing the muscle fibers. The chemical reaction is triggered by a motor nerve impulse. An individual muscle fiber contracts fully (*fires*) when it receives a nerve impulse; there is no partial contraction. However, a muscle may contract only a few fibers, many, or nearly all at once; the degree of tension in the muscle depends on how many fibers contract at once.

Skeletal muscles in motion.

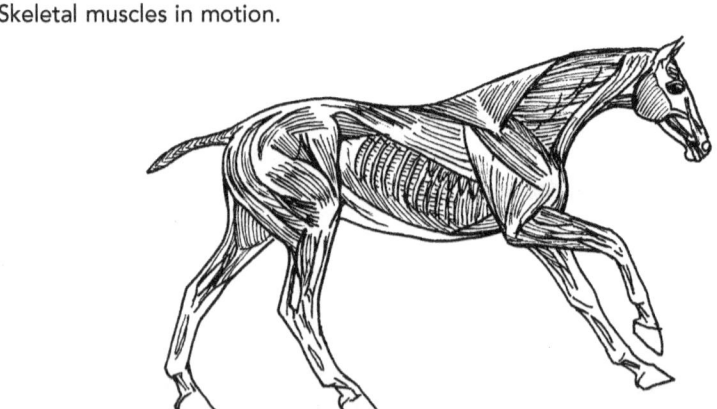

Muscle structures.

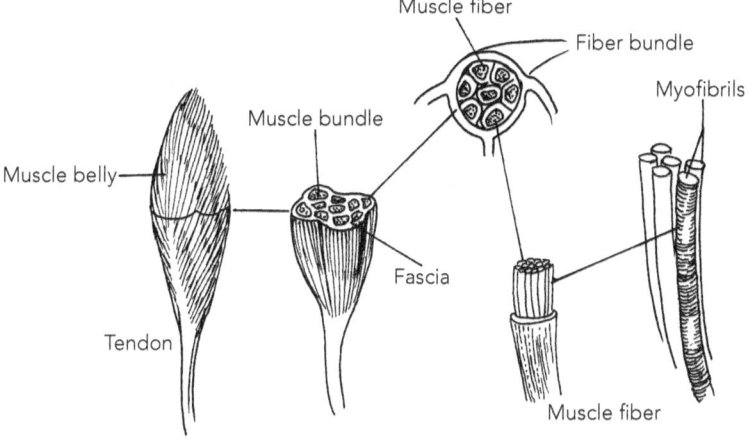

Myofibrils, contracted and relaxed.

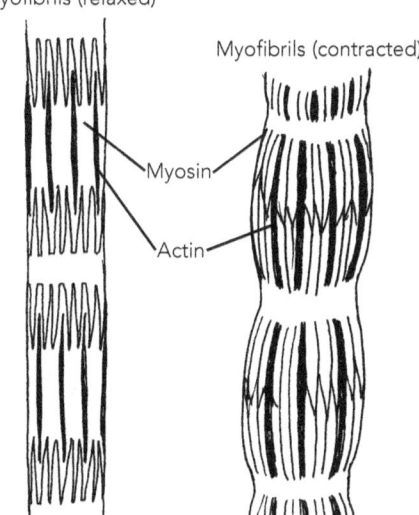

# Types of Muscle Contraction

**Isometric contraction:** The muscle has tension or *tone* but does not change in length. This is important in maintaining the horse's *core strength*.

**Concentric contraction:** The muscle shortens and gains tension. This causes joint extension or flexion, depending on which muscles are contracting.

**Eccentric contraction:** The muscle lengthens as it gains tension. These types of contractions help counteract the force of gravity on the horse's muscles, allowing him to have a controlled gait. Collected gaits and working downhill activate this type of contraction.

## Muscle Metabolism and Energy Production

Muscle contractions require energy, and the amount depends on the specific energy and the duration of the exercise. Energy metabolism is the result of a complex chemical process within the cells, of turning stored food energy (*glycogen*) into a molecule called *adenosine triphosphate* (*ATP*), which is then broken down to provide usable energy for cellular processes.

Energy for the muscles is produced in one of three different ways. The type of *metabolism* (energy production) utilized by the muscles depends on characteristics of the individual horse (breed, muscle fiber type distribution, and fitness level), as well as the intensity and duration of the exercise performed.

**Aerobic metabolism.** Uses *oxygen* and *glycogen* (fuel created primarily from carbohydrates and fats) to create energy to move muscles. It produces energy at a fairly low rate, which can be sustained for long periods of time. Examples of aerobic exercise include endurance and distance riding, foxhunting, and the roads and tracks phase of eventing.

**Anaerobic alactic metabolism.** *Anaerobic* means "without oxygen" and *alactic* means "without lactate." *Anaerobic alactic metabolism* produces energy using *creatinine phosphokinase* (a substance present in limited amounts in the muscle cells) and *glycogen*. It produces a short but intense burst of energy that lasts for only about 10 to 20 seconds, and ends when the muscle's stores of creatinine phosphokinase is exhausted. This energy is used for brief, intensive efforts like short sprints, breaking into a run from a standing start, or jumping.

**Anaerobic lactic metabolism.** Produces energy *without oxygen,* using *glycogen* (carbohydrates) as fuel. This process produces *lactate* (*lactic acid*), a toxic waste product. The lactate is carried away by the circulatory system, but as more lactate is produced than can be carried away, it builds up in the muscle tissues and results in a burning sensation and fatigue. Most activities that require strenuous exertion for more than 20 seconds involve anaerobic lactic metabolism, such as racing, polo, dressage, show jumping, and eventing.

Muscle cells create energy differently, depending on the amount of oxygen available to them from the respiratory and cardiovascular systems. To sustain a contraction, muscle cells require more energy, which is created through *aerobic metabolism* using oxygen. *Anaerobic metabolism,* which does not require oxygen, uses less energy and can be used if a muscle can contract and relax rapidly. This comes at a price to the muscle cells, as they require some oxygen for normal cell function. If they are depleted of oxygen for too long, they will fatigue and fail to contract properly. In addition, the lactic acid produced as a by-product of anaerobic metabolism is harmful to muscle cells and is the cause of muscle soreness and fatigue after a hard workout.

## Types of Muscle Fibers

There are two main types of muscle fibers: *type 1 (slow-twitch fibers)* and *type 2 (fast-twitch fibers)*. Type 2 fibers are further divided into subtypes A and X. Hybrid fiber types also exist (for example, 2AX). Every skeletal muscle in a horse's body has some amount of both types of fibers, but the amount and ratio depends on the primary function of the muscle and the horse's genetic heritage, conformation or body type, and conditioning level.

One goal of conditioning is to increase the *oxidative capacity* of the muscles involved in locomotion, which is the ability to provide oxygen to muscles and for the muscles to effectively use that oxygen. This is accomplished in two ways: changing the ratio of type 1 to type 2 fibers and changing the muscle fibers' size.

> **Type 1 fibers (slow-twitch):** These fibers are slow to contract, require a lot of oxygen (aerobic metabolism), and are slow to fatigue (can sustain a contraction). Horses with a high proportion of type 1 fibers have greater stamina, which is important for endurance and event horses. Type 1 fibers are also involved in muscles involved in sustained contractions to maintain posture. All horses can benefit from increasing the size of these type 1 fibers, to increase their stamina when performing.
>
> **Type 2 fibers (fast-twitch):** These fibers contract faster than type 1 fibers, require little or no oxygen (anaerobic metabolism), and fatigue more quickly. There are two types: *type 2A fibers* have intermediate contraction speeds and have some oxidative capacity allowing them to resist fatigue, while *type 2X fibers* have fast contraction speeds and fatigue rapidly. The quicker the energy burst required, the faster the fibers need to contract, and the less oxygen is required to create energy. These fibers can function without oxygen by using anaerobic metabolism, but this can only be sustained for a short time before muscle cells fatigue and possibly are damaged.

In horses, anaerobic exercise typically occurs at heart rates greater than 150 to 180 beats per minute. A good example of the use of fast-twitch muscles is in a sprinter; he can go fast for a short period of time, but cannot maintain his speed due to muscle fatigue. Sprinters, reiners, jumpers, and eventers require a high to moderate proportion of these fibers in order to perform well.

In training for most horse sports, the goal is to increase the size of type 1 and 2A fibers while decreasing the cross-sectional area of type 2X fibers. Increasing the ratio of type 2A fibers in relation to type 2X fibers is also desirable. This allows a horse to be able to move quickly as needed, but also have the ability to sustain his energy. Normally, type 2 fibers are larger than the type 1 fibers, but when muscle wasting or loss occurs secondarily to disease, injury, or lack of fitness, the type 2 fibers decrease in size to be similar or smaller than the type 1 fibers. With *neurogenic muscle atrophy* (muscles decrease in size due to a problem with the nerves suppling them), both the type 1 and type 2 muscle fibers may decrease in size.

### Chart 12-1: Summary of Muscle Types

| Muscle Type | Energy Mechanism | Heart Rate Needed to Achieve | Type of Work |
| --- | --- | --- | --- |
| Type 1 (slow-twitch). Slow to contract. Want large size with conditioning. | Aerobic (oxygen) | 150–180 bpm | Greater stamina. Dressage, endurance, and event horses. |
| Type 2 (fast-twitch). Contract faster than type 1. Want larger size 2A with conditioning and small area of 2X. Horses have high amounts (70–95%), depending on breed, condition, and muscle type. | Anaerobic (no oxygen) | Over 150–180 bpm | Quickness and power but muscle fatigue occurs earlier. Sprinters, reiners, jumpers, and event horses. |

## Effects of Conditioning

With conditioning, muscles increase in size and strength. The respiratory system improves its ability to exchange oxygen for carbon dioxide, and the cardiovascular system becomes more efficient at delivering oxygen and nutrients and removing waste products from the muscles, because the capillaries become larger and more numerous. Overall, this allows the muscle cells to function more efficiently. The nerve pathways that govern muscular efforts become more efficient, so specific movements become easier, more fluent, and efficient. The muscles also become better able to tolerate the effects of lactate. Muscle tissue shows the effects of conditioning sooner and more dramatically than other body tissues.

## Effects of Conditioning on Bone and Cartilage

While most pronounced in younger growing horses, the types of exercises that a rider performs with her horse changes the structure of bone and cartilage within the horse's joints. For example, faster speed work will cause the bone to thicken on the front (dorsal) aspect of the cannon bone to accommodate the stress placed on the bone when a horse gallops. This change is most pronounced in race horses.

Overall, younger horses have more cartilage and greater bone turnover (bone is broken down and systematically replaced) compared to older horses, as they are adapting to the increased weight and workload placed on their limbs and skeleton as they grow. Ideally, in younger horses that are properly conditioned, the amount of bone and cartilage that is broken down and subsequently replaced to accommodate increasing stress is balanced in order to maintain normal joint and bone function. When it becomes unbalanced, as with disease conditions or with improper conditioning, break down of cartilage and bone can outweigh replacement. This ultimately causes microscopic bone fractures and cartilage damage, and may result in lameness or blemishes, such as osteoarthritis or bucked shins.

## Conditioning the Cardiovascular System

During exercise, the cardiovascular system (heart and blood vessels) must pump blood through the blood vessels at an increased rate, to deliver oxygen and fuel to the cells and remove waste products. The heart is made of muscle that must also become stronger to create stronger and more efficient contractions to increase the blood supply to the far-away muscles. During exercise, the large skeletal muscles help to pump blood throughout the body by rhythmically squeezing the elastic blood vessels as they contract and relax with each stride.

During exercise, the heart rate increases dramatically, from a resting rate of about 35 beats per minute up to 250 beats per minute or higher during maximum exertion to adequately supply the muscles with oxygen.

> **Measuring heart rate:** Heart rate during exercise can be measured most accurately by using an onboard heart rate monitor, which uses electrodes under the saddle or girth to read and display the working heart rate to the rider on a readout device. Methods that involve measuring the heart rate immediately after exercise (such as taking the pulse manually or with a stethoscope) are much less accurate, as the heart rate drops very quickly (within 15 to 30 seconds) after pulling up from a gallop.
>
> **The spleen:** The horse's spleen serves as a reservoir for extra red blood cells, which are released into circulation during exercise. This increases the red cell volume and the amount of oxygen that can be

transported during exercise. In addition, the spleen detects and screens out red blood cells that are used up or damaged, and removes them from circulation for recycling.

**Effects of conditioning:** With conditioning, the heart becomes stronger and more efficient. It can pump more blood with each beat, can achieve a higher maximum heart rate, and drops to a normal resting rate more quickly. The capillaries become larger and greater in number, which makes the exchange of oxygen, carbon dioxide, nutrients, and waste products more efficient. The blood contains more red blood cells, which are higher in hemoglobin, making them better able to transport oxygen and nutrients.

## Conditioning the Respiratory System

Exercise creates a greater demand for oxygen. The job of the respiratory system is to take in oxygen by breathing fresh air into the lungs and to expel waste gases (chiefly carbon dioxide).

**Gas exchange:** Gas exchange refers to the exchange of oxygen for carbon dioxide, which takes place in the alveoli and small blood vessels of the lungs.

**Respiration rate and stride rate:** At the canter and gallop, the mechanics of the stride cause the horse to breathe once during each stride. This "locks" the respiration rate to the stride rate. At other gaits, the horse does not have to breathe in unison with each stride, but he is more aerobically efficient when he moves at a regular stride rate, which allows him to breathe evenly in rhythm with his strides. At the trot, horses often breathe once every two strides.

At the canter and gallop, the movement of the hind legs, gut, diaphragm, chest, and neck are interconnected. During the first phase of the stride, as the hind legs are gathered under the horse, the neck rises, the ribs expand, the gut contents move backward in the abdomen, and the diaphragm is drawn backward, creating more space in the lungs and causing the horse to inhale. During the second half of the stride, the neck is extended and lowered, the rib cage is compressed, the hind legs extend backward, and the gut contents move forward, pushing against the diaphragm and lungs and causing the horse to exhale. The horse can often be heard to snort with every stride.

With conditioning, the respiratory system becomes more efficient at taking in oxygen and expelling carbon dioxide, and the horse becomes more aerobically efficient during exercise. This effect is noticed as an improvement in "wind"; the horse can go farther at a faster speed without tiring or running out of breath.

Breathing mechanism in gallop stride.

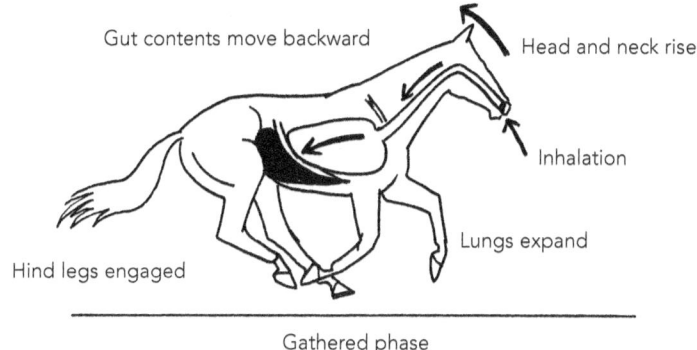

Gathered phase

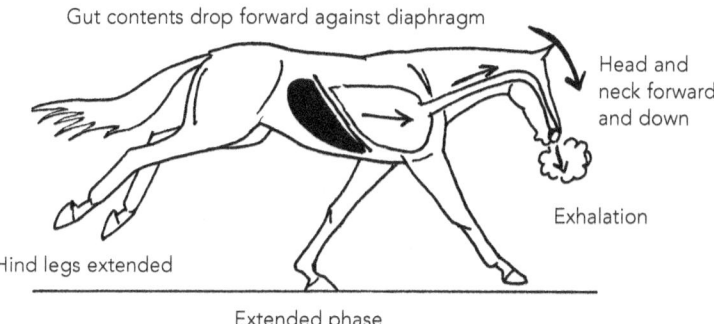

Extended phase

## Conditioning Principles

*Conditioning* is the process of training the body to become physically fit.

*Training* (in the context of conditioning) refers to physical development, which takes place at the cellular level. All the systems of the body are involved in the training (conditioning) process, but some systems (muscular, cardiovascular, and respiratory) are more directly affected than others.

Work creates a *demand* for more oxygen and fuel in the cells of the body. Over time, the body adapts to this demand by increasing the number of red blood cells and improving its efficiency in delivering oxygen and fuel to the cells, removing waste products, and producing energy. In conditioning, the purpose of exercise is to increase demand enough to stimulate a training effect.

The *duration of exercise* is the length of time your horse is working. It can refer to the time taken for your whole ride or the time spent in a specific exercise (galloping, maintaining shoulder-in, working on circles, and so on).

The *frequency of exercise* can refer to the number of times certain exercises are performed each week or to the number of times an exercise is performed during an exercise session.

*Rest* is necessary for conditioning. A brief period of rest (recovery) between efforts allows the body to recover and prepare for a new effort. Rest between workouts is essential for replenishing, repairing, and strengthening body tissues. Insufficient rest results in overloading and damage.

*Progressive loading* increases fitness by alternating between increasing the volume of exercise (by varying duration, distance, or speed) with a period of adaptation in which the workload stays the same. Only the right amount of exercise will have a training effect. Too little does not create a demand and stimulate conditioning; too much leads to overloading, injuries, and breakdowns.

*Overloading or overtraining* occurs when the body or some part of the body is subjected to work or stress beyond its limits. Instead of stimulating a training effect, injury or breakdown occurs. This causes a setback in the conditioning process and may result in permanent damage. Signs of overtraining include poor appetite, dull coat, weight loss, lack of energy, disinterest in work and/or sourness, and heat and/or filling in the legs. Overtraining detrimentally affects the horse's body condition and causes stress. Stress may compromise his immune system, making him vulnerable to injury and illness.

*Interval training* is a conditioning method where work periods are set apart by rest time periods to allow the muscles, heart rate, and respiratory rate to partially recover prior to beginning another period of work.

Proper *nutrition* is essential to provide fuel for energy, protein for building body tissues, water for fluid balance and cooling, and essential vitamins and minerals to regulate metabolic processes. During conditioning, the horse's nutritional needs change with his work and condition.

As a horse's workload increases, his energy needs increase. A horse doing strenuous work may require an increase in concentrates (grain) from a maintenance ration. The ration must be at least 50 percent roughage in order to keep the gut functioning efficiently, but the roughage may need to be of a higher quality than for maintenance or light work. His protein requirements remain approximately the same, although growing horses and aged horses may need slightly higher levels of protein. (For more information on nutrition during conditioning, see Chapter 13, "Feeds and Nutrition.")

*Muscles* show the effects of conditioning most quickly; visible effects may be seen in a few weeks. However, *tendons, ligaments,* and *joints* may take several months to strengthen or remodel, and *hooves* and *bones* require the most time (up to a year) to condition. Because of this, it is important not to mistake early signs of muscular conditioning for overall fitness and risk injuring less well-conditioned structures with too much strenuous work too soon.

*Cardiovascular* and *respiratory conditioning* develops stamina and "wind"; this takes place gradually over weeks and months.

A horse's condition cannot continue to increase past a certain point, or remain at a high level indefinitely. Systematic training will improve it to a *peak* or optimum level, and then it declines somewhat. When conditioning for a particular event, it is important to pace the conditioning process so that the horse achieves peak condition at the time of competition and does not reach his peak too early or too late. The goal is to achieve the maximum amount of fitness, conditioning, and agility at the time when it is most needed (often for a competition). Peaking too early may mean that the horse is over-conditioned for the event and may be at risk for lameness, while peaking too late may mean that he may not be conditioned optimally and will tire too easily.

*Tapering* is reducing exercise or fitness work just prior to a big competition, to enhance performance by providing extra energy at the competition and avoid overtraining.

It is important to record and monitor fitness in order to be able to evaluate a horse's fitness and conditioning progress. You should know and record your horse's *temperature, pulse, and respiratory rate (TPR)* at rest, immediately after exercise, and again at 5 minutes and 10 minutes after exercise. If your horse is in good condition, his pulse (heart rate) should drop to 80 beats per minute 10 minutes after exercise (100 beats per minute for high-intensity intervals). The maximum heart rate after intense work should be 210 to 280 beats per minute; maximum respiration should be 80 to 100 breaths per minute, and maximum temperature 103°F (temperature may continue to rise for 5 to 10 minutes after intense exercise).

In your daily conditioning records, you should also include a description of the weather, the terrain, and the workout (number of sets, speed, rest, vital signs, and recovery rate), as well as an assessment of how the horse handled the work and recovery.

No conditioning program, however technically correct, can succeed without a foundation of excellent daily care, observation, and horse management. Success also depends on the vigilance, good judgment, and good communication between the rider and the team. Some aspects of horse care and management that are important in the conditioning process are:

- Daily routine, including feeding, watering, grooming, exercise, aftercare, and turnout according to a schedule.
- Daily palpation of the feet and legs, and daily observation of the horse's behavior, noticing any changes from the normal. A good horse person knows the horse so well that any small change is noticed immediately.
- Regularly scheduled veterinary, dental, and farrier care, and careful daily attention to any required treatments or medication.
- Good communication among those who ride, train, and care for the horse, including the groom, stable manager, rider, trainer, and coach or instructor, along with the veterinarian and farrier. Anything observed by one (such as the horse failing to clean up his feed, a difference in

movement, or a change in behavior) should be promptly communicated to the others.
- Good record-keeping (feeding, shoeing, veterinary records, and conditioning log).
- Attention to details, including the fit and function of equipment, warming up, cooling out, and after-care (such as wrapping or poulticing), and the horse's mental state as well as his physical development.

# Types of Conditioning

## Aerobic Conditioning

*Aerobic conditioning* is conditioning carried out at a level *below the anaerobic threshold,* at which the horse can function aerobically (his muscles burn oxygen to produce energy). Aerobic conditioning increases the body's ability to deliver oxygen to the tissues efficiently and to produce energy aerobically. This results in improved cardiovascular efficiency and produces greater stamina.

## Conditioning for Stamina

Long, slow distance work (LSD) or continuous training is *aerobic conditioning*. It usually involves trotting and slow cantering, with some periods of walking. As the horse becomes more fit, the distance traveled and the length of the workouts are gradually increased, rather than increasing the speed. Long, slow distance work lays the foundation for all other conditioning, providing a *base* of cardiovascular fitness and endurance.

## Anaerobic Conditioning

*Anaerobic conditioning* is work carried out at a pace *above the anaerobic threshold* (the point at which muscles produce energy anaerobically, without burning oxygen). It is used to strengthen muscles and develop specific skills and speed. Anaerobic conditioning should be added only after the horse has developed a base of fitness through aerobic conditioning.

## Conditioning for Muscle Skills

Conditioning for skills specific to various disciplines, and for muscle strength, coordination, and agility, requires anaerobic conditioning.

Two types of such training are:

> **Skill drills.** Muscles must be prepared for the demands of a particular activity by practice in that skill. For example, jumping horses need

to jump, while dressage horses must practice specific movements. Skill practice conditions specific muscles anaerobically and improves strength, coordination, and fluency in specific skills.

**Speed play.** Speed play is an anaerobic training technique that helps to develop strength, coordination, balance, and quickness. It consists of brief sprints and changes of speed and direction in a random pattern, sometimes incorporating uphill and downhill terrain. It is especially useful for jumpers, eventers, polo ponies, and horses in specialties that require quick responses.

## Conditioning for Strength

Strength increases as the horse's muscles develop, enabling him to move and carry his rider with less muscle fatigue. Exercises that build strength place demands on specific muscle groups, requiring muscle fibers to fire together.

Some exercises to build muscle strength are:

- Gymnastic jumping, performed in interval format (improves agility, power, and specific skills)
- Jumping a few larger fences (improves power)
- Jumping uphill steps (develops explosive power, especially in the hindquarters)
- Riding downhill (aids muscle contraction in front legs)
- Riding over demanding surfaces such as sand or water (causes horse to exert greater muscular effort)
- Riding different slopes, directions, and speeds (increases muscle use and balance)
- Asking for greater collection in dressage (improves strength and specific skills)
- Trotting over a grid of raised cavaletti (builds quadriceps muscles)

## Conditioning for Flexibility and Core Muscle Building

*Flexibility* is the suppleness of the horse's muscles, tendons, and ligaments and their ability to resist injury under stress. Some individuals and certain body types may have more natural muscular-skeletal flexibility or *range of motion*. Like riders, horses need to have flexibility and core body strength to achieve success in various disciplines.

Exercises for flexibility include:

- Passive suppling and stretching (leg extensions, "carrot stretches")
- Dynamic suppling exercises (turns, circles, lateral movements, uphill and downhill work, work over cavaletti)

The following stretches and exercises can be done in hand to stretch specific muscles and activate the horse's core muscles. They can be used to improve and maintain a horse's flexibility and muscle tone while in work or while recovering from an injury.

All of these exercises should be started slowly and progress gradually, preferably with the assistance of a massage therapist or an expert in this field. While performing these exercises, be careful, tactful, and aware of the horse's attitude and response, as some horses may kick.

- **Carrot stretches:** These are used to maintain a horse's flexibility and muscle tone while in work or while recovering from an injury by encouraging the horse to flex his head and neck to either side, reaching toward his hip or hind fetlock (activates oblique abdominal muscles), reach with his head between his front legs (activates rectus abdominus muscles), or to extend his neck (stretches the back muscles along his spine).

    These stretches should be performed slowly as the horse reaches for a carrot or other treat held toward his hip or between his front legs. The horse should stand still and stretch his head and neck, not move his feet. Try not to let the horse bend his knees as he stretches down to his chest, so that he achieves a better stretch. He only needs to hold each stretch for a few seconds.

    Begin with only a few stretches to each side (alternating sides). Be patient in beginning sessions because the horse may be stiff. After a couple of weeks the horse will stretch farther and closer to the hip.

- **Tail pulls:** Place the horse standing square behind and stand close to the side of his hind leg. Be aware of the horse's reactions, and be careful not to get kicked. Gently grasp the tail about halfway down and slowly pull the tail toward you until you see his quadriceps muscles (the muscles just above his stifle) contract. Hold this position for 10 to 30 seconds to maintain the contraction. Repeat this several times on both sides. This is a good exercise for horses that have problems with locking patella due to quadriceps muscle weakness or hip issues.

- **Rocking back/shoulder push:** Pick up the horse's front leg so that it is flexed at the knee. With your other hand, gently push on the horse's shoulder on the same side to "rock" his weight back onto his haunches. You should see his gluteal muscles bulge while doing this. Hold for 10 to 30 seconds and repeat on the other side. This is a great exercise for retraining Thoroughbreds who have been on the track to develop their gluteal and biceps femoris muscles, which are needed for hindquarter engagement and, later on, collected work.

- **Sternal lift:** With the horse standing square, place your hands on his midline at the back of the sternum (just behind the girth area) and lift upward. The horse should lift his back and topline in response, strengthening his abdominal muscles (which are contracting) and stretching his back muscles. Be aware of the horse's attitude and be tactful when performing this lift, as some horses may cow-kick.
- **Pelvic flexion:** For this exercise, you must stand directly behind the horse, so it should not be done on horses that are likely to kick. Use your fingers to scratch the area on either side of the horse's tail head (*ischium*) so that he flexes at the LS joint and tucks his hindquarters. An alternative approach is to use thumb pressure on the spine in the croup area until he rounds up his haunches. This helps develop his gluteal muscles and stretch his lumbosacral spine.
- **Exercise bands:** To encourage a horse to activate his core and walk more actively, an elastic band (such as a wide Ace bandage or two polo wraps connected with Velcro) can be attached to the saddle pad and around his hindquarters, below the point of the buttock. The band encourages the horse to bring his hind legs under his body, activating his core abdominal, gluteal, and biceps femoris muscles.

Before attaching an exercise band, rub it gently against the horse's hindquarters to accustom the horse to the feel of the band on its hindquarters. The horse should be warmed up first, and should be worked in hand or longed wearing the band before he is ridden with it.

# Interval Training

*Interval training* is a conditioning method based on the principle of progressive loading. It consists of several *work intervals* at a measured speed and distance, which raise the horse's heart rate to a certain level. Each work interval is followed by a short rest period in which the heart rate is allowed to recover to a specified level (usually around 100 to 125 beats per minute). The number of *sets* (work and rest intervals) and the speed and distance of each work interval must be carefully determined, keeping in mind the horse's heart rate, recovery rate, and response to the conditioning process. It is the total amount of work, connected by recovery periods, which results in conditioning benefits.

Interval training is a powerful tool for developing cardiovascular fitness. Using interval training, a horse can do more fast work, aimed at more specific conditioning goals than in traditional galloping work, with less risk of injury. However, interval training requires precise measurement of speed, distance, and heart rate (preferably with an *onboard heart rate monitor*), along with a high degree of experience, knowledge, and judgment on the part of the rider or trainer.

Interval training for eventers, which is carried out at a controlled gallop, should not be confused with repeated short sprints, a technique used by some race horse trainers to sharpen short-distance speed.

## Heat and Conditioning

Hot and/or humid conditions add to the stress of conditioning. If horses are expected to compete in hot or humid conditions, they need to become acclimated to them. However, this requires care and attention to conditions, so as not to overstress horses working in hot weather.

The *heat index* is a measure of air temperature and humidity. Heat and humidity increase stress on horses, especially horses that are unfit or working strenuously, and can make it difficult for them to cool down. You can find out the heat index by checking the local weather report or by using a heat index chart. (See pages 237–239 of the *USPC C Level Manual* for a heat index chart, and more information on the effects of heat and humidity and cooling out horses in hot and humid conditions.)

*Panting* is a response that helps the horse dissipate heat. He takes shallow, fast breaths (120 to 140 breaths per minute). Panting for longer than 10 minutes may be a sign of respiratory/heart rate inversion (see below).

*Inversion* occurs when a horse's respiratory rate is higher than his heart rate. This is a sign that he is too hot and is trying to get rid of some of the heat via his respiratory tract by panting. This should last no longer than 10 minutes; otherwise, it is a sign of distress and veterinary intervention may be needed. Respiratory/heart rate inversion is an indication that the horse is stressed and may be unfit for the amount of exercise he has been asked to perform or the conditions (especially extreme heat and humidity).

*Anhidrosis* is a condition in which a horse sweats very little or not at all, which means he cannot cool down quickly enough. The onset may be sudden; the horse will have an elevated pulse and respiration, increased temperature, and may be distressed or lethargic after working in hot, humid weather. Recovery and cool-down is slow, and the horse may need veterinary assistance. The cause of anhidrosis is unknown, but it happens most often in hot, humid climates.

# Part 3

# Horse Care and Stable Management

# 13

# Feeds and Nutrition

## Essential Nutrients for Horses

There are six types of essential nutrients. These are provided in water, sunlight, and different kinds of feed.

## Types of Nutrients

### Water

Water is an essential part of every cell and of all vital fluids that support the cells (including blood), which carry nutrients to all parts of the body, pick up waste products, and help to eliminate them. Water in the body is needed to lubricate the joints, as a component of sweat, serves as a built-in cooling system as a component of sweat in hot weather, and as a component of the circulatory system, helps keep the body warm in cold weather. Water will not wash food out of the stomach or cause digestive upsets, and it should not be restricted when a horse is cooling down.

Lack of water in the body is called *dehydration*. This is very serious and can weaken or even kill a horse. Horses may become dehydrated if they are not given enough clean, pure water often enough. They may also become dehydrated as the result of being sick. An adult horse needs at least 10 to 12 gallons of water daily or 1 gallon per 100 pounds (50 ml/kg). Water should be available at all times. It is important to know how much each horse is drinking, and if he is not drinking a normal amount, to find out why. Dehydration is a serious problem that requires veterinary care (see Chapter 14, "Health Care, Diseases, and Veterinary Knowledge").

## Carbohydrates

*Carbohydrates* make up most of the fuel a horse uses for energy. They are found in hays, grains, and pasture grasses. Carbohydrates are the cheapest and most abundant source of energy for a horse. The energy generated by *carbohydrate metabolism* (the chemical process of breaking down and using carbohydrates) keeps the horse's body temperature normal, which is especially important in cold weather. It also gives him the energy for fast, hard work.

Carbohydrates refer to a broad spectrum of molecules that must include *carbon, hydrogen,* and *oxygen*. These come in different forms. Some have simple structures, while others are much more complex. More simple carbohydrates are known as *non-structural carbohydrates* (*NSC*) and the more complex carbohydrates are known as *structural carbohydrates* (that is, fiber). Carbohydrates come from plants and are created during a process called *photosynthesis.* Non-structural carbohydrates provide the plant with energy, while structural carbohydrates provide structural components to the plant. The horse is able to utilize both kinds of carbohydrate as an energy source.

Cereal grains mostly provide *starch*, a non-structural or *simple carbohydrate* that is digested in the small intestine by *amylase* and absorbed into the bloodstream as *glucose*, a form of sugar. Glucose is used by all cells in the body as the primary energy source to allow for normal cellular functions, something like gasoline for a car. Excess glucose is made into *glycogen* in the liver and stored in the liver and muscle tissue. Glycogen is a very important energy source because it is the only energy source a horse can use during anaerobic work. Once the horse has reached his limit of glycogen storage, remaining carbohydrates are converted into fat and stored in fat tissue throughout the body.

While grasses and hays provide a small amount of non-structural carbohydrates, the greatest proportion of their carbohydrates are in the form of *structural carbohydrates*. As grass grows, it requires a greater proportion of structural carbohydrates to hold its stem upright. These structural carbohydrates (for example *cellulose, hemicelluloses*, and *lignin*) cannot be digested in the small intestine by a horse's enzymes, and instead are broken down by the bacteria living in the large intestine. These bacteria have enzymes that can break down structural carbohydrates and then use them for energy. As the bacteria break down the structural carbohydrates, *volatile fatty acids* are produced, which are then utilized by the horse for energy. The process of breaking down structural carbohydrates gives off heat, which helps to maintain the horse's body temperature. For this reason it is beneficial to feed more hay during cold weather.

## Proteins

*Proteins* are the building blocks of life. They are essential components of every cell in the body and are needed for growth, maintenance, and repair of the body's tissues.

Proteins are made up of long chains of *amino acids*. While the composition of proteins and amino acids can vary greatly, they all contain *nitrogen*. The guaranteed analysis of crude protein for a particular feed is simply a test of nitrogen content. Think of proteins as long chains with each link in the chain being an amino acid. In the horse's small intestine, *enzymes* (which are also made of protein) break down protein, releasing amino acids that are absorbed into the bloodstream. These amino acids are then made available to the cells to create new proteins necessary for cellular functions and tissue maintenance.

Some amino acids are made by the horse, while others known as *essential amino acids* must be provided by the diet. Of the 24 existing amino acids, 10 are essential amino acids, meaning that the horse must ingest them through his diet. *Lysine* and *methionine* are two essential amino acids that are most often deficient in horses' diets and are very important for young growing horses.

The *quality of protein* in a feed is determined by the proportion of essential amino acids that it supplies. While certain hays may provide adequate *total protein*, the proportion of essential amino acids may be low, making the protein a lower quality than a protein source (such as soybean meal) that contains a higher proportion of essential amino acids. If the ration does not provide enough of an essential amino acid, it negatively impacts the horse's ability to utilize all other amino acids to build proteins, even if there are plenty of these other amino acids available. Therefore, it is possible that a diet could provide ample protein but be lacking in a necessary amino acid, resulting in conditions such as poor hoof quality or poor muscling (often noticed as lack of top line muscle). While we say that horses have a *protein requirement*, in reality their requirement is for amino acids.

The horse's protein requirement is measured in *grams*. In the ration it is often expressed as a percentage of the whole diet. For example, a growing foal may need a protein content of 16 percent of his daily ration, while a mature horse in light work might only need 10 percent. The protein content of feed is given as *crude protein*. For the crude protein content of common feeds, refer to the tables on pages 454 and 463.

Protein should not be relied upon as an energy source. While it can be used for energy, it is a very inefficient process and feeding excess energy results in calories being burned unnecessarily. When proteins are processed by the body, urea and ammonia, chemicals containing nitrogen, are produced as a by-product of amino acid breakdown in the liver, filtered from the blood in the kidneys, and eliminated from the body in the urine. When proteins are fed in excess, extra urea and ammonia must be excreted in urine. The horse may need to create more urine to rid the body of these harmful products, which indirectly increases the horse's water requirement. Excess ammonia in the urine creates a strong urine smell that can be harmful to the respiratory tract of both humans and horses in poorly ventilated barns. Overfeeding protein is also costly as it is a relatively expensive feed ingredient.

## Fats (Lipids)

*Fats*, often referred to as *lipids*, play an important role in the horse's body. They affect skin and coat condition, but are also a major component of the outer layer of cells and play a vital role in the absorption of *fat-soluble vitamins*. While the horse's natural diet provides relatively little fat (about 5 to 6 percent), horses actually do very well when fat is added as an energy source. This, combined with the fact that fat provides 2.25 times more calories than an equal amount of carbohydrates, makes it a useful means of increasing calories in the ration without having to feed large amounts of grain.

Using fat as an energy source reduces some of the risks associated with feeding high amounts of grain, such as insulin dysregulation and disruption of the bacterial population in the large intestine. Fat is thought of as a source of "cool" calories, as some horses appear to behave better when fed additional calories from fat than they do when fed grain. Care must be taken not to feed too much fat, as it can cause digestive upsets such as loose manure.

Feeds with high fat content spoil easily and become rancid, especially in hot weather. They lose essential fatty acids, smell and taste bad, and are no longer good for horses. Feeds high in fat should be kept away from heat and light, stored in small quantities, and used up quickly.

## Vitamins

*Vitamins* are organic chemical compounds that are required in small amounts to regulate certain chemical reactions in the body. These reactions are involved in mineral metabolism (vitamin D), provide antioxidant functions (vitamin E), and various enzymatic reactions (vitamin B).

There are two types of vitamins: *fat-soluble* (those that are carried in fat and require fat for absorption from the intestine) and *water-soluble* (those that are carried by and absorbed in water).

Fat-soluble vitamins can be stored in the liver or in body fat, and called up for use when the body needs them. They include vitamins A, D, E, and K. Water-soluble vitamins, including the B-complex vitamins and vitamin C, are produced by the horse. B-complex vitamins are produced by bacteria in the intestine from plant sources and cannot be stored in the body. B-complex vitamins include $B_1$ (thiamine), $B_2$ (riboflavin), $B_3$ (niacin), $B_5$ (pantothenic acid), $B_6$ (pyroxidine), $B_7$ (biotin), $B_9$ (folic acid), and $B_{12}$ (cyanocobalamin). Vitamin C (ascorbic acid) is also a water-soluble vitamin; however, unlike other water-soluble vitamins, it is made in the liver from glucose.

### Fat-Soluble Vitamins
**Vitamin A** may be provided in the diet directly as vitamin A, also known as *retinol*, or in the form of *beta-carotene,* which the horse converts to active vitamin A. Beta-carotene is found in green leafy plants, such as legume hay. Sufficient amounts are provided by fresh pasture and good-quality hay. Horses are able to store enough vitamin A to last about 2 months, which can sustain them during periods when forage quality is poor (for example, during the winter or a drought). If green forage is lacking for longer periods, supplemental sources of vitamin A may be necessary. Vitamin A plays an important role in the health and growth of a growing horse. The eyes, skin, nerves, and hooves, and the reproductive, gastrointestinal, and immune systems, all depend on vitamin A for normal function. Symptoms of vitamin A deficiency include night blindness, excessive tear production, hardening of the skin and cornea (cloudy corneas), and respiratory and reproductive problems. Excess vitamin A is harmful and toxicity can occur when vitamin A is fed as a supplement. Horses will avoid toxicity by converting less beta-carotene into vitamin A. Symptoms of vitamin A toxicity include reduced appetite and growth, anemia, and poor hair and skin.

**Vitamin D** is synthesized when *7-dehydrochelesterol* in the horse's skin is converted to vitamin D from ultraviolet radiation or from eating sun-cured hay. Vitamin D functions as a binding protein required for calcium absorption. Calcium deficiency can result from a horse being deficient in vitamin D. However, feeding vitamin D as a supplement is not recommended, nor beneficial, unless a horse does not have access to the outdoors during the summer or is not fed good-quality hay in the winter. Typically, a vitamin premix will contain vitamins A, D, and E since vitamins E and D enhance vitamin A absorption and storage. Vitamin D plays a vital role in calcium utilization and therefore plays a major role in bone development. Vitamin D deficiency symptoms are the same as in calcium deficiency, including stiffness, lameness, swollen joints, and brittle and porous bones. Toxic levels of vitamin D can result in soft tissue calcifications and excess bone formation, causing bone abnormalities.

**Vitamin E** is a powerful antioxidant involved in removing damaging chemicals called *oxygen free radicals* from the body that form during normal cellular processes. The antioxidant functions of vitamin E work in conjunction with selenium. Vitamin E also protects cell membranes, is essential for DNA synthesis, is a cofactor for vitamin C synthesis, enhances vitamin A absorption and storage, contributes to fertility, and is involved in normal muscle function.

Vitamin E can be stored for several months in the horse. Young green plants are a high source of vitamin E; however, it is easily oxidized and sensitive to moisture, grinding, storage, and heat. Therefore, while vitamin E levels in fresh pasture are quite high, harvesting forage into hay reduces the vitamin E content, and it continues to drop during storage. Horses without unlimited good-quality pasture may require vitamin E supplementation.

Vegetable oils such as corn and soybean oil are relatively high in vitamin E, and commercial supplements are also available. Vitamin E deficiency relates to the vitamin's ability to protect cell membranes and often occurs in combination with *selenium deficiencies*, resulting in muscle and nervous system abnormalities such as *white muscle disease* or *equine degenerative myeloencephalopathy*.

**Vitamin K** is responsible for proper clotting of the blood (*coagulation*). However, there is no requirement for vitamin K in the horse's diet because it is synthesized by the *microflora* in the large intestine. Horses on prolonged antibiotic use without access to good hay or horses receiving very poor nutrition may need supplementation under recommendations of a veterinarian. Vitamin K deficiency has only been reported in horses eating moldy sweet clover, but non-moldy sweet clover poses no problems.

### Water-Soluble Vitamins

**Vitamin C (ascorbic acid)** is synthesized in the horse's liver. It is a powerful antioxidant that plays an important role in the immune systems as well as in the formation of collagen. It also has a role in hormone synthesis and bone calcification. Healthy horses appear to produce adequate amounts of vitamin C, but those suffering from liver disease may require supplementation on recommendation of a veterinarian.

**B-complex vitamins** are synthesized by bacteria in the horse's intestine. These vitamins are not stored in the body because they are highly toxic. Surplus B-complex vitamins are excreted in the urine.

**$B_1$ (thiamine)** is involved in carbohydrate and protein metabolism. It is necessary for appetite stimulation and normal nervous system function. It is the only B vitamin that has a defined dietary requirement in the horse. Deficiency of thiamine can result from bracken fern poisoning, which contains an enzyme that breaks down thiamine, resulting in weight loss, depression, and neurologic signs.

**$B_2$ (riboflavin)** is involved in metabolism of fats, protein, and, especially, carbohydrates acting as a cofactor in various enzymatic reactions.

**$B_3$ (niacin)** is involved in metabolism of fats, protein, and carbohydrates, cholesterol synthesis, and DNA repair.

**$B_5$ (pantothenic acid)** is necessary for synthesis of *Coenzyme A*, an enzyme needed for fat, protein, and carbohydrate metabolism.

**$B_6$ (pyroxidine)** is involved in metabolism of fats, protein, and carbohydrates. It assists in balancing potassium and sodium levels and formation of red blood cells, and is essential for the production of various neurotransmitters.

**$B_7$ (biotin)** is involved in metabolism of fats, protein, and carbohydrates, acting as a cofactor in various enzymatic reactions. It is important for cell proliferation, leading to its association with impaired hoof growth if it is deficient (a very rare condition). Supplementing 10mg to 30mg per day may improve hoof growth when combined with zinc supplementation, although visible improvement can take many months to appear.

**$B_9$ (folic acid)** aids in formation of red blood cells. It is necessary for DNA synthesis and repair and normal nervous system function.

**$B_{12}$ (cobalamin)** is important for normal nervous system function, red blood cell formation, cellular metabolism, and DNA synthesis.

**Choline** is necessary for cell membrane formation, normal nerve function, and fat metabolism.

Horses get most of the vitamins they need from good-quality hay and green, growing pasture grass. During the winter or when pasture grass is poor, it may help to feed a vitamin supplement. Ask your veterinarian or an equine nutritionist before adding any supplement to your horse's feed. Follow the manufacturer's directions, and don't mix supplements or feed more than one. Vitamin B supplementation may be practical when feed intake is limited, horses are ill or heavily parasitized, heavily exercised or stressed, or on a prolonged course of antibiotics.

## Minerals

Minerals are *inorganic elements* (substances not including carbon, oxygen, or hydrogen).

While minerals make up a very small percentage of the horse's diet by weight, they are vitally important to a number of body functions from enzymes involved in cellular metabolism to maintenance of the skeleton. Some amino acids, hormones, and vitamins cannot function without specific minerals.

Most of a horse's mineral needs are provided by the forages and other feedstuffs in their diet. However, the mineral content of these feeds depends on the mineral content of the soils in which they are grown. If the soil is low in a certain mineral, the feed from plants grown in that soil will be low in that mineral. In different areas of the country, the soil may be high in certain minerals and deficient in others. It is important to know where your feed and hay comes from and which minerals it contains. You can determine this by having hay or soil tested, or by checking the ingredients tag on feed bags. Read the sections on types of feed and balancing a ration for information about the mineral content of specific feeds and how to balance the minerals in a ration.

Minerals are classified into two groups: *macrominerals* and *micro- or trace minerals*. The horse's requirement for macrominerals (calcium, phosphorus, magnesium, sodium, potassium, chloride, sulfur) is measured in *grams*. (For example, a 1,100-pound horse in light work requires 30 g of calcium and 18 g of phosphorus a day.) In comparison, the trace minerals (iron, copper, zinc, manganese, iodine, selenium, cobalt) are required in milligram amounts, so the copper requirement for a 1,100-pound horse is 100 mg each day.

The amount of macrominerals in feeds and supplements is often reported as a percentage, so a supplement may say that it contains 12 percent calcium. To calculate the number of grams of calcium provided, you must determine the serving size and then calculate 12 percent of that amount. For example, a 1-ounce serving, which is equal to 28 g, would provide 3.36 g of calcium (28 g × 0.12).

Trace mineral quantities are sometimes given as *parts per million (ppm)*, which is equivalent to *milligrams per kilogram (mg/kg)*. This means that for every kilogram (2.2 pounds) that you feed, you would be providing so many milligrams of that mineral. For example, if a product provides 150 ppm per serving of copper, 150 mg of copper is provided for each kilogram of the supplement or feed. If the serving size is 1 ounce (28 g), it would provide only 4.2 mg of copper (1 kg = 1,000 g, so 1,000 g / 28 g = 35.7 and 150 mg / 35.7 = 4.2 mg).

Because of the different ways in which mineral quantities can be described, it is vital to read mineral supplement product labels carefully to be certain you are selecting the right product for your horse's needs and feeding the appropriate amount.

## Macrominerals

**Sodium** is important for propagation of nerve impulses that cause muscle contraction and maintaining the correct pH in the blood. It is extremely important for fluid regulation within the body, both in and out of the cells, by contributing to the *osmolarity,* or *solute concentration,* in the fluids of the body, including blood. Therefore, it is one of the most important regulators of blood pressure. Increased concentration of sodium in the blood stimulates the thirst reflex, while decreased concentration increases urine production to maintain a constant fluid volume within the body. For this reason, ensuring that your horse consumes adequate sodium is vitally important for maintaining hydration; this is why horses should always have access to salt (sodium chloride).

A 1,100-pound horse has a maintenance sodium requirement of 10 g per day, which is met by consuming 1 ounce of salt each day (equal to a 2-pound block of salt per month). The feeds your horse consumes contains most of his sodium requirement, but may not provide the total amount needed. Supplementation with some form of salt (usually a salt block) should be provided. Horses will eat salt only if their sodium needs are not being met in their diet. Horses lose large quantities of sodium and other electrolytes in sweat, so horses in work may require electrolyte supplementation that contains sodium. Further information about electrolyte supplementation may be found in the "Supplements" section, later in this chapter.

**Calcium and phosphorus** are essential for sound bones, especially in young, growing horses. Ninety-nine percent of the calcium and 80 percent of the phosphorus in the body is found in the bones. Magnesium is closely associated with calcium and phosphorus. Vitamin D is necessary for the absorption of calcium from the intestine.

Calcium is also important for rapid small adjustments in the blood pH, nervous system function, and all types of muscle contraction (cardiac, smooth, and skeletal).

Phosphorus is a major component of DNA, RNA, and cell membranes and transports cell energy in the form of *adenosine triphosphate* (ATP).

To use calcium and phosphorus, a horse must have the right amount of each mineral, but the minerals must also be in balance. If he has too much of one, he cannot use either mineral properly.

Depending on a horse's use and stage of development (growth, lactating, breeding, performance, maintenance), the calcium-to-phosphorus ratio should be within the range of 1:1 to 2:1.

Hays and grasses contain calcium and phosphorus amounts near the ideal ratio stated above (this is why horses can easily survive eating only hay or grass). Alfalfa hay has an increased amount of calcium compared to phosphorus, while cereal grains have significantly more phosphorus than calcium.

Calcium is only absorbed from the intestines (with the help of vitamin D) if the horse needs it. Any extra calcium consumed in the diet passes through the digestive tract unabsorbed, so horses cannot develop calcium toxicity. However, phosphorus is more readily absorbed, and if consumed in excess it can cause an imbalance in the calcium-to-phosphorus ratio that may affect the utilization of calcium. Calcium and phosphorus deficiencies are rare, although horses with colic often have low levels of calcium due to lack of feed intake. Deficiencies in calcium and phosphorus affects bones and muscle function.

**Potassium** is important in maintaining the pH (*acid-base balance*) and, along with sodium, the fluid level inside the cells. It is also important for nerve impulse transmission and muscle contraction. Potassium levels tend to be high in most forages, providing enough to easily meet the average horse's needs. Horses that work hard and sweat heavily may lose potassium, especially in hot weather. Giving electrolytes containing potassium in the right mixture may help replace losses, but this must be done under the supervision of a veterinarian. Potassium is readily excreted in the urine, but it is very dangerous if it exceeds normal levels in the blood, leading to heart irregularities and muscle dysfunction (see Chapter 14 for more information).

About 60 percent of **magnesium** in the body is found in bone, with much of the remaining amount in the muscles where, with calcium, it plays an important role in all types of muscle contractions. It is also important for many enzymatic reactions within the body, including DNA and ATP synthesis. Signs of magnesium deficiency include muscle tremors and nervousness. Magnesium may be administered to horses that suffer from muscle tension or to "relax" a spooky horse. However, its use for behavior modification is ethically questionable and illegal for use in horses showing under USEF rules. Sadly, horses have died from unintentional overdose of magnesium used for this purpose. Therefore, its use as a supplement should only be done with the guidance of your veterinarian or equine nutritionist.

### *Microminerals*

Most trace minerals are supplied by a horse's normal diet. Some salt blocks come with trace minerals added. Discuss your horse's needs with your veterinarian or equine nutritionist before supplementing, as feeding too much of certain minerals may cause more harm than overfeeding other nutrients.

**Iodine** is a trace mineral that helps regulate thyroid activity as it is a primary component in thyroid hormone. Thyroid hormone is necessary for regulation of *basal metabolic rate* and growth and maintenance of tissues. Only small amounts are necessary. In some areas, the soil may be deficient in iodine; therefore, any feed grown in it will also be deficient. Feeding iodized salt will take care of your horse's iodine needs. Iodine deficiency is rare in horses, but can result in "goiter" formation as a result of enlargement of the thyroid gland.

**Iron** is necessary for the formation of *hemoglobin,* which is necessary for the transport of oxygen in blood. It is often supplemented in the hopes of improving performance; however, the high levels of iron found in most forages provides more than enough of this mineral to meet the horse's requirements.

**Copper** is essential for a number of important enzymes involved in the synthesis of cartilage, as well as in the mobilization of iron stored within the body. Foals born to mares whose diets are low in copper during pregnancy may be at greater risk of *osteochondritis dessicans* (see Chapter 10). Forages and grains tend to be low in copper, so a fortified feed or supplement should be provided to ensure that daily needs are met in pregnant mares and growing foals.

**Manganese** is a cofactor for many enzymatic reactions involved in carbohydrate, amino acid, and cholesterol metabolism. It is an antioxidant and important for nervous system function. It is mostly stored in the bones. Manganese is commonly included in joint supplements containing *chondroitin* as it is involved in cartilage formation, and its antioxidant abilities may reduce pain associated with arthritis. In some areas of the country the levels of manganese in forages is very high. A deficiency of manganese may have an impact on bone and cartilage formation in growing horses.

**Selenium** plays a role in *thyroid gland* and *thyroid hormone* function. It also creates antioxidant enzymes that protect cells from harmful *oxygen free radicals,* often in combination with vitamin E. The level of selenium in forages varies greatly by geographic region and the acidity of the soil. Some states such as those in the upper Midwest tend to have very high levels of selenium, and some plants can accumulate large enough quantities to become toxic if eaten. Other areas such as the Pacific Northwest have very low soil levels of selenium and horses eating forages grown there may suffer from selenium deficiency.

Selenium can be toxic in small amounts, leading to hair loss, hoof defects, and even death. Alternatively, selenium deficiency can result in muscle disorders, such as *recurrent rhabdomyolysis.* Testing hay for selenium, as well as testing your horse's blood serum selenium concentration, is recommended before supplementing selenium, which should only be done in consultation with your veterinarian or equine nutritionist.

**Zinc** is a cofactor for many enzymes important to metabolism. Zinc levels in most forages and grains tend to be low and supplementation may be necessary. Seek help from your equine nutritionist or veterinarian if you are concerned about zinc levels in your horse's diet.

# Horse Feeds

Horse feeds can be classified as roughages, concentrates, and supplements. There are many varieties within each category, each with its own characteristics and nutritional values.

## Roughages

Roughages are feeds that are high in fiber and relatively low in energy, while forages are considered pasture and hays (parts of vegetation ready to be consumed). They are the most natural feed for horses, so they should make up the greater part of any ration. Horses should be provided with 1.5 to 2 percent of their body weight in forages or roughages, and never less than 1 percent. At least 1 percent of body weight is required to maintain a well-balanced population of microbes in the digestive tract. Roughages take longer to consume than concentrates, providing the horse with a more natural eating pattern.

## Pasture

Good-quality pasture (with free access to salt and water) can meet all or nearly all of the horse's basic nutritional requirements. Good pasture is high in energy, fiber, protein, essential fatty acids, minerals, and vitamins. These nutrients may be lacking in horses kept in confinement without access to fresh forage. Horses whose diets are comprised solely of pasture may be lacking some trace minerals, especially copper, zinc, and, in some geographic areas, selenium. For this reason, horses maintained on pasture should be provided with a trace mineral ration balancer or supplement similar to that provided to horses maintained on hay. Pasture is especially important for young growing horses, senior horses, and some idle horses because it provides open space to move and a continuous source of feed that helps to reduce boredom.

Although pasture is a good food source for most horses, there are some exceptions. Modern pastures are often *improved,* meaning that they produce large yields of rich grass that may not be suitable for all horses. Easy keepers (horses that are prone to becoming overweight, for example, Morgans, Arabians, Paso Finos, Mustangs, ponies, and miniature horses), horses suffering from metabolic problems, or any horse already overweight are at increased risk of developing laminitis from pasture grass.

This risk is particularly high in the spring when the grass grows quickly and contains large quantities of easily available *non-structural carbohydrates*. However, these types of carbohydrates are also increased in the grass when pastures are stressed. For example, when cool-season grass species (such as orchard, timothy, fescue, or brome) experience nighttime temperatures below 40° F or when pastures are overgrazed, under-irrigated, or under-fertilized, they stop growing (reduce structural carbohydrate production) and store energy as non-structural carbohydrates. Therefore, even when pastures look sparse (possibly due to drought or overgrazing), they can still pose a risk to sensitive horses. At-risk animals should have limited access to pasture and may need to wear a grazing muzzle to reduce their intake of grass. Horses and ponies that have previously suffered laminitis after grazing on pasture may not safely be able to have any access to pasture. Instead, they should be confined to a dry (dirt) lot and fed hay as their source of forage.

Horses doing moderate to hard work generally cannot get enough energy from pasture grass to meet their energy needs. They require supplementary feeding, usually in the form of concentrates. In addition, horses require plenty of grazing time to take in adequate nutrition from pasture. If a horse is frequently kept away from pasture for long periods, he will need supplementary feeding to make up for lost grazing time.

To evaluate the nutritional value of a pasture, walk over it and note the main varieties of grass and the condition of the pasture. Soil testing (available through your local Cooperative Extension or agricultural college) may reveal a need for lime or fertilizer. Cutting down weeds and reseeding bare areas, rotating or resting pastures, and removing manure regularly can make a great difference in the quality of the nutrition available in a pasture.

## Cool-Season and Warm-Season Grasses

The terms *cool-season* and *warm-season* are broad categories used to classify different types of grasses. Cool-season grasses such as timothy, orchard, brome, rye, and fescue grow best in the spring and fall, when temperatures are cooler. Warm-season grasses such as Bermuda, Teff, and Tifton grow best in the summer months and are better able to withstand hot dry weather. One major nutritional difference between the two is that cool-season grasses store excess carbohydrates as *fructan sugars;* whereas warm-season grasses store excess carbohydrates as starch. The amount of starch that warm-season grasses can store is limited, while cool-season grasses are able to store an unlimited amount of fructan.

## Chart 13-1: Pasture Grasses and Nutritional Values

| Forage | Digestible Energy (Mcal/lb) | Crude Protein % | Fiber % | Ca % | P % | Dry Matter % |
|---|---|---|---|---|---|---|
| Alfalfa, late growth | 0.31 | 5.0 | 5.6 | 0.40 | 0.07 | 23.2 |
| Alfalfa, full bloom | 0.25 | 4.6 | 7.2 | 0.28 | 0.06 | 23.8 |
| Bermuda grass | 0.33 | 3.6 | 8.7 | 0.15 | 0.08 | 30.3 |
| Birdsfoot trefoil | 0.19 | 4.0 | 4.1 | 0.33 | 0.05 | 19.3 |
| Bluegrass | 0.33 | 3.8 | 8.6 | 0.15 | 0.14 | 30.8 |
| Brome, smooth, early growth | 0.31 | 5.6 | 6.0 | 0.14 | 0.12 | 26.1 |
| Brome, smooth, mature | 0.40 | 3.4 | 19.1 | 0.14 | 0.09 | 54.9 |
| Clover, early growth | 0.22 | 4.1 | 4.6 | 0.44 | 0.07 | 19.6 |
| Clover, full bloom | 0.27 | 3.8 | 6.8 | 0.26 | 0.07 | 26.2 |
| Fescue | 0.32 | 4.7 | 7.7 | 0.16 | 0.12 | 31.3 |
| Lespedeza | 0.25 | 4.1 | 8.0 | 0.30 | 0.07 | 25.0 |
| Orchard grass, early bloom | 0.24 | 3.0 | 7.5 | 0.06 | 0.09 | 23.5 |
| Orchard grass, midbloom | 0.25 | 2.8 | 9.2 | 0.09 | 0.05 | 27.4 |
| Ryegrass | 0.23 | 4.0 | 4.7 | 0.15 | 0.09 | 22.6 |
| Timothy, early growth | 0.29 | 3.3 | 8.6 | 0.11 | 0.07 | 26.7 |
| Timothy, mid-bloom | 0.07 | 2.7 | 9.8 | 0.11 | 0.09 | 29.2 |

(For more about pasture management and maintenance, see the *USPC C Level Manual*, pages 130–131.)

# Nutrition for Horses at Grass

## Nutritional Value of Pasture

The nutritional value of a pasture depends on many factors, including the variety of grasses and weeds, soil fertility and mineral content, weather, condition of the pasture, the point in the growing cycle, the number of horses, and length of time the pasture has been grazed. Pastures are most nutritious in the spring, when the grass grows quickly and is new, tender, and high in protein, non-structural carbohydrates (NSC), and other nutrients. As the grasses mature, they become more coarse and stemmy, and the nutritional value drops. Pastures that are damaged by overgrazing, high traffic, drought, or flooding, or that are choked with weeds or covered with snow, may have almost no nutritional value. In these cases, supplementary hay and possibly concentrates must be fed. (See the previous table.)

## Seasonal Variations in Care and Feeding of Horses at Grass

Seasonal changes in care and feeding depend on the climate and the part of the country in which you live. In some parts of the country, such as in the South, winter may be a growing season or summer may be a poor grazing season due to lack of rainfall. You must adjust your feeding according to the seasonal changes where you live.

### *Spring*
In the spring, the grass grows quickly and has a high water content, high levels of NSC, and high levels of protein. This lush grass can cause diarrhea and colic in horses that are not used to it. When horses are first turned out on grass, limit their grazing time to an hour a day, and increase it gradually over two to three weeks.

Obese horses, small ponies, and animals that have had previous attacks of laminitis may develop laminitis from overeating lush grass, especially in spring. These horses should also have their grazing time limited, although some may not be able to tolerate any amount of new grass.

As the nutritional value of the pasture increases, supplementary hay feeding can be cut back. Use hay consumption as a guideline; if horses are eating all the hay you give them, they still need it. When they begin to leave hay, it can safely be cut back.

### *Summer*
Salt should be available free choice throughout the year, but it is especially important during hot weather when horses lose salt as they sweat.

Keep track of the condition and nutritional value of the pasture. If it is damaged by drought or overgrazing, or if it becomes choked with weeds, supplementary hay feeding will be necessary. Also, if a pasture is stressed by drought or overgrazing, the percent of NSC in the grass increases, which can put horses with metabolic disorders at risk.

Check water sources daily to be sure they are not dried up.

Horses may be worked harder and more often during the summer. They may need additional concentrates to provide energy for work.

Horses must be dewormed as needed throughout the year to prevent internal damage from parasites, improve digestion and efficient use of feed, and keep pastures from being contaminated with parasite eggs and larvae. (For more about parasite control, see Chapter 14.) Horses at pasture are at greatest risk of parasite infestation as many parasites (for example, small strongyles) are ingested by the horse as it grazes.

### Fall

In temperate and northern regions, the nutritional value of the pasture drops in the late summer and fall as plants and grasses mature and go to seed. Supplementary feeding of hay is often necessary.

When nighttime temperatures drop below 40° F, cool-season grasses store NSC. This can trigger metabolic problems in sensitive horses.

Check pastures for toxic plants. As pasture grasses deteriorate, horses are more likely to eat toxic plants if they are present.

Horses that live outdoors through the winter will do better if they carry a little extra fat in the fall. Horses that are underweight are more severely stressed by wet or cold weather and may be more vulnerable to disease.

### Winter

When pasture grass is covered with snow and of low nutritional value, supplementary feeding of hay is essential. The process of digesting fiber (structural carbohydrates) generates heat and helps horses maintain their body temperature during cold weather.

Horses require more calories to handle the stress of extreme cold or wet weather, especially if they are aged, pregnant, very young, or debilitated. Reduce stress by providing shelter from wind, cold, and rain, and by increasing the energy content of the feed.

Make sure that horses have free access to water during cold weather. This may mean breaking ice twice a day or more often, insulating stock tanks, or using stock tank heaters or heated automatic waterers. Insufficient water intake can result in colic.

Make regular checks of the condition of horses kept on pasture during the winter. Long hair coats may hide the first signs of weight loss. It can be hard to reverse the process of weight loss if you do not notice it early.

## Poisonous Plants

It is important to be able to identify poisonous plants that grow in your area, know when they are most toxic, and recognize the common symptoms of poisoning. Reactions to poisoning vary from very serious consequences, including sudden death, cardiac arrest, or kidney failure, to milder allergic reactions.

Pastures and landscaping around homes and stables should be checked carefully, as many landscaping plants are toxic to horses. Most poisonous plants are not appetizing to horses and they will avoid them if they have other choices. However, they may eat them if there is nothing else readily available, if pastures become poor and overgrazed, or if they are undernourished or have a mineral deficiency. Certain plants (such as locoweed) become addictive once horses develop a taste for them. It is important to check pastures frequently, as weed seeds may be introduced via birds or by the wind. Some plants and trees cause problems in certain situations (for example, when the leaves are wilting or if branches have blown down after storms).

Most toxic plants are native to specific geographic areas, so check with your local agricultural extension service and your veterinarian concerning poisonous plants in your area. You can also find information and pictures of toxic plants on many websites, especially those associated with veterinary programs at major universities and local county agriculture extension services.

### PREVENTING POISONING
- Examine pastures regularly, as plants grow at different times of the year.
- Check fences, hedgerows, landscape plants, and nearby roadsides.
- Promptly remove fallen branches and trees, especially after storms.
- Carefully monitor horses that have gotten loose as they may have eaten toxic plants while off the property.
- Check hay sources for poisonous plants that may get baled into hay.

### GENERAL SIGNS OF POISONING
- Weight loss
- Loss of appetite
- Colic
- Drooling
- Incoordination
- Depression
- Diarrhea

The following table lists some basic information on some common plants that are poisonous to horses, but you will need to research toxic plants common to your area through your Cooperative Extension Services (which can be found online), and keep current so that your animals are safe.

## Chart 13-2: Common Poisonous Plants

| Plant | Where | Description | Symptoms |
|---|---|---|---|
| Lupine (*Digitalis spp.*) | Throughout U.S.—mainly west of Rockies and south; grows wild and in gardens. | 100 varieties in U.S.; single tall stem 1'–4'; leaves palmate (looks like a fan with 7–11 leaflets) ; blue, purple, white pealike flowers. | Affects nervous system: Behavior change; difficulty breathing and moving; depression; incoordination; eventually convulsions and coma; death by respiratory paralysis. Diarrhea. |
| Castor Bean (*Rininus spp.*) | Throughout U.S., especially south and east; wild & cultivars. | Shrublike plant with large umbrella-like leaves that have 5–9 pointed fingerlike lobes; 5'–12' tall; long purple stem attached to center of leaf; green-white flower or red-brown flower in spire; 3-lobed green and red oval seed looks like fat tick. | Colic; bloody diarrhea; incoordination; increased heart rate; fever; sweating; convulsions. Fatal in small amounts. |
| Larkspur (*Delphinium spp.*) | Cultivated and wild; throughout U.S. | Flowers have 5 sepals and 1 is elongated into a spur; 1'–5' tall; thin leaves palmately lobed; usually purple flowers; sometimes palatable. | Incoordination; wide-based stance with arched back; abnormal heart rate; constipation; difficulty breathing; death from cardiac and respiratory failure. |
| Foxglove (*Digitalis spp.*) | Cultivar from Europe. Grows throughout U.S.; wild in west. | 2'–6' tall; oblong thin leaves; tubular hanging flowers; pink, yellow, purple with spots; biennial so reseeds; many varieties. | Weakness; head lowers and becomes edematous; colic; bloody diarrhea; slow heart rate; difficulty breathing. |

| Plant | Where | Description | Symptoms |
|---|---|---|---|
| Privet (*Ligustrum* spp.) | Throughout most of U.S. because of cultivars. Non-native species has become invasive. | 15' tall shrub; simple opposite short evergreen leaves; small white flowers; 1–2 seeded black blueberry-type fruit. | Colic; diarrhea; incoordination; weak pulse; convulsions; death. |
| Laurel (*Kalmia* spp.) | Northern half of U.S. | Many varieties; woody shrub; glossy evergreen leaves; pink flowers. | Colic; salivation; nasal discharge; weakness; muscle tremors; incoordination; increased heart and respiratory rates; ataxia; coma; death. |
| Locoweed-Crazyweed (*Astragulus* spp. or *Oxytropis* spp.) | Western U.S. from Great Plains to Rockies. | 20 toxic varieties that look similar; stem or stemless herb; white, cream, or purple flower; pods; seeds; kidney-bean shape; alternate compound leaves; palatable at certain stages. | Incoordination; bobbing head; depression or nervousness; abortion; weight loss; poor coat; poor vision; salivation; unpredictable signs; possibly addictive. |

# Hay

Hay is the primary source of all nutrients (except water) for many horses. Good-quality hay also provides an adequate amount of fiber and energy, a considerable amount of the horse's protein, macro and micro mineral needs, and vitamins. Much of the carbohydrates in hay are *structural carbohydrates*. Structural carbohydrates (cellulose, hemicelluloses, and lignin) cannot be digested through *enzymatic digestive processes* that allow simple carbohydrates to be absorbed from the small intestine. Instead, these *complex structural carbohydrates* have to be broken down in the large intestine by a population of beneficial microbes including bacteria, protozoa, and fungi in a process known as *bacterial fermentation*. During this process the bacteria release by-products called *volatile fatty acids* (*VFAs*), which are absorbed through the wall of the large intestine into the bloodstream and utilized by the horse as a source of energy. This fermentation process generates heat, so feeding plenty of hay helps horses maintain their body temperature during cold weather.

## Factors Affecting Quality, Palatability, and Nutritional Value of Hay

**Type of hay.** Various plant species contain different levels of nutrients and vary in palatability. For instance, legume hays are higher in protein, energy, and calcium than grass hays.

**Soil and growing conditions.** Plants derive nutrients from the soil in which they grow. Drought, infertile soil, or soil deficient in minerals can affect the quality of hay.

**Stage of plant growth at harvest.** The stage of growth at which plants are harvested determines their maturity and the amount of structural carbohydrate as well as some other nutrients. The more mature the plant, the lesser the nutritional value, the greater the structural carbohydrates, and the more coarse, stemmy, and less palatable the hay will be. For example, early-bloom alfalfa contains approximately 21 percent crude fiber, while late-bloom alfalfa contains about 27 percent. Easy keepers and sedentary horses (those doing light or no work) may benefit from being fed hay that is more mature, while young, growing horses or performance horses need less mature, more easily digestible hay.

**Harvesting and curing.** Properly harvested and cured hay retains most of its nutritional value. Weather damage (for example, being rained on), improper handling, or baling when wet can result in moldy, dusty, or less nutritious hay.

**Moisture level.** Baled hay should have a moisture level of 9 percent to 12 percent. Before cutting, the moisture level is usually 25 to 27 percent or higher; this must be reduced by proper drying. If the hay is baled or stored too damp, it develops mold, which can be toxic to horses. Hay that is excessively dry may suffer from *leaf shatter*, where the leaves crumble and fall off, leaving only the stems. This occurs most commonly in legume hays. Ideally, the leaf-to-stem ratio is at least 1:1. The higher the leaf to stem ratio (the more leaves), the higher the nutrient value of the hay.

**Storage.** Hay stored while damp generates heat, which can lead to spontaneous combustion. Baled hay exposed to inclement weather during storage loses its nutritional value, at least in the outer layers of hay. Heat, overexposure to sunlight, and long periods of storage diminish vitamin levels, especially vitamins A and D.

**Non-nutritious and toxic matter.** Hay must be clean and free from weeds, trash, toxic plants, or foreign objects. Many plants and weeds are poisonous to horses (see the previous section). It is important to check hay for weeds and other foreign objects such as trash and dead

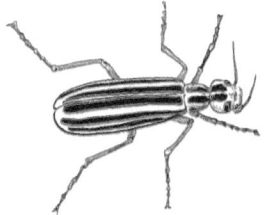

Blister beetle.

animals. Animal carcasses accidentally baled in hay can be a source of botulism, especially in large round bales. Alfalfa hay grown in the South, West, and Southwest must be checked for blister beetles. A single blister beetle can cause inflammation and blistering to your horse's skin within a few hours of contact and if ingested with hay, can cause severe colic.

# Types of Hay

### Grass Hays
*Grass hays* contain more fiber and lower levels of protein than legume hays and provide fewer calories per pound, so they are less likely to be overfed. Therefore, they are a good choice for easy keepers and sedentary horses doing little or no work. Horses that are working harder, growing, or lactating should be fed high-quality grass hay, but it may need to be supplemented with legume hay or concentrate feed to meet those horses' nutritional and energy needs.

There are many different varieties of grass hays grown in different regions of North America; some of the most common are timothy, brome grass, orchard grass, coastal Bermuda grass, and oat hay.

### Legume Hays
The *legume hays* are alfalfa, clover, and birdsfoot trefoil. Legumes are plants that have special roots that capture and store nitrogen in *nodules,* which allow them to produce more protein than grass hays. They have comparably high levels of non-structural carbohydrates which, combined with the higher protein, results in a higher calorie content per pound than grass hay. Alfalfa also contains a significantly higher concentration of calcium than phosphorus, which can make it difficult to correctly balance the calcium-to-phosphorus ratio in diets that include more than 50 percent alfalfa hay. Because of the high calcium content, horses are at increased risk of developing urinary stones if they are fed a diet high in alfalfa.

### Chart 13-3: Types of Hay and Nutritional Values

| Hay | Digestible Energy (Mcal/lb) | Crude Protein % | Ca % | P % |
|---|---|---|---|---|
| Legume hay, immature | 1.00 | 17.3 | 1.31 | 0.26 |
| Legume hay, mid-mature | 0.92 | 17.5 | 1.15 | 0.25 |
| Legume hay, mature | 0.84 | 14.9 | 1.02 | 0.23 |
| Peanut | 0.90 | 10.7 | 1.39 | 0.16 |
| Alfalfa cubes and pellets | 1.09 | 18.5 | 1.52 | 0.24 |
| Grass hay cool season, immature | 0.90 | 15.1 | 0.60 | 0.29 |
| Grass hay cool season, mid-mature | 0.83 | 11.1 | 0.55 | 0.24 |
| Grass hay cool season, mature | 0.78 | 9.1 | 0.40 | 0.22 |
| Oat hay | 0.89 | 8.5 | 0.32 | 0.21 |
| Bermuda grass | 0.94 | 10.7 | 0.49 | 0.20 |
| Grass hay cubes | 0.92 | 12.0 | 0.76 | 0.22 |
| Grass hay pellets | 1.02 | 14.3 | 0.82 | 0.29 |

## Types of Bales

**Small square bales.** Wire bales (65 to 125 pounds) or string bales (35 to 50 pounds) are commonly available and easy to handle. They should be stacked tightly to save space. If the moisture content of the bales is too high, they should be stacked more loosely to let air circulate among bales. Because of their smaller size, it is easier to control their quality, but each batch of hay should be evaluated carefully when it is baled in the field or delivered.

**Round bales.** These are often used to feed horses during the winter or in dry lot management to allow for free-choice feeding. They should be acquired from a trusted source as their quality can be inferior, both nutritionally and in moisture content, to small square bales. There is a slight risk of a horse acquiring botulism from round bales from endemic areas (see Chapter 14). Appropriate farm equipment is necessary to move these large bales around a farm, as 6-feet-tall bales weigh upward of 2,000 pounds. Ideally, round bales should be fed from *horse-safe* round bale feeders or covered in a special net product to reduce waste, as one of the primary disadvantage of round bales is hay wastage. Like small square bales, hay must be properly dried before it is baled in order to reduce mold development. Because of their large size, round bales are often stored outside, which may affect their quality if they are not covered. However, they may be stored uncovered with the outside of the bale being considered as waste and the inside of the bale still containing good-quality hay.

**Large square bales.** These bales weigh less than round bales (up to 1,000 pounds for a 4' × 4' × 8' bale), but they still require appropriate farm equipment to move them around. The hay breaks off in large flakes, as in small square bales; however, one flake from a large square is equivalent to 3 to 6 small square flakes. Because large square bales break into flakes they may be fed a portion at a time, thereby reducing hay wastage. As with round bales, storage can be a challenge.

## Processed Hay

Hay, usually alfalfa, may be processed for ease in storage, handling, and transportation to reduce waste, and to combine it with concentrates for mixed feeds or complete rations. Processing increases digestibility as it increases the surface area on which digestive enzymes and bacteria can act. Processed hay benefits horses with poor *dentition* (teeth) or *malabsorption* (inadequate absorption of nutrients) disorders. However, processing also reduces the amount of time spent eating, which reduces saliva production and the release of buffering substances into the stomach. Reduced time spent chewing may also lead to boredom and stereotypic behaviors such as wood chewing. The more heavily processed the hay, the easier it is to digest and the greater the reduction in chewing.

It is often recommended that hay pellets and cubes be soaked in an equal amount of water for 15 minutes before feeding in order to reduce the risk of choke. (For more information, see the *USPC C Level Manual*, pages 168–169.)

**Cubes (range cubes).** Hay (usually alfalfa) is chopped and run through a press, making cubes about 1½ inches square. Horses fed hay cubes or pellets should have water available to reduce the risk of choke.

**Pellets.** Hay (usually alfalfa) is ground and processed into pellets; often combined with grain as part of a complete pelleted ration. Pellets reduce waste and are convenient to store and transport. As with hay cubes, horses should have water available to reduce the risk of choke.

**Chopped hay, chop, and chaff.** This is a variety of dried forage chopped into small pieces. It is easier to chew and adds fiber to the diet. It can sometimes slow down greedy eaters when mixed with concentrates. (See the *USPC C Level Manual*, page 169.)

**Haylage.** Haylage is produced by immediately storing freshly cut hay in plastic under *anaerobic* (no oxygen) conditions. If ensiled properly, the anaerobic bacteria will ferment the fiber in the hay and produce *volatile fatty acids* (*VFAs*) similar to those produced in the hind gut of the horse. Proper techniques include not compromising the plastic cover and maintaining pH below 4.5. If properly produced, haylage should smell good.

**Silage.** Produced by controlled fermentation of high-moisture forage, often used for cattle feed. Toxins produced in spoiled or moldy silage can be fatal to horses and are hard to detect. Therefore, silage is not recommended as a horse feed.

### Evaluating Hay Quality

| Characteristics of Good-Quality Hay | Signs of Poor-Quality Hay |
| --- | --- |
| Low moisture content (9% to 12%). | Damp. Too-high moisture causes mold and may cause spontaneous combustion. |
| Green in color. | Brown or yellow indicates age or sun bleaching. Gray or black indicates mold. |
| Sweet smelling, like newly cut grass. | Musty, moldy, or fermented odor. |
| Free of mold and dust. | Dusty. Moldy hay is unacceptable. |
| Fine stems, high proportion of leaf to stems. | Coarse, with woody stalks and more stems than leaves. |
| Cut before maturity: grass hays, before seed heads mature; alfalfa, cut early in bloom. | Cut late: Mature seed heads or gone to seed; alfalfa cut late in bloom. |
| Free from weeds, poisonous plants, blister beetles, trash, or foreign objects. | High weed content, poisonous plants, blister beetles, animal carcasses baled in hay. |

Hay samples can be tested in a laboratory to determine the levels of nutrients. For information about hay testing, contact your county extension agent, feed mill, nearest agricultural college, or equine nutritionist.

# Other Roughages

## Beet Pulp

Beet pulp is a by-product process of the sugar from sugar beets. Beet pulp comes either shredded or pelleted; some horses find it less palatable than hay. It is considered a roughage as it is very fibrous. Beet pulp has a similar nutrient profile to grass hay, with comparable digestible energy, 10 percent crude protein, higher calcium (0.4 percent), and lower phosphorus (0.2 percent). The calcium-to-phosphorus ratio is similar to that of grass hay, about 2:1. Beet pulp is highly digestible compared to long-stemmed hay. It's an alternative for horses that may need extra energy, to gain weight, or that require a dust-free feed for diseases such as heaves or allergies.

Beet pulp is considered to be low in non-structural carbohydrates because most of the sugar is removed during the processing, although this varies by each company's processing of the sugar beet. Beet pulp that has not had molasses added is a very good source of extra calories for horses and ponies with metabolic issues such as *pituitary pars intermedia dysfunction* or *Equine Cushings* (see Chapter 14).

Eating dry beet pulp may cause choke. Shredded beet pulp should be soaked with an equal amount of water (1 part water to 1 part beet pulp) until all water has been absorbed. This generally takes 12 hours or overnight if you're using tap water or 1 to 2 hours if you're using boiling water. The soaked beet pulp should be kept in a cool place and consumed within 12 hours. Pelleted beet pulp requires three times as much water (3 parts water to 1 part beet pulp). When feeding soaked beet pulp, take care that it does not ferment, especially in the summer, by keeping at a temperature lower than 80° F. Beet pulp that has started to ferment may smell like vinegar.

## Fruit Pomace

Citrus pulps are the pulp (peel, pit, and seed) from citrus fruits after the juices and sugars are extracted. Limestone is added to remove the acid from the pulp, and it is dried and pelleted. These pulps are similar to beet pulp and other roughages, providing energy to the horse in the form of fiber.

# Concentrates

Concentrates are either feeds that are relatively high in energy and low in fiber, which includes grains, mixed, or processed feeds, or concentrated sources of one or more of the five nutrients, excluding water.

## Cereal Grains

Different types of *cereal grains* are commonly added to rations fed to horses. They have several characteristics in common other than their relatively higher energy content. They all contain large amounts of non-structural carbohydrates in the form of *starch,* which is digested and absorbed in the small intestine. Starch availability differs with the type of grain (oat starch is the most digestible). Any starch not absorbed in the small intestine (where it should be) will reach the hind gut, where it can disrupt microbial fermentation and lead to issues such as colic or diarrhea, and indirectly to laminitis. Diets high in cereal grains also predispose horses to developing gastric ulcers (see Chapter 14). For these reasons, grain must be carefully added to the ration and, as a general rule, should never be fed in quantities greater than 0.5 percent of body weight at any one meal (for example, 5.5 pounds for a 1,100-pound horse).

Grains also contain more phosphorus than calcium, which can impact the calcium-to-phosphorus ratio if grains are fed as a large percentage of the whole diet. If the calcium-to-phosphorus ratio is severely inverted (phosphorus is significantly higher than calcium), bone disorders may develop because the regulation of calcium in the blood is more important than phosphorus. When the blood calcium level is low and the phosphorus level is high, calcium is removed from the bones at the expense of the structure of the bones.

Grains are often processed (rolled, crimped, steamed, or flaked) to improve the availability of the nutrients. Rolling and crimping change particle size, increasing the surface area on which digestive enzymes can work, to increase digestibility. Processing with heat affects the structure of the starch within the grain, making it more digestible, but may result in a shorter shelf life.

## Oats

Oats are the most widely fed horse grain in North America. Oats contain more fiber (9 percent) and less concentrated nutrients than most other grains, which makes them less easy to overfeed. They also have a better amino acid profile and higher fat content than other grains commonly fed to horses. Oats are quite palatable and generally contain about 9 to 12 percent protein and 1.3 Mcal energy per pound.

Oats should be clean, plump, and heavy. Good-quality oats weigh 32 to 40 pounds per bushel. Avoid dusty oats or oats containing small black kernels that resemble mouse droppings, as they may be contaminated with ergot, a fungus that can be toxic to horses. Oats should be stored 3 to 4 months after harvest to allow nitrogen levels to drop before feeding.

Oats may be fed whole, crimped (slightly crushed), or rolled (flattened). Crimping or rolling may improve digestibility for very young or aged horses whose teeth may be less able to break the oat husks, which is important to allow digestive enzymes access to the kernel.

## Barley

Barley is similar to oats in nutritional value but is lower in fiber (6 percent) and somewhat more concentrated. Barley contains about 10 to 14 percent protein and 1.55 to 1.75 Mcal energy per pound.

Because barley kernels are harder than those of oats, it should be rolled (slightly crushed). Barley starch is not easily digestible unless it is heat-treated; therefore, it should be steamed or cooked during processing to reduce the risk of undigested starch reaching the hind gut.

Good-quality whole barley weighs approximately 48 pounds per bushel and rolled barley weighs about 40 pounds per bushel. Like oats, kernels should be plump, heavy, sweet-smelling, and free from dust. Barley is a heavier feed than oats; therefore, it should be fed by weight, not volume.

## Corn

Corn is the most energy-dense of the cereal grains. It is a rather poor source of protein, generally containing less than 10 percent, but a good source of energy, containing 1.7 to 1.8 Mcal energy per pound. It contains significant amounts of carotene. Corn is low in *lysine*, an essential amino acid.

Corn comes in various forms, but it should be ground or heat processed (for example, steam-flaked) to ensure proper digestion of the starch. Cracking is not an adequate form of processing for horses as it does not improve nutrient availability. Whole-ear ground corn contains the ground cobs as well as the grain, so it contains more fiber and reduces the energy per pound to about 1.3 Mcal.

Good-quality corn is plump, clean, firm, dry, and weighs about 56 pounds per bushel. The moisture content should be below 14 percent. It should smell sweet, not musty, and should not have black spots or feel sticky or oily. Corn should be checked under ultraviolet light at the feed mill for evidence of mold, often referred to as *mycotoxins*. The mycotoxin *fumonisin* (a poisonous substance produced by fungus) can cause moldy corn disease, which can cause serious neurologic symptoms and death.

In the past, some horse owners believed that corn was a "hot" feed and would cause horses to sweat, especially if fed in hot weather. This is not true; however, corn is highly concentrated and hence can easily be overfed. Overfeeding corn (or any other grain) can cause a horse to become overweight, which can itself lead to excessive sweating. More importantly, overfeeding corn may predispose horses to metabolic diseases, such as insulin resistance.

## Grain By-Products

### Wheat Bran

Wheat bran is the ground-up outer coating of wheat kernels. It contains about 15.5 to 19.5 percent protein and 1.25 to 1.6 Mcal energy per pound. Often considered a source of fiber, it actually contains only 10 to 12 percent crude fiber, which is considerably less than other sources such as beet pulp and hay. However, wheat bran is a good source of B vitamins and is high in energy. Wheat bran is very high in phosphorus and low in calcium. Feeding large amounts of bran can cause overfeeding of phosphorus, which makes it impossible for the horse to utilize calcium and leads to *calcium deficiency disease* ("Big Head" or "Bran" disease). For this reason, bran should make up no more than 10 percent of the total ration.

Wheat bran is often fed as a laxative in the form of a mash made with boiling water. Enough water is added to create the desired consistency (similar to oatmeal) and the mixture is then covered and left to steep for about 15 minutes. Prior to feeding, other ingredients that may tempt the horse to eat are added, such as salt and chopped apples and carrots. The laxative properties of a bran mash may not be due to the bran itself, but rather digestive upset caused by a sudden change of diet. Despite this potentially negative side effect, feeding a bran mash can be a useful tool for temping picky eaters.

Good bran is light, flaky, and free-flowing. It should not contain dust, clumps, or cobweb-like strands (evidence of weevils) or smell musty.

### Rice Bran

Rice bran is high in fat (approx. 20 percent) and contains a similar amount of starch to wheat bran. It provides about 1.4 Mcal of energy per pound and 14 percent crude protein. Like wheat bran, rice bran is exceptionally high in phosphorus and low in calcium. In order to make it safer to feed, commercial rice bran products often contain added calcium. They are also commonly stabilized to increase shelf life and reduce the risk of becoming rancid, which reduces palatability and can cause digestive upset.

### Brewers Grains

Brewers grains (corn, rye, or barley) are by-products of the process of distilling alcohol or brewing beer. They usually contain about 27 to 29 percent protein and about 1.25 Mcal energy per pound. They are a good source of nutrients from which bacteria make B vitamins, and often contain remnants of the yeast used to brew the beer, which may serve as type of probiotic for the horse's microbial flora in the large intestine.

Brewers grains are usually found as a component of commercially mixed feeds or pelleted rations and are rarely fed alone. They are used as a source of protein and are quite palatable to horses.

### *Fats, Oils, and Meals*

Fats are frequently included in rations as a source of energy as they provide 2.25 times more energy per pound than an equal amount of digestible starch. Although a horse's natural diet is relatively low in fat, horses can absorb up to 90 percent of the fat added to their diet. However, the total percentage of calories from fat added to the diet should not exceed 20 percent, or more than three cups of oil. Fats are a safe way to increase the calories in the ration, especially for horses suffering from metabolic problems.

Fats are typically added to rations in the form of oil or a high-fat ingredient such as flax or rice bran. Feeding diets high in fat makes it easier to meet the horse's energy needs with less volume of feed. However, oils provide no additional protein, vitamins, or minerals, so a reduction in total feed intake can result in protein, mineral, and vitamin deficiencies. When feeding fats and oils, it is especially important to balance the ration and ensure that all the horse's nutritional needs are being met.

Common plant-based oils fed to horses include corn oil, soybean oil, and canola oil. Plant-based oils are ground from the seeds of the plant. While corn oil is the most palatable, it is not the best form of oil for horse rations because of its high *omega-6 fatty acid* content and lack of *omega-3 fatty acids*. Soybean and canola oils are also high in omega-6 fatty acids, but they do provide a small amount of omega-3 fatty acids. For this reason they are the preferred oils used in premium horse feeds.

Fat should be introduced into the diet slowly (over a period of 7 to 10 days) as a sudden introduction of large amounts of fat can cause loose and oily manure. In addition, because horses do not have a bile duct, changes in bile production, as required to process increased fats in the diet, takes time (up to 6 months).

**Soybean meal** comes from ground soybeans. It provides 1.6 Mcal of energy per pound and is an excellent source of protein (44 to 48 percent), containing a relatively large proportion of the essential amino acid lysine. It is commonly added to commercial feeds to improve the amino acid profile, especially in feeds for growing horses whose growth rate may be negatively impacted if lysine is deficient.

**Cottonseed meal** comes from ground cottonseed. While it provides 1.4 Mcal of energy per pound and is 36 to 48 percent crude protein, it is not commonly included in horse feeds because the amino acid profile is inferior compared to other protein sources, such as soybean meal.

**Flaxseed or linseed** comes from the same oilseed (flax) but differs in how it has been processed. The raw flaxseeds contain about 40 percent fat and 35 percent crude protein. The meal is what remains after the fat has been removed and it is fed solely as a protein source.

Flax is generally fed for its fat content and, in particular, its high omega-3 fatty acid content. This form of fatty acid is abundant in fresh forage but not in hay, so horses on a hay, grain, and concentrate diet benefit from a supplemental source of omega-3 fatty acids. Omega-3 fatty acids have anti-inflammatory properties, which benefit horses doing hard work or those that suffer from inflammatory conditions.

About 3 to 4 ounces of whole flaxseeds can be fed each day. It is best to grind the seeds immediately prior to feeding. A coffee grinder works well for this. If left whole, the seeds pass through the horse, providing less nutritional value. Traditionally, flaxseeds were soaked or cooked in boiling water to form a thick, gelatinous soup, but this is no longer recommended because flax contains *neurotoxic cyanogenic glycosides* that form *cyanide* when exposed to water or air. This is why the seeds should be ground immediately prior to feeding. Commercially ground forms of flax that have been stabilized to prevent the formation of cyanide are also available.

**Canola meal** comes from ground rapeseed and contains about 35 to 44 percent crude protein. Its amino acid profile is similar to soybean meal, although with slightly less lysine and more methionine. This makes it a suitable protein supplement to feed to all classes of horses.

### Other Feed Components

**Alfalfa meal and pellets.** Alfalfa meal not only provides a source of roughage to commercial rations, but is also added for its moderately high protein content (approximately 15 to 17 percent). Ground and pelleted alfalfa is often added to commercially mixed feeds and is pazrticularly common in complete senior horse feeds. These feeds are formulated to provide all the necessary roughage in the diet for older horses with poor teeth. It is not suitable as the sole source of protein for young growing horses as it does not contain adequate lysine to support growth. It provides approximately 1 Mcal of energy per pound, which is similar to alfalfa hay. As with alfalfa hay, the calcium content (1.3 to 1.4 percent) is high relative to phosphorus, which makes it a good choice when balancing rations containing high phosphorus grains.

**Molasses.** Molasses is a by-product of the processing of sugar cane or sugar beets. It is used to sweeten feeds, making them more palatable to horses, and to reduce dust in feeds. Molasses is typically mixed with water and/or oil but supplies little or no energy, protein, or phosphorus.

Cane molasses is a good source of calcium. Molasses can be added to feed in dry or syrup form.

## Chart 13-4: Types of Concentrates and Nutritional Values

| Concentrate | DE (Mcal/lb) | Crude Protein % | Ca % | P % | Fat % |
|---|---|---|---|---|---|
| ENERGY FEEDS: GRAINS | | | | | |
| Barley, rolled | 1.52 | 11.3 | 0.05 | 0.35 | 2.0 |
| Corn, steam-flaked | 1.55 | 8.3 | 0.04 | 0.26 | 3.7 |
| Oats, rolled | 1.34 | 11.9 | 0.10 | 0.36 | 4.6 |
| ENERGY FEEDS: GRAIN BY-PRODUCTS | | | | | |
| Wheat bran | 1.30 | 15.4 | 0.12 | 1.05 | 3.8 |
| Rice bran | 1.38 | 14.0 | 0.06 | 1.61 | 13.8 |
| Brewers dried grains | 1.17 | 26.5 | 0.27 | 0.61 | 4.7 |
| Beet pulp | 1.2 | 9.4 | 0.94 | 0.08 | 1.3 |
| ENERGY FEEDS: FATS AND OILS | | | | | |
| Vegetable oil | 4.12 | 0 | 0 | 0 | 0 |
| PROTEIN FEEDS | | | | | |
| Alfalfa meal 17% CP | 1.00 | 17.3 | 1.33 | 0.25 | 2.2 |
| Soybean meal 44% CP | 1.42 | 44.4 | 0.36 | 0.63 | 1.4 |
| CALCIUM AND PHOSPHORUS SUPPLEMENTS | | | | | |
| Dicalcium phosphate | 0 | 0 | 22.00 | 19.3 | 0 |
| Monosodium phosphate | 0 | 0 | 0 | 22.5 | 0 |
| Calcium carbonate | 0 | 0 | 39.39 | 0 | 0 |

# Mixed Feeds and Processed Feeds

Commercially mixed feeds are formulated with different levels of nutrients for different purposes. There are mixed feeds with various levels of protein and energy, formulated to be fed in combination with forage, or complete feeds that contain the forage portion of the diet as well as the concentrate portion. When choosing a commercial feed, check the feed label and manufacturer's information detailing the type of feed, its intended purpose, nutrient levels, and feeding directions.

Feeds intended for cattle, hogs, and other livestock should not be used for horses. Some livestock and cattle feeds may contain drugs such as *monensin* or other antibiotics, which can be toxic to horses.

## Types of Processing

**Pelleted feeds** consist of feed ingredients that are ground and pressed into pellets. They may be mixed-ingredient pellets, hay pellets, or pelleted supplements. Pellets prevent the horse from sorting out the ingredients and eating only some and leaving others. They increase the efficiency with which the feed is digested.

**Extruded feeds** are similar to pelleted feeds in that ingredients are ground, but then they are *extruded* by cooking them at high temperatures under steam pressure, and then forced through a machine with small holes (a *dye*), which makes the feed product look similar to kibbled dog food. The heating process makes some components, such as starch, more easily digestible and increases the surface area to further improve digestibility. Extruded feed has greater volume and is less dense than pellets or grains, so it takes a horse longer to consume the same level of nutrients, reducing overeating.

**Ration balancers** are now offered by many feed companies. Ration balancers are pelleted feed that has a small recommended serving size (1 to 2 pounds per day). They are formulated to complement diets based on forage as the primary calorie source by providing quality protein, vitamins, and minerals that are often lacking in a forage diet. Ration balancers have a range of uses, including for horses that are able to maintain themselves on forage alone but need a source of additional trace minerals and vitamins, performance horses being fed straight grains (not pelleted or processed) as their primary energy source, or whenever a horse is fed a commercial mixed feed at levels below the manufacturer's recommended daily intake.

## Types of Processed Feeds

**Pelleted complete feed** contains both grain and roughage (usually alfalfa, sometimes beet pulp) ground and pelleted. It is fully balanced to provide all required nutrients to maintain a horse that does not eat hay. It is most commonly used to feed senior horses that cannot adequately chew hay as a primary source of calories. It may also be used when a diet requires less bulk from roughage for various medical reasons (for example, following colic surgery).

**Textured feeds** are loose mixes that include a variety of ingredients such as oats, beet pulp, soybean hulls, wheat middlings, and/or alfalfa meal. They often contain pellets with added protein, vitamins, and minerals. There are different textured feeds for a range of purposes, from feeds for growing horses to performance blends and senior feeds.

Often these mixes are referred to as *sweet feeds* because traditionally they contain molasses, which increases palatability, reduces dust, and adds calories. Textured feeds still frequently contain molasses, although the amount has been reduced in most products due to a desire to reduce the overall starch and sugar content of many equine rations. The protein and other nutrient content of the feed depends on the specific mix.

Sweet feeds attract flies, so feed tubs should be kept clean and spilled feed cleaned up promptly.

## Feed Label Information

Commercial feeds and supplements are required by state law to provide specific information on the feed tag or label. This is where the most useful information about the feed may be found. Examine feed labels when making purchasing decisions. The information may differ by state, but in general, the following information is required:

- Product name and manufacturer
- Purpose statement and feeding directions
- Guaranteed analysis, feed ingredients, net weight
- Active drug ingredients, precautionary statement
- Company name and mailing address

The guaranteed analysis must indicate the minimum percentages of crude protein and fat and the maximum percentage of crude fiber. Vitamin and mineral levels are not required to be listed unless specific claims are made on the label, or the mineral content exceeds specified levels.

Ingredients should be listed in order of highest concentration to lowest concentration. This means that the first ingredient on the list is included in the feed in a greater amount than the second ingredient, and so on down the list.

Ingredients may be named by their common names in one of two ways. Some states require that each ingredient be named precisely—for example, oats, barley, or corn. This results in a *fixed formula/fixed ingredient feed*. The ingredients are exactly the same from one bag to another, which means the cost to the consumer may increase if ingredient costs increase. However, other states allow the use of *collective terms* such as "grain products," "plant protein products," or "processed grain by-products," among others.

The use of collective terms allows manufacturers to take advantage of computer formulation and use alternative ingredients to provide the same levels of nutrients while keeping production costs down. This is known as *least cost ration formulation*. The exact ingredients in different bags or batches of feed may differ, although the guaranteed nutrient levels remain the same. Some manufacturers provide fixed formula/fixed ingredient feeds even in states that allow the use of collective terms.

Feeding directions on feed tags are not standardized and may be stated in a number of ways; for example, as the total number of pounds to be fed by body weight and work level, a certain amount per 100 pounds of body weight, or a percentage of body weight. It is important to follow these feeding directions to be sure that your horse is getting all the nutrients he needs. Feeding less than the recommended amount may result in nutritional deficiencies, while feeding more could lead to excesses. If feeding a product at the recommended amount causes a horse to gain too much weight or

Example of feed label.

| Scientifically formulated for mature horses in heavy work | |
|---|---|
| GUARANTEED ANALYSIS | |
| Crude Protein, Minimum | 14.00% |
| Lysine, Minimum | 0.76% |
| Methionine, Minimum | 0.24% |
| Threonine, Minimum | 0.53% |
| Crude Fat, Minimum | 14.00% |
| *NSC (Starch and Sugar) | 23.00% |
| Crude Fiber, Maximum | 14.00% |
| Calcium, Minimum          0.6% Maximum | 1.10% |
| Phosphorus, Minimum | 0.50% |
| Potassium, Minimum | 0.90% |
| Copper, Minimum | 50 ppm |
| Selenium, Minimum | 0.6 ppm |
| Zinc, Minimum | 130 ppm |
| Vitamin A, Minimum | 7000 IU/lb |
| Vitamin D, Minimum | 700 IU/lb |
| Vitamin E, Minimum | 200 IU/lb |
| Ascorbic Acid (Vitamin C), Minimum | 50 IU/lb |
| Biotin, Minimum | 400 mcg/lb |
| Omega 6 Fatty Acids, Minimum | 6.55% |
| Omega 3 Fatty Acids, Minimum | 1.35% |

(* Not recognized by AAFCO as an essential nutrient.)

**INGREDIENTS**
Wheat Middlings, Soybean Hulls, Heat Processed Soybeans, Ground Corn, Oat Mill By-Product, Dried Beet Pulp, Heat Processed Wheat, Dehydrated Alfalfa Meal, Heat Processed Flaxseed, Soybean Meal, Whole Oats, Brewers Rice, L-Lysine, DL Methionine, Cane Molasses, Vegetable Oil, Calcium Carbonate, Calcium Phosphate, Salt, Potassium Chloride, Potassium Sulfate, Magnesium Sulfate, Magnesium Oxide, Manganous Oxide, Ferrous Sulfate, Copper Sulfate, Zinc Sulfate, Manganese Proteinate, Iron Proteinate, Copper Proteinate, Zinc Proteinate, Cobalt Sulfate, Ethylenediamine Dihydriodide, Calcium Iodate, Selenium Yeast, Sodium Selenite, *Saccharomyces cerevisiae* Yeast Culture, Brewers Dried Yeast, Vegetable Fat Product (Feed Grade), Lecithin, Glycerin, Phosphoric Acid, Proprionic Acid, Sodium Benzoate, Sulfuric Acid, Vitamin A Supplement, Vitamin D3 Supplement, Vitamin E Supplement, Niacin, Riboflavin, d-Calcium Pantothenate, Pyridoxine Hydrochloride, Folic Acid, Biotin, Thiamine Mononitrate, Vitamin B12, Choline Chloride, Ascorbyl-2-Polyphosphate, Anise Flavor.

become unmanageable, choose a different feed with a smaller recommended daily serving size.

Because the actual ingredients can vary from one batch of feed to another, it is nearly impossible for the horse owner to evaluate the quality of grains used in commercially processed feeds. Therefore, it makes sense to buy from a feed company that has a good reputation for quality control.

Further information on commercial feeds, ingredients, and nutrition recommendations is available from feed companies, feed stores, and feed salespersons. Other sources of information are county agents, Cooperative Extension services, agricultural colleges, and equine nutritionists.

# Supplements

Feed supplements are concentrated substances that are added to a ration to make up for a deficiency in a specific nutrient.

Supplements add to the cost of feeding and can cause problems if they are overfed. Feeding more than one supplement or feeding excessive doses of any supplement can result in excessive levels of vitamins, minerals, or protein.

Supplements may be helpful when feeding lower-quality hay or pasture is unavoidable (for example, under drought conditions, when hay has been stored for a year or longer, or when it is impossible to obtain good-quality, green hay) or for horses under stress. You should check the nutritional balance of the ration and consult your veterinarian or an equine nutritionist prior to starting a horse on supplements.

## Types of Supplements

**Ration balancing supplements.** These are similar to ration balancer feeds in that they provide a concentrated source of key nutrients, typically a mix of vitamins and minerals, in an even smaller serving size than ration balancer feeds (often as little as 3 to 6 ounces per day). This makes them beneficial for use with very easy keepers, where even the relatively low calorie content of a ration balancer may provide too many additional calories. They may contain a range of other beneficial ingredients in addition to minerals and vitamins, such as yeast and biotin.

**Vitamin supplements.** The fat-soluble vitamins A, D, and K rarely require supplementation as they are available in normal horse feeds or made by the horse.

Vitamin E supplementation may be necessary for horses with limited access to fresh pasture, especially those doing hard work or broodmares in their last trimester of pregnancy. Supplemental vitamin E should be in the form of *natural d-alpha tocopherol* to ensure maximum absorption. The average horse may be supplemented with approximately 2,000 IU per day. Horses suffering from tying up or neurological conditions may require higher doses; consult your veterinarian or equine nutritionist. If you select a vitamin E supplement that also contains selenium, take care that it does not cause an excess of selenium in the ration.

Fat-soluble vitamin supplements come in various forms (pellets, powders, and liquids) that should be stored away from exposure to heat, light, and air as these can cause deterioration. They have a shelf life of approximately 30 to 60 days.

As B vitamins are created by the bacteria in the horse's hind gut, their supplementation is rarely necessary. However, if hind gut fermentation is functioning less than optimally, supplementation of B vitamins may be beneficial, especially in senior horses, those that are not maintaining weight, or horses doing intense work.

**Mineral supplements.** Individual minerals are available for purchase to correct deficiencies and imbalances in the ration. The most common are forms of calcium and phosphorus, such as *calcium carbonate* (*limestone*) and *dicalcium phosphate*, or forms of magnesium, such as *magnesium oxide* and *magnesium sulfate*. Trace minerals are typically provided by broad spectrum supplements, which contain multiple minerals in one supplement. However, in areas where selenium is deficient in the soil, a supplemental source may be recommended by your veterinarian.

Mineral imbalances and overdoses can cause serious problems, so mineral supplementation should not be undertaken without checking the mineral levels supplied in the ration, including commercial and locally grown feeds, and obtaining the advice of your veterinarian or an equine nutritionist.

**Electrolytes.** Electrolytes are *mineral salts* (forms of sodium, chloride, potassium, calcium, and magnesium) that help to maintain the correct fluid balance (called *osmolarity*) in the blood. Heavy sweating, especially during hard work in hot weather, may cause horses to lose large amounts of electrolytes, which need to be replaced.

Electrolyte supplements should match the concentration of electrolytes found in sweat, including 5.3 g chloride, 2.8 g sodium, 1.4 g potassium, 0.12 g calcium, and 0.05 g magnesium per liter of sweat. The first ingredient in many commercial products is *dextrose* (sugar), sometimes in amounts greater than 15 percent. Dextrose is added to improve palatability and aid in the passage of sodium out of the digestive tract. However, when it is included at more than 15 percent, there will not be enough chloride provided in the product to meet the horse's needs. Ideally, the product should be at least 45 percent chloride and the *sodium:potassium:chloride ratio* should be similar to that of sweat (2:1:3.8).

Electrolytes are best offered added to water and mixed according to the manufacturer's directions. Plain water should also be offered as some horses refuse to drink electrolyte water and may become dehydrated. Ask your veterinarian for advice before giving electrolytes. (For more about electrolytes, see Chapter 12, "Conditioning and Exercise Physiology.")

**Protein supplements.** These are sometimes helpful for horses with increased need for protein, such as weanlings and yearlings, pregnant and lactating mares, aged horses, horses doing hard work, and horses under stress. Protein supplements include vegetable protein sources (such as soybean meal, oilseed meals, and legume meals) and milk protein (dried skimmed milk or milk replacers). Amino acid supplements that provide the most commonly lacking essential amino acids, such as lysine and methionine, are also available.

Avoid feeding excess protein. Horses fed excessive protein have been shown to have poorer performance due, in part, to increased heat production.

**Fat supplements.** These serve as a source of concentrated calories to promote weight gain without increasing bulk in the ration. Their supplementation also promotes healthy skin and a shiny hair coat through the production of *sebum* or skin oils.

Traditionally, corn oil has been used as a cheap and readily available fat supplement, but it provides only omega-6 fatty acids and no omega-3 fatty acids. Both forms of fatty acids are essential nutrients and must be provided in the horse's diet. However, omega-6 fatty acids are considered to be pro-inflammatory, while omega-3 fatty acids are considered to be anti-inflammatory. The horse's natural diet of fresh forage is higher in omega-3 fatty acids than omega-6 fatty acids. Canola oil or soybean oil is preferred to corn oil because, while either is still high in omega-6 fatty acids, it also provides some omega-3 fatty acids. Flax is commonly added to rations to ensure adequate omega-3 fatty acids in the diet (for more information on feeding flaxseed, see page 461).

Regardless of the source, fats can turn rancid and lose their palatability if stored too long or exposed to heat and light.

**Calming supplements.** Calming supplements have become increasingly popular for horses that are nervous and spooky, especially under saddle. Common ingredients in calming supplements include magnesium, vitamin $B_1$ (thiamine), the amino acid L-tryptophan, and herbs such as valerian and red raspberry leaf.

Before using a calming supplement, you should eliminate all potential physical causes for poor behavior, such as ill-fitting tack, pain, or lameness. Additionally, eliminate the way the horse is managed and fed.

Little, if any, research is currently available on calming supplements, although magnesium deficiency has been linked to nervousness and spooky behavior, and L-trypotophan is known to be a precursor to the hormone *serotonin,* which increases the feeling of well-being and contentment. Herbs such as valerian and red raspberry leaf are believed to even out hormonal fluctuations and reduce muscle tension and cramping, so they are sometimes used with mares.

Take care when selecting a calming supplement, as some ingredients such as valerian may be banned by some competitive disciplines and will test positive on a drug test. It is important to consult the drug rules if you are considering using a calming supplement for a horse that is showing or competing. Which ingredients, if any, will work for an individual horse depends on that horse, and success can vary between horses.

**Hoof supplements.** Most horses should be able to grow healthy hooves with a correctly balanced diet that provides adequate protein, trace minerals, and fatty acids. However, some individuals need additional help in the form of a hoof supplement. These supplements provide nutrients required for healthy hoof growth: the essential amino acid *methionine*, the B vitamin *biotin*, the trace minerals *zinc* and *copper*, and a source of fatty acids such as *lecithin*.

Methionine contains sulfur, required for the formation of the cross linkages between the fibers in the hoof, which makes the hoof strong and flexible. Zinc is required for *keratin* formation, a protein that increases the hoof's hardness. Long-term biotin supplementation over many months has been shown to improve hoof health in horses with previously poor hooves. Fatty acids may improve the moisture content of the hoof as well as its pliability, so hoof supplements may provide fatty acids from various sources, including flax and soy.

It can take many months to see an improvement in hoof health, even when using a quality hoof supplement.

**Digestive aids.** Digestive aids are broadly defined as either *prebiotics* or *probiotics*. They may be included as a regular part of the horse's daily diet as an ingredient in the feed or given as a supplement, or they may be administered in response to a specific incident (for example, after deworming or giving antibiotics).

Prebiotics are products with non-digestible food ingredients that benefit the horse by providing beneficial substrates for certain beneficial types of bacteria residing in the horse's intestinal tract. These specific bacteria (*lactic acid bacteria*) are able to utilize these ingredients for their own growth in order to support a healthy microbial population, which in turn aids the horse's ability to fully utilize his diet. Examples of prebiotics include *Fructo-oligosaccharides (FOS)* and *Mannanoligosaccharides (MOS)*. There is some evidence that prebiotics may help support the immune system and intestinal function.

Probiotics are *live microbial cultures*. Lactic acid bacteria (such as *Lactobacillus acidophilus* and *Streptococcus faecium*) and *Bacillus subtilis* are commonly included bacteria. Fungi such as *Aspergillus* and yeast strains such as *Saccharomyces cerevisiae* may also be included. When included in feeds or given daily as supplements, probiotics reintroduce beneficial strains of microbes that may otherwise become depleted during various digestive disturbances, thus improving the utilization of the overall diet.

Most healthy horses do not need probiotics. However, they may be beneficial for horses having trouble with weight gain, older horses, horses on antibiotic therapy, those in stressful situations, and those with a history of diarrhea or colic. Specifically, yeasts have been shown to improve milk production when fed to lactating mares and improve performance in growing young stock.

**Joint supplements.** Oral joint supplements are nutraceuticals given for both prevention and treatment of joint problems. While controlled scientific data on the effectiveness of joint supplements is limited and sometimes conflicting, a large body of anecdotal evidence suggests that these supplements may benefit some horses. Many joint supplements such as chondroitin sulfate have low *bioavailability,* meaning they are not absorbed well in the intestine. It is important that oral joint supplements contain a sufficient amount of their active ingredient in order to have any beneficial effects. See Chapter 14 for more information on specific joint supplements.

**Nutraceuticals.** *Nutraceutical* combines the words *nutrient* and *pharmaceutical*. This is a growing field with a broad list of products and a broad array of claims. Most of these claims are made without proper data to support the product's safety or efficacy. Nutraceuticals are not really food or drugs, so they don't fall under any the regulations of either. Therefore, there is no regulation of their claims of effectiveness, how they list their ingredients, or their guaranteed analysis. They contain natural products, but they may or may not be safe. Doubling the dose doesn't give you twice the benefit, and it could be toxic.

Some examples of nutraceuticals are Methylsulfonylmethane (MSM), chondroitin sulfate, glucosamine, glucosamine hydrochloride, sodium hyaluronate, gamma oryzanol, beta-hydroxy beta-methyl butyrate (HMB), N-dimethylglycine (DMG), garlic, echinacea, devil's claw, nettles, yucca, willow bark, black cohosh, and valerian. It would be wise to discuss their use, and any interactions these may have with other medications your horse may be taking, with your veterinarian. If your horse is showing or competing, check the governing body's drug rules, as some of these substances are banned in certain organizations and could result in a positive drug test.

# Feeding Different Ages and Types of Horses

Horses' nutritional needs differ according to their age, work level, and other special circumstances like pregnancy or lactation. Nutritional charts and recommendations are only guidelines that include a range of estimated nutritional requirements. Each horse must be fed as an individual, adapting the feeding program to meet his needs, which may change from week to week or even daily. There is no substitute for close observation of each individual horse and intelligent application of basic feeding principles.

# Factors to Consider When Adjusting the Daily Ration

**Current condition.** Does the horse need to maintain his present weight, put on weight, or lose weight? Is he getting fit, maintaining fitness, or letting down? A horse's current condition is best assessed using the body condition scale (see the *USPC C Level Manual*, pages 223–224). A horse that is overweight will need to consume fewer calories, expend more calories through increased work, or both. A horse with a lower-than-ideal body score should have his caloric intake increased. Your veterinarian or equine nutritionist can help you determine how best to alter the ration to achieve the ideal condition for an individual horse.

**Physical type.** Tall, lean, "rangy" horses usually require more feed per 100 pounds of body weight than compact, chunky, "easy keepers." Small ponies and certain individuals are prone to becoming overweight and need their feed intake carefully monitored to prevent the development of metabolic disease.

**Temperament.** Is the horse high-strung and nervous, aggressive, or lazy? Feeding high-energy feeds can affect behavior and rideability, especially for school horses, small ponies, miniature horses, or horses ridden by inexperienced riders.

**Appetite and feeding behavior.** Some horses have excessive appetites and need their feed intake controlled to prevent too much weight gain. Shy feeders may refuse to eat if they are intimidated by other horses or disturbances. Picky eaters should be encouraged to eat by providing the most palatable feed frequently, in small amounts.

**Health.** Horses that are ill, debilitated, or confined to a stall for long periods need special feeding. Follow your veterinarian's recommendations.

**How the horse is kept.** Horses kept stabled, stabled with some paddock turnout, at grass, or in a dry lot require different feeding. In addition, the management of how feed is provided must be considered (for example, feed on the ground or in a plastic feed bin) for each management scenario.

**Daily work variations.** The grain ration need not be cut back on a rest day, unless a horse is receiving a large grain ration or is predisposed to *Recurrent Exertional Rhabdomyolysis* (*RER*). If the grain is cut back, the horse should receive extra roughage—about 3 pounds of grass hay for every pound of grain cut from his regular ration.

**Seasonal variations.** Horses need more energy, provided in the form of non-structural carbohydrates, in order to maintain their body heat during cold weather. The amount of work and turnout time may vary according to the season and climate, so the feeding program should be adjusted accordingly.

## Guidelines for Feeding Horses

**Mature idle horses and ponies (maintenance ration).** A maintenance ration is one that maintains the horse at his current health and condition without allowing for additional needs such as work or growth. It contains enough protein for maintenance of body tissues and sufficient energy, vitamins, and minerals for normal body functions.

Idle horses and ponies (on long-term rest or not being ridden) often do best on a maintenance ration of 100 percent good-quality roughage (good hay or pasture) with free access to salt and water. This will provide the required energy and protein and adequate sodium to encourage the horse to drink and maintain hydration. However, roughages may not provide the required amounts of all the trace minerals and vitamins; for example copper, zinc, and vitamin E. For this reason, roughages should be tested for vitamin and mineral content to determine if it is necessary to feed a vitamin/mineral supplement to complement the types of forages provided.

Aged horses, "hard keepers," or horses kept on poor-quality pasture may not be able to maintain their body condition without the addition of a small amount of concentrated feed (grain or other calorie supplements). Small ponies, miniature horses, and animals that tend to put on excessive weight should not have unlimited access to lush pastures.

**Mature horses and ponies at work.** A horse or pony at work needs enough nutrients to meet his maintenance requirements, plus enough energy for the work he does, and protein, vitamins, and minerals to provide for maintenance and repair of tissues under increased stress.

As a horse's work level increases from light to moderate to heavy, and finally, to intense, his energy requirements increase by approximately 120 percent, 140 percent, 160 percent, to just over 200 percent of his average maintenance energy needs. By comparison, his protein requirements only increase by 110 percent, 122 percent, 137 percent, and 160 percent over his maintenance needs. It is common for people to misguidedly overfeed protein to working horses, which may have negative consequences on performance and needlessly waste money.

Working horses may also have an increased need for macrominerals, especially the electrolytes lost in sweat, including sodium and chloride. Calcium may also require supplementation due to its importance in bone remodeling and muscle function. Trace mineral requirements also increase, but rarely require supplementation. Consult with your veterinarian or equine nutritionist prior to supplementing a horse with macro- or trace minerals.

Definitions of the four work levels, as defined by the NRC, can be found in Table 1-10 on page 26 of the 2007 *NRC Nutrition Manual*.

### Chart 13-5: Levels of Work

| Exercise Category | Average Heart Rate | Description | Types of Events |
|---|---|---|---|
| Light | 80 beats/min | 1–3 hours/week; 40% walk, 50% trot, 10% canter | Recreational riding<br>Beginning of training program<br>Show horses (occasional) |
| Moderate | 90 beats/min | 3–5 hours/week; 30% walk, 55% trot, 10% canter; 5% low jumping | School horses<br>Recreational riding<br>Beginning of training<br>Cutting, other skill work/breaking in<br>Show horses (frequent)<br>Polo<br>Ranch work (heavy) |
| Heavy | 110 beats/min | 4–5 hours/week; 20% walk, 50% trot, 15% canter, 15% gallop, jumping, other | Ranch work<br>Polo<br>Show horses skill work (frequent, strenuous events)<br>Low-medium-level eventing<br>Race training (middle stages) |
| Very heavy | 110-115 beats/min | Various; ranges from 1 racing hour per week speed work to 6–12 hours per week slow work | Racing (Thoroughbred, Quarter Horse, Standardbred, Endurance)<br>Elite three-day eventing |

*Average heart rate over the entire exercise session.

**These are general descriptions based on weekly totals of work and do not include all combinations of work intensity and duration. The hours of work performed in any particular category could be much more than the estimate given, if the work intensity was much lower. For example, horses in the light category would be exercised more than 3 hours per week if the work intensity was much lower (see Table 1-9) and horses in the moderate category could be exercised for more than 5 hours per week if the work intensity was lower than the average heart rate given.

**Young horses (foals to 2 years).** Young growing horses have special nutritional needs for growth and development of their musculoskeletal system. They are more vulnerable to deficiency diseases and nutritional imbalances than mature horses. The calcium-to-phosphorus ratio is especially critical, as overfeeding phosphorus or underfeeding either mineral can cause musculoskeletal problems.

It is just as important not to overfeed young horses as it is to avoid deficiencies, because overfeeding (with a diet too high in calories) can lead to undesirable rapid growth and developmental problems. Large pastures with plenty of free exercise is essential for healthy bone and hoof formation.

Foals initially receive all the nutrition they need from the mare's milk. Newborn foals are unable to digest forage and grain because their digestive tracts are not yet populated with the necessary bacteria. Gradually, over their first weeks of life, their digestive tracts become populated with beneficial bacteria from their environment as well as from eating manure, a practice known as *coprophagy*. During this process, they begin to consume and digest other feeds such as pasture grass and some of the mare's hay and grain. For this reason, all feeds fed to the mare should be balanced and appropriate for a growing foal. Alternatively, starting at around 4 to 6 weeks, foals may be creep-fed, where they are given free access to their own grain via a "creep feeder" that excludes the mare.

When the foal reaches about 4 months, its needs are no longer met by milk alone and it begins to depend more heavily on additional sources of nutrition. Due to their slowly developing digestive tracts, foals should be fed very high-quality, easily digestible hay, if access to good-quality pasture is not available. Overall, the diet should have a crude protein content of approximately 16 percent and a calcium-to-phosphorus ratio of approximately 1.5 to 2 times more calcium than phosphorus.

Foals should be introduced to the feeds they will be fed after weaning well before weaning takes place, as this helps reduce digestive upset. Ultimately, weanlings should show steady, consistent weight gain.

Crude protein requirements gradually decrease to 14 percent by 1 year of age, and to 10 percent by the time the foal is 2 years old. Caloric requirements also decrease, although they remain slightly higher than that of a mature idle horse of the same size. It is still important to keep the calcium-to-phosphorus ratio correct (from 1.5:1 to 2:1) and provide plenty of exercise. Alfalfa should be fed cautiously to young horses, because even though it provides a good source of protein, it is high in calcium and calories. This can result in an unbalanced calcium-to-phosphorus ratio where calcium is too high, and excess calories which may contribute to DOD.

**Broodmares.** Pregnant mares' nutritional needs start to gradually increase in the second trimester (fifth month) because additional nutrients are needed to support the development of the uterus, placenta, and fetus. The third trimester (eighth month) of pregnancy is when the foal grows the most rapidly *in utero*. Mares should be maintained at a body condition score of between 6 and 7 to ensure that they have enough body stores of energy to support lactation. Weight gain should be clearly visible during the third trimester.

It is important to meet calcium and phosphorus needs while keeping the calcium-to-phosphorus ratio balanced in order to properly support the developing foal. Providing adequate trace minerals during pregnancy is also important, as deficiencies in trace minerals may increase the risk of the foal developing DOD.

Lactating mares require the most feed volume, energy, protein, vitamins, and minerals of all horses. A lactating mare should be fed enough to keep her in good flesh, especially if she is bred back while nursing a foal.

At the peak of lactation (6 to 8 weeks after foaling), a mare can consume up to 3 percent of her body weight in feed per day (30 pounds for a 1,000-pound mare). She will need almost 3 Mcal of energy and 140 g of protein per 100 pounds body weight, as well as extra calcium (.52 percent) and phosphorus (.34 percent).

**Breeding stallions.** Stallions that are not actively being bred require slightly more energy (1.65 Mcal per 100 pounds of body weight) than other mature horses at rest. During the breeding season, this requirement increases to 2 Mcal per 100 pounds of body weight. Breeding stallions also have an increased requirement for vitamins A and E, which are important for fertility. Stallions that are also worked under saddle should be provided with the additional requirements associated with the increased exerciser.

**Aged horses.** Horses today live longer, with many horses living well in their mid to late 20s. As horses age, their nutrient requirements also change due to age-related changes in their digestion, absorption, and metabolism. Additionally, older horses may suffer from one or more age-related diseases that can affect the way they should be fed.

Physical signs of aging include chronically low body condition; loss of muscling over the top line; the appearance of a swayed back; graying of the coat, especially on the face; pronounced hollowing of the sockets above the eyes; and dental disease. Deterioration of the teeth (partially due to completion of eruption) may inhibit an older horse's ability to chew long-stemmed hay, requiring processed forage (such as hay pellets), which require less chewing, to be fed. Depending on their health status, senior horses may require higher levels of protein in their diet than other adult horses; this is reflected in the higher protein content (14 percent) of many commercial senior feeds.

Hard keepers require additional calories above those provided by forage. Often sources of fat such as rice bran and plant-based oils are added to the diet (up to 1 to 3 cups per day) to supplement calories. Soybean oil and canola oil are preferred to corn oil, as they have a better fatty acid profile. *Super fibers* such as beet pulp and soybean hulls are also excellent feeds for senior horses, as they provide a source of highly fermentable fiber that yields more calories per pound than hay or grass.

Some senior horse feeds are *complete* feeds that can be fed in place of hay and grain, providing all the nutrients the horse needs, including fiber. Complete feeds are beneficial for horses that are unable to chew hay. However, such feeds have large serving sizes and are often misfed at amounts below the manufacturer's recommendations with the false belief that they are providing the horse with a balanced diet. Complete senior feeds will only provide a balanced diet when fed at the amounts recommended by the manufacturer.

## Nutritional Management of Health Conditions

### Polysaccharide Storage Myopathy (PSSM)

Horses with PSSM have a genetic defect that causes abnormal accumulation of *glycogen* and storage of *polysaccharides* in the muscle. These horses must be fed a special diet low in non-structural carbohydrates (NSC), such as grains, which should make up less than 30 percent of their diet. Fats, such as canola oil or corn oil, should provide at least 20 percent of the daily caloric intake, replacing the calories from NSC. Oil may gradually be added to the feed, up to 3 cups maximum per day. Even though rice bran has a high fat content, it may not be suitable for horses with PSSM because it also has a relatively high NSC content (approximately 25 percent). Some high-fat commercial feeds may also be high in NSC, so check the NSC content of any feed mix to be sure it is low enough before feeding to horses with PSSM.

As with all horses, the diet for horses with PSSM should be forage-based. Hay should be fed at a rate of 1.5 to 2 percent and not less than 1 percent of body weight daily. Hay should be tested to ensure that the NSC content is 12 percent or less; the lower the amount of NSC, the better. Affected horses with access to pasture need to be managed carefully when pasture NSC levels are high, especially during periods of rapid grass growth in the spring, during stressful periods in late summer, or during droughts. Some horses may need to have their access to pasture grass restricted or be removed from pasture altogether.

Horses suffering from PSSM tend to be easy keepers. Care must be taken to manage the horse's body weight and ensure that they do not become obese, as feeding extra fat can easily be converted to body fat if fed in excess. Grazing muzzles and other aids to slow eating, such as special hay nets, may also reduce overeating.

For more information about PSSM, see Chapter 14, "Health Care, Diseases, and Veterinary Knowledge."

### Recurrent Exertional Rhabdomyolysis (RER)

Horses with RER, also called *tying up*, have no difficulty utilizing NSC, but it is still recommended that they be fed diets that are lower in NSC. Their tying-up episodes are potentially triggered by stress and/or excitement. Research has shown that low-starch diets with fat supplementation may reduce tying-up episodes, especially in fit horses, possibly because horses tend to be calmer when fed low-starch diets.

The diet should provide adequate minerals and vitamins, especially selenium and vitamin E. Ideally, grass or grass-alfalfa mix hay should be fed at 1 to 2 percent of body weight daily. If alfalfa hay is fed, it should make up no more than 50 percent of the forage in the ration. The daily ration should provide approximately 15 percent of the digestible energy from fat and no more than 20 percent calories from NSC. (See Chapter 14 for more information on RER.)

### Equine Metabolic Syndrome (EMS) or Insulin Resistance (IR)

Horses with EMS or IR have a genetic predisposition to this disease and must have a carefully managed diet. Grain, especially with molasses, should be avoided. If they require supplemental energy in their diet, it should be in the form of fat or structural carbohydrates. A ration balancer product (concentrated protein, minerals, and vitamins) may be fed to provide essential nutrients without NSC. Feedings high in NSC cause significant spikes in blood glucose and insulin, which may lead to the development of laminitis in susceptible individuals.

Generally, these types of horses need a reduced-calorie diet consisting of no grain and very little roughage. This may mean keeping them on a dry lot, using a grazing muzzle, or limiting grazing time. If they have access to pasture, it must be managed carefully when pasture NSC levels are high, especially during periods of rapid grass growth and stressful conditions such as drought. It is also important to maintain an ideal body condition score. (See Chapter 14 for more information.)

### Pituitary Pars Intermedia Dysfunction (PPID)

Horses with PPID (also known as Cushing's disease) have a tumorlike growth in their pituitary gland. They may or may not be insulin-resistant. They need diets that are less than 10 to 20 percent of total digestible energy, and should be fed a limited amount of NSC.

Their diet should consist of high fiber (hay, hay cubes, pasture, beet pulp), being careful to monitor the NSC levels of the fiber sources. Affected horses with access to pasture must be managed carefully when pasture NSC levels are high (especially during periods of rapid grass growth and drought) and may need to have their pasture access restricted or be removed from pasture altogether. Avoid feeding grains if possible, especially those with molasses, and high-sugar treats. If more calories are needed to maintain an ideal body condition score, it should be provided in quality forage or a low-NSC supplement, such as fat. (See Chapter 14 for more information.)

## Chart 13-6: Recommended Nutrient Concentrations in Total Diet
### FOR HORSES AND PONIES (DRY MATTER BASIS)

| Type of Horse | Digestible Energy (Mcal/lb in total ration) | Crude Protein (% of daily ration) | Calcium (% of daily ration) | Phosphorus (% of daily ration) |
|---|---|---|---|---|
| MATURE HORSES AND PONIES | | | | |
| Maintenance | .9 Mcal/lb | 8.0 | 0.24 | 0.17 |
| Light work | 1.2 Mcal/lb | 9.8 | 0.30 | 0.22 |
| Moderate work | 1.2 Mcal/lb | 10.4 | 0.31 | 0.22 |
| Intense work | 1.3 Mcal/lb | 11.4 | 0.35 | 0.25 |
| AGED HORSES AND PONIES | | | | |
| From | .9 Mcal/lb | 9.8 | 0.24 | 0.17 |
| To | 1.2 Mcal/lb | 12.0 | 0.24 | 0.17 |
| MATURE BREEDING HORSES AND PONIES | | | | |
| Stallions | 1.1 Mcal/lb | 9.6 | 0.29 | 0.21 |
| Pregnant mares | 1.0 Mcal/lb | 10.0 | 0.43 | 0.32 |
| Lactating mares | 1.2 Mcal/lb | 13.2 | 0.52 | 0.34 |
| GROWING HORSES AND PONIES | | | | |
| Weanlings (6 months) | 1.4 Mcal/lb | 14.5 | 0.56 | 0.31 |
| Yearlings (12 months) | 1.3 Mcal/lb | 12.6 | 0.43 | 0.24 |
| Yearlings (18 months) | 1.15 Mcal/lb | 11.3 | 0.34 | 0.19 |
| 2-year-olds | 1.2 Mcal/lb | 10.4 | 0.31 | 0.17 |

Reprinted with permission from *Nutrient Requirements of Horses*, fifth revised edition. Copyright 1989 by the National Academy of Sciences. Courtesy of National Academy Press, Washington, D.C.

# Balancing a Ration

A balanced ration is a mixture of feeds that not only provides a horse with his daily nutritional requirements, but does so in a way that specific nutrient ratios are maintained.

Sometimes a horse's needs can be met with a simple ration (for instance, a mature, idle horse on good pasture, with free access to water and salt, receiving a ration-balancing supplement). In other cases, it may be necessary to mix several different kinds of feeds to provide a ration that is balanced, palatable, easy to digest, and meets the horse's nutritional requirements.

Feed companies and animal nutritionists formulate rations using computer programs. They factor in fluctuating market prices and adjust feed components to provide specified levels of nutrients at the lowest cost. The average horse owner or stable manager does not need to analyze his horse's ration to this degree of complexity. However, it is important to know your horse's nutritional needs to ensure that your feeding program meets them adequately without deficiencies or overfeeding, and does so as economically as possible. Balancing a ration requires a little math (a calculator is helpful), nutritional charts, and knowing your horse's weight so you can feed by weight, not volume.

## How to Balance a Ration

When researching how to balance a ration, you can consult the NRC (National Research Council) website. There you will find some useful information on how to develop the right nutritional plan for your horse.

Before you can balance a ration for a horse, you must know his weight, age, how much and what kind of work he is doing, and if your horse has any special nutritional needs such as growth, lactation, or pregnancy.

To help determine whether your horse's daily nutritional requirements are being met in his ration, go to the NRC website or other equine nutrition websites and follow the directions to enter your horse's weight, age, physiological state, work level, and other required information. The program can determine the nutritional requirements for that horse, including energy, protein, major minerals, vitamins, and trace minerals. You can then enter the nutrient content of the feeds in your horse's ration, along with the amount fed each day. This allows you to compare your horse's daily nutritional requirements with the nutrients supplied in the ration you have entered.

### *Equine Nutritional Software*

There is computer software that will allow you to determine your horse's nutritional needs based on his weight, age, physiological state, workload, and other factors, determine the nutrient content of the feeds in his ration, and compare his nutritional needs with what the ration provides.

An online search for equine nutritional software programs may help you find new programs, both proprietary and free, that can help you determine your horse's daily nutritional requirements and balance a ration.

## Steps in Developing a Balanced Ration
1. **Assemble information on your horse:**
   a. Weight
   b. Age
   c. Exercise level
      1. See Chart 13-5, page 474.
   d. Other factors:
      1. Growth
      2. Lactation
      3. Pregnancy (trimester)
      4. Other factors such as health, condition, etc.
2. **Determine your horse's total daily nutrient requirements.**

   Your horse's total daily nutrient requirements will depend on his weight and physiological state. (For pregnant mares and growing young stock, nutritional needs can change from month to month.)

   You can use a chart (See Chart 13-6, page 479) or the NRC website.
3. **Determine what kind and how much roughage is in the daily ration.**
4. **Determine how much of each nutrient is supplied by the daily roughage ration:**
   a. Energy (Mcal):
   b. Protein (kg):
   c. Calcium (grams):
   d. Phosphorus (grams):

   **Also important to determine:**

   e. Which nutrients are inadequate and need to be made up by grain and/or supplements?
   f. Calcium-to-phosphorus ratio

The first nutrient of interest when building a ration is energy (Mcal). Ideally, the majority of the energy requirement should be met from feeding forage. Generally, the entire energy requirement for horses at maintenance and doing light work can be met from forage alone. However, as the work level intensifies or energy demands increase due to pregnancy, lactation, or growth, it can be hard to meet energy demands without exceeding the horse's ability or willingness to eat forage. Horse can typically eat up to 3 to 3.5 percent of their body weight in forage per day. If more than this amount of forage is needed each day to meet energy demands, it is a good indicator that a more energy-dense form of feed is needed in the ration.

Next, determine your horse's daily nutritional requirements (see Chart 13-6). You will need to multiply the nutritional values given on the chart by the amount of your horse's total daily ration (TDR) in order to calculate the amount of energy (Mcal), protein (pounds), calcium (pounds), and phosphorus (pounds) he needs per day.

Chart 13-6 also gives recommended daily amounts of concentrates and hay for horses of various ages and classifications.

Next, determine what type of roughage you will feed and in what amount per day. (This varies with the horse's age, work, and other factors.) From this, you can estimate the amount of each nutrient supplied by hay (for more accurate calculations, the hay should be analyzed) and whether it meets the horse's daily nutritional needs. It makes sense to start with hay because roughage should make up the majority of any horse's diet, and because hay is usually bought in bulk, there are generally fewer options available compared to concentrates.

You will need to calculate the amounts of energy (Mcal), protein, calcium, and phosphorus (pounds) contained in your horse's hay ration, using Chart 13-3 and the worksheet on the following page: "Balancing a Ration."

Compare the nutrient amounts supplied in the hay with your horse's daily nutritional requirements. Are they adequate, below required levels, or do they exceed requirements? Is the calcium-to-phosphorus ratio correct, or is the phosphorus too high? This will tell you whether your horse needs additional nutrients supplied by grain and/or supplements and how much.

Finally, you need to determine the kind and amount of concentrates necessary to provide any nutrients that are lacking, without overfeeding any nutrient (see Chart 13-4).

Once you have balanced your horse's ration, you can make adjustments as necessary without going through all the calculations again. For instance, if your horse's work increases and hence his energy requirements increase, you can add grain with a higher energy percentage. Whenever adjusting the ration by adding concentrates, assess the nutritional values of the grain you are adding or increasing to be sure that you have not seriously altered the protein, calcium, or phosphorus levels. This helps you make intelligent decisions about which grain or supplement to use. (For example, if you added several pounds of bran to the ration, it would increase the energy but would also increase the phosphorus level, possibly enough to throw the calcium-to-phosphorus ratio out of balance. Another grain, like barley or corn, might be a better choice.)

## Worksheet: Balancing a Ration

**Horse**_____ _____ **Age**_____**Height**_____**Weight**_____
**Condition:** poor, thin, moderately thin, good, slightly fat, fat, obese

**Special needs:** pregnancy (month_____), growth, getting fit, other:
_____

**Work:** idle, light, moderate, intense _____Hours/Day_____Days/Week
**Other considerations** (temperament, health, etc.):
_____

1. Daily Ration (see Chart 13-6), expressed in lbs, using **lbs per 100 lbs of body weight.**
   Weight (_____lbs) - 100=_____(100 lbs body weight)
   _____(100 lbs) X_____recommended lbs hay =_____**lbs Daily Hay Ration**
   _____(100 lbs) X_____recommended lbs grain =_____**lbs Daily Grain Ration**
   Add_____lbs daily hay and_____lbs daily grain =_____**Total Daily Ration (TDR)**

2. Daily Nutritional Requirements (see Chart 13-1), expressed in Mcals and lbs, using **total body weight.**
   _____lbs TDR    X_____Mcal  =_____Mcal/day (energy)
                         X_____%     =_____lbs/day (protein)
                         X_____%     =_____lbs/day (calcium)
                         X_____%     =_____lbs/day (phosphorus)

3. Calculate nutrients available in **Total Daily Hay Ration** (see Chart 13-3), considering type of hay (see Chart 13-3).
   _____lbs hay X_____Mcal/lb (energy)
   _____lbs hay X_____% (protein)
   _____lbs hay X_____% (calcium)
   _____lbs hay X_____% (phosphorus)

4. Compare nutrients supplied in hay to daily nutrient requirements.
   Daily energy req.   =_____Mcal  Hay supplies_____ Mcal  _____Mcal needed
   Daily protein req.  =_____lbs   Hay supplies_____ lbs   _____lbs needed
   Daily calcium req.  =_____lbs   Hay supplies_____ lbs   _____lbs needed
   Daily phos. req.    =_____lbs   Hay supplies_____ lbs   _____lbs needed

5. Determine type, amount, and nutrient value of concentrates (see Chart 13-4).

|  | | Energy | | | |
|---|---|---|---|---|---|
| Grains fed in concentrate ration | | Mcals/lb | Protein % | Calcium % | Phos. % |
| (grain type)_____ | ___lbs | _____ | _____ | _____ | _____ |
| (grain type)_____ | ___lbs | _____ | _____ | _____ | _____ |
| (grain type)_____ | ___lbs | _____ | _____ | _____ | _____ |
| (grain type)_____ | ___lbs | _____ | _____ | _____ | _____ |

**Total Grain Ration:** _____lbs

6. For each grain, calculate energy, protein, calcium, and phosphorus supplied in amount fed; add totals of each nutrient and compare with Recommended Daily Grain Ration (step 1).

   **Total energy** supplied in **grain ration** = _____Mcals
   **Total protein** supplied in **grain ration** = _____lbs
   **Total calcium** supplied in **grain ration** = _____lbs
   **Total phosphorus** in **grain ration** = _____lbs

7. For each nutrient (energy, protein, calcium, phosphorus), add total amount supplied in hay to total supplied in grain.

   **Total nutrients supplied in Total Daily Ration (hay plus grain):**

   Total energy in Total Daily Ration = _____Mcals total
   Total protein supplied in Total Daily Ration = _____lbs
   Total calcium supplied in Total Daily Ration = _____lbs
   Total phosphorus in Total Daily Ration = _____lbs

8. Compare total amounts supplied in ration to daily nutritional requirements.
   Daily Nutritional Requirements (from step 2):
   _____Mcal/day (energy)
                          _____lbs/day (protein)
                          _____lbs/day (calcium)
                          _____lbs/day (phosphorus)
   Does ration meet nutritional needs of horse? _____Yes _____No
   Ration is too high in _____
   Ration is too low in _____

*Note:* For calcium and phosphorus, it is not enough to meet daily requirements. These minerals must be supplied in proper balance, or neither can be used by the horse and nutritional deficiency disease may result. For mature horses, the ratio of calcium to phosphorus should be from 1.5:1 to 2:1. Never feed more phosphorus than calcium and always meet minimum daily requirement of each.

# Feeding Principles and Practices

*Feed only good-quality, clean, low-dust, mold-free feeds.* Spoiled or contaminated foods may cause colic, laminitis, or other problems. Dusty and moldy feeds (especially hay) can lead to respiratory disease such as *recurrent airway obstruction* (*heaves*). Monitor the quality of the feed, especially when you get new batches of feed, to make sure it is free from poisonous insects, plants, or dangerous debris. Poor-quality feed will not provide the nutritional value your horse needs, making it difficult to maintain your horse's ideal body condition.

*Avoid feeding horses directly on sandy ground or limestone.* When fed on these surfaces, horses tend to ingest sand or limestone with their hay, which can accumulate in the large intestine, leading to colic.

*Always use clean buckets and tubs for feed and water*, to prevent horses from refusing to eat and to prevent the spread of diseases.

*Make sure plenty of clean water is available to horses at all times.*

*Don't work horses strenuously immediately after feeding.* During strenuous exercise, the digestive tract motility slows down, which may lead to colic. Ideally, a horse should not be worked strenuously (for example, go cross-country) for up to 3 hours after feeding. It is also important to let a horse completely cool down after work before you feed him. For horses doing mild to moderate work, free-choice hay and grain fed at less than 0.5 percent of body weight may be fed prior to work.

*Feed horses at regular intervals and maintain a routine schedule.* Horses thrive on routine. Regular interval feeding also keeps consistent amounts of food in the horse's digestive tract, thereby reducing the risk of colic and gastric ulcers.

*Feed grain in small meals* of no more than 5 pounds per meal for a 1,100-pound horse. If larger meals are necessary, feeds with low-starch content, ideally less than 20 percent, should be fed.

*Make roughage the primary component of a horse's diet.* Roughage provides much of the horse's energy from the by-product of hay fermentation in the hind gut. (See page 444 for guidelines on roughage requirements.)

*Maintain each horse's ideal weight* (*body condition*). This is important for many reasons. Excessive weight is hard on the joints, heart, and lungs, and can increase the risk of developing laminitis or metabolic diseases such as insulin resistance (see page 478). Horses in poor condition (either obese or very thin) may lack the stamina to perform, and poor condition makes it difficult to fit tack. It is important to tailor the feeding program to each horse's body type and level of exercise (energy output). See pages 480–484 for more information on balancing a horse's diet.

*Feed each horse based on his level of conditioning and the amount of exercise he is receiving.* A horse's caloric intake should be adjusted according to his current condition and whether he needs to gain, lose, or maintain his current condition. Fit horses that are exercised strenuously require more calories than horses performing little or no work. Calories to meet a high energy demand usually come from concentrates, which supply more calories per pound than roughage. Horses may require different feeds as they age (especially age 15 or older) due to a reduced ability to chew hay and changing metabolic demands. See page 476 for more information.

*Feed horses small feedings frequently, rather than a large amount at one time.* As grazing animals, horses are designed to have feed in their digestive tract at all times. Prolonged periods between meals may result in the formation of gastric ulcers. Their stomach is small and not designed for ingesting a large amount of feed at one time.

*Make changes to your horse's diet slowly, over the course of 1 to 2 weeks,* to allow the bacteria in the horse's large intestine to adjust to their new source of nutrition. If changes are made too quickly, the bacterial population is disrupted, which can result in colic.

*In winter, feed horses more calories as needed to maintain their body weight.* These calories should come from roughage, like hay, because the process of hay fermenting in the large intestine helps to maintain a horse's body temperature even in the coldest weather.

*Succulents* offer a variety of tastes and may also offer a range of different nutrients that may not be in the diet when the same feeds are fed every day. Horses are designed to live on grass; therefore, any amount of grass is better than none. Grass adds moisture and nutrients to the diet.

*Be sure your horse is receiving adequate vitamins and minerals in his diet.* Certain regions of the country are deficient in some minerals (and therefore, the grass, hay, grains, and other plants that grow there). Soil samples and samples from non-commercial feeds can be submitted to labs (usually county or university extension offices) to determine if the soil in your area is deficient in specific minerals, which may mean that your horse requires additional mineral supplementation. All horses benefit from free-choice salt supplementation. See page 436 and 440 for more information on vitamins and minerals.

*Follow your veterinarian's instructions carefully when feeding a sick or lame horse.* Sick horses are often reluctant to drink water, but never try to force a horse to drink by putting a hose in its mouth. You may offer the horse electrolytes in the water along with a bucket of water without electrolytes, offer warm water, soak his hay and/or grain (especially pelleted feeds) in water, or even add a tablespoon of salt to his grain occasionally to increase water intake. If a horse has a sickness other than colic, offer appetizing foods such as fresh grass (if available) and good-quality hay. Do not drastically change his diet in order to encourage him to eat, as this could lead to colic. If a horse suddenly requires stall rest (for lameness, for example), monitor him carefully for fecal output and signs of colic, as a sudden change in activity can decrease gut motility, leading to impaction.

*When a horse's exercise level drastically changes* (for example, due to lameness or at the end of the competition season when he is "roughed off"), his energy requirement decreases and so should his energy intake. This involves a gradual reduction in grain over approximately 2 weeks, depending on his fitness level and feed amounts. Roughage intake requires less adjustment, and should be adjusted gradually over the course of a few weeks to maintain ideal body weight while the horse not working.

*When a horse has a day off from work,* it is important to keep his feeding routine as consistent as possible. It is generally not necessary to reduce the amount of concentrates on days off unless a horse is in a strenuous exercise program and receiving a very high level of concentrate feeding (greater than 2 pounds of concentrates per day) or has a history of recurrent exertional rhabdomyolysis (RER) (tying up). If the concentrates are decreased, the horse should receive additional roughages—about 3 pounds of grass hay for every pound of grain cut from his regular ration.

# 14

# Health Care, Diseases, and Veterinary Knowledge

This chapter covers veterinary information for horse owners, including dental care, determining age by teeth, parasite control, ailments and disease processes, preventing the spread of disease, and drugs and medications. While you must not make decisions and administer treatments that should be determined by a veterinarian, you should be informed about current medications and treatment, including sedation and other methods of restraint. As further research is done and we learn more about horse health, recommended treatments and medications may change. You should stay up to date on the best methods of horse health care through reading about current developments and consulting with your veterinarian.

The *USPC C Level Manual* covers information basic to this chapter, and should also be reviewed.

## Teeth and Dental Care

Basic anatomy of the mouth and teeth and routine dental care are covered in the *USPC C Level Manual*.

# Determining a Horse's Age by His Teeth

The horse's teeth *erupt*, or appear to grow, continuously over his lifetime; the tables (wearing surfaces) of the teeth wear down at the same rate as the teeth grow out. This causes changes in the appearance, shapes, and markings of the teeth (particularly the incisors), which appear at certain ages. The incisor teeth erupt in pairs, with the central incisors first, then the intermediates, and finally the corner incisors. Marks of wear appear and disappear in these pairs in the same order.

By examining the incisor teeth, you can determine a horse's age quite accurately up to the age of 9 or 10. After this age, the changes are less consistent and age can only be estimated.

A foal is born with both sets of teeth (temporary and permanent) present in the jaws. The temporary teeth (deciduous or milk teeth) are smaller and whiter, with shorter roots than permanent teeth. The temporary incisors

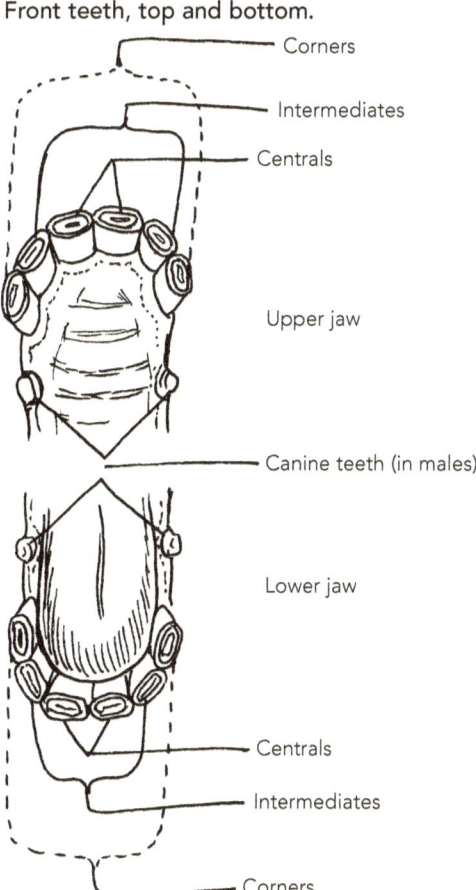

Front teeth, top and bottom.

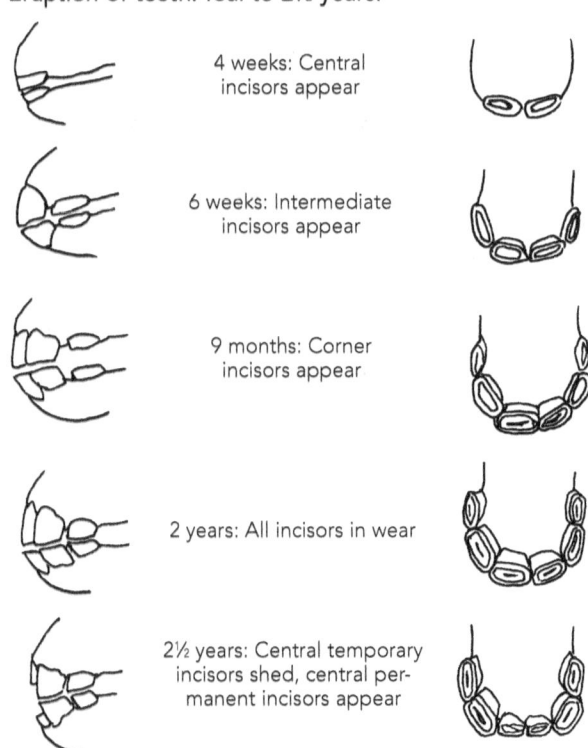

Eruption of teeth: foal to 2½ years.

- 4 weeks: Central incisors appear
- 6 weeks: Intermediate incisors appear
- 9 months: Corner incisors appear
- 2 years: All incisors in wear
- 2½ years: Central temporary incisors shed, central permanent incisors appear

erupt through the gums in the same order as permanent incisors. Temporary premolars (six upper and six lower premolars) are also present at birth.

At about 2½ years of age, permanent molars erupt and push the temporary teeth out. The remains of a temporary tooth is called a cap. Caps usually fall out as the permanent teeth grow near the gum line, but occasionally one may need to be removed to allow the permanent tooth to grow in.

Permanent incisors appear in pairs at fairly consistent intervals. The central incisors appear at 2½ years, intermediates at 3½ years, and corner incisors 4½ years. Canine teeth appear in males between 4 and 5 years. Approximately 20 to 25 percent of mares will also have canine teeth, which are often smaller than those found in male horses. When all permanent teeth are present (at approximately 5 years), the horse is said to have a "full mouth."

Molars and premolars also erupt during this period and all molars are in wear at 5 years of age.

| Tooth | Age at Eruption Time |
|---|---|
| PM1* | 5–6 months |
| PM2 | 2–2½ years |
| PM3 | 3 years |
| PM4 | 4 years |
| M1 | 1 year |
| M2 | 2 years |
| M3 | 3½–4 years |

PM = premolar, M = molar, * Wolf teeth. These may not all erupt.

## Determining Age by Permanent Teeth (2½ to 10 Years)

As each tooth erupts and meets its corresponding tooth, the "tables" or tooth surfaces come into wear. The shape of the tooth changes and marks appear at certain ages as the teeth wear down to a certain level. With experience, you can determine the horse's age by the appearance, shape, and marks of the teeth.

**Cups.** These appear as a hollow oval or rectangle on the tables of the permanent incisors. Cups are present in the permanent teeth when they emerge, and disappear at specific ages as the teeth wear down. The cups are worn away in the lower central incisors at 6 years, the intermediates at 7, and the corner incisors at 8. The upper central cups are gone at 9, the intermediates at 10, and the corners by 11. When all cups are worn away, the horse is called "smooth mouthed."

**Dental star (pulp mark).** As the tooth wears down enough to expose the central pulp cavity, the dental star or pulp mark appears. It appears as a brown or yellow line in front of the cups in the lower central incisors. (Don't confuse dental stars with cups, which are found only in younger teeth.) Dental stars may begin to appear at 6, although their appearance is quite variable. As the cup disappears, the dental star becomes larger and its shape becomes oval, and later, round. Dental stars are usually visible in the central incisors at 8 years and may appear in the intermediates at 9, and the corners by 10 to 12 years.

**Hook or notch on upper corner incisor.** A hook or notch may appear on the upper corner incisor at age 7, and disappear at 8. A similar hook or notch may also appear at 11 years, and disappears around 13. Hooks are quite variable, so they should always be compared with the tables of the incisors, and should not be used as a sole means of estimating age.

### Cups and dental stars.

5 years: Cup; tooth coming into wear

7–8 years: Dental star beginning to show above cup

12 years and older: Dental star; cup has disappeared

### Hook or notch on upper corner incisor.

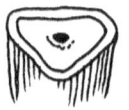

### Cross section of tooth.

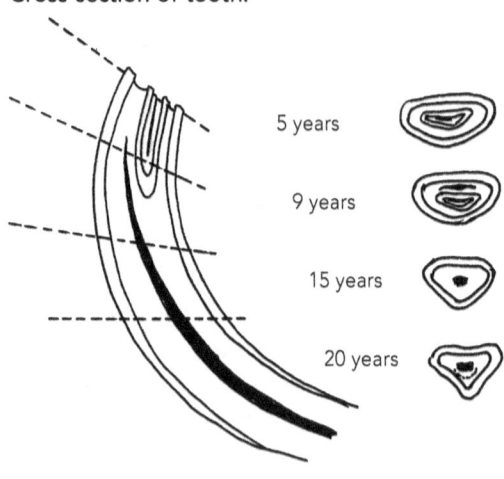

5 years

9 years

15 years

20 years

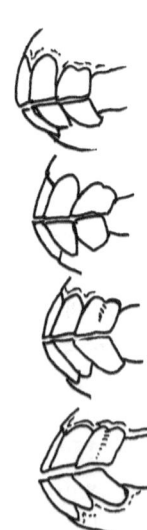

## Estimating Age in Older Horses

In older horses (after age 10), the changes in the appearance of the teeth appear at a less predictable rate, and age cannot be determined as accurately as in younger horses. Factors such as the horse's dental care over his lifetime, the kind of feed he eats, cribbing, and mouth abnormalities can affect the rate of wear and appearance of his teeth.

Some clues to look for are:

> **Shape and angle of incisors.** The shape and angle of the incisors change as they wear down. The first portion of the tooth is oval-shaped and vertical. Between 8 and 13 years of age, the tables become rounder in shape, and the teeth begin to slant forward. In old age, the shape of the tables becomes triangular, and the teeth slant forward at an acute angle.

Appearance and wear of permanent teeth.

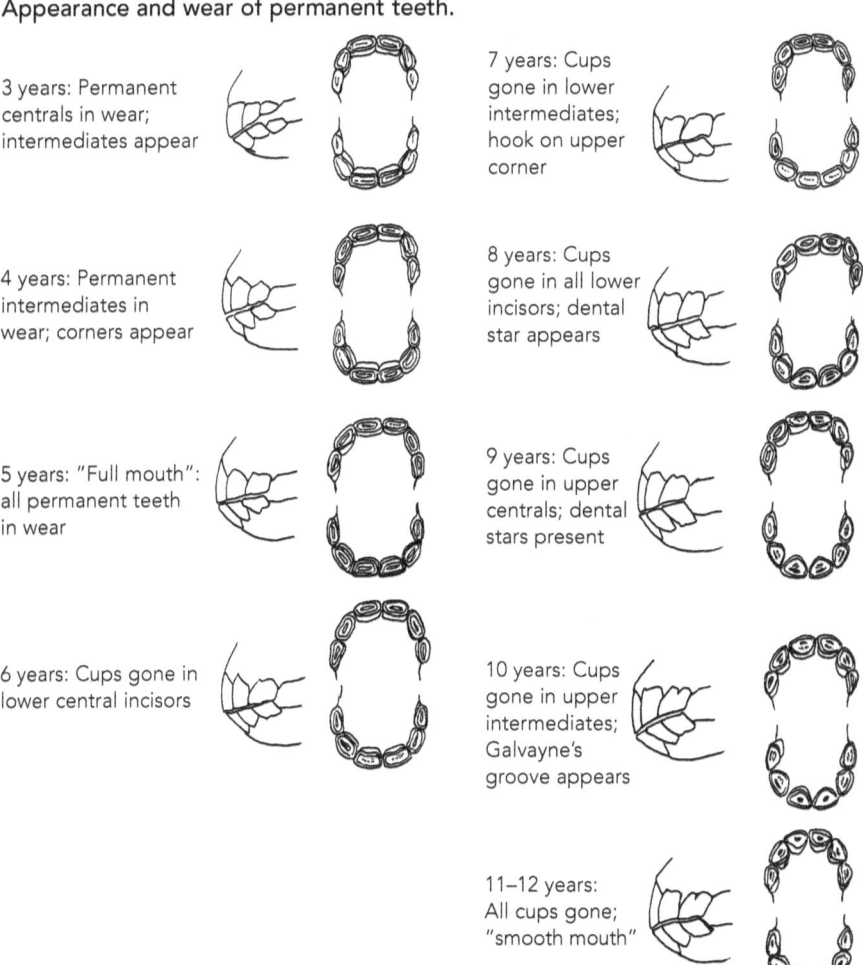

3 years: Permanent centrals in wear; intermediates appear

4 years: Permanent intermediates in wear; corners appear

5 years: "Full mouth": all permanent teeth in wear

6 years: Cups gone in lower central incisors

7 years: Cups gone in lower intermediates; hook on upper corner

8 years: Cups gone in all lower incisors; dental star appears

9 years: Cups gone in upper centrals; dental stars present

10 years: Cups gone in upper intermediates; Galvayne's groove appears

11–12 years: All cups gone; "smooth mouth"

Appearance of teeth in older horses.

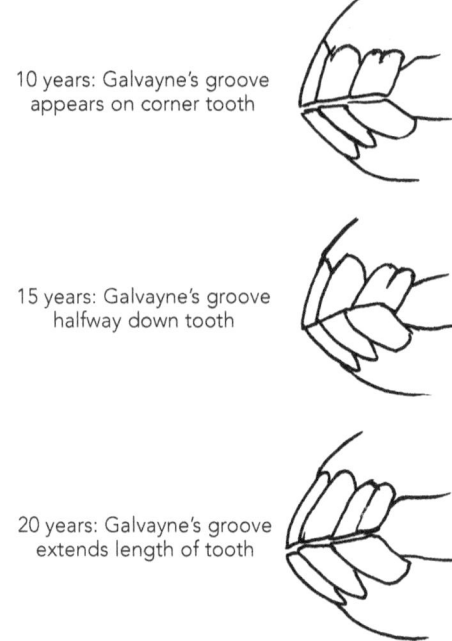

10 years: Galvayne's groove appears on corner tooth

15 years: Galvayne's groove halfway down tooth

20 years: Galvayne's groove extends length of tooth

Teeth become more triangular and slanted with age.

**Galvayne's groove.** This is a vertical groove that appears on the upper corner incisor teeth, beginning at 10 years of age. The groove appears as the horse ages, due to the continuous eruption of the corner incisors. It disappears as the tooth is ground off with age. It reaches halfway down the tooth at 15, and extends the full length of the tooth at 20. After 20, Galvayne's groove begins to disappear, beginning at the top of the tooth, and is gone at 30 years.

### Wolf Teeth

Traditionally, veterinarians have recommended that wolf teeth (small first premolars) be removed from horses at an early age to avoid issues with the bit. Upper wolf teeth that are in a normal position (just in front of the second premolar) may not have contact with the bit and may not need to be removed. An older horse that has wolf teeth but no signs of bitting issues (tossing the head) usually does not need to have them removed.

## Tooth and Mouth Problems

Some horses have abnormalities of the mouth, teeth, or jaws that can affect their dental health and ability to eat. Teeth problems should be suspected if

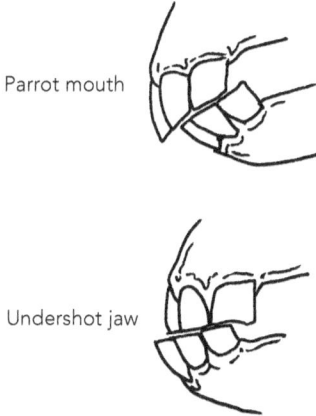

Parrot mouth

Undershot jaw

a horse is eating slowly, quidding (discarding chewed masses of hay), or underweight. Horses with mouth abnormalities need their teeth checked and floated more often than other horses.

### Parrot Mouth (Overshot Jaw) and Undershot Jaw
A parrot mouth is an abnormality in which the upper teeth project forward over the lower teeth. An undershot jaw occurs when the lower teeth project forward ahead of the upper teeth. Both are hereditary defects that make it difficult for the horse to graze normally. Because the jaw is misaligned, the cheek teeth usually wear abnormally, which can result in large hooks where the cheek teeth are not directly opposed.

### Step Mouth, Wave Mouth
These are abnormalities of the dental arcade (the back rows of molars and premolars). A step mouth occurs when one or more teeth are longer than the rest, creating a sharp "step." This is almost always due to loss of opposing teeth; one tooth continues to erupt because it is not worn down by the grinding action of the opposing tooth.

A wave mouth describes an irregular surface of the entire arcade. It tends to occur most often in older animals. It may occur from poor mouth conformation (parrot mouth or undershot jaw), or from unusual chewing motion that may develop due to a painful condition such as an abscessed or fractured tooth or sharp points due to poor dental care. It may also result from improper tooth floating, where some teeth are ground down more than they should be.

These conditions make it difficult for the horse to chew properly, and may require special dental treatment.

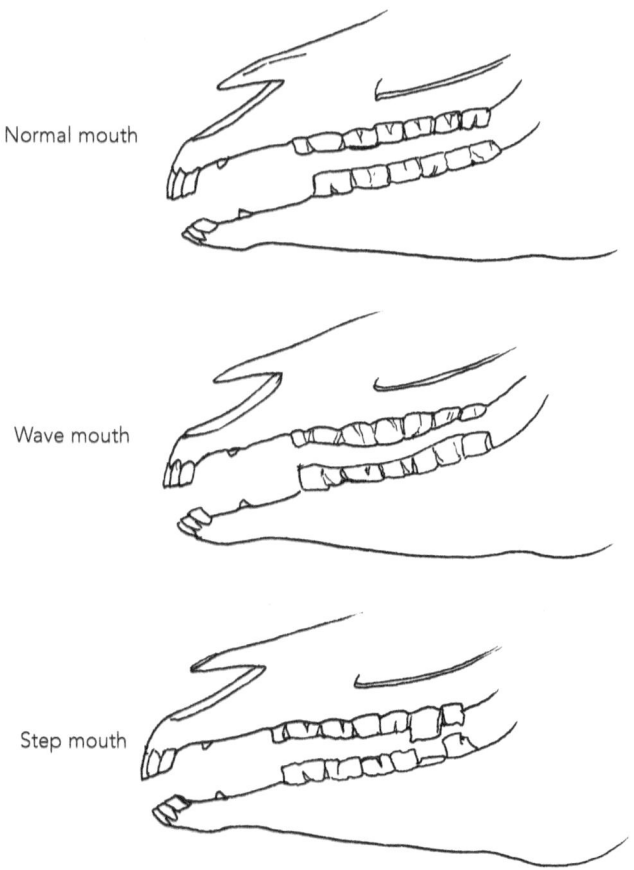

Normal mouth

Wave mouth

Step mouth

### Abscessed Tooth

Horses, like humans, can get cavities, but they are often overlooked and usually don't cause the horse discomfort. However, an abscess can develop at the root of a tooth if a cavity extends deep into the tooth or a tooth fractures. Signs of an abscessed tooth include bad breath; thick, smelly nasal discharge from one nostril; and sometimes swelling in the jaw or skull overlying the abscessed tooth. Bad breath is not normal for horses, and usually indicates an abscess or infection in the mouth, guttural pouch, or nasal cavity; it should be investigated by a veterinarian.

### Hooks and Ramps

Hooks and ramps are large pointy overgrowths of the first and last cheek teeth, which can develop on the front of the upper second premolars and the back of the lower third molars due to normal wear patterns or misalignment of the upper and lower jaw. If the jaw is severely misaligned, they can

### Hooks, ramps, retained caps, bit seat.

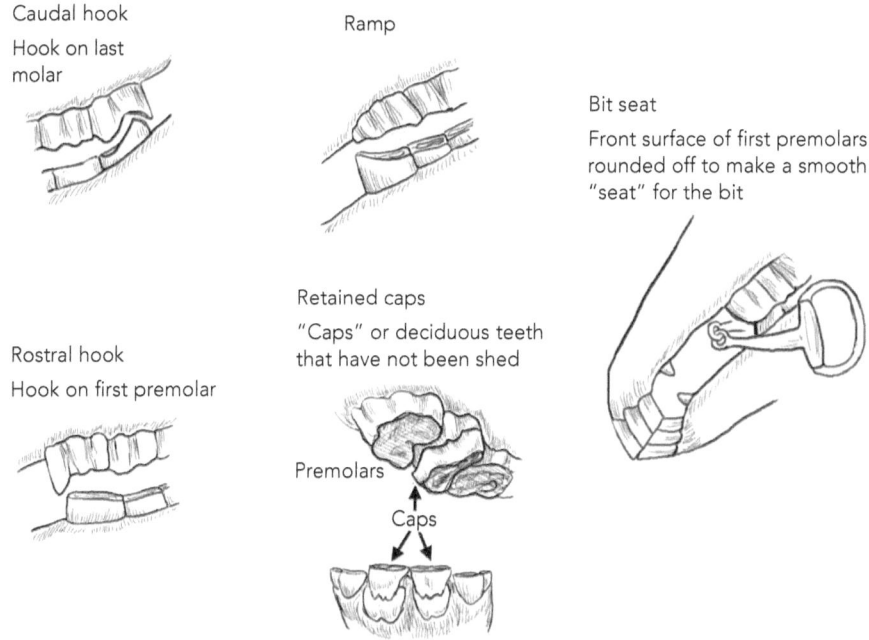

become so large that they poke into the opposing gums, causing pain. They are removed during routine floating.

***Retained caps:*** These occur in young horses when a temporary premolar remains in place on top of the permanent premolar after it has erupted. They should be removed by a veterinarian or certified equine dentist.

***Aged horses:*** As horses age, they become more susceptible to developing dental problems. It is important to monitor aged horses' teeth closely as they are more likely to develop hooks and ramps or tooth disease, which may require a tooth to be pulled. The rate of tooth eruption slows with age.

***Bit seat***: A practice in floating teeth, in which the front edges of the upper and lower second premolars are rounded in order to prevent contact between the bit and the soft tissues of the cheeks. Caution should be used in this practice, as research indicates that the bit has minimal contact with these teeth, and too-aggressive tooth removal can lead to damaging the root pulp, resulting in tooth death and need for removal.

## *Cribbing*

Cribbing causes the front surface of the incisor teeth to be worn down in a characteristic pattern, which makes it possible to detect the habit. Severe cribbing can also result in inflamed gums or even broken front teeth.

Wear pattern of cribber.

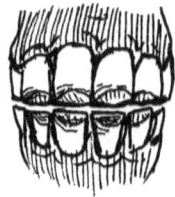

## Controlling Internal Parasites

All horses have internal parasites to some degree. Internal parasites live primarily in the horse's gastrointestinal tract, although the parasites' life cycles may take them to other internal organs. They can damage their host by stealing nutrients, causing tissue damage when migrating through internal organs, or obstructing blood vessels supplying the intestines or the digestive tract itself.

Very young horses, old horses, and those in poor condition are most vulnerable to parasite damage. Outward signs of parasite infestation include colic (often chronic), weight loss, lethargy, poor appetite, pot belly, rough coat, poor growth in young horses, diarrhea, and tail rubbing. Some parasites such as bots, ascarids, small strongyles, or pinworms may be visible in the manure; however, an infested horse may suffer extensive internal damage before any visible signs appear. A fecal parasite float and egg count (microscopic examination of a fecal sample) is the best way to estimate the type and amount of internal parasites present in your horse.

## Common Internal Parasites and Their Life Cycles

Effective parasite control depends on knowing the various internal parasites' life cycles because treatment is aimed at disrupting the life cycle, thereby preventing parasites from maturing to adults.

### Large Strongyles (S. Vulgaris, S. Edentatus, S. Equinus), "Bloodworms"

**General:** These worms are fairly large (¾ to 2 inches long). *S. vulgaris* migrates through the arteries supplying the gastrointestinal tract. *S. edentatus* and *S. equinus*, which are less common, migrate through the liver and cause less damage than *S. vulgaris*. Historically, large strongyles were the most prevalent internal parasite in horses; however, their prevalence has diminished with modern deworming practices.

**Life cycle** (*S. vulgaris*): Adults live in the cecum and large colon, where they produce eggs. Eggs are passed in manure. The eggs hatch and develop into infective larvae 1 to 3 weeks later. Infective larvae crawl up stems of

Life cycles of large strongyles.

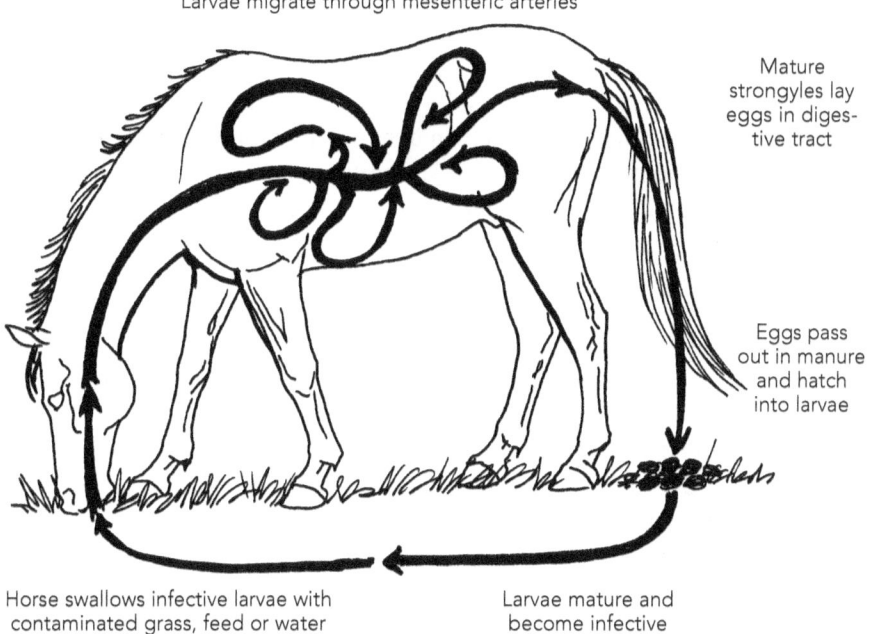

grass and are ingested during grazing. Larvae pass to the small intestine, where they burrow into walls of the arteries supplying the intestine. The larvae travel via the arteries to the cecum and large colon, causing arterial damage. Larvae develop into adults in the cecum and large colon.

**Damage caused:** Arterial damage can lead to thromboembolic colic (portions of the intestine die due to lack of blood supply because the arteries supplying the intestine have been compromised by migrating parasites). This type of colic is severe and often fatal. In addition, horses may demonstrate unthriftiness, anorexia, fever, chronic mild colic, and diarrhea.

**Prevention strategy:** Large strongyles take a relatively long time to complete their life cycle (approximately 6 months). Deworming twice per year with an ivermectin product effectively controls this parasite, and is the reason that they are now an uncommon cause of parasitism in domestic horses.

## *Small Strongyles (Cyathostomins)*
**General:** These internal parasites have become the most prevalent species that infest modern horses. At ¼ to 1 inch long, they are considerably smaller than large strongyles and are usually reddish in color. It is difficult to determine the amount that a horse is infested with as they can encyst (become enclosed in a cyst) in the large colon. When the larvae become encysted, they burrow into the large intestine and their life cycle goes dormant. This results in small number of adults and low fecal egg counts despite significant infestation.

Small strongyle larvae require water to move in the environment, so they are most likely to infect a horse when the grass is covered with dew. For this reason, they are more likely to be acquired from pasture grass and less likely to be acquired in stalls or dry lots. They can survive freezing, but cannot survive in hot and dry weather conditions. Some horses are less susceptible to this parasite, so only a small percentage of a herd (approximately 20 percent) will shed the majority of small strongyle eggs. Therefore, it is important to use fecal egg counts to determine which horses need to be treated against this parasite to prevent the development of resistance.

**Life cycle:** Adults live in the large intestine and lay eggs. Eggs pass in manure and hatch into infective larvae. Larvae are ingested when the horse eats from the ground (usually grass). Larvae form cysts in walls of the large intestine (persisting for weeks to months). They emerge (often in the springtime) and develop into adults in the large intestine.

**Damage caused:** Small strongyles can cause acute (sudden) onset of fever, colic, and diarrhea if they emerge from the intestinal wall all at once. This is a serious consequence of infestation with small strongyles. They can also cause chronic diarrhea, weight loss, and edema due to protein loss through the large intestinal walls.

**Prevention strategy:** Parasite prevention programs are primarily aimed at controlling this parasite. The only drug class that is almost always effective against the encysted stage is moxidectin. Ivermectin is effective against the non-encysted stage and may have some residual activity to kill small strongyles as they emerge from cysts. The life cycle of small strongyles is considerably faster than that of large strongyles, generally completed within 2 months, although if they become encysted, the cycle will be longer.

### Ascarids (Parascaris Equorum), "Roundworms"
**General:** These are large, white, spaghetti-like worms (6 to 8 inches). Adult horses are considered immune to them and they usually infest young horses less than 2 years of age (most are less than 12 months old). The eggs are very hardy and can survive up to 15 years in the outside environment. Therefore, it is difficult to clean a contaminated pasture. There is a growing concern about these parasites becoming resistant to ivermectin and moxidectin (the most commonly used broad spectrum anthelmentics).

**Life cycle:** Adults lay eggs in the small intestine that are passed in manure. Eggs are ingested while grazing and hatch into larvae in the small intestine. Larvae penetrate the intestinal wall and migrate to the liver, then to the lungs via the bloodstream. They are coughed up into the pharynx, where they are swallowed. They pass into the small intestine and develop into adults.

**Damage caused:** Foals that are infested are unthrifty, having a rough hair coat and pot belly, and sometimes mild diarrhea. Following deworming of a foal that is heavily infested, dead worms can become impacted in the small

## Life cycle of ascarid.

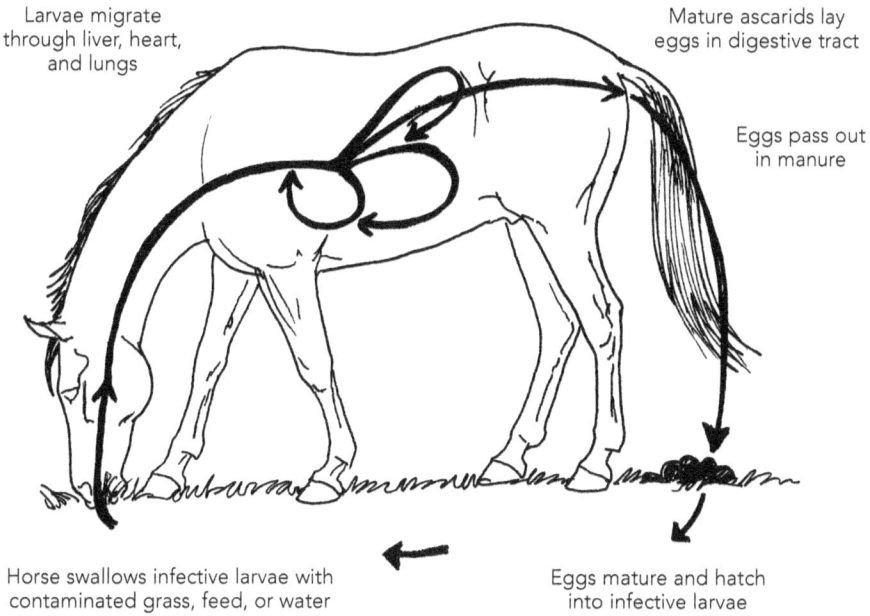

- Larvae migrate through liver, heart, and lungs
- Mature ascarids lay eggs in digestive tract
- Eggs pass out in manure
- Eggs mature and hatch into infective larvae
- Horse swallows infective larvae with contaminated grass, feed, or water

intestine, resulting in serious colic. They can also cause respiratory signs known as "summer colds," consisting of coughing, fever, and nasal discharge, due to migration of larvae through the lungs.

**Prevention strategy:** Foals should be dewormed four times during the first 15 months of life (depending on parasite level on the individual farm) to prevent a heavy infestation that might cause severe colic. The recommended schedule for deworming foals is at 2½ to 3 months of age, at weaning (around 5 to 6 months of age), during the following spring (8 to 10 months of age), and midway through the foal's first grazing season (13 to 15 months of age). The best products to use are ivermectin and fenbendazole.

### Tapeworms (Anoplocephala Magna, A. Perfoliata, Paranoplocephala mamillana)

**General:** These segmented worms can become quite large (up to 2 feet) and are made up of many square sections. Traditionally, they were considered to be less important than other parasites, but recently they have been linked to horses that experience chronic colic. Similar to small strongyles, they can only be acquired from grazing on pasture, because that is where horses may ingest a mite carrying the tapeworm larvae. It is difficult to determine the level of infestation, as the eggs are rarely passed in the feces, so traditional fecal egg counts are useless for this parasite and specialized tests (serum antibodies) are needed to determine levels of infestation.

**Life cycle:** Adults live in the small intestine. Sections of the adult worms containing eggs are passed in manure. Eggs are released and ingested by beetle mites. They hatch into infective larvae within the mites. Horses ingest mites containing infective larvae, usually while grazing on pasture. Larvae develop into adults in the small intestine.

**Damage caused:** Tapeworms can cause colic (especially chronic colic) from inflammatory bowel disease or acute colic if they become impacted in the ileum. They may also cause a horse to appear unthrifty.

**Prevention strategy:** Tapeworms can be controlled with a double dose (twice the amount) of pyrantel pamoate or a product containing praziquantel. Generally, horses only need to be treated once a year. Tapeworms are more common in certain areas of the country, so ask your veterinarian for recommendations for controlling this parasite on your farm.

### Pinworms (Oxyuris Equi)

**General:** These worms are quite small (1 to 2 inches). They may be seen around the horse's anus when they are laying eggs and appear white and rice-like. The eggs dehydrate and die fairly quickly outdoors, so pinworm infestations are usually seen in stabled horses.

**Life cycle:** Adults live in the end of the large intestine. Females crawl out to lay eggs, attaching them to horse's perineum and anus. Larvae develop within the eggs while attached to the horse. The eggs eventually fall off and hatch

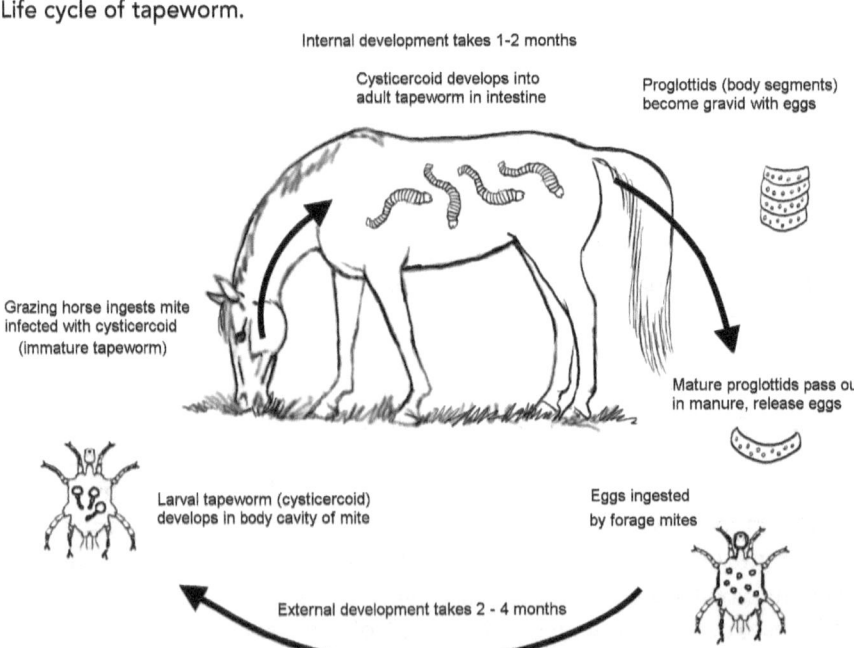

Life cycle of tapeworm.

Life cycle of pinworm.

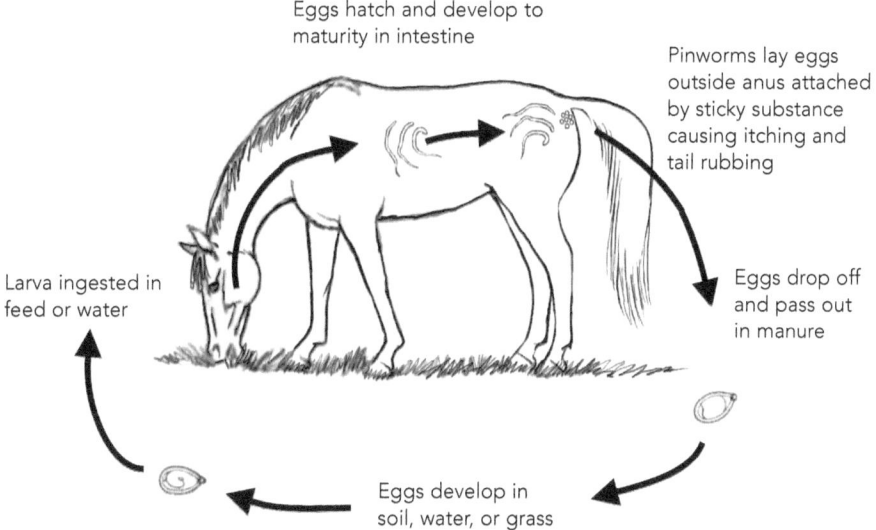

into infective larvae. The infective larvae are ingested when the horse eats from the ground. Larvae travel to the large intestine and mature into adults.

**Damage caused:** These parasites only cause damage from local irritation around the anus, resulting in horses rubbing their tails and damaging the hairs at the top of their tail head. They cause little or no intestinal damage.

**Prevention strategy:** These parasites are susceptible to most common dewormers and are controlled with an effective deworming program. Ivermectin is the dewormer of choice.

### Bots (Gastrophilus)

**General:** This is the only parasite where the adult parasite does not live within the horse. Adult botflies look like small honeybees and larvae look like prickly red maggots.

**Life cycle:** Adult botflies deposit yellow eggs on a horse's legs, shoulders, or belly (depending on the fly species). Horses ingest eggs while grooming themselves or scratching. Once in the mouth, warmth, moisture, and friction cause the eggs to hatch. Larvae burrow into the tongue and gums for 2 to 4 weeks, then re-emerge. Larvae are swallowed and attach to the stomach lining, where they live 8 to 10 months. Larvae pass in manure in the spring or early summer. Larvae pupate for 5 to 6 weeks and turn into adult flies outside the horse.

**Damage caused:** In general, this parasite causes little damage to the horse. Heavy infestations may result in gastric discomfort (mild colic) and unthriftiness. Mouth sores and irritation possibly occur when larvae are burrowing into gums.

**Prevention strategy:** These parasites are easily controlled by ivermectin. Ivermectin should be administered at the end of the adult fly season (after

Life cycle of botfly.

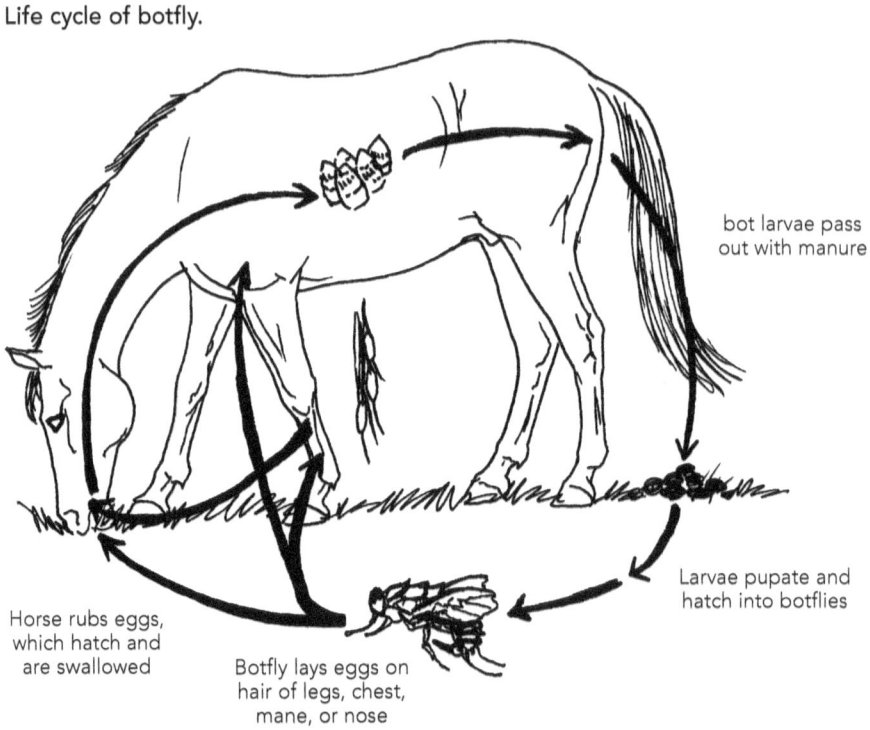

bot larvae pass out with manure

Larvae pupate and hatch into botflies

Botfly lays eggs on hair of legs, chest, mane, or nose

Horse rubs eggs, which hatch and are swallowed

the first frost in northern climates) to kill larvae that may have infested the horse. Treatment with ivermectin should be repeated approximately 6 months later (in the spring in northern climates) to kill any remaining larvae. Ivermectin and moxidectin are the only dewormers that kill bots.

## Assessing the Level of Parasite Infestation

The first step in designing a parasite control program is to assess the level of parasite infestation in your herd. A *fecal float and egg count* (microscopic examination of a fecal sample) shows the number and types of parasite eggs present in a horse and reports the result in *eggs per gram* of feces. However, fecal egg counts only estimate the amount of mature, egg-laying strongyles and ascarids infesting a horse. They do not reveal migrating larvae (which are often more damaging) or other parasites.

An annual fecal egg count can be done in early summer (northern climates) or early fall (southern climates), when the adult parasite population is theoretically the greatest, to assess individual horse's resistance to parasitism. It is important to perform these tests after an appropriate amount of time since the last deworming (4 weeks for fenbendazole, 8 weeks for ivermection, 12 weeks for moxidection) to accurately assess a horse's natural susceptibility to parasite infestation. New horses should also be tested, especially if they show signs of parasite infestation.

Once the level of parasite infestation has been estimated, horses can be dewormed according to their individual level of parasitism (see the *USPC C Level Manual*, page 188). Fecal egg counts should also be performed after deworming (8 to 10 days) to assess the development of resistance to a specific dewormer. Your veterinarian can help determine the best time to perform a repeat fecal egg count based on the targeted parasites' life cycle and effectiveness of the dewormer.

## Choosing an Appropriate Dewormer

Dewormers have medical ingredients that target some internal parasites more efficiently than others. A dewormer should be chosen to target the parasite at a point in its life cycle when it is most vulnerable to being killed by the active ingredient. For example, bot larvae are only present in the horse's stomach over the winter. To target this parasite, a dewormer effective against bots (such as ivermectin) should be given after botflies have died in the fall, generally after the last frost, and again in the spring to kill any larvae that may have remained in the horse's stomach over the winter. You should consult your regular veterinarian to design a deworming program for your herd.

### Chart 14-1: Dewormers

| Active Ingredient | Brand Name(s) | Form(s) | Effective Against |
|---|---|---|---|
| Ivermectin | Zimecterin®, Eqvalan®, Equimectrin®, Ivercare® | Paste, liquid | Large strongyles (adults and larvae)†, small strongyles (adults and non-encysted larvae only), ascarids*, bots†, pinworms† |
| Moxidectin | Quest® | Gel | Large strongyles (adults and larvae), small strongyles (adults and encysted larvae†), ascarids*, bots Caution: Do not use in foals under 6 months. |
| Fenbendazole | Panacur®, Safeguard® | Paste, suspension, granules | Large strongyles* (adults and larvae), small strongyles (adults and non-encysted larvae only), ascarids†, some pinworms* |
| Fenbendazole 5-day dose | Panacur® Powerpak | Paste | Large strongyles* (adults and larvae), ascarids, pinworms* |

| Active Ingredient | Brand Name(s) | Form(s) | Effective Against |
|---|---|---|---|
| Oxibendazole | Anthelcide EQ®, Equipar® | Paste, suspension | Large strongyles (adults and larvae), small strongyles (adults and non-encysted larvae only) |
| Oxfendazole | Benzelmin®, Equicide® | Powder, suspension | Large strongyles (adults and larvae), small strongyles (adults and non-encysted larvae only), ascarids |
| Pyrantel pamoate | Strongid-T®, Antehlban® | Paste, powder, suspension | Large strongyles (adults only), small strongyles* (adults and non-encysted larvae only), ascarids*, pinworms; double dose for tapeworms |
| Pyrantel tartrate | Strongid-C® | Top dress pellets | Large strongyles (adults only), small strongyles (adults only), ascarids; only to be used in specific situations to avoid development of resistance |
| Praziquantel | Not available for horses as Praziquantel only; available in combination with Ivermectin or Moxidectin (see below) | | Tapeworms† |
| Ivermectin + Praziquantel | Zimecterin Gold®, Equimax® | Gel | Large strongyles (adults and larvae), small strongyles (adults and non-encysted larvae only), ascarids*, bots, pinworms, tapeworms |
| Moxidectin + Praziquantel | Quest Plus® | Gel | Large strongyles (adults and larvae), small strongyles (adults and encysted larvae), ascarids, bots, tapeworms  Caution: Do not use in foals under 6 months. |

*Parasite resistance is common
†Preferred dewormer for this parasite

## Reducing Exposure to Internal Parasites

Good management practices can minimize parasite exposure. These center on good hygiene, preventing the contamination of pastures and feed by parasite eggs and larvae, and measures that break parasites' life cycles and reduce their numbers.

# HEALTH CARE, DISEASES, AND VETERINARY KNOWLEDGE

Some recommendations include the following:

- New horses should have a fecal test to assess baseline level of parasitism and should be dewormed appropriately based on veterinarian recommendation.
- Avoid overcrowding and overgrazing of pastures. The more horses (and manure) kept per acre, the greater the potential for parasite infestation.
- Keep feed, hay, and water from becoming contaminated with manure. Avoid feeding from the ground; use feeders instead.
- Manure should be removed from highly concentrated areas, such as paddocks, regularly.
- Manure should not be spread directly onto pastures that are in use. Composting kills some eggs and larvae due to the high heat generated, however, large strongyle larvae can survive for several weeks and small strongyle larvae for up to 8 months in compost.

Further information on parasite control, deworming, and horse management to control parasite infestation can be found in the *USPC C Level Manual*, Chapter 6.

## Basic Health Examination

A knowledgeable horse person is capable of recognizing the signs of a healthy versus an unhealthy horse. The signs of an unhealthy horse may be obvious, such as those seen in a colicky horse, or they may be subtle, requiring observation over time for an abnormality to be confirmed. The discerning horse person evaluates his horse every day for signs of abnormalities. A horse should be evaluated daily for:

- Weight gain or loss
- Abnormal hoof growth (for example, ridges in the hoof wall) or hoof wear (for example, blunted toe)
- Abnormal swelling in the legs or any other areas of the body
- Wounds
- Hair coat abnormalities
- Lameness or comfort when walking
- Type and amount of manure and urine being passed
- Appetite or food and water consumption
- Overall attitude

If abnormalities are noticed in the outward signs of normal body function, then further evaluations should be performed. These include:

- Temperature
  - **Normal:** 98.5–101°F (average is 100°F).
  - See the *USPC C Level Manual* pages 194–195 for methods of taking temperature.
- Pulse or heart rate
  - **Normal:** 30–45 beats per minute (average is 36 beats per minute).
  - See the *USPC C Level Manual* page 196 for methods of taking pulse or heart rate.
- Respiratory rate
  - **Normal:** 8–16 breaths per minute (average is 12 breaths per minute).
  - See the *USPC C Level Manual* page 197 for methods of taking the respiratory rate.
- Gut sounds
  - Ideally, these are evaluated with a stethoscope listening to areas around the flank, but you can also lay your head along the side of the horse's abdomen near the flank to listen to obvious sounds.
  - **Normal:** Some sounds on both sides of the abdomen that are easily heard with a stethoscope and faintly heard with the naked ear.
  - **Abnormal:** Increased or decreased sounds may indicate digestive abnormalities.
- Color and texture of the gums (mucous membranes)
  - To assess *capillary refill* time, press a finger to the gums above the top incisors for 1 second, enough to make the gums white, then remove your finger. The refill time is the time it takes for the area to return to its previous color.
  - **Normal:** Light pink color, moist, capillary refill time (CRT) less than 2 seconds.
  - **Abnormal:** A prolonged CRT may indicate that your horse is dehydrated. Abnormal colors include white (may indicate shock or blood loss), yellow (may indicate liver or red blood cell problems), bright red (may indicate bacterial toxins have been released from the intestine), or dark brown or blue (may indicate that red blood cells are not oxygenated properly).

- Skin tent test
  - This is a basic test for hydration.
  - Use either the point of the shoulder (not the middle of the neck) or the upper eyelid for this test, as areas with loose skin can give a false reading.
  - Use your fingers to tent or pinch the skin at the point of the shoulder or upper eyelid. The skin should return to its normal appearance within 1 second. If it takes longer, this could mean that the horse is dehydrated.
- Examination for overt lameness
  - Walk and/or trot a horse on straight lines and circles.
  - If severe lameness is noted, a veterinarian should be called and the horse should be confined to a stall.

Any concerns should be addressed by a veterinarian. Certain abnormalities should alert the astute horse owner to impending problems. These are discussed below in the following section.

Following are signs that a horse is in distress and requires immediate veterinarian attention:

- Symptoms of colic
- Symptoms of tying up
- Symptoms of choke
- Symptoms of laminitis
- Diarrhea
- Arterial bleeding
- Severe swelling
- Non-weight-bearing lameness
- Large lacerations or any laceration near a joint or synovial structure
- Any eye injury
- A horse that is down and will not get up
- Refusal to eat or drink
- Inability to urinate or defecate
- Significantly elevated temperature, respiratory rate, or pulse
- Severe allergic reaction (hives)

# Disease Processes

## Shock

Shock is the body's response to trauma. It is an acute and progressive failure of the peripheral circulation (blood circulation to outer body parts such as the legs and head) that takes place as the body tries to conserve its resources to deal with a serious injury.

Signs of shock include:

- Trembling, sweating, cool skin
- Depression, apathetic attitude
- Cold extremities (ears and legs), subnormal temperature
- Rapid, weak pulse; low or falling blood pressure
- Pale or bluish mucous membranes
- Weakness; collapse

Shock can be caused by massive bleeding, severe trauma, burns, major infections, intestinal obstructions, dehydration, heart failure, and anaphylactic shock (severe allergic reaction). Shock can progress until blood pressure falls dangerously low and death follows.

Shock must be treated promptly by a veterinarian because it requires intravenous replacement of fluids to restore blood volume and blood pressure. First-aid measures include keeping the horse quiet and warm (but not raising his temperature, which worsens shock), controlling bleeding, and avoiding dehydration. It is important to call the veterinarian before shock progresses to a dangerous point. Do not administer any drugs to a horse in shock without veterinary approval.

## Fever

Fever is an abnormal rise in body temperature that is not caused by exercise, diet, or environment. It may be the result of toxins that accompany an infection or tissue destruction. Fever is a by-product of the process by which a horse's body fights infectious diseases or toxins, but high fevers can lead to weakness, dehydration, and tissue damage. One or more degrees above the horse's normal temperature (from 98.5°F to 101°F) indicates fever. Signs of fever include depression and decreased appetite. Sometimes horses also have a mildly increased heart rate/pulse, show signs of mild colic, or have a raised or fluffy hair coat.

Very high fevers (greater than 5 degrees Fahrenheit above normal) can be life-threatening.

Because fever is usually a sign of infection or disease, a veterinarian should be called to determine the cause of the fever and treat the horse. Antibacterial drugs may be used to control an infection, and the veterinarian may use non-steroidal anti-inflammatory drugs to lower the fever if it is high enough to be dangerous.

## Dehydration

Dehydration occurs when the body's water level becomes deficient. This can happen when the body loses too much water (as in heavy sweating or diarrhea) or fails to take in enough water (as in failure to drink enough). Dehydration is serious because sufficient water is essential for vital functions such as the circulation of the blood, digestion, cooling, and maintaining chemical balance in the cells of the body.

Dehydration can be caused by sweating heavily, which is usually obvious, or continuous sweating that dries rapidly, which is not so noticeable (this can occur during travel in hot weather). Failure to water horses often enough can lead to dehydration. This can easily happen during the winter when water sources may freeze or horses may not drink enough because the water is cold. Dehydration can lead to hard, dry manure, slow digestion, impaction, and colic.

Hydration can be roughly estimated by performing a skin tent test and evaluating the horse's gums for color, texture, and capillary refill time.

Dehydration is treated by encouraging the horse to drink. Ways to encourage a horse to drink include placing a small amount (2 to 4 tablespoons) of table salt on grain or hay, offering a bucket with electrolytes in addition to a normal bucket of water, or offering warm water in cold weather. *Do not* attempt to force water into a horse through his mouth. This can cause the horse to aspirate the water into the trachea rather than swallowing it, which could cause pneumonia.

In severe cases, a veterinarian may have to administer fluids by a nasogastric tube or intravenously.

## Inflammation

Inflammation is the body's natural defensive response to injury or infection. When a part of the body is injured or invaded by an infectious organism, the body responds by increasing circulation at the site, delivering defense cells (white blood cells and antibodies) and carrying away cellular debris. The defense cells attempt to destroy, dilute, or wall off the irritating agents, and the increased circulation helps to carry away the debris left by dead or damaged cells and foreign material. Material such as fluid, cells, and cellular debris is exuded, or escapes out of the capillaries into the surrounding tissues; this material (*exudate*) may include blood, serum, pus, fibrin, or mucus, depending on the location and type of inflammatory reaction. Eventually inflammation leads to healing and repair of the damaged tissues.

Inflammation may be caused by injuries, wounds, burns, disease-causing organisms (*pathogens*) and the toxins they produce, poisons, venoms, and *antigens* (substances against which the animal possesses antibodies).

Five signs of inflammation are:

- Heat (from increased blood supply to the inflamed area)
- Pain (from swelling and nerve irritation)
- Swelling (from fluid portions of blood seeping into tissues)
- Redness (not always visible)
- Loss of function in the inflamed area (because of pain and swelling)

Inflammation is an essential part of the healing process. Normal inflammation should be adequate to heal the wound, defeat the infection, and repair damaged tissue, but excessive inflammation can result in damage to the body, proud flesh, excessive scar tissue, and loss of function. First aid for sprains, strains, and bruises includes the application of cold and immobilizing the part, which reduces the initial inflammatory reaction.

Sometimes the body's natural defenses are inadequate to defeat an infection and help may be necessary in the form of antibiotics. These should only be used on the advice of a veterinarian; improper use of antibiotics can be dangerous and can lead to the development of antibiotic-resistant organisms.

Certain drugs (corticosteroids, and non-steroidal anti-inflammatory drugs like phenylbutazone) can reduce inflammation. These must be used with the advice and supervision of a veterinarian, as misuse of these drugs can suppress healing and leave the horse vulnerable to infection or further injury.

## Pain

Because horses are prey animals, they tend to not demonstrate overt signs of pain until it becomes severe. Generally, if horses are in pain, they do not come to greet you at the stall normally, but tend to stay to the back of the stall and may even face away from the door. They may keep their ears slightly back and have a dull look in their eye. They may also demonstrate signs of a specific painful condition such as colic or laminitis. These are discussed later in this chapter.

## Edema

Edema is non-specific swelling or accumulation of excess fluid in the tissues. In non-inflammatory edema, the swelling is cool and painless. If pressed with a finger, a *pit* or imprint remains. Edema may show up along the midline of the abdomen and in the sheath. Lack of exercise may result in *stocking up* or edema in the hind legs, or in all four legs.

Edema may be caused by certain illnesses, parasite infestation, inactivity, or heart or kidney disorders that interfere with normal circulation or filtration of the blood and lymph. Edema is related to low pressure in the veins and an abnormal protein or salt content in the blood. To treat edema, the veterinarian must look for and treat the underlying cause.

Stocking up is common in horses confined to stalls, especially older horses. It occurs due to inefficient lymphatic drainage of the lower limb, which is dependent on movement of the limbs to properly circulate blood and lymph. The inefficient drainage results in an accumulation of fluid in the tissues of the lower limb. It does not cause lameness and usually disappears quickly with gentle exercise or bandaging. Measures to prevent stocking up include use of stable bandages, access to a turnout paddock, and regular exercise.

## Abnormal Wound Healing

Horses are unique in that they are prone to abnormal wound healing, especially on wounds below the elbow and stifle. When a wound heals abnormally, it results in *excessive* or *exuberant granulation tissue* formation, otherwise known as *proud flesh*. Proud flesh is more likely to develop in areas where a wound experiences excessive motion, if a wound is bandaged beyond the time when it has filled in with normal *granulation tissue* (bright pink spongy tissue), or if irritating substances are applied to a wound. Proud flesh looks like a rough-surfaced, pink tumor growing out of the wound and is prone to bleeding. Proud flesh will slow or even stop normal wound healing, so it is important to have a veterinarian evaluate a wound as soon as possible if proud flesh is suspected. In addition, it is important to ask your veterinarian for advice when dealing with large wounds on the lower limbs.

Wounds will also heal abnormally if there is a foreign object or infected piece of bone left in a wound. In this case, the wound will have continuous drainage and the granulation tissue will not completely cover the wound. The horse may or may not be lame. Again, consult your veterinarian in cases where wounds are healing slowly or incompletely.

Wounds that occur near a synovial structure such as a joint or tendon sheath can be very serious. It is important to know what structures are near a wound that is sustained in the lower limb. Call your veterinarian immediately if you suspect a wound involves a joint or a synovial structure, as septic arthritis may develop, which can lead to severe lameness and possible loss of athletic use, and can even be fatal.

# Common Diseases and Disorders

The following diseases and disorders are listed according to the system(s) they affect.

## Musculoskeletal System

### Laminitis

**Etiology:** Laminitis is a devastating disorder that affects horses. In order to understand laminitis, one must know the anatomy of the horse's hoof; specifically, that the coffin bone is suspended in the hoof by a Velcro-like structure called the lamina. It is similar to how your fingernail is attached to its nail bed. During laminitis, the laminae become inflamed and damaged, sometimes irreparably. Once they become damaged, the connecting structure loosens, resulting in movement of the coffin bone in relation to the hoof wall. Because the *deep digital flexor tendon* is much stronger than the common digital extensor tendon (both of which attach on the coffin bone), the coffin bone rotates so that the tip of the toe points downward due to the pull of the deep digital flexor tendon. Laminitis is extremely painful and because of the mechanical forces that the hoof, coffin bone, and deep digital flexor tendon are under, the damage is irreversible. If a horse recovers from laminitis, he will be predisposed to developing it again later in life. The true cause of why the laminae become inflamed is still unknown, but certain circumstances are known to predispose a horse to laminitis.

- **Endotoxins** released into the blood from certain bacteria. This has its own list of causes:
    - Overeating grain or lush grass
    - Strangulating colic
    - Retained placenta after a mare foals
    - Horses that develop diarrhea
- **Mechanical overload,** usually from a horse bearing excessive weight on one leg due to a serious injury in the opposite leg. The leg that bears the most weight is affected.
- **Equine metabolic syndrome.** The exact reason horses develop laminitis with this syndrome is unknown. These horses are "easy keepers" and will have cresty necks.
- **Equine Cushing's disease.** The exact reason that horses with this syndrome develop is unknown.
- **Exposure to black walnut shavings.** Black walnut shavings are toxic to horses and may cause laminitis when used as bedding.

**Signs and symptoms:** Horses with laminitis show very distinct symptoms, based on the severity of the damage to the laminae. The front feet are more commonly affected than the hind feet. The symptoms of laminitis are listed in order from least to most severe:

- Shifting weight
- Increased digital pulse
- Increased warmth in the hoof
- Reluctance to lift the feet when you ask the horse to pick them up
- Reluctance to walk
- Shifting the weight back on the haunches while keeping the front feet out in front
- Lying down for long periods of time
- If hind legs are affected, horses will walk with a high stepping gait in the rear limbs and may seem to move awkwardly

**Immediate care:** If you think a horse may be developing laminitis, call your veterinarian *IMMEDIATELY.* Put him in a deeply bedded stall and do *not* force him to walk. Try to stand the horse in ice water that goes above the fetlock.

**Prevention:** Keep grain locked away from horses to prevent laminitis from grain overload. Monitor intake of pasture grass, especially when transitioning to pasture from stable, and limit or prevent grazing in at-risk horses. Never bed horses with black walnut shavings.

## Rhabdomyolysis (Polysaccharide Storage Myopathy or PSSM, Exertional Rhabdomyolysis or ER, "Tying Up")

**Etiology:** This is a disorder of muscle metabolism. The problem can originate from improper storage or improper use of carbohydrates in large muscles, resulting in damage to the muscles. It can also be caused by mineral (selenium) deficiencies and electrolyte imbalances in the diet. PSSM and recurrent ER seem to have a genetic cause in some breeds (draft horses, Quarter Horses, Warmbloods, and Thoroughbreds). Some horses will develop rhabdomyolysis from extremely strenuous work (for example, event horses and endurance horses) due to metabolic exhaustion of the muscle cells. Horses fed diets with high amounts of grain are potentially at increased risk.

**Signs and symptoms:** Common signs of rhabdomyolysis are listed below from least to most severe.

- Stiffness or short-striding, especially in the hind legs
- Reluctance to move
- Hard, quivering hindquarter muscles

- Profuse sweating
- Inability to move
- Distress
- Dark urine, from the kidneys filtering the by-products of muscle damage (this occurs hours after the episode)
- Kidney damage

**Immediate care:** If you think a horse is "tying up," do *not* force him to move any more than necessary. Try to keep him quiet, and in cold weather, put a blanket or cooler on him to prevent him from getting chilled. Call a veterinarian immediately. Once a horse has an episode, he is generally at greater risk for another episode unless appropriate management changes are made.

**Prevention:** In horses that are genetically at risk, it is important to manage their diet. Generally, these horses are maintained on low-starch, high-fat diets. In elite event and endurance horses, it is important that they are supplemented with electrolytes and properly conditioned for their level of competition.

## Respiratory System

### Heaves (Recurrent Airway Obstruction or RAO)

**Etiology (cause or causative agent and transmission):** Non-contagious inflammation of the lower airways (*bronchioles*), usually with an allergic component. Long-standing inflammation leads to decreased lung capacity and elasticity, causing the inability to exhale air out of the lungs efficiently. Breathing becomes increasingly difficult. Heaves is generally associated with horses kept in dusty environments and indoor stables, although a pasture form of heaves is seen in some cases, usually in southern regions. There may be a genetic component, making some horses more susceptible to developing the disease.

**Signs and symptoms:** Coughing during exercise, at feeding time, or in certain environments (for example, while stabled in a dusty barn). Affected horses have a higher than normal resting respiratory rate that increases with exercise and hot weather. They may exhibit exercise intolerance (prolonged recovery from exercise or inability to exercise at their normal capacity for level of fitness). Late in the disease a horse may appear to *double exhale* as he is trying to exhale air out of the lungs, which may cause the development of a *heave line,* or increased size of the abdominal muscles from working to exhale.

**Immediate care:** If you are concerned that a horse is developing heaves, contact your veterinarian. The disease is managed by altering the horse's environment to prevent activating the inflammation in the lungs. This includes increasing pasture turnout, feeding wet hay or replacing hay with other less dusty forms of roughage (such as pellets or hay cubes), using bedding that is less dusty (such as cardboard or paper), and keeping the barn clean and well ventilated. Corticosteroids may be used during severe heave episodes or long term in severe cases. Long-term therapy may include inhalers to help open the airways and decrease the inflammation that is present. Clenbuterol (Ventipulmin) is a drug that helps to relieve bronchiole constriction and open the airways; it is commonly used to help athletic horses suffering from heaves.

**Prevention:** Good-quality, clean stabling with proper ventilation or full-time pasture turnout is the best way to prevent the development of heaves (other than the pasture form).

### Roaring (Left Laryngeal Hemiplegia)

**Etiology:** This respiratory disorder is caused by gradual paralysis of one of the main nerves supplying the muscles of the left side of the larynx. The laryngeal muscles work to increase its diameter when breathing, especially during hard exercise. As the nerve becomes paralyzed, the horse is unable to open part of the laryngeal cartilage during inspiration. The cartilage blocks the airway, causing the horse to make noise, a roaring sound, when breathing in (especially when exercising), and can eventually decrease the amount of air the horse takes in so much that it results in *exercise intolerance* (tiring early). Large horses, especially those with long necks such as draft horses, Thoroughbreds, and Warmbloods, tend to be more likely to develop this problem.

**Signs and symptoms:** Horses make a "roaring" noise on inspiration when exercised. In advanced cases exercise intolerance may develop.

**Immediate care:** Horses suspected of being "roarers" are diagnosed with upper airway endoscopy. A surgery called a *tie-back* can be performed to decrease the clinical signs by suturing the cartilage back into a more normal position.

**Prevention:** There is no prevention other than avoiding breeding horses that are "roarers," as there is a suspected genetic link.

### Rhinopneumonitis

**Etiology:** Equine herpes virus (EHV). There are primarily two types that can cause respiratory disease, EHV-1 and EHV-4, although EHV-2 and EHV-5 can cause mild respiratory disease. This respiratory disease most commonly infects young adult horses and horses that travel frequently (such as race horses and show horses). It is transmitted by indirect contact (aerosol transmission/droplets in the air, or contaminated clothing or equipment) and direct contact with an infected horse (nose to nose). It can also cause neurologic disease and abortion in mares. (These forms of the disease are discussed later in this chapter, in the sections "Nervous System" and "Reproductive System," respectively.)

**Signs and symptoms:** Cold-like symptoms, including watery to thick nasal discharge (nickname for the disease is "snots"), mild to high fever, depression, and lack of appetite. Coughing and secondary bacterial infections are also possible.

**Immediate care:** A veterinarian should be called if a horse is suspected of having EHV. Treatment is generally supportive. Horses should be quarantined to prevent the spread to other horses (see "Preventing the Spread of Contagious Disease" later in this chapter). They should also be monitored closely for the development of neurologic signs, as the virus may mutate into the more serious neurologic form.

**Prevention:** There are multiple types of vaccines available. A modified live vaccine is best to prevent or decrease the severity of the respiratory form. It is administered frequently (every 2 to 3 months) as the immunity it creates is short-lived. Pregnant mares should *not* be given the modified live vaccine as it can cause abortion but should instead be given a killed vaccine.

### Influenza

**Etiology:** Equine influenza virus; there are multiple strains of this virus. Similar to rhinopneumonitis, it most commonly infects young adult horses and horses that travel frequently. It is transmitted by indirect contact (aerosol transmission or by contaminated clothing or equipment) and direct contact with an infected horse (nose to nose).

**Signs and symptoms:** Influenza causes respiratory infection symptoms similar to EHV such as coughing, clear nasal discharge, fever (usually high), depression, and lack of appetite. This viral infection may progress to bacterial pneumonia.

**Immediate care:** Horses suspected of having influenza should immediately be quarantined and any horses that were exposed should be monitored for the development of the disease. Treatment is supportive.

**Prevention:** There are many types of vaccines available. The most effective is a modified live intranasal vaccine. It may not completely prevent the development of the disease, but it will lessen the symptoms. It is effective for about 6 months, so horses at risk should receive boosters accordingly.

### Strangles

**Etiology:** *Streptococcus equi* bacteria. It is easily transmitted by indirect contact (aerosol transmission or by contaminated clothing or equipment) and direct contact with an infected horse (nose to nose). It most commonly affects young horses and horses that are exposed frequently to other horses (for example, race and show horses and horses at sale barns). It can become endemic in certain farms, meaning that horses can become infected from the environment. Also, horses can become carriers of strangles if bacteria get into the guttural pouch.

**Signs and symptoms:** The bacteria infect the upper respiratory tract and lymph nodes, usually around the head and neck. The disease got its name from its tendency to cause severe swelling due to pus accumulation in the lymph nodes around the larynx, resulting in blocking airflow or "strangling" the horse. In very severe cases, a horse might go into respiratory distress if he is not receiving enough oxygen, which is an emergency situation. Normally, it causes thick nasal discharge, swelling due to *abscesses* (pus accumulation) of the lymph nodes under and behind the jaw, fever (may be high), depression, and lack of appetite. The abscesses usually mature, then break open, drain, and heal on their own. Complications include infection in the guttural pouches or abscesses of lymph nodes in other areas of the body causing chronic infection (called *bastard strangles*). Very rarely, the body reacts inappropriately to the bacteria and an immune-mediated disease called *purpura hemorrhagica* occurs that can be life-threatening.

**Immediate care:** As with other respiratory diseases, the first step should be to quarantine affected horses, as this disease spreads rapidly. A veterinarian will determine how to care for affected horses. Sometimes horses are treated with antibiotics, although these have been known to prolong the course of the disease. More commonly, horses are just given supportive therapy and the disease is allowed to run its course.

**Prevention:** The best prevention is to prevent the spread and decrease the exposure to the disease. There are vaccines available, but they are generally ineffective at completely preventing the disease. The most effective vaccine is an intranasal product.

### Equine Viral Arteritis (EVA)

**Etiology:** The equine viral arteritis virus is very contagious and spreads through direct or indirect contact with respiratory secretions from an infected horse or through sexual transmission during breeding. This virus is testosterone-dependent, so only stallions can remain carriers. However, all genders can be transiently infected.

EVA also affects the circulatory and reproductive systems. For more information, see the sections on "Circulatory System" and "Reproductive System" later in this chapter.

**Signs and symptoms:** Clinical signs vary from mild to severe disease. Respiratory symptoms are cold-like: clear nasal discharge, cough, fever (may be high), depression, conjunctivitis (eye discharge or pinkeye). Horses often will have limb and ventral edema along their belly. Abortion is also possible in pregnant mares.

**Immediate care:** Horses should be isolated immediately. Otherwise, care is supportive to let the virus run its course.

**Prevention:** There is a modified live vaccination available but it is not extensively used, as outbreaks are fairly rare.

## Circulatory System

### Equine Infectious Anemia (EIA)

**Etiology:** The equine infectious anemia virus is similar in behavior to the human HIV virus. The virus is transmitted through blood, usually via biting flies. It can also be transmitted by dirty needles or surgical instruments. When a horse becomes infected, he is infected for life.

**Signs and symptoms:** There are various forms of this disease. In the acute form, horses have fever, depression, lack of appetite, and swelling of the legs and belly (ventral edema). In the chronic form, horses go through episodes of sickness but then seem to recover only to get sick again. They lose weight and look unthrifty. There is a *carrier* form where horses do not show any symptoms, but can still transmit the disease.

**Immediate care:** Horses that are infected are either euthanized or kept in strict quarantine (away from other horses and from biting insects that spread the disease) for the remainder of their life.

**Prevention:** There is no vaccine or prevention for this disease other than good fly-prevention practices. Fortunately, it is a very uncommon disease because most horses are routinely tested with a Coggins test, which prevents its spread by identifying infected horses before they can spread it to other horses.

### Equine Viral Arteritis (EVA)

**Etiology:** The equine viral arteritis virus is very contagious and spreads through direct or indirect contact with respiratory secretions from an infected horse or through sexual transmission during breeding. It attacks the lining of small arteries, inflaming them, and small amounts of protein and fluid (not blood cells) leak out of them.

See the previous section, "Respiratory System," and "Reproductive System," later in this chapter, for the implications of EVA on those systems.

**Signs and symptoms:** Horses can become very sick with this virus. The primary signs are limb and ventral edema (swelling along the underside of the belly) from the inflamed leaky arteries. Horses become "achy" and may develop colic. Respiratory symptoms are cold-like: clear nasal discharge, cough, mild fever, depression, and conjunctivitis (eye discharge or pinkeye).

**Immediate care:** Horses should be isolated immediately as this virus is *very* contagious. Otherwise, care is supportive to let the virus run its course.

**Prevention:** There is a modified live vaccine and a killed vaccine available, but they are not extensively used as outbreaks are fairly rare.

## Digestive System

### Tooth Problems

**Etiology:** Tooth problems are not very common in young horses, but may become more common as the horse ages. The cause is often unknown or it could be part of normal tooth wear, due to trauma, or due to poor mouth conformation (parrot mouth or undershot jaw). Because the roots of the upper back cheek teeth are encased in a sinus, tooth root abscesses can lead to sinus infections.

**Signs and symptoms:** Horses with teeth problems usually have trouble eating, which is demonstrated by weight loss, dropping feed, quidding, whole pieces of grain in the manure, and even colic. If they also have a sinus infection, a thick, smelly discharge comes from the nostril on the same side as the affected tooth. Horses with problems of the cheek teeth will generally have foul breath.

**Immediate care:** A veterinarian should be called if a horse is suspected of having a tooth problem. He will do a thorough oral exam and may even take radiographs of the horse's skull and teeth to better assess the roots of the teeth.

**Prevention:** Routine dental care, as discussed in the *USPC C Level Manual*, page 193, is the best way to prevent tooth problems, although they can develop despite excellent dental care.

## Colic

**Etiology:** Colic is one of the most common medical problems suffered by horses. The term *colic* means pain in the belly or abdomen. Fortunately, most episodes of colic are quite mild and only require a single visit from the veterinarian. However, occasionally the problem is so severe that the horse requires surgery. There have been significant advances made in colic surgery on horses, making the survival rates much higher and the complication rates much lower.

There are many cases of colic in the horse. Following are the common types and causes of colic.

**Spasmodic colic or "cramps":** This is the most common type of colic. The exact cause is generally unknown, but is most likely due to a mild disturbance of the gastrointestinal bacterial population. It may resolve on its own without treatment by a veterinarian. Some horses seem to be more prone to spasmodic colic than other horses.

**Flatulent or "gas" colic:** This type of colic occurs most frequently with a sudden change in diet that causes the bacteria in the intestines to produce gas. It will usually resolve after treatment by a veterinarian. This type of colic can be quite painful for horses, which they show by rolling violently. If a colicky horse wants to roll, try to prevent it by walking him until the veterinarian arrives. If he rolls violently he may injure himself or others, and could suffer a twisted gut.

**Impaction colic:** This type of colic occurs when horses do not drink enough water, are fed coarse or poor-quality hay, have tooth problems, or sometimes for no apparent reason. Feed or sand accumulates in the large intestine and causes a blockage, resulting in intestinal distension and pain. Horses fed on sandy ground can develop a sand impaction. Horses are also at risk of impaction colic if they have a sudden change in their exercise or if they undergo general anesthesia for surgery. Horses with this type of colic are off-and-on colicky and have reduced fecal production. This type of colic requires prompt veterinary treatment. Sometimes, impactions are so severe that horses have to undergo colic surgery to relieve them.

**Intestinal displacement:** This type of colic often starts with an impaction and results in the large intestine twisting on itself, resulting in further obstruction. Horses with this type of colic show more severe signs of colic and may require colic surgery to correct the problem.

**Intestinal strangulation:** This type of colic results from the blood supply to the intestines becoming cut off by the intestine twisting on itself or, perhaps the most common cause, by a *strangulating lipoma,* a benign fatty tumor commonly found in older horses, twisting around the small intestine. Horses that crib have been shown to be at increased risk for a specific type of small intestinal strangulation called an *epiploic foramen entrapment.* Horses with intestinal strangulation show severe colic signs and always require colic surgery to correct the problem.

**Inflammation of the intestines (enteritis):** This type of colic can occur when the intestines become inflamed from something a horse ingests such as medications or toxic plants, from an overgrowth of bacteria, or from a dysfunction of the immune cells in the intestines.

**Gastric ulcers:** Horses that are kept in stalls and fed infrequently throughout the day are at high risk of developing stomach ulcers. Horses show a wide range of symptoms when they have gastric ulcers, which may include mild colic. This ailment is discussed in "Gastric Ulcers," later in the chapter.

**Parasites:** Parasites can cause inflammation of the intestines (enteritis). In the past, large strongyles were a common cause of colic when they damaged the blood vessels supplying the intestines. Fortunately, large strongyles are extremely rare in modern horse populations. Today, small strongyles are more of a problem in our horse populations. These intestinal parasites encyst in the large colon and can cause inflammation and changes in motility, leading to signs of colic. In foals, the small intestine can become blocked with dead ascarids if a foal is dewormed while carrying a heavy worm burden.

**Overeating grain:** This is a serious, life-threatening problem if a horse eats a large amount of grain at one time. The sudden change in diet will severely impact the bacterial population in the intestines, leading to toxins being released into the bloodstream from dying bacteria. Call a veterinarian immediately if a horse eats a large amount of grain at one time. Keep the horse in the stall, keep him quiet, and ice all four feet continuously until the vet arrives, because laminitis can also be a consequence.

**Signs and symptoms:** Following is a list of common colic signs, in order from least severe to most severe:

- Uninterested in feed
- Decreased manure production
- Lying down quietly for abnormally long periods of time
- Lifting top lip ("Flehman" response), yawning, or some other odd behavior
- Stretching out as if to urinate
- Acting restless
- Looking at or kicking at his flanks and/or belly
- Pawing
- Lying down and getting back up
- Rolling
- Lying down and will not get up
- Throwing himself on the ground and rolling (use care in handling horses that are demonstrating this high level of pain)

**Immediate care:** Call a veterinarian immediately if you think a horse has colic. Be prepared to give the vet the horse's temperature, pulse rate (most important), respiratory rate, time of last defecation, appetite, length of colic signs, diet history, work history, and signs of distress the horse is exhibiting. Walk the horse (especially if he is restless) and do not let him eat (but offer him water) until the veterinarian arrives.

**Prevention:** Fortunately, the chance of a horse developing colic can be dramatically decreased by good horse management practices:

- Feed good-quality feed that is consistent in its origin.
- Feed smaller amounts of feed frequently, rather than a large amount of feed infrequently. This is particularly true of grain, where no more than 5 pounds of grain should be fed at any one feeding (less for horses weighing less than 1,100 pounds). Horses are designed to graze most of the day, so try to mirror your feeding schedule after this.
- Do not make sudden feed changes. The bacteria in a horse's intestines need time to adjust to feed changes. The population of bacteria can become disrupted when feed changes are made rapidly, resulting in gas production or changes in gut motility.
- Provide fresh, clean water at all times.
- Keep grain locked safely away so that a horse cannot get into it.
- Develop an appropriate deworming program.

- Provide horses with plenty of turnout and exercise. Horses are used to moving and grazing constantly. They are more likely to develop colic if they are kept confined most of the time.

### Choke

**Etiology:** In horses, *choke* refers to obstruction of the esophagus, usually with some type of feed. (This is not the same as choking or obstruction of the airway in humans, as the horse can breathe.) The cause of choke is often due to horses eating inappropriate or poor-quality feed, such as coarse hay or grass, pelleted feed, or unsoaked beet pulp. Horses with tooth problems that chew their feed poorly may be predisposed. Choke can also be caused by a horse eating too large an object (a large apple or carrot) or eating too fast without properly chewing the food. Once a horse has choked, there may be damage to the esophagus that predisposes the horse to choke in the future.

**Signs and symptoms:** Horses are generally distressed and may even act like a horse with colic. They may hold their head and neck in a different position than normal, such as stretching their neck out. They usually have saliva and feed coming out of the mouth and nostrils because they cannot swallow them. Strangely, the horse may continue to attempt to eat and drink despite being choked.

**Immediate care:** Sometimes a choke resolves without treatment, but if it has not resolved within an hour, or if it appears severe, you should call your veterinarian. Remove *all* feed and water immediately. ***Do not*** try to force water down the horse's throat to try to break up the choke. When a horse is choked, the food and water he takes in through the mouth will likely go down the trachea and into the lungs since it cannot go down the esophagus, leading to severe, life-threatening pneumonia.

**Prevention:** To prevent choke, horses should be fed high-quality feed. Beet pulp and other expandable feeds should be soaked prior to feeding. Treats should be cut to an easily chewable size. Routine dental care should be performed to allow the horse to properly chew his food. Horses that bolt their grain (eat too fast) should have fist-size rocks placed in their feed bin to slow them down. Once a horse has been choked, it may require a major change in his diet to prevent him from choking again.

### Potomac Horse Fever (PHF)

**Etiology:** *Neorickettsia risticii* bacteria. Transmission involves the passage of a parasite larva called a *trematode* that carries the bacteria through aquatic snails. The horse may ingest the snail or its droppings and acquire the bacteria. Aquatic insects (such as mayflies or caddis flies) also feed on the snail droppings, so if a horse ingests them, they may acquire the bacteria that causes the disease. Some areas of the country have higher numbers of outbreaks than others.

**Signs and symptoms:** The signs of Potomac horse fever progress very rapidly. Initially, the horse is depressed, lacks appetite, and has a fever, which may be high. Within 24 hours, profuse *pipe stream diarrhea* develops (however, some horses do not develop diarrhea). The horse may or may not be colicky prior to the onset of diarrhea. Ventral and limb edema develops as protein is lost in the diarrhea. Many horses that develop severe Potomac horse fever also develop life-threatening laminitis.

**Immediate care:** It is important to monitor horses daily for signs of any type of sickness, as discussed earlier in this chapter. Any time a horse develops diarrhea, it should be considered an emergency and a veterinarian should be contacted immediately.

**Prevention:** There is a vaccine available that does not prevent the disease, but may lessen the severity of the symptoms. It tends to work better in some areas of the country than others.

### Gastric Ulcers

**Etiology:** Gastric ulcers are generally a result of how horses are managed, although horses on pasture can develop ulcers, too. Factors that predispose horses to the development of ulcers include anatomy of the stomach, diet, restricted feed intake (long intervals between meals), strenuous exercise, stress, and using NSAIDs.

**Signs and symptoms:** Horses display a wide range of clinical signs when they have gastric ulcers. Many horses do not show any overt signs. Others show signs such as mild, low-grade colic, decreased performance, change in behavior, back pain, and weight loss.

**Immediate care:** A veterinarian can diagnose a horse with gastric ulcers by passing an endoscope into the stomach. Horses with ulcers are treated with omeprazole (GastroGard™).

**Prevention:** The prevention of gastric ulcers is aimed at removing or reducing the causative factors such as stress, lack of turnout, and long intervals between meals. In addition, a low dose of omeprazole may be given to horses at risk of developing gastric ulcers (for example, competing horses).

## Nervous System

### Rhinopneumonitis (Herpes Myeloencephalopathy)

**Etiology:** Mutation of equine herpes virus. When the respiratory form of this virus mutates (see "Respiratory System" earlier in this chapter), it infects the nervous system, causing debilitating neurologic signs. The mutated virus can be directly and indirectly passed from horse to horse and cause neurologic disease.

**Signs and symptoms:** Neurologic signs include incoordination and weakness, especially in the hind limbs; decreased tail tone; *incontinence* (inability to control bladder); and *recumbency* (inability to stand) in the late stages, which often leads to death. Generally, the horse has a high fever at some point, but once neurologic signs are present, there is often no fever. If a horse can recover, he usually regains normal neurologic function without lasting damage.

**Immediate care:** Quarantine the horse immediately and call your veterinarian. Horses that have potentially been exposed should also be quarantined for at least 2 weeks (consult your veterinarian) and should have their temperatures taken twice daily to watch for fever spikes for at least 7 days after exposure. Anti-viral drugs used to treat herpes in humans can be administered under a veterinarian's supervision; however, they are extremely expensive and do not cure the disease, only lessen the clinical signs. It is possible that the horse will require hospitalization for intensive supportive care.

**Prevention:** There is no prevention for the mutant neurologic form other than preventing the spread of this communicable disease (which can be difficult). Vaccinating with the modified live vaccine to decrease the spread of the respiratory form could potentially decrease the spread of the neurologic form.

### Encephalomyelitis (Eastern, Western, Venezuelan)

**Etiology:** There are three types of equine encephalomyelitis virus: Eastern (EEE), Western (WEE), and Venezuelan (VEE). Eastern and Western are the most common types in the United States, but the Venezuelan type is found occasionally in the southern United States. This virus is spread from birds to horses by mosquitoes, so horses can only acquire the disease during mosquito season. Although humans can contract this disease, they cannot get it directly from horses.

**Signs and symptoms:** This virus affects the nervous system, especially the brain. This disease is also known as *sleeping sickness* because horses may become severely depressed and act like they are sleeping. They may show signs of incoordination and weakness. They may continuously circle one direction or press their head against the wall, and have a very high fever. In severe cases, the horse is unable to stand and may become paralyzed. If a horse recovers from the disease, he usually regains normal neurologic function. The Eastern strain has a very high mortality rate (75 to 90 percent), followed by the Venezuelan form (40 to 90 percent) and Western form (20 to 50 percent).

**Immediate care:** A veterinarian should be called immediately; it is likely that the horse will require hospitalization for intensive supportive care.

**Prevention:** A vaccine is available that is very effective. Horses in areas where mosquitoes are present all year round should be vaccinated every 6 months; otherwise, horses should be vaccinated 1 month prior to the start of mosquito season.

## West Nile Virus

**Etiology:** Like encephalomyelitis, West Nile virus is passed from birds to horses by mosquitoes. (Although humans can contract this disease, they cannot get it directly from horses.) It has spread from the eastern to western states and is currently found in every continental state. It can only be acquired during mosquito season, although horses generally become sick in late summer/early fall.

**Signs and symptoms:** The signs are very similar to Eastern or Western encephalomyelitis. Horses may also have muscle twitching in addition to the neurologic signs. Horses may not be as depressed compared to encephalomyelitis, but they generally show signs of incoordination and weakness. Also, horses generally, but not always, have a high fever. In severe cases, horses are unable to stand and may become paralyzed. If a horse recovers from the disease, he usually regains normal neurologic function; however, the virus can be fatal.

**Immediate care:** A veterinarian should be called immediately; it is likely that the horse will require hospitalization for intensive supportive care.

**Prevention:** Different types of vaccines are available that are very effective. Horses in areas where mosquitoes are present all year round should be vaccinated every 6 months; otherwise, horses should be vaccinated 1 month prior to the start of mosquito season.

## Equine Protozoal Myeloencephalitis (EPM)

**Etiology:** Microscopic parasite-like organism (*protozoa*) called *Sarcocystis neurona*. The exact mechanism by which horses become infected is unknown, although it is likely that opossums are a carrier of the protozoa. It is known that horses ingest the organism, likely from feed contaminated with opossum feces. Then the organism can migrate to the fluid that surrounds the brain and spinal cord, causing inflammation and damage to those structures. Depending on their geographic location, many horses are exposed to EPM, but only a small number of those actually develop neurological disease. This makes testing horses for EPM difficult.

**Signs and symptoms:** Horses have variable neurologic signs that may be mild to severe. Often they become incoordinated or weak on one side of the body or in one leg, resulting in long-term weakness and decreased muscle mass on the affected side. Horses may have an unusual gait that is mistaken for lameness. In severe cases, horses may go blind, become paralyzed, or have seizures. Unfortunately, horses that are treated and recover generally have residual neurologic signs, though generally more mild, from permanent damage that the protozoa have caused.

**Immediate care:** A veterinarian should be consulted. Many treatment regimens are available aimed at killing the organism, with variable success rates.

**Prevention:** The current method of prevention is to prevent contamination of feed sources. Research is ongoing to develop further preventative and treatment measures. Not all diagnostic tools are 100 percent accurate.

### Tetanus

**Etiology:** Toxin from bacteria *Clostridium tetani*. Horses are very sensitive to this bacterial toxin, compared to other animals. This bacterium normally lives in the soil and horses acquire tetanus through deep wounds, especially puncture wounds. The bacteria enter through a break in the skin and are pushed deep into the muscle tissues. Once the skin heals over, there is little air in the wound, producing an ideal environment for these *anaerobic* bacteria to start reproducing because they live without air. They produce toxins that cause nerves to constantly fire because of dysfunction at the neuromuscular junctions, resulting in continuous muscle spasms that paralyze the horse (see Chapter 9, "Systems of the Horse"). It is the toxin, not the bacteria, that causes the symptoms. People can also get tetanus from their environment, so it is important to stay up to date on your tetanus booster when working around horses.

**Signs and symptoms:** Tetanus causes severe stiffness (*rigid paralysis*) that causes the horse to assume a "sawhorse" stance. The horse is unable to open his mouth, which is why the disease is also called *lockjaw*. This results in the inability to eat or drink. The third eyelid may cover the eye and the lips may be drawn back into a sneer or grimace due to contraction of the mouth muscles. The horse is jumpy and sensitive to sound and light. The tail may remain lifted. Eventually the diaphragm is affected, which prevents breathing, and the horse dies. This disease is almost always fatal.

**Immediate care:** If a horse sustains a large wound or puncture wound, he should be boostered with a tetanus toxoid vaccination unless he has been vaccinated within the last 2 months. If you suspect a horse has tetanus, call your veterinarian immediately. They may give the horse tetanus *antitoxin* to try to neutralize the toxins in the body, but this is not very effective if the toxins have already started to affect the horse. The horse will likely require hospitalization to receive intensive veterinary care.

**Prevention:** This disease is almost 100 percent preventable with vaccination. Horses should be vaccinated with *tetanus toxoid* once a year. This vaccination is usually given in combination with the encephalomyelitis vaccine.

### Botulism

**Etiology:** Toxin from bacteria *Clostridium botulinum*. Horses generally acquire the toxin from ingesting feed (especially round bales) contaminated with animal carcasses that contain the organism. It is more common in some areas of the country than others.

**Signs and symptoms:** Unlike tetanus, horses with botulism generally show signs of *flaccid* (floppy) paralysis because the toxin prevents the release of acetylcholine at the neuromuscular junctions (see Chapter 9), preventing muscle cells from contracting. The horse may have muscle tremors and appear weak. The horse often drools because he cannot swallow. As the disease progresses, the horse becomes recumbent. Eventually the muscles involved in breathing are paralyzed and the horse suffocates. The disease is almost always fatal unless promptly treated.

**Immediate care:** A veterinarian should be called immediately and horses often will require hospitalization. An antitoxin is available, as for tetanus, but it is difficult to acquire in some areas and is very expensive.

**Prevention:** A vaccine is available that should be administered in *endemic* areas (where the disease is common).

### Rabies

**Etiology:** The rabies virus is spread through the saliva of an infected or *rabid* animal, which is often a wild animal. Many mammals can acquire rabies, including humans, and it is fatal in most animals. Some of the most common wildlife sources of rabies include skunks, raccoons, coyotes, and bats.

**Signs and symptoms:** The symptoms of rabies are highly variable in horses, which makes it difficult to recognize the disease quickly before people are exposed. It affects the nervous system differently in each case. The area that was bitten by the rabid animal becomes swollen and may itch, but many times there is no obvious bite wound. Neurologic signs often develop days to weeks after the initial bite. One of the first signs is change in behavior, either depression or excitement with aggression. The horse is often incoordinated and may be unable to eat and drink properly. He may become paralyzed or frantic and have muscle tremors. Most infected animals, including horses, salivate excessively (the virus is transferred to other animals through saliva). A horse may also have a fever.

**Immediate care:** *DO NOT* handle a horse that is suspected of having rabies. Call your veterinarian immediately.

**Prevention:** A vaccine is available that is very effective and should be administered to susceptible companion animals (dogs, cats, horses) in endemic areas (where the virus is common in the wildlife).

## Endocrine System and Metabolic Diseases

### Pituitary Pars Intermedia Dysfunction or PPID (Equine Cushing's Disease)

**Etiology:** This disease is caused by a benign tumor-like growth in the pituitary gland that occurs in many horses over 15 years old. It results in an overproduction of ACTH (*adrenocorticotropic hormone*), which stimulates the adrenal glands to overproduce *cortisol*. Horses with PPID may or may not also be insulin-resistant.

**Signs and symptoms:** A classic sign of PPID in horses is the long hair coat that does not shed or takes longer to shed in the spring and summer. Horses also lose weight due to decreased muscle mass (cortisol causes protein in muscles to break down), while accumulating fat in key areas including the crest of the neck, tail head, sheath, and depression above the eye. Affected horses often drink too much and urinate more frequently than normal. They are also more prone to infections and parasite infestation. Most importantly, horses with this disease are at high risk of developing laminitis.

**Immediate care:** A veterinarian should examine a horse if PPID is suspected. Sometimes the clinical signs are present before the veterinarian is able to diagnose the disease with blood work, so treatment may be started even without abnormalities in blood work. In addition, ACTH secretion goes through a naturally occurring seasonal increase in the late summer and early fall, which might alter the results of blood work during those time periods, making diagnosis difficult. Currently the most effective treatment is with a human drug called pergolide; although it will not cure the disease, it will lessen the clinical signs.

**Prevention:** There is no prevention for this disease.

### *Equine Metabolic Syndrome (EMS) or Insulin Resistance (IR)*

**Etiology:** Certain breeds of horses and ponies that develop this disease are thought to have a genetic predisposition that is exacerbated by improper management. The initial stage of equine metabolic syndrome is the development of insulin resistance (similar to type 2 diabetes in people), whereby cells do not respond appropriately to insulin released following a meal, resulting in decreased uptake of glucose into cells and increased insulin levels in the blood. If the IR is not managed, the EMS disease complex progresses, with the horse becoming increasingly obese and showing signs of regional fat deposits. Unfortunately, it is associated with the development of laminitis, which is a career- and life-threatening disorder.

**Signs and symptoms:** Horses at risk of developing IR and EMS have a classic appearance due to typical fat accumulation. These horses are generally overweight and are considered "easy keepers." They accumulate extra fat in the crest of their neck, over the withers, in the sheath, and over the tail head. If the disease is not managed properly or if there is an episode that exacerbates the problem (for example, eating spring grass), these horses often develop laminitis. Once they have developed laminitis, they are more at risk for recurring episodes of laminitis.

**Immediate care:** Horses suspected of being at risk for this disease should have a closely managed diet to prevent obesity. The goal is to create a diet low in simple carbohydrates. This may involve keeping the horse on a dry lot and only feeding small amounts of grass hay or using a grazing muzzle to limit grass intake. Remember that grasses have increased levels of sugars during certain times of the year (early spring during rapid growth and late summer when preparing for winter), so horses with EMS or IR should be kept off of pastures during these times. These horses should almost never be fed grain; if they need supplemental energy in their diet, it should be provided in the form of fat, not carbohydrates.

**Prevention:** As discussed above, dietary management is useful in preventing the development and progression of the disease. Horses and ponies at risk for this condition should be evaluated for body condition regularly and management changes made accordingly. The primary goal is to prevent the development of laminitis, which is accomplished through strict dietary management.

## Reproductive System

### *Rhinopneumonitis*
**Etiology:** Equine herpes virus 1. This is the most common cause of infectious abortion in mares. It is transmitted by direct contact or indirect contact like the respiratory form (see "Respiratory System" earlier in this chapter), but it can also be transferred by a placenta, placental fluids, or aborted fetus from an infected mare.

**Signs and symptoms:** Mares infected with this virus abort in the last trimester (7 to 11 months) of pregnancy or have a foal that dies within a few days of birth.

**Immediate care:** Horses should be isolated immediately as this virus is contagious. Otherwise, care is supportive to let the virus run its course.

**Prevention:** Pregnant mares should be vaccinated with a *killed* vaccine product at the fifth, seventh, and ninth months of pregnancy.

### *Equine Viral Arteritis (EVA)*
**Etiology:** The equine viral arteritis virus is spread through direct or indirect contact with respiratory secretions from an infected horse or through sexual transmission during breeding. Stallions can be carriers of the disease and can shed the virus in semen. See also "Respiratory System" and "Circulatory System" earlier in this chapter.

**Signs and symptoms:** Mares infected with this virus abort during the fifth to tenth months of pregnancy.

**Immediate care:** Horses should be isolated immediately as this virus is contagious. Otherwise, care is supportive to let the virus run its course. Suspected EVA should be reported to your veterinarian.

**Prevention:** A modified live vaccine and a killed vaccine are available, but they are not extensively used as outbreaks are fairly rare. If a stallion is vaccinated, he may become *seropositive*, meaning that he was exposed to the virus, but it is difficult to determine if it was from an infection or the vaccination. This can make it difficult to determine if a stallion is a carrier. *Seronegative* mares should not be bred to seropositive stallions, but *seropositive* mares may be bred to *seropositive* stallions. Mares can only pass the virus to foals if they are actively infected. They pass it through inhalation, not milk. Only stallions can be carriers that can pass it on without being actively infected. If vaccinated, breeding horses may have difficulty being exported out of the U.S. due to import restrictions in other countries.

## Urinary System

### Rhabdomyolysis (Tying Up)
Horses can develop kidney failure after a severe episode of tying up, because the muscle breakdown products released into the bloodstream are filtered by the kidneys and, in large amounts, they can damage the kidney. The muscle breakdown products cause the urine to become dark brown in color. The muscle breakdown products are high in nitrogen and urea, and so the term *azoturia*, meaning increased urea in the urine, was formerly applied to the disease. For more information, see "Musculoskeletal System" earlier in this chapter.

## Integumentary System (Skin Problems)

### Rain Rot (Rain Scald)
**Etiology:** This disease is caused by *Dermatophilus congolensis*, a bacteria found on the skin of normal horses that are considered to be *carriers*. It is unknown whether a carrier horse is contagious to other horses. Rain rot occurs in wet weather conditions such as during the winter and spring. When the skin is constantly wet it cracks, allowing the bacteria to invade the upper layer of skin. The areas that are affected tend to be where water collects on the skin when it rains—the back and croup. It may also affect the legs. Horses with equine Cushing's disease are more likely to develop an infection like this, due to a long hair coat and weakened immune system.

**Signs and symptoms:** Crusty areas appear along the affected skin (back, croup, or legs) that peel off like scabs, leaving a small patch of hairless skin. The horse may be itchy.

**Immediate care:** You should consult a veterinarian, but treatment is aimed at eliminating the bacteria and allowing the skin to heal. Horses should be kept in a dry area until the infection has resolved and given betadine or chlorhexidine baths every other day, working gently to remove the crusts. Severe cases may require treatment with systemic antibiotics or other treatments as recommended by a veterinarian.

**Prevention:** Make sure that horses have access to shelter in the rain. Do not share grooming brushes or blankets from affected horses.

### Ringworm

**Etiology:** Ringworm is caused by a fungus called *Trichophyton*. It is very contagious by direct contact among horses and other animals, including humans. It is most commonly seen in horses that are not well taken care of. It resolves on its own without treatment within 1 to 4 months.

**Signs and symptoms:** Distinct hairless circles appear on the horse's body, most commonly on the neck, shoulders, and barrel. They may itch.

**Immediate care:** Do not touch the areas with bare hands as you can contract the disease from the horse. Horses should be isolated and separate equipment used until they are over the infection. Horses can be bathed with betadine, chlorhexidine, or antifungal shampoos to help clear the infection faster. Oral antifungal medications may be used, but their effectiveness is questionable and they are expensive.

**Prevention:** Keep the horse away from other horses until the ringworm is healed. You will need to disinfect his equipment once the horse is over the disease. In general, do not share grooming tools and equipment. Make sure your horse is properly cared for.

### Scratches (Mud Fever, Greasy Heel)

**Etiology:** This skin disease is caused by a mix of bacteria and possibly fungi invading the skin. Similar to rain rot, the organisms are normally found on the skin. When the skin is damaged from too much moisture, the organisms invade the deeper layers of the skin. The immune system tries to get rid of the organisms and inflammation results. This condition occurs most commonly in the muddy conditions of winter and spring, but it can also occur if a horse's legs are washed frequently and not properly dried. Scratches occur most commonly on the back of the pasterns, but can spread down toward the heel bulbs (called greasy heel) or up over the fetlocks in severe cases.

**Signs and symptoms:** Crusty, painful areas on the lower legs may ooze serum or even pus. Horses generally resent having the crusts removed, as it is painful. In severe cases, it can make the horse lame and cause swelling of the lower legs.

**Immediate care:** Many different regimens exist for treating scratches, so consult your veterinarian for recommendations. The primary goal is to allow the area to properly dry so the skin can heal. The hair in the area should be clipped (some horses resent this, because it hurts) and the skin should be kept clean and dry. The scabs should be softened with antibacterial creams and gently removed to facilitate healing. Sometimes an antibiotic and corticosteroid cream is applied to decrease inflammation while killing bacteria. If fungi are part of the problem, antifungal medications should be included in the treatment regimen.

**Prevention:** Keep horse's legs clean and dry as much as possible. Some horses are prone to getting scratches and should receive extra attention to prevent the disease. Avoid washing legs too often. Avoid letting horses stand in deep mud and flooded lots.

### Equine Sarcoid
**Etiology:** The exact cause of equine sarcoids, a type of benign skin tumor, is unknown. They may be caused by a cow skin virus or may be a dysfunction of how the equine skin heals.

**Signs and symptoms:** Sarcoids have various appearances ranging from flat and black hairless patches to large wart or tumor-like masses. They may increase in size or may stay stable.

**Immediate care:** Sarcoids are a cosmetic blemish unless they are in an area that interferes with tack such as the girth area, or an important structure such as the eye. Consult your veterinarian if you are concerned about a sarcoid on your horse.

**Prevention:** There is no prevention.

### Melanoma
**Etiology:** This is a skin tumor that occurs almost exclusively in grey horses that have black skin. They are usually benign, but can be very invasive. Melanomas can occur in internal organs as well as the skin.

**Signs and symptoms:** These masses covered by black skin vary in size and location, but tend to form around the anus, eyes, and other black-skinned hairless areas. They may only be a blemish unless they are in an area that interferes with tack such as the girth area, or an important structure such as the eye.

**Immediate care:** Consult your veterinarian if you are concerned about a melanoma.

**Prevention:** There is no prevention, but a melanoma vaccine is newly available that may be used to treat horses with the disease.

### Warts
**Etiology:** Equine papilloma virus. It is extremely contagious by direct contact. Horses older than 5 years of age are generally immune to the virus, so it tends to infect only young horses. Horses that have warts are not allowed to travel across state lines.

**Signs and symptoms:** Warts develop around the muzzle, and rarely, in other areas of the head. They dry up and fall off on their own as the horse's immune system kills the virus.

**Immediate care:** The warts go away on their own without treatment. Because horses are contagious while they have warts, they should be isolated from other horses until the warts have resolved.

**Prevention:** The best way to prevent this disease is to avoid sharing equipment among horses and avoid direct contact with strange horses.

Quarantine any young horses coming from a sale barn, as this a common place that warts are acquired.

### Summer Sores (Cutaneous Habronemiasis)
**Etiology:** Summer sores are caused by the larvae of Habronema. This parasite spends part of its life cycle in a fly's digestive tract. When a fly carrying Habronema larvae feeds on an open sore on a horse, tears in the eye, or excretions from the male reproductive tract, the Habronema larvae can travel into the area.

**Signs and symptoms:** When a wound is infected with Habronema larvae it fails to heal normally. It may form exuberant granulation tissue that enlarges like a tumor. Pink, bumpy, tumor-like masses can also develop around the eyes and on the penis. Sometimes, rice-sized yellow dead larvae are found within the tumor-like mass.

**Immediate care:** A horse with summer sores should be dewormed with ivermectin. More extensive treatment by a veterinarian, such as surgical removal, may be required.

**Prevention:** Prevention includes good fly control and appropriate wound care. In addition, horses that are dewormed regularly are less likely to contract this disease.

## Eye

### Conjunctivitis
**Etiology:** Conjunctivitis means inflammation of the conjunctiva, the tissues surrounding the eyeball. Horses can develop conjunctivitis for multiple reasons ranging from infection (EVA), a foreign body within the eye, allergies, an eye injury, or a corneal ulcer.

**Signs and symptoms:** Symptoms vary according to the cause of the conjunctivitis. Generally, the horse squints his eye and does not want to open it completely. There may be mucus discharge or tears coming from the eye. If the conjunctiva is normally pink (some horses have dark brown conjunctiva), it appears red and possibly swollen. The horse is sensitive to light and may resent you touching the eye area.

**Immediate care:** Any time you notice an abnormality in a horse's eye you should call your veterinarian immediately, even if it is after hours. Horses have delicate eyes, and any abnormalities should be treated immediately. Before the veterinarian arrives, move the horse to a dark area to make him more comfortable.

**Prevention:** There is no way to prevent conjunctivitis from eye injuries or allergies.

### Corneal Ulcers
**Etiology:** Corneal ulcers occur from anything rubbing the surface of the eyeball. They are usually sustained when a horse is unattended, so the exact cause may not be discovered. If a horse develops a corneal ulcer it may become infected with bacteria, or even worse, fungi, leading to eye-threatening disease.

**Signs and symptoms:** A horse with a corneal ulcer demonstrates the same signs as a horse with conjunctivitis, but may not have mucus discharge. He generally tears excessively and squints his eye, and is sensitive to bright light.

**Immediate care:** Any time you notice an abnormality in a horse's eye, call your veterinarian immediately, even if it is after hours. Horses have delicate eyes and abnormalities should be treated immediately. Before the vet arrives, move the horse to a dark area to make him more comfortable.

**Prevention:** Corneal ulcers are difficult to prevent. A fly mask can be applied when there are dusty conditions or debris in the air (for example, in the trailer or windy days) to decrease the chances of a corneal ulcer occurring.

### Eye Injuries
**Etiology:** Eye injuries are usually caused by some kind of trauma, such as the horse hitting his eye on something or lacerating the eyelid on a sharp object.

**Signs and symptoms:** Signs are similar to those listed for conjunctivitis and corneal ulcers. Eyelid lacerations are obvious.

**Immediate care:** A veterinarian should be called immediately if any abnormality is noticed in the eye or if a horse sustains an eyelid laceration.

**Prevention:** Keeping the horse in a safe environment free of sharp objects or surfaces that might injure the eye is the best prevention.

### Recurrent Uveitis (Periodic Ophthalmia, Moon Blindness)
**Etiology:** *Uveitis* means inflammation in the inner part of the eyeball. The exact cause of this disease is under investigation, and there may be several different causes that result in the same disease. One possible cause is from an infection with the bacteria *Leptospira,* which results in an immune-mediated attack on the eye. Other immune-mediated diseases may also cause recurrent uveitis. Appaloosa horses are predisposed to recurrent uveitis.

**Signs and symptoms:** Initially, the horse looks like he has a painful eye. One or both eyes may be affected. Generally, if it occurs in one eye, the other eye eventually develops the disease. The eye(s) tears and the horse may squint. As the eye becomes damaged from continual inflammation, it becomes cloudy and eventually the horse becomes blind. This disease is progressive, although it can sometimes be slowed with medical treatment.

**Immediate care:** A veterinarian should be called immediately any time an abnormality is noted in a horse's eye. Anti-inflammatories, like NSAIDs or corticosteroids, that are administered into the eye may be prescribed to decrease the immune response.

**Prevention:** There is currently no known prevention for this disease.

# Preventing the Spread of Contagious Diseases

When a horse suffers from a contagious disease, you must care for him while preventing exposure to other horses. Good horse management practices can decrease the spread of many types of diseases.

Some precautions are:

- Keep in mind that the immune systems of horses stressed by travel, new surroundings, or competition are lowered, so these horses are more susceptible to diseases that can be acquired from other horses, such as influenza, strangles, rhinopneumonitis, and equine viral arteritis (EVA). Horses that have returned from a competition or are new in the barn should be kept separated from the herd and closely monitored, including taking temperatures daily for a week.

- Stable sick horses away from healthy horses during a disease outbreak. Decrease or eliminate the movement of horses and people on and off of the farm property while the disease is ongoing. Infectious organisms can be carried to other stables on people's shoes and clothing.

- Use separate tack, stable equipment, utensils, buckets, feed tubs, feed measures, and any other equipment for the sick horses. Try to use disposable materials to avoid labor-intensive and possibly ineffective cleaning. Thoroughly clean and disinfect all equipment after horses have recovered from illness. Ask your veterinarian which disinfectant to use for each particular disease.

- Monitor healthy horses regularly (usually once or twice a day, including taking temperatures) and separate them if they develop signs of disease (for example, an increase in temperature). Your veterinarian will determine how often healthy horses should be checked.

- Change clothes and footwear and wash your hands after handling the sick horses, and BEFORE handling healthy horses. It is best to handle all healthy horses first and the sick horses last.

- Limit the number of people caring for sick horses to decrease the likelihood of disease spread. Have one person work with the sick horse(s), if possible.

- Ask your veterinarian whether unaffected horses would benefit from vaccination boosters or any other prophylactic treatments.

## Vaccinations

Vaccinations are discussed in *USPC D* and *C Level Manuals*, which should be reviewed. Some points to remember about vaccinations in regard to management of a stable are:

- Consult your veterinarian about which diseases to vaccinate against, considering the age and type of horse, risk of exposure, and incidence of disease in your area. Horses that travel or compete usually need different vaccination programs than those that remain at home.
- Consult with your veterinarian to determine how long and how many vaccinations it takes to establish initial immunity in an unvaccinated horse and when booster shots are required. A basic guide is provided in the *USPC C Level Manual*, pages 181–183. A good resource for current vaccination guidelines is on the website for the American Association of Equine Practitioners (www.aaep.org).
- There are different types of vaccines available for horses. Killed vaccines contain an infectious agent that is intact but has been killed. Modified live vaccines contain an infectious agent that has been genetically modified to be non-infectious but is still alive.
- There are different methods of administering vaccines including in the muscles (intramuscular or IM) or a squirt up the nose (intranasal or IN).
- Keep records up to date for individual horses and for the stable.
- Note dates when boosters are due on the stable calendar.
- Horses may have a reaction, go off feed, or be sore for a day or two after vaccination. Schedule vaccinations so horses can have a day or two off if necessary, not right before a competition.
- Vaccines must be stored at the correct temperature, prepared properly, and administered in the proper dosage, according to manufacturer's specifications. For this reason, they should be administered by a veterinarian.

## Drugs and Medications

Horse owners and stable managers often keep certain drugs and medications on hand for use in emergencies, or to treat minor ailments or chronic conditions. However, any medication strong enough to have potential benefits also has the potential to do harm if misused. Drugs and prescription medications should be given only on orders from the veterinarian. It is dangerous to assume that because a certain medication was used successfully in one case it can safely be given in another.

In some cases, the veterinarian may prescribe certain drugs or medications for you to administer, or he may leave a supply of a drug to be used under certain circumstances. Here are some guidelines for using medications safely:

- Keep on hand only those drugs and medications that your veterinarian agrees you should have. They should be given only with the advice and approval of your veterinarian. He should give you instructions regarding any medications he approves for you to use on your own.
- When a drug is prescribed, get (and write down) complete information on how to administer it, how often, for how long, and any symptoms or side effects to watch out for. Be sure the veterinarian knows about any other drugs or medications the horse has been given recently, including dewormers.
- Drugs are administered by the weight of horse in pounds (lb) or kilograms (kg). Recommended drug dosages are given in milligrams per pound (mg/lb) or milligrams per kilogram (mg/kg). Drug bottles have the concentration of drug listed in milligrams (mg) per unit volume; for example, milliliters (ml) or cubic centimeter (cc). It is very important to check the concentration if your veterinarian gives you a dose in volume only.
- Many drugs are currently available in generic form because their patent has expired. It is important to learn actual drug names, not just trade names.
- Have your veterinarian teach you how to administer medications by mouth and by intramuscular injection, including necessary precautions.
- Most drugs should be stored at a consistent temperature near room temperature (60 to 80°F). Some drugs should not be exposed to light while stored; these generally come in dark-colored glass bottles. Some drugs require refrigeration (such as procaine penicillin and vaccines). If you are unsure how a drug or vaccine should be stored, consult the product label or ask your veterinarian.
- Before using any drug, check its expiration dates (stamped on the vial or box). Drugs will not work as effectively or can be dangerous if used after their expiration date. Dispose of all drugs past their expiration date.
- The possession of needles, syringes, and certain drugs is regulated by law; regulations vary from state to state. You should have a prescription for any controlled items, and they must be kept under lock and key and disposed of properly after use.

## Types of Drugs and Medications

There are many more types and classifications of drugs than can be covered here. Some of the drugs more commonly used by horse owners and managers are tranquilizers, pain relievers, anti-inflammatory drugs, and antibiotics.

### Tranquilizers and Sedatives

Tranquilizers and sedatives are drugs that produce a calming effect by working on the brain or the central nervous system. They are used to calm and restrain horses during veterinary treatment and for clipping, shipping, and other procedures. Tranquilizers raise the horse's pain threshold due to behavioral modification, whereas sedatives modify behavior and reduce pain (analgesic). A tranquilized or sedated horse can still feel pain and may kick, jump, or react violently to a startling or painful stimulus.

Tranquilizers and sedatives work best when administered while the horse is calm. The horse should be allowed to remain undisturbed for 5 to 15 minutes, or until the drug takes effect. Individual horses' sensitivity to tranquilizers can vary greatly.

A tranquilized or sedated horse may be unsteady on his feet and may fall more easily than usual. Keep this in mind when holding a horse for veterinary work or other procedures. If a horse must be tranquilized for shipping, the dose must be carefully calculated to avoid putting him at risk for falling during loading, travel, and unloading. Heavily sedated horses may have difficulty swallowing. They should not be allowed to eat or drink until they have returned to normal alertness, or choke may result.

Tranquilizers may be recommended by your veterinarian to keep a horse calm when he is on stall rest or reintroduced to turnout. Tranquilizing horses for training purposes is not recommended, because tranquilizers block conditioned responses and learned behavior. In addition, a tranquilized horse's reflexes and balance are impaired, so he is more likely to stumble or fall, and his reactions are unpredictable. *Never ride a tranquilized horse; this is dangerous for both horse and rider!*

The use of tranquilizers and sedatives is illegal for most competitive horse sports. Each medication has a different withdrawal time (or time from last administration to elimination from the body). A positive drug test may result in elimination from a competition or other penalties, so make sure your veterinarian is aware of drug withdrawal times before administering a drug when it is close to a show.

Commonly used tranquilizers and sedatives include the following.

**Acepromazine (PromAce®, Promazine® Granules):** A tranquilizer that depresses the central nervous system, resulting in a tranquilizing effect and decreased response to environmental stimuli. It does not provide relief from pain and will not prevent a horse from moving or kicking if he is startled or feels pain. It may be administered intramuscularly, intravenously, or as granules added to feed. **Dangers:** Acepromazine causes a drop in blood pressure, and *must not* be given to horses that are in shock, dehydrated, septic (severe infections), in poor condition (malnutrition), or suffering from colic. Accidental injection into an artery (especially the carotid artery) can produce signs ranging from excitement and disorientation to seizures and death. Acepromazine can, rarely, cause paralysis of the penis. Its use should be avoided in stallions for this reason.

**Xylazine (Rompun®):** This drug works on the sympathetic nervous system, causing sedation and relieving pain for a short amount of time (30 to 45 minutes). It also slows the heart rate and causes horses to sweat. It causes horses to drop their heads and assume a wide-based stance with their limbs, which is helpful for performing veterinary procedures such as dental work. At high doses, it can result in dangerous ataxia (uncoordinated movement). It also decreases the swallowing reflex and slows smooth muscle contractions in the gastrointestinal tract, which may result in choke if a horse eats while still sedated. It is an excellent short-term pain reliever for pain originating from the gastrointestinal tract resulting in colic. Xylazine is administered intravenously or intramuscularly on the advice of a veterinarian. In case of over-sedation, a reversal agent called yohimbine can be administered. **Dangers:** Horses sedated with xylazine may appear sedated and immobile, but can suddenly strike or kick at inappropriate times. In addition, some horses have abnormal reactions to xylazine resulting in severe changes in behavior (becoming aggressive) or incoordination. As with acepromazine, xyalzine injected into an artery can cause serious side effects that may result in death. **Caution:** Xyalzine is extremely toxic to humans in very tiny amounts if it gets into the mouth or eyes or is accidentally injected, resulting in severe respiratory depression. If exposure occurs, the person should be taken to the hospital immediately.

**Detomidine (Dormosedan®):** This sedative is in the same class as xylazine, so it has very similar effects and is administered in the same methods (IV or IM). It lasts longer (45 to 60 minutes) and tends to cause fewer inappropriate responses than xylazine. It is also a stronger reliever of gastrointestinal pain. It is commonly combined with butorphanol (Torbugesic) to achieve a higher degree of sedation and decrease voluntary movement (causing the horse to plant his feet).

**Romifidine (Sedivet®):** This sedative is also in the same class as xyalzine. It has an intermediate length of action and is preferred by some veterinarians. It is also administered intravenously or intramuscularly.

### *Analgesics (Pain-Relieving Drugs)*

Analgesics are drugs that relieve pain by blocking the sensation of pain, but not other sensations. The painful area does not become numb, as it would with an anesthetic, but pain is decreased or relieved.

Narcotics are powerful pain-relieving drugs that act on the central nervous system. They may cause serious drug reactions or side effects. Narcotics must be used *only* by veterinarians, and their possession is regulated by law in all states.

Non-narcotic and non-steroidal anti-inflammatory drugs (called *NSAIDs*) are drugs that relieve pain by reducing inflammation. Some may be prescribed by a veterinarian for the horse owner to administer.

Similar to tranquilizers and sedatives, the use of analgesics is regulated by most competitive bodies. Check with your governing body's rules prior to using analgesics in horses that are actively competing.

**Butorphanol (Torbugesic®):** This is a narcotic analgesic (class C). It is a controlled substance, so it must be administered by a veterinarian or by veterinarian orders. It is used alone for relieving pain, especially colic pain, although its effect is variable. Most commonly, it is used in combination with *detomidine*, to create more profound sedation and for relief of severe pain. A side effect of this drug is mild nervous system excitement known as "torb jerks" that commonly causes head jerking or other muscle twitching. It is usually administered intravenously, but can be given intramuscularly for longer-lasting effects.

### *Non-Steroidal Anti-Inflammatory Drugs (NSAIDs)*

Non-steroidal anti-inflammatory drugs reduce pain by controlling inflammation. They are used to treat a variety of musculoskeletal problems, including sprains, strains, overuse of muscles, joint injuries, and arthritis. They are also used to decrease inflammation and pain in other areas of the body, including the gastrointestinal system, the eye, and the reproductive system. They are also anti-pyretics (anti-fever), and may be used to reduce fever when a horse suffers from a bacterial or viral infection.

NSAIDs do not cure musculoskeletal problems, nor do they block pain in the same way that an anesthetic does. They may be given to make it more comfortable for the horse to move, which helps to keep the affected area from "scarring down" and losing its range of motion during healing. However, pain control and exercise must be carefully balanced, under veterinary supervision, to avoid overstressing the area, re-injuring it, and worsening the original injury.

NSAIDs (especially *phenylbutazone,* or *bute*) are often used to help older, arthritic horses continue to work more comfortably. However, NSAIDs can be abused if used to suppress symptoms for hard work or competition, without regard to the horse's long-term soundness. For this reason, NSAIDs should only be used on the advice of a veterinarian who is familiar with the horse's history, and the level of work must be appropriate for the horse.

NSAIDs tend to be hard on the gastrointestinal tract, and overdosage or prolonged usage can result in ulcers forming in the stomach and large intestine, especially in foals. Horses that are extra-sensitive to the side effects of NSAIDs or that receive an overdose of NSAIDs may develop colic and diarrhea. If you notice this in a horse receiving NSAIDs, call your veterinarian immediately. In addition, the use of NSAIDs should be avoided in dehydrated horses because they can cause serious damage to the kidneys. Kidney damage may also occur if a horse receives an overdose of an NSAID, especially if it is multiple doses in a short period of time.

Commonly used NSAIDs include the following.

**Phenylbutazone ("Bute," Pro-Bute®, other trade names):** Acts directly on inflamed tissues. It is widely used for relief of musculoskeletal disorders, including strains, sprains, muscle overuse, tendonitis, acute joint injuries, and arthritic conditions. It is also used to control pain from injuries, infections, laminitis, and other painful conditions, and to control fever associated with bacterial or viral infections. Phenylbutazone is not especially effective against colic pain.

Phenylbutazone can be given as oral gel or paste, in tablets or powder, or intravenously. It is very irritating to tissues and can cause severe tissue damage if injected outside a vein, or if repeated injections are made into the same vein. It should *never* be injected in the muscle.

Overdoses of phenylbutazone can cause mouth and tongue ulcers, gastrointestinal ulcers, and kidney damage.

Using two NSAIDs at once (*stacking*) occurs on horse-show circuits, but is not advisable as it compounds the side effects of the drugs and could cause toxic levels to be reached. Most local and national horse show associations allow horses to show on low levels of phenylbutzone, but prohibit its use in conjunction with *flunixin meglumine (Banamine®)*. Horses competing at international (FEI) levels are not allowed to compete on any NSAIDs. Ask your veterinarian about drug use in actively competing horses.

**Flunixin meglumine (Banamine®):** Similar to phenylbutazone, flunixin meglumine is a potent anti-inflammatory agent that is primarily used for problems affecting soft tissues, such as the gastrointestinal tract (especially colic), respiratory system, or the eye. It is generally the preferred NSAID for reducing fevers. It is available as a paste for oral administration or an injectable form that is best given intravenously (IV). When given intramuscularly, it can cause severe muscle abscesses, so this route of administration should be avoided.

**Diclofenac (Surpass®):** This is a topical NSAID that is absorbed through the skin. It is used to treat musculoskeletal problems locally by spreading the cream over the specific structure that is injured or inflamed. Because it is absorbed through the skin, it is important to wear gloves when handling it and to clip the horse's hair in the area in order for it to reach the skin.

**Firocoxib (Equioxx®):** This is a selective NSAID designed to inhibit only one part of the inflammatory cascade in order to have less effect on normal body functions, thereby decreasing many of the harmful side effects, such as gastrointestinal ulcers, associated with other NSAIDs. It is available as a paste that should be administered according to manufacturer's directions or with veterinary advice.

### Corticosteroids

Corticosteroids are among the most powerful anti-inflammatory drugs. The body produces natural corticosteroids when the adrenal gland is stimulated by *adrenocorticotrophic hormone (ACTH)*, released by the pituitary gland. When administered as drugs, corticosteroids are used to control inflammation. They may be given orally, intramuscularly, or intravenously, and may be injected directly into a joint.

While reducing inflammation, corticosteroids suppress immune responses, both locally and throughout the body. This makes the horse more vulnerable to infections of all kinds. Other possible side effects are suppression of the body's ability to produce natural corticosteroids, depressed calcium and potassium levels, weakness, loss of muscle mass, and laminitis.

Corticosteroids are sometimes injected into inflamed joints. There is some risk involved when a horse's joints are injected, because bacteria could be introduced into the joint and cause a joint infection that can be career- or even life-threatening. Veterinarians take precautions such as making the injection point as sterile as possible prior to injection and injecting antibiotics into the joint. Repeated joint injections contribute to the deterioration of the joint's cartilage, so they should be performed judiciously.

Because of their potential for harmful side effects, corticosteroids should never be given except on a veterinarian's orders. Horse owners should realize that corticosteroids can reduce pain, heat, and swelling and can make an injury *appear* better very quickly, but it is not healed and is extremely vulnerable to further damage if the horse is worked inappropriately. Abuse of corticosteroids can cause permanent damage.

Corticosteroids include the following:

**Dexamethazone (Azium®):** This general, powerful, quick-acting anti-inflammatory is used to treat allergic reactions (such as hives), inappropriate inflammatory responses (proud flesh on wounds), life-threatening swelling (brain swelling), and chronic inflammatory conditions that are not due to infection (heaves). When used chronically, it increases a horse's chance of developing an infection due to suppression of the immune system, and there is a risk of developing laminitis. This drug is used most frequently in its generic form, which comes in varying concentrations (mg/ml). It is important to treat horses in milligrams, not just milliliters (ml) or cubic centimeters (cc) when using this drug. It is available in a pill or powder for oral administration or in an injectable form that can be given intravenously or intramuscularly.

**Methylprednisolone acetate (Depo-medrol®):** This long-acting corticosteroid is commonly injected into the lower hock joints to alleviate inflammation associated with osteoarthritis.

**Triamcinolone (Vetalog®, Kenalog®):** This is a medium- to long-acting corticosteroid that is injected into joints to decrease inflammation associated with osteoarthritis.

### Joint Therapeutics

Joint therapeutics are substances that encourage the production and improve the quality of joint components such as cartilage, joint fluid, and its components. Some are injected directly into the joint or administered as intramuscular injections, while others are fed to the horse as nutraceuticals. Their purpose is to prevent, reduce, or heal inflammation in joints, and to help the horse build stronger joints and move freely without pain.

**Hyaluronic acid (Legend®, MAP-5®, Hyvisc®):** Hyaluronic acid is a primary component of joint fluid. It also has mild anti-inflammatory properties. When a joint becomes arthritic or inflamed, its hyaluronic acid is degraded rapidly by inflammatory substances. The goal of treating horses with hyaluronic acid either systemically (through intravenous injection or orally) or directly into the joint (through intra-articular injection) is to supplement this component of the joint fluid while the body is attempting to replace it. It is often injected with corticosteroids into the joint so that the corticosteroids decrease the inflammation in the joint and allow the body to catch up with joint fluid production. Your veterinarian will advise you as to the interval of dosing and which product to use, as some products are used systemically, while others are designed for joint injection only.

**Polysulfated glycosaminoglycans or PSGAGs (Adequan®):** PSGAGs are a primary component of cartilage. They are administered intramuscularly with the goal of providing more of this building block for the body to use in repairing damaged cartilage that occurs with osteoarthritis. Similar to hyaluronic acid, your veterinarian will recommend the correct dosing interval for your horse, as there is a lot of variability in how this drug is used.

**Glucosamine and chondroitin sulfate (Cosequin®, Flex Free®):** Similar to PSGAGs, the goal of the oral supplements containing these compounds is to provide cartilage building blocks for the body to repair damaged cartilage and maintain the integrity of the cartilage within the joints.

These compounds are not readily absorbed from the horses' gastrointestinal tract, so supplements must contain high amounts to have any therapeutic benefit. They are available in a wide range of oral products ranging from powders to liquids to gels. They generally require administration of a loading dose for some amount of time to build up high enough levels to be therapeutic. Follow the manufacturers' directions for correct dosing.

There is a huge amount of variability in the amounts of glucosamine and chondroitin sulfate contained in various products because they are supplements, not drugs, and therefore are not subject to the same quality controls as drugs.

**Methylsulfonylmethane (MSM):** Considered a mild anti-inflammatory, MSM is thought to be converted to an important component of connective tissue. There currently is no scientific data to support its use in horses.

## Other Drugs

### Ulcer Drugs

**Omeprazole (GastroGard®, UlcerGard®, Neigh-Lox®):** This drug acts to decrease the acidity of the stomach. This allows gastric ulcers to heal if they have already formed, or helps to prevent them from forming when the drug is used at a lower dose. It is administered as an oral paste. Follow the instructions on the product label or check with your veterinarian for dosing intervals.

### Antibiotics

Antibiotics are drugs that kill bacteria. They are only effective against bacterial infections, *not* against viral infections. Specific antibiotics are only effective against certain types of bacteria. A culture may have to be grown in the laboratory to determine which antibiotics work best against a particular organism.

Antibiotics are often misused by horse owners, which can lead to problems. Giving antibiotics unnecessarily (for instance, for viral infections), in too-small doses, or for too short a period to be effective can cause bacteria to become resistant to certain antibiotics. This is a concern because bacterial resistance to antibiotics is a growing problem in both human and veterinary medicine. As horse owners, we should work to prevent the development of bacterial resistance by using antibiotics judiciously and with the guidance of a veterinarian. In addition, some antibiotics may produce serious side effects.

Antibiotics should be used only on the advice of a veterinarian. It is important to follow the recommended schedule and to continue giving the medication for as long as it was prescribed. The most serious side effect of antibiotic administration in horses is antibiotic-induced diarrhea, which can be life-threatening. You should contact a veterinarian immediately if a horse develops diarrhea after receiving antibiotics.

Some antibiotics are forbidden substances under competition rules, especially if they contain procaine. Consult your organization's drug rules prior to competing with a horse on antibiotics.

Some examples of antibiotics are penicillin, gentamicin, streptomycin, sulfonamides, and tetracycline.

# Restraining Horses

Sometimes horses must be restrained in order to perform veterinary treatment or diagnostic procedures, to medicate minor wounds, or for clipping or other purposes. In using restraints, the following principles are most important:

- Any restraint must be safe for the handler and for the veterinarian or person working on the horse.
- The restraint must be safe for the horse and applied humanely.
- Minimize stress on the horse by using the least severe restraint that will work safely under the circumstances, and for no longer than necessary.
- Plan ahead. Teach horses to accept routine handling procedures, have suitable restraint equipment and experienced help, and work in a safe and appropriate area.
- Restraints must be used with good judgment, taking into account the situation, the individual horse, and the experience of the handler. Apply them kindly but firmly, and *never* lose your temper!

## Types of Restraints

### Distracting the Horse

In many cases, holding a horse safely while distracting him from the procedure is sufficient. Some ways to distract a horse's attention are:

- Patting or scratching him on the neck, between the jawbones, or around the base of the ears.
- Cupping one hand over an eye (to prevent the horse from seeing a needle, for example).
- Holding the upper lip and/or the ear with the fingers. (Do not twist the ear or interfere with the horse's breathing.)
- Gripping the loose skin at the shoulder.

### Using a Chain-End Lead Shank

A chain-end lead shank is one of the simplest and most effective forms of restraint. It should be used with a sturdy, properly fitted halter. The handler should stand at the horse's shoulder (never directly in front of a horse), out of the way of the head and front feet, on the same side as the veterinarian or person working on the horse. For safety, hold the shank, not the chain.

When held quietly, a chain shank does not bother the horse. A short tug or two will get his attention; never hang on a shank with continuous hard pressure. Severe jerking on a chain shank is abusive and dangerous; it can cause a horse to run backward, rear, or resist violently.

Some ways of using a chain-end lead shank are:

**Chain under chin:** Tends to make the horse raise his head.

**Chain over nose:** Adjust so that the opposite side of the halter is not drawn into the horse's eye. Severe use can cause damage to the nose.

**Chain in mouth:** More severe method that can injure the mouth if misused. However, some horses respect this restraint more than any other.

**Chain across gum, under upper lip:** Severe method sometimes used when a horse cannot be twitched or tranquilized. It may cause bleeding if the horse fights it, but is almost as effective as a twitch because, like a twitch, it causes endorphin release if slight pressure is constantly maintained. Ideally, the chain should be wrapped with Vetrap or tape to prevent injury to the gums.

### Holding Up a Foreleg

Holding up a foreleg is a simple restraint that works well to keep a horse from fidgeting or picking up his legs. Hold up the foreleg on the same side the veterinarian or other person is working on, using a toe hold. Don't rely on this restraint to stop a horse from violently kicking or struggling. Also, it is dangerous to use this type of restraint on sedated horses as they may fall down due to lack of coordination. Sometimes when they start to fall, they will leap back up violently and hurt nearby handlers.

### Using a Twitch

A twitch is used to apply pressure to the upper lip. It was once thought that the pain inflicted by a twitch distracted the horse from the procedure. Recent research has shown that pressure of the twitch on the nerves of the upper lip causes the horse to release natural substances called endorphins into the bloodstream, which alleviate pain and help to calm the horse. Some horses will fight when a twitch is applied; the calming effect only begins to work after the horse submits to the twitch. The calming effect begins 3 to 5 minutes after application and usually lasts about 15 minutes.

A twitch must never be applied to any place but the upper lip, and should not be left on longer than 15 to 20 minutes. The horse should be held with a lead shank, never by a twitch alone. It is important to always hold onto the twitch securely as it can become a dangerous projectile if it is let go while a horse is struggling.

There are several types of twitches, including short and long wood-handled twitches, and tongs or clamp twitches that can be fastened to the halter.

Use of chain-end lead shank for restraint.

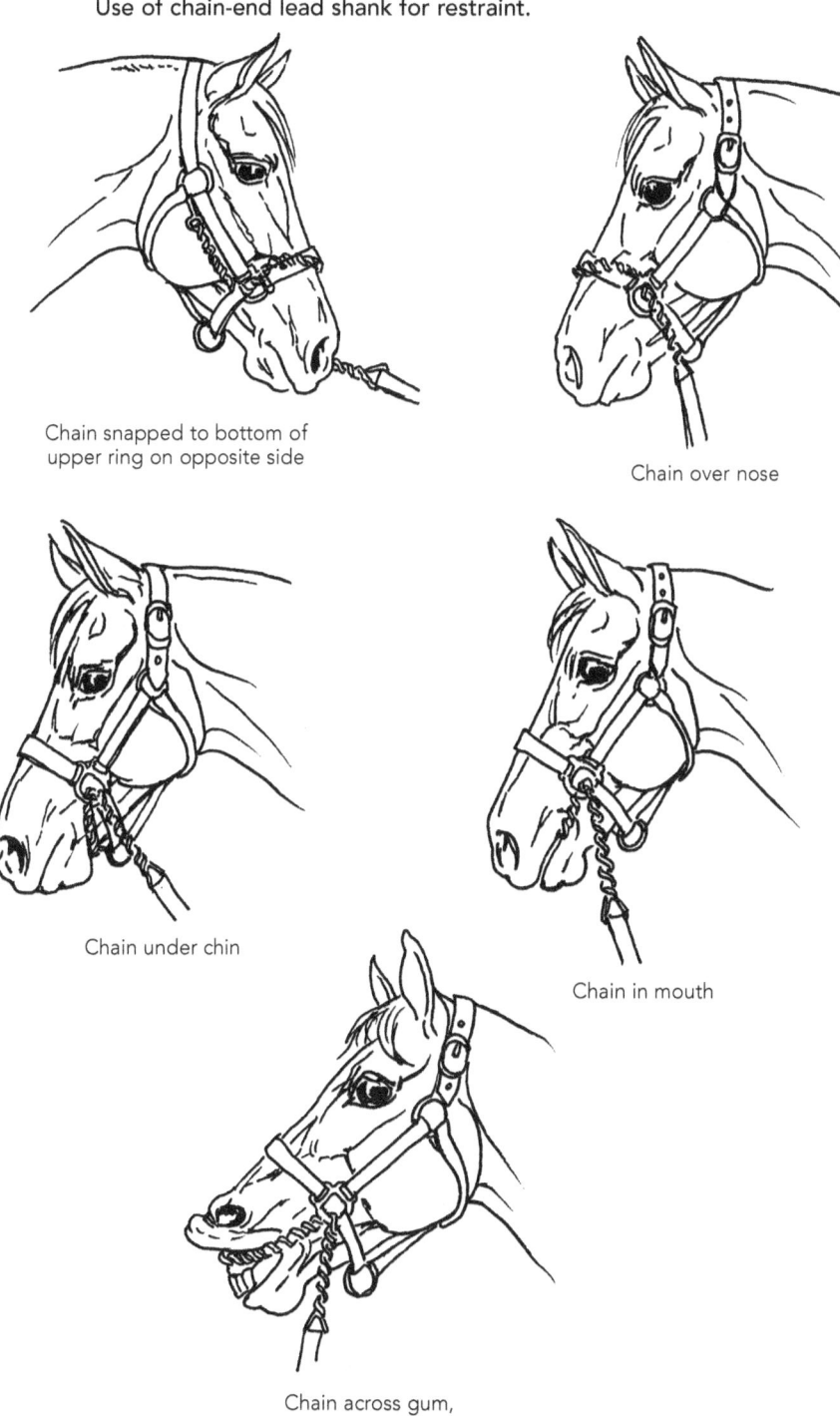

Chain snapped to bottom of upper ring on opposite side

Chain over nose

Chain under chin

Chain in mouth

Chain across gum, under upper lip

## Horse restraints.

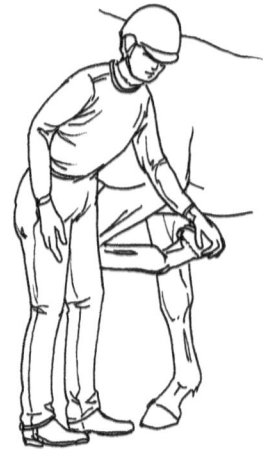

Holding foreleg with toe hold

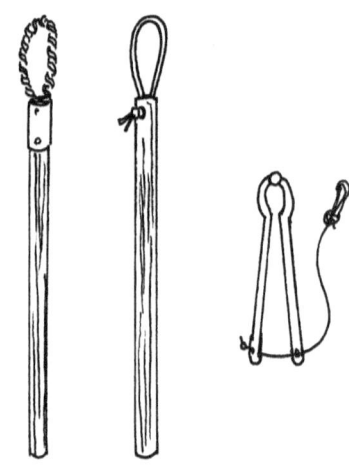

Twitches

## Restraining horse with a twitch.

Apply a twitch: Place loop over thumb and three fingers

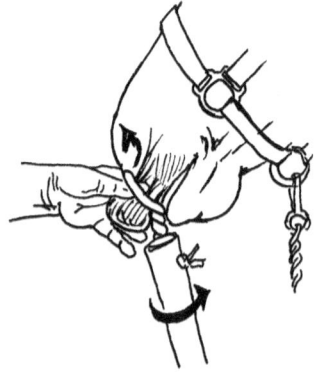

Grasp upper lip, slip twitch over lip, and twist toward horse

Tighten enough for safe and effective restraint

Hold twitch with both hands; stand to one side; always hold horse with halter shank as well as twitch

## Helping a Cast Horse

A horse becomes "cast" when he is lying against a wall or other immovable structure that prevents him from positioning his legs properly (front legs out in front, hind legs underneath belly) to stand up. This may occur with or without an underlying medical condition. Young horses that have recently been stalled may become cast if they roll into the stall wall because they aren't used to small spaces. This could also occur if a large horse is placed in a smaller stall than he is used to. Sometimes, horses become cast when they are severely colicking because they are not concerned with their surroundings while they are rolling from pain, or if they have developed neurologic deficits due to a neurologic disease.

When a horse is cast, he may panic due to his flight instincts. *Never* go into a stall where a horse is struggling violently, as he can inadvertently injure you. In these cases, a veterinarian should be called to sedate the horse. Getting a cast horse up is a very dangerous situation and should only be done by an experienced horse person.

A person can carefully restrain a horse in a lying position by sitting on the back of the head/front of the neck. This should ONLY be done by an experienced person who weighs enough to overcome the strength of a horse's neck muscles.

Often, a horse will lie quietly once he realizes he cannot get up. In this case, human assistance can be provided to reposition the horse in order to allow him to get up. A strong person may be able to grab a horse's tail and move the rear end around enough to give him room to stand. If the horse is very close against the wall, long ropes can be used to roll him over. They should be applied very carefully to the down forelimb and, if the horse is quiet, the down rear limb, at the level of the pastern or just above the fetlocks. Ideally, the ropes are secured with a quick-release knot so that they can be removed immediately after the horse is standing. Once in place, one or two people can pull the horse over, taking care to move out of the way of the horse's limbs. If the horse starts to struggle at any point, it is best to stop and wait for a veterinarian to sedate the horse.

# 15

# Stable and Facility Management

Managing a stable requires more than horse care and routine chores. As a stable manager, you are responsible for the horses, the facility, and the economical operation of the stable. You must organize a program of horse care and facility maintenance, budget your time and money, and be aware of the overall picture as well as the details of getting the work done. It is also your responsibility to stay current (veterinary information, nutrition, and so on), to be environmentally responsible whenever you can, and to protect the natural environment.

## Efficiency and Organization

Efficiency and good organization are the hallmarks of a well-run stable or program. Efficiency means making the most intelligent use of available resources (including time) and to do the job without wasting time, effort, or money. Organization means planning and putting together different elements into a smoothly working whole. Disorganization and inefficiency make you work harder to accomplish less, often leading to slipshod and substandard horse care, dangerous situations, and becoming harried, frustrated, and overworked to the point of burnout.

Here are some tips for organizing stable management:

- Define your job. What are your most important goals and responsibilities? Which are of secondary importance?
- List the work that must be done: daily chores, weekly chores, and occasional jobs.
- What does each job require in skills, equipment, and time? Is there a more efficient way to do it?
- Consider how to make the best use of the resources you have, including yourself and other workers. Trying to do everything yourself is less efficient and more stressful than delegating some responsibilities when appropriate.
- Budget your time. Set up a schedule that allows you to do your essential work at the best time for you to accomplish it. Try to identify "time stealers"—people or activities that frequently waste your productive time—and change your schedule to avoid them.
- Communicate with those you work with; have regular meetings to discuss plans, keep everyone informed, and get important input. Post schedules, notes, tasks, and assignments.
- Relying on memory is inefficient and can lead to mistakes. Make it a habit to carry a notebook and write down everything you need to take care of. Check off tasks as they are completed.
- Set aside a time for office duties such as keeping up records, paying bills, and making phone calls.

## Stable Management Records

Good records are essential for the business and financial aspects of stable management, and for keeping track of horse information, health and farrier care, and other management activities. For records to be useful, they must be complete and accurate. It's important to keep records in a form that is easy to use and in a convenient place, and to keep them up to date. If records are kept on a computer, they must be backed up, or a hard copy (paper copy) of all records should be kept.

Horse management records might include:

**Individual horse records:** A file for each horse, containing:

- Name, description, and identification information.
- Registration papers.
- Health record (inoculations, deworming, vet notes, and so on).

- Vital signs (resting pulse, temperature, and respiration rates).
- Feeding schedule; noting frequency, amount, supplements or medications regularly administered, and any changes.
- Shoeing record (dates; notes on type of shoes or special needs).
- Breeding record.
- Insurance documents.
- Individual horse notes: tack and equipment used, any unusual behaviors, buddies to be turned out with or not to be turned out with.
- Emergency contacts, including vet, farrier, owner, insurance agent, and so on.

**Stable log:** Book for daily notes, including work done, medications and treatments, training notes, vet or farrier visits, and so on.

**Planning calendar:** Shows when inoculations, worming, shoeing, and other periodic maintenance are due, and the time of competitions and other events.

**Shoeing chart:** Lists all horses with individual shoeing notes, dates of farrier visits, and what was done for various horses.

**Vehicle and machinery records:** Registrations, warranties, and service records for farm vehicles and equipment.

Business and financial records may include (depending on nature of business):

- Bookkeeping system for recording expenses and income; essential for paying bills promptly and for tax purposes. If clients are billed for stable services, these must be posted and bills sent out on time. File paid bills and receipts in an orderly manner so they are available for accounting and tax purposes.
- If you have employees, you will need to keep employee records, including payroll and tax records, and be in compliance with state and federal employment laws.
- Loan, lease, or mortgage and tax records.
- Insurance policies, plus inventory of tack, equipment, and machinery, including value and registration numbers. (Keep a separate copy in a safe deposit box.)
- Contracts and release forms, including sales, services, and charges; boarding, training, or lesson contracts; and liability release forms (as recommended by your attorney and insurance agent). Many contracts and forms can be found online for free.

- Client records that include name, address, phone number, and pertinent information for boarders, students, and so on.
- List of vendors and suppliers from whom you obtain feed, bedding, supplies; repairmen and service facilities; professionals (veterinarians, farriers) with whom you do business.

# Safe and Efficient Horse Facilities

The first impression you get upon entering a stable or horse facility is often a true one. The way a barn is set up and kept says a lot about the competence and horsemanship of the people in charge. A horse facility need not be elaborate to be excellent; a simple, workman-like facility that is well organized, neat, clean, and intelligently managed provides a better working environment than a fancy facility that is poorly planned or operated.

## General Considerations

A horse facility must be designed with *horses* in mind—taking into account the size, behavior, and nature of horses, and the safety of people and horses. It should also be designed for durability, efficiency, simplicity, neatness, and the environment.

## Location, Zoning, and Planning

Before starting, buying, or expanding a horse facility, check with your local building department and zoning board to find out whether local ordinances, zoning restrictions, or homeowner covenants might affect your plans or even prohibit such a facility. Land values, property taxes, utilities, and the cost of compliance with local requirements (such as manure disposal and environmental laws) will affect operating costs.

It is important to consider your neighbors, especially in suburban or semirural areas. If your acreage is small or your facility is close to the property line, neighbors may be annoyed by noise, flies, dust, odors, traffic, straying horses, or the appearance of your property. If you are close to a residential area, trespassing children may pose a problem. These factors can lead to legal disputes, liability issues, and increased costs in insurance and security measures. Secure fencing, good sanitation, maintaining a clean and attractive facility, and consideration and good public relations are essential in maintaining a good relationship with your neighbors.

## Land

The topography of the land (flat, rolling, or steep) and the type of soil (clay, adobe, loam, gravel, or sandy) affect the drainage, the grass and hay grown, footing, and usefulness for a horse facility. Stables, riding areas, paddocks, and pastures must be located on well-drained soil. Wet or swampy ground and areas prone to poor drainage, runoff, or flooding are unhealthy for horses, subject to damage and deterioration, and extremely difficult to maintain. They also breed flies and mosquitoes.

Stables and outside pens must be built on a well-drained site, ideally on top of a knoll or hill. If located below a hill or on poorly drained soil, more site preparation, grading, or filling may be required.

## Access

A horse facility needs a hard-surfaced road or driveway capable of handling trucks, farm machinery, vet and farrier vehicles, and trailers. Parking and traffic patterns (including vehicles, trailers, pedestrians, riders, and led horses) should be taken into account in planning the layout.

## Security

Two major security concerns are keeping horses safely confined and keeping control of who can enter your facility. A perimeter fence with a gate barring access to the highway is a safety factor. A security light, mounted on the barn or in the yard, makes it easier to check on the horses and discourages intruders at night; a dog can also be a security measure. The stable itself should never be locked because of the danger of fire, but tack rooms, feed rooms, garages, and storage areas should be secure.

## Design and Materials

Designing a horse facility involves many aspects of planning to be successful. The entire facility should be drawn out and planned in advance, including the barn, turnout areas, pastures, dry lots, riding areas, driveways, and walkways. The floor plan of the barn may include stalls, aisles, feed and hay storage, bedding storage, tack room, grooming areas, windows, doors, and so on. Decisions must be made regarding materials, stall fittings, watering, ventilation, and other important aspects. Feeding systems and turnout methods will be important in certain aspects of the design. Your facility design must also take into account the climate and weather in all seasons. Keep fire safety in mind as you plan, and consult fire safety experts. A facility should also include a place for quarantining two to three horses.

## Ventilation

Stabled horses require a constant supply of fresh air for health and comfort, but should not be exposed to drafts. Good ventilation provides fresh air and carries away excess moisture, ammonia fumes, and odors, and prevents condensation of moisture in cold weather. Horses are healthier and more comfortable in a cool but airy stable (even if blanketing is required) than in a warm barn that is closed up tightly. In hot areas, a well-ventilated stable that takes advantage of shade and prevailing winds is important. Consider the following when planning for effective ventilation:

- Manure, urine, and soiled bedding produce ammonia fumes, which pollute the air and damage the eyes and respiratory system.
- A horse gives off up to two gallons of moisture daily into the air as he breathes. In cold weather, this moisture condenses and may freeze or drip. The resulting dampness favors the growth of fungus and bacteria, aggravates arthritis and stiffness, and contributes to respiratory ailments.
- Constant exposure to dust, especially when hay is stored in an overhead loft or when the stalls face an indoor arena, can cause or aggravate chronic respiratory problems such as heaves.

A stabled horse needs a minimum of 1,600 square feet of air space. High ceilings, open stall partitions, and windows and doors placed for cross-ventilation help to achieve this. In hot climates, stall partitions are usually made of open gridwork as much as possible, and stall gates may be used instead of solid doors, to promote the free flow of air.

Means of providing ventilation include:

**Windows:** Placed high, opening at the top or louvered, to direct air upward instead of creating a direct draft on the horse. Windows should be placed at least 4 feet from the floor, or 5 feet for larger horses. Windows should be unbreakable (Plexiglass or safety glass) and protected by a grid.

**Roof peak ventilation;** Openings along the ridge of the roof that allow stale air to escape.

**Louvers:** Overlapping boards set at an angle with an air passage in between. They may be installed in the upper wall, in the soffits (eaves), or in the gables. They direct fresh air upward and stale air outward.

**Exhaust fan:** Power-driven fan in the roof peak, removes stale air.

**Stall fans:** In very hot, humid conditions, stalls may be equipped with individual box fans, installed high, with both the fan and the electric cord well out of reach of the horse.

Ventilation methods for stables.

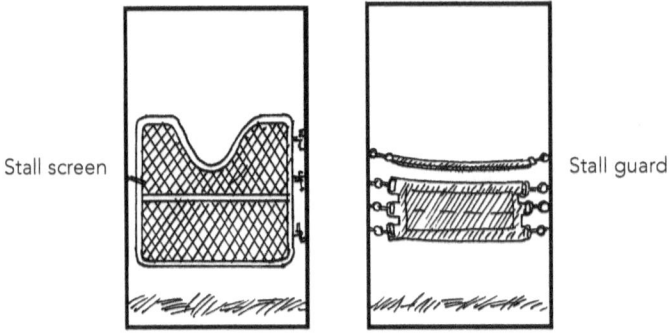

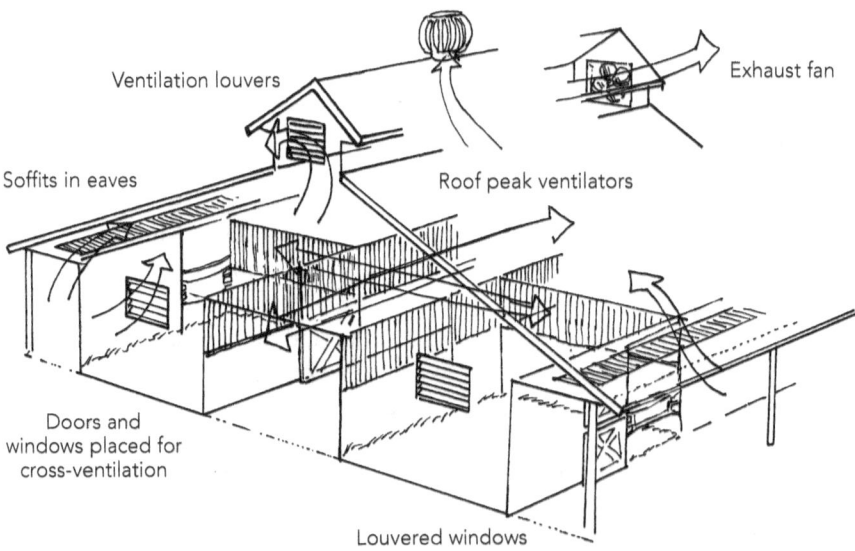

## Drainage

Good drainage is essential for a horse facility. Poor drainage can result in constant dampness, mud, and flooding, and can contaminate groundwater, adversely affecting fish and aquatic wildlife. Such conditions are unhealthy, inefficient, and can lead to damage that is difficult and costly to repair. Solving drainage problems can be expensive, especially if construction is necessary. Expert advice during planning and site preparation and when solving drainage problems can save time, money, and inconvenience.

# STABLE AND FACILITY MANAGEMENT

Drainage depends on location, soil, terrain, rainfall level and snow load, and on the design, engineering, and maintenance of the facility. Important factors in regard to drainage include:

- Stables and manure piles must be located on well-drained ground, but not where runoff can contaminate groundwater or streams.
- Areas under eaves and gutters need good drainage and drain pipes that divert rainwater away from the foundation of the building. A 48' × 36' roof without gutters will put over 5,000 gallons of water on the ground in a 1-inch rainfall. Consider installing rain barrels, and recycle the water regularly.
- Stall floors need good drainage for cleanliness, the health of the horse, and to minimize odors and fly population. Methods of providing drainage in stall floors include:
  - Dig floor down and fill with a 24-inch layer of rocks (approximately 1½ to 2 inches in diameter), then a 12-inch layer of ¾-inch crushed stone. Top with a 6-inch layer of clay, leveled and well tamped down.
  - Fill and level stall floor with a 6-inch layer of "blue stone," decomposed limestone, or road base.
  - Sand, limestone, or dirt floors can be kept level by installing a stall floor grid, which prevents horses from digging holes.
  - Hard-surfaced floors (concrete, brick, or asphalt) may be sloped slightly toward a concrete gutter at the front or rear, or toward a

Stall flooring and subsoil.

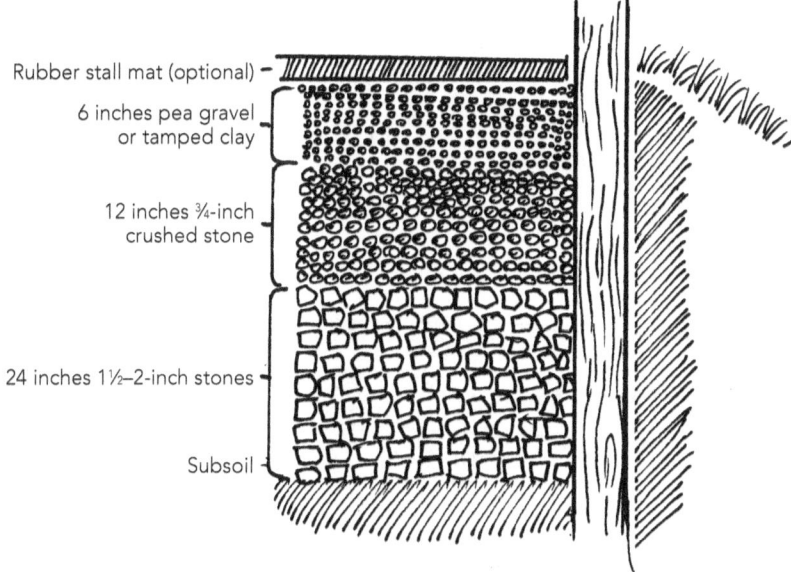

center drain. These surfaces are better for aisles and wash stalls than for stall floors.

- Drainage problems in large areas such as riding arenas and paddocks may require drainage ditches or a French drain (a ditch filled with crushed rock).

## Utilities

A reliable supply of clean water is essential. In cold climates, pipes must be buried below the frost line, and frost-free hydrants should be installed. Decisions must be made regarding where to locate water faucets, how many, and if there will be a wash rack and bathroom.

Electric service must meet local fire codes. Wiring must be properly grounded and protected from chewing by horses or rodents. Explosion-proof light fixtures (protected by a glass cover and metal cage) should be used. Stall light fixtures should use LED or standard light bulbs. Compact florescent bulbs cannot tolerate the heat generated inside the plastic safety fixture and do not light up well in cold environments. Fluorescents may work in safer areas outside the stall, but you may have to buy cold weather–compatible bulbs, depending on your climate. LED and energy-efficient fluorescent bulbs consume the least energy and save money. Fluorescent bulbs contain mercury and must be disposed of at recycling centers. You will need to decide where outlets will be located, and if there will be one near each stall.

Frost-free hydrant.

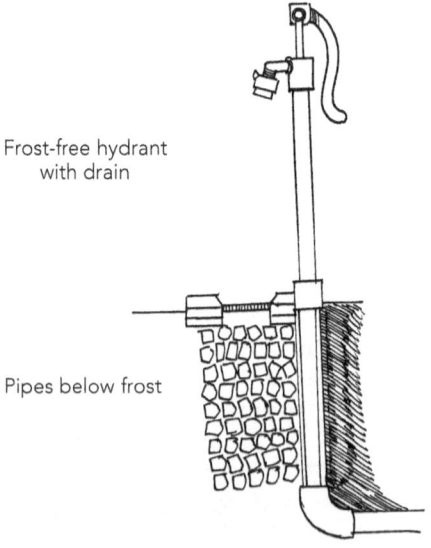

Here are some other tips for saving money and electricity:

- Consider solar-powered electric fences.
- Turn off lights when not in use.
- Use a broom instead of a hose or leaf blower.
- Use natural ventilation instead of fans whenever possible.
- Use industrial-grade fans for safety.
- Put timers on light switches.
- Turn down the water heater temperature and insulate the pipes.
- Unplug appliances and tools that are not in use (coffee pot, clippers, and so on).
- Consider solar powered landscaping lights and motion-activated lights.
- Install solar panels on the barn roof.
- Use wind-powered generators.

# Stalls

Most modern stables employ box stalls, which allow horses freedom to move and lie down. A standard horse stall is 12' × 12' (10' × 10' for ponies), but sometimes 10' × 12' works well for smaller horses and requires less space, less bedding, and takes less time to clean. Consider a larger stall if horses are stalled 24 hours a day, or for very large horses. For foaling stalls, 12' × 16' is a good size. Straight or standing stalls are sometimes used for day stalls in riding school stables where horses and ponies are kept in pasture.

Stall fittings must be designed and installed so as to prevent a horse from getting caught on them. There must be no gaps in which a horse could catch a leg. (See the *USPC C Level Manual*, page 120.)

### Chart 15-1: Stall Size

| Type of Stall | Small Pony | Small Horse | Large Horse | Foaling Stall |
|---|---|---|---|---|
| Box | 9' × 9' | 10' × 10' | 12' × 12' | 16' × 16' |
| Standing | 4' × 8' | 5' × 10' | 6' × 12' | |

Your feeding system (feed tubs, hay fed on the floor or in hay racks) will also play in a role in how stalls are designed.

## Quarantine Area

A quarantine area should be established in every stable. New horses, horses that are sick, suspected of being sick, or those that have recently returned from an event where they may have come in close contact with unknown horses, should be placed here for two to three weeks so they cannot come into physical contact with resident horses. While horses are in the quarantine area, you should do the following:

- Take the horse's temperatures daily (a good precaution when a horse returns from a competition).
- Do not share buckets, feeding tubs, grooming equipment, or tack while in quarantine or while competing. Be sure such equipment is disinfected when the quarantine is over.
- Do not share water troughs.
- Require visiting horses to be in good health and show a current Coggins test and proof of inoculations.
- Keep visiting horses isolated from resident horses. Strip and disinfect stalls before arrival and after their departure.
- Attend to quarantined horses after caring for resident horses, and disinfect or change clothing and boots after any visit to the quarantine area. Germs can be carried on hands, clothing, and boots as well as on equipment.
- Give quarantined horses their own turnout area, which should be well separated from other turnout areas.
- Thoroughly disinfect the stall after it is used. Concrete is the easiest to disinfect. If stall mats are used, remove them and clean underneath. For a dirt or sand floor, the disinfectant must reach the depth of the contamination or the floor material will need to be removed and replaced (especially in case of Salmonella).

## Aisles, Gates, and Doors

Aisles should be wide enough to allow for safe handling of horses and to accommodate a tractor and manure spreader (8 feet minimum; 10 to 12 feet is better). Keep aisles clear of obstructions. The end door for a barn should be at least 8 feet high.

Gates and doors must be wide enough for a horse and handler (minimum 4 feet wide; 4½ feet is better), without any projecting hardware that can injure a horse or catch on tack or blankets. Swinging doors and gates should open outward (except for metal stall gates designed to hang on the inside of the door). Sliding doors must have a guard to prevent them from being pushed outward at the bottom, creating a dangerous gap.

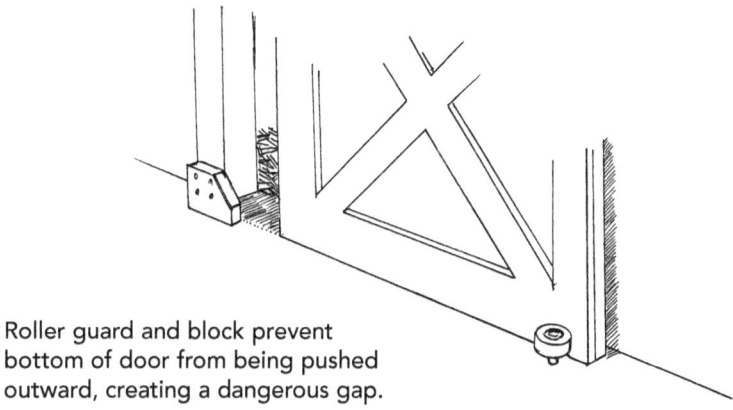

Roller guard and block prevent bottom of door from being pushed outward, creating a dangerous gap.

The barn must have a place to groom horses safely. If this is to be done in the aisle, the area needs to be free of hazards, have quick-release cross-ties for safety, and possibly a mat to provide a safe, nonslip surface. The next set of cross-ties in the aisle should be a safe distance away. One or more grooming stalls add both convenience and safety.

# Floors

Floors may be made of several materials; each has good points and drawbacks. Durability, drainage, comfort, maintenance, and cost of installation and upkeep are important factors.

### Chart 15-2: Floor Materials

| Material | Suitable For | Drainage | Notes |
| --- | --- | --- | --- |
| Concrete | Aisles, tack rooms, feed rooms, wash stalls | Needs slope or drain | Too hard for stall floors. Use texturized concrete for nonslip surface. Should be at least 4" thick to prevent cracking and weak spots. |
| Asphalt | Aisles (porous asphalt may be used for stall floors) | Needs slope or drain | Easy to sweep but can be slippery. Should be at least 2" deep to prevent weak spots, which can develop into holes. If used in stalls, floor mats offer added cushion. |
| Dirt | Stalls, pens | May be muddy; needs at least 4" of gravel underneath for drainage | Horses create holes and uneven surface; needs frequent maintenance; odors linger. Hard to disinfect. |

| Material | Suitable For | Drainage | Notes |
| --- | --- | --- | --- |
| Clay | Stalls | Slow to dry; needs at least 4" of gravel underneath for drainage | Same as dirt. Works well with stall mats on top. |
| Sand | Pens, outdoor aisles | Good; needs at least 4" of gravel underneath for drainage | Horses may ingest sand along with hay and feed, resulting in sand colic. Heavy; difficult to clean when wet. Compacted sand with stall mats on top works well. |
| Wood | Tack room, office | Needs spaces between boards to drain | Not suitable for aisles and stalls because it is hard and slippery, rots and breaks up, and harbors pests. |
| Bricks | Aisles, tack room | Needs drain or slope | Expensive to install but durable and attractive. Hard to sweep. |
| Gravel (pea gravel) | Stall base, outdoor aisle | Excellent | Good traction; hard to keep clean. Stalls require mats over gravel. |
| Road base (limestone/ gravel/dirt mix) | Stalls, aisles | Good | Can be dusty. May develop holes or uneven surface. |
| Rubber mats | Stalls, aisles, wash stalls; can also be used outside on muddy walk areas | Depends on base underneath | Good over concrete, gravel, or dirt in aisles; over dirt, sand, gravel, or other base in stalls. Prevents holes, but requires bedding to absorb urine. |
| Stall floor grid | Stalls | Plastic grid to retain stall floor material and keep flooring level | Use with dirt, gravel, road base, or limestone. |

## Feed and Bedding Storage

It is more economical and often more environmentally friendly to purchase feed and bedding in large quantities or bulk. This requires planning, careful comparison shopping, and additional secure storage space. Buying in bulk may mean less packing material. Buying in paper instead of plastic is also better for the environment. Buying in bulk also saves gas and/or delivery fees. Try to purchase locally when possible, too.

Begin with each horse's daily ration, and estimate how much feed will be consumed per week and per month. Estimate the amount of bedding used. Take into account variations in weather or health, such as feeding more hay during the winter months, or if a horse is kept inside for health reasons.

For a large stable, consider having your basic feed ration custom-mixed at the feed mill. Prices fluctuate with the market, season, demand, and other factors. Sweet feeds and feeds with a high-fat content are somewhat perishable, especially in hot, humid climates, and can freeze in cold weather. In hot weather these should be purchased in smaller quantities so that they are used within two weeks. As a general rule, use the oldest feed bags first. Always check expiration dates on feeds, supplements, and medications, and do not use any feed that has a rancid or fermented odor.

The feed room should be secured at all times. Feed storage containers must be kept clean, dry, and safe from rodents and bugs (and loose horses!). Grain containers should have tight, secure-fitting lids of metal, heavy plastic, or wood. They should prevent mold and spoilage from dampness or exposure to weather and water leaks. Feed bags should be stored on wooden pallets instead of directly on concrete or dirt floors to reduce the possibility of mold. Supplements and medications must also be secure. A feed room should have a scale, measuring containers, and an up-to-date feeding chart. Large stables may use bulk feed bins equipped with feed chutes or dispensers. Keep all areas neat and swept so as not to attract rodents and flies.

Because of the danger of fire (spontaneous combustion and flammable materials), hay should ideally be stored in a hay barn, shed, or stack separate from the stable. Storing hay over the stalls also increases exposure to dust and spores, which may aggravate respiratory ailments. Hay should be stacked on pallets, not directly on the ground or on concrete, or it will mold from the moisture. Bedding, being flammable, ideally should also be stored in another building and should be stacked on wooden pallets. Green sawdust can generate heat, so it should not be piled near a building.

## Manure Disposal

A stabled horse produces approximately 35 to 50 pounds of manure per day (up to 10 tons per year). Manure, urine, and soiled bedding must be removed daily. Manure and urine harbor bacteria and parasites; draw flies; are destructive to horses' feet; release ammonia gas, which is detrimental to lungs and eyes of horses and humans; and cause tack, paint, and wood to deteriorate.

Manure can be hauled away (by a farmer, nursery, or mushroom grower), spread on cropland (but not horse pastures, to prevent contamination), or composted. Composting reduces the size of the manure pile by at least 50 percent, generates enough heat to kill parasites and weed seeds, reduces flies and odor, and produces valuable compost. With good management, it can be used to enrich the soil and improve the environment.

## Manure Pile Maintenance

The manure pile should be kept at a distance from the stable, house, and neighbors to avoid flies and odor. It should be on high ground, well-drained or on a concrete base, with 4-feet walls. Do not put the manure pile near a building, as it creates heat as it decomposes. Ideally, there should be three manure piles: a working pile that you are currently adding manure to daily, one in the process of breaking down, and a finished pile ready for use as fertilizer.

Another method is to keep adding fresh manure to the end of a pile about 6 feet high and 6 feet wide. It requires oxygen to decompose, because it relies on aerobic microbes (microbes that need oxygen to live). The more oxygen the manure pile gets, the faster it decomposes (taking 3 to 6 months versus 6 to 12 months) and the less odor it produces. Providing air to a manure pile can be done by turning the manure by hand, using a tractor, or by inserting multiple 5-foot PVC pipes with holes drilled a few inches apart along the pipe into the center of the pile with the ends sticking out like chimneys. In wet environments, it is necessary to cover the piles to keep them dry and to prevent the rain from washing away all the nutrients. You should develop a plan that works best for your facility.

Plant a buffer strip of native plants (native species specific to the area are best) to improve water quality, provide a filter, and reduce water runoff. Native plants can also be planted near the shore of a water source and 10 to 20 feet (or two mowers width) from the manure pile. This will slow the runoff, filter the water, and help reduce flooding.

## Fly Control

Fly control measures include:

- Sanitation, including cleaning stalls, removing trash, and keeping the stable area swept clean.
- Keeping the manure pile covered and at a distance from the stable.
- Insecticides (fogging, periodic automatic sprayers, residual fly sprays, fly bait). Because insecticides are poisonous and can pollute the environment, it is essential to read the directions, take all recommended precautions, and obey environmental laws when using and disposing of them.
- Fly traps, fly strips, and flypaper.

- Feed-through fly control products (substances treated to pass through the horse and release insecticide in the manure).
- Fly predators, which are beneficial insects that destroy fly eggs and larvae in the manure pile. They can be purchased from biological fly control companies.
- Fly repellents and fly masks can be used to protect the horse during turnout and work. Horses can be turned out at night or when flies are not biting, and kept in during the day. Shade or a dark area like a stall or barn provides relief from flies.

## Tack Room and Equipment Storage

Tack must be stored in a dry environment, away from direct heat (which cracks leather) and excessive humidity (which causes mildew), and protected from dirt, dust, and rodents. Racks should be designed to allow saddle pads and blankets to air-dry, and saddles and bridles to keep their shape. All racks, trunks, and hooks should be labeled for easy identification. In winter, heating the tack room to 55 or 60°F helps keep tack in good condition and provides a better working environment. If used, heaters must be safely designed and installed because of the danger of fire.

A tack room needs cabinets and shelves for storage of supplies, a locked cupboard or small refrigerator for medications, and counter space for a work area. If the tack room also serves as an office, a desk, chair, and file cabinet will be needed.

To prevent theft, tack rooms must be secure, with solid wood or metal doors, security locks, and windows inaccessible from outside. The tack room should be locked when staff is not present. A utility room, containing a deep sink with hot and cold water, washing machine, and additional storage space, is helpful, as is a space for storing trunks, blankets, and other large items. Tools, wheelbarrows, muck baskets, and similar equipment must be kept neat and accessible, but out of the way.

## Vehicles and Machinery

A horse facility may have some or all of the following maintenance vehicles and machinery:

> **Tractor:** Preferably a mid-sized tractor (25 to 27 horsepower) or farm tractor (40 to 70 horsepower), ideally equipped with a power takeoff (PTO) and hydraulically operated three-point hitch for farm machinery. Attachments such as a bucket loader, auger, and blade make a tractor more versatile. A diesel or gasoline tractor may be preferable, depending on fuel costs and availability in your area.

**Manure spreader:** Ground-driven (powered by turning of the wheels when towed) or powered by the tractor's PTO.

**Mower (rotary, sickle bar, or bush hog):** For mowing, clearing, and maintaining pastures.

**Discs, harrow, or chain drag:** For maintaining arena surfaces and pastures.

**Utility trailer, flatbed trailer, wagon, or dump cart:** For hauling and dumping feed, hay, dirt, stones, and other chores. A flatbed trailer or wagon can be used for hauling hay and transporting jumps.

**Post-hole digger:** For building and repairing fences.

**Hay elevator:** For loading bales in mow or high stacks.

**Caution:** Tractors and farm machinery can be dangerous! Operators must be trained in proper operation and safety practices, and must be aware of hazards to themselves and others. Never remove safety guards or operate or ride on machinery in a way for which it was not designed. Machinery and vehicles must be serviced regularly, kept in safe operating condition, and stored in a safe location. Machinery workshops, sheds, and garages should be separate from the stable.

## Arenas and Riding Areas

Riding areas include outdoor rings and jumping fields, trails, and indoor arenas. They must be designed for safety, kept neat, and properly maintained. Important factors include:

**Size:** Suitable for purpose and number of riders:

- All-purpose outdoor ring: 100 × 200 feet or larger.
- Small dressage arena (also suitable for beginner or small group lessons): 66 × 132 feet (20 × 40 meters).
- Large dressage arena: 66 × 198 feet (20 × 60 meters).
- Jumping field: 150 × 300 feet or larger.
- Longeing ring: 60 feet in diameter.

**Footing:** Level, well-drained, without holes, rocks, wet places, or obstructions. Footing should be secure and provide traction. Too-hard footing causes soreness and concussion and may be slippery; too-soft or deep footing causes strain on tendons and ligaments.

There is no universal arena footing surface. The type of footing should be determined by the intended use, environment, and cost of materials. Footing is in constant change as it is used, and will need to be amended every few years; it may need to be completely replaced every 5 to 10 years, depending on use. Good footing is no better than the solid base and sub-base that it sits upon. The base (4 to 6 inches) should be a hard-packed material, similar to road base, with the option of landscape fabric placed underneath.

When selecting arena footing, it is important that the material remains loose without compacting. Compaction happens when voids between particles fill with smaller particles and it all becomes tightly packed, so attention must be paid to the size of particles. Sharply angular particles tend to pack more easily, and round particles pack the least.

The major components of most footing is a mixture of silt, clay, and sand. Sometimes the native soil is used instead. Additives may be used, such as particle coatings, synthetic fibers, or pieces of rubber. Materials and their names vary greatly in different areas, which makes it difficult to create guidelines and formulas. Quarries standardize gravel and footing material by the size of the particles, which is helpful.

## Types of Footing

**Natural turf:** Traction and drainage varies, not dusty, not abrasive on hooves, water retention is good, and cost is low. It can be slippery when wet, will freeze, requires maintenance, and is not very durable as it is easily chopped up with hard use.

**Soil:** Compaction, traction, dust, drainage, and water retention varies according to location and type of soil; cost is low. It may be rocky or uneven, can be slippery and muddy when wet, will freeze, requires a significant amount of maintenance. Sometimes native soil is combined with 70 to 90 percent sand, or the soil may already contain a lot of sand. This combination is a good surface for western reining and speed events.

**Sand:** Low dust, does not compact, adequate traction, good drainage, low water retention, not slippery, doesn't freeze, durable and low maintenance, cost is middle range. Sand is abrasive to hooves and if it's too deep it can cause fatigue, muscle soreness, and tendon strains. Start with 2 inches and add ½ inch at a time, as it can easily become too deep. Six inches is usually too deep.

Select medium to coarse, hard, sharp sand, cleaned and screened, so that it will not quickly compact. Sand alone may provide too loose a footing for riding that requires sharp turns and quick stops, such as some western disciplines.

**Stone dust:** Adequate cushion with high traction, lots of dust, good drainage with low water retention, not slippery when wet, low freezing potential, durable, abrasive on hooves, low-medium cost, requires regular maintenance (watering and harrowing). This is a good surface for quick changes of directions, speed, and jumping.

**Wood surfaces (fiber, shavings, sawdust, tanbark):** Good cushion, adequate traction, medium drainage, high water retention, dust varies, adequate durability, not abrasive to hooves, medium maintenance, and cost is low to medium. It is more resilient than sand but somewhat more slippery; less suitable for jumping. Wood eventually becomes dusty as it breaks down into small particles.

Start with 1 inch of small wood fiber mixed with finer wood. Wood breaks down and decomposes, so every few years you will need to add more; hardwood products last longer than soft wood. Wood can be added to sand to increase traction, and for cushioning and moisture retention. **Caution:** Black walnut or black cherry products are toxic to horses and should not be used.

**Rubber particles:** Good cushioning, adequate traction, low dust, high drainage with low water retention so not slippery when wet, doesn't usually freeze, adequate durability, not abrasive on hooves, low maintenance but high cost. It is often mixed with sand or installed over a sand base. Rubber can be added to sand to increase the cushion. Require a guarantee from the supplier that the footing contains no metal pieces. Rubber may float to the top in rain, so will need to be mixed again. Rubber is usually mixed with stone dust or sand at a rate of 1 to 2 pounds of rubber per square foot.

**Stall waste:** Average cushion with low traction, not abrasive on hooves, low cost but very dusty, poor drainage and high water retention, slippery when wet, will freeze, low durability and high maintenance. In indoor arenas, has potential to cause breathing problems and create poor air quality.

**Mixed footings:** Sand mixed with wood, rubber, fibers, or other particles to provide more stability than lighter materials, more resilient than sand alone. One successful recipe: Mix 3 inches of sand and 2 inches of sawdust, or 2 inches of sand and 1 inch of sawdust.

New footing materials are constantly being developed, both for indoor and outdoor applications, so it is a good idea to stay current with new information.

## Dust Control

Dust in arenas can be a problem for both horses and people, and can cause or exacerbate respiratory problems. Horses kept in stalls that open onto an indoor arena are subject to more dust in their environment.

Dust can be controlled by watering (by hand, lawn sprinklers, or automatic watering system). Some footings (dirt, sawdust, sandy loam) can be oiled annually or biannually to keep down dust, using environmentally friendly oils such as palm, coconut, mineral, or soybean oils. Salt can also be added to the footing, as it collects and holds moisture and keeps it from freezing in the winter. The most commonly used products are calcium chloride and magnesium chloride, as they are less expensive and hold moisture well. Salt is hard on the arena and on horses' hooves and legs, so horses' feet and legs should be cleaned after riding.

## Arena Maintenance

Arenas should be dragged with a harrow, chain drag, or arena leveler as often as necessary to prevent the footing from becoming hard-packed or uneven, especially along the track, in the corners, and around jumps. Turf arenas and jumping fields are easily damaged by overuse, especially in wet weather; they need mowing, rolling, fertilizing, and rotating jumps to prevent wearing out the turf. It is also a good idea to pick up manure promptly, so keep a manure bucket and pitchfork nearby to encourage this habit.

# Facility Maintenance

Maintenance is one of the most important aspects of stable management. Horses and people are hard on equipment and their environment. Major and minor breakages occur, and daily wear and tear takes its toll. Without constant maintenance, a facility quickly deteriorates and becomes unsafe. Neglecting small repairs or maintenance jobs can result in breakdowns, accidents, or damage and deterioration requiring a costly major overhaul. Taking care of what you have saves money and waste, and is better for the environment.

In order to maintain the facility, property, and equipment, someone must be responsible for carrying out routine maintenance and repairs. This person needs to have the necessary skills and knowledge, the proper tools, and time.

## Routine Maintenance

Daily maintenance chores depend on the size and complexity of the facility and the season. A facility should have a workshop, tools, and necessary maintenance supplies. Routine maintenance jobs in many stables might include the following:

- Check stalls, aisles, fences, and working areas daily; fix minor items (pulling out a nail or fixing a faulty latch).
- Check pastures and paddocks (fences, water supply, operation of electric fence), and make any necessary repairs.
- Clean, sweep, dust, remove cobwebs, remove trash.
- Drag/level arena footing.
- Clean public and office areas, bathrooms, and so on.
- Maintain landscaping (mowing, snow plowing, and maintaining drives, walkways, and parking lot).

- Check and service vehicles and machinery.
- Make repairs and improvements to the facility and rebuilding as needed.
- Winterize and perform other seasonal maintenance of buildings, pastures, vehicles, and machinery.
- Clean and organize feed rooms, tack rooms, storage areas, and so on.

## Pasture Management

Maintaining the quality of pastures is important, including regular mowing of tall areas and weeds, especially just before they go to seed. In small areas, weeds can be pulled by hand. Let grassy fencerows go, as this saves time, fuel, and provides a place for wildlife. Grass and weeds should be trimmed away from electric fences so that the fences do not short out. In areas where water stands or runs after rainfall, it may be necessary to fence it off temporarily or permanently to avoid damage. Standing water is a breeding ground for mosquitoes, so these areas should be emptied or filled in when possible.

Soil testing should be performed to assess what type of fertilizer should be applied to your pastures. Local feed mills or your county extension agent can perform such analysis. Samples should be taken from the top 3 to 6 inches of soil from several different areas of the pasture. The analysis will tell you if it is necessary to apply lime or nitrogen to the soil. Correctly seeding with grasses and legumes is beneficial. It is helpful to seek the advice of an agricultural extension agent or knowledgeable feed mill or farm store employee when renovating your pasture for horses. She can help you select the variety of grasses that will grow well in your area and climate and are best for horses and advise you on the best time to seed and treat pastures.

It is important not to overgraze pastures to keep them healthy, so you must regulate how many horses use each pasture and paddock. You may need to prevent damage to pastures by keeping horses off the pasture when the ground is too soft or covered with water. Pasture grass should not be grazed down below 3 inches. Rotating pastures and paddocks can give the grass time to recover from intensive grazing.

For specific recommendations about grazing and turnout in your geographic area, contact your county agent.

## Pasture Feeding

Sometimes it is necessary to give supplementary feed to horses in pastures or to feed horses outside in dry lots. Some factors to consider are safety, herd behavior, making sure each horse gets enough food, and preventing sand ingestion and hay wastage. All baling twine, baling wire, and plastic should be removed from the hay feeder and pasture to prevent horses from becoming entangled in or ingesting small pieces of it.

The simplest way to feed hay to horses in a pasture or dry lot is to place piles of several flakes of hay on the ground, at least 20 feet apart, with one or two more piles than there are horses. If a horse is chased away from one hay pile, he can go to another. It is safer and easier to set out the hay when the horses are not in the field. This method should not be used on loose sandy soil, as horses will ingest sand along with the hay, which may lead to sand colic. In such areas, it is better to feed hay in a hay rack or hay feeder, or on an area covered with stall mats.

Another method of feeding hay is placing one or more large round or square bales in the pasture or paddock. This method is convenient but involves more waste, as horses will use the bale area as a shelter, pull out extra hay, lie down in it, and contaminate the spilled hay with urine and manure. The pasture ground may be damaged by heavy traffic and trodden-in hay.

Using a round bale feeder reduces wastage, but it is important that the feeder is designed to be safe for horses and that a horse cannot catch his head or leg in the feeder.

There are also slow hay feeders designed for round or square bales. These are made like a large hay net with very small holes, which require horses to take smaller amounts of hay and slows their consumption. This type of feeder can be beneficial for horses that are overweight or need to have their hay consumption restricted. The feeders must be secured correctly to prevent horses from pulling them off and getting entangled in them.

It is not recommended to feed grain to horses that are loose in a field. This often leads to kicking and biting, is dangerous for the person who distributes the grain, and can result in some horses getting more grain than they need while others go hungry. It is better to bring horses into stalls to feed grain, or to tie them at individual feeding stations, well separated, while they eat their grain.

## Dry Lots or Sacrifice Areas

There may be times when horse owners need to use dry lots or sacrifice areas. These are a few reasons for their use:

- Used on rainy days to save pasture from being damaged.
- This may be the only access to the outside available for some horses.
- Pasture is not large enough for full-time grazing (grass should not be grazed shorter than 3 inches).
- To preserve a dormant pasture during winter.
- When a horse is recovering from an injury and is not allowed free pasture exercise, or when a horse's access to grass must be restricted.

- Used in the spring when horses are being acclimated to new grass.

A dry lot should be placed in a high area that drains away from the barn. Adequate drainage creates less mud and decreases pollution of surface water. If the proposed area is too low or muddy, some material may need to be removed prior to building the area up with new dirt. If the original soil is prone to holding water or slippery, a layer of geotextile fabric may be laid down before putting the new footing on top.

After building the area up to an acceptable level with native dirt, gravel of various sizes can be added to form a base underneath the footing. The size of the gravel and the amount that should be laid down varies by the soil conditions in the area. For top footing, it is best to put down at least 3 to 6 inches of ⅜-inch to ⅝-inch crushed rock (stone aggregate) in high-traffic areas. Gravel larger than ¾ inch is hard on horses' feet and will not sift through pitchfork tines when picking up manure. Stone dust or mats can also be used on top of the crushed rock to provide a better surface. Consider adding gutters and downspouts to nearby structures to collect rainwater and aid in drainage issues.

Planting native plants, shrubs, and trees in nearby areas will further help any runoff issues and drainage problems. They slow the flow of water, absorb it, and filter out the sediments and pollutants. Native plants are hardy, acclimated to local weather, do not need fertilizers or pesticides, and once established, don't require water or maintenance. They also benefit the environment by providing habitat for birds and small animals.

It is convenient if dry lots or sacrifice areas can be placed between the stable and a larger pasture. This makes it easier to confine horses to the dry lot when necessary, and the gate can be opened to release horses into the larger pasture.

## Pasture Shelters

Although horses are not bothered by most kinds of weather, pastures should have some kind of shelter. A run-in shed with three sides is a simple structure that works well. Generally, 150 square feet is adequate for one horse. Wider is better than deeper, because this makes it more difficult for a dominant horse to block the entrance. It is important to consider herd dynamics when determining the size, and sometimes it is better to build several small run-in sheds throughout a field rather than one big one. It is usually not a good idea to feed inside the shed, as it is difficult to ensure that all horses are getting fed.

A 12' × 18' run-in shed usually works well for three horses that get along with each other. For more horses, a larger shed or multiple sheds may be necessary. One hundred and fifty square feet per animal is recommended. In very cold areas, a deeper shed (up to 24 feet deep) may be needed. The shed interior should be at least 10 feet high with a strong wood kick board wall at least 4 feet high along all sides.

The pitch in the roof should be 4 to 4½ inches for every horizontal foot, with the rise toward the front, creating a taller wall at the front of the shed. The front may be sided at the top to shield against sun and precipitation. The opening of the shed should face away from the prevailing winds, usually facing south. The opening should be at least 10 feet wide and 8 feet high. In hot climates, a two-sided shed may be used so that there is a constant breeze, which reduces heat and flies.

The site, which may be slightly elevated, should be well drained and kept level. The ground surface may be augmented with 4 inches of Class 1 sand, stone dust, or similar material on top of geotextile fabric, which helps reduce sand loss. This also provides for drainage and is easy to clean. Another option that provides good drainage is to use geotextile fabric, number 4 crushed stone, and then a dense-grade aggregate.

Remember to check with your local building code inspector regarding building code compliance. Sheds mounted on skids may be classified differently from permanent structures.

Pasture shelters require regular cleaning and maintenance, including removing manure and replacing footing material as needed.

## Stable Routine

Every farm is different in design and size, but there should be a clear routine so that things are not forgotten and boarders (clients) and horses know what to expect. Here are some things you might include in a morning routine:

- Walk through the barn and/or pastures, checking to make sure all horses are okay and there are no problems.
- Make sure all horses have clean water, including pasture water supply.
- Feed hay according to feed chart.
- Feed grain and supplements according to feed chart.
- Apply any medications or treatments required, and check for vet or farrier appointments.
- Turn horses out (if applicable).
- Clean stalls.
- Set up hay and feed for next feeding.
- Leave stable and area clean and neat, and feed room secured.

In the evening before you leave the barn, these things should be checked (you may have other items to check):

- Feed hay (if required) and set up hay and feed for morning.
- Fill water buckets (including pasture water supply if horses are out at night) and turn off water.
- Put away all tack, equipment, buckets, and so on.
- Sweep aisles and walkways.
- Feed and care for any other pets (such as barn cats).
- Secure and lock tack and feed rooms.
- Check that all stalls and gates are closed and securely latched.
- Check each stall to be sure each horse is safe and comfortable.
- Turn off all heaters and unplug appliances that are not in use.
- Turn off lights; turn on alarm (if applicable).

## Disaster Preparedness

A barn manager should be prepared for emergency situations, potential crises, fires (see the *USPC C Level Manual,* pages 140–144) and natural disasters that may occur in your area (blizzards, hurricanes, tornadoes, floods, mudslides, and wildfires). These disasters can cause building damage, power loss, road closure, and a lack of water and supplies. Being prepared includes planning for and going over all emergency procedures with everyone involved, practicing drills, and working with the fire department or other emergency services.

Every plan will be different, depending on your location and the type of natural disaster. Emergency and essential phone numbers should be posted in the barn and programmed into your phone: EMT, fire, ambulance, veterinarian, farrier, snow removal company, tree removal company, electrician, feed mill, animal shelter, and neighbors. Post the physical address of the barn as well as the cross street or other significant landmarks, so emergency personnel can easily locate the facility.

Consider adding to your plan the location and procedure for shutting off gas, water, and electricity at the source.

Your disaster plan should include ways to be informed of impending natural disasters, preparation, evacuation or other disaster plans, and a plan to deal with the aftermath of a disaster and immediate recovery process. See the USPC website (www.ponyclub.org) and the FEMA website for more information on ways to prepare and recover from disasters.

Being in charge of a barn requires you to be aware of any local weather dangers. A weather radio or other means of staying informed is essential. Check the weather daily and note any potential severe weather. Lightning can strike 10 miles ahead of a storm. When you hear thunder, it is time to stop riding and other outdoor activities and move indoors. Tornados and flash floods can occur miles from a rainstorm, so know if you are in an area where these are likely to occur.

Other weather danger strategies:

- Learn the signs of potential weather dangers in your area or any area you are visiting.
- Have a plan for each type of weather and/or natural disasters.
- Stop lessons, training, and outdoor riding and take cover as soon as you hear thunder or see lightning.
- In strong winds, seek cover in a large building, vehicle, or very low area or ditch. Do not seek shelter under any tall, solitary objects such as trees.
- Do not stand in water or puddles, or hold anything metal or with an antenna, which can be dangerous in case of lightning.

## Land Conservation

All horse people should be concerned about land conservation and take an active role in this effort, as it affects their future. In 2011, approximately 6,000 acres of agriculture, forest, and other lands were lost *each day* in the United States. This loss of land affects the horse industry and has a huge impact on horse sports and recreation in the United States. Land is critical for horse sports, for riding, for growing crops that feed our horses, and more.

Horse people need to become involved in what their local government is doing with area lands, parks, and conservation areas in order to support the conservation of land for the horse industry. This might mean organizing an equestrian community group to help with land conservation issues. Lobby at your local, state, and national levels for support of land conservation and liability measures that impact equine business and sports. Find out what your community land-use plan is, and be sure there is a place for horses. Get involved in the protection of farmland, which is essential for growing horse feed and for open space. Become active in maintaining trails, and educate others in proper land use. Help support stables that are in danger of being closed due to land development. Local, county, state, and regional organizations such as the Farm Bureau, the Grange, and State Horse Councils may be active in staying aware of zoning, land use, equine liability legislation, and other issues important to horse owners.

You can help by responding to and supporting equestrian or land-use issues in the news. Teach land conservation issues to younger Pony Club members and educate students, boarders, and clients about these issues. For more information, contact the Equine Land Conservation Resource (www.elcr.org/index.php) and American Trails (www.americantrails.org).

As responsible horse people, we must begin by taking care of our own farms in a positive manner, being environmentally friendly, working to develop a positive rapport with our neighbors, and thinking globally about our environment. This can mean:

- Keeping your farm in good repair and attractive.
- Controlling water runoff problems.
- Processing and disposing of manure properly.
- Maintaining trails.
- Writing thank-you notes to those who support horse sports or permit riding on their land.
- Recycling everything possible.
- Reducing your impact on the environment.
- Reducing or eliminating pesticides and fertilizers.
- Planting more native species and preserving wildlife habitat.

We need to preserve native species of wildlife, especially birds, on horse farms and facilities. Bluebirds, warblers, cedar waxwings, swifts, barn swallows, and other birds eat mosquitoes and flies. Bats eat more than 1,000 mosquitoes a night. Hawks and owls hunt mice, and snakes reduce rodent populations. Some barns have put up raptor houses or nesting boxes to attract these natural predators. Leaving farm hedgerows and wooded areas in a natural state provides habitat for small animals such as rabbits, foxes, and other species. It is also important to learn about pesticides and other farm chemicals, and to prevent accidental impact on birds and wildlife by misuse of chemicals. Ask your county extension agent for information on local native wildlife species and what you can do to preserve their habitat.

# 16

# Bandaging

This chapter covers bandaging materials and techniques for special purposes, including tail wraps and various types of specialty or treatment bandages. An introduction to bandaging, including shipping and stable bandages, is found in the *USPC C Level Manual,* pages 270–280.

## Bandaging Materials

In addition to the bandage materials discussed in the *USPC C Level Manual*, pages 271–280, the following sections discuss materials that may be used for special-purpose bandages.

### Bandages (Wraps)

**Co-adhesive bandage (Vetrap®, other brands).** Self-adhering elastic bandage sold in tack shops. Excellent for bandaging hard-to-reach areas such as heel grabs, and using as hoof wraps and pressure bandages.

**Ace bandage.** Elastic bandage sold in drugstores and tack shops. Because it is very stretchy, care must be taken not to pull it so tightly that it cuts off circulation. The 6-inch width works well with an ice pack, as it will contract as the ice melts. Well-worn Ace bandages that have lost most of their stretch are commonly used for grooming tail wraps, especially to cover a braided tail.

**Elastic adhesive bandage (Elastoplast® or Elastikon®).** Strong elastic adhesive bandage, used mainly for bandaging wounds. It can be used to wrap around a foot that has thrown a shoe to prevent the wall from chipping. Available in several widths from veterinarians, drugstores, and tack shops.

**Conforming gauze.** Gauze rolls of various widths, with some ability to stretch. It conforms gently to the contours of even hard-to-bandage areas, and is used mostly to hold wound dressings in place.

## Padding and Dressing Materials

**Roll cotton sheets.** These materials are made of a high-quality cotton blend that is very absorbent. They are commonly used by veterinarians to bandage wounds.

**Sheet cottons.** Sheet cottons (which are often polyester) are used for leg padding. Multiple sheets can be folded together to create a custom wrap to a desired thickness and height, which can be covered with cheesecloth or single-knot stretch fabric to increase durability. See the *USPC C Level Manual*, page 272.

**Cotton, polyester, or cotton/poly blend (low loft) quilt batting.** Used in place of sheet cottons for leg padding. Available at fabric and large discount stores, this is often cheaper and more versatile than traditional sheet cottons, as they come in larger sheets and can be custom-fitted to a horse and bandage.

**Nonstick sterile gauze dressings.** Available in roll form or in square pads; 4 × 4 inches is most useful. Applied to a wound after cleaning and medication, they keep the healing wound from adhering to the bandage.

**Quilts.** Durable quilted cotton pads, available ready-made or can be made from quilted mattress covers. Ready-made leg quilts are often too short for shipping bandages, and the sewn seams or binding may cause ripples that prevent the pad from conforming to the leg, creating pressure points. Also, many ready-made quilted pads are too thin to provide sufficient padding to protect the tendons from injury.

**Packaged paddings.** Ready-made packaged paddings are sold in tack stores. They come in a variety of materials including No-Bows, "pillow" pads, foam-lined bandage pads/wraps/liners, fiber-filled pads, synthetic felt, and combinations. Most are machine washable.

**Sterile compress and bandage.** Large sterile wound dressing made of cotton between a layer of paper and muslin, available from surplus stores and some tack shops. It is inexpensive, large, and thick enough to serve as a shipping bandage, but cannot be washed or reused.

**Disposable diapers.** Large-size square type (without elastic edges) can be used for a variety of padding purposes. The plastic backing can be used to make a sweat bandage, but must be removed for other types of bandages.

**Terrycloth towels.** Effective padding for wet applications, such as cold-water bandages or ice packs.

**Sanitary napkins.** Thick, clean, and absorbent, they make an effective first-aid pad to stop bleeding, and can be especially helpful in bandaging a heel grab.

## Special-Purpose Bandages

**Polo wraps.** Washable synthetic fleece bandages that have some stretch. Used to protect polo ponies against accidental mallet blows, they are also popular for protection during work, longeing, and turnout.

The drawbacks of polo wraps are that they are used without padding underneath, which can result in "cording" or tendon damage if improperly applied. They are more likely to slip or come unfastened if not properly applied and fastened or used in inclement conditions involving water or mud.

**Foam-padded elastic bandage.** Specialized bandage with foam rubber adhered to the inside of the elastic, used for exercise bandages.

**Gel packs and cooling wraps.** Made of a special gel that retains cold, these items can be cooled in a freezer and applied in place of an ice pack.

## Tail Wraps

Tail wraps are used to protect the hair of the dock during shipping. They are also used to confine the tail hairs out of the way during breeding, foaling, and body clipping, and to shape the hair of the dock or to protect a braided tail before a show.

Tail wraps may be cotton or synthetic stockinette knitted bandages, or co-adhesive bandages. Ace® bandages are sometimes used, but must never be applied too tightly or for too long, because they can cut off circulation and cause damage to the dock. The same cautions for Ace bandages apply to co-adhesive bandages: They must not be applied too tightly or left on for more than an hour.

Tail wraps should be fastened with Velcro, pins, or tape—not string ties, which may cause a ring of pressure around the dock.

## Tail Wrap to Shape Top of Tail/ Protect Braided Tail

MATERIALS NEEDED:
- Stretchy bandage such as a cotton or polyester knitted track bandage, co-adhesive bandage, or Ace bandage. (Well-worn Ace bandages that have lost most of their stretch are preferred.)

    **Caution:** An Ace bandage should not be left on the tail for more than an hour.
- Fasteners: Velcro closure or strips of masking tape.

Tail bandage (to lay hair of dock).

Remove tail bandage.

PROCEDURE:
1. Dampen the tail hair slightly. **Caution:** Do not wet the bandage, as it may shrink.
2. Start the bandage close to the top of the tail. Wrap around once to secure the end of the bandage, then wrap up to the very top of the tail.
3. Wrap downward to the end of the dock, then upward to the end of the bandage.
4. Fasten with strips of tape or Velcro closure, but not tightly.
5. To remove the bandage from an unbraided tail, grasp the bandage firmly with the fingers hooked over the top of the bandage and pull straight down. For a braided tail, unwrap the bandage.

## Nonslip Tail Wrap to Protect Tail During Shipping

This tail wrap must be secure so that it won't slip down and allow the tail to be rubbed. A tail guard may be used as an alternative to a tail wrap for shipping.

MATERIALS NEEDED:
- Stretchy bandage such as a cotton or polyester knitted track bandage, co-adhesive bandage, or Ace bandage. (A cotton or polyester stockinette bandage is preferred.)

PROCEDURE:
1. Start as with the tail wrap above and wrap downward for 8 to 10 inches.
2. To prevent the bandage from slipping off, separate a few hairs from the side of the tail and hold them upward while taking one wrap over them. Then fold the hairs downward over the last wrap, and wrap over them again. Repeat this once or twice more.
3. To keep the skirt clean and tangle-free during shipping:
   - Slip a nylon stocking over the skirt; fasten it to the tail bandage with safety pins.
   - Bandage over the skirt of the tail. A second bandage may be used if the first is not long enough.

Nonslip tail bandage (for shipping).

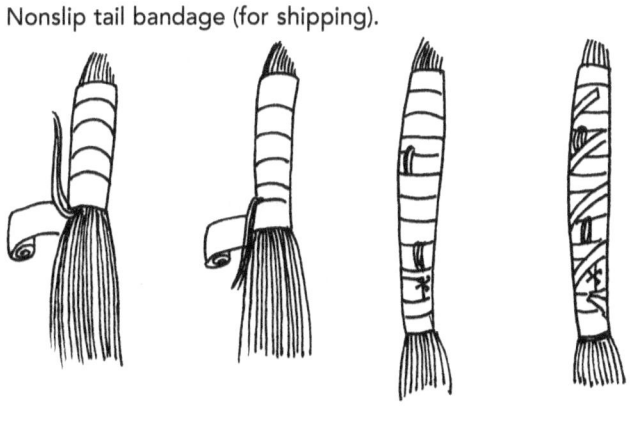

Tail bandage to cover skirt of tail.

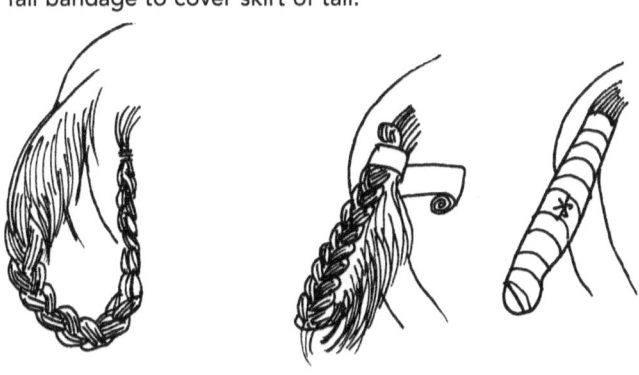

**Caution:** Tail wraps must not be left on for extended periods or they can cause loss of hair, tissue damage, sores, and in extreme cases, gangrene, requiring amputation of the tail. Do not use tail wraps for long trips; for this purpose, a tail guard (made of padded leather or synthetic material) is safer.

## Tail Wrap to Cover Skirt of Tail

This bandage is used to contain the tail hairs when necessary for foaling, breeding, or body clipping.

MATERIALS NEEDED:
- Stretchy bandage such as a cotton or polyester knitted track bandage, co-adhesive bandage, or Ace bandage. (A co-adhesive bandage such as Vetrap works best.)

PROCEDURE:
1. Braid the skirt of the tail into a long single braid and fold it up over the dock.
2. Wrap the tail as you normally would, wrapping over the dock and braided skirt.

# Polo Wraps

Polo wraps are often used for longeing, schooling, turnout, and ring work. They are not recommended for jumping or cross-country work because they are not as secure or as protective as correctly applied exercise bandages or galloping boots. Polo wraps may absorb water from water jumps or streams. This makes the bandage heavier and may cause the bandage to shift or shrink if allowed to dry on the legs, which may contribute to injury.

Polo wraps are only allowed in certain USPC competitions. Please check the current rulebooks for specific USPC disciplines.

MATERIALS NEEDED:
- Four fleece polo or Sandown bandages (usually used on all four legs).

PROCEDURE:
1. Start on the center third of the cannon bone, by placing the end of the bandage in the tendon groove, close to the cannon bone, on the outside of the leg.
2. Take one turn around the leg to anchor the first wrap.

Polo bandage.

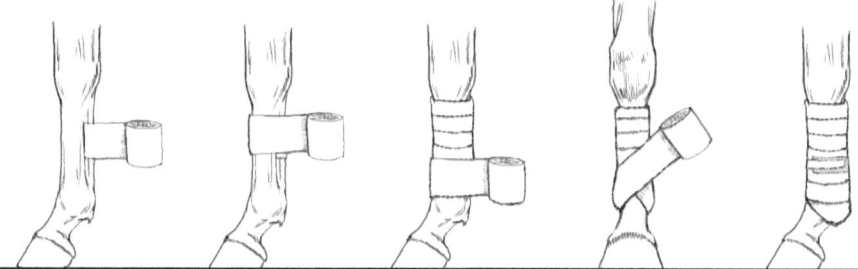

3. Wrap downward over the bandage end, keeping each wrap parallel to the last, overlapping half the width of the bandage and keeping the tension even.
4. At the fetlock joint, drop half the width of the bandage down underneath the joint, bringing it up in front to form an upside-down "V." It should not be loose, but must not be tight enough to restrict movement of the fetlock joint.
5. Wrap upward and finish the bandage on the outside of the cannon bone (not on the tendon, shin, or fetlock joint). Most polo wraps have Velcro closures. These can be reinforced with pins or tape.

An alternative method is:

1. Unroll 8 to 10 inches of bandage. Starting at the back of the knee or hock, hold the bandage end diagonally across the outside of the knee or hock, with the end toward the front of the horse.
2. Take one turn around the leg, over the base of the diagonal bandage end.
3. Fold the bandage end downward, over the first wrap and down the back of the flexor tendons. This cushions the tendons and keeps the bandage from slipping.
4. Wrap downward, over the bandage end, keeping each wrap parallel to the last, overlapping half the width of the bandage and keeping the tension even.
5. Continue wrapping and finish the bandage as above.

This method creates more padding over the tendons, but standard polo wraps may not be long enough, especially on large horses.

## Specialty Bandages or Treatment Bandages

Specialty bandages or treatment bandages are used to treat and protect wounds, sprains, strains, and other injuries, or to prevent swelling caused by a recent injury.

Before bandaging a wound, the wound should be cleaned and treated and a dressing applied. The padding and bandage should be applied in the direction that best supports closure of the wound.

Treatment bandages may be left in place for varying periods, depending on their purpose. Wound dressings are usually not removed more often than once a day, to avoid disturbing the healing surface too often. Ice packs and cold-water bandages are usually used for relatively short periods (20 minutes to several hours), while a sweat or a poultice may be left on for 12 hours or so.

Follow the veterinarian's instructions on when wounds require bandaging and how often to change treatment bandages. Bandaging incorrectly or when it is not indicated can do more harm than good.

**Caution:** The following are special-purpose bandages that must be applied by an experienced person, along with the proper course of treatment.

## Pressure Bandage

A pressure bandage is used to stop bleeding, prevent swelling caused by a recent injury, or inhibit the formation of proud flesh. It is applied snugly, with sufficient padding to create a uniform counter-pressure that prevents swelling or stops hemorrhage.

MATERIALS NEEDED:
Depending on the kind of wound and the purpose of the pressure bandage, any of the following materials may be used:

- Dressing or pressure pad (sterile nonstick gauze pads are preferable); sanitary napkins are good for stopping bleeding
- Leg padding: Sheet cotton or equivalent, folded to fit
- Wraps: Elastic adhesive tape (preferred for bandaging heel grabs), Ace bandage, or knit stockinette "track" bandage
- Fasteners: Velcro, safety pins, and/or strips of masking tape
- Duct tape: Used to protect the bottom of a bandage used on the hoof

PROCEDURE:
1. If a wound is present, apply wound dressing as directed by your veterinarian, under sterile nonstick gauze pads secured with roll gauze bandage. Apply padding thick enough to protect the leg when the bandage is

applied with a greater amount of tension than normal. Wrap with the selected bandage material using firm, even pressure.

2. To stop bleeding, a pressure bandage must be applied quickly and proficiently. The wound should usually be cleaned first, but if bleeding is serious, skip this step and apply pressure at once. Apply an appropriate padding (such as dressing or pressure pads, sterile nonstick gauze pads, sanitary napkins, or baby diapers) over the wound and apply the bandage (elastic adhesive tape or Vetrap) directly over the pad. If blood soaks through the pad and bandage, do not remove the first pad, but add more over it. Removing the pad may cause bleeding to start again; this should be left to a veterinarian. This type of pressure bandage should not be left in place for more than a few hours, and must not cut off circulation.

3. To treat a heel grab (over-reach injury), clean the wound and apply a mild topical antimicrobial ointment. Cover with a sterile gauze dressing (sanitary napkins work especially well for heel grabs), then wrap the heel, coronary band, and foot with elastic adhesive tape, being careful to not wrap too tightly. When wrapping with a co-adhesive bandage, the bandage should be applied lightly enough to only slightly remove the wrinkles, never tightly enough to remove all wrinkles. The bottom part of the wrap, over the hoof, can be protected with duct tape, but do not use duct tape above the coronary band.

Pressure bandage to control bleeding.

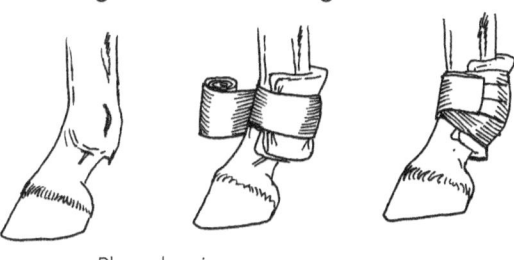

Place dressing pad over wound

Pressure bandage for heel grab (over-reach injury).

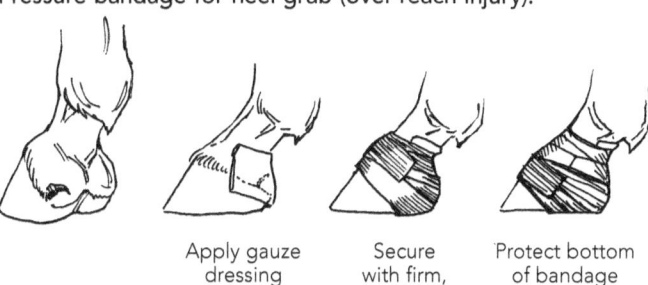

Apply gauze dressing over wound

Secure with firm, even wraps

Protect bottom of bandage with duct tape

## Poultices for Legs

A poultice draws infection or inflammation from wounds such as puncture wounds, or reduces the inflammation (pain, heat, and swelling) that accompany a sprain or bruise. Poultices are sometimes used on tendons as a precautionary measure to prevent swelling or "filling," after especially hard work. A hot or warm poultice is used to increase circulation; a cold one is used to decrease heat and inflammation.

MATERIALS NEEDED:
- Poultice material such as poultice powder or paste (there are several brands)
- Brown paper bag or newspaper
- Bandage and leg padding (of a type suitable for the area to be poulticed)
- 4" gauze pad (unfolded) or gauze material
- Plastic food wrap or disposable diaper with plastic lining left intact (for a hot/warm poultice, to keep in the warmth)
- One leg cut from a pair of pantyhose (optional)

Applying a poultice.

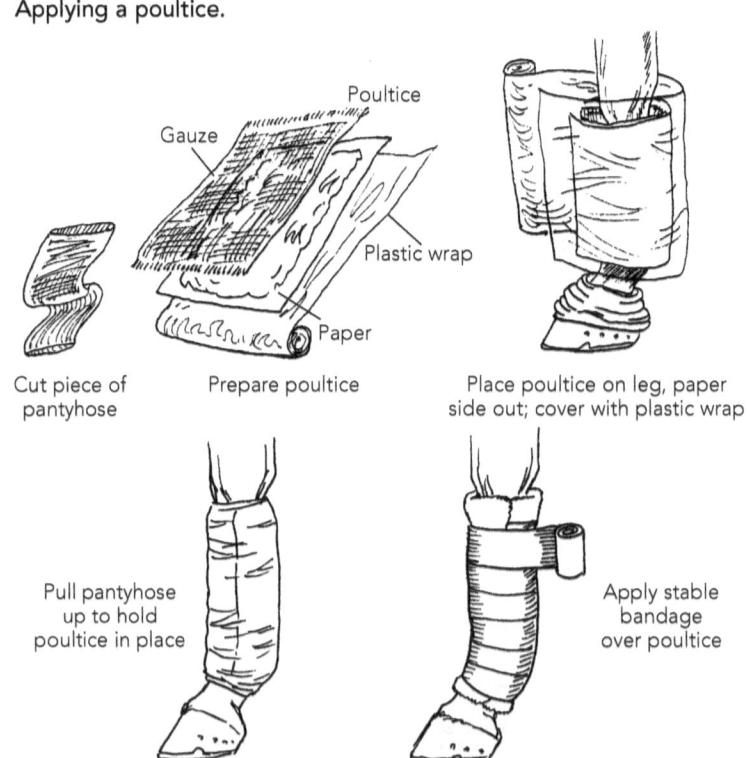

PROCEDURE:
1. Prepare the poultice according to manufacturer's directions. For a hot poultice, mix poultice powder with warm water, heat in a double boiler, or place poultice on brown paper and heat in a microwave oven. The poultice must be warm, not hot, as it will hold heat for a considerable length of time and can burn the leg if it is too hot.
2. Cut paper to the size of the padding. Apply the poultice to the paper and form it to the size and shape of the area to be covered, ¼-inch thick. To make removal easier, cover the poultice with gauze material.
3. Clean the horse's leg and for easy application you can place pantyhose over the foot. Then apply the entire pack (gauze side next to the horse) to the area to be poulticed. Cover with plastic wrap to keep in the moisture and heat. Pull up the pantyhose, which will help keep the poultice in place as you bandage.
4. Place padding over the wrap and bandage.
5. Leave on for 12 to 24 hours. When the poultice is removed, any remaining poultice material should be washed off the leg with soap and water.

## Poultice for Hoof Abscess

Hoof abscesses are very painful, and horses usually show a quick onset of severe lameness. It is helpful to work with your vet and/or farrier. Sometimes the shoe is removed. Sometimes the abscess can be located and a very small hole is made in the sole with the hoof knife to allow for drainage and provide relief from the pressure. If the point of origin is not located, then the abscess may progress up to the coronary band and the pus or infection will drain from there. A poultice will help draw out the infection or inflammation.

MATERIALS NEEDED:
- Commercial poultice or Epsom salts
- Diaper, sheet cottons, or gamgee
- Co-adhesive bandage (such as Vetrap)
- Duct tape

PROCEDURE:
1. Thoroughly clean and wash the hoof and sole.
2. Prepare the poultice. If you don't have a ready-made medicated poultice, you can mix your own. An example of one formula you can make uses 2 parts wheat bran to 1 part Epsom salts mixed with water to make a paste.
3. Cover the sole of the hoof with the poultice.

4. Cover the sole and hoof with the diaper, sheet cottons, and/or gamgee. Fold up the diaper or cottons.
5. Secure the padding by wrapping with the co-adhesive bandage over the hoof and coronet band.
6. Cover the hoof with duct tape for durability, especially on the sole, but not on the coronet band.

This bandage should be redone daily, usually for 3 to 10 days, or as directed by your veterinarian.

## Sweat Bandage

A sweat bandage is used to reduce swelling by increasing blood circulation through heat application. Sweats are usually used for swelling that is more than 48 hours old; a fresh injury usually benefits more from cold applications. A sweat is left on for 8 hours and then removed. It can be repeated if necessary.

Sweat bandages should not be applied over liniments, blistering agents, or leg paints, or they may cause blistering of the skin. **Caution:** When ambient temperatures are greater than 80°F, sweat bandages can become too hot and cause severe skin blistering.

MATERIALS NEEDED:
- Sweat medication approved by your veterinarian
- Plastic food wrap, brown paper bag, newspaper, or disposable diaper with the plastic liner left intact
- Leg padding and bandage suitable for area to be sweated

PROCEDURE:
1. Wash the leg and allow it to dry.
2. Apply nitrofurazone ointment or sweat medication, rubbing it in as directed.
3. Cover the area lightly with plastic wrap, newspaper, or brown paper or diaper, and do not pull it tight.
4. Place padding over the leg and apply and secure the bandage with Velcro or other fastener.

## Ice Packs

An ice pack is used to reduce pain, heat, and swelling due to a recent injury, especially sprains, strains, and bruises. For best effect, ice packs should be applied to the injury as soon as possible and left on for 20 to 30 minutes at a time, repeating as often as necessary. Cold applications are most effective immediately after an injury and for the first 48 hours.

MATERIALS NEEDED:
- Chopped ice or gel cooling packs (a bag of frozen peas or corn works well as an ice pack, as it conforms easily to the shape of the leg).
- Two plastic bags with zipper closures, or freezer tape. Use the food storage size bag (1 gallon or smaller) that fits the area affected; there are many to choose from.
- Padding (terrycloth towels are most effective).
- Two Ace bandages, each 6" wide.
- Fasteners: Velcro, duct tape, or safety pins.

PROCEDURE:
1. If using ice, double-bag the plastic bags; fill the bags with chopped ice, and seal them or tape them shut with freezer tape. Gel cooling packs must be placed in the freezer to cool them before use.
2. Apply the cold pack to the injured area and wrap with several layers of terrycloth towel for insulation as well as padding.
3. Wrap one Ace bandage firmly over the ice and towels, and fasten with Velcro, tape, or safety pins.
4. When the ice begins to melt, wrap the second Ace bandage over the first to keep the whole application from sagging away from the injury site, fastening as above.
5. Remove the entire wrap as soon as the ice is melted, or it will become a sweat wrap, producing heat instead of cold. Apply fresh ice packs as often as necessary.

## Cold-Water Bandages

Cold-water bandages are used to apply cold and pressure to an inflamed leg. They are most effective when applied after cold-hosing.

Cold-water bandages must be kept wet. If allowed to dry, they may shrink and cause excessive or uneven pressure, compounding the injury. For this reason, they cannot be left on overnight or until they dry. Check on the bandage periodically to make sure it is still wet.

MATERIALS NEEDED:
- Petroleum jelly
- Padding that is durable when wet (preferably terrycloth towels)

- Knit stockinette "track" wrap
- Fasteners other than tape (safety pins are best)

PROCEDURE:
1. Apply petroleum jelly to the skin of the heels and pastern to protect against chapping.
2. Soak the padding in ice water until it is thoroughly wet and cold.
3. Without wringing it out, apply the padding to the leg. Bandage snugly, as pressure is part of the purpose of this wrap. Fasten with pins.
4. Frequently run cold water over the entire wrap, especially between the leg and the padding. Keep the entire bandage wet.

# Bandaging the Knee and Hock

Bandaging joints such as the knee and hock present special problems. It is more difficult to achieve uniform pressure, and a bandage must not bind or apply excessive pressure to bony prominences like the back of the knee or the point of the hock. In some cases, the purpose of the bandage is to restrict or prevent movement of the joint; in others, the bandage must remain in place without slipping even though there will be some movement.

## Figure-Eight Bandage

A figure-eight bandage is used to wrap the joints of the knee or hock to keep a wound clean or to keep medication in place. It allows some mobility in the joint, so it is not suitable for an immobilizing bandage.

MATERIALS NEEDED:
- Wrap and padding for a stable bandage, to be applied below the figure-eight bandage.
- Dressing and/or medication, as needed.
- Sufficient padding for the joint; terrycloth towels, packaged padding or sheet cottons.
- Several long bandages (knit stockinette "track" bandages in 4"–5" width work best).
- When applying to the hock joint: Two 1" diameter, 4"–6" long rolls of gauze bandage or co-adhesive bandage to place in the hollows of the hock over the first layer of padding. Two 4" pieces of 1" foam pipe insulation also work well to protect the Achilles tendon and point of hock from pressure.
- Fasteners: Duct tape, white medical tape, or safety pins.

## PROCEDURE:

1. Apply a stable bandage to the leg below the joint to prevent swelling of the lower leg and to keep the figure-eight bandage from slipping down.
2. Apply wound dressing and/or medication, as indicated.
3. Place padding around the joint, from mid-cannon to mid-forearm or mid-gaskin.
4. Begin wrapping at the bottom of the padding. Make several turns to secure it, working upward and overlapping each wrap by half the width of the bandage.
5. For the hock: Pass the bandage diagonally upward, across the front of the hock. Take one complete wrap around the gaskin. Then pass the bandage diagonally downward, across the front of the hock, and make a complete wrap around the base of the hock. This forms a figure eight, with the crossover point on the front of the hock, allowing the joint to remain mobile.

Figure-eight bandage (knee).

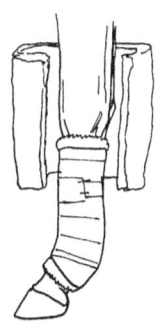
Apply stable bandage to lower leg

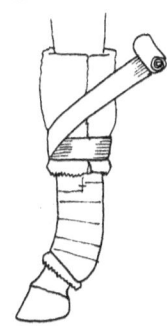
Apply cotton padding from center of lower leg to above joint

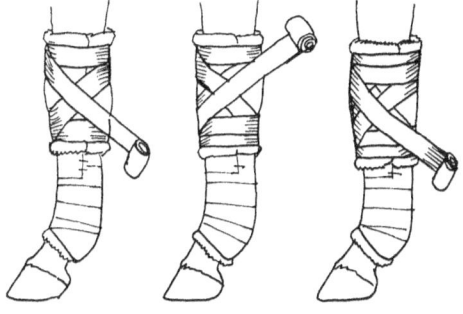
Anchor bandage and apply in crossover pattern

Fasten bandage on outside of leg; crossover point should be opposite to site of injury

Place a 1-inch diameter roll of cotton gauze (or a roll of used co-adhesive bandage) on each side in the hollow of the hock, over the first layer of padding. This helps to keep the bandage pressure off the point of the hock and the Achilles tendon. In addition, take care not to pull too hard across the back of the gaskin.

Repeat the wrapping process (diagonally upward, complete wrap, diagonally downward, and complete wrap) until you reach the end of the bandage. Try to finish the bandage at the bottom of the wrap, making one or two wraps to complete the bandage.

6. For the knee: When bandaging a knee, the same method is used. The crossover point may be on the front of the knee, on either side of the knee, or on both sides of the knee, but it should never cross over the back of the knee, as this puts pressure on the accessory carpal bone. Crossovers on the inside and outside of the knee allow for greater mobility of the joint than crossing over the front of the knee.

## Stack Bandage

A stack bandage is commonly used to reduce swelling that involves the entire leg (for example, cellulitis) or an area around the knee or hock; to protect a wound involving the knee, forearm, hock, or gaskin; or as the padding for a splint. It has slightly less padding than an immobilizing bandage.

MATERIALS NEEDED:
- Sufficient padding, depending on the application. Thick commercial bandages (for example, pillow wraps), sheet cottons, gamgees, or medical cotton padding work well.
- Several track or flannel bandages with Velcro fasteners.
- When applying to the hock joint: Two 1" diameter, 4"–6" long rolls of gauze bandage or co-adhesive bandage (Vetrap), to place in the hollows of the hock over the first layer of padding. Two 4" pieces of 1" foam pipe insulation also work well to protect the Achilles tendon and point of hock from pressure.
- Fasteners: Velcro, duct tape, white medical tape, or masking tape.

PROCEDURE:
1. Apply a stable bandage from just below the knee or hock to the midway down the hoof (no need to protect the heels). (For directions on applying a stable bandage, see the *USPC C Level Manual*, pages 276–279.)
2. Apply another bandage on top of the first (overlapping very little to not at all with the lower bandage), over the knee or hock. When bandaging

Stack bandage.

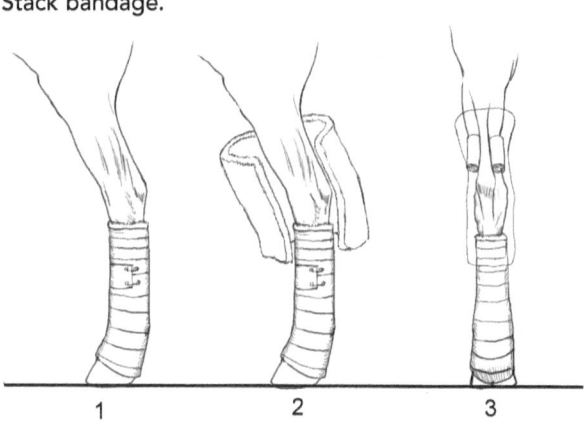

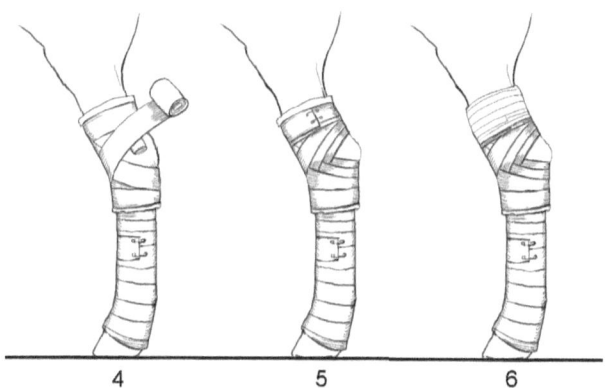

over these joints, use a figure-eight pattern (as previously described) to avoid applying excessive pressure on the point of the hock or the accessory carpal bone at the back of the knee. When the bandage is complete, secure the bandage with your fastener.

3. For bandaging the forearm or gaskin, stack a third bandage on top of the second. Apply it like a normal stable bandage, with even tension and sufficient padding, and secure it with fasteners.

## Spider Bandage

A spider bandage is used to provide limited mobility to an injured knee or hock. It requires a significant amount of padding over the joint. A variety of materials may be used.

**MATERIALS NEEDED:**
- Spider bandage, made from a large piece of fabric such as medium-weight stretchy material, lightweight stretch denim, kitchen towel, or very heavy T-shirt material. It should measure 24" × 30". The two ends are cut into 10" strips roughly 1½" wide, leaving a 10"–12" section in the middle. When cutting the tie strips, fold the fabric in half to cut the tails two at a time. This will ensure that you have the same number and width of tie strips cut on each side of the bandage.
- Wound dressings and medications, if needed.
- Sufficient padding to protect bony prominences on the knee or hock; terrycloth towels or sheet cottons work well.
- Leg pad and wrap for stable bandage, to be applied below the spider bandage.

**PROCEDURE:**
1. Apply a stable bandage to the leg below the knee or hock to be bandaged. This keeps the spider bandage in place and helps prevent swelling of the leg below the joint.
2. Apply dressing and medication as needed and cover it with nonstick gauze so it won't stick to the cotton. Then cover the joint with padding (terrycloth towels or sheet cottons) that extends from mid-cannon to mid-forearm or mid-gaskin. There must be sufficient padding to prevent pressure damage to the Achilles tendon above the hock, the point of the hock, or the bony prominence at the back of the knee.
3. Place the spider bandage over the joint with the middle of the bandage over the front of the knee, or over the back of the hock. The "tails" or tie strips will be tied on the outside of the joint. The bottom edge of the spider bandage padding may be stacked on top of the stable bandage or overlap it. If the bandage is going to be worn overnight or for several days, check with your veterinarian on how often you should change the bandage. It is advisable to stack it so that a pressure point is not created.
4. Start by tying at the middle to hold the bandage in place. Then begin at the top, tying each set of ties in a square knot. Tuck the ends of the previous knot under the next one to eliminate loose ends.

   Another method is to braid the ties, using a French braid as in braiding a tail. This method conforms better to the leg as it moves, and is less likely to cause pressure points than knots.

   Surgical knots can be used instead of square knots to secure the bandage over the padding. Surgical knots start like a square knot, but instead of tying "right over left, left over right," you tie "right over left"

Spider (many-tailed) bandage for knee or hock.

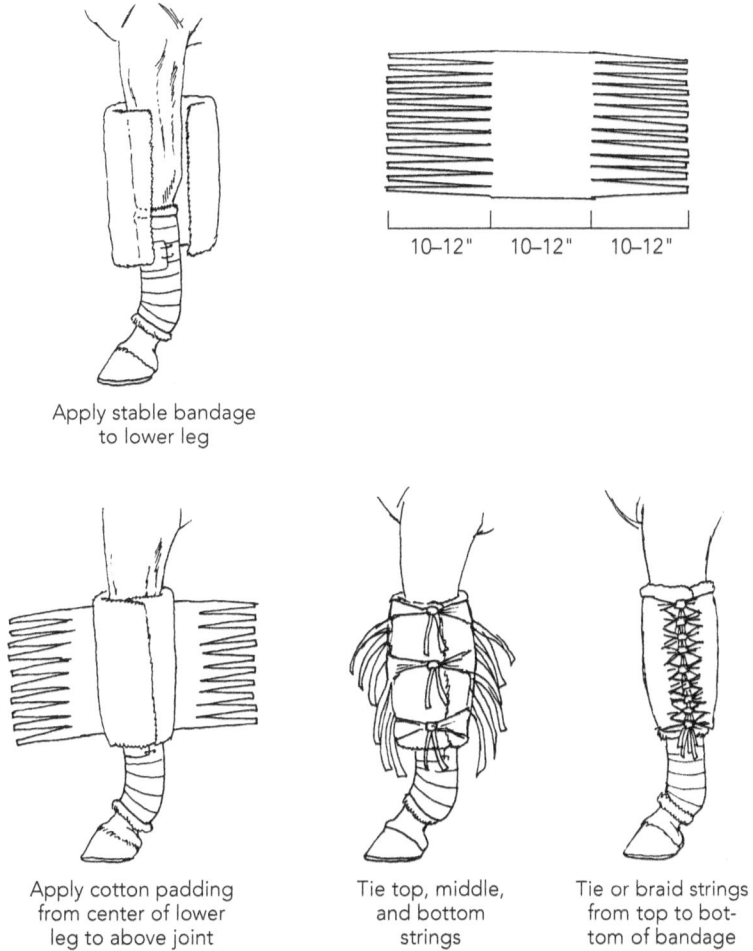

(just like starting to tie your shoelaces) twice, then pull the knot as tightly as you can. Tuck the "tails" of the tie strips under each new surgical knot as you make it to secure the bandage. Square knots can tighten greatly, sometimes to the point where they cannot be untied and the spider bandage must be cut off, which makes it impossible to reuse. Surgical knots make it easier to remove and then reuse the bandage.

5. If you need to increase the immobilizing properties of a spider bandage on the knee, apply a regular stable bandage to the lower portion of the limb. Then apply a second stable bandage above the knee to create a "stacking" of the two stable bandages. Apply padding over the knee and then the spider bandage as directed in step 4.

## Immobilizing Bandage (Robert Jones Bandage)

An immobilizing bandage is used to prevent movement of a joint or as a temporary emergency measure to stabilize the leg if a fracture is suspected.

It should be used cautiously so it does not cause more harm to the horse, as it makes it difficult for him to move and could result in loss of balance. The splints must be properly padded to avoid injury to the leg.

MATERIALS NEEDED:
- Many layers of padding, depending on the application. Pillow wraps, large amounts of rolled cotton, or gamgee work well.
- Several track or flannel bandages, Ace bandages, or a spider bandage (see above).
- Splints (suitable lengths of PVC pipe cut to ¾–½ their circumference or an appropriate length of a 2 × 4 board): These should be applied only on the recommendation of a veterinarian because of the danger of cutting off circulation or puncturing the joint if the splint should break.
- Fasteners: Duct tape or white medical tape (preferred), Velcro, or industrial masking tape.
- Materials to hold splint in place: Duct tape, elastic adhesive tape, or wide white medical tape.

PROCEDURE:
1. Apply a stack bandage as described in the procedure above. The bandage over the knee and hock should be applied in a figure-eight pattern to reduce pressure on the accessory carpal bone and point of hock; however, because many layers are applied, there will not be an obvious area of padding showing as in a regular figure-eight or stack bandage. Ideally, after the bandage has been applied, the circumference should be three to five times that of the normal leg. To increase the thickness of the bandages, apply multiple layers of an entire bandage (padding plus bandages). This approach ensures that there is enough tension to keep the bandage in place and provides greater strength to the bandage construction to immobilize a joint.
2. Apply the splint as directed by your veterinarian. In case of a fracture, the joints above and below the fracture must be immobilized.

# 17

# Travel Safety

This chapter includes information on trailering, trailer and tow vehicle maintenance, training horses to load, and tips for transporting horses that are difficult travelers. You can find more information on travel preparation, long-distance trips, and safe loading and unloading in the travel safety chapters of the *USPC D* and *C Level Manuals*.

## Trailer Care and Maintenance

If you have your own trailer or are trailering with someone else, you should learn how to check the trailer and tow vehicle before a trip. Proper trailer maintenance not only keeps your trailer safer, but keeps it in good condition, makes it easier to operate, and maintains its value. Even if you are not yet old enough to drive or trailer horses yourself, you can be responsible for (or at least help with) regular trailer maintenance chores such as the following:

- Clean out the trailer after every trip. (Leaving manure and urine in the trailer will rot wooden floorboards, rust walls, and corrode metal floors.)
- Check air pressure in the tires, and check the tires for cuts, bulges, or uneven wear (once a week, and before a trip).
- Pull out the floor mats, clean the mats and the floor underneath, and inspect the floor. (If you can push a penknife blade into wooden floorboards, there may be a rotten spot. You should always check the floor

before using a trailer, because a rotten board might give way under a horse and a corroded metal floor could collapse.)
- Check and lubricate the trailer nose wheel, jack, hitch coupler, tailgate, ramp, or trailer doors (especially if the trailer is stored outside). Lubricate butt bars where they are attached to the wall, joints, and all divider pins to make them easy to remove in case of an accident.
- Check and lubricate the hitch receiver and electrical receptacle on the tow vehicle to keep them free from rust and corrosion.
- Check the breakaway brake connector and battery to be sure they are functioning properly.
- Examine the safety chains to ensure that the chains, the connection to the trailer, and the hooks to the tow vehicle are strong and in working order.
- Wash and wax the trailer and clean the interior with soap and water frequently. Diluted dishwashing soap works well for the inside of the trailer.
- Wood floors can be sealed with wood preservative. Aluminum floors should be washed and sprinkled with baking soda to neutralize the corrosiveness of urine.
- Check that all lights (running lights, brake lights, turn signals) and brakes are working properly before every trip.

## Tow Vehicle and Trailer Hitch

A vehicle used to tow a horse trailer must be in excellent running condition and capable of the task. Subcompacts or "mini" vehicles are not suitable for this purpose, especially in hilly terrain. A full-sized 1-ton or ¾-ton vehicle with a heavy-duty towing package is the best choice. Too light a vehicle may lack the braking capacity and stability to handle a heavy trailer, and the engine, drive train, and transmission will quickly wear out if overloaded.

The tow vehicle must be equipped with a Class III or stronger heavy-duty hitch, and the trailer must be balanced so that it is level when it is hitched. When pulling a tow-behind trailer, a weight-distributing hitch, equipped with torsion bars, distributes the tongue weight over all four vehicle wheels instead of placing it mainly over the rear wheels. This results in less wear and tear on the tow vehicle and better control of the trailer, with less tendency for the trailer to sway. Gooseneck trailers require a special hitch installed in the bed of a pickup truck. All trailer hitches must be designed for the specific tow vehicle (requirements vary for different years and models) and the weight of the trailer, and should be installed by an expert.

The trailer hitch should be adjusted so that the trailer, hitch, and tow vehicle are level when loaded. If the trailer is high in front, it increases the wear on the tow vehicle and forces the horses to ride on a sloping surface, which is tiring. A trailer that is low in front is even worse, as this increases the likelihood of sway and may result in loss of control in an emergency. If the leverage of the trailer's tongue weight is so heavy as to lift the front of the tow vehicle, this reduces the vehicle's steering stability and makes the vehicle more likely to sway in difficult conditions.

The tow vehicle and trailer should be checked and serviced regularly, especially before a long trip. Towing puts more strain on the engine, cooling system, transmission, brakes, and tires than ordinary driving, so these points are especially important. A breakdown is a problem at any time, but when towing horses, it can become a much larger problem. Be sure to carry the necessary equipment (see the trailer equipment list later in this chapter) to handle any problems that might occur while on the road.

## Yearly Maintenance Program for a Trailer or Horse Van

Horse vans, trailers, and tow vehicles must be well maintained for the safety of people and horses. You probably don't tow your trailer or drive a horse van as frequently as you drive your car, and when you do, you may be concentrating on the horses or the event you are going to instead of the vehicle. If you neglect to maintain the trailer or van until you need to use it, it is a perfect setup for a costly and potentially dangerous breakdown that can put both drivers and horses at risk beside the highway. Maintenance must be done on a regular schedule, even if the trailer or van is used irregularly.

Some vans and trailers are used heavily during the competition or hunting season, and out of service for the winter. Your yearly maintenance schedule should take into account seasonal changes in storage, use, climate, and road conditions.

Here are some points to remember about year-round van and trailer maintenance:

- Use the trailer safety checklist (see the next section) for your van or trailer and tow vehicle before *every* trip, no matter how short.
- Clean and check the trailer or van after each trip and attend to any minor repairs or maintenance chores promptly.

Weight-distributing hitch with torsion bars.

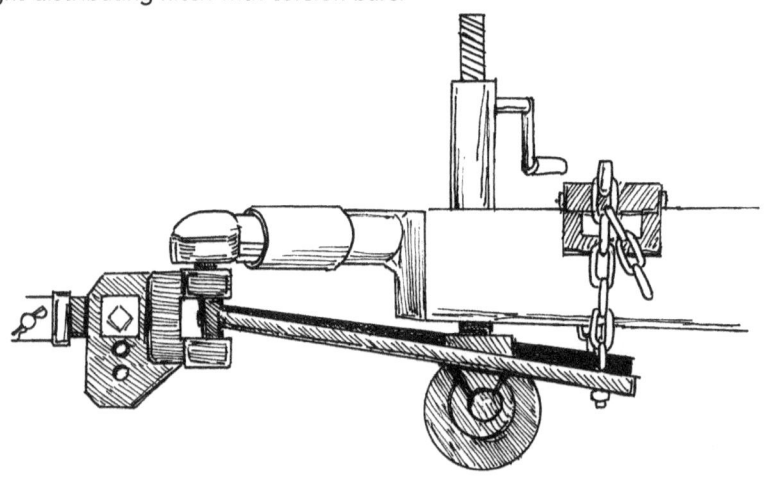

Balance of trailer and tow vehicle.

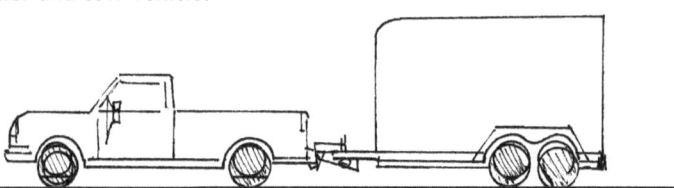

Right: trailer and tow vehicle level

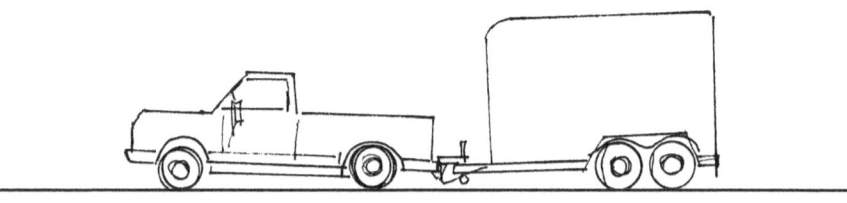

Wrong: trailer low in front (unsafe)

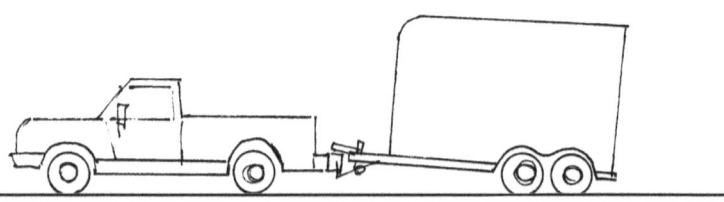

Wrong: trailer high in front (unsafe)

- Set up a yearly maintenance plan with a mechanic who knows your vehicle, including the following points:
  - Annual State inspection, including brakes, lights, signals, and wheel bearing packing and hitch safety devices, as required by your state vehicle code.
  - Renew insurance, trailer license, and inspection sticker, if applicable.
- Your annual safety inspection, should be scheduled before using the trailer (usually in spring). This should include:
  - Check floor (interior and exterior), supports, and braces. Wood floors must be checked for rot and aluminum floors for pitting and corrosion.
  - Check interior for loose welds, rust, sharp edges, or exposed wiring. Examine the ventilation doors (ceiling or walls) for leaks, broken hinges, or missing parts.
  - Check partitions, doors, latches, butt bars, and tailgate for soundness, security, and proper operation.
  - Check axles, spindles, and suspension or springs; lubricate as needed. Check undercarriage: subframe, springs, shackle hangers, welds, stress points, and beams.
  - Check brake system and its operation, including emergency breakaway braking system.
  - Check coupler for proper operation, correct size ball, safety chains, and locking pins; lubricate as needed.
  - Check electrical plug, receptacle, and wiring. Use protective spray to protect contacts against corrosion.
  - Check balance of trailer and hitch when hitched to tow vehicle; have height of hitch and torsion bars adjusted so that hitch and trailer are level. Riding uphill puts more strain on the tow vehicle; riding downhill causes poor balance of trailer and can be dangerous.
  - Check lights (brake lights, turn signals, running lights, and interior lights) and the electrical coupling. Use a product designed for light-bulb lubrication; do not use household products, WD-40, or petroleum jelly on lightbulbs or sockets.
  - Check trailer brakes and breakaway brake. Battery for breakaway brake may have to be replaced.
  - Check tires for wear, balance, and proper inflation (including the spare). Have tire-changing equipment (jack, blocks, tire iron) in trailer.
  - Clean and repack trailer wheel bearings.

Check tire dates, as even "new" tires may have been in storage for some time and may be older than 5 years (the recommended life span of a tire). Since 2000, the week and year the tire was produced is included in last four digits of the Tire Identification Number. The first two digits identify the week of production, and the last two digits immediately preceding those identify the year.

For example:

| DOT U2LL LMLR 5107 | |
|---|---|
| **51 =** | Manufactured during the 51st week of the year |
| **07 =** | Manufactured during 2007 |

A horse van is essentially a large truck. It should be maintained and serviced regularly by a truck mechanic who can help you set up a regular maintenance program with special attention to the engine, transmission, tires, suspension, and chassis.

If possible, park a van or trailer under cover, on a hard, dry surface. Exposure to weather (especially strong sunlight) causes the tires and exterior finish to deteriorate. If a trailer is parked in the sun when not in use, it is highly recommended to replace the tires every 4 to 5 years regardless of their apparent condition to avoid tire failure due to cracked or weakened sidewalls. Wash and wax the van or trailer regularly (frequency depends on use, climate, and exposure to mud and road salt).

## Trailer Safety Checklist

The following items should be checked on the trailer and tow vehicle *every time* you tow a trailer, even for short trips. (You may want to copy this list and keep it in the tow vehicle.)

On the tow vehicle, check:

- Fluid levels: Oil, transmission fluid, brake fluid, and radiator fluid. Check engine belts and hoses. Fill up fuel.
- Tire pressure: Check tire pressure when tires are cold. Examine tires for cracks, bulges, or signs of excessive wear. (For trucks with dual tires: Strike the inside tire with a hammer. If the air pressure is okay, the hammer will bounce back.) Even a few pounds of difference in tire pressures from one tire to another can make your trailer tow roughly or unevenly, especially if a horse moves around inside.

- Hitch and receiver (no rust, loose bolts, or cracked welds; ball is correct size for trailer and is tight within the coupling or the hitch).
- Electrical connectors and wiring on both vehicles (no loose connectors or broken wires).
- With the trailer hitched, test the brakes and trailer brake controller, and adjust trailer brakes for the load. Check running lights, turn indicators, and brake lights.

On the trailer, check:

- Hitch and coupling (be sure coupler fastens securely over ball). Older trailers often took a 2-inch ball, whereas most new ones require a 2⅝-inch ball. Make sure the nose wheel or nose jack is cranked all the way up.
- The battery and cable of the trailer's breakaway system. Check safety chains, hooks, and points where they connect.
- Tire pressure and condition of all tires. Check tire pressure when tires are cold. Check lug nuts on wheels. Most flat tires result from low pressure, excessive weight loads, and/or excessive speed.
- Signal and brake lights, running lights, and emergency flashers.
- Trailer floor for soundness (no signs of dry rot); mats in place.
- Any loose, rattling parts have been tightened and secured.
- Interior for wasp or hornet nests. (These can appear within a day!)

Be sure you have:

- Spare tires and tire-changing equipment for tow vehicle and trailer. Carry a length of 2-inch diameter steel pipe or tubing that will slip over the lug wrench to increase leverage to loosen tight lug nuts. Most tires are now put on with air wrenches and can be very hard to loosen.
- Registration for both tow vehicle and trailer, with current inspection stamp; insurance card.
- Maps, directions, and GPS if you own one. However, don't rely solely on GPS, as in remote areas with no cell signal you will have to refer to printed maps.
- Important phone numbers: Program into your phone and/or carry a list: veterinarian, farrier, tow company, insurance company, destination phone number, cell numbers of friends also going to same destination.
- Coggins test, health papers, and any other transport papers required for horses, especially if you are crossing state lines.
- Tool kit (see the next section) and first-aid kits (horse and human).

- Auto club membership, towing insurance, or other arrangements for emergency road service that covers the trailer and tow vehicle. A credit card may be necessary for major repairs on the road. A cell phone is helpful in case of emergency.

## Trailer Equipment List

The following items should always be carried in the trailer:

- Spare tire and jack for trailer and tow vehicle.
- Jumper cables, tow strap, or chain.
- Road flares or warning signal and road cones in case of breakdown.
- Blocks (two) to put behind front and back tires when parked (the type of block that can serve as a ramp for changing a tire is especially useful).
- Longe line, extra lead rope and halter, sheet or blanket, extra cotton and leg wraps, pins, masking tape.
- Chain-end lead shank for every horse in the trailer, to be used in case horses must be unloaded or handled by strangers in an emergency. These, plus extra halters, should be carried in the tow vehicle, not in the trailer.
- Large container of water (can be used for drinking water, first aid, or some vehicle problems).
- Small pail with sponge or cloth.
- Water and feed buckets, hay net (fastened so it won't swing or drop too low), with fresh hay for every trip.
- Broom, shovel, rake, fork, muck basket, manure disposal bags. (Leave parking areas clean!)
- First-aid kits (horse and human). Please refer to *USPC C Level Manual*, pages 216–218, for the equine first-aid kit.
- Tool kit, containing:
  - Rechargeable battery charger/tire inflator power pack
  - Flashlight and extra batteries
  - Screwdrivers, pliers, hammer, wrenches, and other basic tools
  - Extra bulbs or light modules for trailer lights, and a small selection of spare fuses that match the tow vehicle
  - Electrical tape and duct tape
  - Fire extinguisher type A or ABC (one in tow vehicle and one in trailer)
  - Extra quart of oil for tow vehicle

- Crowbar and hacksaw (essential in case you need to remove center divider quickly)
- Sturdy, sharp knife (to cut tie ropes in an emergency)
- WD-40, grease, or lubricating oil
- Can of bee/wasp/hornet spray
- Work gloves and waterless hand cleaner

## Safe Trailer Loading Checklist

Before a trip, make sure that your horse (and any other horses you are hauling) is used to loading, traveling, and unloading quietly. Pack the trailer and tow vehicle and check off all items before loading the horses.

Review safe loading and unloading procedures (see the *USPC D Level Manual*, pages 239–242).

When hauling only one horse in a two-horse trailer, load him on the driver's side. This makes the trailer tow better, and is more comfortable for the horse since the road is crowned in the center.

When hauling two horses, put the larger one on the driver's side. Use a barrier or hay net to keep their heads apart so they cannot nip each other, but don't tie them so tightly that they cannot ride comfortably.

Be aware of airflow patterns in your trailer at highway speed: If you use bedding to reduce slipping on floor mats, check that the wind isn't blowing the shavings around during the drive, or wet down the shavings to reduce dust.

Load and unload with the trailer parked on level ground, on good footing, and in a clear area away from traffic. If it is necessary to unload at a rest stop or beside a road, put a longe line on the horse as well as a lead rope. If he should pull back, he is less likely to get loose.

Be quiet, patient, and confident when loading and handling horses. Get the horse's attention by practicing proper leading, walking, halting, and backing before asking him to load.

Never enter an enclosed trailer stall (without an escape door) with a horse.

When loading, *always* fasten the rear chain or butt bar before tying the horse's head. When unloading, *always* untie the horse's head before unfastening the rear chain or butt bar, or opening the trailer door or tailgate.

Keep fingers clear of the trailer door, hinges, latches, and tailgate. Wear gloves when loading or unloading horses.

Keep the rear door or tailgate closed when the horse is standing in the trailer (for example, between classes at a show or at a rest stop). Some smaller horses or ponies can back out under a butt bar or rear chain.

# Training Horses to Load and Unload

Entering a trailer, traveling, and unloading quietly are skills that must be taught. It goes against a horse's natural instincts to step up into an enclosed box with a floor that may sound hollow or move slightly under his feet. Proper preparation, good training, unhurried practice, and calm, patient handling produce a horse that is obedient, confident, and relaxed during loading, travel, and unloading. The worst possible approach is to attempt to force a green horse to load when you are in a hurry to get somewhere.

## Safety Precautions When Loading Green or Difficult Horses

Always wear gloves when loading horses.

Work in a quiet, secure area (not on a road) away from crowds and distractions. Any helpers must be competent and experienced horse handlers who will follow your instructions.

Park the trailer on level ground with good footing, hitched to a tow vehicle with the brake on for stability. A step-in trailer should be placed so that the step is as low as possible. A ramp should be firmly supported, not wobbly.

The trailer should be made as light and inviting as possible:

- Open escape doors and windows; turn on interior lights.
- Swing the partition to one side for maximum room.
- Cover the floor with several inches of shavings (dampened if dusty or windblown).
- Place a flake of hay and a small feed of grain in the manger or front of the trailer. Dampen hay if possible, to cut down on dust, unless the local climate creates a mold risk.

Parking the trailer beside a wall or fence can prevent the horse from escaping sideways. Don't create a dangerous gap between the fence and the ramp.

Assemble any equipment and have it in place before you begin loading.

If available, a quiet, familiar horse that loads easily may be loaded first and give the green horse confidence.

The horse should wear shipping boots or bandages, a poll guard, a tail guard if he sits against the butt bar, and a strong, well-fitting breakaway halter.

Use equipment that permits safe control. A chain-end lead shank can help keep the horse's attention. A longe line attached to the halter makes it less likely for a horse to get loose if he should pull back unexpectedly.

Work quietly, calmly, and patiently, and use good judgment to prevent accidents to yourself, your helpers, or the horse. Never wrap a rope around your hand or any part of your body; keep fingers clear of hinges and trailer posts, and never enter an enclosed trailer stall with a horse. If the horse becomes upset or resists violently, stop and think before the situation gets worse!

## Steps in Trailer Training

**Work in hand.** Before trailer training can begin, the horse must be taught to lead properly without crowding, hanging back, or pulling; to move forward, stop, turn, and back up on command; and to pay attention to his handler. This is essential for safe handling and control during trailer training.

Teaching the horse to walk over a large piece of plywood on the ground is good practice for trailer training.

**Familiarization with trailer and equipment.** The horse should be accustomed to travel equipment (particularly shipping boots or bandages) before trailer training. Let him investigate the trailer; feed him a little grain from the tailgate or trailer floor. Loading a quiet, familiar horse first may give him confidence.

**Loading.** Lead the horse straight toward the trailer entrance, moving forward briskly and with confidence. Keep him straight; don't let him turn his head or veer away. If he hesitates, halt and wait. Don't allow him to back up or turn away from the trailer, but don't try to force him forward. Instead, wait until he is relaxed, then ask him to move forward.

The horse should be asked to move forward with a familiar signal: a voice command or cluck, with the handler in the leading position. A 48-inch training whip (used to touch or tap, not for punishment) can be helpful. A longe line placed around the hindquarters can be used to keep the horse straight, encourage forward movement, and discourage backing up (see trailer loading diagram on page 612). Any such aids must be used to signal and encourage the horse to move forward, not to force him into the trailer. Forceful methods are dangerous for horses and handlers, and can create long-term loading and trailering problems.

When asking the horse to step onto the ramp or into the trailer, it may help to have an assistant pick up the horse's foot and place it on the ramp or trailer floor. When the horse puts his head inside the trailer, allow time for his eyes to adjust to the darker interior.

If the horse backs away from the trailer at any time, *do not* try to restrain him forcibly by pulling on his head. This scares a horse and can cause him to resist harder and toss his head up into the doorway frame. Instead, go with him, stop him, then lead him forward again; try to return to the place where he backed up.

When the horse first goes into the trailer, reward him and let him stand for a few minutes before unloading him. Do not close him in immediately, and *never* tie him unless the back chain or bar has been fastened and the door or tailgate is closed.

**Teaching a horse to unload quietly.** Unloading, like loading, should be taught in small steps. Ask the horse to put one foot in the trailer (or on the ramp), stand for 30 seconds or so, and then back out quietly. Practice this several times, then have him put both front feet in the trailer, wait, then back out. With patience and practice, he will learn to back out one step at a time.

## Loading Difficult Horses

Loading a difficult horse requires patience, experience, tact, and confidence. A horse may be reluctant to load because he is unfamiliar with or afraid of the trailer or loading, he is too large for the trailer, he has suffered from a bad trailering experience or poor handling, or he needs trailer training. The approach chosen must fit the individual; methods that might work on a calm but stubborn horse could be all wrong for a fearful horse. The handler must never get impatient or let her temper get the better of her.

For the safety of all, it is essential to stay cool and calm, and always to work below the horse's panic level. Using force can provoke violent resistance, endangering handlers and the horse, or cause the horse to enter the trailer in such a state of tension that he "blows up" once inside. If the horse (or handler) begins to get excited, stop and let him calm down.

Some techniques for difficult loaders are:

**Linking arms.** If the horse is gentle and not too big, two helpers can link arms behind his hindquarters and "boost" him into the trailer. This often works well with foals and ponies.

**Caution:** Never attempt this with a "kicky" animal!

**Single longe line.** A longe line or cotton rope is attached to one side of the trailer and passed behind the horse's hindquarters. It can be used to discourage the horse from moving sideways or backing up. Brief tugs on the longe line can be used to encourage forward movement.

**Caution:** If the horse rushes backward, the longe line must be released, or it may cause him to fall over backward.

**Double longe lines.** Two longe lines are attached to the sides of the trailer to form a chute to keep the horse from moving sideways. Each longe line is handled by an assistant. They cross behind the

Using longe line in trailer loading.

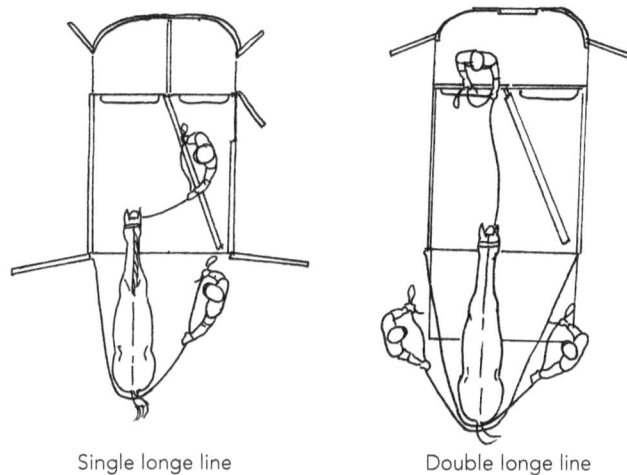

Single longe line   Double longe line

horse to keep him straight and discourage backward movement. As with a single longe line, both lines must be released if the horse should rush backward.

Some horses that are extremely difficult to load in a two-horse trailer will load in a stock trailer. This is also useful for horses that ride poorly in a regular trailer stall.

## Poor Travelers

Horses that travel badly may sweat up, kick the trailer, lean on the divider, or scramble, especially on turns. This behavior is due to fear and tension, which may be caused by bad driving (especially taking turns too fast), or a previous bad experience in the trailer. However, the most common cause is inability to balance securely because of lack of foot room.

Try moving the partition over, using a half-partition (one that does not reach to the floor), or removing it entirely, giving the horse the entire width of the trailer. Some poor travelers ride better in a slant-load trailer, a stock trailer, or facing backward.

Poor travelers should be especially well protected with shipping boots or bandages, a head bumper, and tail wrap or tail guard. Bell boots may offer better protection to the heels than ordinary shipping bandages.

## Transporting a Mare with a Foal

Special measures are necessary when transporting a mare with a foal. A young foal cannot be tied by the halter like an older horse, and he may lie down. The foal must be prevented from getting underneath the mare, or he may be stepped on and injured. Foals may try to climb out of a trailer stall, so the trailer must be completely enclosed. Be sure to provide adequate ventilation, especially in hot weather.

A small foal can be hauled in the front of a trailer with breast bars, with the front area partitioned off with plywood to form a box stall. This lets the mare see, smell, and touch her foal, and the foal can lie down safely.

A foal can also be hauled loose in a trailer stall with a full partition, or in a stock trailer.

On long trips, rest stops should be planned in order to allow the foal to nurse.

## Care of Horses While Traveling

We need to be able to travel with our horses, but we also need to do it in a manner that keeps them as comfortable and healthy as possible. Trailering causes stress on horses, which affects their immune system, and the longer the trip, the longer it takes a horse to return to normal. This can increase a horse's risk of becoming sick after traveling.

Trailering is very strenuous on a horse's body. A 5-hour trailer ride is like a 5-hour walk for a horse, yet he cannot walk, move around, or lie down. Good shipping bandages can offer some support and comfort to his legs during a trailer trip.

Horses do not eat or drink as well when traveling, which adds to dehydration and weight loss, affects gut mobility, and can contribute to stress. In a moving trailer, a horse may sweat and dry almost continuously as he travels, which may contribute to stress and dehydration. In hot weather, horses are also exposed to heat from the trailer floor, especially in aluminum-floor trailers. While a trailer may be comfortable when it is moving, it can quickly reach very high temperatures when parked in the sun, so it is important to park in the shade, open the doors and windows, and monitor the trailer temperature during stops. It may also be wise to check for road construction areas and avoid them. In cold weather, while ventilation is necessary, a moving trailer can result in drafts and wind chills on the horse. However, closing up the trailer and over-blanketing can cause a horse to sweat heavily, further increasing his stress, so you need to manage ventilation and blanketing correctly for the conditions.

It is important to ensure that your trailer has good ventilation. This doesn't mean letting your horse stick his head out of the window (this is not safe!), but having proper venting to let in the fresh air and window screens to keep out flying road debris. If you don't have window screens, consider having your horse wear a fly mask to protect his eyes when traveling.

If you are hauling horses in hot weather, try to drive at night when the temperatures are cooler. Two mats on the floor will better insulate your horse's feet from heat from the road and the trailer floor, and provide additional cushioning. A safety thermometer in the trailer lets you see what temperature your horse is contending with. High temperatures should not necessarily make you change your travel plans, but you should take more breaks to stop and offer your horse water.

Horses must keep their heads up during travel in order to eat from their hay feeder and to balance themselves. This prevents the normal clearance of mucus draining out of the nose, and can have a negative effect on the respiratory system, contributing to shipping-associated respiratory disease. Stopping for breaks to allow horses to stretch their heads down, and not tying their heads higher than necessary, can help.

Horses that travel or compete are more susceptible to communicable diseases such as influenza, strangles, rhinopneumonitis, and equine viral arteritis (EVA). At least 4 to 6 weeks before a trip or competition, make sure that your horse receives all inoculations or boosters far enough in advance to provide immunity before traveling. Before you leave, take and record your horse's vital signs to make sure he is healthy and ready to travel. Don't work a horse excessively the day before travel. Maximal exercise can decrease immune function, so it is best for him not to start out already stressed and tired. Give the horse plenty of hay the night before traveling, and you may want to decrease his grain meal slightly.

Encourage a horse to drink plenty of water before, during, and after traveling. You may use a water flavoring, like horse teas, Gatorade, or anything that encourages your horse to drink. Stop and offer water frequently while traveling—at least every 2 hours. Check your horse's vital signs and demeanor, and do a skin pinch test as a quick dehydration test.

Be sure your horse is bandaged and blanketed appropriately for the weather and for safety, and bring along sheets or blankets of different weights in case weather conditions and temperatures change. Check the temperature in the trailer, especially if it is closed up with more than one horse inside, as they can heat up the trailer more than you would expect.

## Health and Biosecurity

It is important to be aware of health and biosecurity challenges when traveling and competing. Travel causes stress and lowers a horse's immune defenses, and he may be exposed to communicable diseases, which he may then carry back to horses at home. Be sure to bring your own equipment for all your needs for the trip, and reduce the chance of your horse coming into contact with other horses or their feed, water, and equipment.

Here are some practices to reduce the chances of exposing your horse to communicable diseases when traveling:

- Bring along your horse's regular feed, hay, and water to help avoid digestive upsets caused by a change of feed.
- Never take water from, or allow your horse to drink from, a water trough away from home.
- Bring your own buckets and equipment. Do not borrow or loan tack, bits, buckets, brushes, blankets, or other equipment.
- Do not allow horses to touch noses or get close to other horses. Do not turn your horse out with other horses.
- Make sure a stall is clean and remove feed tubs and water buckets before stabling your horse in it. Consider disinfecting the stall before using it.
- Take your horse's temperature daily while traveling and after arrival at home. Be aware of fever or other symptoms.
- Quarantine your horse for 2 weeks after arriving home from a competition or a long trip.

## Driving with a Horse Trailer— Be an Aware Driver

Towing a horse trailer is an important responsibility because, as a driver, you are responsible for the safety of yourself and others as well as the welfare and safety of your horses. Remember the following guidelines:

- Practice hitching up and pulling an empty horse trailer before you try to haul horses.
- Program important numbers into your cell phone before the trip: veterinarian, insurance company, emergency road service, stable, destination, and friends.
- *Do not* use your cell phone or text while driving. Pull over to a protected area before making a call, texting, or answering the phone. This is the law in most states.
- Do a final walk around the trailer before you drive off (and after every refueling stop or rest stop) to check that the doors and ramp are secure, the windows are up, the tires look okay (touch every tire and wheel bearing to check for unequal heat), and the hitch is safely latched. Check that brake lights, turn signals, and running lights are working.

- Never allow a horse to put his head out the window unless the trailer is stopped in a safe place. Window screens keep horses' heads safely inside and prevent flying debris from entering the trailer.
- Remember that you cannot brake or accelerate quickly with a trailer. Because of the weight of the trailer, it takes much longer to accelerate or slow down than when not towing, so allow for this. This is not only safer for the horses, but saves wear and tear on your tow vehicle.
- Signal for turns earlier, and prepare for stops such as traffic lights. Brake early, gently, and smoothly, and use the trailer brake controller to slow the trailer on downgrades or when coming to a stop.
- Do not exceed the speed limit, and slow down on curves and downhill grades.
- Maintain a safe distance between your vehicle and the one in front of you—1 second for every 10 mph.
- Be aware of other drivers who may cut into the lane in front of you.
- Stop every 2 to 4 hours to let your horse rest, offer water, and allow him to stretch his head down to clear congestion. If a trip is 12 hours or more, it is best to plan for an overnight stay.

# Index

Acepromazine, 364, 540–541
Aerobic conditioning, 426
Aids:
    advanced use of, 39–42, *39, 40, 41*
    inside and outside, 53–54
    making the connection, *41*, 47–48, *48*, 76
    on the, 39, 76
    timing, 55–57, *57, 58, 59, 59*
Aisles, in horse facility, 562–563
Alfalfa hay, 453–454
Alfalfa meal and pellets, 455, 462, 463
Anaerobic conditioning, 426–427
Analgesics, 541–542
Anatomy and physiology:
    circulatory system, 350–352
    digestive system, 354–358
    endocrine system, 360–362
    of exercise, 415–420, *416, 417*
    foot, 394–395, *396*
    immune and lymphatic system, 352–353
    integumentary system, 368–370
    movement, biomechanics of, 4–13
    muscular system, 337–346
    nervous system, 358–360
    overview, 327–328
    reproductive system, 363–366
    respiratory system, 346–349
    skeletal system, 329–337
    terminology, 328
    urinary system, 366–368
Angle fences, 198–199, 200, *200*

Angles, evaluating conformation of, 373–376, *374, 375*
Angles, rider's, 121, *122, 123*
Antibiotics, 546
Arenas, 66, *67*, 568–571
Arthritis, 383–384, 386, 387, 389–390
Ascarids, 500–501, *501*
Azoturia. *See* Recurrent Exertional Rhabdomyolysis

Balance:
    in cross-country riding, 180–182, *182*, 190
    evaluating conformation, 378
    in jumping, 116, 122, 147, 190
    lateral, 51, 71–73, *74*
    longeing, 228, 232–235, 307
    longitudinal, 73–74, *74*
    outline (frame), 82–83
Balanced seat, 36–37, *37*, 117
Bandage bows, 386
Bandaging:
    knee and hock, 592–598
    materials, 579–581
    polo wraps, 581, 584–585, *585*
    specialty or treatment, 586–592
    tail wraps, 581–584, *582, 583*
Banks, jumping, 191, *192*, 202–204, *202, 203, 204*
Barley, 459, 463
Bedding, 564–565
Beet pulp, 456–457, 463
Bending (lateral balance), 51–53, *52, 53*, 71–73

Bending lines, 148, *149*, 161–162, *162*
Biomechanics. *See* Movement
Bitless bridles, 266–267, *267*
Bits and bitting:
   *See also* Bridles
   accepting the bit, 48–51, *49*, *50*, 75, *76*, 76, 235
   bit guards, 265, 276, *276*
   ill-fitting, adjustments for, 275–276, *276*
   longeing with the bit, 209–210, *210*, 235
   mouthpiece materials, 250–251
   pressure points, 248–249, *250*
   selecting, 251–252
   severity of, 249–250
   types of, 253–262
Blemishes, 380
Blood, 350
Blood vessels, 351–352, *352*, 421–422
Bloodworms (strongyles), 498–500, *499*, 522
Body awareness, 35–36, *36*
Bones, 329–333, *330*, *332*, 421
Bots, 503–504, *504*
Botulism, 528–529
Bounce fences, 202, *202*
Braiding, 281–282
Breastplates and breast collars, 269–271, *271*
Breathing, 188, 348, 422, *423*
Bridges, *127*, *175*, 179, *179*, *180*
Bridles:
   accessories, 264–265
   figure eight, storage of, 277–278, *278*
   ill-fitting, adjustments for, 275–277, *275*, *276*
   types of, 259, *260*, 261–262, *262*, 266–267, *267*
Bucked shins, 386
Butorphanol, 542

Calming supplements, 469–470
Canter:
   aids for, 56, *58*, 59, *59*, 61–63, *63*
   biomechanics of, 26–28, *27*, *28*
   cavaletti work, 113–114
   counter-canter, 104–105, *106*, 151
   cross-country, 185–186
   departs, 61–63, *63*, *64*
   half-halts, 59
   leads and lead changes, 105–107, 150–151
   lengthening stride in, 77, 86
   longeing, 233–234, 236, 241–242
   paces within, 77, 86–87, *86*
   transitions, 61–64, *63*, *64*
Carbohydrates, 434–435
Cardiovascular system, 350–352, *351*, *352*, 421–422
Cartilage, 334, 337, 421
"Cast" horses, 551
Cavaletti and ground pole work, 111–114, *112*, *113*, 142–147, *144*, *145*
Chain-end lead shank, 547–548, *549*
Chevron fences, 199, *199*
Chewing the bit out of the rider's hands, 52–53, *54*
Choke, 524
Chondroitin sulfate, 545–546
Circulatory system, 350–352, 351, *352*, 421–422, 520
Clips, 412, *412*
Coffin canter, 185–186, 195
Coffin jumps, 185–186, 194–196, *197*
Cold-water bandages, 591–592
Colic, 521–524
Collection, 81–82, *81*
Combination jumps, 139–142, *141*, 160–161, *161*, 194–197, *197*, 200–202, *202*, 207
Concentrates, 457–463
Conditioning:
   effects, 420–422, *423*
   heat and humidity, 430
   nutritional needs, 424, 473–474, 479, 486, 487
   physiology of, 415–420, *416*, *417*
   principles, 423–426
   types, 426–430
Conformation:
   angles, 373–376, *374*, *375*
   evaluating, 378–379, *379*
   hindquarter, 376–378, *376*, *377*, *378*
   lameness, 383–393, 514–515
   overview, 371
   proportions, 372, *372*, 378–379
   soundness, and effects of defects on, 380–383
Conjunctivitis, 535

Connection, *41*, 47–48, *48*, 76
Contact, 47–48, *48*, 74–76, *75*, *76*
Corn, 459, 463
Corneal ulcers, 536
Corner fences, 198–199, 200, *201*
Corticosteroids, 544–545
Counter-canter, 104–105, *106*, 151
Cribbing, 497, *498*
Crookedness. *See* Straightness
Cross-country courses, 205–207, *206*
Cross-country riding:
    balance, 180–182, *182*
    control, 178–180, *179*, *180*, *181*
    fundamentals of, 172–177
    galloping, 177–178, *180*, 184–188
    jumping, 188–207
    rider fitness, 34–35, *35*, 173
    schooling your horse, 183–184
Cruppers, 271, *272*
Curb bits, 252, 256–258, *257*, *258*, *259*

Dehydration, 433–434, 511, 613
Detomidine (Dormosedan), 364, 541, 542
Developmental Orthopedic Disease
    (DOD), 384–385
Deworming, 504–506
Dexamethazone, 544
Diclofenac, 543
Digestive aids, 470–471
Digestive system, 354–358, 520–525
Direction, changes in, 87
Direct-pressure bits and mouthpieces, 253–256, *253*, *255*
Disaster preparedness, 576–577
Diseases and disorders:
    nutritional management, 477–479, 486–487
    preventing spread of, 537
    processes, 510–513
    and travel, 613–614
    types of, 514–537
    vaccinations, 538
Distance, measuring, 162–163, *163*, 186–187
Ditches, jumping, 138–139, 191, 194–195, *196*, *202*
Doors and gates, stable, 562–563, *563*
Double bridle (Weymouth), 259, *260*
Double longeing, 225–226, *226*, 610–611, *611*

Downhill jumps, 193, *194*
Drainage, stable, 558–560, *559*
Draw reins, 268
Dressage and training:
    arenas, 66, *67*
    biomechanics of, 13–19
    cavaletti and ground pole exercises, 111–114
    lateral movements, 89–90, 96–104, *98*, *99*, *100*, *101*, *102*, *104*
    open, work in the, 110–111
    other movements, 104–108
    paces within the gaits, 83–87
    principles and goals, 66–68
    qualities developed through, 68–83
    schooling figures, 87–89
    stages of, 109–110
    two track exercises, 89, 90–96, *91*, *93*, *95*, *96*
Drop jumps, 191, *192*, 193, 202–204, *204*
Drugs, 538–546
Dry lots, 573–574
Dust control, 570

Edema, 512–513
Elasticity, 71
Elastic poll pressure device, 269
Electrolytes, 468
Encephalomyelitis, 526
Endocrine system, 360–362, 529–531
Engagement, 16–17, *16*, 74, 230–231, *231*
Equine Cushing's disease, 529–530
Equine herpes virus (EHV), 517–518, 525–526, 531
Equine infectious anemia (EIA), 520
Equine metabolic syndrome (EMS), 530–531
Equine protozoal myeloencephalitis (EPM), 527–528
Equine sarcoid, 534
Equine viral arteritis (EVA), 519, 520, 531–532
Equitation courses, 165–167, *166*
Exercise. *See* Conditioning
Eye problems, 535–537

False collection, *31*, 32
False extension, *31*, 32–33
False frame, 50
Fats (lipids), 436, 469

Feeding:
  balanced rations, 479–484
  considerations and guidelines, 471–477
  and exercise levels, 424, 473–474, 479, 486, 487
  health conditions, management of, 477–479, 486–487
  nutrients, types of, 433–444
  principles and practices, 485–487
  seasonal variations, 447–448, 473
Feeds:
  buying, 564–565
  concentrates, 457–463
  label information, 465–466
  processed, 455–456, 463–467
  roughages, 444–457, 485
  storage, 452, 454–455, 565
  supplements, 467–471
Fences. *See* Jumping
Fever, 510–511
Figure-eight bandages, 592–594, *593*
Firocoxib, 543–544
Fitness, of rider, 34–35, *35*, 122–123, 173
Flat work, 34–65
Flexibility, 234, 427–429
Floor materials, stable, 563–564
Flunixin meglumine, 543
Fly control, 566–567
Flying changes of leads, 106–107, 151–152, *151*, *153*
Foals:
  corrective trimming, 407
  longeing, 226–227
  nutrition for, 475–476, 479
  teeth, 489–490, *490*
  transporting, 611–612
Foot:
  anatomy, 394–395, *396*
  functions, 396–398, *397*
  hoof conformation, 379
  hoof supplements, 470
  lamenesses of, 391–393, 514–515
  movement of, 399–402, *399*, *400*, *401*
  poultices for, 589–590
  shoeing and trimming, 402–414
Foot flight patterns, 399–402, *399*, *400*, *401*
Footing, in riding areas, 569–570
Forehand, on the, 29–30, *31*

Frame (outline), 82–83, *82*
Fruit pomace, 457
Full seat, 118, *119*, 120, 174

Gag bits, 261, *262*
Gaits:
  biomechanics of, 13, *14*, 23–29
  lead, changes of, 105–106
  lengthening and shortening strides, 77, 85, *85*, 86, 240–241
  paces within, 83–87
  rhythms, 69–70, 73, 229–230
  transitions, 59–64, 73, 74, 233–234
Galloping, 28–29, *29*, *117*, 177–178, *180*, *182*, *182*, 183–188
Galloping fences, 197–198, *199*
Gastric ulcers, 522, 525, 546
Gates and doors, stable, 562–563, *563*
German martingale, 269
Glucosamine, 545–546
Grain by-products, 460–461, 463
Grains, 457–459, 463
Grass, pasture. *See* Pasture feeding
Grass hays, types of, 453, 454
Greasy heel, 533–534
Gridwork, 142–147, *144*, *145*
Ground pole work, 111–114, *112*, *113*, 142–147, *144*, *145*
Gymnastic jumping, 142–147, *144*, *145*

Hackamores, 266–267, *267*
Half-halts:
  flat work, 57, 59, 60, *60*, 61
  jumping, 132–133, *132*
Half-pass, 103–104, *104*
Half-seat, 118, *119*, 120, 132, 174
Haunches, turn on, 100, 102, *102*, *103*
Haunches-in (travers), 97, 99, *100*, *101*
Haunches-out, 99–100, *101*
Hay:
  bales, 454–455
  overview, 451
  pasture feeding, 572–573
  processed, 455–456
  quality of, 452–453, 456
  storage, 452, 454–455, 565
  types of, 453–454

# INDEX

Health care:
    *See also* Bandaging; Diseases and disorders
    basic examination, 507–509
    "cast" horses, 551
    corrective shoeing or trimming, 406–408
    lameness, 391–393, 514–515
    medications, 538–546
    parasites, 448, 498–507, 522, 524–525, 535
    restraining horses, 547–548, *549, 550*
    teeth and dental care, 488–497
    vaccinations, 538
Heart, 350–352, *351, 352*, 421
Heat and humidity, 430, 612–613
Heaves, 516–517
Hollow back, 30–33, *31*, 37–38, *38*
Hoof. *See* Foot
Hooks and ramps, 496–497, *497*
Hormones, 360–362, 363, 364, 365, 369–370, 442–443
Horsemanship, teaching:
    approaches to, 291–294
    beginners, 303–305
    emergency procedures, 315–319
    jumping, 305–307
    longeing, 307–310
    mounted lessons, 299–310
    overview, 285
    principles and methods, 286–291
    problems, 319–323
    safety, 291–292, 297, 311–319
    techniques, 295–299
Horses, unfamiliar, 65, 228
Horse trailers. *See* Travel
Hunter courses, 164–165, *164*, 165
Hyaluronic acid, 545

Ice packs, 590–591
Illness. *See* Health care
Immobilizing bandages, 598
Immune system, 352–353, 537
Impulsion, 16–17, 74, 76–78, 147, 230–231, *231*
Inflammation, 511–512
Influenza, 518
Inside rein, releasing, 54–55, *55*
Insulin resistance (IR), 530–531

Integumentary system, 368–370, 532–535
Interval training, 424, 429–430
Inverted horses, 30–32, *31*

Joints, anatomy of, 4, 5–6, 333–335, *334*, 376, *376*
Joints, bandaging, 592–598
Joints, diseases and injuries of, 383–385, 386–387, 389–391
Joint supplements, 471
Joint therapeutics, 545–546
Jumping:
    approaches to fences, 147–150, *149, 150*
    biomechanics of, 19–23, *21*
    bits for, 261, 262
    challenges and corrections, 133–136, *135*
    courses, elements of, 157–162, *158, 159, 161, 162*
    courses, types of, 163–171
    cross-country, 188–207
    distance, measuring, 162–163, *163*
    good performances, qualities of, 115–116, *116*
    gymnastics and ground poles, 142–147, *144, 145*
    half-halts, 132–133, *132*
    hands and releases, 126–131, *127, 128, 129, 130*
    leads and lead changes, 150–152, *151, 153*
    lessons in, 305–307
    obstacles, types of, 136–142, 190–205
    rider errors, correcting, 123–126, *126*
    rider's angles, 118, 120, 121, *122, 123*
    rider strength and fitness, 122–123
    seat and position, 116–121, *117, 119*, 153–154
    turns, 153–157, *154, 155, 157*, 161–162, *162*
Jumping (jumper) courses, 167–171, *167, 168, 170*

Kimberwicke bits, 252, 259–261

Lameness, 383–393, 514–515
Laminitis, 514–515

Land, and facility management, 555–556, 577–578
Lateral movements, 89–90, 96–104, *98, 99, 100, 101, 102, 103, 104*
Leads and lead changes, 105–108, *108,* 150–152, *151, 153*
Leg aids, 39, *39,* 55–57, *57, 58,* 153–154
Legs, bandaging, 584–589, 590–598
Legume hays, 453, 454
Leg-yielding, 93–96, *95, 96*
Leverage bits, 252, 256–258, *257, 258, 259*
Ligaments, 6, *6,* 10–11, *10,* 12, *12,* 335–337, *336, 337,* 388–389, 391
Light seat, 118–119, *119,* 132, 174
Longeing:
    with bit, 209–210, *210,* 235
    circle, importance of, 223–225
    double, 225–226, *226,* 610–611, *611*
    equipment, 209–218
    handling the whip, 222–223
    lessons in, 307–310
    overview, 208
    problems, 242–246
    teaching horse to, 236–242
    techniques, 218–222, *219, 221*
    various purposes of, 227–236
    young horses, 226–227
Longe lines, 209–210, *210,* 218–222, *219, 221,* 610–611, *611*
Lymphatic system, 352–353

Machinery, farm, 567–568
Manure disposal, 565–566
Market Harborough martingale, 269
Medications, 538–546
Melanoma, 534
Mental preparation, 35–36, *36*
Metabolic diseases, 478, 529–531
Metabolism, 360–362, 418–419
Methylprednisolone acetate, 545
Methylsulfonylmethane, 546
Minerals, 440–444, 468, 486
Moon blindness, 536–537
Mound jumps, 193, *193*
Mouthpieces, 250–251, 253, 254–256, *255, 257, 258,* 259
Movement:
    anatomy and biomechanics of, 3–13
    conformation defects, 380–393
    dressage horse, 13–19
    and gaits, 13, *14,* 23–29
    jumping horse, 19–23, *21*
    longeing, improving with, 229–235
    problems, 29–33, *31*
    stride, phases of, 13, *14*
Mud fever, 533–534
Muscle contractions, 416–418, *417*
Muscle fibers, 416, *417,* 419–420
Muscles, and conditioning, 416–420, 424, 426–429
Muscles, biomechanics of, 4–13, 14–16, 17–20
Muscles, circle of, 5–11, *7, 8, 9, 10, 11,* 214
Muscular system, 337–346, 514–516

"Neck-stretchers," 269
Nervous system, 358–360, 525–529
Non-leverage bits, 253–256, *253, 255*
Non-steroidal anti-inflammatory drugs (NSAIDs), 542–544
Nosebands, 262–264, *265,* 266, *267*
Nutraceuticals, 471
Nutrition. *See* Feeding; Feeds

Oats, 458, 463
Obedience, 68, 228–229, 243
Obstacles. *See* Jumping
Omeprazole, 546
Ophthalmia, periodic, 536–537
Option fences, 165, 197, *198,* 200–201, 207
Outline (frame), 82–83, *82*
Outside rein, riding into, 51–52, *53*
Oxers. *See* Spread fences

Pace, 147, 185–187
Paces with the gaits, 83–87
Pads, under shoes, 411–412, *411*
Pain, 512
Parasites, 448, 498–507, 522, 524–525, 535
Parrot mouth, 383, 495, *495*
Pasture feeding, 444–451, 572–573
Pasture management, 572–575
Pelham bits, 252, 258, 259–260, 259
Phenylbutazone, 542, 543
Physical education, 290–291
Pinworms, 502–503, *503*

Pituitary pars intermedia dysfunction (PPID), 529–530
Poisonous plants, 449–451
Polo wraps, 581, 584–585, *585*
Polysulfated glycosaminoglycans (PSGAGs), 545
Position. *See* Seat and position
Potomac horse fever (PHF), 524–525
Poultices, 588–590, *588*
Presentation, 279–284, *283*
Pressure bandages, 586–587, *587*
Preventative health care, 506–507, 537, 538
Processed feeds, 455–456, 463–467
Proportions, 372, *372*, 378–379
Proteins, 435–436, 468–469
Proud flesh, 513

Quarantine area, 562

Rabies, 529
Rain rot (rain scald), 532
Reciprocal apparatus, 344, *345*
Recurrent Airway Obstruction (RAO), 516–517
Recurrent Exertional Rhabdomyolysis, 443, 472, 478, 487, 515–516, 532
Rein aids:
  five rein effects, 42–45, *43*, *44*, *45*
  hands, action of, 41–42
  indirect reins of opposition, 46–47, *46*, *47*
  longeing, 220–221
  overview, 40–41
  releasing the inside rein, 54–55, *55*
  riding into the outside rein, 51–52, *53*
Rein-back, 107–108, *108*
Reins, temporary adjustments for, 277
Related distances, 158–160, *158*, *159*, 171, 197
Relaxation, 70–74, 227–228, 230
Releases, in jumping, 126–131, *127*, *128*, *129*, *130*
Releasing the inside rein, 54–55, *55*
Renvers, 99–100, *101*
Reproductive system, 363–366, 531–532
Respiratory system, 346–349, 422, 423, 516–519
Restraints, 547–548, 549, 550

Rhabdomyolysis, 443, 478, 515–516, 532
Rhinopneumonitis, 517–518, 525–526, 531
Rhythm, 69–70, 73, 229–230
Riding areas, 568–571
Riding "in position," 79, *80*
Riding lessons. *See* Horsemanship, teaching
Riding strange horses, 65
Ring figures, 87–88
Ringworm, 533
Roaring, 517
Robert Jones bandages, 598
Roll-back turns, 155–156, *155*
Rollers, 211
Romifidine (Sedivet), 364, 541
Roughages, 444–457, 485
Roundworms, 500–501, *501*
Running reins, 268

Saddles, ill-fitting, 273–274, *274*
Safety:
  cross-country riding and jumping, 172–173
  stable management, 555–568, *558*, *559*, *560*, *563*
  in teaching horsemanship, 291–292, 297, 311–319
  and travel, 599–615
Sale, presentation for, 280–284
Schooling figures, 87–89
Scratches, 533–534
Seasonal variations in feeding, 447–448, 473
Seat aids, 40, *40*
Seat and position:
  cross-country, 174–176, *175*, *176*, *177*, 178
  on the flat, 36–37, *37*
  jumping, 116–121, *117*, *119*, 153–154
  riding "in position," 79, *80*
Sedatives, 364, 540–541
Shock, 510
Shoeing:
  corrective or therapeutic, 406–408
  materials and sizes, 406
  optional features, 411–414, *411*, *412*, *413*, *414*
  principles of, 402–404, *402*, *403*, *404*
  removal, 404–406, *405*

tools, 404
types of, 408–410, *409*
Shoulder-fore, 80, *81*
Shoulder-in, 96–97, *98*, *99*, *101*
Show jumping, 167–170, *168*, *169*, *170*
Side reins, 211–215, *212*, *213*, *214*, *216*
Single fences, 158, *158*, 161
Skeletal system, 329–337, 514–515
Skin, 368–370, 532–535
Sliding side reins, 215, *216*
Snaffle bits, 252, 253–256, *253*, *255*
Soundness, 380–383
Speed, 70, 147, 185–187
Spider bandages, 595–597, *597*
Spiraling in and out, 92–93, *93*, 234–235, 241
Sport psychology, 291
Spread fences, 137–139, *137*, *139*, 140–141, *141*
Stable and facility management:
    arenas and riding areas, 568–571
    disaster preparedness, 576–577
    efficiency and organization, 552–553
    land conservation, 577–578
    maintenance, 571–575
    record-keeping, 553–555
    routines, 575–576
    safety and design, 555–568, *558*, *559*, *560*, *563*
Stack bandages, 594–595, *595*
Stadium jumping, 169–171, *169*, *170*
Stalls, 557, *558*, 559–560, *559*, 561, 563–564
Stamina, conditioning for, 426
Stay apparatus, 343–344, *345*
Steeplechase fences, 197–198, *199*
Step mouth, 495, *496*
Steps, 191, *192*
Stirrups, in cross-country riding, 174–175, *175*, 178
Stirrups, in jumping, 117–118, *117*, 120
Stirrups, riding without, 38, 310
Straightness, 33, 51, 71, 78–80, *79*, *80*, *81*, 145–146, *145*, 234–235
Strangles, 518–519
Strength conditioning, 427
Stretching down, 52–53, 54, 88, *88*, *89*, 231–232, *233*
Stride, lengthening, 77, 85, *85*, *86*, 240–241

Stride, phases of, 13, *14*
Strongyles, 498–500, *499*, 522
Submission, 68, 76
Summer sores, 535
Sunken roads, 202–203, *203*
Supplements, 467–471
Suppleness, 71, 74, 234–235, 307, 427–429
Surcingles, 211
Suspensory apparatus, 4, 11–13, *12*, 344
Sweat bandages, 590
Sweet feeds, 464

Tack:
    adjustments to ill-fitting, 272–277
    buying, 278–279
    presentation, 279–280
    reclaiming, neglected, 279
    storing, 277–278, *278*, 567
Tack rooms, 277, 567
Tail wraps, 581–584, *582*, *583*
Tapeworms, 501–502, *502*
Teeth:
    dental care, 488
    determining age of horse by, 489–494
    problems, 494–498, 520–521
Tempo, 69–70, 229–230
Tendons, 11–13, *12*, 342–343, *342*, 344, 385–386, 389, 391
Tetanus, 528
3-point position, 118, *119*, 120, 174
Throughness, 48, 68, 77
Traction devices, 413–414, *413*, *414*
Tractors and machinery, 567–568
Trailers, horse. *See* Travel
Training. *See* Dressage and training; Horsemanship, teaching
Training devices or aids, 216–218, *218*, 268–269
Trakehners, 194
Tranquilizers, 364, 540–541
Transitions, 59–64, 73, 74, 233–234
Travel:
    care of horses while, 612–614
    safe driving, 614–615
    special measures for, 611–612
    tow vehicles and hitch, 600–601, *602*
    trailer care and maintenance, 599–600, 601, 603–604
    trailer equipment checklist, 606–607

trailer loading and unloading, 607–611
trailer safety checklist, 604–606
Travers (haunches-in), 97, 99, *100*, *101*
Triamcinolone, 545
Trimming, hoof, 402–404, *402*, *403*, *404*, 406–407
Trot:
  cavaletti work, 111–113, *112*, *113*, 143, *144*
  lead, changes of, 105, 151
  lengthening stride in, 77, 85, *85*, 86
  longeing, 240
  paces within, 84–86, *85*
  posting, aids for, 56, *58*, 92
  sitting, 37–38, *38*
  transitions, 61, 64
Turn on the haunches, 100, 102, *102*, *103*
Turnout. *See* Presentation
Turns, jumping, 153–157, *154*, *155*, *157*, 161–162, *162*
Twitches, 548, *550*
2-point position, 118, *119*, 120, 132, 174
Two track exercises, 89, 90–96, *91*, *93*, *95*, *96*
Tying up (rhabdomyolysis), 443, 478, 515–516, 532

Undershot jaw, 383, 495, *495*
Uphill jumps, 193–194, *195*
Urinary system, 366–368, 532
Utilities, stable, 560, *560*
Uveitis, recurrent, 536–537

Vaccinations, 538
Ventilation, stable, 557, *558*
Vertical fences, 136–137, *137*, 139, 140–141, *141*
Vitamins, 436–439, 467–468, 486

Walk, 23–24, *24*, 56, 83–84, *84*, 111, *112*
Warm-up, 64–65, 297
Warts, 534–535
Water, as nutrient, 433–434
Water jumps, 138–139, *140*, 203–205, *204*, *205*
Water supply, in horse facility, 560, *560*
Wave mouth, 495, *496*
West Nile virus, 527
Weymouth bridle, 259, *260*

Whip, longe, 222–223
Wound healing, abnormal, 513
Wraps. *See* Bandaging

Xylazine (Rompun), 364, 541

Zigzag fences, *196*, 199